# CISSP®

# Certified Information Systems Security Professional

## Study Guide

### Fifth Edition

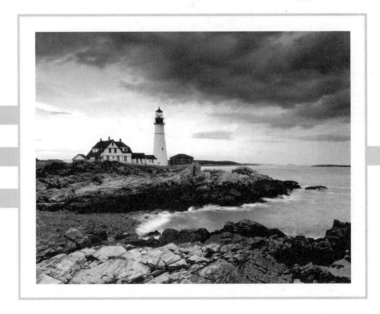

# CISSP®
# Certified Information Systems Security Professional

## Study Guide

## Fifth Edition

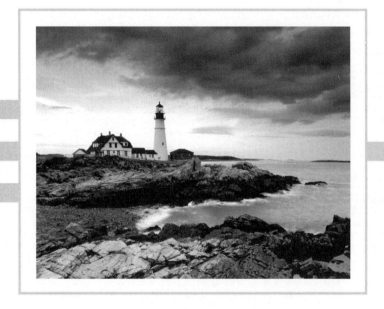

James Michael Stewart

Ed Tittel

Mike Chapple

WILEY

Wiley Publishing, Inc.

Acquisitions Editor: Jeff Kellum
Development Editor: Rob Truhn
Technical Editor: Darril Gibson
Production Editor: Eric Charbonneau
Copy Editor: Judy Flynn
Editorial Manager: Pete Gaughan
Production Manager: Tim Tate
Vice President and Executive Group Publisher: Richard Swadley
Vice President and Publisher: Neil Edde
Media Project Manager 1: Laura Moss-Hollister
Media Associate Producer: Shawn Patrick
Media Quality Assurance: Marilyn Hummel
Book Designer: Judy Fung
Proofreader: Nancy Bell
Indexer: Nancy Guenther
Project Coordinator, Cover: Katie Crocker
Cover Designer: Ryan Sneed

Dear Reader,

Thank you for choosing *CISSP: Certified Information Systems Security Professional Study Guide*. This book is part of a family of premium-quality Sybex books, all of which are written by outstanding authors who combine practical experience with a gift for teaching.

Sybex was founded in 1976. More than 30 years later, we're still committed to producing consistently exceptional books. With each of our titles, we're working hard to set a new standard for the industry. From the paper we print on, to the authors we work with, our goal is to bring you the best books available.

I hope you see all that reflected in these pages. I'd be very interested to hear your comments and get your feedback on how we're doing. Feel free to let me know what you think about this or any other Sybex book by sending me an email at nedde@wiley.com. If you think you've found a technical error in this book, please visit http://sybex.custhelp.com. Customer feedback is critical to our efforts at Sybex.

Best regards,

Neil Edde
Vice President and Publisher
Sybex, an Imprint of Wiley

*To Cathy, whenever there is trouble, just remember "Some beach, somewhere . . ."*
—James Michael Stewart

*To my Mom, Cecilia Katherine: the world is not as bright without you in it anymore, and we all still miss you every day.*
—Ed Tittel

*To my family: Renee, Richard, Matthew, and Christopher, who lovingly put up with me during the hours I spent buried in my laptop writing this book.*
—Mike Chapple

# Acknowledgments

I hope our efforts to improve this study guide will lend themselves handily to your understanding and comprehension of the wide berth of CISSP concepts. I'd like to express my thanks to Sybex for continuing to support this project. Thanks to Ed Tittel and Mike Chapple for continuing to contribute to this project. Also thanks to all my CISSP course students who have provided their insight and input to improve my training courseware and ultimately this tome. Extra thanks to the 5th Edition Technical Editor, Darril Gibson, who performed amazing feats in guiding us to improve this book.

To my wonderful wife, Cathy, our life together is just getting started. To my son, Xzavier Slayde, and daughter, Remington Annaliese, may you grow to be more than we could imagine. To my parents, Dave and Sue, thanks for your love and consistent support. To Mark, as best friends go, it could've been worse. And finally, as always, to Elvis—all hail the King!

*—James Michael Stewart*

Thanks to both Michael Stewart and Mike Chapple for continuing to keep me involved in this project. Michael continues to teach CISSP courses with amazing frequency, which provides us with a lifeline to the hard-working professionals in the trenches for whom this credential means so much. Congrats again to Michael on another addition to his family; my son, Gregory, is now in first grade and the time just keeps flying by. May the months and years slip by as pleasantly and painlessly for you as they have for us. Next, thanks to the folks at Sybex, especially Jeff Kellum for rounding us all up and keeping us headed in the same direction and for his excellent view of where we need to take this book. Finally, I'd like to thank my loving and lovely wife, Dina, for all the great things she does to make family life so comfortable, clean, interesting and fun.

*—Ed Tittel*

Special thanks go to the information security team at the University of Notre Dame. Gary Dobbins, Bob Winding, David Seidl, and Robert Riley provided hours of interesting conversation and debate on security issues that inspired and informed much of the material in this book.

I would like to thank the team at Wiley who provided invaluable assistance throughout the book development process. I also owe a debt of gratitude to my literary agent, Carole Jelen of Waterside Productions. My coauthors, Ed Tittel and James Michael Stewart, have worked with me ever since we published the first edition of this book together eight years ago. I'd also like to thank the many people who participated in the production of this book but whom I never had the chance to meet: the graphics team, the production staff, and all of those involved in bringing this book to press.

*—Mike Chapple*

# About the Authors

**James Michael Stewart,**CISSP, has been writing and training for more than 16 years, with a current focus on security. He has been teaching CISSP training courses since 2002, not to mention other courses on Windows security and ethical hacking/penetration testing. He is the author of several books and courseware sets on security certification, Microsoft topics, and network administration. More information about Michael can be found at his website: www.impactonline.com.

**Ed Tittel** is a full-time freelance writer, trainer, and consultant specializing in matters related to information security, markup languages, and networking technologies. He is a regular contributor to numerous TechTarget websites (and keeps updating his security certification survey for SearchSecurity.com), teaches online security and technology courses for HP, and enjoys his occasional gigs as an expert witness on Web technologies from the mid-1990s when he was lucky enough to write a raft of books in that arena. Ed's professional bio and other information are available at www.edtittel.com.

**Mike Chapple,**CISSP, PhD, is an IT professional with the University of Notre Dame. In the past, he was chief information officer of Brand Institute and an information security researcher with the National Security Agency and the U.S. Air Force. His primary areas of expertise include network intrusion detection and access controls. Mike is a frequent contributor to TechTarget's SearchSecurity site and the author of several information security titles including *The GSEC Prep Guide* from Wiley and *Information Security Illuminated* from Jones and Bartlett Publishers.

# Contents at a Glance

# Contents

# Introduction

The *CISSP: Certified Information Systems Security Professional Study Guide, 5th Edition,* offers you a solid foundation for the Certified Information Systems Security Professional (CISSP) exam. By purchasing this book, you've shown a willingness to learn and a desire to develop the skills you need to achieve this certification. This introduction provides you with a basic overview of this book and the CISSP exam.

This book is designed for readers and students who want to study for the CISSP certification exam. If your goal is to become a certified security professional, then the CISSP certification and this study guide are for you. The purpose of this book is to adequately prepare you to take the CISSP exam.

Before you dive into this book, you need to have accomplished a few tasks on your own. You need to have a general understanding of IT and of security. You should have the necessary five years of experience (or four years if you have a college degree) in one of the 10 domains covered by the CISSP exam. If you are qualified to take the CISSP exam according to (ISC)$^2$, then you are sufficiently prepared to use this book to study for the CISSP exam. For more information on (ISC)$^2$, see the next section.

## (ISC)$^2$

The CISSP exam is governed by the International Information Systems Security Certification Consortium (ISC)$^2$ organization. (ISC)$^2$ is a global not-for-profit organization. It has four primary mission goals:

- Maintain the Common Body of Knowledge (CBK) for the field of information systems security.

- Provide certification for information systems security professionals and practitioners.

- Conduct certification training and administer the certification exams.

- Oversee the ongoing accreditation of qualified certification candidates through continued education.

The (ISC)$^2$ is operated by a board of directors elected from the ranks of its certified practitioners. You can obtain more information about (ISC)$^2$ from its website at www.isc2.org.

## CISSP and SSCP

(ISC)$^2$ supports and provides two primary certifications: CISSP and SSCP. These certifications are designed to verify the knowledge and skills of IT security professionals across all industries. The Certified Information Systems Security Professional credential is for security professionals responsible for designing and maintaining security infrastructure within an organization. The System Security Certified Practitioner (SSCP) is a credential for security professionals responsible for implementing or operating a security infrastructure in an organization.

The CISSP certification covers material from the 10 CBK domains:

- Access Control
- Telecommunications and Network Security
- Information Security Governance and Risk Management
- Application Development Security
- Cryptography
- Security Architecture and Design
- Operations Security
- Business Continuity and Disaster Recovery Planning
- Legal, Regulations, Investigations, and Compliance
- Physical (Environmental) Security

The SSCP certification covers material from seven CBK domains:

- Access Controls
- Administration
- Audit and Monitoring
- Cryptography
- Data Communications
- Malicious Code/Malware
- Risk, Response, and Recovery

The content for the CISSP and SSCP domains overlap significantly, but the focus is different for each set of domains. The CISSP focuses on theory and design, whereas the SSCP focuses more on implementation and best practices. This book focuses only on the domains for the CISSP exam.

## Prequalifications

(ISC)$^2$ has defined several qualification requirements you must meet to become a CISSP. First, you must be a practicing security professional with at least five years' experience or with four years' experience and a recent IT or IS degree. Professional experience is defined as security work performed for salary or commission within one or more of the 10 CBK domains.

Second, you must agree to adhere to a formal code of ethics. The CISSP Code of Ethics is a set of guidelines the (ISC)$^2$ wants all CISSP candidates to follow to maintain professionalism in the field of information systems security. You can find it in the Information section on the (ISC)$^2$ website at www.isc2.org.

(ISC)$^2$ also offers an entry program known as an Associate of (ISC)$^2$. This program allows someone without any or enough experience to qualify as a CISSP to take the CISSP exam anyway and then obtain experience afterward. Associates are granted six years to obtain five years of security experience. Only after providing proof of such experience, usually by means of endorsement and a resume, can the individual be awarded CISSP certification.

To sign up, visit the (ISC)$^2$ website, and follow the instructions listed there for registering to take the CISSP exam (the link reads "Register Now for CISSP Certification Exams"). You'll provide your contact information, payment details, and security-related professional experience. You'll also select one of the available time and location settings for the exam. Once (ISC)$^2$ approves your application to take the exam, you'll receive a confirmation email with all the details you'll need to find the testing center and take the exam.

# Overview of the CISSP Exam

The CISSP exam consists of 250 questions, and you have six hours to complete it. The exam is still administered using a paper booklet and answer sheet. This means you'll be using a pencil to fill in answer bubbles.

The CISSP exam focuses on security from a 30,000-foot view; it deals more with theory and concept than implementation and procedure. It is very broad, but not very deep. To successfully complete this exam, you'll need to be familiar with every domain in the CBK but not necessarily be a master of each domain.

You'll need to register for the exam through the (ISC)$^2$ website at www.isc2.org.

(ISC)$^2$ administers the exam itself. In most cases, the exams are held in large conference rooms at hotels. Existing CISSP holders are recruited to serve as proctors or administrators for these exams. Be sure to arrive at the testing center around 8 a.m., and keep in mind that absolutely no one will be admitted into the exam after 8:30 a.m. Once all test takers are signed in and seated, the exam proctors will pass out the testing materials and read a few pages of instructions. This may take 30 minutes or more. Once that process is finished, the 6-hour window for taking the test will begin.

## CISSP Exam Question Types

Every question on the CISSP exam is a four-option, multiple-choice question with a single correct answer. Some are straightforward, such as asking you to select a definition. Some are a bit more involved, such as asking you to select the appropriate concept or best practice. And some questions present you with a scenario or situation and ask you to select the best response. Here's an example:

1. What is the most important goal and top priority of a security solution?

    **A.** Preventing disclosure

    **B.** Maintaining integrity

    **C.** Maintaining human safety

    **D.** Sustaining availability

You must select the one correct or best answer and mark it on your answer sheet. In some cases, the correct answer will be very obvious to you. In other cases, several answers may seem correct. In these instances, you must choose the best answer for the question asked. Watch for general, specific, universal, superset, and subset answer selections. In other cases, none of the answers will seem correct. In these instances, you'll need to select the least incorrect answer.

 By the way, the correct answer for this sample question is C. Protecting human safety is always your first priority.

## Advice on Taking the Exam

The CISSP exam consists of two key elements. First, you need to know the material from the 10 CBK domains. Second, you must have good test-taking skills. With six hours to complete a 250-question exam, you have just less than 90 seconds for each question. Thus, it is important to work quickly, without rushing but also without wasting time.

One key factor to remember is that guessing is better than not answering a question. If you don't answer a question, you will not get any credit. But if you guess, you have at least a 25 percent chance of improving your score. Wrong answers are not counted against you. So, near the end of the sixth hour, be sure an answer is selected for every line on the answer sheet.

You can write on the test booklet, but nothing written on it will count for or against your score. Use the booklet to make notes and keep track of your progress. We recommend circling each answer you select before you mark it on your answer sheet.

To maximize your test-taking activities, here are some general guidelines:

- Answer easy questions first.
- Skip harder questions, and return to them later. Consider creating a column on the front cover of your testing booklet to keep track of skipped questions.
- Eliminate wrong answers before selecting the correct one.
- Watch for double negatives.
- Be sure you understand what the question is asking.

Manage your time. You should try to complete about 50 questions per hour. This will leave you with about an hour to focus on skipped questions and double-check your work.

Be very careful to mark your answers on the correct question number on the answer sheet. The most common cause of failure is making a transfer mistake from the test booklet to the answer sheet.

Be sure to bring food and drink to the test site. You will not be allowed to leave to obtain sustenance. Your food and drink will be stored against one wall of the testing room. You can eat and drink at any time, but only against that wall. Be sure to bring any medications or other essential items, but leave all things electronic at home or in your car. Wear a watch, but make sure it is not a programmable one. Bring pencils, a manual sharpener, and an eraser.

If English is not your first language, you can register for one of several other language versions of the exam. Or, if you choose to use the English version of the exam, a translation dictionary is allowed. You must be able to prove that you need such a dictionary; this is usually accomplished with your birth certificate or your passport.

> Occasionally, small changes are made to the exam or exam objectives. When that happens, Sybex will post updates to its web site. Visit www.sybex.com/go/cissp5thedition before you sit for the exam to make sure you have the latest information.

## Study and Exam Preparation Tips

We recommend planning for a month or so of nightly intensive study for the CISSP exam. Here are some suggestions to maximize your learning time; you can modify them as necessary based on your own learning habits:

- Take one or two evenings to read each chapter in this book and work through its review material.

- Take all the practice exams provided in the book and on the CD. Complete the written labs from each chapter, and use the review questions for each chapter to help guide you to topics where more study or time spent working through key concepts and strategies might be beneficial.

- Review the (ISC)²'s study guide from www.isc2.org.

- Use the flashcards found on the CD to reinforce your understanding of concepts.

> We recommend spending about half of your study time reading and reviewing concepts and the other half taking practice exams. Students have reported that the more time they spent taking practice exams, the better they retained test topics. You might also consider visiting resources such as www.cccure.org, www.cissp.com, and other CISSP-focused websites.

## Completing the Certification Process

Once you have been informed that you successfully passed the CISSP certification, there is one final step before you are actually awarded the CISSP certification. That final step is known as *endorsement*. Basically, this involves getting someone familiar with your work history to sign and submit an endorsement form on your behalf. The endorsement form is sent to you as an attachment to the email notifying you of your achievement in passing the exam. Simply send the form to a CISSP in good standing along with your resume. The endorser must review your resume, ensure that you have sufficient experience in the 10 CISSP domains, and then submit the signed form to (ISC)² via fax or post mail. You must have submitted the endorsement files to (ISC)² within 90 days after receiving the confirmation of passing email. Once (ISC)² receives your endorsement form, the certification process will be completed and you will be sent a welcome packet via post mail.

If you happen to fail the exam, you may take the exam a second time as soon as you can find another open slot in a testing location. However, you will need to pay full price for your second attempt. In the unlikely case you need to test a third time, (ISC)² requires that you wait six months.

## Post-CISSP Concentrations

(ISC)² has added three concentrations to its certification lineup. These concentrations are offered only to CISSP certificate holders. The (ISC)² has taken the concepts introduced on the CISSP exam and focused on specific areas, namely, architecture, management, and engineering. These three concentrations are as follows:

**Information Systems Security Architecture Professional (ISSAP)**   Aimed at those who specialize in information security architecture. Key domains covered here include access control systems and methodology; cryptography; physical security integration; requirements analysis and security standards, guidelines, and criteria; technology-related aspects of business continuity planning and disaster recovery planning; and telecommunications and network security. This is a credential for those who design security systems or infrastructure or for those who audit and analyze such structures.

**Information Systems Security Management Professional (ISSMP)**   Aimed at those who focus on management of information security policies, practices, principles, and procedures. Key domains covered here include enterprise security management practices; enterprise-wide system development security; law, investigations, forensics, and ethics; oversight for operations security compliance; and understanding business continuity planning, disaster recovery planning, and continuity of operations planning. This is a credential for those professionals who are responsible for security infrastructures, particularly where mandated compliance comes into the picture.

**Information Systems Security Engineering Professional (ISSEP)**   Aimed at those who focus on the design and engineering of secure hardware and software information systems, components, or applications. Key domains covered include certification and accreditation, systems security engineering, technical management, and U.S. government information assurance rules and regulations. Most ISSEPs work for the U.S. government or for a government contractor that manages government security clearances.

For more details about these concentration exams and certifications, please see the (ISC)² website at www.isc2.org.

# Notes on This Book's Organization

This book is designed to cover each of the 10 CISSP Common Body of Knowledge domains in sufficient depth to provide you with a clear understanding of the material. The main body of this book comprises 19 chapters. The first nine domains are each covered by two chapters, and the final domain (Physical Security) is covered in Chapter 19. The domain/chapter breakdown is as follows:

**Chapters 1 and 2**   Access Control

**Chapters 3 and 4**   Telecommunications and Network Security

**Chapters 5 and 6**   Information Security Governance and Risk Management

**Chapters 7 and 8**   Application Development Security

**Chapters 9 and 10**   Cryptography

**Chapters 11 and 12**   Security Architecture and Design

**Chapters 13 and 14**   Operations Security

**Chapters 15 and 16**   Business Continuity and Disaster Recovery Planning

**Chapters 17 and 18**   Legal, Regulations, Investigations, and Compliance

**Chapter 19**   Physical (Environmental) Security

Each chapter includes elements to help you focus your studies and test your knowledge, detailed in the following sections.

## The Elements of This Study Guide

You'll see many recurring elements as you read through this study guide. Here's a description of some of those elements:

**Key Terms and Glossary**   In every chapter, we've identified *key terms,* which are important for you to know. You'll also find these key terms and their definitions in the Glossary. Note that the Glossary is included as a PDF on the Companion CD.

**Summaries**   The summary is a brief review of the chapter to sum up what was covered.

**Exam Essentials**   The Exam Essentials highlight topics that could appear on one or both of the exams in some form. While we obviously do not know exactly what will be included in a particular exam, this section reinforces significant concepts that are key to understanding the body of knowledge area and the test specs for the CISSP exam.

**Chapter Review Questions**   Each chapter includes practice questions that have been designed to measure your knowledge of key ideas that were discussed in the chapter. After you finish each chapter, answer the questions; if some of your answers are incorrect, it's an indication that you need to spend some more time studying that topic. The answers to the practice questions can be found at the end of the chapter.

**Written Labs**   Each chapter includes written labs that synthesize various concepts and topics that appear in the chapter. These raise questions that are designed to help you put together various pieces you've encountered individually in the chapter and assemble them to propose or describe potential security strategies or solutions.

**Real World Scenarios**   As you work through each chapter, you'll find at least two descriptions of typical and plausible workplace situations where an understanding of the security strategies and approaches relevant to the chapter content could play a role in fixing problems or in fending off potential difficulties. This gives readers a chance to see how specific security policies, guidelines, or practices should or may be applied to the workplace.

## What's on the CD?

We worked really hard to provide some essential tools to help you with your certification process. All of the following gear should be loaded on your workstation when studying for the test.

## The Sybex Test Preparation Software

The test preparation software, made by experts at Sybex, prepares you for the CISSP exam. In this test engine, you will find all the review and assessment questions from the book, plus additional bonus exams that appear exclusively on the CD. You can take the assessment test, test yourself by chapter, take the practice exams, or take a randomly generated exam comprising all the questions.

## Electronic Flashcards

Sybex's electronic flashcards include hundreds of questions designed to challenge you further for the CISSP exam. Between the review questions, practice exams, and flashcards, you'll have more than enough practice for the exam!

## *CISSP Study Guide* in PDF

Sybex offers the *CISSP Study Guide* in PDF format on the CD so you can read the book on your PC or laptop. So if you travel and don't want to carry a book, or if you just like to read from the computer screen, Adobe Acrobat is also included on the CD.

## Bonus Exams

Sybex includes bonus exams on the CD, each comprising questions meant to survey your understanding of key elements in the CISSP CBK.

# How to Use This Book and CD

This book has a number of features designed to guide your study efforts for the CISSP certification exam. It assists you by listing at the beginning of each chapter the CISSP body of knowledge domain topics covered in the chapter and by ensuring that each topic is fully discussed within the chapter. The practice questions at the end of each chapter and the practice exams on the CD are designed to test your retention of the material you've read to make you aware of areas in which you should spend additional study time. Here are some suggestions for using this book and CD:

- Take the assessment test before you start reading the material. This will give you an idea of the areas in which you need to spend additional study time as well as those areas in which you may just need a brief refresher.

- Answer the review questions after you've read each chapter; if you answer any incorrectly, go back to the chapter and review the topic, or utilize one of the additional resources if you need more information.

- Download the flashcards to your handheld device, and review them when you have a few minutes during the day.

- Take every opportunity to test yourself. In addition to the assessment test and review questions, there are bonus exams on the CD. Take these exams without referring to the chapters and see how well you've done—go back and review any topics you've missed until you fully understand and can apply the concepts.

Finally, find a study partner if possible. Studying for, and taking, the exam with someone else will make the process more enjoyable, and you'll have someone to help you understand topics that are difficult for you. You'll also be able to reinforce your own knowledge by helping your study partner in areas where they are weak.

# Assessment Test

1. Which of the following type of access control seeks to discover evidence of unwanted, unauthorized, or illicit behavior or activity?

   **A.** Preventive

   **B.** Deterrent

   **C.** Detective

   **D.** Corrective

2. Define and detail the aspects of password selection that distinguish good password choices from ultimately poor password choices.

   **A.** Difficult to guess or unpredictable

   **B.** Meet minimum length requirements

   **C.** Meet specific complexity requirements

   **D.** All of the above

3. Which of the following is most likely to detect DoS attacks?

   **A.** Host-based IDS

   **B.** Network-based IDS

   **C.** Vulnerability scanner

   **D.** Penetration testing

4. Which of the following is considered a denial-of-service attack?

   **A.** Pretending to be a technical manager over the phone and asking a receptionist to change their password

   **B.** While surfing the Web, sending to a web server a malformed URL that causes the system to consume 100 percent of the CPU

   **C.** Intercepting network traffic by copying the packets as they pass through a specific subnet

   **D.** Sending message packets to a recipient who did not request them simply to be annoying

5. At which layer of the OSI model does a router operate?

   **A.** Network layer

   **B.** Layer 1

   **C.** Transport layer

   **D.** Layer 5

6. Which type of firewall automatically adjusts its filtering rules based on the content of the traffic of existing sessions?

   **A.** Static packet filtering

   **B.** Application-level gateway

   **C.** Stateful inspection

   **D.** Dynamic packet filtering

7. A VPN can be established over which of the following?

   **A.** Wireless LAN connection

   **B.** Remote access dial-up connection

   **C.** WAN link

   **D.** All of the above

8. Email is the most common delivery vehicle for which of the following?

   **A.** Viruses

   **B.** Worms

   **C.** Trojan horse

   **D.** All of the above

9. The CIA Triad comprises what elements?

   **A.** Contiguousness, interoperable, arranged

   **B.** Authentication, authorization, accountability

   **C.** Capable, available, integral

   **D.** Availability, confidentiality, integrity

10. Which of the following is not a required component in the support of accountability?

   **A.** Auditing

   **B.** Privacy

   **C.** Authentication

   **D.** Authorization

11. Which of the following is not a defense against collusion?

   **A.** Separation of duties

   **B.** Restricted job responsibilities

   **C.** Group user accounts

   **D.** Job rotation

12. A data custodian is responsible for securing resources after _____ has assigned the resource a security label.

    **A.** Senior management

    **B.** Data owner

    **C.** Auditor

    **D.** Security staff

13. In what phase of the Capability Maturity Model for Software (SW-CMM) are quantitative measures utilized to gain a detailed understanding of the software development process?

    **A.** Repeatable

    **B.** Defined

    **C.** Managed

    **D.** Optimizing

14. Which one of the following is a layer of the ring protection scheme that is not normally implemented in practice?

    **A.** Layer 0

    **B.** Layer 1

    **C.** Layer 3

    **D.** Layer 4

15. What is the last phase of the TCP/IP three-way handshake sequence?

    **A.** SYN packet

    **B.** ACK packet

    **C.** NAK packet

    **D.** SYN/ACK packet

16. Which one of the following vulnerabilities would best be countered by adequate parameter checking?

    **A.** Time-of-check-to-time-of-use

    **B.** Buffer overflow

    **C.** SYN flood

    **D.** Distributed denial of service

**17.** What is the value of the logical operation shown here?

```
X:        0 1 1 0 1 0
Y:        0 0 1 1 0 1
_____

X ∨ Y:      ?
```

   **A.** 0 1 1 1 1 1
   **B.** 0 1 1 0 1 0
   **C.** 0 0 1 0 0 0
   **D.** 0 0 1 1 0 1

**18.** In what type of cipher are the letters of the plain-text message rearranged to form the cipher text?

   **A.** Substitution cipher
   **B.** Block cipher
   **C.** Transposition cipher
   **D.** One-time pad

**19.** What is the length of a message digest produced by the MD5 algorithm?

   **A.** 64 bits
   **B.** 128 bits
   **C.** 256 bits
   **D.** 384 bits

**20.** If Renee receives a digitally signed message from Mike, what key does she use to verify that the message truly came from Mike?

   **A.** Renee's public key
   **B.** Renee's private key
   **C.** Mike's public key
   **D.** Mike's private key

**21.** Which of the following statements is true?

   **A.** The less complex a system, the more vulnerabilities it has.
   **B.** The more complex a system, the less assurance it provides.
   **C.** The less complex a system, the less trust it provides.
   **D.** The more complex a system, the less attack surface it generates.

**22.** Ring 0, from the design architecture security mechanism known as protection rings, can also be referred to as all but which of the following:

  **A.** Privileged mode

  **B.** Supervisory mode

  **C.** System mode

  **D.** User mode

**23.** Which of the following is not a composition theory related to security models?

  **A.** Cascading

  **B.** Feedback

  **C.** Iterative

  **D.** Hookup

**24.** The collection of components in the TCB that work together to implement reference monitor functions is called the _____.

  **A.** Security perimeter

  **B.** Security kernel

  **C.** Access matrix

  **D.** Constrained interface

**25.** Audit trails, logs, CCTV, intrusion detection systems, antivirus software, penetration testing, password crackers, performance monitoring, and cyclic redundancy checks (CRCs) are examples of what?

  **A.** Directive controls

  **B.** Preventive controls

  **C.** Detective controls

  **D.** Corrective controls

**26.** System architecture, system integrity, covert channel analysis, trusted facility management, and trusted recovery are elements of what security criteria?

  **A.** Quality assurance

  **B.** Operational assurance

  **C.** Life cycle assurance

  **D.** Quantity assurance

**27.** Which of the following is a procedure designed to test and perhaps bypass a system's security controls?

  **A.** Logging usage data

  **B.** War dialing

  **C.** Penetration testing

  **D.** Deploying secured desktop workstations

**28.** Auditing is a required factor to sustain and enforce what?

    **A.** Accountability

    **B.** Confidentiality

    **C.** Accessibility

    **D.** Redundancy

**29.** What is the formula used to compute the ALE?

    **A.** ALE = AV * EF * ARO

    **B.** ALE = ARO * EF

    **C.** ALE = AV * ARO

    **D.** ALE = EF * ARO

**30.** What is the first step of the business impact assessment process?

    **A.** Identification of priorities

    **B.** Likelihood assessment

    **C.** Risk identification

    **D.** Resource prioritization

**31.** Which of the following represent natural events that can pose a threat or risk to an organization?

    **A.** Earthquake

    **B.** Flood

    **C.** Tornado

    **D.** All of the above

**32.** What kind of recovery facility enables an organization to resume operations as quickly as possible, if not immediately upon failure of the primary facility?

    **A.** Hot site

    **B.** Warm site

    **C.** Cold site

    **D.** All of the above

**33.** What form of intellectual property is used to protect words, slogans, and logos?

    **A.** Patent

    **B.** Copyright

    **C.** Trademark

    **D.** Trade secret

**34.** What type of evidence refers to written documents that are brought into court to prove a fact?

   **A.**  Best evidence

   **B.**  Payroll evidence

   **C.**  Documentary evidence

   **D.**  Testimonial evidence

**35.** Why are military and intelligence attacks among the most serious computer crimes?

   **A.**  The use of information obtained can have far-reaching detrimental strategic effects on national interests in an enemy's hands.

   **B.**  Military information is stored on secure machines, so a successful attack can be embarrassing.

   **C.**  The long-term political use of classified information can impact a country's leadership.

   **D.**  The military and intelligence agencies have ensured that the laws protecting their information are the most severe.

**36.** What type of detected incident allows the most time for an investigation?

   **A.**  Compromise

   **B.**  Denial of service

   **C.**  Malicious code

   **D.**  Scanning

**37.** If you want to restrict access into or out of a facility, which would you choose?

   **A.**  Gate

   **B.**  Turnstile

   **C.**  Fence

   **D.**  Mantrap

**38.** What is the point of a secondary verification system?

   **A.**  To verify the identity of a user

   **B.**  To verify the activities of a user

   **C.**  To verify the completeness of a system

   **D.**  To verify the correctness of a system

# Answers to Assessment Test

1.  C. Detective access controls are used to discover (and document) unwanted or unauthorized activity. For more information, please see Chapter 1.

2.  D. Strong password choices are difficult to guess, unpredictable, and of specified minimum lengths to ensure that password entries cannot be computationally determined. They may be randomly generated and utilize all the alphabetic, numeric, and punctuation characters; they should never be written down or shared; they should not be stored in publicly accessible or generally readable locations; and they shouldn't be transmitted in the clear. For more information, please see Chapter 1.

3.  B. Network-based IDSs are usually able to detect the initiation of an attack or the ongoing attempts to perpetrate an attack (including DoS). They are, however, unable to provide information about whether an attack was successful or which specific systems, user accounts, files, or applications were affected. Host-based IDSs have some difficulty with detecting and tracking down DoS attacks. Vulnerability scanners don't detect DoS attacks; they test for possible vulnerabilities. Penetration testing may cause a DoS or test for DoS vulnerabilities, but it is not a detection tool. For more information, please see Chapter 2.

4.  B. Not all instances of DoS are the result of a malicious attack. Errors in coding OSs, services, and applications have resulted in DoS conditions. Some examples of this include a process failing to release control of the CPU or a service consuming system resources out of proportion to the service requests it is handling. Social engineering and sniffing are typically not considered DoS attacks. For more information, please see Chapter 2.

5.  A. Network hardware devices, including routers, function at layer 3, the Network layer. For more information, please see Chapter 3.

6.  D. Dynamic packet-filtering firewalls enable the real-time modification of the filtering rules based on traffic content. For more information, please see Chapter 3.

7.  D. A VPN link can be established over any other network communication connection. This could be a typical LAN cable connection, a wireless LAN connection, a remote access dial-up connection, a WAN link, or even an Internet connection used by a client for access to the office LAN. For more information, please see Chapter 4.

8.  D. Email is the most common delivery mechanism for viruses, worms, Trojan horses, documents with destructive macros, and other malicious code. For more information, please see Chapter 4.

9.  D. The components of the CIA Triad are confidentiality, availability, and integrity. For more information, please see Chapter 5.

10. B. Privacy is not necessary to provide accountability. For more information, please see Chapter 5.

11. C. Group user accounts allow for multiple people to log in under a single user account. This allows collusion because it prevents individual accountability. For more information, please see Chapter 6.

**12.** B. The data owner must first assign a security label to a resource before the data custodian can secure the resource appropriately. For more information, please see Chapter 6.

**13.** C. The Managed phase of the SW-CMM involves the use of quantitative development metrics. The Software Engineering Institute (SEI) defines the key process areas for this level as Quantitative Process Management and Software Quality Management. For more information, please see Chapter 7.

**14.** B. Layers 1 and 2 contain device drivers but are not normally implemented in practice. Layer 0 always contains the security kernel. Layer 3 contains user applications. Layer 4 does not exist. For more information, please see Chapter 7.

**15.** B. The SYN packet is first sent from the initiating host to the destination host. The destination host then responds with a SYN/ACK packet. The initiating host sends an ACK packet, and the connection is then established. For more information, please see Chapter 8.

**16.** B. Parameter checking is used to prevent the possibility of buffer-overflow attacks. For more information, please see Chapter 8.

**17.** A. The ∨ symbol represents the OR function, which is true when one or both of the input bits are true. For more information, please see Chapter 9.

**18.** C. Transposition ciphers use an encryption algorithm to rearrange the letters of the plaintext message to form a cipher-text message. For more information, please see Chapter 9.

**19.** B. The MD5 algorithm produces a 128-bit message digest for any input. For more information, please see Chapter 10.

**20.** C. Any recipient can use Mike's public key to verify the authenticity of the digital signature. For more information, please see Chapter 10.

**21.** B. The more complex a system, the less assurance it provides. More complexity means more areas for vulnerabilities exist and more areas must be secured against threats. More vulnerabilities and more threats mean that the subsequent security provided by the system is less trustworthy. For more information, please see Chapter 11.

**22.** D. Ring 0 has direct access to the most resources, thus user mode is not an appropriate label because user mode requires restrictions to limit access to resources. For more information, please see Chapter 11.

**23.** C. Iterative is not one of the composition theories related to security models. Cascading, feedback, and hookup are the three composition theories. For more information, please see Chapter 12.

**24.** B. The collection of components in the TCB that work together to implement reference monitor functions is called the security kernel. For more information, please see Chapter 12.

**25.** C. Examples of detective controls are audit trails, logs, CCTV, intrusion detection systems, antivirus software, penetration testing, password crackers, performance monitoring, and CRCs. For more information, please see Chapter 13.

26. B. Assurance is the degree of confidence you can place in the satisfaction of security needs of a computer, network, solution, and so on. Operational assurance focuses on the basic features and architecture of a system that lend themselves to supporting security. For more information, please see Chapter 13.

27. C. Penetration testing is the attempt to bypass security controls to test overall system security. For more information, please see Chapter 14.

28. A. Auditing is a required factor to sustain and enforce accountability. For more information, please see Chapter 14.

29. A. The annualized loss expectancy (ALE) is computed as the product of the asset value (AV) times the exposure factor (EF) times the annualized rate of occurrence (ARO). This is the longer form of the formula ALE = SLE * ARO. The other formulas displayed here do not accurately reflect this calculation. For more information, please see Chapter 15.

30. A. Identification of priorities is the first step of the business impact assessment process. For more information, please see Chapter 15.

31. D. Natural events that can threaten organizations include earthquakes, floods, hurricanes, tornados, wildfires, and other acts of nature as well. Thus options A, B, and C are correct because they are natural and not man made. For more information, please see Chapter 16.

32. A. Hot sites provide backup facilities maintained in constant working order and fully capable of taking over business operations. Warm sites consist of preconfigured hardware and software to run the business, neither of which possesses the vital business information. Cold sites are simply facilities designed with power and environmental support systems but no configured hardware, software, or services. Disaster recovery services can facilitate and implement any of these sites on behalf of a company. For more information, please see Chapter 16.

33. C. Trademarks are used to protect the words, slogans, and logos that represent a company and its products or services. For more information, please see Chapter 17.

34. C. Written documents brought into court to prove the facts of a case are referred to as documentary evidence. For more information, please see Chapter 17.

35. A. The purpose of a military and intelligence attack is to acquire classified information. The detrimental effect of using such information could be nearly unlimited in the hands of an enemy. Attacks of this type are launched by very sophisticated attackers. It is often very difficult to ascertain what documents were successfully obtained. So when a breach of this type occurs, you sometimes cannot know the full extent of the damage. For more information, please see Chapter 18.

36. D. Scanning incidents are generally reconnaissance attacks. The real damage to a system comes in the subsequent attacks, so you may have some time to react if you detect the scanning attack early. For more information, please see Chapter 18.

**37.** B.  A turnstile is a form of gate that prevents more than one person from gaining entry at a time and often restricts movement to one direction. It is used to gain entry but not exit, or vice versa. For more information, please see Chapter 19.

**38.** D.  Secondary verification mechanisms are set in place to establish a means of verifying the correctness of detection systems and sensors. This often means combining several types of sensors or systems (CCTV, heat and motion sensors, and so on) to provide a more complete picture of detected events. For more information, please see Chapter 19.

# Chapter

# 1

# Accountability and Access Control

---

## THE CISSP EXAM TOPICS COVERED IN THIS CHAPTER INCLUDE:

✓ **Access Control**

  ▪ Control access by applying the following concepts/methodology/techniques:

    ▪ Policies; types of controls (e.g., preventative, detective, corrective); techniques (e.g., nondiscretionary, discretionary and mandatory); identification and authentication; decentralized/distributed access control techniques; authorization mechanisms; logging and monitoring

The Access Control domain in the Common Body of Knowledge (CBK) for the CISSP certification exam deals with topics and issues related to monitoring, identifying, and authorizing or restricting user access to resources. Generally, an *access control* is any hardware, software, or organizational administrative policy or procedure that grants or restricts access, monitors and records attempts to access, identifies users attempting to access, and determines whether access is authorized.

In this chapter and in Chapter 2, "Attacks and Monitoring," we discuss the Access Control domain. Be sure to read and study the materials from both chapters to ensure complete coverage of the essential material for this domain of the CISSP certification exam. We've called this chapter "Accountability and Access Control" because accountability and access control are interrelated concepts and share overlapping principles even though CISSP course materials reference only access control.

# Access Control Overview

Controlling access to resources is one of the central themes of security. Access control addresses more than just controlling which users can access which files or services. Access control is about the relationships between subjects and objects. The transfer of information from an object to a subject is called *access*. However, access is not just a logical or technical concept: Don't forget about the physical realm where access can involve disclosure, use, or proximity. A basic principle of access control is to deny access by default if access is not granted explicitly to a subject.

Subjects are active entities that, through the exercise of access, seek information about or data from passive entities, or objects. A *subject* can be a user, program, process, file, computer, database, and so on. An *object* can be a file, database, computer, program, process, file, printer, storage media, and so on. The subject is always the *entity* that receives information about or data from the object. The subject is also the entity that alters information about or data stored within the object. The object is always the entity that provides or hosts information or data. The roles of subject and object can switch back and forth while two entities, such as a program and a database or a process and a file, interact to accomplish a task. For example, when a program interacts with a database, the program begins as the subject and the database as the object when the program passes a query to the database. But when the database posts a reply to the program, the roles reverse because the database generates data that it returns to the program.

# Types of Access Control

Access controls are necessary to protect the *confidentiality*, *integrity*, and *availability* of objects (and by extension, their information and data). Taken together, these three essential security principles are known as the CIA Triad. Confidentiality addresses access control in the sense that it ensures that only authorized subjects can access objects. Integrity addresses the preservation of information in that unauthorized or unwanted changes to objects are denied (and checked). Availability addresses the ability to obtain access within a reasonable amount of time upon request, in the sense that authorized requests for objects must be granted as quickly as system and network parameters allow. The term *access control* describes a broad range of controls, from forcing a user to provide a valid username and password to log on to preventing users from gaining access to a resource outside their sphere of access.

Access controls can be divided into the following seven categories of function or purpose. You should notice that some security mechanisms may acquire labels from multiple categories. Thus, for example, a fence can be both a preventive control and a deterrent control.

**Preventive access control**   A preventive access control (sometimes called a preventative access control in CISSP materials) is deployed to stop unwanted or unauthorized activity from occurring. Examples of preventive access controls include fences, locks, biometrics, mantraps, lighting, alarm systems, separation of duties, job rotation, data classification, penetration testing, access control methods, encryption, auditing, presence of security cameras or closed circuit television (CCTV), smart cards, callback, security policies, security awareness training, and antivirus software.

**Deterrent access control**   A deterrent access control is deployed to discourage violation of security policies. Deterrent controls pick up where prevention leaves off. A deterrent doesn't stop with trying to prevent an action; instead, it goes further to exact consequences in the event of an attempted or successful violation. Examples of deterrent access controls include locks, fences, security badges, security guards, mantraps, security cameras, trespass or intrusion alarms, separation of duties, work task procedures, awareness training, encryption, auditing, and firewalls.

Notice that *fences* (among others) are both preventive and deterrent access controls. This is true for many security items that appear in more than one category. For example, an 8-foot perimeter fence acts as a preventive access control by restricting open access and deters anyone without adequate means from scaling up and over it.

**Detective access control**   A detective access control is deployed to discover unwanted or unauthorized activity. Often detective controls operate after the fact rather than in real time. Examples of detective access controls include security guards, guard dogs, motion detectors, recording and reviewing of events captured by security cameras or CCTV, job rotation, mandatory vacations, audit trails, honeypots or honeynets, intrusion detection systems, violation reports, supervision and reviews of users, incident investigations, and intrusion prevention systems.

**Corrective access control**   A corrective access control is deployed to restore systems to normal after an unwanted or unauthorized activity has occurred. Usually corrective controls are simple, such as terminating access or rebooting a system. Corrective controls have only minimal capability to respond to access violations. Examples of corrective access controls include intrusion detection systems, antivirus solutions, alarms, mantraps, business continuity planning, and security policies.

**Recovery access control**   A recovery access control is deployed to repair or restore resources, functions, and capabilities after a violation of security policies. Recovery controls have more advanced or complex abilities to respond to access violations than corrective access controls. For example, recovery access can repair damage as well as prevent further damage. Examples of recovery access controls include backups and restores, fault-tolerant drive systems, server clustering, antivirus software, and database or virtual machine shadowing.

**Compensation access control**   A compensation access control is deployed to provide various options to other existing controls to aid in enforcement and support of security policy. Examples of compensation access controls include security policy requirements or criteria, personnel supervision, monitoring, and work task procedures.

Compensation controls can also include controls used instead of more desirable or damaging controls. For example, if a guard dog cannot be deployed owing to proximity of a residential area, a motion detector with a spotlight and a barking sound playback device can be used instead.

**Directive access control**   A directive access control is deployed to direct, confine, or control the actions of subjects to force or encourage compliance with security policies. Examples of directive access controls include security guards, guard dogs, security policy requirements or criteria, posted notifications, escape route exit signs, monitoring, supervision, work task procedures, and awareness training.

Access controls can be further categorized by how they are implemented. Where matters of implementation are concerned, the related categories are administrative, logical/technical, and physical:

**Administrative access controls**   Administrative access controls are the policies and procedures defined by an organization's security policy to implement and enforce overall access control. Administrative access controls focus on two areas: personnel and business practices (for example, people and policies). Examples of administrative access controls include policies, procedures, hiring practices, background checks, data classification, security training, vacation history, reviews, work supervision, personnel controls, and testing.

**Logical/technical access controls**   Logical access controls and technical access controls are the hardware or software mechanisms used to manage access to resources and systems and also provide protection for those resources and systems. Examples of logical or technical access controls include encryption, smart cards, passwords, biometrics, constrained interfaces, access control lists (ACLs), protocols, firewalls, routers, intrusion detection systems, and clipping levels.

 We use the words *logical* and *technical* interchangeably within this concept.

**Physical access controls**   Physical access controls are physical barriers deployed to prevent direct contact with systems or areas within a facility. Examples of physical access controls include guards, fences, motion detectors, locked doors, sealed windows, lights, cable protection, laptop locks, swipe cards, guard dogs, video cameras, mantraps, and alarms.

## Access Control in a Layered Environment

No single access control mechanism is ever deployed on its own. In fact, combining various types of access controls is the only means by which a reasonably secure environment can be developed. Often multiple layers or levels of access controls are deployed to provide layered security, or defense in depth.

This idea is depicted using concentric circles of protection, which surround your assets and resources with logical circles of security protection. Thus, intruders or attackers need to overcome multiple layers of defense to reach protected assets. Layered security, or defense in depth, is considered a more logical approach to security than a traditional fortress mentality. In a fortress mentality, a single giant master wall is built around the assets, like the massive rock walls of a castle. The major flaw in such an approach is that large massive structures often have minor weakness and flaws; are difficult if not impossible to reconfigure, adjust, or move; and are easily seen and avoided by would-be attackers (in other words, they find easier ways into protected areas).

In a *layered security* (or *defense-in-depth*) deployment, your assets are surrounded by a layer of protection provided for by administrative access controls, which in turn is surrounded by a layer of protection consisting of logical or technical access controls, which is finally surrounded by a layer of protection that includes physical access controls. This concept of defense in depth highlights two important points. First, an organization's security policy ultimately provides the first or innermost layer of defense for your assets. Without a security policy, there is no real security that can be trusted. Security policies are one element of administrative access controls. Second, people are your last line of defense. People or personnel are the other focus for administrative access control. Only with proper training and education can your personnel implement, comply with, and support security elements defined in your security policy.

# The Process of Accountability

One important purpose of security is to be able to hold people accountable for activities that their online personae (in other words, their user accounts) perform within the digital world of a computer network. The first step in this process is identifying the subject. In fact, several steps lead up to the ability to hold a person accountable for online actions: identification, authentication, authorization, auditing, and accountability.

## Identification

*Identification* is the process by which a subject professes an identity and accountability is initiated. A user provides a username, a logon ID, a personal identification number (PIN), or a smart card to represent an identification process. Providing a process ID number also represents an identification process. Once a subject has identified itself, the claimed identity becomes accountable for any further actions undertaken by that subject. Information technology (IT) systems track activity by identities, not by subjects themselves. A computer doesn't know one human from another, but it does know that your user account is different from all other user accounts.

## Authentication

*Authentication* is the process of verifying or testing that a claimed identity is valid. Authentication requires that a subject provide additional information that must correspond exactly to the identity professed. The most common form of authentication is a password, which is the first of three information factors ("something you know") used for authentication:

**Type 1**   A Type 1 authentication factor is *something you know.* It is any string of characters you have memorized and can reproduce on a keyboard when prompted. Examples include a password, PIN, lock combination, passphrase, mother's maiden name, and so on.

**Type 2**   A Type 2 authentication factor is *something you have.* It is a physical device that you possess and must have on your person at the time of authentication. Examples include a smart card, token device, memory card, USB drive, and so on. This can also include your physical location, referred to as the *somewhere you are* factor.

> The main difference between a memory card and a smart card is that a memory card is used only to store information, while a smart card has the ability to process data. We'll discuss these security methods in more detail in Chapter 19, "Physical Security Requirements."

**Type 3**   A Type 3 authentication factor is *something you are.* It is a body part or a physical characteristic of your person. Examples of this factor include fingerprints, voice prints, retina patterns, iris patterns, face shapes, palm topology, hand geometry, and so on. This factor is often labeled as a *biometric*, or a *biometric factor*. (We discuss these in more detail shortly.)

Each type of authentication factor is roughly the same in terms of the level of security provided in that only a single attack must succeed to overcome any single such factor. However, by number, each type is more secure than the one before it. For instance, a Type 3 factor is the most difficult to breach of the three just described. Nevertheless, a biometric factor may be overcome by creating a fake duplicate (like a gummi fingerprint). A Type 2 factor, the next most difficult to breach, can be overcome by physical theft, and a Type 1 factor can be overcome by a password attack. As you can see, a Type 3 factor is slightly more secure than a Type 2 factor, which is in turn more secure than a Type 1 factor.

These three basic factors ("something you know," "something you have," and "something you are") are the most common elements in a fully functional security system. However, a few other factors also apply to the same security scenario in different ways, and with very different implications.

## "Something" and "Somewhere"

In addition to these three commonly recognized factors, there are at least two others. One is *something you do,* such as writing a signature, typing a passphrase (keyboard dynamics), or speaking a phrase. Something you do is often included in the "something you are," or Type 3, category.

Another factor, mentioned earlier, is *somewhere you are,* such as the computer terminal from which you log in or the phone number (identified by caller ID) or country (identified by your IP address) from whence you connect. Controlling access by physical location forces a subject to be present rather than connecting remotely. "Somewhere you are" is often included in the "something you have," or Type 2, category.

## Logical Location

Logical location can combine the ideas of "somewhere you are," "something you have," and "something you know." A *logical location* access control restricts access based upon some form of logical identification, such as IP address, MAC address, client type, or protocol used. However, please note that logical location control should not be the only factor used because any type of address information can be spoofed using hacking tools.

Access can further be restricted to date and time of day or by transaction type. The former prevents access except within defined time periods. The latter is a content- or context-dependent control where access is dynamic based on transactions a subject wants to complete.

## Multiple-Factor Authentication

*Two-factor authentication* occurs when two different factors are required to provide authentication. For example, when using a debit card at the grocery store, you must usually swipe the card ("something you have") and enter a PIN ("something you know") to complete the transaction. Strong authentication is simply any authentication that requires two or more factors, but these are not necessarily factors of different types. As a general rule, when factors of different types are combined, the resultant authentication is more secure.

The concept behind two-factor authentication is that when two of the same factors are used together, the strength of the system is no greater than it would be if just one of the factors was used alone. More specifically, the same attack that could steal or obtain one instance of the factor could obtain all instances of the factor. For example, using two passwords together is no more secure than using a single password because a password-cracking attempt could discover both in a single successful attack. However, when two or more different factors are employed, two or more different types or methods of attack must succeed to collect all relevant authentication elements. For example, if a token, a password, and a biometric factor are all used for authentication, then a physical theft, a password crack, and a biometric duplication attack must all succeed simultaneously to gain entry into the system.

Once logon credentials of a proffered identity and its authentication factor(s) are supplied to a system, they are checked against a database of identities on that system. If an identity is located and correct authentication factor(s) supplied, the subject is authenticated.

## Authorization

Once a subject is authenticated, its access must be *authorized*. The process of authorization ensures that the requested activity or object access is possible given the rights and privileges assigned to the authenticated identity (which we refer to as the *subject* from this point forward). Authorization indicates who is trusted to perform specific operations. In most cases, the system evaluates an access control matrix that compares the subject, the object, and the intended activity (we discuss the access control matrix in greater detail in Chapter 11, "Principles of Computer Design"). If the specific action is allowed, the subject is authorized; if disallowed, the subject is not authorized.

Keep in mind that just because a subject has been identified and authenticated, that does not automatically mean it has been authorized. It is possible for a subject to log onto a network (in other words, be identified and authenticated) yet be blocked from accessing a file or printing to a printer (in other words, by not being authorized to perform such activities). Most network users are authorized to perform only a limited number of activities on a specific collection of resources. Identification and authentication are "all-or-nothing" aspects of access control. Authorization occupies a wide range of variations between all and nothing for each individual subject or object within the environment. For example, a user may be able to read a file but not delete it. A user may be able to print a document but not alter the print queue. A user may be able to log onto a system but not be allowed to access any resources.

It is important to understand the differences between identification, authentication, and authorization. Although they are similar and are essential to all security mechanisms, they are distinct and must not be confused.

## Auditing and Accountability

*Auditing* is the process by which online activities of user accounts and processes are tracked and recorded. Auditing produces audit trails. Audit trails can be used to reconstruct events and to verify whether a security policy or authorization was violated. When contents of audit trails are compared with authorization against authenticated user accounts, people associated with accounts can be held *accountable* for their online actions.

According to the National Institute of Standards and Technology (NIST) in its Minimum Security Requirements for Federal Information and Information Systems (FIPS 200), audit data recording must comply with the following requirements:

- Create, protect, and retain information system audit records to the extent needed to enable the monitoring, analysis, investigation, and reporting of unlawful, unauthorized, or inappropriate information system activity.

- Ensure that the actions of individual information system users can be uniquely traced to those users so they can be held accountable for their actions.

An earlier standard promulgated by NIST (NISTIR5153) is now superseded by the preceding document, but it spells these requirements out in more (and more useful) detail:

- The system shall provide a mechanism for generating a security audit trail that contains information to support after-the-fact investigation of loss or impropriety and appropriate management response.

- The system shall provide end-to-end user accountability for all security-relevant events.

- The system shall protect the security audit trail from unauthorized access.

- The system shall provide a mechanism to dynamically control, during normal system operation, the types of events recorded.

- The system shall protect the audit control mechanisms from unauthorized access.

- The system shall, by default, cause a record to be written to the security audit trail for numerous specific security-related events.

- The system shall provide a privileged mechanism to enable or disable the recording of other events into the security audit trail.

- For each recorded event, the audit record shall identify several specific data points at a minimum.

- The character strings input as responses to password challenges shall not be recorded in the security audit trail.

- The audit control mechanism shall provide an option to enable or disable the recording of invalid user IDs during failed user authentication attempts.

- Audit control data (for example, audit event masks) shall survive system restarts.

- The system shall provide a mechanism for automatically copying security audit trail files to an alternative storage area after a customer-specifiable period of time.

- The system shall provide a mechanism for the automatic deletion of security audit trail files after a customer-specifiable period of time.

- The system shall allow site control of the procedure to be invoked when audit records are unable to be recorded.

- The system shall provide tools to monitor the activities (in other words, capture the keystrokes) of specific terminals or network connections in real time.

 This list is based on the NISTIR 5153 document, but we have paraphrased only a small excerpt. To view all the details see document NISTIR 5153 at http://csrc.nist.gov. You can download the FIPS 200 document from http://csrc.nist.gov/publications/fips/fips200/FIPS-200-final-march.pdf.

An organization's security policy can be properly enforced only if accountability is maintained. In other words, security can be maintained only if subjects are held accountable for their actions. Effective accountability relies on the capability to prove a subject's identity and track its activities. Thus, accountability builds on the concepts of identification, authentication, authorization, access control, and auditing.

# Identification and Authentication Techniques

Identification is a fairly straightforward concept. A subject must provide an identity to a system to start the authentication, authorization, and accountability processes. Providing an identity might entail typing a username, swiping a smart card, waving a token device, speaking a phrase, or positioning your face, hand, or finger for a camera or scanning device. Without an identity, a system has no way to correlate an authentication factor with the subject. A subject's identity is typically considered to be public information.

Authentication verifies the identity of the subject by comparing one or more factors against a database of valid identities (in other words, user accounts). The authentication factor used to verify identity is typically considered to be private information. The ability of the subject and system to maintain the secrecy of the authentication factors for identities directly reflects the level of security of that system.

Identification and authentication always occur together as a single two-step process. Providing an identity is the first step, and providing the authentication factor(s) is the second step. Without both, a subject cannot gain access to a system—neither element alone is useful.

A subject can provide several types of authentication information (for example, "something you know," "something you have," and so on). Each authentication technique or factor has its unique benefits and drawbacks. Thus, it is important to evaluate each mechanism in light of the environment in which it will be deployed to determine viability.

# Passwords

The most common authentication technique is the use of *passwords*, but they are also considered the weakest form of protection. Passwords are poor security mechanisms for several reasons:

- Users typically choose passwords that are easy to remember and therefore easy to guess or crack.

- Randomly generated passwords are hard to remember; thus, many users write them down.

- Passwords are easily shared, written down, and forgotten.

- Passwords can be stolen through many means, including observation, recording and playback, and security database theft.

- Passwords are often transmitted in clear text or with easily broken encryption protocols.

- Password databases are often stored in publicly accessible online locations.

- Short passwords can be discovered quickly in brute-force attacks.

## Password Selection

Passwords can be effective if selected intelligently and managed properly. There are two types of passwords: static and dynamic. *Static* passwords always remain the same. *Dynamic* passwords change after a specified interval of time or use. One-time passwords or single-use passwords are a variant of dynamic passwords that change every time they are used. One-time passwords are considered the strongest password type, at least in concept. Humans can't remember an infinite series of lengthy random character strings, which have only a single-attempt use before expiring. Thus, one-time passwords are often implemented with Type 2 factors using a processing device known as a *token* (we discuss tokens later in this chapter).

As the importance of maintaining security increases, so does the need to change passwords more frequently. The longer a password remains static and the more often the same password is used, the more likely it is that it will be compromised or discovered.

In some environments, initial passwords for user accounts are generated automatically. Often the generated password is a form of composition password. A *composition password* is a password constructed from two or more unrelated words joined together with a number or symbol in between. Composition passwords are easy for computers to generate, but they should not be used for extended periods of time because they are vulnerable to password-guessing attacks. If the algorithm for computer-generated passwords is discovered, all passwords created by the system are in jeopardy of being compromised.

A password mechanism that is slightly more effective than a basic password is a *passphrase*. A passphrase is a string of characters usually much longer than a password. Once a passphrase is entered, the system converts it into a virtual password for use by the authentication process. Passphrases are often modified natural-language sentences to simplify memorization. Here's an example: "She $ell$ C shells ByE the c-shor." Using a passphrase has several benefits. It is difficult to crack a passphrase using a brute-force tool, and it encourages the use of a lengthy string with numerous characters yet is still easy to remember.

Another interesting password mechanism is the cognitive password. A cognitive password is usually a series of questions about facts or predefined responses that only a subject should know. For example, three to five questions such as these might be asked of the subject:

- What is your birth date?
- What is your mother's maiden name?
- What is the name of your division manager?
- What was your score on your last evaluation exam?
- Who was your favorite player in the 1984 World Series?

If all questions are answered correctly, the subject is authenticated. The most effective cognitive password systems ask a different set of questions each time. The primary limitation for cognitive password systems is that each question must be answered at the time of user enrollment (in other words, user account creation) and answered again during the logon process, which increases the time to complete that process. Cognitive passwords are often employed for phone- or web-based authentication at financial organizations, such as your bank. However, this type of password is considered to be inappropriate and insecure when it comes to protecting IT.

Many systems include password policies that restrict or dictate password characteristics. Common requirements include minimum length, minimum age, maximum age, requiring three or four character types (uppercase, lowercase, numbers, and symbols), and preventing password reuse. As needs for security increase, such restrictions should be tightened.

However, even with strong software-enforced password restrictions, it remains possible to create passwords that may be easily guessed or cracked. An organization's security policy must clearly define both the need for strong passwords and what a strong password is. Users need to be trained about security so they will respect an organization's security policy and adhere to its requirements. If end users create their own passwords, offer suggestions like the following to help them create strong ones:

- *Don't* reuse any part of your name, logon name, email address, employee number, Social Security number, phone number, extension, or other identifying name or code.
- *Don't* use dictionary words, slang, or industry acronyms.
- *Do* use nonstandard capitalization and spelling.
- *Do* switch letters and replace letters with numbers.

## Password Security

When a malicious user or attacker seeks to obtain passwords, they can employ several methods, including network traffic analysis, password file access, brute-force attacks, dictionary attacks, and social engineering. *Network traffic analysis* (also known as *sniffing*) is the process of capturing network traffic when a user is entering a password for authentication. Once a password is discovered, the attacker attempts to replay the packet containing the password against the network to gain access. If an attacker can gain access to the password database file, it can be copied and a password-cracking tool can be used against it to extract usernames and passwords.

Brute-force and dictionary attacks are types of password attacks that can be waged against a stolen password database file or a system's logon prompt. In a *dictionary attack*, the attacker uses a script of common passwords and dictionary words to attempt to discover an account's password. In a *brute-force attack*, a systematic trial of all possible character combinations is used to discover an account's password. Finally, a *hybrid attack* attempts a dictionary attack and then performs a type of brute-force attack. The follow-up brute-force attack is used to add prefix or suffix characters to passwords from the dictionary to discover one-upped-constructed passwords, two-upped-constructed passwords, and so on. A *one-upped-constructed* password is a password where a single character differs from its form in the dictionary. For example, "password1" is one-upped from "password," and so are "Password," "1password," and "passXword." This approach is often used to generate so-called rainbow tables, which map known passwords to equivalent hash values to speed password-cracking efforts. (Rainbow tables are discussed in more detail in Chapter 2, under the heading "Brute-Force and Dictionary Attacks.")

No matter what type of password attack is used, only read access is required for the password database. Write access is not required. Therefore, a wider number of user accounts can be employed to launch password-cracking attacks. From an intruder's perspective, this makes finding a weak user account more attractive than attacking an administrator or root account from the get-go to gain system access.

A *social-engineering attack* is an attempt by an attacker to obtain logon capabilities. It involves deceiving a user, sometimes over the telephone, into performing specific actions on a system, such as changing the password for an executive who is on the road or creating a user account for a new fictitious employee.

You can improve the security of passwords in several ways. *Account lockout* is a mechanism used to disable a user account after a specified number of failed logons. Account lockouts stop brute-force and dictionary attacks against a system's logon prompt. Once the logon attempt limit is reached, a message displaying the time, date, and location (in other words, the computer name or IP address) of the last successful or failed logon attempt appears. Users who suspect that their account is under attack or has been compromised can report this to a system administrator. Auditing can be configured to track logon success and failure. An intrusion detection system can easily identify logon prompt attacks and notify administrators.

Here are some other options to improve the security offered by password authentication:

- Use the strongest form of one-way encryption available for password storage.

- Never allow passwords to be transmitted over the network in clear text or with weak encryption.

- Use password verification tools and password-cracking tools against your own password database file. Require that weak or discovered passwords be changed.

- Disable idle user accounts for short periods of inactivity, such as a week or a month. Delete accounts no longer in use.

- Properly train users about the necessity of maintaining security and the use of strong passwords. Prohibit writing down or sharing passwords. Offer tips to prevent shoulder surfing or keyboard logging to capture passwords. Offer tips and techniques for creating strong passwords:
  - Require that users change passwords regularly. The more secure or sensitive the environment, the more frequently passwords should be changed.
  - Never display passwords in clear form on any screen or within any form. Instead, mask the display of the password at all times. This is a commonly recognized feature of software, such as displaying asterisks instead of letters when someone is typing a password into a logon dialog box.
  - Longer passwords, such as those with 16 characters or more, are harder for a brute-force password-cracking tool to discover. However, it's harder for people to remember longer passwords, which often leads users to write them down. Your organization should have a standard security awareness rule that no passwords should ever be written down. The only possible exception to that rule is that long, complex passwords for the most sensitive accounts, such as administrator or root, can be written down and stored in a vault or safety deposit box.
  - Create lists of passwords users should avoid. Easy-to-memorize passwords are often easily discovered by password-cracking tools.
  - If a root or administrator password is ever compromised, every password for every account should be changed. (In a high-security environment, a compromised system can never be fully trusted again. Thus, it may require formatting the drives and rebuilding the entire system from scratch.)
  - Hand out passwords in person after a user proves their identity. Never transmit passwords via email.

## Biometrics

Another common authentication and identification technique is the use of *biometric factors*. Biometric factors fall into the Type 3, "something you are," authentication category. A biometric factor is a behavioral or physiological characteristic that is unique to a subject. There are many types of biometric factors, including fingerprints, face scans, iris scans, retina scans, palm scans (also known as *palm topography* or *palm geography*), hand geometry, voice patterns, signature dynamics, and keystroke patterns (keystroke dynamics).

We now discuss biometric factors in more detail, taking into account the human body part they utilize and the information that each quantifies in order to make the most accurate identification possible:

**Fingerprints**    The *macroscopic* (in other words, visible to the naked eye) patterns on the last phalange of fingers and thumbs make fingerprinting so effective for security. A type of fingerprinting known as *minutia matching* examines the microscopic view of the fingertips.

Unfortunately, minutia matching is affected by small changes to the finger, including temperature, pressure, and minor surface damage (such as sliding your fingers across a rough surface).

**Face scans**   Face scans utilize the geometric patterns of faces for detection and recognition. They employ recognition technology known as *eigenfeatures* (facial metrics) or *eigenfaces*. (The German word *eigen* refers to recursive mathematics used to analyze intrinsic or unique numerical characteristics.)

**Retina scans**   Retina scans focus on the pattern of blood vessels at the back of the eye. They are the most accurate form of biometric authentication (and are able to differentiate between identical twins), but also the least acceptable because retina scans can reveal medical conditions, such as high blood pressure and pregnancy. In addition, these types of scans often require a subject to use a cup reader that blows air directly into the eye.

**Iris scans**   Focusing on the colored area around the pupil, iris scans are the second most accurate form of biometric authentication. However, iris scans cannot differentiate between identical twins. Iris scans are often recognized as having a longer useful authentication life span than other biometric factors. This is because the iris remains relatively unchanged throughout a person's life (barring eye damage or illness). Every other type of biometric factor is more likely to change over time. Iris scans are considered acceptable by general users because they don't involve direct contact with a reader and don't reveal personal medical information.

**Palm scans**   Also known as *palm topography* or *palm geography*, palm scans utilize the whole area of the hand, including the palm and fingers. Palm scans function as a hand-sized fingerprint by analyzing the grooves, ridges, and creases as well as the fingerprints themselves.

**Hand geometry**   Hand geometry recognizes the physical dimensions of the hand. This includes the width and length of the palm and fingers. This can be a mechanical or image-edge (in other words, visual silhouette) graphical solution.

 Skin scans are not used as a form of biometric authentication because they cannot differentiate among all individuals.

**Heart/pulse patterns**   This involves measuring the user's pulse or heartbeat to ensure that a real person is providing the biometric factor. This is often employed as a secondary biometric to support another type.

**Voice pattern recognition**   This type of biometric authentication relies on the sound of a subject's speaking voice. This is different from speech recognition, which extracts communications from sound (in other words, automatic dictation software). Specifically, voice pattern recognition differentiates between one person's voice and another, while speech recognition differentiates between words within any person's voice.

Voice pattern recognition is often thought to have numerous benefits, such as its reliability and its function as a "natural" biometric factor. However, the idea of speech recognition is commonly confused with voice pattern recognition. Remember, voice pattern recognition differentiates between one person's voice and another, while speech recognition differentiates between words within any person's voice. The benefits of speech recognition include flexibility, hands- and eyes-free operation, reduced data entry time, elimination of spelling errors, and improved accuracy.

**Signature dynamics**    This recognizes how a subject writes a string of characters. Signature dynamics examine how a subject performs the act of writing as well as features in a written sample. The success of signature dynamics relies upon pen pressure, stroke pattern, stroke length, and the points in time when the pen is lifted from the writing surface. However, the speed at which the written sample is created is usually not an important factor.

**Keystroke patterns (keystroke dynamics)**    Keystroke patterns measure how a subject uses a keyboard by analyzing flight time and dwell time. *Flight time* is how long it takes between key presses, and *dwell time* is how long a key is pressed. Using keystroke patterns is inexpensive, nonintrusive, and often transparent to the user (for both use and enrollment). Unfortunately, using keystroke patterns for security is subject to wild variances. Simple changes in user behavior greatly affect this biometric, such as using only one hand, being cold, standing rather than sitting, changing keyboards, or sustaining an injury to the hand or a finger.

Biometric factors can be used as an identifying or authentication technique. Using a biometric factor instead of a username or account ID as an identification factor requires a one-to-many search of the offered biometric pattern against a stored database of enrolled and authorized patterns. As an identification technique, biometric factors are used in physical access controls. Using a biometric factor as an authentication technique requires a one-to-one match of the offered biometric pattern against a stored pattern for the offered subject identity. As an authentication technique, biometric factors are used in logical access controls.

The use of biometrics promises universally unique identification for every person on the planet. Unfortunately, biometric technology has yet to live up to this promise. For biometric factors to be useful, they must be extremely sensitive. The most important aspect of a biometric device is its accuracy. To use biometrics for identification, a biometric device must be able to detect minute differences in information, such as variations in the blood vessels in a person's retina or tones and timbres in their voice. Because most people are basically similar, the level of detail required to authenticate a subject often results in false negative and false positive authentications.

## Biometric Factor Ratings

Biometric devices are rated for performance in producing false negative and false positive authentications. Most biometric devices have a sensitivity adjustment so they can be tuned to be more or less sensitive. When a biometric device is too sensitive, a Type 1 error occurs. A Type 1 error occurs when a valid subject is not authenticated. The ratio of Type 1 errors to valid authentications is known as the *false rejection rate (FRR)*. When a biometric device is not sensitive enough, a Type 2 error occurs. A Type 2 error occurs when an invalid subject is authenticated. The ratio of Type 2 errors to valid authentications is called the *false acceptance rate (FAR)*.

The FRR and FAR are usually plotted on a graph that shows the level of sensitivity adjustment against the percentage of FRR and FAR errors (see Figure 1.1). The point at which the FRR and FAR are equal is known as the *crossover error rate (CER)* or the *equal error rate (ERR)*; these terms are used interchangeably. The CER level is used as a standard assessment point from which to measure the performance of a biometric device. The CER is used for a single purpose: to compare the accuracy of similar biometric devices (in other words, those focusing on the same biometric factor) from different vendors or different models from the same vendor. On the CER graph, the device with the lowest CER is overall the most accurate. In some situations, making a device more sensitive than the CER rate is preferable, such as on a metal detector at an airport.

**FIGURE 1.1**   Graph of FRR and FAR errors indicating the CER point

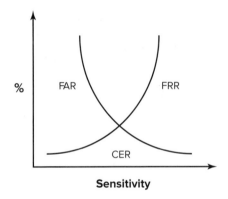

**Biometric Registration**

In addition to issues concerning the sensitivity of biometric devices, several other factors may make them less effective—namely, enrollment time, throughput rate, and acceptance. For a biometric device to work as an identification or authentication mechanism, subjects must be enrolled or registered. This means a subject's biometric factor must be sampled and stored in the device's database. The stored sample of a biometric factor is called a *reference profile* or a *reference template*.

The time required to scan and store a biometric factor varies greatly according to which physical or performance characteristic is measured. The longer it takes to enroll using a biometric mechanism, the less willingly the user community accepts the inconvenience. In general, enrollment times over 2 minutes are unacceptable. If you use a biometric characteristic that changes over time, such as a person's voice tones, facial hair, or signature pattern, re-enrollment must occur at regular intervals.

Once subjects are enrolled, the amount of time the system requires to scan and process them is the *throughput rate*. The more complex or detailed a biometric characteristic, the longer processing takes. Subjects typically accept a throughput rate of about six seconds or faster.

A subject's acceptance of a security mechanism depends upon many subjective perceptions, including privacy, invasiveness, and psychological or physical discomfort. Subjects may be concerned about transferring body fluids or may have health concerns about biometric-scanning devices.

## Appropriate Biometric Usage

When selecting a biometric solution for a specific environment, you must consider numerous aspects. These aspects include which type of biometric factor is most suitable as well as the effectiveness and acceptability of the biometric factor. When comparing different types of biometric factors, a Zephyr chart is often used. A Zephyr chart rates various aspects, functions, or features of different biometric controls together on a single easy-to-read diagram (see Figure 1.2).

**FIGURE 1.2**   An example Zephyr chart

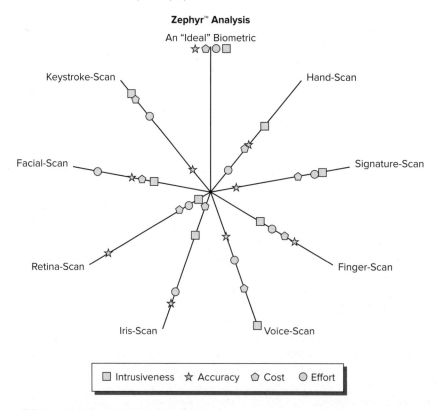

©Copyright, International Biometric Group.
This image is used with permission of the International Biometric Group. www.biometricgroup.com

The *effectiveness* of access controls, specifically biometric controls, depends on how accurate one type of biometric factor is in comparison to others. Here is the common order of accuracy from most to least:

- Palm scan
- Hand geometry
- Iris scan
- Retina pattern
- Fingerprint
- Voice verification
- Facial recognition
- Signature dynamics
- Keystroke dynamics

The *acceptance* of biometrics is a rating of how well people accept use of specific biometric factors in their environment. An acceptance rating incorporates a person's view of how invasive and easy to use some specific biometric factor is and the level of health risk it presents. Here is the usual order of acceptance level from most to least:

- Iris scan
- Keystroke dynamics
- Signature dynamics
- Voice verification
- Facial recognition
- Fingerprint
- Palm scan
- Hand geometry
- Retina pattern

 This list comes from work by A. K. Jain, a distinguished professor in the departments of computer science and engineering at Michigan State University. It is available through his Biometric Recognition website at http://biometrics.cse.msu.edu.

## Tokens

*Tokens* (or *smart tokens*) are password-generating devices that subjects must carry with them. A token device is an example of a Type 2 factor, or "something you have." A token can be a static password device, such as an ATM card or other memory card. To use an ATM card, you must supply the token (the ATM card itself) and your PIN. Tokens can also be one-time or dynamic password devices that look like small calculators, or they might even be smart cards (to read more about smart cards, see Chapter 19). The device displays a string of characters (a password) for you to enter into the system.

There are four types of token devices:

- Static tokens

- Synchronous dynamic password tokens

- Asynchronous dynamic password tokens

- Challenge-response tokens

A *static token* can be a swipe card, a smart card, a floppy disk, a USB RAM dongle, or even something as simple as a key for a physical lock. Static tokens offer a physical means to prove identity. Static tokens often require an additional factor to provide authentication, such as a password or biometric factor. Most device static tokens host a cryptographic key, such as a private key, digital signature, or encrypted logon credentials. A cryptographic key can be used as an identifier or as an authentication mechanism. A cryptographic key is much stronger than a password because it is pre-encrypted using strong encryption, is significantly longer, and resides only in the token. Static tokens are used more as identification devices than as authentication factors.

A *synchronous dynamic password token* generates passwords at fixed time intervals. Time interval tokens require synchronizing the clock on an authentication server with the clock on the token device. The subject enters a generated password into the system along with a PIN, passphrase, or password. This generated password provides identification, and the PIN/password provides authentication.

An *asynchronous dynamic password token* generates passwords based on occurrence of some event. An event token requires the subject to press a key on the token and on the authentication server. This advances to the next password value. The generated password and the subject's PIN, passphrase, or password are entered into the system for authentication.

---

### One-Time Password Generators

As we discussed earlier, one-time passwords are dynamic passwords that change every time they are used. They can be effective for security purposes, except that humans can rarely remember passwords that change so frequently. *One-time password generators* create passwords for your users and make one-time passwords reasonable to deploy. Users need a token device (in other words, a password generator), must understand the logon procedure, and often need to memorize a short PIN, depending on which generator they use. With device-based authentication systems, an environment can benefit from the strength of one-time passwords without relying on users' memorization skills.

The five widely recognized one-time password generator systems are synchronous, PIN synchronous, asynchronous, PIN asynchronous, and transaction synchronous. Systems that use a PIN require entry of an additional memorized key sequence to complete the authentication process.

*Challenge-response tokens* generate passwords or responses based on instructions from the authentication system. The authentication system displays a challenge, usually a code or a passphrase. This challenge is entered into the token device. The token responds to the challenge, and its response is keyed into the system for authentication.

Using token authentication systems offers much stronger security than using password authentication alone. Token systems use two or more factors to establish identity and provide authentication. In addition to knowing the username, password, PIN, code, and so on, the subject must be in physical possession of the token device.

However, token systems do have failings. If the battery dies or the device breaks, the subject is unable to gain access. Token devices can get lost or stolen. Tokens must be stored and managed intelligently because if a token system is compromised, it can be difficult and expensive to replace. Furthermore, human factors can render tokens less secure than they are designed to be. First and foremost, if a user writes the access code or PIN on the token device, the security of the token system is compromised. Users must recognize that loaning a token and PIN, even to a co-worker, violates security.

## Tickets

*Ticket authentication* is a mechanism that employs a third-party entity to prove identification and provide authentication. The most common and well-known ticket system is Kerberos. Kerberos was developed under Project Athena at MIT. We'll discuss Kerberos and its tickets later in this chapter.

 The Kerberos name is borrowed from Greek mythology. A three-headed dog named Kerberos guards the gates to the underworld, but in the myth, the three-headed dog faces inward, preventing escape rather than denying entrance.

## Single Sign-On

*Single sign-on* (SSO) is a mechanism that allows a subject to be authenticated only once on a system yet remain able to access resource after resource unhindered by repeated authentication prompts. With SSO, once a subject is authenticated, it can roam the network freely and access resources and services without further authentication challenges.

The primary disadvantage to SSO is that once an account is compromised, a malicious subject gains unrestricted access. In other words, a maximum level of unauthorized access is gained simply through password disclosure. SSO typically supports stronger passwords because a subject must memorize only a single password. Furthermore, SSO eases administration by reducing the number of locations on which an account must be defined for the subject. You can enable SSO through authentication systems or through scripts that provide logon credentials automatically when prompted.

Kerberos, SESAME, KryptoKnight, NetSP, thin clients, directory services, and scripted access are examples of SSO mechanisms. Two or more SSO mechanisms can be combined into a single security solution. It is typical for Kerberos to be combined with another SSO mechanism. For example, under Windows Server 2008 (as well as Windows Server 2003), it is possible to employ the native directory service (Active Directory), which is integrated with Kerberos and other SSO options, including thin clients (in other words, Terminal Services) and scripted access (in other words, logon scripts).

## Kerberos

*Kerberos* is a trusted third-party authentication protocol that can be used to provide a single sign-on solution and to provide protection for logon credentials. Kerberos relies upon symmetric-key cryptography (also known as private-key cryptography), specifically, Advanced Encryption Standard (AES), and it provides end-to-end security for authentication traffic between the client and the key distribution center (KDC). Kerberos provides confidentiality and integrity for authentication traffic.

The Kerberos authentication mechanism centers on a trusted server (or servers) that hosts the functions of the KDC, a ticket-granting service (TGS), and an authentication service (AS). Generally, the Kerberos central server that hosts all these services is simply referred to as the KDC. Kerberos uses symmetric-key cryptography to authenticate clients to servers. All clients and servers are registered with the KDC, so it maintains the secret keys for all network members.

A complicated exchange of tickets (in other words, cryptographic messages) between clients, network servers, and the KDC is used to prove identity and provide authentication. This allows a client to request resources from the server with full assurance that both client and server are who they claim to be. An exchange of encrypted tickets also ensures that no logon credentials, session keys, or authentication messages are ever transmitted in clear text.

Kerberos tickets have specific lifetimes and usage parameters. Once a ticket expires, a client must request a renewal or a new ticket to continue communications with any server.

The Kerberos logon process is as follows:

1.    The user types a username and password into the client.

2.    The client encrypts the credentials with AES for transmission to the KDC.

3.    The KDC verifies the user credentials.

4.    The KDC generates a TGT by hashing the user's password.

5.    The TGT is encrypted with AES for transmission to the client.

6.    The client installs the TGT for use until it expires.

The Kerberos server or service access process is as follows:

1.    The client sends its TGT back to the KDC with a request for access to a server or service.

2.    The KDC verifies the ongoing validity of the TGT and checks its access control matrix to verify that the user has sufficient privilege to access the requested resource.

3.    A service ticket (ST) is generated and sent to the client.

**4.**   The client sends the ST to the server or service host.

**5.**   The server or service host verifies the validity of the ST with the KDC.

**6.**   Once identity and authorization is verified, Kerberos activity is complete. The server or service host then opens a session with the client and begins communications or data transmission.

## Limitations of Kerberos

Kerberos is a versatile authentication mechanism that works over local LANs, local logons, remote access, and client-server resource requests. However, Kerberos presents a single point of failure—the KDC. If the KDC is compromised, the secret key for every system on the network is also compromised. Also, if a KDC goes offline, no subject authentication can occur.

Kerberos has other limitations or problems:

- Dictionary and brute-force attacks on the initial KDC response to a client may reveal a subject's password. In fact, direct password-guessing attacks can be waged against a KDC unimpeded. A countermeasure to such attacks is to deploy a preauthentication service to check logon credentials and watch for access attacks before granting a subject access to the KDC.

- Issued tickets are stored in memory on the client and server.

- Malicious subjects can replay captured tickets if they are reused within their lifetime window.

- Issued tickets, specifically the TGT, are based on a hash of the user's password with an added time stamp for expiration.

- Kerberos encrypts only authentication traffic (in other words, mechanisms for proving identity); it does not provide security for subsequent communication sessions or data transmissions.

## Other Examples of Single Sign-On

Although Kerberos may be the most widely recognized (and deployed) form of single sign-on, it is not the only one of its kind. In this section, we summarize other SSO mechanisms you may encounter.

The Secure European System for Applications in a Multivendor Environment (SESAME) is a system developed to address weaknesses in Kerberos. However, it did not compensate for all problems with Kerberos completely. Eventually later Kerberos versions and various vendor implementations resolved its initial problems. In the professional security world, SESAME is no longer considered a viable product.

KryptoKnight is a peer-to-peer authentication solution developed by IBM. It was incorporated into the NetSP product. Like SESAME, KryptoKnight and NetSP never took off and are no longer widely used.

*Thin clients* are low-end client systems that connect over a network to a server system. Thin clients originated in the mainframe world where host-terminal connections enabled dumb terminals to interact with and control centralized mainframes. These terminals had no processing or storage abilities. The idea of thin clients has been replicated on modern client-server environments using interface software applications that act as clients to server-hosted environments. All processing and storage takes place on the server, while the client provides an interface for the subject through a local keyboard, mouse, and monitor. Some thin clients are also called *remote control tools*, used for remote desktop access and remote assistance, or "on the fly" remote connectivity tools such as DameWare.

A *directory service* is a centralized database of objects that includes information about resources available to a network along with information about subjects such as users and computers. It can be understood as a telephone directory for network services and assets. Users, clients, and processes consult the directory service to learn where a desired system or resource resides. Then once this address or location is known, access can be directed toward it. A directory service must be authenticated to before queries and lookup activities can be performed. Even after authentication, the directory service will reveal only certain information to a subject based on that subject's assigned privileges. Directory services are often based on the Lightweight Directory Access Protocol (LDAP). Some well-known directory services include Microsoft's Active Directory and Novell's NetWare Directory Services (NDS), now known as eDirectory.

*Scripted access* or *logon scripts* are used to establish communication links by providing an automated process by which logon credentials are transmitted to resource hosts at the start of a logon session. Scripted access can often simulate SSO even though the environment still requires a unique authentication process to connect to each server or resource. Scripts can be used to implement SSO in those environments where true SSO technologies are not available. However, scripts and batch files should be stored in a protected area because they usually contain access credentials.

# Access Control Techniques

Once a subject has been identified and authenticated and accountability has been established, it must be authorized to access resources or perform actions. Authorization can occur only after a subject's identity has been verified through authentication. Systems provide authorization through the use of access controls. Access controls manage the type and extent of access subjects have to objects. There are two primary categories for access control techniques: discretionary and nondiscretionary. Nondiscretionary can be further subdivided into specific techniques, such as mandatory, role-based, and task-based access controls.

There are several forms of access controls that define how subjects access and interact with objects in a variety of ways. Each system has its own security properties that individually distinguish and differentiate it from all others. The types of access control systems are described in the following sections.

# Discretionary Access Controls

A system that employs *discretionary access controls (DACs)* allows the owner or creator of an object to control and define subject access to that object. That is, access control is based on the discretion (in other words, a decision) of the owner. Access is granted or denied in a discretionary environment based on the identity of the subject (which is typically the user account name). For example, if a user creates a new spreadsheet file, that user is the owner of that file. As the owner of the file, that user can modify the permissions on that file to grant or deny access to other subjects.

DACs are often implemented using access control lists on objects. Each ACL defines the types of access granted or restricted to individual or grouped subjects. Discretionary access control does not offer a centrally controlled management system because owners can alter the ACLs on their objects at will. Thus, access is more dynamic than it is with mandatory access controls.

DAC environments can be extended beyond just controlling the type of access between subjects and objects via ACLs by including or applying time controls, transaction controls, and other forms of ID-focused controls (in other words, device, host, protocol, address, and so on). Within a DAC environment, users' privileges can be suspended while they are on vacation, resumed when they return, or terminated when they leave an organization.

> The U.S. government labels access controls that do not rely upon policy to define access as discretionary; however, corporate environments and nongovernmental organizations will often label such environments as *need to know*.

# Nondiscretionary Access Controls

*Nondiscretionary access controls* are used in a rule-based system in which a set of rules, restrictions, or filters determines what can and cannot occur on the system, such as granting subject access, performing an action on an object, or accessing a resource. Access is not based on administrator or owner discretion and does not focus on user identity. (Thus, nondiscretionary access control is the opposite of discretionary in much the same way as non-A is the opposite of A.) Rather, a static set of rules that governs the whole environment is used to manage access (in other words, nondiscretionary access implies a centrally controlled management system).

In general, rule-based access control systems are more appropriate for environments that experience frequent changes to data permissions (in other words, changing the security domain or label for objects). This is because rule-based systems can implement sweeping changes just by changing centralized rules without having to manipulate or "touch" every subject and/or object in the environment. However, in most cases, once rules are established, they remain fairly static and unchanged throughout the life of the environment.

In rule-based access control systems, control is based on a specific profile created for each user. A common example of such a system is a firewall. A firewall is governed by a set of rules or filters defined by the administrator. Users are able to communicate across the firewall because they have initiated transactions that are allowed by the defined rules. Users are able to accomplish this because they have client environments configured to permit some transactions and to deny all others; these are their specific profiles. A formal definition of a rule-based access control (or specifically, a *rule-based security policy*) is found in RFC 2828, "Internet Security Glossary." This document includes the following definition for the term *rule-based security policy*: "A security policy based on global rules imposed for all users. These rules usually rely on comparison of the sensitivity of the resource being accessed and the possession of corresponding attributes of users, a group of users, or entities acting on behalf of users."

## Mandatory Access Controls

*Mandatory access controls* rely upon the use of classification labels. Each classification label represents a security domain or a realm of security. A *security domain* is a realm of common trust that is governed by a specific security policy for that domain. Subjects are labeled by their level of clearance (which is a form of privilege). Objects are labeled by their level of classification or sensitivity. For example, the military uses the labels of top secret, secret, confidential, sensitive but unclassified (SBU), and unclassified (see Chapter 5, "Security Management Concepts and Principles").

NOTE    Despite the title just cited for Chapter 5 in this book, the corresponding domain in the CISSP common body of knowledge is now known as "Information Security Governance and Risk Management," and it stresses the key role that risk assessment and management, and best practices in security governance, play in managing security of all kinds.

In a mandatory access control system, subjects are able to access objects that have the same or a lower level of classification. An expansion of this access control method is known as *need to know*. Subjects with higher clearance levels are granted access to highly sensitive resources only if their work tasks require such access. If they don't have a need to know, even if they have sufficient clearance, they are denied access.

Mandatory access control (MAC) is prohibitive rather than permissive. If access is not specifically granted, it is forbidden. MAC is generally recognized as being more secure than DAC but neither as flexible nor as scalable. The relative scale for security is evident in the ISO Standard Common Criteria for Computer Security (ISO 15408), a standard used to permit users to specify security requirements, vendors to specify security attributes for products, and evaluators to determine if such products embody claimed attributes. The Common Criteria, often abbreviated as CC, includes evaluation criteria and specifies mandatory protection as a higher level of security than discretionary protection (for more information about CC, see Chapter 12, "Principles of Security Models").

Using security labels in mandatory access controls presents some interesting problems. First, for a mandatory access control system to function, every subject and object must have a security label. Depending on the environment, security labels can refer to sensitivity, value to the organization, need for confidentiality, classification, department, project, and so on. The military security labels mentioned earlier range from highest sensitivity to lowest: top secret, secret, confidential, sensitive but unclassified (SBU), and unclassified. Common corporate or commercial security labels are confidential, proprietary, private, sensitive, and public. Security classifications indicate a hierarchy of sensitivity, but each level is distinct.

Classifications within a MAC environment are of three types:

**Hierarchical environments**   Hierarchical environments relate various classification labels in an ordered structure from low security to medium security to high security. Each level or classification label in the structure is related. Clearance in one level grants the subject access to objects in that level as well as to all objects in all lower levels but prohibits access to all objects in higher levels.

**Compartmentalized environments**   In compartmentalized environments, there is no relationship between one security domain and another. To gain access to an object, the subject must have specific clearance for its security domain.

**Hybrid environments**   A hybrid environment combines both hierarchical and compartmentalized concepts so that each hierarchical level may contain numerous subdivisions that are isolated from the rest of the security domain. A subject must not only have the correct clearance but also the need to know for a specific compartment to gain access to the compartmentalized object. Possessing the need to know for one compartment within a security domain does not grant a subject access to any other compartment. Each compartment has its own unique and specific need to know. If you have a need to know (based on your assigned work tasks), then you are granted access. If you don't have a need to know, your access is blocked. A hybrid MAC environment provides more granular control over access but becomes increasingly difficult to manage as the size of the environment (in other words, number of classifications, objects, and subjects) increases.

## Role-Based Access Control

Systems that employ role-based or task-based access controls define a subject's ability to access an object via subject roles (in other words, job descriptions) or tasks (in other words, work functions). If a subject occupies a management position, it will have greater access to resources than a subject who is in a temporary job. Role-based access controls are useful in volatile environments with frequent personnel changes because access depends on a job description (in other words, a role or task) rather than on subject identity.

*Role-based access control* (RBAC) and groups within a DAC environment may serve a similar purpose, but they differ in their deployment and use. They are similar in that both serve as containers to collect users into manageable units. However, a user can belong to more than one group. In addition to collecting rights and permissions from each group, individual user accounts may also be directly assigned rights and permissions.

In a DAC system, even with groups, access is still based on the discretion of an owner and focuses control on the identity of the user. When an RBAC system is employed, a user may have only a single role, but users may also be assigned multiple roles. Users have only the rights and permissions that belong to such roles, and there are no additional individually assigned rights or permissions. Furthermore, access is not determined by owner discretion; it derives from the inherent responsibilities of an assigned role (in other words, job description). Also, access focuses on the assigned role, not on user identity. Two different users with the same assigned role will have the same access and privileges.

RBAC is becoming increasingly attractive to corporate entities with high rates of employee turnover. It also allows company-specific security policies to be directly mapped and enforced to map directly into an organization's hierarchy and management structure. This implies that roles or job descriptions within an RBAC system are often hierarchical, meaning that roles are related in a low-to-high fashion so that higher roles are created by adding access and privileges to lower ones. Often, RBAC solutions can replace MAC and DAC environments.

Another method related to RBAC is called *task-based access control* (TBAC). TBAC is basically the same as RBAC, but instead of being assigned a single role, each user is assigned an array of tasks. These items all relate to assigned work tasks for the person associated with a user account. Under TBAC, access remains based on rules (in other words, on work tasks) and focuses on controlling access by tasks assigned rather than by user identity.

## Lattice-Based Access Controls

Some, if not most, nondiscretionary access controls can be labeled as *lattice-based access controls*. Lattice-based access controls define upper and lower bounds of access for every relationship between a subject and an object. These boundaries can be arbitrary, but they usually follow military or corporate security label levels.

A subject with the lattice permissions shown in Figure 1.3 can access resources up to private and down to sensitive but cannot access confidential, proprietary, or public resources. Subjects under lattice-based access controls acquire a *least upper bound* and a *greatest lower bound* of access to labeled objects based on their assigned lattice positions. Lattice-based access controls were originally developed to address information flow, which primarily concerns itself with confidentiality. A common example of a lattice-based access control is a mandatory access control.

**FIGURE 1.3**   A representation of the boundaries provided by lattice-based access controls

## Access Control Methodologies and Implementation

There are two primary access control methodologies: centralized and decentralized (or distributed). *Centralized* access control implies that all authorization verification is performed by a single entity within a system. *Decentralized* access control, or *distributed* access control, implies that various entities located throughout a system perform authorization verification.

### Centralized and Decentralized Access Control

Centralized and decentralized access control methodologies offer the same benefits and drawbacks found in any centralized or decentralized system. A small team or individual can manage centralized access control. Administrative overhead is lower because all changes are made in a single location and a single change affects the entire system. However, centralized access control also presents a single point of failure. If system elements are unable to access the centralized access control system, subjects and objects cannot interact. Two examples of centralized access control are Remote Authentication Dial-In User Service (RADIUS) and Terminal Access Controller Access Control System (TACACS).

Decentralized access control often requires several teams or multiple individuals. Administrative overhead is higher because changes must be implemented across numerous locations. Maintaining homogeneity across a system becomes more difficult as the number of access control points increases. Changes made to any individual access control point affect only aspects of the systems that rely upon that specific access control point. Decentralized access control has no single point of failure. If an access control point fails, other access control points may be able to balance the load until the control point is repaired; in addition, objects and subjects that don't rely upon the failed access control point can continue to interact normally. Domains and trusts are commonly used in decentralized access control systems.

A domain is a realm of trust or a collection of subjects and objects that share a common security policy. Each domain's access control operates independently from those of other domains. This results in decentralized access control when multiple domains are involved. To share resources from one domain to another, a trust is established. A trust is simply a security bridge established between two domains that allows users from one domain to access resources in another. Trusts can be one way only, or they can be two way.

## RADIUS and TACACS

RADIUS centralizes authentication for remote dial-up connections. A network that employs a RADIUS server is configured so the remote access server passes dial-up user logon credentials to the RADIUS server for authentication. This process is similar to the process used by domain clients sending logon credentials to a domain controller for authentication. Using an authentication server such as RADIUS or TACACS that is separate from the primary remote access server system provides the benefit of keeping auditing and access settings on a system other than the remote access server, thus providing greater security. RADIUS and other remote authentication protocols and services are designed to transport authentication, authorization, and session configuration information between a remote access server (aka a *network access server*) and a centralized authentication server (often known as a *domain controller*). Note also that a single RADIUS or TACACS server can support many remote access servers and acts as a central clearinghouse for such servers.

RADIUS was defined in RFC 2138 and is now covered in RFC 2865. It is used primarily to provide an additional layer of protection against intrusions via dial-up connections. RADIUS supports dynamic passwords and callback security. It acts as a proxy for remote clients because it acts on behalf of clients to obtain authentication on the network. RADIUS acts as a client for the network by requesting authentication in much the same way that a typical client would. Likewise, within the RADIUS architecture, a remote access server is configured as a RADIUS client.

Owing to the success of RADIUS, an enhanced version of RADIUS named DIAMETER was developed; it is designed to support all forms of remote connectivity, not just dial-up. However, RADIUS and DIAMETER are not interoperable. Eventually, DIAMETER's features were added back into RADIUS. Today, only a version of RADIUS that supports all types of remote access is available.

TACACS is an alternative to RADIUS. TACACS is available in three versions: original TACACS, extended TACACS (XTACACS), and TACACS+. TACACS integrates the authentication and authorization processes. XTACACS keeps the authentication, authorization, and accounting processes separate. TACACS+ improves XTACACS by adding two-factor authentication. TACACS and RADIUS operate similarly, and TACACS provides the same functionality as RADIUS. However, RADIUS is based on an Internet standard, whereas TACACS is more proprietary (although widely used). TACACS is defined in RFC 1492.

These forms of centralized access control, specific to remote access, provide an additional layer of security for a private network. They prevent LAN authentication systems and domain controllers from being attacked directly by remote attackers. When a separate system for remote access users is deployed, even if that system is compromised, only remote access users are affected; the rest of the LAN still functions unhindered.

# Access Control Administration

*Access control administration* is the collection of tasks and duties assigned to an administrator to manage user accounts, access, and accountability. A system's security is based on effective administration of access controls. Remember that access controls rely upon four principles: identification, authentication, authorization, and accountability. As they relate to access control administration, these principles transform into three main responsibilities:

- User account management
- Activity tracking
- Access rights and permissions management

## Account Administration

User account management involves creating, maintaining, and closing user accounts. Although these activities may seem mundane, they are essential to a system's access control capabilities. Without properly defined and maintained user accounts, a system is unable to establish identity, perform authentication, provide authorization, or track accountability.

### Creating New Accounts

Creating new user accounts is a simple process, but it must be protected and secured via organizational security policy procedures. User accounts should not be created at an administrator's whim or in response to some particular request. Rather, account management should follow a stringent procedure that flows from the HR department's hiring or promotion procedures.

The HR department should make a formal request for a user account for a new employee. That request should include the classification or security level to be assigned to the new employee's user account. The new employee's department manager and the organization's security administrator should verify that security assignment. Once the request is verified, only then should a new user account be created. Creating user accounts outside established security policies and procedures creates holes and oversights that can be exploited by malicious subjects. A similar process for increasing or decreasing an existing user account's security level is also required.

As part of the hiring process, new employees should be trained on organization security policies and procedures. Before hiring is complete, employees must sign an agreement committing to uphold the organization's security standards. Many organizations opt to craft a document that stipulates that violating security policy is grounds for dismissal as well as grounds for prosecution under federal, state, and local laws. When passing on the user account ID and temporary password to a new employee, organizations should conduct a review of the password policy and acceptable use restrictions at that time.

The initial creation of a new user account is often called an *enrollment*. The enrollment process creates a new identity and establishes the factors the system needs to perform authentication. It is critical that the enrollment process be completed fully and accurately. It is also critical that the identity of the individual being enrolled be proved through whatever means your organization deems necessary and sufficient. Photo ID, birth certificate, background check, credit check, security clearance verification, FBI database search, and even calling references are all valid forms of verifying a person's identity before enrolling them in any secured system.

## Account Maintenance

Throughout the life of a user account, ongoing maintenance is required. Organizations with fairly static organizational hierarchies and low employee turnover or promotion will conduct significantly less account administration than an organization with a flexible or dynamic organizational hierarchy and high employee turnover and promotion rates. Most account maintenance deals with altering rights and privileges. Procedures similar to those used when creating new accounts should be established to govern how access is changed throughout the life of a user account. Unauthorized increases or decreases in an account's access capabilities can cause serious security repercussions.

When employees leave an organization, their user accounts should be disabled, deleted, or revoked. Whenever possible, this task should be automated and tied into the HR department. In most cases, when someone's paychecks are stopped, that person should no longer have logon capabilities. Temporary or short-term employees should have specific expiration dates programmed into their user accounts. This maintains a degree of control established at the time of account creation without requiring ongoing administrative oversight.

# Account, Log, and Journal Monitoring

Activity auditing, account tracking, and system monitoring are also important aspects of access control management. Without these capabilities, it is impossible to hold subjects accountable. Through the establishment of identity, authentication, and authorization, tracking the activities of subjects (including how many times they access objects) offers direct and specific accountability. We discuss auditing and monitoring as an aspect of operations security and as an essential element in a secure environment in Chapter 14, "Auditing and Monitoring."

User accounts, event logs, and system journals help piece together the state of affairs for a server at any referenced point along the timeline of its operation. Event logs and system journals capture events, changes, messages, and other data that describe what activities occurred on a system. Thus, they are commonly used to support conclusions drawn about any incidents that might warrant investigation. When an account is obtained after an outside attacker exploits a vulnerable service, you can bet the server documented some aspects of that incident in its event logs and system journals.

# Access Rights and Permissions

Assigning access to objects is an important part of implementing an organizational security policy. Not all subjects should be granted access to all objects. Not all subjects should have the same functional capabilities on objects. A few specific subjects should access only some objects; likewise, certain functions should be accessible only to a few specific subjects.

For instance, the data entry department in any given organization does not require explicit access to the resources and information found in the accounting department. Therefore, not all subjects (those in data entry) require access to particular objects (in this case, accounting). Only managers within the accounting department may access financial data, and only supervisors are responsible for creating and maintaining that data.

## The Principle of Least Privilege

The *principle of least privilege* arises from the complex structure that results when subjects are granted access to objects. This principle states that subjects should be granted only as much access to objects as is required to accomplish their assigned work tasks. The principle has a converse that should be followed as well: Subjects should be blocked from accessing objects that are not required by their work tasks. The principle of least privilege is most often linked with DAC, but this concept applies to all types of access control environments, including non-DAC, MAC, RBAC, and TBAC.

We utilize acronyms throughout this book to conserve space and to make terms easier to memorize. On the exam, you will be tested with all terms and acronyms spelled out, so there will be no confusion between a rule-based access control (RBAC) system and a role-based access control (RBAC) system. Study each system and its defining characteristics carefully.

Keep in mind that the idea of privilege usually means the ability to write, create, alter, or delete data. Thus, limiting and controlling privilege based upon this concept can be a protection mechanism for data integrity. If users can change only those data files that their work tasks require them to change, then the integrity of all other files in the environment is protected.

This principle relies on the assumption that all users have a definite and distinct job description that is well defined and understood. Without a specific job description, it is not possible to know what privileges a user does or does not need.

## Need-to-Know Access

A related principle in the realm of mandatory access control environments is known as *need to know*. Within a specific classification level or security domain, some assets or resources may be sectioned off or compartmentalized. Such resources are restricted from general access even to subjects with otherwise sufficient clearance. Compartmentalized resources require an additional level of formalized access approval before they can be used by subjects. Subjects are granted access when they can justify their work-task-related reason for access or their need to know. Often, need to know is determined by a domain supervisor and is granted only for a limited period of time.

Determining which subjects have access to which objects is a function of the organizational security policy, the organizational hierarchy of personnel, and the implementation of an access control model. Thus, the criteria for establishing or defining access can be based on identity, roles, rules, classifications, location, time, interfaces, need to know, and so on. Access control models are formal descriptions of a *security policy*, which is a document that encapsulates the security requirements for an organization and prescribes the steps necessary to achieve the desired security. Access control models (or security models) are used in security evaluations and assessments as well as in tools used to validate security.

---

### Excessive Privilege and Creeping Privileges

It's important to guard against two problems related to access control: excessive privilege and creeping privileges. *Excessive privilege* is when a user has more access, privilege, or permission than assigned work tasks dictate. If a user account is discovered to have excessive privilege, additional and unnecessary privileges should be immediately revoked. *Creeping privileges* involve a user account accumulating privileges over time as job roles and assigned tasks change. This can occur because new tasks are added to a user's job and the related or necessary privileges are added as well but no privileges are ever removed, even if a related work task is no longer associated with or assigned to that user. Creeping privileges result in excessive privilege. You can prevent both of these issues by applying the principle of least privilege properly and stringently.

## Users, Owners, and Custodians

When discussing access to objects, three subject labels are used: user, owner, and custodian. A *user* is any subject who accesses objects on a system to perform some action or accomplish a work task. An *owner*, or information owner, is the person who has final corporate responsibility for classifying and labeling objects and protecting and storing data. The owner may be liable for negligence if they fail to perform due diligence in establishing and enforcing security policies to protect and sustain sensitive data. A *custodian* is a subject who has been assigned or delegated the day-to-day responsibility of properly storing and protecting objects.

A user is any end user on the system. The owner is typically the CEO, president, or department head. The custodian is typically the IT staff or the system security administrator.

## Separation of Duties and Responsibilities

The separation of duties and responsibilities is a common practice that prevents any single subject from being able to circumvent or disable security mechanisms. When core administration or high-authority responsibilities are divided among several subjects, no one subject has sufficient access to perform significant malicious activities or to bypass imposed security controls.

A separation of duties creates a checks-and-balances system where multiple subjects verify each other's actions and must work in concert to accomplish necessary work tasks. Separating duties makes perpetration of malicious, fraudulent, or otherwise unauthorized activities much more difficult and broadens the scope of detection and reporting. It is easy for individuals to perform unauthorized acts if they think they can get away with it. Once two or more people are involved, the committal of an unauthorized activity requires that each person agrees to keep a shared secret. This typically serves as a significant deterrent rather than as a means to corrupt a group en masse. The separation of duties can be static or dynamic. The static separation of duties is accomplished by assigning privileges based on written policies that don't change often. The dynamic separation of duties is used when security requirements cannot be determined until the system is active and functioning.

An example of a properly enforced separation of duties is to prevent the security administrator from being able to access system administration utilities or to perform changes to system configuration not related to security. For example, a security administrator needs no more than read access to system logs. In this manner, a separation of duties helps prevent conflicts of interest in the types of privileges assigned to administrators as well as users in general. Figure 1.4 illustrates common privileges that should not be combined with others in order to properly enforce a separation of duties.

**FIGURE 1.4**   A segregation of duties control matrix

| | Control Group | Systems Analyst | Application Programmer | Help Desk and Support Mgr. | End User | Data Entry | Computer Operator | DB Administrator | Network Administrator | System Administrator | Security Administrator | Tape Librarian | Systems Programmer | Quality Assurance |
|---|---|---|---|---|---|---|---|---|---|---|---|---|---|---|
| Control Group | | X | X | X | | X | X | X | X | X | | | X | |
| Systems Analyst | X | | | X | X | | X | | | | | X | X | |
| Application Programmer | X | | | X | X | X | X | X | X | X | X | X | X | |
| Help Desk and Support Mgr. | X | X | X | | X | X | | X | X | X | | X | X | |
| End User | | X | X | X | | | X | X | X | | | X | X | X |
| Data Entry | X | | X | X | | | X | X | X | X | X | | X | |
| Computer Operator | X | X | X | | X | X | | X | X | X | X | | X | |
| DB Administrator | X | | X | X | X | X | | | X | X | | | X | |
| Network Administrator | X | | X | X | X | X | X | X | | | | X | | |
| System Administrator | X | | X | X | | X | X | X | | | | X | | |
| Security Administrator | | X | X | | X | X | | | | | | X | X | |
| Tape Librarian | | X | X | X | X | | | X | X | X | | | X | |
| Systems Programmer | X | | X | X | X | X | X | X | | | X | X | | X |
| Quality Assurance | | | | X | | | | | | | | X | X | |

X—Combination of these functions may create a potential control weakness.

**NOTE**   The segregation of duties control matrix is not an industry standard; rather, it's a guideline that indicates which positions should be separated and require compensating controls if combined. This matrix illustrates potential segregation of duties and should not be viewed or used as an absolute mandate; instead, use it to help identify potential conflicts so proper questions may be asked to identify compensating controls.

# Summary

The first domain of the CISSP CBK is Access Control. Access controls are central to establishing a secure system. They rely upon identification, authentication, authorization, and accountability. Access control is the management, administration, and implementation of granting or restricting subject access to objects.

The first step in access control is verifying the identities of subjects on the system, commonly known as authentication. Other methods are available to authenticate subjects, including passwords and passphrases, biometric scans, tokens, and tickets.

Once a subject is authenticated, their access must be managed (authorization) and their activities logged so ultimately the person can be held accountable for the user account's online actions. Again, this is why we believe accountability and access control are mutually dependent, equally important components of a much larger and reliable security framework.

There are various models for access control or authorization. These include discretionary and nondiscretionary access controls. There are at least three important subdivisions of nondiscretionary access control: mandatory, role-based, and task-based access control.

Access can be managed for an entire network at once. Such systems are known as single sign-on solutions. Remote access clients pose unique challenges to LAN security and often require specialized tools such as RADIUS or TACACS.

Access control administration represents the collection of tasks and duties assigned to an administrator as they relate to managing user accounts, access, and accountability. This includes user account management, activity tracking, and access rights and permissions management, all of which are subject to life cycle considerations related to their creation, ongoing maintenance, and deletion or removal at the end of their useful lives.

Account, log, and journal monitoring also play an important role in managing access control because they provide the mechanisms and the data necessary to hold subjects accountable for their actions.

Assigned access to objects is a key aspect of implementing organizational security policy. This is where the principle of least privilege comes into play; it dictates that subjects should only obtain as much access as is required to accomplish assigned work tasks. This also explains need to know as a mandatory access control mechanisms designed to restrict access to information only to those whose job responsibilities require them to possess that information.

When access to objects is under discussion, three key subject labels are often used—namely, user, owner, and custodian. The user is a subject who accesses objects on a system pursuant to performing an action or accomplishing some work task. The owner is the subject responsible for classifying and labeling objects and protecting and storing data. A custodian is a subject to whom responsibility for properly storing and protecting objects is assigned or delegated.

Separation of duties provides a necessary set of checks and balances whereby multiple subjects must verify each other's actions on objects and work together to accomplish necessary work tasks. Separation of duties helps to reduce the possibility (and the perpetration) of malicious, fraudulent, and other unauthorized uses of objects. Proper separation and segregation of duties ensures that no single individual obtains sufficient access to violate security policy without involving other individuals.

# Exam Essentials

**Know the various types of access control.**   Access controls may be preventive (to stop unwanted or unauthorized activity from occurring), deterrent (to discourage violation of security policy), detective (to discover unwanted or unauthorized activity), corrective (to restore systems to normal after an unwanted or unauthorized activity has occurred), recovery (to repair or restore resource, functions and capabilities after a violation of security policy has occurred), compensation (to provide various options to other existing controls to aid in enforcement and support of security policy), directive (to direct, confine, or control the action of subjects to force or encourage compliance with security policy), administrative (policies or procedures to implement and enforce overall access control), logical/technical (hardware or software mechanisms used to manage access to resources and systems and to provide protection for those resources and systems), and physical (physical barrier deployed to prevent direct contact with systems or areas within a facility).

**Know the common access control techniques.**   Common access control techniques include discretionary, mandatory, nondiscretionary, rule based, role based, and lattice based. Access controls are used to manage the type and extent of access subjects have to objects. This is important to system security because such controls define who has access to what.

**Understand access control administration.**   Securely creating new user accounts, managing and maintaining user accounts on an ongoing basis, auditing/logging/monitoring subject activity, and assigning and managing subject access are important aspects of keeping a system secure. Security is an ongoing task, and administration is how you keep a system secure over time.

**Know details about each of the access control models.**   There are two primary categories of access control techniques: discretionary and nondiscretionary. Nondiscretionary can be further subdivided into specific techniques, such as mandatory, role-based, and task-based access control.

**Understand the processes of identification and common identification factors.**   The processes of identification include subject identity claims by using a username, user ID, PIN, smart card, biometric factors, and so on. They are important because identification is the first step in authenticating a subject's identity and proper access rights to objects.

**Understand the processes of authentication and the various authentication factors.** Authentication involves verifying the authentication factor provided by a subject against the authentication factor stored for the claimed identity, which could include passwords, biometrics, tokens, tickets, SSO, and so on. In other words, the authentication process ensures that a subject is who they claim to be and grants object rights accordingly.

**Understand the processes of authorization.** Authorization ensures that the requested activity or object access is possible given the rights and privileges assigned to the authenticated identity. This is important because it maintains security by providing proper access rights for subjects.

**Understand the strengths and weaknesses of passwords.** Users typically choose passwords that are easy to remember and therefore easy to guess or crack, which is one weakness often associated with passwords. Another is that randomly generated passwords are hard to remember, and thus many users write them down. Passwords are easily shared and can be stolen through many means. Additionally, passwords are often transmitted in clear text or with easily broken encryption protocols, and password databases are often stored in publicly accessible online locations. Finally, short passwords can be discovered quickly in brute-force attacks. On the other hand, passwords can be effective if selected intelligently and managed properly. It is important to change passwords frequently; the more often the same password is used, the more likely it will be compromised or discovered.

**Know the two access control methodologies and implementation examples.** Access control methodologies include centralized access control, in which authorization verification is performed by a single entity within a system, and decentralized access control, in which authorization verification is performed by various entities located throughout a system. Remote authentication mechanisms such as RADIUS and TACACS are implementation examples; they are used to centralize the authentication of remote dial-up connections.

**Understand the use of biometrics.** Biometric factors are used for identification or authentication. FRR, FAR, and CER are important aspects of biometric devices. Fingerprints, face scans, iris scans, retina scans, palm topography, palm geography, voice pattern, signature dynamics, and keystroke patterns are often used along with other authentication factors, such as a password, to provide an additional method to control authentication of subjects.

**Understand single sign-on.** Single sign-on (SSO) is a mechanism that allows a subject to be authenticated only once on a system and be able to access resource after resource unhindered by further authentication prompts. Kerberos, SESAME, KryptoKnight, NetSP, thin clients, directory services, and scripted access are all SSO mechanisms.

**Understand access control administration.** Access control administration breaks down into three areas of administrative responsibility: user account management, activity tracking, and access rights and permission management. It's important to understand the tasks and activities related to each of these three areas and how they can impact security.

**Appreciate how account, log, and journal monitoring enforce accountability.**   Managing access control also means holding subjects accountable for their actions. Account, log, and journal monitoring and auditing tools provide the means whereby accountability may be assigned to specific subjects.

**Understand key concepts involved in assigning object access.**   The principle of least privilege dictates that subjects be granted no more permissions than they absolutely need to perform their assigned work duties. Need to know means the subjects should only be granted object access when they require such access to do their jobs (and adds a specific dimension to individual objects that general security classification schemes cannot provide). In general, the default access rule for objects should be to deny access unless specific subjects require access to do their jobs (and then such access should permit only those actions that the job entails and no more).

**Be able to explain these subject labels: user, owner, and custodian.**   A user is a subject who accesses objects in the course of performing some action or accomplishing a work task. The owner is the subject responsible for classifying and labeling objects and for protecting and storing data on any system. A custodian is a subject to whom the protect and store role for some object or collection of objects has been delegated or assigned.

**Understand why separation or segregation of duties is important.**   When subjects have permissions that enable them to conduct entire transactions, change general security settings, or alter policy, they have the ability to transgress against policy without necessarily setting off alarms or alerts about potential or actual policy violations. By design, separation or segregation of duties breaks up permissions and access necessary to make such sweeping changes across multiple job roles so that no single individual should be able to undertake such activities.

# Written Lab

1.   Name at least seven access control types.
2.   Describe the three primary authentication factor types.
3.   Identify at least three access control techniques.
4.   What is the principle of least privilege?

# Answers to Written Lab

1. Access control types include preventive access control, deterrent access control, detective access control, corrective access control, recovery access control, compensation access control, directive access control, administrative access control, logical or technical access control, and physical control.

2. A Type 1 authentication factor is "something you know." A Type 2 authentication factor is "something you have." A Type 3 authentication factor is "something you are."

3. Discretionary access controls, nondiscretionary or rule-based access controls, mandatory access controls, role-based access controls, and lattice-based access controls.

4. The principle of least privilege defines the access permissions that are granted to a given user to achieve some specified tasks. It is the security concept and best practice of allowing only the necessary permissions to achieve such tasks.

# Review Questions

1. What is access?
   - **A.** Functions of an object
   - **B.** Information flow from objects to subjects
   - **C.** Unrestricted admittance of subjects on a system
   - **D.** Administration of ACLs

2. Which of the following is true?
   - **A.** A subject is always a user account.
   - **B.** The subject is always the entity that provides or hosts the information or data.
   - **C.** The subject is always the entity that receives information about or data from the object.
   - **D.** A single entity can never change roles between subject and object.

3. Which of the following types of access control uses fences, security policies, security awareness training, and antivirus software to stop an unwanted or unauthorized activity from occurring?
   - **A.** Preventive
   - **B.** Detective
   - **C.** Corrective
   - **D.** Authoritative

4. _____ access controls are the hardware or software mechanisms used to manage access to resources and systems and to provide protection for those resources and systems.
   - **A.** Administrative
   - **B.** Logical/technical
   - **C.** Physical
   - **D.** Preventive

5. What is the first step of access control?
   - **A.** Accountability logging
   - **B.** ACL verification
   - **C.** Subject authorization
   - **D.** Subject identification

6. _____ is the process of verifying or testing the validity of a claimed identity.

A. Identification

B. Authentication

C. Authorization

D. Accountability

7. Which of the following is an example of a Type 2 authentication factor?

A. "Something you have," such as a smart card, ATM card, token device, and memory card

B. "Something you are," such as fingerprints, voice print, retina pattern, iris pattern, face shape, palm topology, and hand geometry

C. "Something you do," such as type a passphrase, sign your name, and speak a sentence

D. "Something you know," such as a password, personal identification number (PIN), lock combination, passphrase, mother's maiden name, and favorite color

8. Which of the following is not a reason why using passwords alone is a poor security mechanism?

A. When possible, users choose easy-to-remember passwords that are easy to guess or crack.

B. Randomly generated passwords are hard to remember, and thus many users write them down.

C. Short passwords can be discovered quickly in brute-force attacks only when used against a stolen password database file.

D. Passwords can be stolen through many means, including observation, recording and playback, and security database theft.

9. Which of the following is not a valid means to improve the security offered by password authentication?

A. Enabling account lockout controls

B. Enforcing a reasonable password policy

C. Using password verification tools and password-cracking tools against your password database file

D. Allowing users to reuse the same password

10. What can be used as an authentication factor that is a behavioral or physiological characteristic unique to a subject?

A. Account ID

B. Biometric factor

C. Token

D. IQ

11. What does the crossover error rate (CER) for a biometric device indicate?

    **A.** The sensitivity is tuned too high.

    **B.** The sensitivity is tuned too low.

    **C.** The false rejection rate and the false acceptance rate are equal.

    **D.** The biometric device is not properly configured.

12. Which of the following is not an example of an SSO mechanism?

    **A.** Kerberos

    **B.** KryptoKnight

    **C.** TACACS

    **D.** SESAME

13. _____ access controls rely upon the use of labels.

    **A.** Discretionary

    **B.** Role-based

    **C.** Mandatory

    **D.** Nondiscretionary

14. A network environment that uses discretionary access controls is vulnerable to which of the following?

    **A.** SYN flood

    **B.** Impersonation

    **C.** Denial of service

    **D.** Birthday attack

15. What is the most important aspect of a biometric device?

    **A.** Accuracy

    **B.** Acceptability

    **C.** Enrollment time

    **D.** Invasiveness

16. Which of the following is not an example of a deterrent access control?

    **A.** Encryption

    **B.** Auditing

    **C.** Awareness training

    **D.** Antivirus software

**17.** Kerberos provides the security services of _____ protection for authentication traffic.

   **A.** Availability and nonrepudiation

   **B.** Confidentiality and authentication

   **C.** Confidentiality and integrity

   **D.** Availability and authorization

**18.** Which of the following forms of authentication provides the strongest security?

   **A.** Password and a PIN

   **B.** One-time password

   **C.** Passphrase and a smart card

   **D.** Fingerprint

**19.** Which of the following is the least acceptable form of biometric device?

   **A.** Iris scan

   **B.** Retina scan

   **C.** Fingerprint

   **D.** Facial geometry

**20.** Why is separation of duties important for security purposes?

   **A.** It ensures that multiple people can do the same job.

   **B.** It prevents an organization from losing important information when they lose important people.

   **C.** It prevents any single security subject (person) from being able to make major security changes without involving other subjects.

   **D.** It helps subjects concentrate their talents where they will be most useful.

# Answers to Review Questions

1.  B. Access is the transfer of information from an object to a subject.

2.  C. The subject is always the entity that receives information about or data from the object. The subject is also the entity that alters information about or data stored within the object. The object is always the entity that provides or hosts information or data. A subject can be a user, a program, a process, a file, a computer, a database, and so on. The roles of subject and object can switch while two entities, such as a program and a database or a process and a file, communicate to accomplish a task.

3.  A. A preventive access control is deployed to stop an unwanted or unauthorized activity from occurring. Examples of preventive access controls include fences, security policies, security awareness training, and antivirus software.

4.  B. Logical/technical access controls are the hardware or software mechanisms used to manage access to resources and systems and to provide protection for those resources and systems. Examples of logical or technical access controls include encryption, smart cards, passwords, biometrics, constrained interfaces, access control lists, protocols, firewalls, routers, intrusion detection systems, and clipping levels.

5.  D. Access controls govern subjects' access to objects. The first step in this process is identifying who the subject is. In fact, there are several steps preceding actual object access: identification, authentication, authorization, and accountability.

6.  B. Authentication is the process of verifying or testing the validity of a claimed identity.

7.  A. A Type 2 authentication factor is "something you have." This could be a smart card, ATM card, token device, or memory card.

8.  C. Brute-force attacks can be used against password database files and system logon prompts.

9.  D. Preventing password reuse increases security by preventing the theft of older password database files, which can be used against the current user passwords.

10. B. A biometric factor is a behavioral or physiological characteristic that is unique to a subject, such as fingerprints and face scans.

11. C. The point at which the FRR and FAR are equal is the crossover error rate (CER). The CER level is used as a standard assessment point from which to measure the performance of a biometric device.

12. C. Kerberos, SESAME, and KryptoKnight are examples of SSO mechanisms. TACACS is a centralized authentication service used for remote access clients.

13. C. Mandatory access controls rely on use of labels. A system that employs discretionary access controls allows the owner or creator of an object to control and define subject access to that object. Nondiscretionary access controls are also called *role-based access controls*. Systems that employ nondiscretionary access controls define a subject's ability to access an object through the use of subject roles or tasks.

**14.**  B.  A discretionary access control environment controls access based on user identity. If a user account is compromised and another person uses that account, they are impersonating the real owner of the account.

**15.**  A.  The most important aspect of a biometric factor is its accuracy. If a biometric factor is not accurate, it may allow unauthorized users into a system.

**16.**  D.  Antivirus software is not a deterrent access control, though it is regarded as an access control that has recovery, corrective, and preventative characteristics.

**17.**  C.  Kerberos provides confidentiality and integrity protection security services for authentication traffic.

**18.**  C.  Among these options, passphrase and a smart card provide the strongest authentication security because they deliver two-factor authentication.

**19.**  B.  Of the options listed, retina scan is the least accepted biometric device because it blows air into the eye and can reveal personal health issues.

**20.**  C.  Of the options listed, separation or segregation of duties is intended to make fraud, theft, or malicious violations of security policy more difficult by involving multiple subjects (people) in making security changes or conducting complete transactions with security or monetary significance.

# Chapter

# 2

# Attacks and Monitoring

---

## THE CISSP EXAM TOPICS COVERED IN THIS CHAPTER INCLUDE:

✓ **Access Control**

- Control access by applying the following concepts/methodology/techniques:

  - Policies; types of controls (e.g., preventative, detective, corrective, etc.); techniques (e.g., nondiscretionary, discretionary, and mandatory); identification and authentication; decentralized/distributed access control techniques; authorization mechanisms; logging and monitoring

- Understand access control attacks

- Assess effectiveness of access controls

✓ **Operations Security**

- Implement and support patch and vulnerability management

- Understand fault tolerance requirements

The Access Control domain in the Common Body of Knowledge (CBK) for the CISSP certification exam deals with topics and issues related to the monitoring, identification, and authorization of granting or restricting user access to resources. Generally, access control is any hardware, software, or organizational administrative policy or procedure that grants or restricts access, monitors and records attempts to access, identifies users attempting to access, and determines whether access is authorized or not.

The Access Control domain is discussed in this chapter and in the previous chapter (Chapter 1, "Accountability and Access Control"), as well as in Chapter 14. Be sure to read and study the materials from all these chapters to ensure complete coverage of the essential material for the CISSP certification exam.

The Operations Security domain in the CBK for the CISSP exam deals with topics and issues related to identifying the controls over hardware, media, and those operators with access privileges to any such resources. Audit and monitoring refer to those mechanisms, tools, and facilities that enable security events to be detected, and for subsequent actions to occur so that key elements are identified and reported appropriately. Operations security is also covered in Chapter 13, "Administrative Management."

# Monitoring

Monitoring is a programmatic means by which subjects are held accountable for their actions while authenticated on a system. It is also the process by which unauthorized or abnormal activities may be detected on a system. Monitoring is necessary to detect malicious actions by subjects as well as to detect attempted intrusions and system failures. It can help reconstruct events, provide evidence for prosecution, and produce problem reports and analysis. Auditing and logging are usually native features in an operating system and for most applications and services. Thus, configuring a system to record information about specific types of events is fairly straightforward.

Using log files to detect problems is another matter. In most cases, when sufficient logging and auditing are enabled to monitor a system, so much data is collected that important details can get lost in the sheer volume of resulting data. You can use numerous tools to search through log files for specific events or ID codes. The art of data reduction is crucial when working with large volumes of monitoring data obtained from log files. The tools used to extract the relevant, significant, or important details from large collections of data are known as *data mining tools*. For true automation and even real-time analysis of events, a specific type of data mining tool is required, namely, an intrusion detection system (IDS, covered in the next section).

Accountability is maintained by recording the activities of subjects and objects as well as core system functions that sustain the operating environment and security mechanisms. The audit trails created by recording system events to logs can be used to evaluate a system's health and performance. System crashes may indicate faulty programs, failing hardware, corrupt drivers, or intrusion attempts. The event logs leading up to a crash can often be used to discover the reason a system failed. Log files provide an audit trail for re-creating a step-by-step history of an event, intrusion, or system failure.

 **Real World Scenario**

**Monitoring Activity**

Accountability is absolutely necessary at every level of business, from the frontline infantry to the high-level commanders overseeing daily operations. Without monitoring the actions and activities of users and their applications on a given system, how can you hold them accountable for any mistakes or misdeeds they might commit?

Meet Alex, a quality assurance supervisor for the data entry department at an oil-drilling data mining company. During his daily routine, he sees many highly sensitive documents and the kind of juicy information that can earn a heavy tip from a greasy palm. He also corrects the kind of mistakes that could cause serious backlash from his company's clientele, because sometimes a minor clerical error can cause serious issues for a client's entire project.

Whenever Alex touches or transfers such information on his workstation, his actions leave an electronic trail of evidence that Brianna, his supervisor, can examine in the event that Alex's actions should come under scrutiny. She can observe where he obtained or placed pieces of sensitive information, when he accessed and modified such information, and just about anything else related to the handling and processing of the data as it flows in from the source and out to the client.

Without the electronic ability to observe and analyze the way Alex handles this highly sensitive information, how can you be certain about what he does with this information both in and out of the workplace? You can't, and that's what makes monitoring important (and required, pursuant to legislation such as the Sarbanes-Oxley Act, HIPAA, EU privacy laws, and so forth for some markets or types of information).

Monitoring is a necessary function of the auditing process through which subjects are held accountable for their actions and activities with regard to other subjects, objects, or functions on any given system. Additionally, you can build up multiple supportive layers of defense around monitoring, auditing, and accounting practices that include real-time detection and deterrence of network-borne attack patterns that originate both inside and outside the perimeter of your business environment.

# Intrusion Detection

An intrusion detection system is a product that automates the inspection of audit logs and real-time system events. IDSs are primarily used to detect intrusion attempts, but they can also be employed to detect system failures and to rate overall performance. IDSs watch for violations of confidentiality, integrity, and availability. The goal of an IDS is to provide perpetrator accountability for intrusion activities and provide a means for a timely and accurate response to intrusions. An IDS can recognize attacks that come from external connections (such as the Internet or partner networks), viruses, malicious code, trusted internal subjects attempting to perform unauthorized activities, and unauthorized access attempts from trusted locations. An IDS is considered one form of technical detective security control.

An IDS can actively watch for suspicious activity, peruse audit logs, and send alerts to administrators as specific events are detected. It can also lock down important system files or capabilities, track slow and fast intrusion attempts, highlight vulnerabilities, identify an intrusion's origination point, and track down the logical or physical location of the perpetrators. In addition, an IDS can terminate or interrupt attacks and intrusion attempts and can reconfigure routers and firewalls to prevent repeats of known attacks. IDS alerts can be sent or communicated with an onscreen notification (the most common) by playing a sound, sending an email notification, alerting a pager, or recording information in a log file.

A response from an IDS can be active, passive, or hybrid:

**Active response.**   Directly affects malicious activity in network traffic or a host application

**Passive response.**   Does not affect malicious activity but records information about the issue and notifies the administrator

**Hybrid response.**   Stops unwanted activity, records information about the event, and possibly even notifies the administrator

Generally, an IDS is used to detect unauthorized or malicious activity originating from inside or outside a trusted network. In general, an IDS has only limited capability to stop current or prevent future attacks. Typical responses an IDS can take against an attack include blocking ports, blocking protocols, blocking source addresses, and disabling all communications over some specific cable segment. Whenever an IDS discovers abnormal behavior (such as spoofed traffic) or violations of its security policy, filters, or rules, it records a log detail of the issue and then drops, discards, or deletes the relevant packets.

---

### 🌐 Real World Scenario

### I Detect an IDS

Chance can't seem to understand why he needs an IDS. Doesn't a firewall take care of everything? Doesn't a firewall provide sufficient security on a business network for every conceivable purpose? Deidre explains to Chance that a firewall is reactive in its approach: It has a basic idea of what is allowed where and from what addresses connections may be made. For example, her firewall blocks illicit connections to unused service ports and authorizes restricted access to publicly accessible mission-critical services.

Chance is left to wonder what else there could possibly be to safeguard against. Isn't it enough to prevent unauthorized access to network resources? Deidre then describes to Chance how an IDS is more responsive because it's "aware" of unusual application behavior patterns that may indicate a possible attack that a firewall does not directly analyze. There may be allowable forms of traffic that include impermissible or potentially harmful protocols or data formats. For example, Deidre once deterred a protocol field attack from executing against a vulnerable network-accessible service because her IDS had a rule set to catch that very attack in place; otherwise, it would have bypassed the firewall and caught them unprotected.

Although Deidre has the real-world experience to grasp the capabilities of an IDS as compared to a firewall, she's not sure Chance appreciates the difference. How might you differentiate an IDS from a firewall so you could explain it to nontechnical personnel (perhaps one of your superiors) and convey its significance and security impact?

The best approach is to emphasize that a firewall responds to traffic and within limits can apply state information to that traffic. On the other hand, an IDS attends to overall patterns of behavior to which a firewall may be oblivious. If you explain how distributed denial-of-service attacks, slow iterations on a password attack, or obvious network scanning and profiling works—and why an IDS can catch such things easily, whereas firewalls may not—you'll be able to make the case without too much effort. You can also make a case that an IDS contributes to layered security or defense in depth in that it goes beyond what firewalls or various security appliances can do.

---

An IDS should be considered one of many components that a well-formed security endeavor employs to protect a network. An IDS is complementary to a firewall. Other security controls, such as physical restrictions and logical access controls, are also necessary components (refer to Chapter 1 for a discussion of those controls).

Intrusion prevention requires adequate maintenance of overall system security, such as applying patches and setting security controls. It also involves responding to intrusions that an IDS discovers by erecting barriers to prevent future occurrences of the same attack. This could be as simple as updating software or reconfiguring access controls, or it could be as drastic as reconfiguring a firewall, removing or replacing an application or service, or redesigning an entire network.

When an intrusion is detected, your first response should be to contain the intrusion. Intrusion containment prevents additional damage to other systems but may allow continued infestation of already compromised systems. Later, once compromised systems are rebuilt from scratch, be sure to double-check compliance with your security policy—including checking ACLs, service configurations, and user account settings—before connecting the reestablished system to your network. Be aware that if you wipe and re-create a system, no parts of the previous system, nor any intrusion footprints, remain behind.

It is considered unethical and risky to actively launch counterstrikes against an intruder or to actively attempt to reverse-hack an intruder's computer system. Instead, rely upon your logging capabilities and sniffing collections to provide sufficient data to prosecute criminals or to simply improve the security of your environment in response.

IDS type and classification define the scope of responsibility and functional role for each system. Among the many variations in type and classification for IDSs there are enough complementary elements that enable two or more systems to combine their efforts toward a single common goal on the network.

# Host- and Network-Based IDSs

IDS types are most commonly classified by their information source. There are two primary types of IDSs: host based and network based. A *host-based* IDS watches for questionable activity on a single computer system, especially by watching audit trails, event logs, and application logs. A *network-based* IDS watches for questionable activity occurring on the network medium by inspecting packets and observing network traffic patterns. You may even occasionally find mention of an application-based IDS, which monitors application activity in a networked environment.

## Host-Based IDS

Because the attention of a host-based IDS is focused on a single computer (whereas a network-based IDS must monitor the activity on an entire network), it can examine events in much greater detail than a network-based IDS can. A host-based IDS is able to pinpoint the files and processes compromised or employed by a malicious user to perform unauthorized activity.

Host-based IDSs can detect anomalies undetected by network-based IDSs; however, a host-based IDS cannot detect network-only attacks or attacks on other systems. Because a host-based IDS is installed on the computer being monitored, attackers can discover the IDS software and disable or manipulate it to hide their tracks. A host-based IDS has some difficulty with detecting and tracking down denial-of-service (DoS) attacks, especially those that seek to consume all available bandwidth. A host-based IDS also consumes resources from the computer being monitored, thereby reducing its performance. A host-based IDS is also limited by the auditing capabilities of the host operating system and applications.

Host-based IDSs are considered more costly to manage than network-based IDSs. Host-based IDSs require that an installation on each server be monitored. They require administrative attention at each point of installation, while network-based IDSs usually require only a single installation point. Host-based IDSs have other disadvantages as well; for example, they degrade host system performance significantly, and they are easier for an intruder to discover and disable.

## Network-Based IDS

Network-based IDSs detect attacks or event anomalies through the capture and evaluation of network packets. A single network-based IDS can monitor a large network if installed on its backbone, where a majority of network traffic travels. Some versions of network-based IDSs use remote agents to collect data from various subnets and report to a central management console. Network-based IDSs are installed onto single-purpose computers. This allows them to be hardened against attack, reduces the number of vulnerabilities in the IDS, and allows the IDS to operate in stealth mode. In stealth mode, an IDS is invisible to the network, and intruders would have to know its exact location and system identification to discover it. A network-based IDS has little negative effect on overall network performance, and because it is deployed on a single-purpose system, it doesn't adversely affect performance on any other computer.

On networks with large volumes of traffic, a network-based IDS may be unable to keep up with the flow of data. This could cause the IDS to miss an attack that occurred during high traffic levels. Network-based IDSs do not usually work well on a switched network, especially if its routers do not have monitoring ports. Network-based IDSs cannot monitor the content of encrypted traffic in transit over the network medium. They are usually able to detect initiation of an attack or ongoing attempts to perpetrate an attack (including DoS), but they are unable to provide information about whether an attack succeeded or about which specific systems, user accounts, files, or applications may have been affected.

Often, a network-based IDS can provide some limited functionality to discover the source of an attack by performing Reverse Address Resolution Protocol (RARP) or reverse Domain Name System (DNS) lookups. However, because most attacks are launched by malicious individuals whose identity is masked through spoofing or by proxy through so-called "zombies," this is not always reliable.

An IDS should not be viewed as a security panacea. It is only one part of a multifaceted security solution for an environment. Although an IDS can offer numerous benefits, there are several drawbacks to consider. A host-based IDS may not be able to examine every detail if the host system is overworked and insufficient execution time is granted to the

IDS processes. A network-based IDS can suffer the same problem if network traffic load is high and it is unable to process packets efficiently and swiftly. A network-based IDS is also unable to examine the contents of encrypted traffic. A network-based IDS is not an effective network-wide solution on switched networks because it is unable to view all network traffic if it is not placed on a *mirrored port* (that is, a port specifically configured to send all data to the IDS). An IDS may initially produce numerous false alarms, and it requires significant management on an ongoing basis.

> A switched network is often a preventative measure against rogue sniffers. Whenever an IDS is attached to a switch, if the switch is not configured to mirror all traffic, then only a small portion of network traffic is accessible to the IDS. However, numerous types of attacks, such as MAC or ARP flooding, can cause a switch to default into hub mode, thus granting the attacker access to all data (as well as greatly reducing the efficiency and throughput of your network).

## Knowledge- and Behavior-Based Detection

An IDS can detect malicious behavior using two common methods. One way is to use *knowledge-based detection* (also called *signature-based detection* or *pattern-matching detection*). Here, the IDS uses a signature database and attempts to match all monitored events to its contents. If a match is made, the IDS assumes that an attack is taking place (or has taken place). The IDS vendor develops a suspect chart by examining and inspecting numerous intrusions on various systems. What results is a description, or *signature*, for common attack methods or behaviors. An IDS using knowledge-based detection functions in much the same way as many antivirus applications.

The primary drawback for a knowledge-based IDS is that it is effective only against known attack methods. New attacks or slightly modified versions of known attacks often go unrecognized by the IDS. This means that a knowledge-based IDS lacks a learning model; that is, it is unable to recognize new attack patterns as they occur. Thus, this type of IDS is only as useful as its signature file is correct and up-to-date. Keeping the signature file current is an important aspect in maintaining the best performance from a knowledge-based IDS.

The second detection type is *behavior-based detection* (also called *statistical intrusion detection*, *anomaly detection*, and *heuristics-based detection*). Basically, behavior-based detection learns about the normal activities and events on your system by watching and tracking what it sees. Once it has accumulated enough data about normal activity, it can detect abnormal and possibly malicious activities or events.

A behavior-based IDS can be labeled an expert system or a pseudo-artificial intelligence system because it can learn and make assumptions about events. In other words, the IDS can act like a human expert by evaluating current events against known events. The more information provided to a behavior-based IDS about normal activities and events, the more accurately it can detect anomalies. A behavior-based IDS can also detect newer attacks that have no signatures and will thus be invisible to a signature-based approach.

The primary drawback for a behavior-based IDS is that it produces many false alarms. Normal patterns of user and system activity can vary widely, and thus establishing a definition of normal or acceptable activity can be difficult. The more a security detection system creates false alarms, the less likely it is that security administrators will heed its warnings, just as in the fable of the boy who cried wolf. Over time, an IDS can become more efficient and accurate, but its learning process takes a long while to become usable. Using known behaviors, activity statistics, and heuristic evaluation of current vs. previous events, a behavior-based IDS can detect unforeseen, new, or unknown vulnerabilities, attacks, and intrusion methods.

Although knowledge-based and behavior-based detection methods do have their differences, both employ an alarm-signal system. When an intrusion is recognized or detected, an alarm is triggered. The alarm system notifies administrators via email or pop-up messages or by executing scripts to send pager messages. In addition to administrator notification, the alarm system can record alert messages in log and audit files as well as generate violation reports detailing the detected intrusions and discoveries of vulnerabilities.

Some IDSs also perform what's called *stateful packet analysis*, which means that they understand enough of the protocols used for communications to monitor potentially dangerous or malicious communications. If a known pattern of unwanted or malicious activity emerges, the IDS can then block further communications of that kind.

Anomaly analysis also adds to an IDS's capabilities in that these devices can recognize and react to sudden increases in traffic volume or activity (which can indicate a direct attack of some kind, if not a denial-of-service attack), multiple failed login attempts (indicative of possible password cracking attacks), logons or program activity outside normal working hours for accounts in use, or sudden increases in error or failure messages (which can also indicate that attacks are underway).

An IDS (or intrusion prevention system, aka IPS) can also respond to unwanted or untoward patterns of behavior by changing ACLs for routers, deliberately dropping suspicious packets, or denying access to suspicious, ill-behaved, or anomalous users. IDSs and IPSs can also help to drive quick, effective responses to unwanted or unexpected behavior, thanks to their abilities to generate instant messages or email alerts, to page on-duty security or administrative staff, and to pop up onscreen alerts in IT department control centers that are manned 24/7/365.

# IDS-Related Tools

Intrusion detection systems are often deployed in concert with other components. These IDS-related tools expand the usefulness and capabilities of IDSs and make them more efficient and less prone to false positives. These tools include honeypots, padded cells, and vulnerability scanners. They are described in the following sections.

## Understanding Honeypots

*Honeypots* are individual computers or entire networks created to serve as a snare for intruders. They look and act like legitimate networks, but they are 100 percent fake. Honeypots tempt intruders by presenting unpatched and unprotected security vulnerabilities as well as by hosting attractive and tantalizing but faux data. They are designed to grab an intruder's attention and direct them into a restricted playground while keeping them away from the legitimate network and confidential resources. Legitimate users never enter the honeypot; there is no real data or useful resources in the honeypot system. Thus, when honeypot access is detected, it is most likely an unauthorized intruder. Honeypots are deployed to keep an intruder logged on and performing malicious activities long enough for the automated IDS to detect the intrusion and gather as much information about the intruder as possible. The longer the honeypot retains the attention of the intruder, the more time an administrator has to investigate the attack and potentially identify the intruder.

A *honeynet* is two or more networked honeypots used in tandem to monitor or re-create larger, more diverse network arrangements. Often, these honeynets facilitate intrusion detection systems.

The use of honeypots raises the issue of enticement vs. entrapment. A honeypot can be legally used as an enticement device if the intruder discovers it through no outward efforts of the honeypot owner. Placing a system on the Internet with open security vulnerabilities and active services with known exploits is *enticement*. Enticement occurs when the opportunity for illegal or unauthorized actions is provided but perpetrators make their own decisions to perform such action. *Entrapment*, which is illegal, occurs when the honeypot owner actively solicits visitors to access the site and then charges them with unauthorized intrusion. In other words, it is considered to be entrapment when you trick or encourage a perpetrator into performing an illegal or unauthorized action.

## Understanding Padded Cells

A *padded cell* system is similar to a honeypot, but it performs intrusion isolation using a different approach. When an IDS detects an intruder, that intruder is automatically transferred to a padded cell. The padded cell has the look and layout of the actual network, but within the padded cell the intruder can neither perform malicious activities nor access any confidential data.

A padded cell is a simulated environment that offers fake data to retain an intruder's interest. The transfer of the intruder into a padded cell is performed without informing the intruder that the change has occurred. Like a honeypot, a padded cell system is heavily monitored and used by administrators to gather evidence for tracing and possible prosecution.

## Understanding Vulnerability Scanners

Another type of IDS-related tool is a *vulnerability scanner*. Vulnerability scanners are used to test a system for known security vulnerabilities and weaknesses. They are used to generate reports that indicate the areas or aspects of the system that need to be managed to improve security. The reports may recommend applying patches or making specific configuration or security setting changes to improve or impose security.

A vulnerability scanner is only as useful as its database of security issues. Thus, the database must be updated from the vendor often to provide a useful audit of your system. The use of vulnerability scanners in cooperation with IDSs may help reduce false positives by the IDS and keep the total number of overall intrusions or security violations to a minimum. When discovered vulnerabilities are patched quickly and often, the system provides a more secure environment.

An extension to the concept of the IDS is the *intrusion prevention system* (IPS), which was mentioned earlier. An IPS seeks to actively block unauthorized connection attempts or illicit traffic patterns as they occur. IPS designs fall under the same type (host and network based) and classification (behavior and signature based) as IDS counterparts, and they are often deployed together for complete network coverage. Additionally, many IPS platforms are capable of dissecting higher-level application protocols in search of malicious payloads. In fact, the line between IDSs and IPSs can be quite blurry in that many self-professed IDSs have IPS capabilities. These days, detection and prevention systems occur together more than they do separately.

# Penetration Testing

In security terms, a *penetration* occurs when an attack is successful and an intruder is able to breach the perimeter around your environment. A breach can be as small as reading a few bits of data from your network or as big as logging in as a user with unrestricted privileges. A primary goal of security is to prevent penetrations.

One common method to test the strength of your security measures is to perform penetration testing, a vigorous attempt to break into your protected network using any means available. It is common for organizations to hire external consultants to perform penetration testing so testers are not privy to confidential elements of the environment's security configuration, network design, and other internal secrets.

Penetration testing seeks to find any and all detectable weaknesses in your existing security perimeter. The operative term is *detectable*; there are undetected and presently unknowable threats lurking in the large-scale infrastructure of network software and hardware design that no amount of penetration testing can directly discover or reveal. Once a weakness is discovered, countermeasures can be selected and deployed to improve security in the environment. One significant difference between penetration testing and an actual attack is that once a vulnerability is discovered during a penetration test, the intrusion attempt ceases before a vulnerability exploit can cause any damage. There are open-source and commercial tools (such as Metasploit and Core IMPACT) that take penetration testing one step further and attempt to exploit known vulnerabilities in systems and networks and may be used by good guys and bad guys alike.

Penetration testing may employ automated attack tools or suites or be performed manually using common network utilities and scripts. Automated attack tools range from professional vulnerability scanners to wild, underground tools discovered on the Internet. Tools are also often used for penetration testing performed manually, but the real emphasis is on knowing how to perpetrate an attack.

Penetration testing should be performed only with the consent and knowledge of management (and security staff). Performing unapproved security testing could cause productivity losses, trigger emergency response teams, or even cost you your job and potentially earn you jail time.

Regularly staged penetration tests are a good way to accurately judge the security mechanisms deployed by an organization. Penetration testing can also reveal areas where patches or security settings are insufficient and where new vulnerabilities have developed. To evaluate your system, benchmarking and testing tools are available for download at www.cisecurity.org.

> We discuss penetration testing further in Chapter 14, "Auditing and Monitoring."

Identifying and repelling attacks require an explicit, well-defined body of knowledge about their nature and occurrence. Some attack patterns leave behind signatures that make them readily apparent to casual observation with IDS instrumentation; other forms of attack are esoteric or not conducive to pattern-matching engines and therefore must be measured against a baseline of acceptable activity.

What elements or properties signify an attack sequence rather than some benign traffic formation? Answering this question depends on keeping up with the latest attacks, vulnerabilities, exploits, and demands that careful, attentive security professionals keep up with security bulletins (like those from the U.S. Computer Emergency Readiness Team at www.us-cert.gov/cas/bulletins or those from the Common Vulnerabilities and Exposures database at http://cve.mitre.org).

# Methods of Attack

As discussed in Chapter 1, one of the goals of access control is to prevent unauthorized access to objects. This includes access into a system (a network, a service, a communications link, a computer, and so forth) or access to data. In addition to controlling access, security seeks to prevent unauthorized alteration and disclosure and to provide consistent availability (remember the CIA Triad in Chapter 1).

However, malicious entities often focus on violating the security perimeter of a system to obtain access to data, alter or destroy data, and inhibit valid access to data and resources. The actual means by which attacks are perpetrated vary greatly. Some are extremely complex and require detailed knowledge of the victimized systems and programming techniques, whereas others are dead simple to execute and require little more than an IP address and the ability to manipulate a few tools or scripts. But even though there are many kinds of attacks, they can be grouped into a handful of classifications or categories.

The following are the most common or well-known access control attacks or attack methodologies (these are listed in alphabetical order):

- Brute-force and dictionary attacks
- Denial-of-service attacks
- Malware: viruses, worms, Trojans, spyware, and more
- Man-in-the-middle attacks
- Sniffers
- Spamming
- Spoofing

All these methods will eventually be attempted on your network. Assessing the severity of each on a case-by-case basis is less relevant than assessing each element as part of a much larger combination of risk potential and threat value.

Simple one-stage attacks (brute-force/dictionary lookups, spoofing, malware, and denial-of-service attacks) are the most common because they're the easiest to mount against a target and require only basic Internet access. Eavesdropping, sniffing, and man-in-the-middle attacks are more complex and involve an intrusion component to propel an attacker inside the network perimeter. They occur less frequently but can have more serious consequences if they succeed. Malware straddles these two categories in that anyone can propagate it, many can assemble kit-based instances, but expert malefactors create the most dangerous malware.

## Brute-Force and Dictionary Attacks

We discuss brute-force and dictionary attacks together because they are waged against the same entity: passwords. Either type of attack can be waged against a password database file or against an active logon prompt.

A *brute-force attack* is an attempt to discover passwords for user accounts by systematically attempting all possible combinations of letters, numbers, and symbols. With the speed of modern computers and the ability to employ distributed computing, brute-force attacks prove successful even against strong passwords. With enough time, all passwords can be discovered using a brute-force attack. Most passwords of 14 characters or less can be discovered within 7 days on a fast system using a brute-force attack program against a stolen password database file (the actual time it takes to discover passwords depends upon the algorithm used to encrypt them).

This window can be exploited in a time-memory trade-off known as *rainbow tables*, often used to speed up and amplify dictionary attacks or hybrid combinations of brute-force and dictionary attacks. Precomputed inputs (passwords and password combinations) are compactly represented in an iterated series of variations that make up a dictionary of possible password hashes. These precomputed hashes are then referenced against target hashes to find a matching entry. Two immediate problems arise: Any given password must be predetermined by some means (dictionary word lists, combinations and variations of alphanumeric elements, and so on) and contain no password salts, which extend the length and complexity of a password entry. Both of these conditions make rainbow tables effective only so long as the target password is knowable and predictably defined. Nevertheless, rainbow tables often play a complementary front-runner role to more exhaustive brute-force methods.

The longer a password (or the greater the number of keys in an algorithm's key space), the more costly and time-consuming a brute-force attack becomes. As the number of possibilities increases, the cost of performing an exhaustive attack goes up. In other words, the longer the password, the more secure it is against brute-force attacks. In addition, some password storage facilities also use a technique called "salting" to add additional bits (and increase complexity) for stored password hash values to stymie such attacks and make password data less susceptible to brute-force methods.

A *dictionary attack* is an attempt to discover passwords by presenting every possible password in a predefined list of common or expected passwords. This type of attack earns it name because the possible password list is so long, it is as if you were using an entire dictionary one word at a time to discover passwords.

Password attacks employ a specific cryptographic attack method known as the *birthday attack*. This attack is also called *reverse hash matching* or the *exploitation of collision*. Basically, the attack exploits the fact that if two messages are hashed and the hash values are the same, then the two messages are probably the same. A way of expressing this in mathematical or cryptographic notation is $H(M)=H(M')$. Passwords are stored in an account's database file on secured systems. Instead of being stored as plain text, though, passwords are hashed and only their hash values retained. This provides a reasonable level of protection. However, using reverse hash matching, a password attacker tool looks for possible passwords (through either brute-force or dictionary methods) with the same hash value as an entry stored in the account's database file. When a hash value match occurs, then the tool is said to have *cracked* the password.

Combinations of these two password attack methodologies can be used as well. For example, a brute-force attack could use a dictionary list as one source for its guesswork.

---

🌐 **Real World Scenario**

### Finesse and Careful Access Controls Beat Brute Force

Brute-force login attacks are relatively simple and rather effective against many types of targets. Claire sees thousands of failed and unauthorized connection attempts on her Internet-facing secure FTP servers, which includes Damien's constant inability to remember his own password. The effectiveness of a brute-force login attack hinges entirely on the notion that people tend to seek the path of least resistance, which in this case means using easily guessed passwords devoid of creativity or variation.

Claire runs a modified version of the secure FTP server that thwarts brute-force attempts and includes a user/group access list for its configuration, but she also wisely deploys an access list of permitted IPs on the firewall. This gives her several layers of protection over less-experienced administrators who don't enforce strong password choices or configurations and rule sets.

She knows that for every Damien in her user group who can't understand why his password is of a certain length and difficulty level, there's an Elaine or Frank on some other network who never forgets their password. Neither does the surreptitious attacker who keeps using their accounts, the passwords for which he found in a dictionary-driven attack.

---

Dictionary attacks often succeed because it's human nature to select passwords based on personal experiences. Unfortunately, those personal experiences are often broadcast to the world simply by the way you live and act on a daily basis. If you are a sports fan, your password might be based on a player's name or a hit record. If you have children, your password might be based on their names or birth dates. If you work in a technical industry, your password might be based on industry acronyms or product names. The more data about a victim that a custom dictionary list includes, whether that data is obtained through intelligence gathering, dumpster diving, or social engineering, the more successful it will be.

Protecting passwords from brute-force and dictionary attacks requires numerous security precautions and rigid adherence to a strong security policy. Here are some key elements to consider:

**Control physical access to systems.**   You must control physical access to your systems. If a malicious entity can gain physical access to an authentication server, they can often steal the password file within seconds. Once a password file is stolen, all passwords should be considered compromised.

**Control electronic access to password files.**   Tightly control and monitor electronic access to password files. End users and those who are not account administrators have no need to access the password database file for regular, daily work tasks. If you discover unauthorized access to the database file, investigate immediately. If you cannot determine that all such access is valid, then consider all passwords compromised.

**Create a strong password policy.**   Craft a password policy that programmatically enforces strong passwords and provides guidance to help end users create stronger passwords. The stronger and longer a password, the longer it will take for it to be discovered in a brute-force attack. However, with enough time, all passwords can be discovered via brute-force methods. Thus, changing passwords regularly is required to maintain security. Static passwords older than 30 days should be considered compromised even if no other aspect of a security breach has been discovered.

**Deploy multifactor authentication.**   Deploy multifactor authentication, such as using biometrics or token devices. If passwords are not the only means used to protect the security of a network, their compromise will not automatically result in a system breach.

**Use account lockout controls.**   Use account lockout controls to prevent brute-force and dictionary attacks against logon prompts. For those systems and services that don't support account lockout controls, such as most FTP servers, employ extensive logging and an IDS to look for attempted fast and slow password attacks.

**Encrypt password files.**   Encrypt password files with the strongest encryption available for your OS. Maintain rigid control over all media that have a copy of the password database file, such as backup tapes and some types of boot or repair disks.

Passwords are a poor security mechanism when used as a sole deterrent against unauthorized access. Brute-force and dictionary attacks show that passwords alone offer little more than a temporary blockade. Don't lose sight of the importance of physical security, multifactor authentication, and constant monitoring of access behaviors and patterns of use.

## Denial-of-Service Attacks

Denial-of-service (DoS) attacks are attacks that prevent a system from processing or responding to legitimate traffic or requests for resources and objects. The most common form of denial-of-service attacks is transmitting so many data packets to a server that it cannot process them all. Other forms of denial-of-service attacks focus on the exploitation of a known fault or vulnerability in an operating system, service, or application. Exploiting the fault often results in system crash or 100 percent CPU utilization. No matter what the actual attack consists of, any attack that renders its victim unable to perform normal activities can be considered a denial-of-service attack. Denial-of-service attacks can result in system crashes, system reboots, data corruption, blockage of services, and more.

Unfortunately, denial-of-service attacks based on *flooding* (that is, sending sufficient traffic to a victim to cause a DoS) are a way of life on the Internet. In fact, there are few means by which you can prevent any and all denial-of-service flood attacks (though individual attacks can be shut down once they're recognized and the source addresses involved identified). Furthermore, because of the ability to spoof packets or exploit legitimate Internet services, it is often impossible to trace the actual origin for such an attack or to apprehend the culprit.

There are several types of DoS flood attacks. The first, or original, type of attack employed a single attacking system flooding a single victim with a steady stream of packets. Those packets could be valid requests that were never completed or malformed or fragmented packets that consume the attention of the victimized system. This simple form of DoS is easy to terminate just by blocking packets from the source IP address.

Another form of attack is called a *distributed denial of service* (DDoS). A distributed denial of service occurs when the attacker compromises several systems and uses them as launching platforms against one or more victims. The compromised systems used in the attack are often called *slaves* or *zombies*, which operate in loose federations called *botnets* (short for "network of robots") managed in the background by shadowy control stations and covert servers. A DDoS attack results in the victims being flooded with data from numerous sources. DDoS attacks can be stopped by blocking packets from the compromised systems. But this can also result in blocking legitimate traffic because the sources of the flood packets are victims themselves and not the original perpetrators of the attack. These types of attacks are labeled as *distributed* because numerous systems are involved in the propagation of the attack against the victim.

A more recent form of DoS, called a *distributed reflective denial of service* (DRDoS), has been discovered. DRDoS attacks take advantage of the normal operation mechanisms of key Internet services, such as DNS and router update protocols. DRDoS attacks function by sending numerous update, session, or control packets to various Internet service servers or routers with a spoofed source address for the intended victim. Usually these servers or routers are part of the high-speed, high-volume Internet backbone trunks. What results is a flood of update packets, session acknowledgment responses, or error messages sent to the victim. A DRDoS attack can result in so much traffic that upstream systems are adversely affected by the sheer volume of data focused on the victim. This type of attack is called a *reflective attack* because the high-speed backbone systems reflect the attack to the victim. Unfortunately, these types of attacks cannot be prevented because they exploit normal functions of the systems involved. Blocking packets from these key Internet systems effectively cuts the victim off from a significant section of the Internet.

Not all instances of DoS result from a malicious attack. Errors in coding operating systems, services, and applications have resulted in DoS conditions. For example, a process failing to release control of the CPU or a service consuming system resources out of proportion to the service requests it is handling can cause DoS conditions. Most vendors quickly release patches to correct these self-inflicted conditions, so it is important to stay informed.

Many forms of DoS attacks have been committed over the Internet. Specific, historically significant examples of denial-of-service attacks are discussed in greater detail in the following sections.

## SYN Flood Attack

*SYN flood* attacks are waged by breaking the standard three-way handshake used by TCP/IP to initiate communication sessions. Normally, a client sends a SYN packet to a server, the server responds with a SYN/ACK packet to the client, and the client then responds with an ACK packet back to the server. This three-way handshake establishes a communication session that is used for data transfer until the session is terminated (using a three-way handshake with FIN and ACK packets). A SYN flood occurs when numerous SYN packets are sent to a server but the sender never replies to the server's SYN/ACK packets with the final ACK.

> A TCP session can also be terminated with an RST (reset) packet. In some instances, attackers forge or counterfeit reset packets in attempts to disconnect other users.

In addition, bogus SYN packets usually have a spoofed source address, so the SYN/ACK response is sent elsewhere, not to the actual originator of the packets. The server waits for the client's ACK packet, often for several seconds, holding open a session and consuming system resources. If a significant number of sessions are held open (for example, through the receipt of a flood of SYN packets), this causes a DoS. A server can be easily overtaxed by keeping sessions that are never finalized open, thus causing a failure. That failure can be as simple as an inability to respond to legitimate requests for communications or as serious as a frozen or crashed system.

One countermeasure to SYN flood attacks is increasing the number of connections a server can support. However, this usually requires additional hardware resources (memory, CPU, and so on) and may not be possible for all operating systems or network services. A more useful countermeasure is to reduce the time-out period while waiting for the concluding ACK packet. However, this can also result in failed sessions for clients connected using slower links or hindered by intermittent Internet traffic jams. Network-based IDSs may offer some protection against sustained SYN flood attacks by noticing that numerous SYN packets originate from one or only a few locations, resulting in incomplete sessions. An IDS could warn of such an attack or dynamically block flooding attempts.

## Smurf Attack

A *smurf* attack occurs when an amplifying server or network is used to flood a victim with useless data. An amplifying server or network is any system that generates multiple response packets, such as Internet Control Message Protocol (ICMP) echo packets or special User Datagram Protocol (UDP) packets, from a single submitted packet.

A common smurf attack method is to send a message to the broadcast address for a subnet or network so that every node on that network produces one or more response packets. The attacker sends information request packets with the victim's spoofed source address to the amplification system. Thus, all the responses are sent to the victim. If the amplification network can produce sufficient response packet volume, the victim's system will experience a DoS.

Figure 2.1 shows the basic elements in a smurf attack. The attacker sends multiple IMCP ping packets with a spoofed source address for the victim (V) and a destination with the broadcast address for the amplification network (AN:B). The amplification network responds with high volumes of echo packets to the victim, thus fully consuming the victim's connection bandwidth. Another DoS attack similar to smurf is called *fraggle*. Fraggle attacks employ spoofed UDP packets rather than ICMP packets.

Countermeasures for smurf attacks include disabling directed broadcasts on all network border routers and configuring all systems to drop ICMP ECHO packets. An IDS may be able to detect this type of attack, but there are no means to prevent the attack other than blocking the addresses of the amplification network. This tactic is problematic because the amplification network is usually also a victim.

**FIGURE 2.1**    A smurf attack

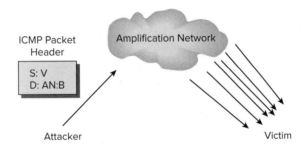

## Ping-of-Death, Stream, Teardrop, and Land Attacks

The attacks named in this section date back as far as the 1990s, but each uses interesting and devastating (at the time of their creation) techniques to subvert how incoming IP data is handled on the unwitting recipient's end. In the interim, specific defenses have been erected so that these attacks are highly unlikely to succeed today.

A *ping-of-death* attack employs an oversized ping packet. Using special tools, an attacker sends numerous oversized ping packets to a victim. In many cases, when the victimized system attempts to process those packets, an error occurs, causing the system to freeze, crash, or reboot. The ping of death is really a buffer-overflow attack, but because it often crashes its target server, it is considered a DoS attack. Countermeasures to this attack include keeping up-to-date with OS and software patches, properly coding in-house applications to prevent buffer overflows, running no untested code with system- or root-level privileges, and blocking ping packets at border routers/firewalls.

A *stream* attack occurs when a large number of packets are sent to numerous ports on a victim system using random source and sequence numbers. The processing performed as the victim system attempts to make sense of the data results in a DoS. Countermeasures include patching the system and using an IDS for dynamic blocking.

A *teardrop* attack occurs when an attacker exploits an operating system bug. This bug exists in the routines used to reassemble (that is, resequence) fragmented packets. An attacker sends numerous specially formatted fragmented packets to the victim, which causes the system to freeze or crash. Countermeasures for this attack include patching the OS and deploying an IDS for detection and dynamic blocking.

A *land* attack occurs when the attacker sends numerous SYN packets to a victim and the SYN packets have been spoofed to use the same source and destination IP address and port number as the victim. This causes the system to think it initiated a TCP/IP session with itself, which causes a system failure along with a system freeze, crash, or reboot. Countermeasures for this attack include patching the OS and deploying an IDS for detection and dynamic blocking.

## Beware the Botnets!

All the attack methods described in the preceding section are well documented today, which grants them zero stealth capability and minimal effectiveness when used against modern computing networks and operating systems. A more troubling trend has, however, emerged in recent years, including the rise of *botnets*. These are coordinated networks of compromised machines used in a cohesive or scheduled manner to attack, compromise, and disrupt other end users or entire networks. They are also widely employed to distribute spam on behalf of third parties who seek to find paying customers through unwanted email or to disseminate phishing lures to part unwary or naive recipients from their hard-earned cash.

For every botnet, there is usually one or more controlling computers, often called *botnet controllers*, which provide cutouts between the actual botnet operator (usually called a *bot herder*) and the compromised machines. This enables bot herders to control larger numbers of computers (many botnets exceed more than 100,000 compromised PCs, and botnets bigger than 10 million machines were reported in 2008) and to protect themselves from discovery even when their botnets are detected and disabled.

With hundreds of thousands to tens of millions of potential attack machines in their corrals, botnet abilities to mount huge and devastating DoS attacks are painfully obvious. As we write this chapter, they've been used recently in attacks against high-profile security organizations such as SANS and the CIA as well as major Web portals such as Google, Yahoo, and MSN.

## Spoofing Attacks

*Spoofing* is the art of pretending to be something you're not. Spoofing attacks consist of replacing a valid source and/or destination IP address and node numbers with false ones. Spoofing is involved in most attacks because it grants attackers the ability to hide their identities through misdirection. Spoofing is employed when an intruder uses a stolen username and password to gain entry, when an attacker changes the source address in a malicious packet, or when an attacker assumes the identity of a client to fool a server into transmitting controlled data.

Two specific types of spoofing attacks are *impersonation* and *masquerading*. Ultimately, these attacks are the same: Someone is able to gain access to a secured system by pretending to be someone else. These attacks often result in unauthorized access to a system through a valid user account that has been compromised. Impersonation is considered a more active attack because it requires the capture of authentication traffic and the replay of that traffic in such a way as to gain access to the system. Masquerading is considered a more passive attack because the attacker uses previously stolen account credentials to log on to a secured system.

Countermeasures for spoofing attacks include patching the OS and software, enabling source/destination verification on routers, and employing an IDS to detect and block attacks. As a general rule, whenever your system detects spoofed information, it should record relevant data elements into a log file; then the system should drop or delete the spoof itself.

## Man-in-the-Middle Attacks

A *man-in-the-middle* attack occurs when a malicious user is able to gain a position between the two endpoints of an ongoing communication. There are two types of man-in-the-middle attacks. One involves copying or sniffing the traffic between two parties; this is basically a sniffer attack (see the next section). The other involves attackers positioning themselves in the line of communication where they act as a store-and-forward or proxy mechanism (see Figure 2.2). The attacker functions as the receiver for data transmitted by the client and the transmitter for data sent to the server. The attacker is invisible to both ends of the communication link and is able to alter the content or flow of traffic. Through this type of attack, the attacker can collect logon credentials or sensitive data as well as change the content of the messages exchanged between the two endpoints.

**FIGURE 2.2**   A man-in-the-middle attack

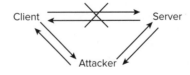

To perform this type of attack, the attacker must often alter routing information and DNS values, steal IP addresses, or falsify ARP lookups to impersonate a server from the perspective of the client and to impersonate the client from the perspective of the server.

An offshoot of a man-in-the-middle attack is known as a *hijack attack*. In this type of attack, a malicious user is positioned between a client and server and then interrupts the session and takes it over. Often, the malicious user impersonates a client to extract data from the server. The server is unaware that any change in the communication partner has occurred. The client is aware that communications with the server have ceased, but there is no indication as to why the communications were terminated, so it's invariably written off as a dropped connection.

Another type of attack, a *replay attack* (also known as a *playback attack*), resembles hijacking. A malicious user records traffic between a client and server; then packets sent from the client to the server are played back or retransmitted to that server with slight variations in the time stamp and source IP address (that is, spoofing). In some cases, this allows a malicious user to restart an old link with a server. Once this communication session is reopened, the malicious user can attempt to obtain data or additional access. Such captured traffic is often authentication traffic (which typically includes logon credentials, such as username and password), but it could be service access traffic or message control traffic. Replay attacks can be prevented by employing complex sequencing rules and time stamps to prevent retransmitted packets from being accepted as valid.

Countermeasures to these types of attacks require improvement in session establishment, identification, and authentication processes. Some man-in-the-middle attacks are thwarted through patching the OS and software. An IDS cannot usually detect man-in-the-middle or hijack attacks, but it can detect abnormal activities occurring over "secured" communication links. Operating systems and many IDSs can often detect and block replay attacks.

## Sniffer Attacks

A *sniffer* attack (also known as a *snooping* attack) is any activity that results in a malicious user obtaining information about a network or the traffic over that network. A sniffer is some kind of packet-capturing program that dumps the contents of packets traveling over a network medium into a file. Sniffer attacks often focus on the initial connections between clients and servers to obtain logon credentials (for example, usernames and passwords), secret keys, and so on. When performed properly, sniffing attacks are invisible to all other entities on the network and often precede spoofing or hijack attacks. A replay attack (discussed in the preceding section) is a type of sniffer attack.

Countermeasures to prevent or stop sniffing attacks require improving the physical access control, actively monitoring for sniffing signatures (such as looking for packet delay, additional routing hops, or lost packets, which can be performed by some IDSs), and using encrypted traffic over internal and external network connections.

## Spamming Attacks

*Spam* is the term that describes unsolicited email, newsgroup, or discussion forum messages. Spam can be as innocuous as an advertisement from a well-meaning vendor or as malignant as floods of unrequested messages with viruses or Trojan horses attached. Aside from emails that carry malicious (malware) payloads, spam is most often perceived as a type of denial-of-service attack, though it is also a significant security threat as well. As the level of spam increases, locating or accessing legitimate messages can be difficult. In addition to its nuisance value, spam consumes a significant portion of Internet resources (in the form of bandwidth and CPU processing), resulting in overall slower Internet performance and lower bandwidth availability for everyone.

Spamming attacks are directed floods of unwanted messages to a victim's email inbox or other messaging system. Such attacks cause DoS issues by filling up storage space and preventing legitimate messages from being delivered. In extreme cases, spamming attacks can cause system freezes or crashes and interrupt the activity of other users on the same subnet or ISP.

Spam attack countermeasures include using email filters, email proxies, and IDSs to detect, track, and terminate spam flood attempts.

## Crackers, Hackers, and Attackers

Crackers are malicious users intent on waging an attack against a person or system. Crackers may be motivated by greed, power, or recognition. Their actions can result in stolen property (data, ideas, and so on), disabled systems, compromised security, negative public opinion, loss of market share, reduced profitability, and lost productivity.

A term commonly confused with *crackers* is *hackers*. Hackers are technology enthusiasts with no malicious intent. Many authors and the media often use the term *hacker* when they are actually discussing issues relating to crackers. To avoid confusion, we use the term *attacker* for malicious intruders throughout this book.

Thwarting an attacker's attempts to breach your security or perpetrate DoS attacks requires vigilant effort to keep systems patched and properly configured. IDSs and honeypot systems often offer means to detect and gather evidence to prosecute attackers once they have breached your controlled perimeter.

# Access Control Compensations

Access control is used to regulate or specify which objects a subject can access and what type of access is allowed or denied. Numerous attacks, discussed in the previous sections, are designed to bypass or subvert access control. In addition to specific countermeasures for each of these attacks, you can use certain measures to help compensate for access control violations. A *compensation measure* does not directly prevent problems but rather provides a means by which you can design resiliency into your environment to support a quick recovery or response.

Backups are the best means of compensation against access control violations. With reliable backups and a mechanism to restore data, any corruption or file-based asset loss can be repaired, corrected, or restored. RAID technology can provide fault tolerance to allow for quick recovery in the event of a failure or severe access violation.

In general, avoiding single points of failure and deploying fault-tolerant systems helps ensure that the loss of use or control over a single system, device, or asset does not directly lead to the compromise or failure of your entire network environment. Fault tolerance countermeasures seek to combat threats to design reliability. Having backup communication routes, mirrored servers, clustered systems, failover systems, and so on can provide instant automatic or quick manual recovery in the event of an access control violation.

Your business continuity plan should include procedures for dealing with access control violations that threaten the stability of your mission-critical processes. Likewise, you should include in your insurance coverage categories of assets for which you may require compensation in the event of severe access control violations.

# Summary

Managing a system's access control involves a thorough understanding of system monitoring and common forms of malicious attacks. Monitoring a system provides the basis for accountability of authenticated users. Audit trails and logging files provide details about valid and unauthorized activities as well as system stability and performance. Using an IDS can simplify the process of examining the copious amount of data gathered through monitoring.

There are two types of IDSs: host based and network based. A host-based IDS is useful for detecting specific intrusions on single systems. A network-based IDS is useful for detecting overall aberrant network activity. There are two types of detection methods employed by IDSs: knowledge based and behavior based. A knowledge-based IDS uses a database of attack signatures to detect intrusion attempts. However, it fails to recognize new attack methods. A behavior-based IDS uses learned patterns of activity to detect abnormal events, but it produces numerous false positives until it gains sufficient knowledge about the system it is monitoring.

Honeypots, honeynets, and padded cells are useful tools to prevent malicious activity from occurring on a production network while enticing intruders to stick around long enough to gather evidence for prosecution.

Vulnerability scanners are signature-based detection tools that scan a system for a list of known vulnerabilities. These tools produce reports enumerating any discovered vulnerabilities and provide recommendations to improve system security.

Penetration testing is a useful mechanism to check the strength and effectiveness of deployed security measures and an organization's security policy. Be sure to obtain management approval before performing a penetration test.

There are numerous methods of attacks that intruders perpetrate against systems. Some of the more common attacks include brute-force, dictionary, denial-of-service, spoofing, man-in-the-middle, spamming, and sniffing attacks. Each type of attack employs different means to infiltrate, damage, or interrupt systems, and each has unique countermeasures to prevent them.

# Exam Essentials

**Understand the use of monitoring in relation to access controls.** Monitoring is used to hold subjects accountable for their actions and to detect abnormal or malicious activities.

**Understand the need for intrusion detection systems (IDSs) and that they are only one component in a security policy.** An IDS is needed to automate the process of discovering anomalies in subject activity and system event logs. IDSs are primarily used to detect intrusions or attempted intrusions. An IDS alone will not secure a system. It must be used in conjunction with access controls, physical security, and maintaining secure systems on the network.

**Know the limits of using host-based IDSs.** Host-based IDSs can monitor activity on a single system only. In addition, they can be discovered by attackers and disabled.

**List the pros and cons of network-based IDSs.** Network-based IDSs can monitor activity on the network medium, and they can be made invisible to attackers. They do not, however, work well on switched networks.

**Know how to explain differences between knowledge-based and behavior-based IDS detection methods.** Knowledge-based detection employs a database of attack signatures. Behavior-based detection learns what is normal about a system and assumes that all unknown activities are abnormal or possible signs of intrusion.

**Understand honeypots, honeynets, and padded cells.** A honeypot is a fake system or network that is designed to lure intruders with fake data to keep them on the system long enough to gather tracking information. A honeynet is a network composed of two or more honeypots. A padded cell is a simulated environment that intruders are seamlessly moved into once they are detected on the system. The simulated environment varies from the real environment only in that the data is fake and therefore malicious activities cause no harm.

**Be able to explain vulnerability scanners and penetration testing.** Vulnerability scanners are used to detect known security vulnerabilities and weaknesses. They are used to generate reports that indicate the areas or aspects of the system that need to be managed to improve security. Penetration testing is used to test the strength and effectiveness of deployed security measures with an authorized attempted intrusion attack.

**Know how brute-force and dictionary attacks work.**   Brute-force and dictionary attacks are carried out against a password database file or the logon prompt of a system. They are designed to discover passwords. In brute-force attacks, all possible combinations of keyboard characters are used, whereas a predefined list of possible passwords is used in a dictionary attack.

**Understand the need for strong passwords.**   Strong passwords make password-cracking utilities less successful. Strong passwords are dynamic passwords and should be strengthened by using two-factor authentication, enabling account lockouts, and using strong encryption on the password database file.

**Know what denial-of-service (DoS) attacks are.**   DoS attacks prevent a system from responding to legitimate requests for service. The two types of DoS attacks are traffic flooding and fault exploitation.

**Be able to explain the SYN flood DoS attack.**   The SYN flood DoS attack takes advantage of the TCP/IP three-way handshake to inhibit a system by requesting numerous connection sessions but failing to provide the final acknowledgment packet.

**Know how the smurf DoS attack works.**   Smurf attacks employ an amplification network to send numerous response packets to a victim.

**Know how ping-of-death DoS attacks work.**   Ping-of-death attacks send numerous oversized ping packets to the victim, causing the victim to freeze, crash, or reboot.

**Understand stream DoS attacks.**   Stream attacks send a large number of packets to numerous ports on the victim system by using random source and sequence numbers. The processing performed by the victim system attempting to make sense of the data will result in a DoS.

**Be able to explain teardrop DoS attacks.**   A teardrop attack occurs when an attacker exploits an operating system bug in the routines used to reassemble fragmented packets. An attacker sends numerous specially formatted fragmented packets to the victim, which causes the system to freeze or crash.

**Understand land DoS attacks.**   A land attack occurs when an attacker sends numerous SYN packets to a victim that have been spoofed to use the victim's own source and destination IP address and port number. This causes the victim to think it sent a TCP/IP session-opening packet to itself, which in turn causes a system failure, usually resulting in a freeze, crash, or reboot.

**Understand botnets, botnet controllers, and botnet herders.**   A botnet is a collection of compromised PCs whose unauthorized software payload includes remote control software that lets a coordinating computer (the botnet controller) issue instructions and schedule and coordinate attacks from those compromised PCs. The botnet herder is the often shadowy person or group in the background who manages the botnet controllers and determines what attacks or activities the botnet computers will undertake.

**Understand spoofing attacks.**   Spoofing attacks are any form of attack that uses modified packets in which the valid source and/or destination IP address and node numbers are replaced with false ones. Spoofing grants attackers the ability to hide their identities through misdirection.

**Understand man-in-the-middle attacks.**   A man-in-the-middle attack occurs when a malicious user is able to gain position between the two endpoints of a communications link. There are two types of man-in-the-middle attacks. One involves copying or sniffing traffic between two parties; this is basically a sniffer attack. The other requires the attacker to position itself in the line of communication and act as a store-and-forward or proxy mechanism between the two endpoints.

**Be able to explain hijack attacks.**   The hijack attack is an offshoot of a man-in-the-middle attack. In this type of attack, a malicious user positions himself between a client and server and then interrupts the session and takes it over. Often, the malicious user impersonates the client to extract data from the server. The server is unaware that any change in the communication partner has occurred.

**Understand replay or playback attacks.**   In a replay attack, a malicious user records traffic between a client and server. Then packets sent from the client to the server are played back or retransmitted to the server with slight variations in the time stamp and source IP address (that is, spoofing). In some cases, this allows a malicious user to restart an old session with a server.

**Know what sniffer attacks are.**   A sniffer attack (or snooping attack) is any activity that results in a malicious user obtaining information about a network or traffic on that network. A sniffer is a packet-capturing program that dumps the contents of packets traveling over the network medium into a file.

**Understand spamming attacks.**   *Spam* is a term describing unsolicited email, newsgroup, or discussion forum messages. Spam can be as innocuous as an advertisement from a well-meaning vendor or as malignant as floods of unrequested messages with viruses or Trojan horses attached. Spam is usually not a security threat but rather a type of denial-of-service attack. As the level of spam increases, locating or accessing legitimate messages can be difficult.

**Be able to list the countermeasures to all types of DoS attacks and to spoofing, man-in-the-middle, sniffer, and spamming attacks.**   Countermeasures include patching the OS for vulnerabilities, using firewalls and routers to filter and/or verify traffic, altering system/protocol configuration, and using IDSs.

# Written Lab

1.   Describe the two primary intrusion detection system types.
2.   Identify and define the three intrusion detection system response types.
3.   What is penetration testing, and why is it necessary?
4.   Name at least four common methods of network-based attack.

# Answers to Written Lab

1. Host-based IDSs examine events on individual computers in great detail, including file activities, accesses, and processes. Network-based IDSs examine general network events and anomalies through traffic evaluation.

2. Active response directly responds to malicious network activity or host process. Passive response observes and reports findings of intrusion or malicious activity but does not take action. Hybrid response halts identified malicious activity, records the event, and potentially notifies administration.

3. Penetration testing is the act of detecting infrastructure or system weakness, identifying vulnerabilities, and possibly exercising exploitative attacks as demonstrative proof.

4. Brute-force and dictionary word list attacks; denial-of-service (DoS) attacks, distributed DoS (DDoS), and distributed reflective DoS (DRDoS); spoofing attacks; botnets; protocol sniffing attacks; spamming; man-in-the-middle attacks; vulnerability exploitation; and resource/service saturation attack.

# Review Questions

1.  What is used to keep subjects accountable for their actions while they are authenticated to a system?

    **A.**   Access controls

    **B.**   Monitoring

    **C.**   Account lockout

    **D.**   Performance reviews

2.  Which of the following tools is most useful in sorting through large log files to search for intrusion-related events?

    **A.**   Text editor

    **B.**   Vulnerability scanner

    **C.**   Password cracker

    **D.**   IDS

3.  An intrusion detection system (IDS) is primarily designed to perform what function?

    **A.**   Detect abnormal activity.

    **B.**   Detect system failures.

    **C.**   Rate system performance.

    **D.**   Test a system for vulnerabilities.

4.  IDSs are capable of detecting which types of abnormal or unauthorized activities? (Choose all that apply.)

    **A.**   External connection attempts

    **B.**   Execution of malicious code

    **C.**   Unauthorized access attempts to controlled objects

    **D.**   None of the above

5.  Which of the following is true for a host-based IDS?

    **A.**   It monitors an entire network.

    **B.**   It monitors a single system.

    **C.**   It's invisible to attackers and authorized users.

    **D.**   It's ineffective on switched networks.

6.  Which of the following types of IDS is effective only against known attack methods?

    **A.**   Host based

    **B.**   Network based

    **C.**   Knowledge based

    **D.**   Behavior based

7. Which type of IDS can be considered an expert system?

    **A.** Host based

    **B.** Network based

    **C.** Knowledge based

    **D.** Behavior based

8. Which of the following is a fake network designed to tempt intruders with unpatched and unprotected security vulnerabilities and false data?

    **A.** IDS

    **B.** Honeynet

    **C.** Padded cell

    **D.** Vulnerability scanner

9. When a padded cell is used by a network for protection from intruders, which of the following is true?

    **A.** The data offered by the padded cell is what originally attracts the attacker.

    **B.** Padded cells are a form of entrapment.

    **C.** The intruder is seamlessly transitioned into the padded cell once they are detected.

    **D.** Padded cells are used to test a system for known vulnerabilities.

10. Which of the following is true regarding vulnerability scanners?

    **A.** They actively scan for intrusion attempts.

    **B.** They serve as a form of enticement.

    **C.** They locate known security holes.

    **D.** They automatically reconfigure a system to a more secure state.

11. When using penetration testing to verify the strength of your security policy, which of the following is not recommended?

    **A.** Mimicking attacks previously perpetrated against your system

    **B.** Performing attacks without management consent

    **C.** Using manual and automated attack tools

    **D.** Reconfiguring the system to resolve any discovered vulnerabilities

12. Which of the following attacks is an attempt to test every possible combination against a security feature in order to bypass it?

    **A.** Brute-force attack

    **B.** Spoofing attack

    **C.** Man-in-the-middle attack

    **D.** Denial-of-service attack

13. Which of the following is not a valid measure to take to improve protection against brute-force and dictionary attacks?

   **A.** Enforce strong passwords through a security policy.

   **B.** Maintain strict control over physical access.

   **C.** Require all users to log in remotely.

   **D.** Use two-factor authentication.

14. Which of the following is not considered a denial-of-service attack?

   **A.** Teardrop

   **B.** Smurf

   **C.** Ping of death

   **D.** Spoofing

15. A SYN flood attack works by what mechanism?

   **A.** Exploiting a packet processing glitch in Windows 95

   **B.** Using an amplification network to flood a victim with packets

   **C.** Exploiting the three-way handshake used by TCP/IP

   **D.** Sending oversized ping packets to a victim

16. Which of the following attacks sends packets with the victim's IP address as both the source and the destination?

   **A.** Land

   **B.** Spamming

   **C.** Teardrop

   **D.** Stream

17. In what type of attack are packets sent to a victim using invalid resequencing numbers?

   **A.** Stream

   **B.** Spamming

   **C.** Distributed denial of service

   **D.** Teardrop

18. Spoofing is primarily used to perform what activity?

   **A.** Send large amounts of data to a victim.

   **B.** Cause a buffer overflow.

   **C.** Hide the identity of an attacker through misdirection.

   **D.** Steal user accounts and passwords.

**19.** Spamming attacks occur when numerous unsolicited messages are sent to a victim. Because enough data is sent to the victim to prevent legitimate activity, it is also known as what?

**A.** Sniffing

**B.** Denial of service

**C.** Brute-force attack

**D.** Buffer-overflow attack

**20.** What type of attack occurs when malicious users position themselves between a client and server and then interrupt the session and takes it over?

**A.** Man-in-the-middle

**B.** Spoofing

**C.** Hijack

**D.** Cracking

# Answers to Review Questions

1.  B.  Accountability is maintained by monitoring the activities of subjects and objects as well as of core system functions that maintain the operating environment and the security mechanisms.

2.  D.  In most cases, when sufficient logging and auditing is enabled to monitor a system, so much data is collected that the important details get lost in the bulk. For automation and real-time analysis of events, an intrusion detection system (IDS) is required.

3.  A.  An IDS automates the inspection of audit logs and real-time system events to detect abnormal activity. IDSs are generally used to detect intrusion attempts, but they can also be employed to detect system failures or rate overall performance.

4.  A, B, C.  IDSs watch for violations of confidentiality, integrity, and availability. Attacks recognized by IDSs can come from external connections (such as the Internet or partner networks), viruses, malicious code, trusted internal subjects attempting to perform unauthorized activities, and unauthorized access attempts from trusted locations.

5.  B.  A host-based IDS watches for questionable activity on a single computer system. A network-based IDS watches for questionable activity being performed over the network medium, can be made invisible to users, and is ineffective on switched networks.

6.  C.  A knowledge-based IDS is effective only against known attack methods, which is its primary drawback.

7.  D.  A behavior-based IDS can be labeled an expert system or a pseudo-artificial intelligence system because it can learn and make assumptions about events. In other words, the IDS can act like a human expert by evaluating current events against known events.

8.  B.  Honeypots are individual computers, and honeynets are entire networks created to serve as a snare for intruders. They look and act like legitimate networks, but they are 100 percent fake. Honeypots and honeynets tempt intruders with unpatched and unprotected security vulnerabilities as well as attractive and tantalizing but faux data.

9.  C.  When intruders are detected by an IDS, they are transferred to a padded cell. The transfer of intruders into a padded cell is performed automatically, without informing the intruder that the change has occurred. The padded cell is unknown to the intruder before the attack, so it cannot serve as an enticement or entrapment. Padded cells are used to detain intruders, not to detect vulnerabilities.

10. C.  Vulnerability scanners are used to test a system for known security vulnerabilities and weaknesses. They are not active detection tools for intrusion, they offer no form of enticement, and they do not configure system security. In addition to testing a system for security weaknesses, they produce evaluation reports and make recommendations.

**11.** B. Penetration testing should be performed only with the knowledge and consent of the management staff. Unapproved security testing could result in productivity loss or trigger emergency response teams. It could even cost you your job.

**12.** A. A brute-force attack is an attempt to discover passwords for user accounts by systematically attempting every possible combination of letters, numbers, and symbols.

**13.** C. Strong password policies, physical access control, and two-factor authentication all improve the protection against brute-force and dictionary password attacks. Requiring remote logons has no direct effect on password attack protection; in fact, it may offer sniffers more opportunities to grab password packets from the data stream.

**14.** D. Spoofing is the replacement of valid source and destination IP and port addresses with false ones. It is often used in DoS attacks but is not considered a DoS attack itself. Teardrop, smurf, and ping of death are all DoS attacks.

**15.** C. A SYN flood attack is waged by breaking the standard three-way handshake used by TCP/IP to initiate communication sessions. Exploiting a packet processing glitch in Windows 95 is a WinNuke attack. The use of an amplification network is a smurf attack. Oversized ping packets are used in a ping-of-death attack.

**16.** A. In a land attack, the attacker sends a victim numerous SYN packets that have been spoofed to use the same source and destination IP address and port number as the victim's. The victim then thinks it sent a TCP/IP session-opening packet to itself.

**17.** D. In a teardrop attack, an attacker exploits a bug in operating systems. The bug exists in the routines used to reassemble (that is, resequence) fragmented packets. An attacker sends numerous specially formatted fragmented packets to the victim, which causes the system to freeze or crash.

**18.** C. Spoofing grants the attacker the ability to hide their identity through misdirection. It is therefore involved in most attacks.

**19.** B. A spamming attack is a type of denial-of-service attack. *Spam* is the term describing unwanted email, newsgroup, or discussion forum messages. It can be an advertisement from a well-meaning vendor or a flood of unrequested messages with viruses or Trojan horses attached.

**20.** C. In a hijack attack, which is an offshoot of a man-in-the-middle attack, a malicious user is positioned between a client and server and then interrupts the session and takes it over.

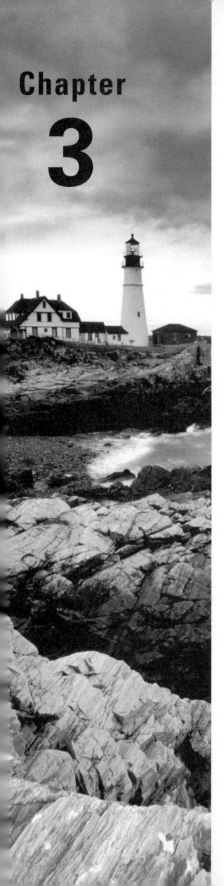

# Chapter

# 3

# ISO Model, Protocols, Network Security, and Network Infrastructure

---

## THE CISSP EXAM TOPICS COVERED IN THIS CHAPTER INCLUDE:

✓ **Telecommunications and Network Security**

- Establish secure data communications

- Understand secure network architecture and design

  - OSI and TCP/IP models; IP networking

- Secure network components

  - Hardware (e.g., modems, switches; routers); transmission media; filtering devices (e.g., firewalls, proxies); end-point security

- Establish secure multimedia communications

  - Voice over IP (VoIP); multimedia collaboration (e.g., remote meeting technology, instant messaging); Virtual Private Networks (VPN); remote access

Computers and networks emerge from the integration of communication devices, storage devices, processing devices, security devices, input devices, output devices, operating systems, software, services, data, and people. The CISSP CBK states that a thorough knowledge of these hardware and software components is an essential element of being able to implement and maintain security. This chapter discusses the OSI model as a guiding principle in networking, cabling, wireless connectivity, TCP/IP and related protocols, networking devices, firewalls, remote access security, encryption and authentication protocols, and avoiding single points of failure.

The Telecommunications and Network Security domain for the CISSP certification exam deals with topics related to network components (primarily network devices and protocols); specifically, how they function and how they are relevant to security. This domain is discussed in this chapter and in Chapter 4, "Communications Security and Countermeasures." Be sure to read and study the materials in both chapters to ensure complete coverage of the essential material for the CISSP certification exam.

# OSI Model

Communications between computers over networks are made possible by protocols. A *protocol* is a set of rules and restrictions that define how data is transmitted over a network medium (e.g., twisted-pair cable, wireless transmission). In the early days of network development, many companies had their own proprietary protocols, which meant interaction between computers of different vendors was often difficult, if not impossible. In an effort to eliminate this problem, the International Organization for Standardization (ISO) developed the OSI Reference Model for protocols in the early 1980s. Specifically, ISO 7498 defines the OSI Reference Model (more commonly called the *OSI model*). Understanding the OSI model and how it relates to network design, deployment, and security is essential in preparing for the CISSP exam.

In order to properly establish secure data communications, it is important to fully understand all of the technologies involved in computer communications. From hardware to software to protocols to encryption and beyond, there are lots of details to know, standards to understand, and procedures to follow. Additionally, the basis of secure network architecture and design is a thorough knowledge of the OSI and TCP/IP models as well as IP networking in general.

# History of the OSI Model

The OSI model wasn't the first or only attempt to streamline networking protocols or establish a common communications standard. In fact, the most widely used protocol today, TCP/IP (which is based upon the DARPA model, also known now as the *TCP/IP model*), was developed in the early 1970s. The OSI model was not developed until the late 1970s.

The OSI protocol was developed to establish a common communication structure or standard for all computer systems. The actual OSI protocol was never widely adopted, but the theory behind the OSI protocol, the OSI model, was readily accepted. The OSI model serves as an abstract framework, or theoretical model, for how protocols should function in an ideal world on ideal hardware. Thus, the OSI model has become a common reference point against which all protocols can be compared and contrasted.

# OSI Functionality

The OSI model divides networking tasks into seven distinct layers. Each layer is responsible for performing specific tasks or operations for the ultimate goal of supporting data exchange (in other words, network communication) between two computers. The layers are always numbered from bottom to top (see Figure 3.1). They are referred to by either their name or their layer number. For example, *layer 3* is also known as the *Network layer*. The layers are ordered specifically to indicate how information flows through the various levels of communication. Each layer communicates directly with the layer above it as well as the layer below it, plus the peer layer on a communication partner system.

**FIGURE 3.1**    A representation of the OSI model

| | |
|---|---|
| Application | 7 |
| Presentation | 6 |
| Session | 5 |
| Transport | 4 |
| Network | 3 |
| Data Link | 2 |
| Physical | 1 |

The OSI model is an open network architecture guide for network product vendors. This standard, or guide, provides a common foundation for the development of new protocols, networking services, and even hardware devices. By working from the OSI model, vendors are able to ensure that their products will integrate with products from other companies and be supported by a wide range of operating systems. If all vendors developed their own networking framework, interoperability between products from different vendors would be next to impossible.

The real benefit of the OSI model is its expression of how networking actually functions. In the most basic sense, network communications occur over a physical connection (whether that physical connection is electrons over copper, photons over fiber, or radio signals through the air). Physical devices establish channels through which electronic signals can pass from one computer to another. These physical device channels are only one type of the seven logical communication types defined by the OSI model. Each layer of the OSI model communicates via a logical channel with its peer layer on another computer. This enables protocols based on the OSI model to support a type of authentication by being able to identify the remote communication entity as well as authenticate the source of the received data.

## Encapsulation/Deencapsulation

Protocols based on the OSI model employ a mechanism called *encapsulation*. Encapsulation is the addition of a header, and possibly a footer, to the data received by each layer from the layer above before it's handed off the data to the layer below. As the message is encapsulated at each layer, the previous layer's header and payload become the payload of the current layer. Encapsulation occurs as the data moves down through the OSI model layers from Application to Physical. The inverse action occurring as data moves up through the OSI model layers from Physical to Application is known as *deencapsulation*. The encapsulation/deencapsulation process is as follows:

1.  The Application layer creates a message.

2.  The Application layer passes the message to the Presentation layer.

3.  The Presentation layer encapsulates the message by adding information to it. Information is usually added only at the beginning of the message (called a *header*); however, some layers also add material at the end of the message (called a *footer*), as shown in Figure 3.2.

**FIGURE 3.2**    A representation of OSI model encapsulation

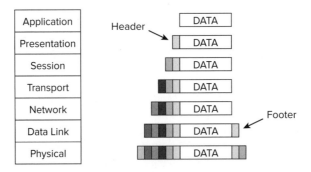

4.  The process of passing the message down and adding layer-specific information continues until the message reaches the Physical layer.

5.  At the Physical layer, the message is converted into electrical impulses that represent bits and is transmitted over the physical connection.

6.  The receiving computer captures the bits from the physical connection and re-creates the message in the Physical layer.

7.  The Physical layer converts the message from bits into a Data Link frame and sends the message up to the Data Link layer.

8.  The Data Link layer strips its information and sends the message up to the Network layer.

9.  This process of deencapsulation is performed until the message reaches the Application layer.

10. When the message reaches the Application layer, the data in the message is sent to the intended software recipient.

The information removed by each layer contains instructions, checksums, and so on that can be understood only by the peer layer that originally added or created the information (see Figure 3.3). This information is what creates the logical channel that enables peer layers on different computers to communicate.

**FIGURE 3.3**  A representation of the OSI model peer layer logical channels

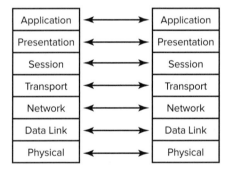

The message sent into the protocol stack at the Application layer (layer 7) is called the *data stream*. It retains the label of data stream until it reaches the Transport layer (layer 4), where it is called a *segment* (TCP protocols) or a *datagram* (UDP protocols). In the Network layer (layer 3), it is called a *packet*. In the Data Link layer (layer 2), it is called a *frame*. In the Physical layer (layer 1), the data has been converted into bits for transmission over the physical connection medium. Figure 3.4 shows how each layer changes the data through this process.

**FIGURE 3.4**    The OSI model data names

| Application | Data stream |
| Presentation | Data stream |
| Session | Data stream |
| Transport | Segment (TCP)/Datagram (UDP) |
| Network | Packet |
| Data Link | Frame |
| Physical | Bits |

## OSI Layers

Understanding the functions and responsibilities of each layer of the OSI model will help you understand how network communications function, how attacks can be perpetrated against network communications, and how security can be implemented to protect network communications. We discuss each layer, starting with the bottom layer, in the following sections.

For more information on the TCP/IP stack, search for *TCP/IP* at Wikipedia (http://en.wikipedia.org).

 **Real World Scenario**

### Remember the OSI

Although it can be argued that the OSI has little practical use and that most technical workers don't use the OSI on a regular basis, you can rest assured that the OSI model and its related concepts are firmly positioned within the CISSP exam. To make the most of the OSI, you must first be able to remember the names of the seven layers in their proper order. One common method of memorizing them is to create a mnemonic from the initial letters of the layer names so they are easier to remember. One of our favorites is Please Do Not Teach Surly People Acronyms. Do take note that this memorization mnemonic works from the Physical layer up to the Application layer. A mnemonic working from the Application layer down is All Presidents Since Truman Never Did Pot. There are many others of these memorization schemes out there; just be sure you know whether they are top-down or bottom-up.

# Physical Layer

The *Physical layer (layer 1)* accepts the frame from the Data Link layer and converts the frame into bits for transmission over the physical connection medium. The Physical layer is also responsible for receiving bits from the physical connection medium and converting them into a frame to be used by the Data Link layer.

The Physical layer contains the device drivers that tell the protocol how to employ the hardware for the transmission and reception of bits. Located within the Physical layer are electrical specifications, protocols, and interface standards such as the following:

- EIA/TIA-232 and EIA/TIA-449
- X.21
- High-Speed Serial Interface (HSSI)
- Synchronous Optical Network (SONET)
- V.24 and V.35

Through the device drivers and these standards, the Physical layer controls throughput rates, handles synchronization, manages line noise and medium access, and determines whether to use digital or analog signals or light pulses to transmit or receive data over the physical hardware interface.

Network hardware devices that function at layer 1, the Physical layer, are network interface cards (NICs), hubs, repeaters, concentrators, and amplifiers. These devices perform hardware-based signal operations, such as sending a signal from one connection port out on all other ports (a hub) or amplifying the signal to support greater transmission distances (a repeater).

# Data Link Layer

The *Data Link layer (layer 2)* is responsible for formatting the packet from the Network layer into the proper format for transmission. The proper format is determined by the hardware and the technology of the network. There are numerous possibilities, such as Ethernet (IEEE 802.3), Token Ring (IEEE 802.5), asynchronous transfer mode (ATM), Fiber Distributed Data Interface (FDDI), and Copper DDI (CDDI). Within the Data Link layer resides the technology-specific protocols that convert the packet into a properly formatted frame. Once the frame is formatted, it is sent to the Physical layer for transmission.

The following list includes some of the protocols found within the Data Link layer:

- Serial Line Internet Protocol (SLIP)
- Point-to-Point Protocol (PPP)
- Address Resolution Protocol (ARP)
- Reverse Address Resolution Protocol (RARP)
- Layer 2 Forwarding (L2F)
- Layer 2 Tunneling Protocol (L2TP)

- Point-to-Point Tunneling Protocol (PPTP)
- Integrated Services Digital Network (ISDN)

Part of the processing performed on the data within the Data Link layer includes adding the hardware source and destination addresses to the frame. The hardware address is the Media Access Control (MAC) address, which is a 6-byte (48-bit) binary address written in hexadecimal notation (for example, 00-13-02-1F-58-F5). The first 3 bytes (24 bits) of the address denotes the vendor or manufacturer of the physical network interface. This is known as the Organizationally Unique Identifier (OUI). OUIs are registered with IEEE, who controls their issuance. The OUI can be used to discover the manufacture of a NIC through the IEEE website at http://standards.ieee.org/regauth/oui/index.shtml. The last 3 bytes (24 bits) represent a unique number assigned to that interface by the manufacturer. No two devices can have the same MAC address.

Among the protocols at the Data Link layer (layer 2) of the OSI model, the two you should be familiar with are Address Resolution Protocol (ARP) and Reverse Address Resolution Protocol (RARP). ARP is used to resolve IP addresses into MAC addresses. Traffic on a network segment (for example, cables across a hub) is directed from its source system to its destination system using MAC addresses. RARP is used to resolve MAC addresses into IP addresses.

The Data Link layer contains two sublayers: the Logical Link Control (LLC) sublayer and the MAC sublayer. Details about these sublayers are not critical for the CISSP exam.

Network hardware devices that function at layer 2, the Data Link layer, are switches and bridges. These devices support MAC-based traffic routing. Switches receive a frame on one port and send it out another port based on the destination MAC address. MAC address destinations are used to determine whether a frame is transferred over the bridge from one network to another.

## Network Layer

The *Network layer (layer 3)* is responsible for adding routing and addressing information to the data. The Network layer accepts the segment from the Transport layer and adds information to it to create a packet. The packet includes the source and destination IP addresses.

The routing protocols are located at this layer and include the following:

- Internet Control Message Protocol (ICMP)
- Routing Information Protocol (RIP)
- Open Shortest Path First (OSPF)
- Border Gateway Protocol (BGP)
- Internet Group Management Protocol (IGMP)
- Internet Protocol (IP)
- Internet Protocol Security (IPSec)

- Internetwork Packet Exchange (IPX)
- Network Address Translation (NAT)
- Simple Key Management for Internet Protocols (SKIP)

The Network layer is responsible for providing routing or delivery information, but it is not responsible for verifying guaranteed delivery (that is the responsibility of the Transport layer). The Network layer also manages error detection and node data traffic (in other words, traffic control).

Routers and brouters are among the network hardware devices that function at layer 3. *Routers* determine the best logical path for the transmission of packets based on speed, hops, preference, and so on. Routers use the destination IP address to guide the transmission of packets. A *brouter*, working primarily in layer 3 but in layer 2 when necessary, is a device that attempts to route first, but if that fails, it defaults to bridging.

---

### Routing Protocols

There are two broad categories of routing protocols: distance vector and link state. *Distance vector* routing protocols maintain a list of destination networks along with metrics of direction and distance as measured in hops (in other words, the number of routers to cross to reach the destination). *Link state* routing protocols maintain a topography map of all connected networks and use this map to determine the shortest path to the destination. Common examples of distance vector routing protocols are RIP, IGRP, and BGP, while a common example of a link state routing protocol is OSPF.

---

## Transport Layer

The *Transport layer (layer 4)* is responsible for managing the integrity of a connection and controlling the session. It accepts a PDU from the *Session layer* and converts it into a segment. The Transport layer controls how devices on the network are addressed or referenced, establishes communication connections between nodes (also known as *devices*), and defines the rules of a session. Session rules specify how much data each segment can contain, how to verify the integrity of data transmitted, and how to determine whether data has been lost. Session rules are established through a handshaking process. (You should recall the discussion of the SYN/ACK three-way handshake for TCP/IP from Chapter 2, "Attacks and Monitoring.")

The Transport layer establishes a logical connection between two devices and provides end-to-end transport services to ensure data delivery. This layer includes mechanisms for segmentation, sequencing, error checking, controlling the flow of data, error correction, multiplexing, and network service optimization. The following protocols operate within the Transport layer:

- Transmission Control Protocol (TCP)
- User Datagram Protocol (UDP)
- Sequenced Packet Exchange (SPX)
- Secure Sockets Layer (SSL)
- Transport Layer Security (TLS)

## Session Layer

The *Session layer (layer 5)* is responsible for establishing, maintaining, and terminating communication sessions between two computers. It manages dialogue discipline or dialogue control (simplex, half-duplex, full-duplex), establishes checkpoints for grouping and recovery, and retransmits PDUs that have failed or been lost since the last verified checkpoint. The following protocols operate within the Session layer:

- Network File System (NFS)
- Structured Query Language (SQL)
- Remote Procedure Call (RPC)

Communication sessions can operate in one of three different discipline or control modes:

**Simplex**   One-way direction communication

**Half-duplex**   Two-way communication, but only one direction can send data at a time

**Full-duplex**   Two-way communication, in which data can be sent in both directions simultaneously

## Presentation Layer

The *Presentation layer (layer 6)* is responsible for transforming data received from the Application layer into a format that any system following the OSI model can understand. It imposes common or standardized structure and formatting rules onto the data. The Presentation layer is also responsible for encryption and compression. Thus, it acts as an interface between the network and applications. It is what allows various applications to interact over a network, and it does so by ensuring that the data formats are supported by both systems. Most file or data formats operate within this layer. This includes formats for images, video, sound, documents, email, web pages, control sessions, and so on. The following list includes some of the format standards that exist within the Presentation layer:

- American Standard Code for Information Interchange (ASCII)
- Extended Binary-Coded Decimal Interchange Mode (EBCDIC)
- Tagged Image File Format (TIFF)

- Joint Photographic Experts Group (JPEG)
- Moving Picture Experts Group (MPEG)
- Musical Instrument Digital Interface (MIDI)

 **Real World Scenario**

**So Many Protocols, So Many Layers**

With seven layers and more than 50 protocols, it may seem daunting to remember the layer in which each protocol resides. One way to learn this is to create flash cards. On the front of each card, write the name of the protocol; then on the back, write the layer name. After shuffling the cards, put each protocol in a pile representing its supposed layer. Once you have placed all the protocols, check your work by viewing the backs of the cards. Repeat this process until you are able to place each one correctly.

## Application Layer

The *Application layer (layer 7)* is responsible for interfacing user applications, network services, or the operating system with the protocol stack. It allows applications to communicate with the protocol stack. The Application layer determines whether a remote communication partner is available and accessible. It also ensures that sufficient resources are available to support the requested communications.

The application is not located within this layer; rather, the protocols and services required to transmit files, exchange messages, connect to remote terminals, and so on are found here. Numerous application-specific protocols are found within this layer, such as the following:

- Hypertext Transfer Protocol (HTTP)
- File Transfer Protocol (FTP)
- Line Print Daemon (LPD)
- Simple Mail Transfer Protocol (SMTP)
- Telnet
- Trivial File Transfer Protocol (TFTP)
- Electronic Data Interchange (EDI)
- Post Office Protocol version 3 (POP3)
- Internet Message Access Protocol (IMAP)
- Simple Network Management Protocol (SNMP)

- Network News Transport Protocol (NNTP)
- Secure Remote Procedure Call (S-RPC)
- Secure Electronic Transaction (SET)

There is a network device (or service) that works at the Application layer, namely, the gateway. However, an Application layer gateway is a specific type of component. It serves as a protocol translation tool. For example, an IP-to-IPX gateway takes inbound communications from TCP/IP and translates them over to IPX/SPX for outbound transmission.

## TCP/IP Model

The TCP/IP model (also called the DARPA or the DOD model) consists of only four layers, as opposed to the OSI Reference Model's seven. The four layers of the TCP/IP model are Application, Transport (previously known as Host-to-Host), Internet (sometimes Internetworking), and Link (although Network Interface and sometimes Network Access are used). Figure 3.5 shows how they compare to the seven layers of the OSI model. The TCP/IP protocol suite was developed before the OSI Reference Model was created. The designers of the OSI Reference Model took care to ensure that the TCP/IP protocol suite fit their model because of its established deployment in networking.

**FIGURE 3.5**   Comparing the OSI model with the TCP/IP model

The TCP/IP model's Application layer corresponds to layers 5, 6, and 7 of the OSI model. The TCP/IP model's Transport layer corresponds to layer 4 from the OSI model. The TCP/IP model's Internet layer corresponds to layer 3 from the OSI model. The TCP/IP model's Link layer corresponds to layers 1 and 2 from the OSI model.

It has become common practice (through confusion, misunderstanding, and probably laziness) to also call the TCP/IP model layers by their OSI model layer equivalent names. The TCP/IP model's Application layer is already using a name borrowed from the OSI, so that one is a snap. The TCP/IP model's Host-to-Host layer is sometimes called the Transport layer (the OSI model's fourth layer). The TCP/IP model's Internet layer is sometimes called the Network layer (the OSI model's third layer). And the TCP/IP model's Link layer is sometimes called the Data Link or the Network Access layer (the OSI model's second layer).

Since the TCP/IP model layer names and the OSI model layer names can be used interchangeably, it is important to know which model is being addressed in various contexts. Unless informed otherwise, always assume the OSI model provides the basis for discussion because it's the most widely used network reference model.

# Communications and Network Security

Establishing security on a network involves more than just managing the operating system and software. You must also address physical issues, including cabling, topology, and technology.

---

### LANs vs. WANs

There are two basic types of networks: LANs and WANs. A *local area network (LAN)* is a network typically spanning a single floor or building. This is commonly a limited geographical area. *Wide area network (WAN)* is the term usually assigned to the long-distance connections between geographically remote networks.

WAN connections and communication links can include private circuit technologies and packet-switching technologies. Common private circuit technologies include dedicated or leased lines and PPP, SLIP, ISDN, and DSL connections. Packet-switching technologies include X.25, Frame Relay, asynchronous transfer mode (ATM), Synchronous Data Link Control (SDLC), and High-Level Data Link Control (HDLC). Packet-switching technologies use virtual circuits instead of dedicated physical circuits. A virtual circuit is created only when needed, which makes for efficient use of the transmission medium and is extremely cost-effective. (We discuss the WAN technologies in Chapter 4.)

# Network Cabling

The type of connectivity media employed in a network is important to the network's design, layout, and capabilities. Without the right cabling or transmission media, a network may not be able to span your entire enterprise, or it may not support the necessary traffic volume. In fact, the most common causes of network failure (in other words, violations of availability) are caused by cable failures or misconfigurations. It is important for you to understand that different types of network devices and technologies are used with different types of cabling. Each cable type has unique useful lengths, throughput rates, and connectivity requirements.

## Coaxial Cable

*Coaxial cable*, also called *coax*, was a popular networking cable type used throughout the 1970s and 1980s. In the early 1990s, its use quickly declined because of the popularity and capabilities of twisted-pair wiring (explained in more detail later). Coaxial cable has a center core of copper wire surrounded by a layer of insulation, which is in turn surrounded by a conductive braided shielding and encased in a final insulation sheath.

The center copper core and the braided shielding layer act as two independent conductors, thus allowing two-way communications over a coaxial cable. The design of coaxial cable makes it fairly resistant to electromagnetic interference (EMI) and makes it able to support high bandwidths (in comparison to other technologies of the time period), and it offers longer usable lengths than twisted-pair. It ultimately failed to retain its place as the popular networking cable technology because of twisted-pair's much lower cost and ease of installation. Coaxial cable requires the use of segment terminators, whereas twisted-pair cabling does not. Coaxial cable is bulkier and has a larger minimum arc radius than twisted-pair. (The arc radius is the maximum distance the cable can be bent before damaging the internal conductors.) Additionally, with the widespread deployment of switched networks, the issues of cable distance became moot because of the implementation of hierarchical wiring patterns.

There are two main types of coaxial cable: thinnet and thicknet. *Thinnet*, also known as 10Base2, was commonly used to connect systems to backbone trunks of thicknet cabling. Thinnet can span distances of 185 meters and provide throughput up to 10 Mbps. *Thicknet*, also known as 10Base5, can span 500 meters and provide throughput up to 10 Mbps.

The most common problems with coax cable are as follows:

- Bending the coax cable past its minimum arc radius and thus breaking the center conductor

- Deploying the coax cable in a length greater than its maximum recommended length (which is 185 meters for 10Base2 or 500 meters for 10Base5)

- Not properly terminating the ends of the coax cable with a 50 ohm resistor

## Baseband and Broadband

The naming convention used to label most network cable technologies follows the syntax *XXyyyyZZ*. *XX* represents the maximum speed the cable type offers, such as 10 Mbps for a 10Base2 cable. The next series of letters, *yyyy*, represents the baseband or broadband aspect of the cable, such as baseband for a 10Base2 cable. Baseband cables can transmit only a single signal at a time, and broadband cables can transmit multiple signals simultaneously. Most networking cables are baseband cables. However, when used in specific configurations, coaxial cable can be used as a broadband connection, such as with cable modems. *ZZ* either represents the maximum distance the cable can be used or acts as shorthand to represent the technology of the cable, such as the approximately 200 meters for 10Base2 cable (actually 185 meters, but it's rounded up to 200) or T or TX for twisted-pair in 10Base-T or 100Base-TX. (Note that 100Base-TX is implemented using two CAT 5 UTP or STP cables—one issued for receiving, the other for transmitting.)

Table 3.1 shows the important characteristics for the most common network cabling types.

**TABLE 3.1**   Important characteristics for common network cabling types

| Type | Max Speed | Distance | Difficulty of Installation | Susceptibility to EMI | Cost |
|------|-----------|----------|----------------------------|-----------------------|------|
| 10Base2 | 10 Mbps | 185 meters | Medium | Medium | Medium |
| 10Base5 | 10 Mbps | 500 meters | High | Low | High |
| 10Base-T (UTP) | 10 Mbps | 100 meters | Low | High | Very low |
| STP | 155 Mbps | 100 meters | Medium | Medium | High |
| 100Base-T/100Base-TX | 100 Mbps | 100 meters | Low | High | Low |
| 1000Base-T | 1 Gbps | 100 meters | Low | High | Medium |
| Fiber-optic | 2+ Gbps | 2+ kilometers | Very high | None | Very high |

## Twisted-Pair

Twisted-pair cabling is extremely thin and flexible compared to coaxial cable. It consists of four pairs of wires that are twisted around each other and then sheathed in a PVC insulator. If there is a metal foil wrapper around the wires underneath the external sheath, the wire is known as *shielded twisted-pair* (STP). The foil provides additional protection from external EMI. Twisted-pair cabling without the foil is known as *unshielded twisted-pair* (UTP). UTP is most often referred to as just 10Base-T.

The wires that make up UTP and STP are small, thin copper wires that are twisted in pairs. The twisting of the wires provides protection from external radio frequencies and electric and magnetic interference and reduces crosstalk between pairs. Crosstalk occurs when data transmitted over one set of wires is picked up by another set of wires due to radiating electromagnetic fields produced by the electrical current. Each wire pair within the cable is twisted at a different rate (in other words, twists per inch); thus, the signals traveling over one pair of wires cannot cross over onto another pair of wires (at least within the same cable). The tighter the twist (the more twists per inch), the more resistant the cable is to internal and external interference and crosstalk, and thus the capacity for throughput (that is, higher bandwidth) is greater.

There are several classes of UTP cabling. The various categories are created through the use of tighter twists of the wire pairs, variations in the quality of the conductor, and variations in the quality of the external shielding. Table 3.2 shows the UTP categories.

**TABLE 3.2**  UTP categories

| UTP Category | Throughput | Notes |
|---|---|---|
| Cat 1 | Voice only | Not suitable for networks, but usable by modems |
| Cat 2 | 4 Mbps | Not suitable for most networks; often employed for host-to-terminal connections on mainframes |
| Cat 3 | 10 Mbps | Primarily used in 10Base-T Ethernet networks (offers only 4 Mpbs when used on Token Ring networks) |
| Cat 4 | 16 Mbps | Primarily used in Token Ring networks |
| Cat 5 | 100 Mbps | Used in 100Base-TX, FDDI, and ATM networks |
| Cat 6 | 155 Mbps | Used in high-speed networks |
| Cat 7 | 1 Gbps | Used on gigabit-speed networks |

Cat 5e is an enhanced version of Cat 5 designed to protect against far-end crosstalk. In 2001, the TIA/EIA-568-B no longer recognized the original Cat 5 specification. Now, the Cat 5e standard is rated for use by 100Base-T and even 1000Base-T deployments.

The following problems are the most common with twisted-pair cabling:

- Using the wrong category of twisted-pair cable for high-throughput networking
- Deploying a twisted-pair cable longer than its maximum recommended length (in other words, 100 meters)
- Using UTP in environments with significant interference

## Conductors

The distance limitations of conductor-based network cabling stem from the resistance of the metal used as a conductor. Copper, the most popular conductor, is one of the best and least expensive room-temperature conductors available. However, it is still resistant to the flow of electrons. This resistance results in a degradation of signal strength and quality over the length of the cable.

Plenum cable is a type of cabling sheathed with a special material that does not release toxic fumes when burned, as does traditional PVC coated wiring. Often plenum-grade cable must be used to comply with building codes, especially if the building has enclosed spaces that could trap gases.

The maximum length defined for each cable type indicates the point at which the level of degradation could begin to interfere with the efficient transmission of data. This degradation of the signal is known as *attenuation*. It is often possible to use a cable segment that is longer than the cable is rated for, but the number of errors and retransmissions will be increased over that cable segment, ultimately resulting in poor network performance. Attenuation is more pronounced as the speed of the transmission increases. It is recommended that you use shorter cable lengths as the speed of the transmission increases.

Long cable lengths can often be supplemented through the use of repeaters or concentrators. A repeater is a signal amplification device, much like the amplifier for your car or home stereo. The repeater boosts the signal strength of an incoming data stream and rebroadcasts it through its second port. A concentrator does the same thing except it has more than two ports. However, using more than four repeaters in a row is discouraged (see the sidebar "5-4-3 Rule").

---

**5-4-3 Rule**

The 5-4-3 rule is used whenever Ethernet or other IEEE 802.3 shared-access networks are deployed in a tree topology (in other words, a central trunk with various splitting branches). This rule defines the number of repeaters/concentrators and segments that can be used in a network design. The rule states that between any two nodes (a node can be any type of processing entity, such as a server, client, or router), there can be a maximum of five segments connected by four repeaters/concentrators, and it states that only three of those five segments can be populated (in other words, have additional or other user, server, or networking device connections).

The 5-4-3 rule does not apply to switched networks or the use of bridges or routers.

---

An alternative to conductor-based network cabling is fiber-optic cable. Fiber-optic cables transmit pulses of light rather than electricity. This has the advantage of being extremely fast and nearly impervious to tapping and interference. However, it is difficult to install and expensive; thus, the security and performance it offers comes at a steep price.

## Wireless Communications and Security

Wireless communications is a quickly expanding field of technologies for networking, connectivity, communication, and data exchange. There are literally thousands of protocols, standards, and techniques that can be labeled as wireless. These include cell phones, Bluetooth, cordless phones, and wireless networking. As wireless technologies continue to proliferate, your organization's security must go beyond locking down its local network. Security should be an end-to-end solution that addresses all forms, methods, and techniques of communication.

### General Wireless Concepts

Wireless communications employ radio waves to transmit signals over a distance. There is a finite amount of radio wave spectrum; thus, its use must be managed properly to allow multiple simultaneous uses with little to no interference. The radio spectrum is measured or differentiated using *frequency*. Frequency is a measurement of the number of wave oscillations within a specific time identified using the unit Hertz (Hz), or oscillations per second. Radio waves have a frequency between 3 Hz and 300 GHz. Different ranges of frequencies have been designated for specific uses, such as AM and FM radio, VHF and UHF television, and so on. Currently, the 900 MHz, 2.4 GHz, and 5 GHz frequencies are the most commonly used in wireless products because of their unlicensed categorization. However, to manage the simultaneous use of the limited radio frequencies, several spectrum-use techniques were developed. This included spread spectrum, FHSS, DSSS, and OFDM.

Most devices operate within a small subsection of frequencies rather than all available frequencies. This is because of frequency-use regulations (in other words, the FCC in the United States), power consumption, and the expectation of interference.

*Spread spectrum* means that communication occurs over multiples frequencies at the same time. Thus, a message is broken into pieces, and each piece is sent at the same time but using a different frequency. Effectively this is a parallel communication rather than a serial communication.

Frequency Hopping Spread Spectrum (FHSS) was an early implementation of the spread spectrum concept. However, instead of sending data in a parallel fashion, it transmits data in a series while constantly changing the frequency in use. The entire range of available frequencies is employed, but only one frequency at a time is used. As the sender changes from one frequency to the next, the receiver has to follow the same hopping pattern to pick up the signal. FHSS was designed to help minimize interference by not using only a single frequency that could be affected. Instead, by constantly shifting frequencies, it minimizes interference.

Direct Sequence Spread Spectrum (DSSS) employs all the available frequencies simultaneously in parallel. This provides a higher rate of data throughput than FHSS. DSSS also uses a special encoding mechanism known as *chipping code* to allow a receiver to reconstruct data even if parts of the signal were distorted because of interference. This occurs in much the same way that the parity of RAID 5 allows the data on a missing drive to be re-created.

Orthogonal Frequency-Division Multiplexing (OFDM) is yet another variation on frequency use. OFDM employs a digital multicarrier modulation scheme that allows for a more tightly compacted transmission. The modulated signals are perpendicular (orthogonal) and thus do not cause interference with each other. Ultimately, OFDM requires a smaller frequency set (aka channel bands) but can offer greater data throughput.

## Cell Phones

Cell phone wireless communications consist of using a portable device over a specific set of radio wave frequencies to interact with the cell phone carrier's network and either other cell phone devices or the Internet. The technologies used by cell phone providers are numerous and are often confusing. One point of confusion is the use of terms like *2G* and *3G*. These do not refer to technologies specifically but instead to the generation of cell phone technology. Thus, 1G is the first generation (mostly analog), 2G is the second (mostly digital, as are 3G and 4G), and so forth. There are even discussions of 2.5G when systems integrate second- and third-generation technologies. Table 3.3 attempts to clarify some of these confusing issues (this is only a partial listing of the technologies).

**TABLE 3.3**  Some wireless telephone technologies

| Technology | Generation |
|---|---|
| NMT | 1G |
| AMPS | 1G |
| TACS | 1G |
| GSM | 2G |
| iDEN | 2G |
| TDMA | 2G |
| CDMA | 2G |
| PDC | 2G |
| HSCSD | 2.5G |
| GPRS | 2.5G |
| W-CDMA | 3G |
| TD-CDMA | 3G |
| UWC | 3G |
| EDGE | 3G |
| DECT | 3G |
| UMTS | 3G |
| HSPDA | 3.5G |
| WINNER | 4G |
| WWRF | 4G |
| WiMax – IEEE 802.16 | 4G |
| XOHM | 4G |
| Mobile Broadband – IEEE 801.20 | 4G |
| LTE (Long Term Evolution) | 4G |

There are a few key issues to keep in mind with regard to cell phone wireless transmissions. First, not all cell phone traffic is voice; often cell phone systems are used to transmit text and even computer data. Second, communications over a cell phone provider's network, whether voice, text, or data, are not necessarily secure. Third, with specific wireless-sniffing equipment, your cell phone transmissions can be intercepted. Fourth, using your cell phone connectivity to access the Internet or your office network provides attackers with yet another potential avenue of attack, access, and compromise.

One important cell phone technology to discuss is Wireless Application Protocol (WAP). WAP is often confused with wireless networking (802.11). This is due to the use of the same acronym, which stands for Wireless Access Point when used in relation to 802.11. However, it is different in that with WAP, portable devices use a cell phone carrier's network to establish communication links with the Internet, while with wireless networking, an organization deploys its own wireless access points to allow its wireless clients to connect to its local network. WAP is not a standard; instead, it is a functioning industry-driven protocol stack. Via WAP-capable devices, users can communicate with the company network by connecting from their cell phone or PDA through the cell phone carrier network over the Internet and through a gateway into the company network. WAP is a suite of protocols working together. One of these protocols is Wireless Transport Layer Security (WTLS), which provides security connectivity services similar to those of SSL or TLS.

One very important security issue to recognize with WAP or with any security service provided by a telco is that you are unlikely to obtain true end-to-end protection from a communications service provider. The U.S. law known as the Communications Assistance for Law Enforcement Act (CALEA) mandates that all telcos, regardless of the technologies involved, must make it possible to wiretap voice and data communications when a search warrant is presented. Thus, a telco cannot provide customers with end-to-end encryption. At some point along the communication path, the data must be returned to clear form before being resecured for the remainder of the journey to its destination. WAP complies with the CALEA restriction as follows: A secure link is established between the mobile device and the telco's main server using WAP/WTLS. The data is converted into its clear form before being reencapsulated in SSL, TLS, IPSec, and so on for its continued transmission to its intended destination. Knowing this, use telco services appropriately, and whenever possible, feed pre-encrypted data into the telco link rather than clear form data.

## Bluetooth (802.15)

Bluetooth or IEEE 802.15 personal area networks (PANs) are another area of wireless security concern. Headsets for cell phones, mice, keyboards, GPS devices, and many other interface devices and peripherals are being connected via Bluetooth. Many of these connections are set up using a technique known as *pairing*, where the primary device scans the 2.4 GHz radio frequencies for available devices, and then, once a device is discovered, a four-digit PIN is used to "authorize" the pairing. This process does reduce the number of accidental pairings; however, a four-digit PIN is not secure (not to mention that the default PIN is often 0000). In addition, there are attacks against Bluetooth-enabled devices. One technique, known as *bluejacking*, is able to transmit SMS-like messages to your device. *Bluesnarfing* allows hackers to connect with your Bluetooth devices without your knowledge and extract information from them. This form of attack can offer attackers access to your contact lists, your data, and even your conversations. *Bluebugging* is an attack that grants hackers remote control over the feature and functions of a Bluetooth device. This could include the ability to turn on the microphone to use the phone as an audio bug. Fortunately, Bluetooth typically has a limited range of 30 feet, but some devices can function from more than 100 meters away. Bluetooth devices sometimes employ encryption, but it is not dynamic and can be usually cracked with modest effort. Use Bluetooth for those activities that are not sensitive or confidential. Whenever possible, change the default PINs on your devices. Do not leave your devices in discovery mode, and always turn off Bluetooth when not in active use.

## Cordless Phones

Cordless phones represent an often-overlooked security issue. Cordless phones are designed to use any one of the unlicensed frequencies, in other words, 900 MHz, 2.4 GHz, or 5 GHz. These three unlicensed frequency ranges are employed by many different types of devices, from cordless phones and baby monitors to Bluetooth and wireless networking devices. The issue that is often overlooked is that someone could easily eavesdrop on a conversation on a cordless phone since its signal is rarely encrypted. With a frequency scanner, anyone can listen in on your conversations.

## Wireless Networking (802.11)

Wireless networking is a popular method of connecting systems for communications because of the ease of deployment and relatively low cost. Historically, wireless networking has been fairly insecure, mainly because of a lack of knowledge by end users and organizations as well as insecure default configurations set by device manufacturers.

Wireless networking is primarily based on the IEEE 802.11 standard. It uses two primary components: an access point and host interfaces. The access point or wireless access point is the radio signal hub for the wireless network. The wireless access point supports associations with host devices with wireless interfaces (wireless NICs). The wireless access point performs a proxy function of converting the radio signal transmissions into cable-based transmissions in order to support communications between the wireless clients and the wired network and often ultimately the Internet.

Wireless networks can be deployed in two primary methods: ad hoc and infrastructure. An *ad hoc*, or *peer-to-peer*, network links wireless clients directly without the use of a wireless access point. *Infrastructure* mode is any wireless network configuration using a wireless access point to connect wireless clients. Within the infrastructure mode concept are several variations, including stand-alone, wired extension, enterprise extended, and bridge. A *stand-alone* mode infrastructure occurs when there is a wireless access point connecting wireless clients to each other, but not to any wired resources. The wireless access point serves as a wireless hub exclusively. A *wired extension* mode infrastructure occurs when the wireless access point acts as a connection point to link the wireless clients to the wired network. An *enterprise extended* mode infrastructure occurs when multiple wireless access points (WAPs) are used to connect a large physical area to the same wired network. Each wireless access point will use the same Extended Service Set Identifier (ESSID) so clients can roam the area while maintaining network connectivity, even while their wireless NICs change associations from one wireless access point to another. A *bridge* mode infrastructure occurs when a wireless connection is used to link two wired networks. This often uses dedicated wireless bridges and is used when wired bridges are inconvenient, such as when linking networks between floors or buildings.

The term *SSID* (which stands for service set identifier) is typically misused to indicate the name of a wireless network. Technically there are two types of SSIDs, namely extended service set identifier (ESSID) and basic service set identifier (BSSID). An ESSID is the name of a wireless network when a wireless base station or WAP is used (i.e., infrastructure mode). A BSSID is the name of a wireless network when in ad-hoc or peer-to-peer mode (i.e., when a base station or WAP is not used). However, when operating in infrastructure mode, the BSSID is the MAC address of the base station hosting the ESSID in order to differentiate multiple base stations supporting a single extended wireless network.

 **Real World Scenario**

**Wireless Channels**

There are so many more topics within wireless networking that we are not addressing because of space limitations and because they're not covered on the exam. For instance, you may want to learn more about wireless channels. Within the assigned frequency of the wireless signal are subdivisions of that frequency known as *channels*. Think of channels as lanes on the same highway. In the United States, there are 11 channels, in Europe there are 13, and in Japan there are 17. The differences stem from local laws regarding frequency management (think international versions of the United States's FCC). Wireless communications take place between a client and access point over a single channel. However, when two or more access points are relatively close to each other physically, signals on one channel can interfere with signals on another channel. One way to avoid this is to set the channels of physically close access points as differently as possible to minimize channel overlap interference. For example, if a building has four access points arranged in a line along the length of the building, the channel settings could be 1, 11, 1, and 11. However, if the building is square and an access point is in each corner, the channel settings may need to be 1, 4, 8, and 11. Think of the signal within a single channel as like a wide-load truck in a lane on the highway. The wide-load truck is using part of each lane to either side of it, thus making passing the truck in those lanes dangerous. Likewise, wireless signals in adjacent channels will interfere with each other.

Wireless networks are assigned a service set identifier (SSID) (either BSSID or ESSID) to differentiate one wireless network from another. If multiple basestations or wireless access points are involved in the same wireless network, an extended station set identifier (ESSID) is defined. The SSID is similar to the name of a workgroup. If a wireless client knows the SSID, they can configure their wireless NIC to communicate with the associated WAP. Knowledge of the SSID does not always grant entry, though, because the WAP can use numerous security features to block unwanted access. SSIDs are defined by default by vendors, and since these default SSIDs are well known, standard security practice dictates that the SSID should be changed to something unique before deployment. The SSID is broadcast by the WAP via a special transmission called a *beacon frame*. This allows any wireless NIC within range to see the wireless network and make connecting as simple as possible. However, this default broadcasting of the SSID should be disabled to keep the wireless network secret. However, attackers can still discover the SSID with a wireless sniffer since the SSID must still be used in transmissions between wireless clients and the WAP. Thus, disabling SSID broadcasting is not a true mechanism of security. Instead, use WPA2 as a reliable authentication and encryption solution rather than trying to hide the existence of the wireless network.

The IEEE 802.11 standard defines two methods that wireless clients can use to authenticate to WAPs before normal network communications can occur across the wireless link. These two methods are open system authentication (OSA) and shared key authentication (SKA). OSA means there is no real authentication required. As long as a radio signal can be transmitted between the client and WAP, communications are allowed. It is also the case that wireless networks using OSA typically transmit everything in clear text, thus providing no secrecy or security. SKA means that some form of authentication must take place before network communications can occur. The 802.11 standard defines one optional technique for SKA known as Wired Equivalent Privacy (WEP).

WEP is a form of encrypted authentication that employs RC4. WEP supports only one-way authentication from client to WAP. WEP is considered insufficient for security because of several deficiencies in its design and implementation. WEP uses static keys, uses initialization vectors improperly, and does not maintain true packet integrity. Because of these factors, attackers have developed techniques to crack WEP in less than a minute. Therefore, WEP should be used only when no other more secure option is available. Fortunately, WEP is optional, and the 802.11 standard allows for add-on security and authentication features.

An early alternative to WEP was WiFi Protected Access (WPA). This technique was an improvement but was itself not fully secure. It is based on the LEAP and TKIP cryptosystem and employs a secret passphrase. Unfortunately, the use of a single static passphrase is the downfall of WPA. An attacker can simply run a brute-force guessing attack against a WPA network to discover the base passphrase. If the passphrase is 14 characters or more, this is usually a time-prohibitive proposition, but not an impossible one. Additionally, both the LEAP and TKIP encryption options for WPA are now crackable using a variety of cracking techniques. While it is more complex than a WEP compromise, WPA no longer provides long-term reliable security.

Eventually, two new methods were developed that are still considered secure. First is the amendment known as 802.11i or WPA-2. It is a new encryption scheme known as the Counter Mode with Cipher Block Chaining Message Authentication Code Protocol (CCMP), which uses the AES encryption scheme. To date, no real-world attack has compromised the encryption of a properly configured WPA-2 wireless network. The second method is the use of 802.1X, a standard port-based network access control that ensures that clients cannot communicate with a resource until proper authentication has taken place. Effectively, 802.1X is a hand-off system that allows the wireless network to leverage the existing network infrastructure's authentication services. Through the use of 802.1X, other techniques and solutions such as RADIUS, TACACS, certificates, smart cards, token devices, and biometrics can be integrated into wireless networks.

Even though wireless networks are often inexpensive to initially deploy, some organizations have decided that the long-term cost to maintain and secure wireless is much more costly than a wired network. If a wireless network is present, you can take several steps to improve its security (these are in order of consideration and application/ installation; additionally, this order does not imply security or importance priority because using WPA-2 is a real security feature as opposed to SSID broadcast disabling):

1. Change the default administrator password.

2. Disable the SSID broadcast.

3. Change the SSID to something unique.

4. Enable MAC filtering if the pool of wireless clients is relatively small (usually less than 20) and static.

5. Consider using static IP addresses, or configure DHCP with reservations (applicable only for small deployments).

6. Turn on the highest form of authentication encryption supported: WEP, WPA, or WPA-2 (802.11i).

7. Treat wireless as remote access, and manage access using 802.1X.

8. Treat wireless as external access, and separate the WAP from the wired network using a firewall.

9. Treat wireless as an entry point for attackers, and monitor all WAP-to-wired-network communications with an IDS.

10. Require all transmissions between wireless clients and WAPs to be encrypted; in other words, require a VPN link.

Often, adding data encryption and other forms of filtering to a wireless link can reduce the effective throughput as much as 80 percent.

**Wireless Attacks**

Even with wireless security present, wireless attacks can still occur. There is an ever-increasing variety of attacks against networks, and many of these work against both wired and wireless environments. A few focus on wireless networks alone. One of these is a collection of techniques to discover that a wireless network is present, commonly called *wardriving*. It basically is the use of a wireless interface or a wireless detector to locate wireless network signals. Once an attacker knows there is a wireless network present, they can use sniffers to gather wireless packets for investigation. With the right tools, an attacker can discover hidden SSIDs, active IP addresses, valid MAC addresses, and even the authentication mechanism in use by the wireless clients. From there, attackers can grab dedicated cracking tools to attempt to break into the connection. The older and weaker your protections, the faster and more successful such attacks become.

Four main 802.11 wireless network amendments define unique frequencies and speeds of transmission (among many other technical details). Table 3.4 lists several of these along with their speed and frequency. The b, g, and n amendments all use the same frequency; thus, they maintain backward compatibility.

**TABLE 3.4**    802.11 wireless networking amendments

| Amendment | Speed | Frequency |
| --- | --- | --- |
| 802.11a | 54 Mbps | 5 GHz |
| 802.11b | 11 Mbps | 2.4 GHz |
| 802.11g | 54 Mbps | 2.4 GHz |
| 802.11n | 200+ Mbps | 2.4 GHz or 5 GHz |

Two final items in the realm of wireless networking are WiMax (802.16) and Mobile Broadband (802.20). These standards are designed to support broadband access over a metropolitan area, in other words, citywide wireless network connectivity. If you want more information on this topic, please visit Wikipedia or the IEEE standards page (http://standards.ieee.org/getieee802/index.html) and follow its external links.

# LAN Technologies

There are three main types of LAN technologies: Ethernet, Token Ring, and FDDI. There are a handful of other LAN technologies, but they are not as widely used as these three. Plus, only these three are potentially addressed on the CISSP exam. Most of the differences between LAN technologies exist at and below the Data Link layer.

## Ethernet

Ethernet is a shared-media LAN technology (also known as a *broadcast technology*). That means it allows numerous devices to communicate over the same medium but requires that the devices take turns communicating and perform collision detection and avoidance. Ethernet employs broadcast and collision domains. A *broadcast* domain is a physical grouping of systems in which all the systems in the group receive a broadcast sent by a single system in the group. A *broadcast* is a message transmitted to a specific address that indicates that all systems are the intended recipients.

A *collision* domain consists of groupings of systems within which a data collision occurs if two systems transmit simultaneously. A data collision takes place when two transmitted messages attempt to use the network medium at the same time. It causes one or both of the messages to be corrupted.

Ethernet can support full-duplex communications (in other words, full two-way) and usually employed using twisted-pair cabling (Note that coaxial cabling was the original cabling type used to support Ethernet, but coax is now a legacy cable type). Ethernet is most often deployed on star or bus topologies. Ethernet is based on the IEEE 802.3 standard. Individual units of Ethernet data are called *frames*. Fast Ethernet supports 100 Mbps throughput. Gigabit Ethernet supports 1000 Gbps throughput.

## Token Ring

Token Ring employs a token-passing mechanism to control which systems can transmit data over the network medium. The token travels in a logical loop among all members of the LAN. Token Ring can be employed on ring or star network topologies. It is rarely used today because of its performance limitations, higher cost compared to Ethernet, and increased difficulty in deployment and management.

Token Ring can be deployed as a physical star using a multistation access unit (MAU). An MAU allows for the cable segments to be deployed as a star, while internally the device makes logical ring connections.

## Fiber Distributed Data Interface (FDDI)

Fiber Distributed Data Interface (FDDI) is a high-speed token-passing technology that employs two rings with traffic flowing in opposite directions. FDDI is often used as a backbone for large enterprise networks. Its dual-ring design allows for self-healing by removing the failed segment from the loop and creating a single loop out of the remaining inner and outer ring portions. FDDI is expensive but was often used in campus environments before Fast Ethernet and Gigabit Ethernet were developed. A less-expensive, distance-limited, and slower version known as Copper Distributed Data Interface (CDDI) uses twisted-pair cables. CDDI is also more vulnerable to interference and eavesdropping.

## Subtechnologies

Most networks comprise numerous technologies rather than a single technology. For example, Ethernet is not just a single technology but a superset of subtechnologies that support its common and expected activity and behavior. Ethernet includes the technologies of digital communications, synchronous communications, and baseband communications, and it supports broadcast, multicast, and unicast communications and Carrier-Sense Multiple Access with Collision Detection (CSMA/CD). Many of the LAN technologies, such as Ethernet, Token Ring, and FDDI, may include many of the subtechnologies described in the following sections.

### Analog and Digital

One subtechnology common to many forms of network communications is the mechanism used to actually transmit signals over a physical medium, such as a cable. There are two types: analog and digital. Analog communications occur with a continuous signal that varies in frequency, amplitude, phase, voltage, and so on. The variances in the continuous signal produce a wave shape (as opposed to the square shape of a digital signal). The actual communication occurs by variances in the constant signal. Digital communications occur through the use of a discontinuous electrical signal and a state change or on-off pulses.

Digital signals are more reliable than analog signals over long distances or when interference is present. This is because of its definitive information storage method employing direct current voltage where voltage on represents a value of 1 and voltage off represents a value of 0. These on-off pulses create a stream of binary data. Analog signals become altered and corrupted because of attenuation over long distances and interference. Since an analog signal can have an infinite number of variations used for signal encoding as opposed to digital's two states, unwanted alterations to the signal make extraction of the data more difficult as the degradation increases.

### Synchronous and Asynchronous

Some communications are synchronized with some sort of clock or timing activity. Communications are either synchronous or asynchronous. Synchronous communications rely upon a timing or clocking mechanism based upon either an independent clock or a time stamp embedded in the data stream. Synchronous communications are typically able to support very high rates of data transfer. Asynchronous communications rely upon a stop and start delimiter bit to manage the transmission of data. Because of the use of delimiter bits and the stop and start nature of its transmission, asynchronous communication is best suited for smaller amounts of data. Public switched telephone network (PSTN) modems are good examples of asynchronous communication.

## Baseband and Broadband

How many communications can occur simultaneously over a cable segment depends on whether you use baseband technology or broadband technology. Baseband technology can support only a single communication channel. It uses a direct current applied to the cable. A current that is at a higher level represents the binary signal of 1, and a current that is at a lower level represents the binary signal of 0. Baseband is a form of digital signal. Ethernet is a baseband technology.

Broadband technology can support multiple simultaneous signals. Broadband uses frequency modulation to support numerous channels, each supporting a distinct communication session. Broadband is suitable for high-throughput rates, especially when several channels are multiplexed. Broadband is a form of analog signal. Cable television and cable modems, ISDN, DSL, T1, and T3 are examples of broadband technologies.

## Broadcast, Multicast, and Unicast

Another technology determines how many destinations a single transmission can reach. The options are broadcast, multicast, and unicast. A broadcast technology supports communications to all possible recipients. A multicast technology supports communications to multiple specific recipients. A unicast technology supports only a single communication to a specific recipient.

## LAN Media Access

Finally, there are at least five LAN media access technologies that are used to avoid or prevent transmission collisions. These technologies define how multiple systems all within the same collision domain are to communicate. Some of these technologies actively prevent collisions, while others respond to collisions.

**Carrier-Sense Multiple Access (CSMA)**   This is the LAN media access technology that performs communications using the following steps:

1. The host listens to the LAN media to determine whether it is in use.

2. If the LAN media is not being used, the host transmits its communication.

3. The host waits for an acknowledgment.

4. If no acknowledgment is received after a time-out period, the host starts over at step 1.

CSMA does not directly address collisions. If a collision occurs, the communication would not have been successful, and thus an acknowledgment would not be received. This causes the sending system to retransmit the data and reperform the CSMA process.

**Carrier-Sense Multiple Access with Collision Avoidance (CSMA/CA)**   This is the LAN media access technology that performs communications using the following steps:

1. The host has two connections to the LAN media: inbound and outbound. The host listens on the inbound connection to determine whether the LAN media is in use.

2. If the LAN media is not being used, the host requests permission to transmit.

3. If permission is not granted after a time-out period, the host starts over at step 1.

4. If permission is granted, the host transmits its communication over the outbound connection.

5. The host waits for an acknowledgment.

6. If no acknowledgment is received after a time-out period, the host starts over at step 1.

AppleTalk and 802.11 wireless networking are examples of networks that employ CSMA/CA technologies. CSMA/CA attempts to avoid collisions by granting only a single permission to communicate at any given time. This system requires a master or primary system to be designated, which responds to the requests and grants permission to send data transmissions.

**Carrier-Sense Multiple Access with Collision Detection (CSMA/CD)**   This is the LAN media access technology that performs communications using the following steps:

1. The host listens to the LAN media to determine whether it is in use.

2. If the LAN media is not being used, the host transmits its communication.

3. While transmitting, the host listens for collisions (in other words, two or more hosts transmitting simultaneously).

4. If a collision is detected, the host transmits a jam signal.

5. If a jam signal is received, all hosts stop transmitting. Each host waits a random period of time and then starts over at step 1.

Ethernet networks employ the CSMA/CD technology. CSMA/CD responds to collisions by having each member of the collision domain wait for a short but random period of time before starting the process over. Unfortunately, allowing collisions to occur and then responding or reacting to collisions causes delays in transmissions as well as a required repetition of transmissions. This results in about 40 percent loss in potential throughput.

**Token passing**   This is the LAN media access technology that performs communications using a digital token. Possession of the token allows a host to transmit data. Once its transmission is complete, it releases the token to the next system. Token passing is used by Token Ring networks, such as FDDI. Token Ring prevents collisions since only the system possessing the token is allowed to transmit data.

**Polling**   This is the LAN media access technology that performs communications using a master-slave configuration. One system is labeled as the primary system. All other systems are labeled as secondary. The primary system polls or inquires of each secondary system in turn whether they have a need to transmit data. If a secondary system indicates a need, it is granted permission to transmit. Once its transmission is complete, the primary system moves on to poll the next secondary system. Synchronous Data Link Control (SDLC) uses polling.

Polling addresses collisions by attempting to prevent them using a permission system. Polling is an inverse of the CSMA/CA method. Both use masters and slaves (or primary and secondary), but while CSMA/CA allows the slaves to request permissions, polling has the master offer permission. Polling can be configured to grant one (or more) system priority over other systems. For example, if the standard polling pattern was 1, 2, 3, 4, then to give system 1 priority, the polling pattern could be changed to 1, 2, 1, 3, 1, 4.

# Network Topologies

The physical layout and organization of computers and networking devices is known as the *network topology*. The *logical topology* is the grouping of networked systems into trusted collectives. The physical topology is not always the same as the logical topology. There are four basic topologies of the physical layout of a network: ring, bus, star, and mesh.

## Ring Topology

A ring topology connects each system as points on a circle (see Figure 3.6). The connection medium acts as a unidirectional transmission loop. Only one system can transmit data at a time. Traffic management is performed by a token. A token is a digital hall pass that travels around the ring until a system grabs it. A system in possession of the token can transmit data. Data and the token are transmitted to a specific destination. As the data travels around the loop, each system checks to see whether it is the intended recipient of the data. If not, it passes the token on. If so, it reads the data. Once the data is received, the token is released and returns to traveling around the loop until another system grabs it. If any one segment of the loop is broken, all communication around the loop ceases. Some implementations of ring topologies employ a fault tolerance mechanism, such as dual loops running in opposite directions, to prevent single points of failure.

**FIGURE 3.6**   A ring topology

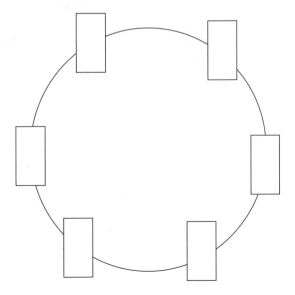

## Bus Topology

A bus topology connects each system to a trunk or backbone cable. All systems on the bus can transmit data simultaneously, which can result in collisions. A collision occurs when two systems transmit data at the same time; the signals interfere with each other. To avoid this, the systems employ a collision avoidance mechanism that basically "listens" for any other currently occurring traffic. If traffic is heard, the system waits a few moments and listens again. If no traffic is heard, the system transmits its data. When data is transmitted on a bus topology, all systems on the network hear the data. If the data is not addressed to a specific system, that system just ignores the data. The benefit of a bus topology is that if a single segment fails, communications on all other segments continue uninterrupted. However, the central trunk line remains a single point of failure.

There are two types of bus topologies: linear and tree. A linear bus topology employs a single trunk line with all systems directly connected to it. A tree topology employs a single trunk line with branches that can support multiple systems. Figure 3.7 illustrates both types. The primary reason a bus is rarely if ever used today is that it must be terminated at both ends and any disconnection can take down the entire network.

**FIGURE 3.7**   A linear topology and a tree bus topology

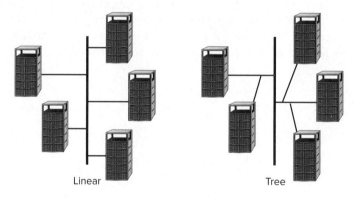

Linear                                   Tree

## Star Topology

A star topology employs a centralized connection device. This device can be a simple hub or switch. Each system is connected to the central hub by a dedicated segment (see Figure 3.8). If any one segment fails, the other segments can continue to function. However, the central hub is a single point of failure. Generally, the star topology uses less cabling than other topologies and makes the identification of damaged cables easier.

**FIGURE 3.8**   A star topology

A logical bus and a logical ring can be implemented as a physical star. Ethernet is a bus-based technology. It can be deployed as a physical star, but the hub or switch device is actually a logical bus connection device. Likewise, Token Ring is a ring-based technology. It can be deployed as a physical star using a multistation access unit (MAU). An MAU allows for the cable segments to be deployed as a star while internally the device makes logical ring connections.

## Mesh Topology

A mesh topology connects systems to other systems using numerous paths (see Figure 3.9). A full mesh topology connects each system to all other systems on the network. A partial mesh topology connects many systems to many other systems. Mesh topologies provide redundant connections to systems, allowing multiple segment failures without seriously affecting connectivity.

**FIGURE 3.9**   A mesh topology

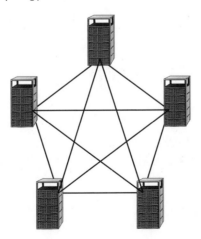

# TCP/IP Overview

The most widely used protocol suite is TCP/IP, but it is not just a single protocol; rather, it is a protocol stack comprising dozens of individual protocols (see Figure 3.10). TCP/IP is a platform-independent protocol based on open standards. However, this is both a benefit and a drawback. TCP/IP can be found in just about every available operating system, but it consumes a significant amount of resources and is relatively easy to hack into because it was designed for ease of use rather than for security.

**FIGURE 3.10**    The four layers of TCP/IP and its component protocols

| Application | | | | | |
|---|---|---|---|---|---|
| Application<br>Presentation<br>Session | Application | FTP | Telnet | SNMP | LPD |
| | | TFTP | SMTP | NFS | X Window |

| Transport | Transport | TCP | | UDP | |
|---|---|---|---|---|---|

| Network | Internet | ICMP | ARP | | RARP |
|---|---|---|---|---|---|
| | | IP | | | |

| Data Link<br>Physical | Link | Ethernet | Fast Ethernet | Token Ring | FDDI |
|---|---|---|---|---|---|

TCP/IP can be secured using VPN links between systems. VPN links are encrypted to add privacy, confidentiality, and authentication and to maintain data integrity. Protocols used to establish VPNs are Point-to-Point Tunneling Protocol (PPTP), Layer 2 Tunneling Protocol (L2TP), and Internet Protocol Security (IPSec). Another method to provide protocol-level security is to employ TCP wrappers. A *TCP wrapper* is an application that can serve as a basic firewall by restricting access to ports and resources based on user IDs or system IDs. Using TCP wrappers is a form of port-based access control.

## Transport Layer Protocols

The two primary Transport layer protocols of TCP/IP are TCP and UDP. TCP is a connection-oriented protocol, whereas UDP is a connectionless protocol. When a communication connection is established between two systems, it is done using ports. TCP and UDP each have 65,536 ports. Since port numbers are 16-digit binary numbers, the total number of ports is $2^{16}$, or 65,536, numbered from 0 through 65,535. A port (also called a *socket*) is little more than an address number that both ends of the communication link agree to use when transferring data. Ports allow a single IP address to be able to support multiple simultaneous communications, each using a different port number.

The first 1,024 of these ports (0–1,023) are called the *well-known ports* or the *service ports*. This is because they have standardized assignments as to the services they support. For example, port 80 is the standard port for web (HTTP) traffic, port 23 is the standard port for Telnet, and port 25 is the standard port for SMTP. You can find a list of ports worth knowing for the exam in the section "Common Application Layer Protocols" later in this chapter. Ports 1024 to 49151 are known as the registered software ports. These are ports that have one or more networking software products specifically registered with the International Assigned Numbers Authority (IANA, www.iana.org) in order to provide a standardized port numbering system for clients attempting to connect to their products. Ports 49152 to 65535 are known as the random, dynamic, or ephemeral ports because they are often used randomly and temporarily by clients as a source port. These random ports are also used by several networking services when negotiating a data transfer pipeline between client and server outside the initial service or registered ports, such as performed by common FTP.

---

### Port Numbers

The IANA recommends that ports 49152 to 65535 be used as dynamic and/or private ports. However, not all OSes abide by this. For example:

- Berkeley Software Distribution (BSD) uses ports 1024 through 4999.

- Many Linux kernels use 32768 to 61000.

- Microsoft, up to and including Windows Server 2003, uses the range 1025 to 5000.

- Windows Vista, Windows 7, and Server 2008 use the IANA range.

- FreeBSD uses the IANA suggested port range since version 4.6.

---

Transmission Control Protocol (TCP) operates at layer 4 (the Transport layer) of the OSI model. It supports full-duplex communications, is connection oriented, and employs reliable sessions. TCP is connection oriented because it employs a handshake process between two systems to establish a communication session. Upon completion of this handshake process, a communication session that can support data transmission between the client and server is established. The three-way handshake process is as follows:

**1.** The client sends a SYN (synchronize) flagged packet to the server.

**2.** The server responds with a SYN/ACK (synchronize and acknowledge) flagged packet back to the client.

**3.** The client responds with an ACK (acknowledge) flagged packet back to the server.

When a communication session is complete, there are two methods to disconnect the TCP session. First, and most common, is the use of FIN flagged packets instead of SYN flagged packets. Each side of a conversation will transmit a FIN flagged packet once all of its data is transmitted, triggering the opposing side to confirm with an ACK flagged packet. Thus, it takes four packets to gracefully tear down a TCP session. Second is the use of an RST flagged packet, which causes an immediate and abrupt session termination. (Please see the discussion of the TCP header flag later in this section.)

The segments of a TCP transmission are sequenced. This allows the receiver to rebuild the original communication by reordering received segments back into their proper arrangement in spite of the order in which they were received. Data communicated through a TCP session is periodically verified with an acknowledgment signal. The acknowledgment is a hash value of all previously transmitted data. If the server's own hash of received data does not match the hash value sent by the client, the server asks the client to resend the last collection of data. The number of packets transmitted before an acknowledge packet is sent is known as the *transmission window*. Data flow is controlled through a mechanism called *sliding windows*. TCP is able to use different sizes of windows (in other words, a different number of transmitted packets) before sending an acknowledgment. Larger windows allow for faster data transmission, but they should be used only on reliable connections where lost or corrupted data is minimal. Smaller windows should be used when the communication connection is unreliable. TCP should be employed when the delivery of data is required. Sliding windows allow this size to vary dynamically because the reliability of the TCP session changes while in use.

The TCP header is relatively complex when compared to its sister protocol UDP. A TCP header is 20 to 60 bytes long. This header is divided into several sections, or fields, as detailed in Table 3.5.

**TABLE 3.5**   TCP header construction (ordered from beginning of header to end)

| Size in Bits | Field |
| --- | --- |
| 16 | Source port |
| 16 | Destination port |
| 32 | Sequence number |
| 4 | Data offset |

| Size in Bits | Field |
|---|---|
| 4 | Reserved for future use |
| 8 | Flags (see Table 3.6) |
| 16 | Window size |
| 16 | Checksum |
| 16 | Urgent pointer |
| Variable | Various options; must be a multiple of 32 bits |

All of these fields have unique parameters and requirements, most of which are beyond the scope of the CISSP exam. However, you should be familiar with the details of the flags field. The flags field can contain a designation of one or more flags, or control bits. These flags indicate the function of the TCP packet and request that the recipient respond in a specific manner. The flag field is 8 bits long. Each of the bit positions represents a single flag, or control setting. Each position can be set on with a value of 1 or off with a value of 0. There are some conditions in which multiple flags can be enabled at once (in other words, the second packet in the TCP three-way handshake when both the SYN and ACK flags are set). Table 3.6 details the flag control bits.

**TABLE 3.6**  The TCP header flag field values

| Flag Bit Designator | Name | Description |
|---|---|---|
| CWR | Congestion Window Reduced | Used to manage transmission over congested links; see RFC 3168 |
| ECE | ECN-Echo (Explicit Congestion Notification) | Used to manage transmission over congested links; see RFC 3168 |
| URG | Urgent | Indicates urgent data |
| ACK | Acknowledgment | Acknowledges synchronization or shutdown request |
| PSH | Push | Indicates need to push data immediately to application |

**TABLE 3.6**   The TCP header flag field values *(continued)*

| Flag Bit Designator | Name | Description |
|---|---|---|
| RST | Reset | Causes immediate disconnect of TCP session |
| SYN | Synchronization | Requests synchronization with new sequencing numbers |
| FIN | Finish | Requests graceful shutdown of TCP session |

An additional important tidbit is that the IP header protocol field value for TCP is 6 (0x06). The protocol field value is the label or flag found in the header of every IP packet that tells the receiving system what type of packet it is. The IP header's protocol field indicates the identity of the next encapsulated protocol (in other words, the protocol contained in the payload from the current protocol layer, such as ICMP or IGMP, or the next layer up, such as TCP or UDP). Think of it as like the label on a mystery-meat package wrapped in butcher paper you pull out of the freezer. Without the label, you would have to open it and inspect it to figure out what it was. But with the label, you can search or filter quickly to find items of interest. For a list of other protocol field values, please visit www.iana.org/assignments/protocol-numbers.

---

 **Real World Scenario**

**Protocol Discovery**

Hundreds of protocols are in use on a typical TCP/IP network at any given moment. Using a sniffer, you can discover what protocols are in use on your current network. Before using a sniffer, though, make sure you have the proper permission or authorization. Without approval, using a sniffer can be considered a security violation because it enables you to eavesdrop on unprotected network communications. If you can't obtain permission at work, try this on your home network instead. Download and install a sniffer, such as Wireshark. Then use the sniffer to monitor the activity on your network. Discover just how many protocols (in other words, subprotocols of TCP/IP) are in use on your network.

Another step in using a sniffer is to analyze the contents of captured packets. Pick out a few different protocol packets, and inspect their headers. Look for TCP, ICMP, ARP, and UDP packets. Compare the contents of their headers. Try to locate any special flags or field codes used by the protocols. You'll likely discover that there is a lot more going on within a protocol than you ever imagined.

User Datagram Protocol (UDP) also operates at layer 4 (the Transport layer) of the OSI model. It is a connectionless "best-effort" communications protocol. It offers no error detection or correction, does not use sequencing, does not use flow control mechanisms, does not use a pre-established session, and is considered unreliable. UDP has very low overhead and thus can transmit data quickly. However, UDP should be used only when the delivery of data is not essential. UDP is often employed by real-time or streaming communications for audio and/or video. The IP header protocol field value for UDP is 17 (0x11).

As mentioned earlier, the UDP header is relatively simple in comparison with the TCP header. A UDP header is 8 bytes long. This header is divided into several sections or fields, as detailed in Table 3.7.

**TABLE 3.7**   UDP header construction

| Size in Bits | Field |
| --- | --- |
| 16 | Source port |
| 16 | Destination port |
| 16 | Message length |
| 16 | Checksum |

## Network Layer Protocols

Another important protocol in the TCP/IP protocol suite operates at the Network layer of the OSI model, namely, Internet Protocol (IP). IP provides route addressing for data packets. It is this route addressing that is the foundation of global Internet communications since it provides a means of identity and prescribes transmission paths. Similar to UDP, IP is connectionless and is an unreliable datagram service. IP does not offer guarantees that packets will be delivered or that packets will be delivered in the correct order, and it does not guarantee that packets will not be delivered more than once. Thus, you must employ TCP on IP to gain reliable and controlled communication sessions.

### IPv4 vs. IPv6

IPv4 is the version of Internet Protocol that is most widely used around the world. However, a new version known as IPv6 is primed to take over and improve network addressing and routing. IPv4 uses a 32-bit addressing scheme, while IPv6 uses 128 bits for addressing. IPv6 offers many new features that are not available in IPv4. Some of IPv6's new features are scoped addresses, autoconfiguration, and QoS priority values.

Scoped addresses give administrators the ability to group and then block or allow access to network services, such as file servers or printing. Autoconfiguration removes the need for both DHCP and NAT. QoS priority values allow for traffic management based on prioritized content.

IPv6 is supported by most operating systems released since 2000 either natively or via an add-in. However, IPv6 has been slowly adopted. Most of the IPv6 networks are currently located in private networks such as large corporations, research laboratories, and universities.

Other protocols at the OSI model Network layer include ICMP and IGMP.

### ICMP

Internet Control Message Protocol (ICMP) is used to determine the health of a network or a specific link. ICMP is utilized by `ping`, `traceroute`, `pathping`, and other network management tools. The `ping` utility employs ICMP echo packets and bounces them off remote systems. Thus, you can use `ping` to determine whether the remote system is online, whether the remote system is responding promptly, whether the intermediary systems are supporting communications, and the level of performance efficiency at which the intermediary systems are communicating. The `ping` utility includes a redirect function that allows the echo responses to be sent to a different destination than the system of origin. Unfortunately, the features of ICMP are often exploited in various forms of bandwidth-based denial-of-service attacks, such as Ping of Death, Smurf, and Ping Floods.

You should be aware of several important details regarding ICMP. First, the IP header protocol field value for ICMP is 1 (0x01). Second, the type field in the ICMP header defines the type or purpose of the message contained within the ICMP payload. There are more than 40 defined types, but only 7 are commonly used (see Table 3.8). You can find a complete list of the ICMP type field values at www.iana.org/assignments/icmp-parameters. It may be worth noting that many of the types listed may also support codes. A code is simply an additional data parameter offering more detail about the function or purpose of the ICMP message payload.

**TABLE 3.8**   Common ICMP type field values

| Type | Function |
| --- | --- |
| 0 | Echo reply |
| 3 | Destination unreachable |
| 5 | Redirect |

| Type | Function |
| --- | --- |
| 8 | Echo request |
| 9 | Router advertisement |
| 10 | Router solicitation |
| 11 | Time exceeded |

### IGMP

Internet Group Management Protocol (IGMP) allows systems to support multicasting. Multicasting is the transmission of data to multiple specific recipients. (RFC 1112 discusses the requirements to perform IGMP multicasting.) IGMP is used by IP hosts to register their dynamic multicast group membership. It is also used by connected routers to discover these groups. Through the use of IGMP multicasting, a server can initially transmit a single data signal rather than a separate initial data signal for each intended recipient. With IGMP, the single initial signal is multiplied at the router if divergent pathways exist to the intended recipients. The IP header protocol field value for IGMP is 2 (0x02).

### ARP and Reverse ARP

Address Resolution Protocol (ARP) and Reverse Address Resolution Protocol (RARP) are essential to the interoperability of logical and physical addressing schemes. ARP is used to resolve IP addresses (32-bit binary number for logical addressing) into Media Access Control (MAC) addresses (48-bit binary number for physical addressing). Traffic on a network segment (for example, cables across a hub) is directed from its source system to its destination system using MAC addresses. RARP is used to resolve MAC addresses into IP addresses.

Both ARP and RARP function using caching and broadcasting. The first step in resolving an IP address into a MAC address, or vice versa, is to check the local ARP cache. If the needed information is already present in the ARP cache, it is used. This activity is sometimes abused using a technique called *ARP cache poisoning* where an attacker inserts bogus information into the ARP cache. If the ARP cache does not contain the necessary information, an ARP request in the form of a broadcast is transmitted. If the owner of the queried address is in the local subnet, it can respond with the necessary information. If not, the system will use its default gateway to transmit its communications. Then, the default gateway (in other words, a router) will need to perform its own ARP or RARP process.

### IP Classes

Basic knowledge of IP addressing and IP classes is a must for any security professional. If you are rusty on addressing, subnetting, classes, and other related topics, take the time to refresh yourself. Table 3.9 and Table 3.10 provide a quick overview of the key details of classes and default subnets. A full Class A subnet supports 16,777,214 hosts; a full class B subnet supports 65,534 hosts; and a full Class C subnet supports 254 hosts. Class D is used for multicasting, while Class E is reserved for future use.

Note that the entire Class A network of 127 was set aside for the loopback address, although only a single address is actually needed for that purpose.

**TABLE 3.9** IP classes

| Class | First Binary Digits | Decimal Range of First Octet |
| --- | --- | --- |
| A | 0 | 1–126 |
| B | 10 | 128–191 |
| C | 110 | 192–223 |
| D | 1110 | 224–239 |
| E | 1111 | 240–255 |

**TABLE 3.10** IP classes' default subnet masks

| Class | Default Subnet Mask | CIDR Equivalent |
| --- | --- | --- |
| A | 255.0.0.0 | /8 |
| B | 255.255.0.0 | /16 |
| C | 255.255.255.0 | /24 |

Another option for subnetting is to use Classless Inter-Domain Routing (CIDR) notation. CIDR uses mask bits rather than a full dotted-decimal notation subnet mask. Thus, instead of 255.255.0.0, a CIDR is added to the IP address after a slash, as in 172.16.1.1/16, for example. One significant benefit of CIDR over traditional subnet-masking techniques is the ability to combine multiple noncontiguous sets of addresses into a single subnet. For example, it is possible to combine several Class C subnets into a single larger subnet grouping. If CIDR piques your interest, see the CIDR article on Wikipedia or visit the IETF's RFC for CIDR at http://tools.ietf.org/html//rfc4632 for more information.

## Common Application Layer Protocols

In the Application layer of the TCP/IP model (which includes the Session, Presentation, and Application layers of the OSI model) reside numerous application- or service-specific protocols. A basic knowledge of these protocols and their relevant service ports is important for the CISSP exam:

**Telnet, TCP port 23**   This is a terminal emulation network application that supports remote connectivity for executing commands and running applications but that does not support transfer of files.

**File Transfer Protocol (FTP), TCP ports 20 and 21**   This is a network application that supports an exchange of files that requires anonymous or specific authentication.

**Trivial File Transfer Protocol (TFTP), UDP port 69**   This is a network application that supports an exchange of files that does not require authentication.

**Simple Mail Transfer Protocol (SMTP), TCP port 25**   This is a protocol used to transmit email messages from a client to an email server and from one email server to another.

**Post Office Protocol (POP3), TCP port 110**   This is a protocol used to pull email messages from an inbox on an email server down to an email client.

**Internet Message Access Protocol (IMAP 4), TCP port 143**   This is a protocol used to pull email messages from an inbox on an email server down to an email client. IMAP is more secure than POP3 and offers the ability to pull headers down from the email server as well as to delete messages directly off the email server without having to download to the local client first.

**Dynamic Host Configuration Protocol (DHCP), UDP ports 67 and 68**   DHCP uses port 67 for server point-to-point response and port 68 for client request broadcast. It is used to assign TCP/IP configuration settings to systems upon bootup. DHCP enables centralized control of network addressing.

**Hypertext Transport Protocol (HTTP), TCP port 80**   This is the protocol used to transmit web page elements from a web server to web browsers.

**Secure Sockets Layer (SSL), TCP port 443 (for HTTP encryption)**   This is a VPN-like security protocol that operates at the Transport layer. SSL was originally designed to support secured web communications (HTTPS) but is capable of securing any Application-layer protocol communications.

**Line Print Daemon (LPD), TCP port 515**   This is a network service that is used to spool print jobs and to send print jobs to printers.

**X Window, TCP ports 6000–6063**   This is a GUI API for command-line operating systems.

**Bootstrap Protocol (BootP), UDP ports 67 and 68**   This is a protocol used to connect diskless workstations to a network through autoassignment of IP configuration and download of basic OS elements. BootP is the forerunner to Dynamic Host Configuration Protocol (DHCP).

**Network File System (NFS), TCP port 2049**   This is a network service used to support file sharing between dissimilar systems.

**Simple Network Management Protocol (SNMP), UDP port 161 (UDP port 162 for trap messages)**   This is a network service used to collect network health and status information by polling monitoring devices from a central monitoring station.

### TCP/IP Vulnerabilities

TCP/IP's vulnerabilities are numerous. Improperly implemented TCP/IP stacks in various operating systems are vulnerable to buffer overflows, SYN flood attacks, various DoS attacks, fragment attacks, oversized packet attacks, spoofing attacks, man-in-the-middle attacks, hijack attacks, and coding error attacks.

In addition to these intrusive attacks, TCP/IP (as well as most protocols) is also subject to passive attacks via monitoring or sniffing. Network monitoring is the act of monitoring traffic patterns to obtain information about a network. Packet sniffing is the act of capturing packets from the network in hopes of extracting useful information from the packet contents. Effective packet sniffers can extract usernames, passwords, email addresses, encryption keys, credit card numbers, IP addresses, system names, and so on.

## Domain Name Resolution

Addressing and naming are important components that make network communications possible. Without addressing schemes, networked computers would not be able to distinguish one computer from another or specify the destination of a communication. Likewise, without naming schemes, humans would have to remember and rely upon numbering systems to identify computers. It is much easier to remember Google.com than 64.233.187.99. Thus, most naming schemes were enacted for human use rather than computer use.

It is reasonably important to grasp the basic ideas of addressing and numbering as used on TCP/IP-based networks. There are three different layers to be aware of. First, the top layer is the domain name. The second or middle layer is the IP address. The third, or bottom, layer is the MAC address. The MAC address, or hardware address, is a "permanent" physical address. The IP address is a "temporary" logical address assigned over or onto the MAC address. The domain name or computer name is a "temporary" human-friendly convention assigned over or onto the IP address.

---

### "Permanent" and "Temporary"

The reason these two adjectives are within quotation marks is that they are not completely accurate. MAC addresses are designed to be permanent physical addresses. However, some NICs support MAC address changes, and most modern operating systems do as well (including Windows and Linux). When the NIC supports the change, the change occurs on the hardware. When the OS supports the change, the change is only in memory, but it looks like a hardware change to all other network entities.

An IP address is temporary because it is a logical address and could be changed at any time, either by DHCP or by an administrator. However, there are instances where systems are statically assigned an IP address. Likewise, computer names or DNS names are logical and thus able to be modified by an administrator.

This system of naming and addressing grants each networking component the information it needs while making its use of that information as simple as possible. Humans get human-friendly domain names, networking protocols get router-friendly IP addresses, and the network interfaces get physical addresses. However, all three of these schemes must be linked together to allow interoperability between them. Thus, the Domain Name System (DNS) and the ARP/RARP system were developed. DNS resolves a human-friendly domain name into its IP address equivalent. Then, ARP resolves the IP address into its MAC address equivalent. Both of these resolutions also have an inverse, namely, DNS reverse lookups and RARP (please see the section "ARP and Reverse ARP" earlier in this chapter).

**Further Reading on DNS**

For an excellent primer to advanced discussion on DNS, its operation, known issues, and the Dan Kaminski vulnerability, please visit "An Illustrated Guide to the Kaminsky DNS Vulnerability" at http://unixwiz.net/techtips/iguide-kaminsky-dns-vuln.html.

For a look into the future of DNS, specifically the defense against the Kaminski vulnerability, visit www.dnssec.net.

# Internet/Intranet/Extranet Components

The Internet is host to countless information services and numerous applications, including the Web, email, FTP, Telnet, newsgroups, chat, and so on. The Internet is also home to malicious people whose primary goal is to locate your computer and extract valuable data from it, use it to launch further attacks, or damage it in some way. You should be familiar with the Internet and able to readily identify its benefits and drawbacks from your own online experiences. Because of the success and global use of the Internet, many of its technologies were adapted or integrated into the private business network. This created two new forms of networks: intranets and extranets.

An *intranet* is a private network that is designed to host the same information services found on the Internet. Networks that rely upon external servers (in other words, ones positioned on the public Internet) to provide information services internally are not considered intranets. Intranets provide users with access to the Web, email, and other services on internal servers that are not accessible to anyone outside the private network.

An *extranet* is a cross between the Internet and an intranet. An extranet is a section of an organization's network that has been sectioned off so that it acts as an intranet for the private network but also serves information to the public Internet. An extranet is often reserved for use by specific partners or customers. It is rarely on a public network. An extranet for public consumption is typically labeled a demilitarized zone (DMZ) or perimeter network.

When you're designing a secure network (whether a private network, an intranet, or an extranet), you must evaluate numerous networking devices. Not all of these components are necessary for a secure network, but they are all common network devices that may have an impact on network security.

## Firewalls

Firewalls are essential tools in managing and controlling network traffic. A *firewall* is a network device used to filter traffic and is typically deployed between a private network and a link to the Internet, but it can be deployed between departments within an organization. Without firewalls, it would not be possible to prevent malicious traffic from the Internet from entering into your private network. Firewalls filter traffic based on a defined set of rules, also called *filters* or *access control lists*. They are basically a set of instructions that are used to distinguish authorized traffic from unauthorized and/or malicious traffic. Only authorized traffic is allowed to cross the security barrier provided by the firewall.

Firewalls are useful for blocking or filtering traffic. They are most effective against unrequested traffic and attempts to connect from outside the private network as well as for blocking known malicious data, messages, or packets based on content, application, protocol, port, or source address. They are capable of hiding the structure and addressing scheme of a private network from the public. Most firewalls offer extensive logging, auditing, and monitoring capabilities as well as alarms and basic intrusion detection system (IDS) functions. Firewalls are typically unable to block viruses or malicious code (i.e., firewalls do not typically scan traffic as an antivirus scanner would) transmitted through otherwise authorized communication channels, prevent unauthorized but accidental or intended disclosure of information by users, prevent attacks by malicious users already behind the firewall, or protect data after it passes out of or into the private network. However, you can add these features through special add-in modules or companion products, such as antivirus scanners and IDS tools. There are firewall appliances that are preconfigured to perform all (or most) of these "add-on" functions natively.

In addition to logging network traffic activity, firewalls should log several other events as well:

- A reboot of the firewall
- Proxies or dependencies being unable to or not starting

- Proxies or other important services crashing or restarting
- Changes to the firewall configuration file
- A configuration or system error while the firewall is running

Firewalls are only one part of an overall security solution. With a firewall, many of the security mechanisms are concentrated in one place, and thus they may be a single point of failure. Firewall failure is most commonly caused by human error and misconfiguration. Firewalls provide protection only against traffic that crosses the firewall from one subnet to another. They offer no protection against traffic within a subnet (in other words, behind a firewall).

There are four basic types of firewalls: static packet-filtering firewalls, application-level gateway firewalls, circuit-level gateway firewalls, and stateful inspection firewalls. There are also ways to create hybrid or complex gateway firewalls by combining two or more of these firewall types into a single firewall solution. In most cases, having a multilevel firewall provides greater control over filtering traffic. Regardless, we'll cover the various firewall types and discuss firewall deployment architectures as well.

## Static Packet-Filtering Firewalls

A *static packet-filtering firewall* filters traffic by examining data from a message header. Usually, the rules are concerned with source, destination, and port addresses. Using static filtering, a firewall is unable to provide user authentication or to tell whether a packet originated from inside or outside the private network, and it is easily fooled with spoofed packets. Static packet-filtering firewalls are known as *first-generation firewalls*; they operate at layer 3 (the Network layer) of the OSI model. They can also be called *screening* routers or *common* routers.

## Application-Level Gateway Firewalls

An *application-level gateway firewall* is also called a *proxy* firewall. A proxy is a mechanism that copies packets from one network into another; the copy process also changes the source and destination addresses to protect the identity of the internal or private network. An application-level gateway firewall filters traffic based on the Internet service (in other words, the application) used to transmit or receive the data. Each type of application must have its own unique proxy server. Thus, an application-level gateway firewall comprises numerous individual proxy servers. This type of firewall negatively affects network performance because each packet must be examined and processed as it passes through the firewall. Application-level gateways are known as *second-generation* firewalls, and they operate at the Application layer (layer 7) of the OSI model.

## Circuit-Level Gateway Firewalls

*Circuit-level gateway firewalls* are used to establish communication sessions between trusted partners. They operate at the Session layer (layer 5) of the OSI model. SOCKS (from *sockets*, as in TCP/IP ports) is a common implementation of a circuit-level gateway firewall. Circuit-level gateway firewalls, also known as *circuit proxies*, manage communications based on the circuit, not the content of traffic. They permit or deny forwarding decisions based solely on the endpoint designations of the communication circuit (in other words, the source and destination addresses and service port numbers). Circuit-level gateway firewalls are considered second-generation firewalls because they represent a modification of the application-level gateway firewall concept.

## Stateful Inspection Firewalls

*Stateful inspection firewalls* (also known as dynamic packet filtering firewalls) evaluate the state or the context of network traffic. By examining source and destination addresses, application usage, source of origin, and relationship between current packets and the previous packets of the same session, stateful inspection firewalls are able to grant a broader range of access for authorized users and activities and actively watch for and block unauthorized users and activities. Stateful inspection firewalls generally operate more efficiently than application-level gateway firewalls. They are known as third-generation firewalls, and they operate at the Network and Transport layers (layers 3 and 4) of the OSI model.

## Multihomed Firewalls

Some firewall systems have more than one interface. For instance, a multihomed firewall must have at least two interfaces to filter traffic (they're also known as *dual-homed* firewalls). All multihomed firewalls should have IP forwarding disabled to force the filtering rules to control all traffic rather than allowing a software-supported shortcut between one interface and another. A bastion host or a screened host is just a firewall system logically positioned between a private network and an untrusted network. Usually, the bastion host is located behind the router that connects the private network to the untrusted network. All inbound traffic is routed to the bastion host, which in turn acts as a proxy for all the trusted systems within the private network. It is responsible for filtering traffic coming into the private network as well as for protecting the identity of the internal client.

 The word *bastion* comes from medieval castle architecture. A bastion guardhouse was positioned in front of the main entrance to serve as a first layer of protection. Using this term to describe a firewall indicates that the firewall is acting as a sacrificial host that will receive all inbound attacks.

A screened subnet is similar to the screened host (in other words, the bastion host) in concept, except a subnet is placed between two routers and the bastion host(s) is located within that subnet. All inbound traffic is directed to the bastion host, and only traffic proxied by the bastion host can pass through the second router into the private network. This creates a subnet where some external visitors are allowed to communicate with resources offered by the network. This is the concept of a DMZ, which is a network area (usually a subnet) that is designed to be accessed by outside visitors but that is still isolated from the private network of the organization. The DMZ is often the host of public web, email, file, and other resource servers.

## Firewall Deployment Architectures

There are three commonly recognized firewall deployment architectures: single tier, two tier, and three tier (also known as *multitier*). As you can see in Figure 3.11, a single-tier deployment places the private network behind a firewall, which is then connected through a router to the Internet (or some other untrusted network). Single-tier deployments are useful against generic attacks only. This architecture offers only minimal protection.

A two-tier deployment architecture may be one of two different designs. One uses a firewall with three or more interfaces. The other uses two firewalls in a series. This allows for a DMZ or a publicly accessible extranet. In the first design, the DMZ is located off one of the interfaces of the primary firewall, while in the second design the DMZ is located between the two serial firewalls. The DMZ is used to host information server systems to which external users should have access. The firewall routes traffic to the DMZ or the trusted network according to its strict filtering rules. This architecture introduces a moderate level of routing and filtering complexity.

**FIGURE 3.11**   Three firewall deployment architectures

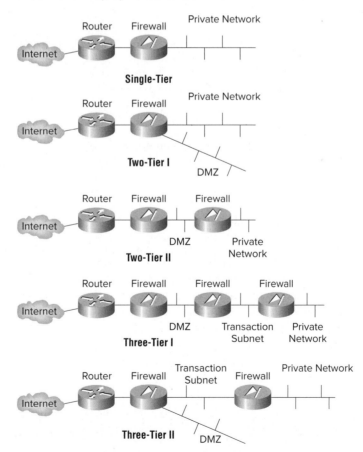

A three-tier deployment architecture is the deployment of multiple subnets between the private network and the Internet separated by firewalls. Each subsequent firewall has more stringent filtering rules to restrict traffic to only trusted sources. The outermost subnet is usually a DMZ. A middle subnet can serve as a transaction subnet where systems needed to support complex web applications in the DMZ reside. The third, or backend, subnet can support the private network. This architecture is the most secure; however, it is also the most complex to design, implement, and manage.

# Other Network Devices

You'll use numerous devices when constructing a network. Strong familiarity with the components of networks can assist you in designing an IT infrastructure that avoids single points of failure and provides strong support for availability.

---

### Collisions vs. Broadcasts

A collision occurs when two systems transmit data at the same time onto a connection medium that supports only a single transmission path. A broadcast occurs when a single system transmits data to all possible recipients. Generally, collisions are always something to avoid and prevent, while broadcasts have useful purposes from time to time. The management of collisions and broadcasts introduces a new term known as *domains*.

A *collision* domain is a group of networked systems that could cause a collision if any two (or more) of the systems in that group transmitted simultaneously. Any system outside the collision domain cannot cause a collision with any member of that collision domain.

A *broadcast* domain is a group of networked systems in which all other members receive a broadcast signal when one of the members of the group transmits it. Any system outside a broadcast domain would not receive a broadcast from that broadcast domain.

As you design and deploy a network, you should consider how collision domains and broadcast domains will be managed. Collision domains are divided by using any layer 2 or higher device, and broadcast domains are divided by using any layer 3 or higher device. When a domain is divided, it means that systems on opposite sides of the deployed device are members of different domains.

---

These are some of the devices in a network:

**Repeaters, concentrators, and amplifiers**   Repeaters, concentrators, and amplifiers are used to strengthen the communication signal over a cable segment as well as connect network segments that use the same protocol. These devices can be used to extend the maximum length of a specific cable type by deploying one or more repeaters along a lengthy cable run. Repeaters, concentrators, and amplifiers operate at OSI layer 1. Systems on either side of a repeater, concentrator, or amplifier are part of the same collision domain and broadcast domain.

**Hubs**  Hubs are used to connect multiple systems in a star topology and connect network segments that use the same protocol. They repeat inbound traffic over all outbound ports. This ensures that the traffic will reach its intended host. A hub is a multiport repeater. Hubs operate at OSI layer 1. Systems on either side of a hub are part of the same collision and broadcast domains. Most organizations have a no-hub security policy to limit or reduce the risk of sniffing attacks.

**Bridges**  A bridge is used to connect two networks together, even networks of different topologies, cabling types, and speeds, in order to connect network segments that use the same protocol. A bridge forwards traffic from one network to another. Bridges that connect networks using different transmission speeds may have a buffer to store packets until they can be forwarded to the slower network. This is known as a *store-and-forward* device. Bridges operate at OSI layer 2. Systems on either side of a bridge are part of the same broadcast domain but are in different collision domains.

**Switches**  Rather than using a hub, you might consider using a switch, or intelligent hub. Switches know the addresses of the systems connected on each outbound port. Instead of repeating traffic on every outbound port, a switch repeats traffic only out of the port on which the destination is known to exist. Switches offer greater efficiency for traffic delivery, create separate collision domains, and improve the overall throughput of data. Switches can also create separate broadcast domains when used to create VLANs. In such configurations, broadcasts are allowed within a single VLAN but not allowed to cross unhindered from one VLAN to another. Switches operate primarily at OSI layer 2. When switches have additional features, such as routing, they can operate at OSI layer 3 as well (such as when routing between VLANs). Systems on either side of a switch operating at layer 2 are part of the same broadcast domain but are in different collision domains. Systems on either side of a switch operating at layer 3 are part of different broadcast domains and different collision domains. Switches are used to connect network segments that use the same protocol.

**Routers**  Routers are used to control traffic flow on networks and are often used to connect similar networks and control traffic flow between the two. They can function using statically defined routing tables, or they can employ a dynamic routing system. There are numerous dynamic routing protocols, such as RIP, OSPF, and BGP. Routers operate at OSI layer 3. Systems on either side of a router are part of different broadcast domains and different collision domains. Routers are used to connect network segments that use the same protocol.

**Brouter**  Brouters are combination devices comprising a router and a bridge. A brouter attempts to route first, but if that fails, it defaults to bridging. Thus, a brouter operates primarily at layer 3 but can operate at layer 2 when necessary. Systems on either side of a brouter operating at layer 3 are part of different broadcast domains and different collision domains. Systems on either side of a brouter operating at layer 2 are part of the same broadcast domain but are in different collision domains. Brouters are used to connect network segments that use the same protocol.

**Gateways**    A gateway connects networks that are using different network protocols. A gateway is responsible for transferring traffic from one network to another by transforming the format of that traffic into a form compatible with the protocol or transport method used by each network. Gateways, also known as *protocol translators*, can be stand-alone hardware devices or a software service (for example, an IP-to-IPX gateway). Systems on either side of a gateway are part of different broadcast domains and different collision domains. Gateways are used to connect network segments that use different protocols. There are many types of gateways, including data, mail, application, secure, and Internet. Gateways typically operate at OSI layer 7.

**Proxies**    A proxy is a form of gateway that does not translate across protocols. Instead, proxies serve as mediators, filters, caching servers, and even NAT/PAT servers for a network. A proxy performs a function or requests a service on behalf of another system and connects network segments that use the same protocol. Proxies are most often used in the context of providing clients on a private network with Internet access while protecting the identity of the clients. A proxy accepts requests from clients, alters the source address of the requester, maintains a mapping of requests to clients, and sends the altered request packets out. This mechanism is commonly known as Network Address Translation (NAT). Once a reply is received, the proxy server determines which client it is destined for by reviewing its mappings and then sends the packets on to the client. Systems on either side of a proxy are part of different broadcast domains and different collision domains.

---

### Network Infrastructure Inventory

If you can gain approval from your organization, perform a general survey or inventory of the significant components comprising your network. See how many different network devices you can locate within your network. Also, do you notice any patterns of device deployment, such as devices always deployed in parallel or in series? Is the exterior of a device usually sufficient to indicate its function, or must you look up its model number?

---

**LAN extender**    A LAN extender is a remote access, multilayer switch used to connect distant networks over WAN links. This is a strange beast of a device in that it creates WANs, but marketers of this device steer clear of the term *WAN* and use only *LAN* and *extended LAN*. The idea behind this device was to make the terminology easier to understand and easier to sell than a normal WAN device with complex concepts and terms tied to it. Ultimately, it was the same product as a WAN switch or WAN router. (We agree with Douglas Adams, who believed the marketing people should be shipped out with the lawyers and phone sanitizers on the first spaceship to the far end of the universe.)

While managing network security with filtering devices such as firewalls and proxies is important, we must not overlook the need for endpoint security. Endpoints are the ends of a network communication link. One end is often at a server where a resource resides, and the other end is often a client making a request to use a network resource. Even with secured communication protocols, it is still possible for abuse, misuse, oversight, or malicious action to occur across the network because it originated at an endpoint. All aspects of security from one end to the other, often called *end-to-end security*, must be addressed. Any unsecured point will be discovered eventually and abused.

# Remote Access Security Management

Telecommuting, or remote connectivity, has become a common feature of business computing. Remote access is the ability of a distant client to establish a communication session with a network. This can take the form of using a modem to dial up directly to a remote access server, connecting to a network over the Internet through a VPN, or even connecting to a terminal server system through a thin-client connection. The first two examples use fully capable clients. They establish connections just as if they were directly connected to the LAN. The last example, with a terminal server, establishes a connection from a thin client. In such a situation, all computing activities occur on the terminal server system rather than on the distant client.

When remote access capabilities are deployed in any environment, security must be considered and implemented to provide protection for your private network against remote access complications. Remote access users should be stringently authenticated before being granted access. Only those users who specifically need remote access for their assigned work tasks should be granted permission to establish remote connections. All remote communications should be protected from interception and eavesdropping. This usually requires an encryption solution that provides strong protection for the authentication traffic as well as all data transmission.

It is important to establish secure communication channels before initiating the transmission of sensitive, valuable, or personal information. Remote access security in general is important, but you should also focus on the specifics of the various work tasks that require secured communications. This can include voice over IP (VoIP) and multimedia collaboration.

VoIP is a technology that encapsulates audio into IP packets in order to support telephone calls over TCP/IP network connections. VoIP has become a popular and inexpensive telephony solution for companies and individuals worldwide. It is important to keep security in mind when selecting a VoIP solution to ensure that it provides the privacy and security you expect. Some VoIP systems are essentially plain-form communications that are easily intercepted and eavesdropped; others are highly encrypted, and any attempt to interfere or wiretap is deterred and thwarted.

Multimedia collaboration is the use of various multimedia-supporting communication solutions to enhance distance collaboration. Collaboration occurs when people can work on a project together. Often, collaboration allows workers to work simultaneously as well as across different time frames. Collaboration can also be used for tracking changes and including multimedia functions. Collaboration can incorporate email, chat, VoIP, videoconferencing, use of a whiteboard, online document editing, real-time file exchange, versioning control, and other tools. Collaboration often is a feature of advanced forms of remote meeting technology. No matter what form of multimedia collaboration is implemented, the attendant security implications must be evaluated. Does the service use strong authentication techniques? Does the communication occur across an open protocol or an encrypted tunnel? Does the solution allow for true deletion of content? Are activities of users audited and logged? Multimedia collaboration can improve the work environment and allow for input from a wider range of diverse workers across the globe, but this is only a benefit if the security of the solution can be ensured.

When outlining your remote access security management strategy, be sure to address the following issues:

**Remote connectivity technology**   Each type of connection has its own unique security issues. Fully examine every aspect of your connection options. This can include modems, DSL, ISDN, wireless networking, and cable modems.

**Transmission protection**   There are several forms of encrypted protocols, encrypted connection systems, and encrypted network services or applications. Use the appropriate combination of secured services for your remote connectivity needs. This can include VPNs, SSL, TLS, Secure Shell (SSH), IPSec, and L2TP.

**Authentication protection**   In addition to protecting data traffic, you must ensure that all logon credentials are properly secured. This requires the use of an authentication protocol and may mandate the use of a centralized remote access authentication system. This can include Password Authentication Protocol (PAP), Challenge Handshake Authentication Protocol (CHAP), Extensible Authentication Protocol (EAP), Remote Authentication Dial-In User Service (RADIUS), and Terminal Access Controller Access Control System (TACACS).

**Remote user assistance**   Remote access users may periodically require technical assistance. You must have a means established to provide this as efficiently as possible. This can include addressing software and hardware issues, user training issues, and so on.

The ability to use remote access or establish a remote connection should be tightly controlled. As mentioned earlier, only those users who require remote access for their work tasks should be granted such access. You can control and restrict the use of remote connectivity by using filters, rules, or access controls based on user identity, workstation identity, protocol, application, content, and time of day. To provide protection and restriction of remote access only to authorized users, you can use callback and caller ID. Callback is a mechanism that disconnects a remote user upon initial contact and then immediately attempts to reconnect to them using a predefined phone number (in other words, the number defined in the user account's security database). Callback does have a user-defined mode. However, this mode is not used for security; it is used to reverse toll charges to the company rather than charging the remote client. Caller ID verification can be used for the same purpose as callback—by verifying the physical location (via phone number) of the authorized user.

It should be a standard element in your security policy that no unauthorized modems be present on any system connected to the private network. You may need to further specify this policy by indicating that those with portable systems must either remove their modems before connecting to the network or boot with a hardware profile that disables the modem's device driver.

# Network and Protocol Security Mechanisms

TCP/IP is the primary protocol suite used on most networks and on the Internet. It is a robust protocol suite, but it has numerous security deficiencies. In an effort to improve the security of TCP/IP, many subprotocols, mechanisms, or applications have been developed to protect the confidentiality, integrity, and availability of transmitted data. It is important to remember that even with the foundational protocol suite of TCP/IP, there are literally hundreds, if not thousands, of individual protocols, mechanisms, and applications in use across the Internet. Some of them are designed to provide security services. Some protect integrity, others protect confidentiality, and others provide authentication and access control. In the next sections, we'll discuss some of the more common network and protocol security mechanisms.

## Secure Communications Protocols

Protocols that provide security services for application-specific communication channels are called *secure communication protocols*. They are as follows:

**Simple Key Management for IP (SKIP)**   This is an encryption tool used to protect sessionless datagram protocols. SKIP was designed to integrate with IPSec; it functions at layer 3. SKIP is able to encrypt any subprotocol of the TCP/IP suite. SKIP was replaced by IKE in 1998.

**SoftWare IP Encryption (SWIPE)**   This is another layer 3 security protocol for IP. It provides authentication, integrity, and confidentiality using an encapsulation protocol.

**Secure Remote Procedure Call (S-RPC)**   This is an authentication service and is simply a means to prevent unauthorized execution of code on remote systems.

**Secure Sockets Layer (SSL)**   This is an encryption protocol developed by Netscape to protect the communications between a web server and a web browser. SSL can be used to secure web, email, FTP, or even Telnet traffic. It is a session-oriented protocol that provides confidentiality and integrity. SSL is deployed using a 40-bit key or a 128-bit key. SSL is superseded by Transport Layer Security (TLS). TLS functions in the same general manner as SSL, but it uses stronger authentication and encryption protocols.

**Secure Electronic Transaction (SET)**   This is a security protocol for the transmission of transactions over the Internet. SET is based on Rivest, Shamir, and Adelman (RSA) encryption and Data Encryption Standard (DES). It has the support of major credit card companies, such as Visa and MasterCard. However, SET has not been widely accepted by the Internet in general; instead, SSL/TLS encrypted sessions are the preferred mechanism for secure e-commerce.

These five secure communication protocols (SKIP, SWIPE, S-RPC, SSL/TLS, and SET) are just a few examples of options available. Keep in mind that there are many other secure protocols, such as IPSec (discussed in Chapter 4).

## Dial-Up Protocols

When a remote connection link is established, a protocol must be used to govern how the link is actually created and to establish a common communication foundation for other protocols to work over. Dial-up protocols such as those described in the following list provide this function, not only for true dial-up links, but also for some VPN links:

**Point-to-Point Protocol (PPP)**   This is a full-duplex protocol used for transmitting TCP/IP packets over various non-LAN connections, such as modems, ISDN, VPNs, Frame Relay, and so on. PPP is widely supported and is the transport protocol of choice for dial-up Internet connections. PPP authentication is protected through the use of various protocols, such as CHAP or PAP. PPP is a replacement for SLIP and can support any LAN protocol, not just TCP/IP.

**Serial Line Internet Protocol (SLIP)**   This is an older technology developed to support TCP/IP communications over asynchronous serial connections, such as serial cables or modem dial-up. SLIP is rarely used but is still supported on many systems. SLIP can support only IP, requires static IP addresses, offers no error detection or correction, and does not support compression.

One of the many proprietary dial-up protocols is Microcom Networking Protocol (MNP). MNP was found on Microcom modems in the 1990s. It supports its own form of error control called Echoplex.

# Authentication Protocols

After a connection is initially established between a remote system and a server or a network, the first activity that should take place is to verify the identity of the remote user. This activity is known as *authentication*. There are several authentication protocols that control how the logon credentials are exchanged and whether those credentials are encrypted during transport:

**Challenge Handshake Authentication Protocol (CHAP)**   This is one of the authentication protocols used over PPP links. CHAP encrypts usernames and passwords. It performs authentication using a challenge-response dialogue that cannot be replayed. CHAP also periodically reauthenticates the remote system throughout an established communication session to verify persistent identity of the remote client. This activity is transparent to the user.

**Password Authentication Protocol (PAP)**   This is a standardized authentication protocol for PPP. PAP transmits usernames and passwords in the clear. It offers no form of encryption; it simply provides a means to transport the logon credentials from the client to the authentication server.

**Extensible Authentication Protocol (EAP)**   This is a framework for authentication instead of an actual protocol. EAP allows customized authentication security solutions, such as supporting smart cards, tokens, and biometrics.

These three authentication protocols were initially used over dial-up PPP connections. Today, these and many other newer authentication protocols and concepts are in use over a wide number of distance connection technologies, including broadband and VPN.

# Centralized Remote Authentication Services

As remote access becomes a key element in an organization's business functions, it is often important to add layers of security between remote clients and the private network. Centralized remote authentication services, such as RADIUS and TACACS, provide this extra layer of protection. These mechanisms provide a separation of the authentication and authorization processes for remote clients from that performed for LAN or local clients:

**Remote Authentication Dial-In User Service (RADIUS)**   This is used to centralize the authentication of remote dial-up connections. A network that employs a RADIUS server is configured so the remote access server passes dial-up user logon credentials to the RADIUS server for authentication. This process is similar to the process used by domain clients sending logon credentials to a domain controller for authentication.

**Terminal Access Controller Access Control System (TACACS)**   This is an alternative to RADIUS. TACACS is available in three versions: original TACACS, Extended TACACS (XTACACS), and TACACS+. TACACS integrates the authentication and authorization processes. XTACACS keeps the authentication, authorization, and accounting processes separate. TACACS+ improves XTACACS by adding two-factor authentication.

If the RADIUS or TACACS servers are ever compromised, then only remote connectivity is affected, not the rest of the network.

# Avoiding Single Points of Failure

Any element in your IT infrastructure, component in your physical environment, or person on your staff can be a single point of failure. A single point of failure is simply any element—such as a device, service, protocol, or communication link—that would cause total or significant downtime if compromised, violated, or destroyed, affecting the ability of members of your organization to perform essential work tasks. To avoid single points of failure, you must design your networks and your physical environment with redundancy and backups by doing such things as deploying dual network backbones. The use of systems, devices, and solutions with fault-tolerant capabilities is a means to improve resistance to single-point-of-failure vulnerabilities. Taking steps to establish a means to provide alternate processing, failover capabilities, and quick recovery will also aid in avoiding single points of failure.

## Redundant Servers

Using redundant servers is one fault-tolerant deployment option. Redundant servers can take numerous forms. Server mirroring is when you deploy a backup system along with the primary system. Every change made to the primary system is immediately duplicated to the secondary system. Electronic vaulting is the collection of changes on a primary system into a transaction or change document. Periodically, the change document is sent to an offsite duplicate server where the changes are applied. This is also known as *batch processing* because changes are duplicated over intervals rather than in real time. Remote journaling is the same as electronic vaulting except that changes are sent immediately to the offsite duplicate server rather than in batches. This provides a more real-time server backup. Database shadowing is remote journaling to more than one destination duplicate server. There may be one or more local duplicates and one or more offsite duplicates.

Another type of redundant server is a cluster. Clustering means deploying two or more duplicate servers in such a way as to share the workload of a mission-critical application. Users see the clustered systems as a single entity. A cluster controller manages traffic to and among the clustered systems to balance the workload across all clustered servers. As changes occur on one of the clustered systems, they are immediately duplicated to all other cluster partners.

## Failover Solutions

When backup systems or redundant servers exist, there needs to be a means by which you can switch over to the backup in the event the primary system is compromised or fails. Rollover, or failover, is redirecting workload or traffic to a backup system when the primary system fails. Rollover can be automatic or manual. Manual rollover, also known as *cold rollover*, requires an administrator to perform some change in software or hardware configuration to switch the traffic load over the down primary to a secondary server. With automatic rollover, also known as *hot rollover*, the switch from primary to secondary system is performed automatically as soon as a problem is encountered. *Fail-secure*, *fail-safe*, and *fail-soft* are terms related to these issues. A system that is fail-secure is able to resort to a secure state when an error or security violation is encountered. Fail-safe is a similar feature, but human safety is protected in the event of a system failure. However, these two terms are often used interchangeably to mean a system that is secure after a failure. Fail-soft describes a refinement of the fail-secure capability: Only the portion of a system that encountered or experienced the failure or security breach is disabled or secured, while the rest of the system continues to function normally.

A specific implementation of a fail-secure system would be the use of TFTP servers to store network device configurations. In the event of a system failure, configuration corruption, or power outage, most network devices (such as routers and switches) can be hard-coded to pull their configuration file from a TFTP server upon reboot. In this way, essential network devices can self-restore quickly.

Power failure is potentially a single point of failure. If electrical power is lost, all electronic devices will cease to function. Addressing this weakness is important if 24/7 uptime is essential to your organization. Ways to combat power failure or fluctuation issues include power conditioners (in other words, surge protectors), uninterruptible power supplies, and onsite electric generators.

# RAID

Within individual systems, storage devices can be a single point of failure. Redundant Array of Independent Disks (RAID) is a storage device mechanism that uses multiple hard drives in unique combinations to produce a storage solution that provides better throughput as well as resistance to device failure. The two primary storage techniques employed by RAID are mirroring and striping. Striping can be further enhanced by storing parity information. Parity information enables on-the-fly recovery or reconstruction of data lost due to the failure of one or more drives. There are several levels or forms of RAID. Table 3.11 lists some of the more common ones.

**TABLE 3.11**   Common RAID levels

| RAID Level | Description |
| --- | --- |
| 0 | Striping |
| 1 | Mirroring |
| 2 | Hamming code parity |
| 3 | Byte-level parity |
| 4 | Block-level parity |

**TABLE 3.11**   Common RAID levels *(continued)*

| RAID Level | Description |
| --- | --- |
| 5 | Interleave parity |
| 6 | Second parity data |
| 10 | RAID levels 1 + 0 |
| 15 | RAID levels 1 + 5 |

RAID can be implemented in hardware or in software. Hardware-based RAID offers more reliable performance and fault tolerance protection. Hardware-based RAID performs all the processing necessary for multidrive access on the drive controllers. Software-based RAID performs the processing as part of the operating system. Thus, system resources are consumed in managing and using RAID when it is deployed through software. RAID 0 offers no fault tolerance, just performance improvements. RAID 1 and 5 are the most common implementations of RAID.

There are three forms of RAID drive swapping: hot, cold, and warm. *Hot-swappable* RAID allows for failed drives to be removed and replaced while the host server remains up and running. *Cold-swappable* RAID systems require the host server to be fully powered down before failed drives can be removed and replaced. *Warm-swappable* RAID allows for failed drives to be removed and replaced by disabling the RAID configuration via software, then replacing the drive, and then reenabling the RAID configuration. RAID is a specific technology example of fault-resistant disk systems (FRDSs).

No matter what fault-tolerant designs and mechanisms you employ to avoid single points of failure, no environment's security precautions are complete without a backup solution. Backups are the only means of providing reliable insurance against minor and catastrophic losses of your data. For a backup system to provide protection, it must be configured to store all data necessary to support your organization. It must perform the backup operation as quickly and efficiently as possible. The backups must be performed on a regular basis, such as daily, weekly, or in real time. And backups must be periodically tested to verify that they are functioning and that your restore processes are adequate. An untested backup cannot be assumed to work.

# Summary

The tasks of designing, deploying, and maintaining security on a network require intimate knowledge of the technologies involved in networking. This includes protocols, services, communication mechanisms, topologies, cabling, and networking devices.

The OSI model is a standard against which all protocols are evaluated. Understanding how the OSI model is used and how it applies to real-world protocols can help system designers and system administrators improve security.

There is a wide range of hardware components that can be used to construct a network, not the least of which is the cabling used to tie all the devices together. Understanding the strengths and weaknesses of each cabling type is part of designing a secure network.

Wireless communications occur in many forms, including cell phone, Bluetooth (802.15), and networking (802.11). Wireless communication is more vulnerable to interference, eavesdropping, denial of service, and man-in-the-middle attacks.

There are three common LAN technologies: Ethernet, Token Ring, and FDDI. Each can be used to deploy a secure network. There are also several common network topologies: ring, bus, star, and mesh.

Most networks employ TCP/IP as the primary protocol. However, there are numerous subprotocols, supporting protocols, services, and security mechanisms that can be found in a TCP/IP network. A basic understanding of these various entities can help you when designing and deploying a secure network.

Remote access security management requires that security system designers address the hardware and software components of the implementation along with policy issues, work task issues, and encryption issues.

In addition to routers, hubs, switches, repeaters, gateways, and proxies, firewalls are an important part of a network's security. There are four primary types of firewalls: static packet filtering, application-level gateway, circuit-level gateway, and stateful inspection.

Avoiding single points of failure includes incorporating fault-tolerant systems and solutions into an environment's design. When designing a fault-tolerant system, you should make sure you include redundant or mirrored systems, use TFTP servers, address power issues, use RAID, and maintain a backup solution.

# Exam Essentials

**Know the OSI model layers and which protocols are found in each.**    The seven layers and protocols supported by each of the layers of the OSI model are as follows:

- *Application*: HTTP, FTP, LPD, SMTP, Telnet, TFTP, EDI, POP3, IMAP, SNMP, NNTP, S-RPC, and SET
- *Presentation*: Encryption protocols and format types, such as ASCII, EBCDIC, TIFF, JPEG, MPEG, and MIDI
- *Session*: NFS, SQL, and RPC
- *Transport*: SPX, SSL, TLS, TCP, and UDP
- *Network*: ICMP, RIP, OSPF, BGP, IGMP, IP, IPSec, IPX, NAT, and SKIP
- *Data Link*: SLIP, PPP, ARP, RARP, L2F, L2TP, PPTP, FDDI, and ISDN
- *Physical*: EIA/TIA-232, EIA/TIA-449, X.21, HSSI, SONET, V.24, and V.35

**Know the TCP/IP model and how it relates to the OSI model.**   The TCP/IP model has four layers: Application, Transport, Internet, and Link.

**Know the different cabling types and their lengths and maximum throughput rates.**   This includes STP, 10Base-T (UTP), 10Base2 (thinnet), 10Base5 (thicknet), 100Base-T, 1000Base-T, and fiber-optic. You should also be familiar with UTP categories 1 through 7.

**Be familiar with the common LAN technologies.**   These are Ethernet, Token Ring, and FDDI. Also be familiar with analog vs. digital communications; synchronous vs. asynchronous communications; baseband vs. broadband communications; broadcast, multicast, and unicast communications; CSMA, CSMA/CA, and CSMA/CD; token passing; and polling.

**Understand the different wireless technologies.**   Cell phones, Bluetooth (802.15), and wireless networking (802.11) are all called wireless technologies, even though they are all different. Be aware of their differences, strengths, and weaknesses. Understand the basics of securing 802.11 networking.

**Know the standard network topologies.**   These are ring, bus, star, and mesh.

**Have a thorough knowledge of TCP/IP.**   Know the difference between TCP and UDP; be familiar with the four TCP/IP layers and how they correspond to the OSI model. In addition, understand the usage of the well-known ports, and be familiar with the subprotocols.

**Know the common network devices.**   Common network devices are firewalls, routers, hubs, bridges, repeaters, switches, gateways, and proxies.

**Understand the different types of firewalls.**   There are four basic types of firewalls: static packet filtering, application-level gateway, circuit-level gateway, and stateful inspection.

**Understand the issues around remote access security management.**   Remote access security management requires that security system designers address the hardware and software components of an implementation along with issues related to policy, work tasks, and encryption.

**Be familiar with the various protocols and mechanisms that may be used on LANs and WANs.**   These are IPSec, SKIP, SWIPE, SSL, SET, PPP, SLIP, PPTP, L2TP, CHAP, PAP, EAP, RADIUS, TACACS, and S-RPC.

**Know the protocol services used to connect to LAN and WAN communication technologies.**   These are Frame Relay, SMDS, X.25, ATM, HSSI, SDLC, HDLC, and ISDN.

**Understand the issues around single points of failure.**   Avoiding single points of failure includes incorporating fault-tolerant systems and solutions into an environment's design. Fault-tolerant systems include redundant or mirrored systems, TFTP servers, and RAID. You should also address power issues and maintain a backup solution.

# Written Lab

1.  Name the layers of the OSI model and their numbers from top to bottom.

2.  Name three problems with cabling and the methods to counteract those issues.

3.  What are the various technologies employed by wireless devices to maximize their use of the available radio frequencies?

4.  Discuss methods used to secure 802.11 wireless networking.

5.  Name the LAN shared media access technologies and examples of their use, if known.

# Answers to Written Lab

1.  Application (7), Presentation (6), Session (5), Transport (4), Network (3), Data Link (2), and Physical (1).

2.  Problems with cabling and their countermeasures include attenuation (use repeaters or don't violate distance recommendations), using the wrong CAT cable (check the cable specifications against throughput requirements, and err on the side of caution), crosstalk (use shielded cables, place cables in separate conduits, or use cables of different twists per inch), cable breaks (avoid running cables in locations where movement occurs), interference (use cable shielding, use cables with higher twists per inch, or switch to fiber-optic cables), and eavesdropping (maintain physical security over all cable runs or switch to fiber-optic cables).

3.  Some of the frequency spectrum-use technologies are spread spectrum, Frequency Hopping Spread Spectrum (FHSS), Direct Sequence Spread Spectrum (DSSS), and Orthogonal Frequency-Division Multiplexing (OFDM).

4.  Methods to secure 802.11 wireless networking include disabling the SSID broadcast; changing the SSID to something unique; enabling MAC filtering; considering the use of static IPs or using DHCP with reservations; turning on the highest form of encryption offered (such as WEP, WPA, or WPA2/802.11i); treating wireless as remote access and employing 802.1X, RADIUS, or TACACS; separating wireless access points from the LAN with firewalls; monitoring all wireless client activity with an IDS; and considering requiring wireless clients to connect with a VPN to gain LAN access.

5.  The LAN shared media access technologies are CSMA, CSMA/CA (used by 802.11 and AppleTalk), CSMA/CD (used by Ethernet), token passing (used by Token Ring and FDDI/CDDI), and polling (used by SDLC, HDLC, and some mainframe systems).

# Review Questions

1. What is layer 4 of the OSI model?

   **A.** Presentation

   **B.** Network

   **C.** Data Link

   **D.** Transport

2. What is encapsulation?

   **A.** Changing the source and destination addresses of a packet

   **B.** Adding a header and footer to data as it moves down the OSI stack

   **C.** Verifying a person's identity

   **D.** Protecting evidence until it has been properly collected

3. Which OSI model layer manages communications in simplex, half-duplex, and full-duplex modes?

   **A.** Application

   **B.** Session

   **C.** Transport

   **D.** Physical

4. Which of the following is the least resistant to EMI?

   **A.** Thinnet

   **B.** 10Base-T UTP

   **C.** 10Base5

   **D.** Coaxial cable

5. Which of the following cables has the most twists per inch?

   **A.** STP

   **B.** UTP

   **C.** 100Base-T

   **D.** 1000Base-T

6. Which of the following is not true?

   **A.** Fiber-optic cable offers very high throughput rates.

   **B.** Fiber-optic cable is difficult to install.

   **C.** Fiber-optic cable is expensive.

   **D.** Communications over fiber-optic cable can be tapped easily.

**7.** If you are the victim of a bluejacking attack, what was compromised?

   **A.** Your car

   **B.** Your switch

   **C.** Your cell phone

   **D.** Your Web cookies

**8.** Which networking technology is based on the IEEE 802.3 standard?

   **A.** Ethernet

   **B.** Token Ring

   **C.** FDDI

   **D.** HDLC

**9.** What is a TCP wrapper?

   **A.** An encapsulation protocol used by switches

   **B.** An application that can serve as a basic firewall by restricting access based on user IDs or system IDs

   **C.** A security protocol used to protect TCP/IP traffic over WAN links

   **D.** A mechanism to tunnel TCP/IP through non-IP networks

**10.** Which of the following protocols is connectionless?

   **A.** TCP

   **B.** UDP

   **C.** IGMP

   **D.** FTP

**11.** By examining the source and destination addresses, the application usage, the source of origin, and the relationship between current packets with the previous packets of the same session, _____ firewalls are able to grant a broader range of access for authorized users and activities and actively watch for and block unauthorized users and activities.

   **A.** Static packet-filtering

   **B.** Application-level gateway

   **C.** Stateful inspection

   **D.** Circuit-level gateway

**12.** _____ firewalls are known as third-generation firewalls.

   **A.** Application-level gateway

   **B.** Stateful inspection

   **C.** Circuit-level gateway

   **D.** Static packet-filtering

**13.** Which of the following is not true regarding firewalls?

   **A.** They are able to log traffic information.

   **B.** They are able to block viruses.

   **C.** They are able to issue alarms based on suspected attacks.

   **D.** They are unable to prevent internal attacks.

**14.** Which of the following is not a routing protocol?

   **A.** OSPF

   **B.** BGP

   **C.** RPC

   **D.** RIP

**15.** A _____ is an intelligent hub because it knows the addresses of the systems connected on each outbound port. Instead of repeating traffic on every outbound port, it repeats traffic only out of the port on which the destination is known to exist.

   **A.** Repeater

   **B.** Switch

   **C.** Bridge

   **D.** Router

**16.** Which of the following is not a technology specifically associated with 802.11 wireless networking?

   **A.** WAP

   **B.** WPA

   **C.** WEP

   **D.** 802.11i

**17.** Which wireless frequency access method offers the greatest throughput with the least interference?

   **A.** FHSS

   **B.** DSSS

   **C.** OFDM

   **D.** OSPF

**18.** What authentication protocol offers no encryption or protection for logon credentials?

   **A.** PAP

   **B.** CHAP

   **C.** SSL

   **D.** RADIUS

**19.** What function does the RARP protocol perform?

    **A.** It is a routing protocol.

    **B.** It converts IP addresses into MAC addresses.

    **C.** It resolves physical addresses into logical addresses.

    **D.** It manages multiplex streaming.

**20.** What form of infrastructure mode wireless networking deployment supports large physical environments through the use of a single SSID but numerous access points?

    **A.** Stand-alone

    **B.** Wired extension

    **C.** Enterprise extension

    **D.** Bridge

# Answers to Review Questions

1.  D.  The Transport layer is layer 4. The Presentation layer is layer 6, the Data Link layer is layer 2, and the Network layer is layer 3.

2.  B.  Encapsulation is adding a header and footer to data as it moves down the OSI stack.

3.  B.  Layer 5, Session, manages simplex (one-direction), half-duplex (two-way, but only one direction can send data at a time), and full-duplex (two-way, in which data can be sent in both directions simultaneously) communications.

4.  B.  10Base-T UTP is the least resistant to EMI because it is unshielded. Thinnet (10Base2) and thicknet (10Base5) are each a type of coaxial cable, which is shielded against EMI.

5.  D.  1000Base-T offers 1000 Mbps throughput and thus must have the greatest number of twists per inch. The tighter the twist (in other words, the number of twists per inch), the more resistant the cable is to internal and external interference and crosstalk and thus the greater the capacity is for throughput (in other words, higher bandwidth).

6.  D.  The statement that fiber-optic cable can be tapped easily is false. Fiber-optic cable is difficult to tap.

7.  C.  A bluejacking attack is a wireless attack on Bluetooth, and the most common device compromised in a bluejacking attack is a cell phone.

8.  A.  Ethernet is based on the IEEE 802.3 standard.

9.  B.  A TCP wrapper is an application that can serve as a basic firewall by restricting access based on user IDs or system IDs.

10. B.  UDP is a connectionless protocol.

11. C.  Stateful inspection firewalls are able to grant a broader range of access for authorized users and activities and actively watch for and block unauthorized users and activities.

12. B.  Stateful inspection firewalls are known as third-generation firewalls.

13. B.  Most firewalls offer extensive logging, auditing, and monitoring capabilities as well as alarms and even basic IDS functions. Firewalls are unable to block viruses or malicious code transmitted through otherwise authorized communication channels, prevent unauthorized but accidental or intended disclosure of information by users, prevent attacks by malicious users already behind the firewall, or protect data after it passed out of or into the private network.

14. C.  There are numerous dynamic routing protocols, including RIP, OSPF, and BGP, but RPC is not a routing protocol.

15. B.  A switch is an intelligent hub. It is considered to be intelligent because it knows the addresses of the systems connected on each outbound port.

**16.** A. Wireless Application Protocol (WAP) is a technology associated with cell phones accessing the Internet rather than 802.11 wireless networking.

**17.** C. Orthogonal Frequency-Division Multiplexing (OFDM) offers high throughput with the least interference. OSPF is a routing protocol, not a wireless frequency access method.

**18.** A. Password Authentication Protocol (PAP) is a standardized authentication protocol for PPP. PAP transmits usernames and passwords in the clear. It offers no form of encryption. It simply provides a means to transport the logon credentials from the client to the authentication server.

**19.** C. Reverse Address Resolution Protocol (RARP) resolves physical addresses (MAC addresses) into logical addresses (IP addresses).

**20.** C. Enterprise extended infrastructure mode exists when a wireless network is designed to support a large physical environment through the use of a single SSID but numerous access points.

# Chapter

# 4

# Communications Security and Countermeasures

---

## THE CISSP EXAM TOPICS COVERED IN THIS CHAPTER INCLUDE:

✓ **Operations Security**

  ▪ Understand fault tolerance requirements

✓ **Telecommunications and Network Security**

  ▪ Establish secure data communications

  ▪ Secure network components

    ▪ Hardware (e.g., modems, switches; routers); transmission media; filtering devices (e.g., firewalls, proxies); end-point security

  ▪ Establish secure multimedia communications

    ▪ Voice over IP (VoIP); multimedia collaboration (e.g., remote meeting technology, instant messaging); virtual private networks (VPN); remote access

  ▪ Understand network attacks

Data residing in a static form on a storage device is fairly simple to secure. As long as physical access control is maintained and reasonable logical access controls are implemented, stored files remain confidential, retain their integrity, and are available to authorized users. However, once data is used by an application or transferred over a network connection, the process of securing it becomes much more difficult.

Communications security covers a wide range of issues related to the transportation of electronic information from one place to another. That transportation may be between systems on opposite sides of the planet or between systems on the same business network. Data becomes vulnerable to a plethora of threats to its confidentiality, integrity, and availability once it is involved in any means of transportation. Fortunately, many of these threats can be reduced or eliminated with the appropriate countermeasures.

Communications security is designed to detect, prevent, and even correct data transportation errors (that is, integrity protection). This is done to sustain the security of networks while supporting the need to exchange and share data. This chapter covers the many forms of communications security, vulnerabilities, and countermeasures.

The Telecommunications and Network Security domain for the CISSP certification exam deals with topics of communications security and vulnerability countermeasures. This domain is discussed in this chapter and in the preceding chapter (Chapter 3, "OSI Model, Protocols, Network Security, and Network Infrastructure"). Be sure to read and study the materials in both chapters to ensure complete coverage of the essential material for the CISSP certification exam.

# Virtual Private Network (VPN)

A *virtual private network* (VPN) is a communication tunnel that provides point-to-point transmission of both authentication and data traffic over an intermediary untrusted network. Most VPNs use encryption to protect the encapsulated traffic, but encryption is not necessary for the connection to be considered a VPN. VPNs are most commonly associated with establishing secure communication paths through the Internet between two distant networks.

VPNs can exist anywhere, however, including within private networks or between end-user systems connected to an ISP. The VPN can link two networks or two individual systems. VPNs can link clients, servers, routers, firewalls, and switches. VPNs are also helpful in providing security for legacy applications that rely upon risky or vulnerable communication protocols or methodologies, especially when communication is across a network.

VPNs can provide confidentiality and integrity over insecure or untrusted intermediary networks. VPNs do not provide or guarantee availability.

# Tunneling

Before you can truly understand VPNs, you must first understand tunneling. Tunneling is the network communications process that protects the contents of protocol packets by encapsulating them in packets of another protocol. The encapsulation is what creates the logical illusion of a communications tunnel over the untrusted intermediary network. This virtual path exists between the encapsulation and the deencapsulation entities located at the ends of the communication.

In fact, sending a letter to your grandmother involves the use of a tunneling system. You create the personal letter (the primary content protocol packet) and place it in an envelope (the tunneling protocol). The envelope is delivered through the postal service (the untrusted intermediary network) to its intended recipient.

## The Need for Tunneling

You can use tunneling in many situations, such as when you're bypassing firewalls, gateways, proxies, or other traffic control devices. The bypass is achieved by encapsulating the restricted content inside packets that are authorized for transmission. The tunneling process prevents the traffic control devices from blocking or dropping the communication because such devices don't know what the packets actually contain.

Tunneling is often used to enable communications between otherwise disconnected systems. If two systems are separated by a lack of network connectivity, a communication link can be established by a modem dial-up link or other remote access or wide area network (WAN) networking service. The actual LAN traffic is encapsulated in whatever communication protocol is used by the temporary connection, such as Point-to-Point Protocol (PPP) in the case of modem dial-up. If two networks are connected by a network employing a different protocol, the protocol of the separated networks can often be encapsulated within the intermediary network's protocol to provide a communication pathway.

Regardless of the actual situation, tunneling protects the contents of the inner protocol and traffic packets by encasing, or wrapping, it in an authorized protocol used by the intermediary network or connection. Tunneling can be used if the primary protocol is not routable and to keep the total number of protocols supported on the network to a minimum.

### Real World Scenario

**The Proliferation of Tunneling**

Tunneling is such a common activity within communication systems that many of us use tunneling on a regular basis without even recognizing it. For example, every time you access a website using a secured SSL or TLS connection, you are using tunneling. Your plain-text web communications are being tunneled within an SSL or TLS session. Also, if you use Internet telephone or VoIP systems, your voice communication is being tunneled inside a VoIP protocol.

How many other instances of tunneling can you pinpoint that you encounter on a weekly basis?

If the act of encapsulating a protocol involves encryption, tunneling can provide a means to transport sensitive data across untrusted intermediary networks without fear of losing confidentiality and integrity.

## Tunneling Drawbacks

Tunneling is not without its problems. It is generally an inefficient means of communicating because most protocols include their own error detection, error handling, acknowledgment, and session management features, so using more than one protocol at a time compounds the overhead required to communicate a single message. Furthermore, tunneling creates either larger packets or additional packets that in turn consume additional network bandwidth. Tunneling can quickly saturate a network if sufficient bandwidth is not available. In addition, tunneling is a point-to-point communication mechanism and is not designed to handle broadcast traffic.

# How VPNs Work

Now that you understand the basics of tunneling, we'll discuss the details of VPNs. A VPN link can be established over any other network communication connection. This could be a typical LAN cable connection, a wireless LAN connection, a remote access dial-up connection, a WAN link, or even a client using an Internet connection for access to an office LAN. A VPN link acts just like a typical direct LAN cable connection; the only possible difference would be speed based on the intermediary network and on the connection types between the client system and the server system. Over a VPN link, a client can perform the same activities and access the same resources they could if they were directly connected via a LAN cable.

VPNs can connect two individual systems or two entire networks. The only difference is that the transmitted data is protected only while it is within the VPN tunnel. Remote access servers or firewalls on the network's border act as the start points and endpoints for VPNs. Thus, traffic is unprotected within the source LAN, protected between the border VPN servers, and then unprotected again once it reaches the destination LAN.

VPN links through the Internet for connecting to distant networks are often inexpensive alternatives to direct links or leased lines. The cost of two high-speed Internet links to local ISPs to support a VPN is often significantly less than the cost of any other connection means available.

## Implementing VPNs

VPNs can be implemented using software or hardware solutions. In either case, there are four common VPN protocols: PPTP, L2F, L2TP, and IPSec. PPTP, L2F, and L2TP operate at the Data Link layer (layer 2) of the OSI model. PPTP and IPSec are limited for use on IP networks, whereas L2F and L2TP can be used to encapsulate any LAN protocol.

SSL can also be used as a VPN protocol, not just as a session encryption tool operating on top of TCP. However, the CISSP exam does not seem to include SSL VPN content at this time.

Point-to-Point Tunneling Protocol (PPTP) is an encapsulation protocol developed from the dial-up protocol Point-to-Point Protocol (PPP). PPTP creates a point-to-point tunnel between two systems and encapsulates PPP packets. PPTP offers protection for authentication traffic through the same authentication protocols supported by PPP:

- Microsoft Challenge Handshake Authentication Protocol (MS-CHAP)
- Challenge Handshake Authentication Protocol (CHAP)
- Password Authentication Protocol (PAP)
- Extensible Authentication Protocol (EAP)
- Shiva Password Authentication Protocol (SPAP)

The initial tunnel negotiation process used by PPTP is not encrypted. (The CISSP exam focuses on the RFC 2637 version of PPTP, not the Microsoft implementation, which was customized using proprietary modifications to support data encryption using Microsoft Point to Point Encryption (MPPE).) Thus, the session establishment packets that include the IP address of the sender and receiver—and can include usernames and hashed passwords—could be intercepted by a third party. PPTP is used on VPNs, but it is often replaced by the Layer 2 Tunneling Protocol (L2TP), which can use IPSec to provide traffic encryption for VPNs.

Cisco developed its own VPN protocol called Layer 2 Forwarding (L2F), which is a mutual authentication tunneling mechanism. However, L2F does not offer encryption. L2F was not widely deployed and was soon replaced by L2TP.

Layer 2 Tunneling Protocol (L2TP) was derived by combining elements from both PPTP and L2F. L2TP creates a point-to-point tunnel between communication endpoints. It lacks a built-in encryption scheme, but it typically relies upon IPSec as its security mechanism. L2TP also supports TACACS+ and RADIUS, whereas PPTP does not.

The most commonly used VPN protocol is now IPSec. IP Security (IPSec) is both a stand-alone VPN protocol and the security mechanism for L2TP, and it can be used only for IP traffic. IPSec provides for secured authentication as well as encrypted data transmission. IPSec has two primary components, or functions:

**Authentication Header (AH)**   AH provides authentication, integrity, and nonrepudiation.

**Encapsulating Security Payload (ESP)**   ESP provides encryption to protect the confidentiality of transmitted data, but it can also perform limited authentication. It operates at the Network layer (layer 3) and can be used in transport mode or tunnel mode. In transport mode, the IP packet data is encrypted but the header of the packet is not. In tunnel mode, the entire IP packet is encrypted and a new header is added to the packet to govern transmission through the tunnel.

Table 4.1 illustrates the main characteristics of VPN protocols.

**TABLE 4.1**   VPN characteristics

| VPN Protocol | Native Authentication Protection | Native Data Encryption | Protocols Supported | Dial-Up Links Supported | Number of Simultaneous Connections |
|---|---|---|---|---|---|
| PPTP | Yes | No | IP only | Yes | Single point to point |
| L2F | Yes | No | IP only | Yes | Single point to point |
| L2TP | Yes | No (can use IPSec) | Any | Yes | Single point to point |
| IPSec | Yes | Yes | IP only | No | Multiple |

A VPN device is a network add-on device used to create VPN tunnels separately from server or client OSs. The use of the VPN devices is transparent to networked systems.

# Network Address Translation

The tasks of hiding the identity of internal clients, masking the design of your private network, and keeping public IP address leasing costs to a minimum are all made simple through the use of Network Address Translation (NAT). NAT is a mechanism for converting the internal IP addresses found in packet headers into public IP addresses for transmission over the Internet. NAT was developed to allow private networks to use any IP address set without causing collisions or conflicts with public Internet hosts with the same IP addresses. In effect, NAT translates the IP addresses of your internal clients to leased addresses outside your environment.

NAT offers numerous benefits, such as being able to connect an entire network to the Internet using only a single (or just a few) leased public IP addresses. NAT allows you to use the private IP addresses defined in RFC 1918 in a private network while still being able to communicate with the Internet. NAT protects a network by hiding the IP addressing scheme and network topography from the Internet. It also provides protection by restricting connections so that only connections originating from the internal protected network are allowed back into the network from the Internet. Thus, most intrusion attacks are automatically repelled.

 **Real World Scenario**

**Are You Using NAT?**

Most networks, whether at an office or at home, employ NAT. You can use at least three ways to tell whether you are working within a NATed network. First, check your client's IP address. If it is one of the RFC 1918 addresses and you are still able to interact with the Internet, then you are on a NATed network. Second, check the configuration of your proxy, router, firewall, modem, or gateway device to see whether NAT is configured. Obviously, this action requires authority and access to the networking device. Third, if your client's IP address is not an RFC 1918 address, then compare your address to what the Internet thinks your address is. You can do this by visiting any of the IP-checking websites; a popular one is http://ipchicken.com. If your client's IP address and the address that http://ipchicken.com claims is your address are different, then you are working from a NATed network.

 Frequently, security professionals refer to NAT when they really mean PAT. By definition, NAT maps one internal IP address to one external IP address. However, Port Address Translation (PAT) maps one internal IP address to an external IP address and port number combination. Thus, PAT can theoretically support 65,536 ($2^{16}$) simultaneous communications from internal clients over a single external leased IP address. So with NAT, you must lease as many public IP addresses as you want to have for simultaneous communications, while with PAT you can lease fewer IP addresses and obtain a reasonable 100:1 ratio of internal clients to external leased IP addresses.

NAT is part of a number of hardware devices and software products, including firewalls, routers, gateways, and proxies. It can be used only on IP networks and operates at the Network layer (layer 3).

## Private IP Addresses

The use of NAT has proliferated recently because of the increased scarcity of public IP addresses and security concerns. With only roughly 4 billion addresses ($2^{32}$) available in IPv4, the world has simply deployed more devices using IP than there are unique IP addresses available. Fortunately, the early designers of the Internet and the TCP/IP protocol had good foresight and put aside a few blocks of addresses for private, unrestricted use. These IP addresses, commonly called the *private IP addresses*, are defined in RFC 1918. They are as follows:

- 10.0.0.0–10.255.255.255 (a full Class A range)
- 172.16.0.0–172.31.255.255 (16 Class B ranges)
- 192.168.0.0–192.168.255.255 (256 Class C ranges)

 **Real World Scenario**

**Can't NAT Again!**

On several occasions we've needed to re-NAT an already NATed network. This occurs when you need to make an isolated subnet within a NATed network and attempt to do so by connecting a router to host your new subnet to the single port offered by the existing network. Another time this might occur is when you have a DSL or cable modem that offers only a single connection but you have multiple computers or want to add wireless to your environment.

By connecting a NAT proxy router or a wireless access point, you are usually attempting to re-NAT what was NATed to you initially. One configuration setting that can either make or break this setup is the IP address range in use. It is not possible to re-NAT the same subnet. For example, if your existing network is offering 192.168.1.x addresses, then you cannot use that same address range in your new NATed subnet. So, change your new router/WAP's configuration to perform NAT on a slightly different address range, such as 192.168.5.x, so you won't have the conflict. This seems obvious, but it is quite frustrating to troubleshoot the unwanted result without this insight.

All routers and traffic-directing devices are configured by default not to forward traffic to or from these IP addresses. In other words, the private IP addresses are not routed by default. Thus, they cannot be directly used to communicate over the Internet. However, they can be easily used on private networks where routers are not employed or where slight modifications to router configurations are made. Using private IP addresses in conjunction with NAT greatly reduces the cost of connecting to the Internet by allowing fewer public IP addresses to be leased from an ISP.

> Attempting to use these private IP addresses directly on the Internet is futile because all publicly accessible routers will drop data packets containing a source or destination IP address from these RFC 1918 ranges.

## Stateful NAT

NAT operates by maintaining a mapping between requests made by internal clients, a client's internal IP address, and the IP address of the Internet service contacted. When a request packet is received by NAT from a client, it changes the source address in the packet from the client's to the NAT server's. This change is recorded in the NAT mapping database along with the destination address. Once a reply is received from the Internet server, NAT matches the reply's source address to an address stored in its mapping database and then uses the linked client address to redirect the response packet to its intended destination. This process is known as stateful NAT because it maintains information about the communication sessions between clients and external systems.

NAT can operate on a one-to-one basis with only a single internal client able to communicate over one of its leased public IP addresses at a time. This type of configuration can result in a bottleneck if more clients attempt Internet access than there are public IP addresses. For example, if there are only five leased public IP addresses, the sixth client must wait until an address is released before its communications can be transmitted over the Internet. Other forms of NAT employ multiplexing techniques in which port numbers are used to allow the traffic from multiple internal clients to be managed on a single leased public IP address.

## Static and Dynamic NAT

You can use NAT in two modes: static and dynamic. Use static mode NAT when a specific internal client's IP address is assigned a permanent mapping to a specific external public IP address. This allows for external entities to communicate with systems inside your network even if you are using RFC 1918 IP addresses. Use dynamic mode NAT to grant multiple internal clients access to a few leased public IP addresses. Thus, a large internal network can still access the Internet without having to lease a large block of public IP addresses. This keeps public IP address usage abuse to a minimum and helps keep Internet access costs to a minimum.

In a dynamic mode NAT implementation, the NAT system maintains a database of mappings so that all response traffic from Internet services is properly routed to the original internal requesting client. Often NAT is combined with a proxy server or proxy firewall to provide additional Internet access and content-caching features. NAT is not directly compatible with IPSec because it modifies packet headers, which IPSec relies upon to prevent security violations. However, there are versions of NAT proxies designed to support IPSec over NAT. Specifically, NAT-Traversal (RFC 3947) was designed to support IPSec VPNs through the use of UDP encapsulation of IKE. IP Security (IPSec) is a standards-based mechanism for providing encryption for point-to-point TCP/IP traffic.

## Automatic Private IP Addressing (APIPA)

Automatic Private IP Addressing (APIPA), not to be confused with the private IP address ranges defined in RFC 1918, assigns an IP address to a system in the event of a DHCP assignment failure. APIPA is primarily a feature of Windows. APIPA assigns each failed DHCP client with an IP address from the range of 169.254.0.1 to 169.254.255.254 along with the default Class B subnet mask of 255.255.0.0. This allows the system to communicate with other APIPA-configured clients within the same broadcast domain but not with any system across a router or with a correctly assigned IP address.

It is a good idea to know how to convert between decimal, binary, and even hexadecimal. Also, don't forget how to convert from a dotted-decimal notation IP address (such as 172.16.1.1) to its binary equivalent (that is, 10101100000100000000000100000001). And it is probably not a bad idea to be able to convert the 32-bit binary number to a single decimal number (that is, 2886729985). Understand that IP addresses and subnet masks are actual binary numbers and through their use in binary all the functions of routing and traffic management occur. Additionally, knowledge of number conversions comes in handy when attempting to identify obfuscated addresses.

 **Real World Scenario**

**The Loopback Address**

Another IP address range that you should be careful not to confuse with the private IP address ranges defined in RFC 1918 is the loopback address. The loopback address is purely a software entity. It is an IP address used to create a software interface that connects to itself via the TCP/IP protocol. The loopback address allows for the testing of local network settings in spite of missing, damaged, or nonfunctional network hardware and related device drivers. Technically, the entire 127.x.x.x network is reserved for loopback use. However, only the 127.0.0.1 address is widely used. Windows XP SP2 (and possibly other OS updates) recently restricted the client to use only 127.0.0.1 as the loopback address. This caused several applications that used other addresses in the upper ranges of the 127.x.x.x network services to fail. In restricting client use to only 127.0.0.1, Microsoft has attempted to open up a wasted Class A address. Even if this tactic is successful for Microsoft, it will affect only the modern Windows systems.

# Switching Technologies

When two systems (individual computers or LANs) are connected over multiple intermediary networks, the task of transmitting data packets from one to the other is a complex process. To simplify this task, switching technologies were developed. The first switching technology was circuit switching.

## Circuit Switching

Circuit switching was originally developed to manage telephone calls over the public switched telephone network. In circuit switching, a dedicated physical pathway is created between the two communicating parties. Once a call is established, the links between the two parties remain the same throughout the conversation. This provides for fixed or known transmission times, a uniform level of quality, and little or no loss of signal or communication interruptions. Circuit-switching systems employ permanent, physical connections. However, the term *permanent* applies only to each communication session. The path is permanent throughout a single conversation. Once the path is disconnected, if the two parties communicate again, a different path may be assembled. During a single conversation, the same physical or electronic path is used throughout the communication and is used only for that one communication. Circuit switching grants exclusive use of a communication path to the current communication partners. Only after a session has been closed can a pathway be reused by another communication.

 **Real World Scenario**

**Real-World Circuit Switching**

There is very little real-world circuit switching in the modern world (or at least in the past 10 to 15 years or so). Packet switching, discussed next, has become ubiquitous for data and voice transmissions. Decades ago we could often point to the public switched telephone network (PSTN) as a prime example of circuit switching, but with the advent of digital switching and VoIP systems, those days are long gone. That's not to say that circuit switching is nonexistent in today's world; it is just not being used for data transmission. Instead, you can still find circuit switching in rail yards, irrigation systems, and even electrical distribution systems.

## Packet Switching

Eventually, as computer communications increased as opposed to voice communications, a new form of switching was developed. Packet switching occurs when the message or communication is broken up into small segments (usually fixed-length packets, depending on the protocols and technologies employed) and sent across the intermediary networks to the destination. Each segment of data has its own header that contains source and destination information. The header is read by each intermediary system and is used to route each packet to its intended destination. Each channel or communication path is reserved for use only while a packet is actually being transmitted over it. As soon as the packet is sent, the channel is made available for other communications.

Packet switching does not enforce exclusivity of communication pathways. It can be seen as a logical transmission technology because addressing logic dictates how communications traverse intermediary networks between communication partners. Table 4.2 compares circuit switching to packet switching.

**TABLE 4.2**   Circuit switching vs. packet switching

| Circuit Switching | Packet Switching |
| --- | --- |
| Constant traffic | Bursty traffic |
| Fixed known delays | Variable delays |
| Connection oriented | Connectionless |
| Sensitive to connection loss | Sensitive to data loss |
| Used primarily for voice | Used for any type of traffic |

## Virtual Circuits

A virtual circuit (also called a *communication path*) is a logical pathway or circuit created over a packet-switched network between two specific endpoints. Within packet-switching systems are two types of virtual circuits:

- Permanent virtual circuits (PVCs)
- Switched virtual circuits (SVCs)

A PVC is like a dedicated leased line; the logical circuit always exists and is waiting for the customer to send data. An SVC is more like a dial-up connection because a virtual circuit has to be created before it can be used and then disassembled after the transmission is complete. In either type of virtual circuit, when a data packet enters point A of a virtual circuit connection, that packet is sent directly to point B or the other end of the virtual circuit. However, the actual path of one packet may be different from the path of another packet from the same transmission. In other words, multiple paths may exist between point A and point B as the ends of the virtual circuit, but any packet entering at point A will end up at point B.

# WAN Technologies

WAN links and long-distance connection technologies can be divided into two primary categories: dedicated and nondedicated lines. A dedicated line (also called a *leased line* or *point-to-point link*) is one that is indefinably and continually reserved for use by a specific customer (see Table 4.3). A dedicated line is always on and waiting for traffic to be transmitted over it. The link between the customer's LAN and the dedicated WAN link is always open and established. A dedicated line connects two specific endpoints and only those two endpoints together.

A nondedicated line is one that requires a connection to be established before data transmission can occur. A nondedicated line can be used to connect with any remote system that uses the same type of nondedicated line.

**TABLE 4.3**   Examples of dedicated lines

| Technology | Connection Type | Speed |
| --- | --- | --- |
| Digital Signal Level 0 (DS-0) | Partial T1 | 64 Kbps up to 1.544 Mbps |
| Digital Signal Level 1 (DS-1) | T1 | 1.544 Mbps |
| Digital Signal Level 3 (DS-3) | T3 | 44.736 Mbps |
| European digital transmission format 1 | EI | 2.108 Mbps |
| European digital transmission format 3 | E3 | 34.368 Mbps |
| Cable modem or cable routers | | 10+ Mbps |

To obtain fault tolerance with leased lines or with connections to carrier networks (that is, Frame Relay, ATM, SONET, SMDS, X.25, and so on), you must deploy two redundant connections. For even greater redundancy, purchase the connections from two different telcos or service providers. However, when you're using two different service providers, be sure they don't connect to the same regional backbone or share any major pipeline. If you cannot afford to deploy an exact duplicate of your primary leased line, consider a nondedicated DSL, ISDN, or cable modem connection. These less-expensive options may still provide partial availability in the event of a primary leased line failure.

Standard modems, DSL, and ISDN are examples of nondedicated lines. Digital subscriber line (DSL) is a technology that exploits the upgraded telephone network to grant consumers speeds from 144 Kbps to 6 Mbps (or more). There are numerous formats of DSL, such as ADSL, xDSL, CDSL, HDSL, SDSL, RASDSL, IDSL, and VDSL. Each format varies as to the specific downstream and upstream bandwidth provided. For the exam, just worry about the general idea of DSL instead of trying to memorize all the details about the various DSL subformats. The maximum distance a DSL line can be from a central office (that is, a specific type of distribution node of the telephone network) is approximately 1,000 meters.

Don't forget about satellite connections. Satellite connections may offer high-speed solutions even in locales that are inaccessible by cable-based, radio-wave-based, and line-of-sight-based communications. However, satellites are considered insecure because of their large surface footprint. Communications over a satellite can be intercepted by anyone, but if you have strong encryption, satellite communications can be reasonably secured. Just think of satellite radio. As long as you have a receiver, you can get the signal anywhere. But without a paid service plan, you can't gain access to the audio content.

Integrated Services Digital Network (ISDN) is a fully digital telephone network that supports both voice and high-speed data communications. There are two standard classes or formats of ISDN service: BRI and PRI. Basic Rate Interface (BRI) offers customers a connection with two B channels and one D channel. The B channels support a throughput of 64 Kbps and are used for data transmission. The D channel is used for call establishment, management, and teardown and has a bandwidth of 16 Kbps. Even though the D channel was not designed to support data transmissions, a BRI ISDN is said to offer consumers 144 Kbps of total throughput. Primary Rate Interface (PRI) offers consumers a connection with multiple 64 Kbps B channels (2 to 23 of them) and a single 64Kbps D channel. Thus, a PRI can be deployed with as little as 192 Kbps and up to 1.544 Mbps. However, remember that those numbers are bandwidth, not throughput, because they include the D channel, which cannot be used for actual data transmission (at least not in most normal commercial implementations).

# WAN Connection Technologies

Numerous WAN connection technologies are available to companies that need communication services between multiple locations and even external partners. These WAN technologies vary greatly in cost and throughput. However, most share the common feature of being transparent to the connected LANs or systems. A WAN switch, specialized router, or border connection device provides all the interfacing needed between the network carrier service and a company's LAN. The border connection device is called the *channel service unit/data service unit (CSU/DSU)*. These devices convert LAN signals into the format used by the WAN carrier network and vice versa. The CSU/DSU contains data terminal equipment/data circuit-terminating equipment (DTE/DCE), which provides the actual connection point for the LAN's router (the DTE) and the WAN carrier network's switch (the DCE). The CSU/DSU acts as a translator, a store-and-forward device, and a link conditioner. A WAN switch is simply a specialized version of a LAN switch that is constructed with a built-in CSU/DSU for a specific type of carrier network. There are many types of carrier networks, or WAN connection technologies, such as X.25, Frame Relay, ATM, and SMDS.

---

 **Real World Scenario**

**Remote Access and Telecommuting Techniques**

There are three main types of remote access techniques:

**Service specific**   Service-specific remote access gives users the ability to remotely connect to and manipulate or interact with a single service, such as email.

**Remote control**   Remote control remote access grants a remote user the ability to fully control another system that is physically distant from them. The monitor and keyboard act as if they are directly connected to the remote system.

**Remote node operation**   Remote node operation is just another name for dial-up connectivity. A remote system connects to a remote access server. That server provides the remote client with network services and possible Internet access.

Telecommuting is performing work at a location other than the primary office. In fact, there is a good chance that you perform some form of telecommuting as part of your current job. Telecommuting clients can use any or all of these remote access techniques to establish connectivity to the central office LAN.

---

## X.25 WAN Connections

X.25 is an older packet-switching technology that was widely used in Europe. It uses permanent virtual circuits to establish specific point-to-point connections between two systems or networks. It is the predecessor to Frame Relay and operates in much the same fashion. However, X.25 use is declining because of its lower performance and throughput rates when compared to Frame Relay or ATM.

## Frame Relay Connections

Like X.25, Frame Relay is a packet-switching technology that also uses PVCs. However, unlike X.25, Frame Relay supports multiple PVCs over a single WAN carrier service connection. Frame Relay is a layer 2 connection mechanism that uses packet-switching technology to establish virtual circuits between communication endpoints. Unlike dedicated or leased lines, for which cost is based primarily on the distance between endpoints, Frame Relay's cost is primarily based on the amount of data transferred. The Frame Relay network is a shared medium across which virtual circuits are created to provide point-to-point communications. All virtual circuits are independent of and invisible to each other.

A key concept related to Frame Relay is the Committed Information Rate (CIR). The CIR is the guaranteed minimum bandwidth a service provider grants to its customers. It is usually significantly less than the actual maximum capability of the provider network. Each customer may have a different CIR that is established and defined in their contract. The service network provider may allow customers to exceed their CIR over short intervals when additional bandwidth is available. This is known as *bandwidth on demand*. Although at first this might sound like an outstanding benefit, the reality is that the customer is charged a premium rate for the extra consumed bandwidth. Frame Relay operates at layer 2 (the Data Link layer) of the OSI model as a connection-oriented packet-switching transmission technology.

Frame Relay requires the use of DTE/DCE at each connection point. The customer owns the DTE, which acts like a router or a switch and provides the customer's network with access to the Frame Relay network. The Frame Relay service provider owns the DCE, which performs the actual transmission of data over the Frame Relay as well as establishing and maintaining the virtual circuit for the customer.

There are two types of virtual circuits: permanent virtual circuit (PVC) and switched virtual circuit (SVC). A PVC is a predefined virtual circuit that is always available. The virtual circuit may be closed down when not in use, but it can be instantly reopened whenever needed. An SVC is more like a dial-up connection. Each time the customer needs to transmit data over Frame Relay, a new virtual circuit is established using the best paths currently available. A PVC is like a two-way radio or walkie-talkie. Whenever communication is needed, you press the button and start talking; the radio reopens the predefined frequency automatically (that is, the virtual circuit). An SVC is more like a shortwave or ham radio. You must tune the transmitter and receiver to a new frequency every time you want to communicate with someone.

## ATM

Asynchronous transfer mode (ATM) is a cell-switching WAN communication technology, as opposed to a packet-switching technology like Frame Relay. It fragments communications into fixed-length 53-byte cells. The use of fixed-length cells allows ATM to be very efficient and offer high throughputs. ATM can use either PVCs or SVCs. ATM providers can guarantee a minimum bandwidth and a specific level of quality to their leased services. Customers can often consume additional bandwidth as needed when available on the service network for an additional pay-as-you-go fee; as mentioned earlier with Frame Relay, this is known as *bandwidth on demand*. ATM is a connection-oriented packet-switching technology.

## SMDS

Switched Multimegabit Data Service (SMDS) is a connectionless packet-switching technology. Often, SMDS is used to connect multiple LANs to form a metropolitan area network (MAN) or a WAN. SMDS was often a preferred connection mechanism for linking remote LANs that communicate infrequently. SMDS supports high-speed bursty traffic and bandwidth on demand. It fragments data into small transmission cells. SMDS can be considered a forerunner to ATM because of the similar technologies used.

### Specialized Protocols

Some WAN connection technologies require additional specialized protocols to support various types of specialized systems or devices. Three of these protocols are SDLC, HDLC, and HSSI:

**SDLC**   Synchronous Data Link Control (SDLC) is used on permanent physical connections of dedicated leased lines to provide connectivity for mainframes, such as IBM Systems Network Architecture (SNA) systems. SDLC uses polling, operates at OSI layer 2 (the Data Link layer), and is a bit-oriented synchronous protocol.

**HDLC**   High-Level Data Link Control (HDLC) is a refined version of SDLC designed specifically for serial synchronous connections. HDLC supports full-duplex communications and supports both point-to-point and multipoint connections. HDLC, like SDLC, uses polling and operates at OSI layer 2 (the Data Link layer). HDLC offers flow control and includes error detection and correction.

**HSSI**   High Speed Serial Interface (HSSI) is a DTE/DCE interface standard that defines how multiplexors and routers connect to high-speed network carrier services such as ATM or Frame Relay. A multiplexor is a device that transmits multiple communications or signals over a single cable or virtual circuit. HSSI defines the electrical and physical characteristics of the interfaces or connection points and thus operates at OSI layer 1 (the Physical layer).

## Dial-Up Encapsulation Protocols

The Point-to-Point Protocol (PPP) is an encapsulation protocol designed to support the transmission of IP traffic over dial-up or point-to-point links. PPP allows for multivendor interoperability of WAN devices supporting serial links. All dial-up and most point-to-point connections are serial in nature (as opposed to parallel). PPP includes a wide range of communication services, including the assignment and management of IP addresses, management of synchronous communications, standardized encapsulation, multiplexing, link configuration, link quality testing, error detection, and feature or option negotiation (such as compression).

PPP was originally designed to support CHAP and PAP for authentication. However, recent versions of PPP also support MS-CHAP, EAP, and SPAP. PPP can also be used to support Internetwork Packet Exchange (IPX) and DECnet protocols. PPP is an Internet standard documented in RFC 1661. It replaced the Serial Line Internet Protocol (SLIP). SLIP offered no authentication, supported only half-duplex communications, had no error detection capabilities, and required manual link establishment and teardown.

# Miscellaneous Security Control Characteristics

When you're selecting or deploying security controls for network communications, you need to evaluate numerous characteristics in light of your circumstances, capabilities, and security policy. We discuss these issues in the following sections.

## Transparency

Just as the name implies, *transparency* is the characteristic of a service, security control, or access mechanism that ensures that it is unseen by users. Transparency is often a desirable feature for security controls. The more transparent a security mechanism is, the less likely a user will be able to circumvent it or even be aware that it exists. With transparency, there is a lack of direct evidence that a feature, service, or restriction exists, and its impact on performance is minimal.

In some cases, transparency may need to function more as a configurable feature than as a permanent aspect of operation, such as when an administrator is troubleshooting, evaluating, or tuning a system's configurations.

## Verifying Integrity

To verify the integrity of a transmission, you can use a checksum called a *hash total*. A hash function is performed on a message or a packet before it is sent over the communication pathway. The hash total obtained is added to the end of the message and is called the *message digest*. Once the message is received, the hash function is performed by the destination system, and the result is compared to the original hash total. If the two hash totals match, then there is a high level of certainty that the message has not been altered or corrupted during transmission. Hash totals are similar to cyclic redundancy checks (CRCs) in that they both act as integrity tools. In most secure transaction systems, hash functions are used to guarantee communication integrity.

---

 **Real World Scenario**

**Checking the Hash**

Checking the hash value of files is always a good idea. This simple task can prevent the use of corrupted files and prevent the accidental acceptance of maligned data. Several IDS systems and system integrity verification tools use hashing as a means to check that files did not change over time. This is done by creating a hash for every file on a drive, storing those hashes in a database, and then periodically recalculating hashes for files and checking the new hash against the historical one. If there is ever any difference in the hashes, then you should investigate the file.

Another common use of hashes is to verify downloads. Many trusted Internet download sites provide MD5 and SHA hash totals for the files they offer. You can take advantage of these hashes in at least two ways. First, you can use a download manager that automatically checks the hashes for you upon download completion. Second, you can obtain a hashing tool, such as md5sum or sha1sum, to generate your own hash values. Then manually compare your generated value from the downloaded file against the claimed hash value from the download site. This mechanism ensures that the file you ultimately have on your system matches the file from the download site to the last bit.

---

Record sequence checking is similar to a hash total check; however, instead of verifying content integrity, it verifies packet or message sequence integrity. Many communications services employ record sequence checking to verify that no portions of a message were lost and that all elements of the message are in their proper order.

## Transmission Mechanisms

Transmission logging is a form of auditing focused on communications. Transmission logging records the particulars about source, destination, time stamps, identification codes, transmission status, number of packets, size of message, and so on. These pieces of information may be useful in troubleshooting problems and tracking down unauthorized communications or used against a system as a means to extract data about how it functions.

Transmission error correction is a capability built into connection- or session-oriented protocols and services. If it is determined that a message, in whole or in part, was corrupted, altered, or lost, a request can be made for the source to resend all or part of the message. Retransmission controls determine whether all or part of a message is retransmitted in the event that a transmission error correction system discovers a problem with a communication. Retransmission controls can also determine whether multiple copies of a hash total or CRC value are sent and whether multiple data paths or communication channels are employed.

# Managing Email Security

Email is one of the most widely and commonly used Internet services. The email infrastructure employed on the Internet primarily consists of email servers using Simple Mail Transfer Protocol (SMTP) to accept messages from clients, transport those messages to other servers, and deposit messages into a user's server-based inbox. In addition to email servers, the infrastructure includes email clients. Clients retrieve email from their server-based inboxes using Post Office Protocol version 3 (POP3) or Internet Message Access Protocol (IMAP). Clients communicate with email servers using SMTP. Many Internet-compatible email systems rely upon the X.400 standard for addressing and message handling.

Sendmail is the most common SMTP server for Unix systems, Exchange is the most common SMTP server for Microsoft systems, and GroupWise is (or at least was) the most common SMTP server for Novell systems. In addition to these three popular products, numerous alternatives exist, but they all share the same basic functionality and compliance with Internet email standards.

If you deploy an SMTP server, it is imperative that you properly configure authentication for both inbound and outbound mail. SMTP is designed to be a mail relay system. This means it relays mail from sender to intended recipient. However, you want to avoid turning your SMTP server into an open relay (also known as *open relay agent* or *relay agent*), which is an STMP server that does not authenticate senders before accepting and relaying mail. Open relays are prime targets for spammers because they allow spammers to send out floods of emails by piggybacking on an insecure email infrastructure.

## Email Security Goals

For email, the basic mechanism in use on the Internet offers the efficient delivery of messages but lacks controls to provide for confidentiality, integrity, or even availability. In other words, basic email is not secure. However, you can add security to email in many ways. Adding security to email may satisfy one or more of the following objectives:

- Provide for nonrepudiation.
- Restrict access to messages to their intended recipients (i.e., privacy and confidentiality).
- Maintain the integrity of messages.
- Authenticate and verify the source of messages.

- Verify the delivery of messages.
- Classify sensitive content within or attached to messages.

As with any aspect of IT security, email security begins in a security policy approved by upper management. Within the security policy, you must address several issues:

- Acceptable use policies for email
- Access control
- Privacy
- Email management
- Email backup and retention policies

Acceptable use policies define what activities can and cannot be performed over an organization's email infrastructure. It is often stipulated that professional, business-oriented email and a limited amount of personal email can be sent and received. Specific restrictions are usually placed on performing personal business (that is, work for another organization, including self-employment) and sending or receiving illegal, immoral, or offensive communications as well as any other activities that would have a detrimental effect on productivity, profitability, or public relations.

Access control over email should be maintained so that users have access only to their specific inbox and email archive databases. An extension of this rule implies that no other user, authorized or not, can gain access to an individual's email. Access control should provide for both legitimate access and some level of privacy, at least from peer employees and unauthorized intruders.

The mechanisms and processes used to implement, maintain, and administer email for an organization should be clarified. End users may not need to know the specifics of how email is managed, but they do need to know whether email is considered private communication. Email has recently been the focus of numerous court cases in which archived messages were used as evidence. Often, this was to the chagrin of the author or recipient of those messages. If email is to be retained (that is, backed up and stored in archives for future use), users need to be made aware of this. If email is to be reviewed for violations by an auditor, users need to be informed of this as well. Some companies have elected to retain only the last three months of email archives before they are destroyed, whereas others have opted to retain email for years. Depending upon your country and industry, there are often regulations that dictate retention policies.

## Understanding Email Security Issues

The first step in deploying email security is to recognize the vulnerabilities specific to email. The protocols used to support email do not employ encryption. Thus, all messages are transmitted in the form in which they are submitted to the email server, which is often plain text. This makes interception and eavesdropping easy. However, the lack of native encryption is one of the least important security issues related to email.

Email is the most common delivery mechanism for viruses, worms, Trojan horses, documents with destructive macros, and other malicious code. The proliferation of support for various scripting languages, autodownload capabilities, and autoexecute features has transformed hyperlinks within the content of email and attachments into a serious threat to every system.

Email offers little in the way of source verification. Spoofing the source address of email is a simple process for even a novice attacker. Email headers can be modified at their source or at any point during transit. Furthermore, it is also possible to deliver email directly to a user's inbox on an email server by directly connecting to the email server's SMTP port. And speaking of in-transit modification, there are no native integrity checks to ensure that a message was not altered between its source and destination.

In addition, email itself can be used as an attack mechanism. When sufficient numbers of messages are directed to a single user's inbox or through a specific STMP server, a denial of service (DoS) can result. This attack is often called *mail-bombing* and is simply a DoS performed by inundating a system with messages. The DoS can be the result of storage capacity consumption or processing capability utilization. Either way, the result is the same: Legitimate messages cannot be delivered.

Like email flooding and malicious code attachments, unwanted email can be considered an attack. Sending unwanted, inappropriate, or irrelevant messages is called *spamming*. Spamming is often little more than a nuisance, but it does waste system resources both locally and over the Internet. It is often difficult to stop spam because the source of the messages is usually spoofed.

## Email Security Solutions

Imposing security on email is possible, but the efforts should be in tune with the value and confidentiality of the messages being exchanged. You can use several protocols, services, and solutions to add security to email without requiring a complete overhaul of the entire Internet-based SMTP infrastructure. These include S/MIME, MOSS, PEM, and PGP. We'll discuss S/MIME further in Chapter 10, "PKI and Cryptographic Applications."

**S/MIME**    Secure Multipurpose Internet Mail Extensions (S/MIME) offers authentication and confidentiality to email through public key encryption and digital signatures. Authentication is provided through X.509 digital certificates. Privacy is provided through the use of Public Key Cryptography Standard (PKCS) encryption. Two types of messages can be formed using S/MIME: signed messages and secured enveloped messages. A signed message provides integrity, sender authentication, and nonrepudiation. An enveloped message provides integrity, sender authentication, and confidentiality.

**MOSS**    MIME Object Security Services (MOSS) can provide authentication, confidentiality, integrity, and nonrepudiation for email messages. MOSS employs Message Digest 2 (MD2) and MD5 algorithms; Rivest, Shamir, and Adelman (RSA) public key; and Data Encryption Standard (DES) to provide authentication and encryption services.

**PEM**   Privacy Enhanced Mail (PEM) is an email encryption mechanism that provides authentication, integrity, confidentiality, and nonrepudiation. PEM uses RSA, DES, and X.509.

**PGP**   Pretty Good Privacy (PGP) is a public-private key system that uses a variety of encryption algorithms to encrypt files and email messages. The first version of PGP used RSA, the second version, IDEA, but later versions offered a spectrum of algorithm options. PGP is not a standard but rather an independently developed product that has wide Internet grassroots support.

 **Real World Scenario**

**Current Free PGP Solution**

PGP started off as a free product for all to use, but it has since split into two divergent products. One is available as a commercial product, and the other is a GNU project now known as GnuPG. If you have not used PGP before, we recommend downloading the appropriate GnuPG version for your preferred email platform. This secure solution is sure to improve your email privacy and integrity. You can learn more about GnuPG at http://gnupg.org. You can learn more about PGP by visiting its pages on Wikipedia.

By using these and other security mechanisms for email and communication transmissions, you can reduce or eliminate many of the security vulnerabilities of email. Digital signatures can help eliminate impersonation. The encryption of messages reduces eavesdropping. And the use of email filters keep spamming and mail-bombing to a minimum.

Blocking attachments at the email gateway system on your network can ease the threats from malicious attachments. You can have a 100 percent no-attachments policy or block only those attachments that are known or suspected to be malicious, such as attachments with extensions that are used for executable and scripting files. If attachments are an essential part of your email communications, you'll need to train your users and your antivirus tools for protection. Training users to avoid contact with suspicious or unexpected attachments greatly reduces the risk of malicious code transference via email. Antivirus software is generally effective against known viruses, but it offers little protection against new or unknown viruses.

**Real World Scenario**

**Fax Security**

Fax communications are waning in popularity because of the widespread use of email. Electronic documents are easily exchanged as attachments to email. Printed documents are just as easy to scan and email as they are to fax. However, you must still address faxing in your overall security plan. Most modems give users the ability to connect to a remote computer system and send and receive faxes. Many operating systems include built-in fax capabilities, and there are numerous fax products for computer systems. Faxes sent from a computer's fax/modem can be received by another computer or by a regular fax machine.

Even with declining use, faxes still represent a communications path that is vulnerable to attack. Like any other telephone communication, faxes can be intercepted and are susceptible to eavesdropping. If an entire fax transmission is recorded, it can be played back by another fax machine to extract the transmitted documents.

Some of the mechanisms that can be deployed to improve the security of faxes include fax encryptors, link encryption, activity logs, and exception reports. A fax encryptor gives a fax machine the capability to use an encryption protocol to scramble the outgoing fax signal. The use of an encryptor requires that the receiving fax machine support the same encryption protocol so it can decrypt the documents. Link encryption is the use of an encrypted communication path, like a VPN link or a secured telephone link, to transmit the fax. Activity logs and exception reports can be used to detect anomalies in fax activity that could be symptoms of attack.

In addition to the security of a fax transmission, it is important to consider the security of a received fax. Faxes that are automatically printed may sit in the out tray for a long period of time, therefore making them subject to viewing by unintended recipients. Studies have shown that adding banners of CONFIDENTIAL, PRIVATE, and so on have the opposite effect and spur the curiosity of passersby. So, disable automatic printing. Also, avoid using faxes employing ribbons or duplication cartridges that retain images of the printed faxes. Consider integrating your fax system with your network so you can email faxes to intended recipients instead of printing them to paper.

# Securing Voice Communications

The vulnerability of voice communication is tangentially related to IT system security. However, as voice communication solutions move on to the network by employing digital devices and VoIP, securing voice communications becomes an increasingly important issue. When voice communications occur over the IT infrastructure, it is important to implement mechanisms to provide for authentication and integrity. Confidentiality should be maintained by employing an encryption service or protocol to protect the voice communications while in transit.

Normal private branch exchange (PBX) or POTS voice communications are vulnerable to interception, eavesdropping, tapping, and other exploitations. Often, physical security is required to maintain control over voice communications within the confines of your organization's physical locations. Security of voice communications outside your organization is typically the responsibility of the phone company from which you lease services. If voice communication vulnerabilities are an important issue for sustaining your security policy, you should deploy an encrypted communication mechanism and use it exclusively.

# Social Engineering

Malicious individuals can exploit voice communications through a technique known as *social engineering*. Social engineering is a means by which an unknown, untrusted, or at least unauthorized person gains the trust of someone inside of your organization. Adept individuals can convince employees that they are associated with upper management, technical support, the help desk, and so on. Once convinced, the victim is often encouraged to make a change to their user account on the system, such as reset their password. Other attacks include instructing the victim to open specific email attachments, launch an application, or connect to a specific URL. Whatever the actual activity is, it is usually directed toward opening a back door that the attacker can use to gain network access.

The people within an organization make it vulnerable to social engineering attacks. With just a little information or a few facts, it is often possible to get a victim to disclose confidential information or engage in irresponsible activity. Social engineering attacks exploit human characteristics such as a basic trust in others, a desire to provide assistance, or a propensity to show off. Overlooking discrepancies, being distracted, following orders, assuming others know more than they actually do, wanting to help others, and fearing reprimands can also lead to attacks. Attackers are often able to bypass extensive physical and logical security controls because the victim opens an access pathway from the inside, effectively punching a hole in the secured perimeter.

 **Real World Scenario**

**Social Engineering Fascination**

Social engineering is a fascinating subject. It is the means to break into the perfectly technically secured environment. Social engineering is the art of using an organization's own people against it. Although not necessary for the CISSP exam, there are lots of excellent resources, examples, and discussions of social engineering that you might not only benefit from in terms of increasing your awareness of this security problem but also find highly entertaining. We suggest doing some searching on the term *social engineering* to discover books and online videos. You'll find the reading informative and the video examples addicting.

The only way to protect against social engineering attacks is to teach users how to respond and interact with voice-only communications. Here are some guidelines:

- Always err on the side of caution whenever voice communications seem odd, out of place, or unexpected.

- Always request proof of identity. This can be a driver's license number or Social Security number, which can be easily verified. It could also take the form of having a person in the office that would recognize the caller's voice take the call. For example, if the caller claims to be a department manager, you could confirm their identity by asking their administrative assistant to take the call.

- Require callback authorizations on all voice-only requests for network alterations or activities.

- Classify information (usernames, passwords, IP addresses, manager names, dial-in numbers, and so on), and clearly indicate which information can be discussed or even confirmed using voice communications.

- If privileged information is requested over the phone by an individual who should know that giving out that particular information over the phone is against the company's security policy, ask why the information is needed and verify their identity again. This incident should also be reported to the security administrator.

- Never give out or change passwords based on voice-only communications.

- Always securely dispose of or destroy all office documentation, especially any paperwork or disposable media that contains information about the IT infrastructure or its security mechanisms.

## Fraud and Abuse

Another voice communication threat is PBX fraud and abuse. Many PBX systems can be exploited by malicious individuals to avoid toll charges and hide their identity. Malicious attackers known as *phreakers* abuse phone systems in much the same way that attackers abuse computer networks. Phreakers may be able to gain unauthorized access to personal voice mailboxes, redirect messages, block access, and redirect inbound and outbound calls.

Countermeasures to PBX fraud and abuse include many of the same precautions you would employ to protect a typical computer network: logical or technical controls, administrative controls, and physical controls. Here are several key points to keep in mind when designing a PBX security solution:

- Consider replacing remote access or long-distance calling through the PBX with a credit card or calling card system.

- Restrict dial-in and dial-out features to only authorized individuals who require such functionality for their work tasks.

- For your dial-in modems, use unpublished phone numbers that are outside the prefix block range of your voice numbers.

- Block or disable any unassigned access codes or accounts.
- Define an acceptable use policy and train users on how to properly use the system.
- Log and audit all activities on the PBX and review the audit trails for security and use violations.
- Disable maintenance modems and accounts.
- Change all default configurations, especially passwords and capabilities related to administrative or privileged features.
- Block remote calling (that is, allowing a remote caller to dial in to your PBX and then dial out again, thus directing all toll charges to the PBX host).
- Deploy Direct Inward System Access (DISA) technologies to reduce PBX fraud by external parties.
- Keep the system current with vendor/service provider updates.

---

 **Real World Scenario**

**DISA: A Disease and the Cure**

An often-touted "security" improvement to PBX systems is Direct Inward System Access (DISA). This system is designed to help manage external access and external control of a PBX by assigning access codes to users. Although great in concept, this system is being compromised and abused by phreakers. Once an outside phreaker learns the PBX access codes, they can often fully control and abuse the company's telephone network. This can include using the PBX to make long-distance calls that are charged to your company's telephone account rather than the phreaker's phone.

DISA, like any other security feature, must be properly installed, configured, and monitored in order to obtain the desired security improvement. Simply having DISA is not sufficient. Be sure to disable all features that are not required by the organization, craft user codes/passwords that are complex and difficult to guess, and then turn on auditing to keep watch on PBX activities.

---

Additionally, maintaining physical access control to all PBX connection centers, phone portals, or wiring closets prevents direct intrusion from onsite attackers.

## Phreaking

As mentioned earlier, phreaking is a specific type of attacking directed toward the telephone system. Phreakers use various types of technology to circumvent the telephone system to make free long-distance calls, to alter the function of telephone service, to steal specialized services, and even to cause service disruptions. Some phreaker tools are actual devices, whereas others are just particular ways of using a regular telephone. No matter what the tool or technology actually is, phreaker tools are referred to as colored boxes (*black box*, *red box*, and so on). Over the years, many box technologies have been developed and widely used by phreakers, but only a few of them still work against today's telephone systems based on packet switching. Here are a few of the phreaker tools you need to recognize for the exam:

- Black boxes are used to manipulate line voltages to steal long-distance services. They are often just custom-built circuit boards with a battery and wire clips.

- Red boxes are used to simulate tones of coins being deposited into a pay phone. They are usually just small tape recorders.

- Blue boxes are used to simulate 2600 Hz tones to interact directly with telephone network trunk systems (that is, backbones). This could be a whistle, a tape recorder, or a digital tone generator.

- White boxes are used to control the phone system. A white box is a DTMF, (Dual-Tone MultiFrequency), generator (that is, a keypad). It can be a custom-built device or one of the pieces of equipment that most telephone repair personnel use.

 As you probably know, cell phone security is a growing concern. Captured electronic serial numbers (ESNs) and mobile identification numbers (MINs) can be burned into blank phones to create clones. When a clone is used, the charges are billed to the original owner's cell phone account. Furthermore, conversations and data transmission can be intercepted using radio frequency scanners. Also, anyone in the immediate vicinity can overhear at least one side of the conversation. So, don't talk about confidential, private, or sensitive topics in public places.

# Security Boundaries

A security *boundary* is the line of intersection between any two areas, subnets, or environments that have different security requirements or needs. A security boundary exists between a high-security area and a low-security one, such as between a LAN and the Internet. It is important to recognize the security boundaries both on your network and in the physical world. Once you identify a security boundary, you need to deploy controls and mechanisms to control the flow of information across those boundaries.

Divisions between security areas can take many forms. For example, objects may have different classifications. Each classification defines what functions can be performed by which subjects on which objects. The distinction between classifications is a security boundary.

Security boundaries also exist between the physical environment and the logical environment. To provide logical security, you must provide security mechanisms that are different from those used to provide physical security. Both must be present to provide a complete security structure, and both must be addressed in a security policy. However, they are different and must be assessed as separate elements of a security solution.

Security boundaries, such as a perimeter between a protected area and an unprotected one, should always be clearly defined. It's important to state in a security policy the point at which control ends or begins and to identify that point in both the physical and logical environments. Logical security boundaries are the points where electronic communications interface with devices or services for which your organization is legally responsible. In most cases, that interface is clearly marked, and unauthorized subjects are informed that they do not have access and that attempts to gain access will result in prosecution.

The security perimeter in the physical environment is often a reflection of the security perimeter of the logical environment. In most cases, the area over which the organization is legally responsible determines the reach of a security policy in the physical realm. This can be the walls of an office, the walls of a building, or the fence around a campus. In secured environments, warning signs are posted indicating that unauthorized access is prohibited and attempts to gain access will be thwarted and result in prosecution.

When transforming a security policy into actual controls, you must consider each environment and security boundary separately. Simply deduce what available security mechanisms would provide the most reasonable, cost-effective, and efficient solution for a specific environment and situation. However, all security mechanisms must be weighed against the value of the objects they are to protect. Deploying countermeasures that cost more than the value of the protected objects is unwarranted.

# Network Attacks and Countermeasures

Communication systems are vulnerable to attacks in much the same way any other aspect of the IT infrastructure is vulnerable. Understanding the threats and possible countermeasures is an important part of securing an environment. Any activity or condition that can cause harm to data, resources, or personnel must be addressed and mitigated if possible. Keep in mind that harm includes more than just destruction or damage; it also includes disclosure, access delay, denial of access, fraud, resource waste, resource abuse, and loss. Common threats against communication system security include denial of service, eavesdropping, impersonation, replay, and modification.

## Eavesdropping

As the name suggests, *eavesdropping* is simply listening to communication traffic for the purpose of duplicating it. The duplication can take the form of recording the data to a storage device or to an extraction program that dynamically attempts to extract the original content from the traffic stream. Once a copy of traffic content is in the hands of a attacker, they can often extract many forms of confidential information, such as usernames, passwords, process procedures, data, and so on.

Eavesdropping usually requires physical access to the IT infrastructure to connect a physical recording device to an open port or cable splice or to install a software-recording tool onto the system. Eavesdropping is often facilitated by the use of a network traffic capture or monitoring program or a protocol analyzer system (often called a *sniffer*). Eavesdropping devices and software are usually difficult to detect because they are used in passive attacks. When eavesdropping or wiretapping is transformed into altering or injecting communications, the attack is considered an active attack.

 **Real World Scenario**

**Eavesdrop on Networks**

Eavesdropping on networks is the act of collecting packets of the communication medium. As a valid network client, you are limited to seeing just the traffic designated for your system. However, with the right tool (and authorization from your organization!), you can see all the data that passes your network interface. Sniffers such as Wireshark and NetWitness and dedicated eavesdropping tools such as T-sight and Paros can show you what is going on over the network. Some tools will display only the raw network packets, while others will reassemble the original data and display it for you in real time on your screen. We encourage you to experiment with a few eavesdropping tools (only on networks where you have the proper approval) so you can see firsthand what can be gleaned from network communications.

You can combat eavesdropping by maintaining physical access security to prevent unauthorized personnel from accessing your IT infrastructure. As for protecting communications that occur outside your network or for protecting against internal attackers, using encryption (such as IPSec or SSH) and one-time authentication methods (that is, one-time pads or token devices) on communication traffic will greatly reduce the effectiveness and timeliness of eavesdropping.

The common threat of eavesdropping is one of the primary motivations to maintain reliable communications security. While data is in transit, it is often easier to intercept than when it is in storage. Furthermore, the lines of communication may lie outside your organization's control. Thus, reliable means to secure data while in transit outside your internal infrastructure is of utmost importance. Some of the common network health and communication reliability evaluation and management tools, such as sniffers, can be used for nefarious purposes and thus require stringent controls and oversight to prevent abuse.

## Impersonation/Masquerading

*Impersonation*, or *masquerading*, is the act of pretending to be someone or something you are not to gain unauthorized access to a system. Impersonation is often possible through the capture of usernames and passwords or of session setup procedures for network services.

Some solutions to prevent impersonation are using one-time pads and token authentication systems, using Kerberos, and using encryption to increase the difficulty of extracting authentication credentials from network traffic.

## Replay Attacks

*Replay attacks* are an offshoot of impersonation attacks and are made possible through capturing network traffic via eavesdropping. Replay attacks attempt to reestablish a communication session by replaying captured traffic against a system. You can prevent them by using one-time authentication mechanisms and sequenced session identification.

## Modification Attacks

*Modification* is an attack in which captured packets are altered and then played against a system. Modified packets are designed to bypass the restrictions of improved authentication mechanisms and session sequencing. Countermeasures to modification replay attacks include using digital signature verifications and packet checksum verification.

## Address Resolution Protocol Spoofing

The Address Resolution Protocol (ARP) is a subprotocol of the TCP/IP protocol suite that operates at the Network layer (layer 3). ARP is used to discover the MAC address of a system by polling using its IP address. ARP functions by broadcasting a request packet with the target IP address. The system with that IP address (or some other system that already has an ARP mapping for it) will reply with the associated MAC address. The discovered IP-to-MAC mapping is stored in the ARP cache and is used to direct packets.

If you find the idea of misdirecting traffic through the abuse of the ARP system interesting, then consider experimenting with attacking tools that perform this function. Some of the well-known tools for performing ARP spoofing attacks include Ettercap and arpspoof. Using these tools in combination with a network sniffer (so you can watch the results) will give you great insight into this form of network attack. However, as always, perform these activities only on networks where you have proper approval; otherwise, your attacker activities could land you in legal trouble.

ARP mappings can be attacked through spoofing. Spoofing provides false MAC addresses for requested IP-addressed systems to redirect traffic to alternate destinations. ARP attacks are often an element in man-in-the-middle attacks. Such attacks involve an intruder's system spoofing its MAC address against the destination's IP address into the source's ARP cache. All packets received from the source system are inspected and then forwarded to the actual intended destination system. You can take measures to fight ARP attacks, such as defining static ARP mappings for critical systems, monitoring ARP caches for MAC-to-IP-address mappings, or using an IDS to detect anomalies in system traffic and changes in ARP traffic.

## DNS Poisoning, Spoofing, and Hijacking

*DNS poisoning* and *DNS spoofing* are also resolution attacks. DNS poisoning occurs when an attacker alters the domain-name-to-IP-address mappings in a DNS system to redirect traffic to a rogue system or to simply perform a denial of service against a system. DNS spoofing occurs when an attacker sends false replies to a requesting system, beating the real reply from the valid DNS server. This is also technically an exploitation of race conditions. Protections against false DNS results caused by poisoning and spoofing include allowing only authorized changes to DNS, restricting zone transfers, and logging all privileged DNS activity.

Recently, a fairly significant vulnerability has been discovered and disclosed to the world by Dan Kaminsky. The vulnerability lies in the method by which local or caching DNS servers obtain information from root servers regarding the identity of the authoritative servers for a particular domain. By sending falsified replies to a caching DNS server for nonexistent subdomains, an attacker can hijack the entire domain's resolution details. For an excellent detailed explanation on how DNS works and how this vulnerability threatens the current DNS infrastructure, visit "An Illustrated Guide to the Kaminsky DNS Vulnerability" located at http://unixwiz.net/techtips/iguide-kaminsky-dns-vuln.html.

The only real solution to this DNS hijacking vulnerability is to upgrade DNS to DNSSEC. For details, please visit dnssec.net.

## Hyperlink Spoofing

Yet another related attack is *hyperlink spoofing*, which is similar to DNS spoofing in that it is used to redirect traffic to a rogue or imposter system or to simply divert traffic away from its intended destination. Hyperlink spoofing can take the form of DNS spoofing or can simply be an alteration of the hyperlink URLs in the HTML code of documents sent to clients. Hyperlink spoofing attacks are usually successful because most users do not verify the domain name in a URL via DNS; rather, they assume that the hyperlink is valid and just click it.

---

🌐 **Real World Scenario**

**Going Phishing?**

Hyperlink spoofing is not limited to just DNS attacks. In fact, any attacking activity that attempts to misdirect legitimate users to malicious websites through the abuse of URLs or hyperlinks could be considered hyperlink spoofing. Spoofing is falsifying information, which includes falsifying the relationship between a URL and its trusted and original destination.

*Phishing* is another attack where hyperlink spoofing is common. The term means fishing for information. Phishing attacks can take many forms, including the use of false URLs.

Be wary of any URL or hyperlink in an email, PDF file, or productivity document. If you want to visit a site offered as such, go to your web browser and manually type in the address, use your own preexisting URL bookmark, or use a trusted search engine to find the site. These methods do involve more work on your part, but it will establish a pattern of safe behaviors that will serve you well. There are too many attackers in the world to be casual or lazy about following proffered links and URLs.

A related attack to phishing is *pretexting*, which is the practice of obtaining your personal information under false pretenses. Pretexting is often used to obtain personal identity details that are then sold to others who actually perform the abuse of your credit and reputation.

---

Protections against hyperlink spoofing include the same precautions used against DNS spoofing as well as keeping your system patched and using the Internet with caution.

# Summary

Maintaining control over communication pathways is essential to supporting confidentiality, integrity, and availability for network, voice, and other forms of communication. Numerous attacks are focused on intercepting, blocking, or otherwise interfering with the transfer of data from one location to another. Fortunately, there are also reasonable countermeasures to reduce or even eliminate many of these threats.

Tunneling is a means by which messages in one protocol can be transported over another network or communications system using a second protocol. Tunneling, otherwise known as *encapsulation*, can be combined with encryption to provide security for the transmitted message. VPNs are based on encrypted tunneling.

NAT is used to hide the internal structure of a private network as well as enable multiple internal clients to gain Internet access through a few public IP addresses. NAT is often a native feature of border security devices, such as firewalls, routers, gateways, and proxies.

In circuit switching, a dedicated physical pathway is created between the two communicating parties. Packet switching occurs when the message or communication is broken up into small segments (usually fixed-length packets depending on the protocols and technologies employed) and sent across the intermediary networks to the destination. Within packet-switching systems are two types of communication: paths and virtual circuits. A virtual circuit is a logical pathway or circuit created over a packet-switched network between two specific endpoints. There are two types of virtual circuits: permanent virtual circuits (PVCs) and switched virtual circuits (SVCs).

WAN links or long-distance connection technologies can be divided into two primary categories: dedicated and nondedicated lines. A dedicated line connects two specific endpoints and only those two endpoints together. A nondedicated line is one that requires a connection to be established before data transmission can occur. A nondedicated line can be used to connect with any remote system that uses the same type of nondedicated line. WAN connection technologies include X.25, Frame Relay, ATM, SMDS, SDLC, HDLC, and HSSI.

When selecting or deploying security controls for network communications, you need to evaluate numerous characteristics in light of your circumstances, capabilities, and security policy. Security controls should be transparent to users. Hash totals and CRC checks can be used to verify message integrity. Record sequences are used to ensure sequence integrity of a transmission. Transmission logging helps detect communication abuses.

Basic Internet-based email is insecure, but you can take steps to secure it. To secure email, you should provide for nonrepudiation, restrict access to authorized users, make sure integrity is maintained, authenticate the message source, verify delivery, and even classify sensitive content. These issues must be addressed in a security policy before they can be implemented in a solution. They often take the form of acceptable use policies, access controls, privacy declarations, email management procedures, and backup and retention policies.

Email is a common delivery mechanism for malicious code. Filtering attachments, using antivirus software, and educating users are effective countermeasures against that kind of attack. E-mail spamming or flooding is a form of denial of service that can be deterred through filters and IDSs. Email security can be improved using S/MIME, MOSS, PEM, and PGP.

Using encryption to protect the transmission of documents and prevent eavesdropping improves fax and voice security. Training users effectively is a useful countermeasure against social engineering attacks.

A security boundary can be the division between one secured area and another secured area, or it can be the division between a secured area and an unsecured area. Both must be addressed in a security policy.

Communication systems are vulnerable to many attacks, including denial of service, eavesdropping, impersonation, replay, modification, ARP, and DNS attacks. Fortunately, effective countermeasures exist for each of these. PBX fraud and abuse and phone phreaking are problems that must also be addressed.

# Exam Essentials

**Know what tunneling is.**   Tunneling is the encapsulation of a protocol-deliverable message within a second protocol. The second protocol often performs encryption to protect the message contents.

**Understand VPNs.**   VPNs are based on encrypted tunneling. They can offer authentication and data protection as a point-to-point solution. Common VPN protocols are PPTP, L2F, L2TP, and IPSec.

**Be able to explain NAT.**   NAT protects the addressing scheme of a private network, allows the use of the private IP addresses, and enables multiple internal clients to obtain Internet access through a few public IP addresses. NAT is supported by many security border devices, such as firewalls, routers, gateways, and proxies.

**Understand the difference between packet switching and circuit switching.**   In circuit switching, a dedicated physical pathway is created between the two communicating parties. Packet switching occurs when the message or communication is broken up into small segments and sent across the intermediary networks to the destination. Within packet-switching systems are two types of communication paths, or virtual circuits: permanent virtual circuits (PVCs) and switched virtual circuits (SVCs).

**Understand the difference between dedicated and nondedicated links.**   A dedicated line is one that is indefinably and continually reserved for use by a specific customer. A dedicated line is always on and waiting for traffic to be transmitted over it. The link between the customer's LAN and the dedicated WAN link is always open and established. A dedicated line connects two specific endpoints and only those two endpoints. Examples of dedicated lines include T1, T3, E1, E3, and cable modems. A nondedicated line is one that requires a connection to be established before data transmission can occur. A nondedicated line can be used to connect with any remote system that uses the same type of nondedicated line. Examples of nondedicated lines include standard modems, DSL, and ISDN.

**Know the various types of WAN technologies.**   Know that most WAN technologies require a channel service unit/data service unit (CSU/DSU). These can be referred to as *WAN switches*. There are many types of carrier networks and WAN connection technologies, such as X.25, Frame Relay, ATM, and SMDS. Some WAN connection technologies require additional specialized protocols to support various types of specialized systems or devices. Three of these protocols are SDLC, HDLC, and HSSI.

**Understand the differences between PPP and SLIP.**   The Point-to-Point Protocol (PPP) is an encapsulation protocol designed to support the transmission of IP traffic over dial-up or point-to-point links. PPP includes a wide range of communication services, including assignment and management of IP addresses, management of synchronous communications, standardized encapsulation, multiplexing, link configuration, link quality testing, error detection, and feature or option negotiation (such as compression). PPP was originally designed to support CHAP and PAP for authentication. However, recent versions of PPP also support MS-CHAP, EAP, and SPAP. PPP replaced the Serial Line Internet Protocol (SLIP). SLIP offered no authentication, supported only half-duplex communications, had no error detection capabilities, and required manual link establishment and teardown.

**Understand common characteristics of security controls.**   Security controls should be transparent to users. Hash totals and CRC checks can be used to verify message integrity. Record sequences are used to ensure sequence integrity of a transmission. Transmission logging helps detect communication abuses.

**Understand how email security works.**   Internet email is based on SMTP, POP3, and IMAP. It is inherently insecure. It can be secured, but the methods used must be addressed in a security policy. Email security solutions include using S/MIME, MOSS, PEM, or PGP.

**Know how fax security works.**   Fax security is primarily based on using encrypted transmissions or encrypted communication lines to protect the faxed materials. The primary goal is to prevent interception. Activity logs and exception reports can be used to detect anomalies in fax activity that could be symptoms of attack.

**Know the threats associated with PBX systems and the countermeasures to PBX fraud.** Countermeasures to PBX fraud and abuse include many of the same precautions you would employ to protect a typical computer network: logical or technical controls, administrative controls, and physical controls.

**Recognize what a phreaker is.**   Phreaking is a specific type of attack in which various types of technology are used to circumvent the telephone system to make free long-distance calls, to alter the function of telephone service, to steal specialized services, or even to cause service disruptions. Common tools of phreakers include black, red, blue, and white boxes.

**Understand voice communications security.**   Voice communications are vulnerable to many attacks, especially as voice communications become an important part of network services. You can obtain confidentiality by using encrypted communications. Countermeasures must be deployed to protect against interception, eavesdropping, tapping, and other types of exploitation.

**Be able to explain what social engineering is.**   Social engineering is a means by which an unknown person gains the trust of someone inside your organization by convincing employees that they are, for example, associated with upper management, technical support, or the help desk. The victim is often encouraged to make a change to their user account on the system, such as reset their password, so the attacker can use it to gain access to the network. The primary countermeasure for this sort of attack is user training.

**Explain the concept of security boundaries.** A security boundary can be the division between one secured area and another secured area. It can also be the division between a secured area and an unsecured area. Both must be addressed in a security policy.

**Understand the various attacks and countermeasures associated with communications security.** Communication systems are vulnerable to many attacks, including eavesdropping, impersonation, replay, modification, ARP, and DNS attacks. Be able to list effective countermeasures for each.

# Written Lab

1. Describe the differences between transport mode and tunnel mode of IPSec.
2. Discuss the benefits of NAT.
3. What are the main differences between circuit switching and packet switching?
4. What are some security issues with email and options for safeguarding against them?

# Answers to Written Lab

1.  IPSec's transport mode is used for host-to-host links and encrypts only the payload, not the header. IPSec's tunnel mode is used for host-to-LAN and LAN-to-LAN links and encrypts the entire original payload and header and then adds a link header.

2.  Network Address Translation (NAT) allows for the identity of internal systems to be hidden from external entities. Often NAT is used to translate between RFC 1918 private IP addresses and leased public addresses. NAT serves as a one-way firewall because it allows only inbound traffic that is a response to a previous internal query. NAT also allows a few leased public addresses to be used to grant Internet connectivity to a larger number of internal systems.

3.  Circuit switching is usually associated with physical connections. The link itself is physically established and then dismantled for the communication. Circuit switching offers known fixed delays, supports constant traffic, is connection oriented, is sensitive only to the loss of the connection rather than the communication, and was most often used for voice transmissions. Packet switching is usually associated with logical connections because the link is just a logically defined path among possible paths. Within a packet switching system, each system or link can be employed simultaneously by other circuits. Packet switching divides the communication into segments, and each segment traverses the circuit to the destination. Packet switching has variable delays since each segment could take a unique path, is usually employed for bursty traffic, is not physically connection oriented but often uses virtual circuits, is sensitive to the loss of data, and is used for any form of communication.

4.  Email is inherently insecure because it is primarily a plain-text communication medium and employs nonencrypted transmissions protocols. This allows for email to be easily spoofed, spammed, flooded, eavesdropped on, interfered with, and hijacked. Defenses against these issues primarily include having stronger authentication requirements and using encryption to protect the content while in transit.

# Review Questions

1. _____ is a layer 2 connection mechanism that uses packet-switching technology to establish virtual circuits between the communication endpoints.
   A. ISDN
   B. Frame Relay
   C. SMDS
   D. ATM

2. Tunnel connections can be established over all except for which of the following?
   A. WAN links
   B. LAN pathways
   C. Dial-up connections
   D. Stand-alone systems

3. _____ is a standards-based mechanism for providing encryption for point-to-point TCP/IP traffic.
   A. UDP
   B. IDEA
   C. IPSec
   D. SDLC

4. Which of the following IP addresses is not a private IP address as defined by RFC 1918?
   A. 10.0.0.18
   B. 169.254.1.119
   C. 172.31.8.204
   D. 192.168.6.43

5. Which of the following cannot be linked over a VPN?
   A. Two distant Internet-connected LANs
   B. Two systems on the same LAN
   C. A system connected to the Internet and a LAN connected to the Internet
   D. Two systems without an intermediary network connection

6. What is needed to allow an external client to initiate a communication session with an internal system if the network uses a NAT proxy?
   A. IPSec tunnel
   B. Static mode NAT
   C. Static private IP address
   D. Reverse DNS

**7.** Which of the following VPN protocols do not offer native data encryption? (Choose all that apply.)

   **A.** L2F

   **B.** L2TP

   **C.** IPSec

   **D.** PPTP

**8.** At which OSI model layer does the IPSec protocol function?

   **A.** Data Link

   **B.** Transport

   **C.** Session

   **D.** Network

**9.** Which of the following is not defined in RFC 1918 as one of the private IP address ranges that are not routed on the Internet?

   **A.** 169.172.0.0–169.191.255.255

   **B.** 192.168.0.0–192.168.255.255

   **C.** 10.0.0.0–10.255.255.255

   **D.** 172.16.0.0–172.31.255.255

**10.** Which of the following is not a benefit of NAT?

   **A.** Hiding the internal IP addressing scheme

   **B.** Sharing a few public Internet addresses with a large number of internal clients

   **C.** Using the private IP addresses from RFC 1918 on an internal network

   **D.** Filtering network traffic to prevent brute-force attacks

**11.** A significant benefit of a security control is when it goes unnoticed by users. What is this called?

   **A.** Invisibility

   **B.** Transparency

   **C.** Diversion

   **D.** Hiding in plain sight

**12.** When you're designing a security system for Internet-delivered email, which of the following is least important?

   **A.** Nonrepudiation

   **B.** Availability

   **C.** Message integrity

   **D.** Access restriction

13. Which of the following is typically not an element that must be discussed with end users in regard to email retention policies?

    **A.** Privacy

    **B.** Auditor review

    **C.** Length of retainer

    **D.** Backup method

14. What is it called when email itself is used as an attack mechanism?

    **A.** Masquerading

    **B.** Mail-bombing

    **C.** Spoofing

    **D.** Smurf attack

15. Why is spam so difficult to stop?

    **A.** Filters are ineffective at blocking inbound messages.

    **B.** The source address is usually spoofed.

    **C.** It is an attack requiring little expertise.

    **D.** Spam can cause denial-of-service attacks.

16. Which of the following is a type of connection that can be described as a logical circuit that always exists and is waiting for the customer to send data?

    **A.** ISDN

    **B.** PVC

    **C.** VPN

    **D.** SVC

17. In addition to maintaining an updated system and controlling physical access, which of the following is the most effective countermeasure against PBX fraud and abuse?

    **A.** Encrypting communications

    **B.** Changing default passwords

    **C.** Using transmission logs

    **D.** Taping and archiving all conversations

18. Which of the following can be used to bypass even the best physical and logical security mechanisms to gain access to a system?

    **A.** Brute-force attacks

    **B.** Denial of service

    **C.** Social engineering

    **D.** Port scanning

**19.** Which of the following is not a denial-of-service attack?

   **A.** Exploiting a flaw in a program to consume 100 percent of the CPU

   **B.** Sending malformed packets to a system, causing it to freeze

   **C.** Performing a brute-force attack against a known user account

   **D.** Sending thousands of emails to a single address

**20.** Which of the following is a digital end-to-end communications mechanism developed by telephone companies to support high-speed digital communications over the same equipment and infrastructure that is used to carry voice communications?

   **A.** ISDN

   **B.** Frame Relay

   **C.** SMDS

   **D.** ATM

# Answers to Review Questions

1.  B. Frame Relay is a layer 2 connection mechanism that uses packet-switching technology to establish virtual circuits between the communication endpoints. The Frame Relay network is a shared medium across which virtual circuits are created to provide point-to-point communications. All virtual circuits are independent of and invisible to each other.

2.  D. A stand-alone system has no need for tunneling because no communications between systems are occurring and no intermediary network is present.

3.  C. IPSec, or IP Security, is a standards-based mechanism for providing encryption for point-to-point TCP/IP traffic.

4.  B. The 169.254.x.x subnet is in the APIPA range, which is not part of RFC 1918. The addresses in RFC 1918 are 10.0.0.0–10.255.255.255, 172.16.0.0–172.31.255.255, and 192.168.0.0–192.168.255.255.

5.  D. An intermediary network connection is required for a VPN link to be established.

6.  B. Static mode NAT is needed to allow an outside entity to initiate communications with an internal system behind a NAT proxy.

7.  A, B, D. L2F, L2TP, and PPTP all lack native data encryption. Only IPSec includes native data encryption.

8.  D. IPSec operates at the Network layer (layer 3).

9.  A. The address range 169.172.0.0–169.191.255.255 is not listed in RFC 1918 as a public IP address range.

10. D. NAT does not protect against nor prevent brute-force attacks.

11. B. When transparency is a characteristic of a service, security control, or access mechanism, it is unseen by users.

12. B. Although availability is a key aspect of security in general, it is the least important aspect of security systems for Internet-delivered email.

13. D. The backup method is not an important factor to discuss with end users regarding email retention.

14. B. Mail-bombing is the use of email as an attack mechanism. Flooding a system with messages causes a denial of service.

15. B. It is often difficult to stop spam because the source of the messages is usually spoofed.

16. B. A permanent virtual circuit (PVC) can be described as a logical circuit that always exists and is waiting for the customer to send data.

**17.** B.  Changing default passwords on PBX systems provides the most effective increase in security.

**18.** C.  Social engineering can often be used to bypass even the most effective physical and logical controls. Whatever activity the attacker convinces the victim to perform, it is usually directed toward opening a back door that the attacker can use to gain access to the network.

**19.** C.  A brute-force attack is not considered a DoS.

**20.** A.  Integrated Services Digital Network (ISDN) is a digital end-to-end communications mechanism. ISDN was developed by telephone companies to support high-speed digital communications over the same equipment and infrastructure that is used to carry voice communications.

# Chapter

# 5

# Security Management Concepts and Principles

---

## THE CISSP EXAM TOPICS COVERED IN THIS CHAPTER INCLUDE:

✓ **Information Security Governance and Risk Management**

- Understand and apply security governance

  - Organizational processes; define security roles and responsibilities; legislative and regulatory compliance; privacy requirements compliance; control frameworks; due care; due diligence

- Understand and apply concepts of confidentiality, availability, and integrity

- Define and implement information classification and ownership

- Understand and apply risk management concepts

  - Identify threats and vulnerabilities; risk assessment/ analysis; risk assignment/acceptance; countermeasure selection

- Evaluate personnel security; Background checks and employment candidate screening; employment agreements and policies; employee termination processes; vendor, consultant and contractor controls

- Develop and implement information system security strategies

The Information Security Governance and Risk Management domain of the Common Body of Knowledge (CBK) for the CISSP certification exam deals with the common and foundational elements of security solutions. These include elements essential to the design, implementation, and administration of security mechanisms.

This domain is discussed in this chapter and in Chapter 6, "Asset Value, Policies, and Roles." Be sure to read and study the materials from both chapters to ensure complete coverage of the essential material for the CISSP certification exam.

# Security Management Concepts and Principles

Security management concepts and principles are inherent elements in a security policy and solution deployment. They define the basic parameters needed for a secure environment. They also define the goals and objectives that both policy designers and system implementers must achieve to create a secure solution. It is important for real-world security professionals, as well as CISSP exam students, to understand these items thoroughly.

The primary goals and objectives of security are contained within the *CIA Triad*, which is the name given to the three primary security principles:

- Confidentiality
- Integrity
- Availability

Security controls are typically evaluated on whether they address these core information security tenets. Overall, a complete security solution should adequately address each of these tenets. Vulnerabilities and risks are also evaluated based on the threat they pose against one or more of the CIA Triad principles. Thus, it is a good idea to be familiar with these principles and use them as guidelines for judging all things related to security.

These three principles are considered the most important within the realm of security. However important each is to a specific organization depends on the organization's security goals and requirements and on the extent to which the organization's security might be threatened.

# Confidentiality

The first principle of the CIA Triad is *confidentiality*. If a security mechanism offers confidentiality, it offers a high level of assurance that data, objects, or resources are restricted from unauthorized subjects. If a threat exists against confidentiality, unauthorized disclosure could take place.

In general, for confidentiality to be maintained on a network, data must be protected from unauthorized access, use, or disclosure while in storage, in process, and in transit. Unique and specific security controls are required for each of these states of data, resources, and objects to maintain confidentiality.

Numerous attacks focus on the violation of confidentiality. These include capturing network traffic and stealing password files as well as social engineering, port scanning, shoulder surfing, eavesdropping, sniffing, and so on.

Violations of confidentiality are not limited to directed intentional attacks. Many instances of unauthorized disclosure of sensitive or confidential information are because of human error, oversight, or ineptitude. Events that lead to confidentiality breaches include failing to properly encrypt a transmission, failing to fully authenticate a remote system before transferring data, leaving open otherwise secured access points, accessing malicious code that opens a back door, or even walking away from an access terminal while data is displayed on the monitor. Confidentiality violations can occur because of the actions of an end user or a system administrator. They can also occur because of an oversight in a security policy or a misconfigured security control.

Numerous countermeasures can ensure confidentiality against possible threats. These include encryption, network traffic padding, strict access control, rigorous authentication procedures, data classification, and extensive personnel training.

Confidentiality and integrity depend on each other. Without object integrity, confidentiality cannot be maintained. Other concepts, conditions, and aspects of confidentiality include sensitivity, discretion, criticality, concealment, secrecy, privacy, seclusion, and isolation.

# Integrity

The second principle of the CIA Triad is *integrity*. For integrity to be maintained, objects must retain their veracity and be intentionally modified by only authorized subjects. If a security mechanism offers integrity, it offers a high level of assurance that the data, objects, and resources are unaltered from their original protected state. This includes alterations occurring while the object is in storage, in transit, or in process. Thus, maintaining integrity means the object itself is not altered and the operating system and programming entities that manage and manipulate the object are not compromised.

Integrity can be examined from three perspectives:

- Unauthorized subjects should be prevented from making modifications.

- Authorized subjects should be prevented from making unauthorized modifications, such as mistakes.

- Objects should be internally and externally consistent so that their data is a correct and true reflection of the real world and any relationship with any child, peer, or parent object is valid, consistent, and verifiable.

For integrity to be maintained on a system, controls must be in place to restrict access to data, objects, and resources. Additionally, activity logging should be employed to ensure that only authorized users are able to access their respective resources. Maintaining and validating object integrity across storage, transport, and processing requires numerous variations of controls and oversight.

Numerous attacks focus on the violation of integrity. These include viruses, logic bombs, unauthorized access, errors in coding and applications, malicious modification, intentional replacement, and system back doors.

As with confidentiality, integrity violations are not limited to intentional attacks. Many instances of unauthorized alteration of sensitive information are because of human error, oversight, or ineptitude. Events that lead to integrity breaches include accidentally deleting files; entering invalid data; altering configurations, including errors in commands, codes, and scripts; introducing a virus; and executing malicious code such as a Trojan horse. Integrity violations can occur because of the actions of any user, including administrators. They can also occur because of an oversight in a security policy or a misconfigured security control.

Numerous countermeasures can ensure integrity against possible threats. These include strict access control, rigorous authentication procedures, intrusion detection systems, object/data encryption, hash total verifications (see Chapter 9, "Cryptography and Symmetric Key Algorithms"), interface restrictions, input/function checks, and extensive personnel training.

Integrity is dependent upon confidentiality. Without confidentiality, integrity cannot be maintained. Other concepts, conditions, and aspects of integrity include accuracy, truthfulness, authenticity, validity, nonrepudiation, accountability, responsibility, completeness, and comprehensiveness.

 **Real World Scenario**

**CIA Priority**

Every organization has unique security requirements. On the CISSP exam, most security concepts are discussed in general terms, but in the real world, general concepts and best practices don't get the job done. The management team and security team must work together to prioritize an organization's security needs. This includes establishing a budget and spending plan, allocating expertise and hours, and focusing the IT and security staff efforts. One key aspect of this effort is to prioritize the security requirements of the organization. Knowing which tenet or asset is more important than another guides the creation of a security stance and ultimately the deployment of a security solution. Often, getting started in establishing priorities is a challenge. A possible solution to this challenge is to start with prioritizing the three primary security tenets of confidentiality, integrity, and availability. Defining which of these elements is most important to the organization is essential in crafting a sufficient security solution. This establishes a pattern that can be replicated from concept through design through architecture through deployment and through maintenance.

Do you know the priority your organization places on each of the components of the CIA Triad? If not, find out.

An interesting generalization of this concept of CIA prioritization is that in many cases military and government organizations tend to prioritize confidentiality above integrity and availability while private companies tend to prioritize availability above confidentiality and integrity. Although such prioritization focuses efforts on one aspect of security over another, it does not imply that the second or third prioritized items are ignored or improperly addressed.

## Availability

The third principle of the CIA Triad is *availability*, which means authorized subjects are granted timely and uninterrupted access to objects. If a security mechanism offers availability, it offers a high level of assurance that the data, objects, and resources are accessible to authorized subjects. Availability includes efficient uninterrupted access to objects and prevention of denial-of-service (DoS) attacks. Availability also implies that the supporting infrastructure—including network services, communications, and access control mechanisms—is functional and allows authorized users to gain authorized access.

For availability to be maintained on a system, controls must be in place to ensure authorized access and an acceptable level of performance, to quickly handle interruptions, to provide for redundancy, to maintain reliable backups, and to prevent data loss or destruction.

There are numerous threats to availability. These include device failure, software errors, and environmental issues (heat, static, flooding, power loss, and so on). There are also some forms of attacks that focus on the violation of availability, including denial-of-service attacks, object destruction, and communication interruptions.

As with confidentiality and integrity, violations of availability are not limited to intentional attacks. Many instances of unauthorized alteration of sensitive information are because of human error, oversight, or ineptitude. Some events that lead to integrity breaches include accidentally deleting files, overutilizing a hardware or software component, underallocating resources, and mislabeling or incorrectly classifying objects. Availability violations can occur because of the actions of any user, including administrators. They can also occur because of an oversight in a security policy or a misconfigured security control.

Numerous countermeasures can ensure availability against possible threats. These include designing intermediary delivery systems properly, using access controls effectively, monitoring performance and network traffic, using firewalls and routers to prevent DoS attacks, implementing redundancy for critical systems, and maintaining and testing backup systems. Most security policies (as well as BCP [Business Continuity Planning] focus on the use of fault-tolerance features at the various levels of access/storage/security (i.e., disk, server, site) with the goal of eliminating single points of failure to maintain availability of critical systems.

Availability depends upon both integrity and confidentiality. Without integrity and confidentiality, availability cannot be maintained. Other concepts, conditions, and aspects of availability include usability, accessibility, and timeliness.

# Standards of Due Care and Due Diligence

*Due care* is using reasonable care to protect the interests of an organization. *Due diligence* is practicing the activities that maintain the due care effort. For example, due care is developing a formalized security structure containing a security policy, standards, baselines, guidelines, and procedures. Due diligence is the continued application of this security structure onto the IT infrastructure of an organization. Operational security is the ongoing maintenance of continued due care and due diligence by all responsible parties within an organization.

In today's business environment, prudence is mandatory: Showing due care and due diligence is the only way to disprove negligence in an occurrence of loss. Senior management must show due care and due diligence to reduce their culpability and liability when a loss occurs.

# Other Security Concepts

In addition to the CIA Triad, you need to consider a plethora of other security-related concepts and principles when designing a security policy and deploying a security solution. The following sections discuss privacy, identification, authentication, authorization, auditing, accountability, and nonrepudiation.

## Privacy

*Privacy* can be a difficult entity to define. The term is used frequently in numerous contexts without much quantification or qualification. Here are some possible partial definitions of privacy:

- Active prevention of unauthorized access to information that is personally identifiable (that is, data points that can be linked directly to a person or organization)

- Freedom from unauthorized access to information deemed personal or confidential

- Freedom from being observed, monitored, or examined without consent or knowledge

When addressing privacy in the realm of IT, it usually becomes a balancing act between individual rights and the rights or activities of an organization. Some claim that individuals have the right to control whether information can be collected about them and what can be done with it. This often brings up the issue of personally identifiable information (PII). PII is any data item that can be easily and/or obviously traced back to the person of origin or concern.

Others claim that any activity performed in public view, such as most activities performed over the Internet or activities performed on company equipment, can be monitored without knowledge of or permission from the individuals being watched and that the information gathered from such monitoring can be used for whatever purposes an organization deems appropriate or desirable.

On one hand, protecting individuals from unwanted observation, direct marketing, and disclosure of private, personal, or confidential details is considered a worthy effort. Likewise, organizations profess that demographic studies, information gleaning, and focused marketing improve business models, reduce advertising waste, and save money for all parties.

Whatever your personal or organizational stance is on the issue of online privacy, it must be addressed in an organizational security policy. Privacy is an issue not just for external visitors to your online offerings but also for your customers, employees, suppliers, and contractors. If you gather any type of information about any person or company, you must address privacy.

In most cases, especially when privacy is being violated or restricted, the individuals and companies must be informed; otherwise, you may face legal ramifications. Privacy issues must also be addressed when allowing or restricting personal use of email, retaining email, recording phone conversations, gathering information about surfing or spending habits, and so on.

## Identification

*Identification* is the process by which a subject professes an identity and accountability is initiated. A subject must provide an identity to a system to start the process of authentication, authorization, and accountability. Providing an identity can be typing in a username; swiping a smart card; waving a proximity device; speaking a phrase; or positioning your face, hand, or finger for a camera or scanning device. Proving a process ID number also represents the identification process. Without an identity, a system has no way to correlate an authentication factor with the subject.

Once a subject has been identified (that is, once the subject's identity has been recognized and verified), the identity is accountable for any further actions by that subject. IT systems track activity by identities, not by the subjects themselves. A computer doesn't know one human from another, but it does know that your user account is different from all other user accounts. A subject's identity is typically labeled as, or considered to be, public information. However, simply claiming an identity does not imply access or authority. The identity must be proven or verified before access to controlled resources is allowed. That process is authentication.

## Authentication

The process of verifying or testing that the claimed identity is valid is *authentication*. Authentication requires from the subject additional information that must exactly correspond to the identity indicated. The most common form of authentication is using a password (this includes the password variations of PINs and passphrases). Authentication verifies the identity of the subject by comparing one or more factors against the database of valid identities (that is, user accounts). The authentication factor used to verify identity is typically labeled as, or considered to be, private information. The capability of the subject and system to maintain the secrecy of the authentication factors for identities directly reflects the level of security of that system. If the process of illegitimately obtaining and using the authentication factor of a target user is relatively easy, then the authentication system is insecure. If that process is relatively difficult, then the authentication system is reasonably secure.

Identification and authentication are always used together as a single two-step process. Providing an identity is the first step, and providing the authentication factor(s) is the second step. Without both, a subject cannot gain access to a system—neither element alone is useful in terms of security.

A subject can provide several types of authentication (for example, something you know, something you have, and so on). Each authentication technique or factor has its unique benefits and drawbacks. Thus, it is important to evaluate each mechanism in light of the environment in which it will be deployed to determine viability. (We discussed authentication at length in Chapter 1, "Accountability and Access Control.")

## Authorization

Once a subject is authenticated, access must be authorized. The process of *authorization* ensures that the requested activity or access to an object is possible given the rights and privileges assigned to the authenticated identity. In most cases, the system evaluates an access control matrix that compares the subject, the object, and the intended activity. If the specific action is allowed, the subject is authorized. If the specific action is not allowed, the subject is not authorized.

Keep in mind that just because a subject has been identified and authenticated does not mean they have been authorized to perform any function or access all resources within the controlled environment. It is possible for a subject to be logged onto a network (that is, identified and authenticated) but be blocked from accessing a file or printing to a printer (that is, by not being authorized to perform that activity). Most network users are authorized to perform only a limited number of activities on a specific collection of resources. Identification and authentication are all-or-nothing aspects of access control. Authorization has a wide range of variations between all or nothing for each object within the environment. A user may be able to read a file but not delete it, print a document but not alter the print queue, or log on to a system but not access any resources. Authorization is usually defined using one of the concepts of access control, such as DAC, MAC, or RBAC (see Chapter 1).

## Auditing

*Auditing*, or monitoring, is the programmatic means by which a subject's actions are tracked and recorded for the purpose of holding the subject accountable for their actions while authenticated on a system. Auditing is also the process by which unauthorized or abnormal activities are detected on a system. Auditing is recording activities of a subject and its objects as well as recording the activities of core system functions that maintain the operating environment and the security mechanisms. The audit trails created by recording system events to logs can be used to evaluate the health and performance of a system. System crashes may indicate faulty programs, corrupt drivers, or intrusion attempts. The event logs leading up to a crash can often be used to discover the reason a system failed. Log files provide an audit trail for re-creating the history of an event, intrusion, or system failure. Auditing is needed to detect malicious actions by subjects, attempted intrusions, and system failures and to reconstruct events, provide evidence for prosecution, and produce problem reports and analysis. Auditing is usually a native feature of operating systems and most applications and services. Thus, configuring the system to record information about specific types of events is fairly straightforward.

For more information on configuring and administrating auditing and logging, see Chapter 14, "Auditing and Monitoring."

## Accountability

An organization's security policy can be properly enforced only if *accountability* is maintained. In other words, you can maintain security only if subjects are held accountable for their actions. Effective accountability relies upon the capability to prove a subject's identity and track their activities. Accountability is established by linking a human to the activities of an online identity through the security services and mechanisms of auditing, authorization, authentication, and identification. Thus, human accountability is ultimately dependent on the strength of the authentication process. Without a strong authentication process, there is doubt that the human associated with a specific user account was the actual entity controlling that user account when the undesired action took place.

To have viable accountability, you must be able to support your security in a court of law. If you are unable to legally support your security efforts, then you will be unlikely to be able to hold a human accountable for actions linked to a user account. With only a password as authentication, there is significant room for doubt. Passwords are the least secure form of authentication, with dozens of different methods available to compromise them. However, using multifactor authentication, such as a password, smart card, and fingerprint scan in combination, there is very little possibility that any other human could have hacked the authentication in order to impersonate the human responsible for the user account's.

### Legally Defensible Security

The point of security is to keep bad things from happening while supporting the occurrence of good things. When bad things do happen, organizations often desire assistance from law enforcement and the legal system for compensation. To obtain legal restitution, you must demonstrate that a crime was committed, that the suspect committed that crime, and that you took reasonable efforts to prevent the crime. This results in the necessity of your organization's security to be legally defensible. If you are unable to convince a court that your log files are accurate and that no other person other than the subject could have committed the crime, you will not obtain restitution. Ultimately, this requires a complete security solution that has unbreachable authentication techniques, solid authorization mechanisms, and impeccable auditing systems. Additionally, you must show that the organization complied with all applicable laws and regulations, that proper warnings and notifications were posted, that both logical and physical security were not otherwise compromised, and that there are no other possible reasonable interpretations of the electronic evidence.

### Nonrepudiation

Nonrepudiation ensures that the subject of an activity or event cannot deny that the event occurred. Nonrepudiation prevents a subject from claiming not to have sent a message, not to have performed an action, or not to have been the cause of an event. It is made possible through identity, authentication, authorization, accountability, and auditing. Nonrepudiation can be established using digital certificates, session identifiers, transaction logs, and numerous other transactional and access control mechanisms. If nonrepudiation is not built into a system and properly enforced, then you will not be able to verify that a specific entity performed a certain action. Nonrepudiation is an essential part of accountability. A suspect cannot be held accountable if they can repudiate the claim against them.

# Protection Mechanisms

Another aspect of security solution concepts and principles is the element of protection mechanisms. These are common characteristics of security controls. Not all security controls must have them, but many controls offer their protection for confidentiality, integrity, and availability through the use of these mechanisms. These mechanisms include using multiple layers or levels of access, employing abstraction, hiding data, and using encryption.

## Layering

*Layering*, also known as *defense in depth*, is simply the use of multiple controls in a series. No one control can protect against all possible threats. Using a multilayered solution allows for numerous, different controls to guard against whatever threats come to pass. When security solutions are designed in layers, most threats are eliminated, mitigated, or thwarted.

Using layers in a series rather than in parallel is important. Performing security restrictions in a series means to perform one after the other in a linear fashion. Only through a series configuration will each attack be scanned, evaluated, or mitigated by every security control. A single failure of a security control does not render the entire solution ineffective. If security controls were implemented in parallel, a threat could pass through a single checkpoint that did not address its particular malicious activity. Serial configurations are very narrow but very deep, whereas parallel configurations are very wide but very shallow. Parallel systems are useful in distributed computing applications, but parallelism is not often a useful concept in the realm of security.

Think of physical entrances to buildings. A parallel configuration is used for shopping malls. There are many doors in many locations around the entire perimeter of the mall. A series configuration would most likely be used in a bank or an airport. A single entrance is provided, and that entrance is actually several gateways or checkpoints that must be passed in sequential order to gain entry into active areas of the building.

Layering also includes the concept that networks comprise numerous separate entities, each with its own unique security controls and vulnerabilities. In an effective security solution, there is a synergy between all networked systems that creates a single security front. Using separate security systems creates a layered security solution.

## Abstraction

*Abstraction* is used for efficiency. Similar elements are put into groups, classes, or roles that are assigned security controls, restrictions, or permissions as a collective. Thus, the concept of abstraction is used when classifying objects or assigning roles to subjects. The concept of abstraction also includes the definition of object and subject types or of objects themselves (that is, a data structure used to define a template for a class of entities). Abstraction is used to define what types of data an object can contain, what types of functions can be performed on or by that object, and what capabilities that object has. Abstraction simplifies security by enabling you to assign security controls to a group of objects collected by type or function.

## Data Hiding

*Data hiding* is exactly what it sounds like: preventing data from being discovered or accessed by a subject by positioning the data in a logical storage compartment that is not accessible or seen by the subject. Keeping a database from being accessed by unauthorized visitors is a form of data hiding, as is restricting a subject at a lower classification level from accessing data at a higher classification level. Preventing an application from accessing hardware directly is also a form of data hiding. Data hiding is often a key element in security controls as well as in programming.

## Encryption

*Encryption* is the art and science of hiding the meaning or intent of a communication from unintended recipients. Encryption can take many forms and be applied to every type of electronic communication, including text, audio, and video files, as well as applications themselves. Encryption is an important element in security controls, especially in regard to the transmission of data between systems. There are various strengths of encryption, each of which is designed and/or appropriate for a specific use or purpose. Encryption is discussed at length in Chapter 9, "Cryptography and Symmetric Key Algorithms," and Chapter 10, "PKI and Cryptographic Applications."

# Change Control/Management

Another important aspect of security management is the control or management of change. Change in a secure environment can introduce loopholes, overlaps, missing objects, and oversights that can lead to new vulnerabilities. The only way to maintain security in the face of change is to systematically manage change. This usually involves extensive planning, testing, logging, auditing, and monitoring of activities related to security controls and mechanisms. The records of changes to an environment are then used to identify agents of change, whether those agents are objects, subjects, programs, communication pathways, or even the network itself.

The goal of change management is to ensure that any change does not lead to reduced or compromised security. Change management is also responsible for making it possible to roll back any change to a previous secured state. Change management can be implemented on any system despite the level of security. It is a requirement for systems complying with the Information Technology Security Evaluation and Criteria (ITSEC) classifications of B2, B3, and A1. Ultimately, change management improves the security of an environment by protecting implemented security from unintentional, tangential, or affected diminishments. Although an important goal of change management is to prevent unwanted reductions in security, its primary purpose is to make all changes subject to detailed documentation and auditing and thus able to be reviewed and scrutinized by management.

Change management should be used to oversee alterations to every aspect of a system, including hardware configuration and OS and application software. Change management should be included in design, development, testing, evaluation, implementation, distribution, evolution, growth, ongoing operation, and modification. It requires a detailed inventory of every component and configuration. It also requires the collection and maintenance of complete documentation for every system component, from hardware to software and from configuration settings to security features.

The change control process of configuration or change management has several goals or requirements:

- Implement changes in a monitored and orderly manner. Changes are always controlled.
- A formalized testing process is included to verify that a change produces expected results.
- All changes can be reversed.
- Users are informed of changes before they occur to prevent loss of productivity.
- The effects of changes are systematically analyzed.
- The negative impact of changes on capabilities, functionality, and performance is minimized.

One example of a change management process is a *parallel run*, which is a type of new system deployment testing where the new system and the old system are run in parallel. Each major or significant user process is performed on each system simultaneously to ensure that the new system supports all required business functionality that the old system supported or provided.

# Data Classification

Data classification is the primary means by which data is protected based on its need for secrecy, sensitivity, or confidentiality. It is inefficient to treat all data the same when designing and implementing a security system because some data items need more security than others. Securing everything at a low security level means sensitive data is easily accessible. Securing everything at a high security level is too expensive and restricts access to unclassified, noncritical data. Data classification is used to determine how much effort, money, and resources are allocated to protect the data and control access to it.

The primary objective of data classification schemes is to formalize and stratify the process of securing data based on assigned labels of importance and sensitivity. Data classification is used to provide security mechanisms for storing, processing, and transferring data. It also addresses how data is removed from a system and destroyed.

The following are benefits of using a data classification scheme:

- It demonstrates an organization's commitment to protecting valuable resources and assets.

- It assists in identifying those assets that are most critical or valuable to the organization.

- It lends credence to the selection of protection mechanisms.

- It is often required for regulatory compliance or legal restrictions.

- It helps to define access levels, types of authorized uses, and parameters for declassification and/or destruction of resources that are no longer valuable.

The criteria by which data is classified vary based on the organization performing the classification. However, you can glean numerous generalities from common or standardized classification systems:

- Usefulness of the data

- Timeliness of the data

- Value or cost of the data

- Maturity or age of the data

- Lifetime of the data (or when it expires)

- Association with personnel

- Data disclosure damage assessment (that is, how the disclosure of the data would affect the organization)

- Data modification damage assessment (that is, how the modification of the data would affect the organization)

- National security implications of the data

- Authorized access to the data (that is, who has access to the data)

- Restriction from the data (that is, who is restricted from the data)
- Maintenance and monitoring of the data (that is, who should maintain and monitor the data)
- Storage of the data

Using whatever criteria is appropriate for the organization, data is evaluated, and an appropriate data classification label is assigned to it. In some cases, the label is added to the data object. In other cases, labeling is simply assigned by the placement of the data into a storage mechanism or behind a security protection mechanism.

To implement a classification scheme, you must perform seven major steps, or phases:

1. Identify the custodian, and define their responsibilities.
2. Specify the evaluation criteria of how the information will be classified and labeled.
3. Classify and label each resource. (The owner conducts this step, but a supervisor should review it.)
4. Document any exceptions to the classification policy that are discovered, and integrate them into the evaluation criteria.
5. Select the security controls that will be applied to each classification level to provide the necessary level of protection.
6. Specify the procedures for declassifying resources and the procedures for transferring custody of a resource to an external entity.
7. Create an enterprise-wide awareness program to instruct all personnel about the classification system.

Declassification is often overlooked when designing a classification system and documenting the usage procedures. Declassification is required once an asset no longer warrants or needs the protection of its currently assigned classification or sensitivity level. In other words, if the asset were new, it would be assigned a lower sensitivity label than it currently is assigned. When assets fail to be declassified as needed, security resources are wasted, and the value and protection of the higher sensitivity levels is degraded.

The two common classification schemes are government/military classification and commercial business/private sector classification. There are five levels of government/military classification (listed here from highest to lowest):

**Top secret**   The highest level of classification. The unauthorized disclosure of top-secret data will have drastic effects and cause grave damage to national security.

**Secret**   Used for data of a restricted nature. The unauthorized disclosure of data classified as secret will have significant effects and cause critical damage to national security.

**Confidential**   Used for data of a confidential nature. The unauthorized disclosure of data classified as confidential will have noticeable effects and cause serious damage to national security. This classification is used for all data between secret and sensitive but unclassified classifications.

**Sensitive but unclassified**   Used for data of a sensitive or private nature, but the disclosure of this data would not cause significant damage.

**Unclassified** The lowest level of classification. This is used for data that is neither sensitive nor classified. The disclosure of unclassified data does not compromise confidentiality or cause any noticeable damage.

 An easy way to remember the names of the five levels of the government or military classification scheme in least secure to most secure order is with a memorization acronym: U.S. Can Stop Terrorism. Notice that the five uppercase letters represent the five named classification levels, from least secure on the left to most secure on the right (or from bottom to top in the preceding list of items).

The classifications of confidential, secret, and top secret are collectively known or labeled as *classified*. Often, revealing the actual classification of data to unauthorized individuals is a violation of that data. Thus, the term *classified* is generally used to refer to any data that is ranked above the sensitive but unclassified level. All classified data is exempt from the Freedom of Information Act as well as many other laws and regulations. The U.S. military classification scheme is most concerned with the sensitivity of data and focuses on the protection of confidentiality (that is, the prevention of disclosure). You can roughly define each level or label of classification by the level of damage that would be caused in the event of a confidentiality violation. Data from the top-secret level would cause grave damage to national security, while data from the unclassified level would not cause any serious damage to national or localized security.

Commercial business/private sector classification systems can vary widely, as they typically do not have to adhere to a standard or regulation. As an example, the CISSP exam focuses on four common or possible business classification levels (listed highest to lowest):

**Confidential** The highest level of classification. This is used for data that is extremely sensitive and for internal use only. A significant negative impact could occur for a company if confidential data is disclosed. Sometimes the label *proprietary* is substituted for *confidential*.

 Another classification often used in the commercial business/private sector is *proprietary*. Proprietary data is a form of confidential information. If proprietary data is disclosed, it can have drastic effects on the competitive edge of an organization.

**Private** Used for data that is of a private or personal nature and intended for internal use only. A significant negative impact could occur for the company or individuals if private data is disclosed.

 Confidential and private data in a commercial business/private sector classification scheme both require roughly the same level of security protection. The real difference between the two labels is that confidential data is used for company data while private data is used only for data related to individuals, such as medical data.

**Sensitive**   Used for data that is more classified than public data. A negative impact could occur for the company if sensitive data is disclosed.

**Public**   The lowest level of classification. This is used for all data that does not fit in one of the higher classifications. Its disclosure does not have a serious negative impact on the organization.

# Planning to Plan

Crafting a security stance for an organization often involves a lot more than just writing down a few lofty security ideals. In most cases, there is a significant amount of planning that goes into developing a solid security policy. Many Dilbert fans may recognize the seemingly absurd concept of holding a meeting to plan a meeting for a future meeting. It turns out that planning for security must start with planning to plan, then move into planning for standards and compliance, and finally move into the actual plan development and design. Skipping any of these "planning to plan" steps can derail an organization's security solution before it even gets started.

One of the first and most important security planning steps is to consider the overall control framework or structure of the security solution desired by the organization. You can choose from several options in regard to security concept infrastructure; however, the one covered on the CISSP exam is Control Objectives for Information and Related Technology (CobiT). CobiT is a documented set of best IT security practices crafted by the Information Systems Audit and Control Association (ISACA) and IT Governance Institute (ITGI). CobiT prescribes goals and requirements for security controls and encourages the mapping of IT security ideals to business objectives. The CobiT system is a complex structure with four main domains: Planning and Organization, Acquisition and Implementation, Delivery and Support, and Monitoring. Each of these domains breaks down into high-level processes (34 in all), which in turn break down into control objects (more than 200). This overwhelming system includes six types of publications to assist an organization in implementing the goals and controls of the CobiT concept. These six publications are *Executive Summary*, *Framework*, *Control Objectives*, *Audit Guidelines*, *Implementation Toolset*, and *Management Guidelines*. CobiT is used not just to organize the IT security of an organization but as a guideline for auditors.

Fortunately, CobiT is only modestly referenced on the exam, so further details are not necessary. However, if you have interest in this concept, please visit the ISACA.org website, or if you want a general overview, read the CobiT entry on Wikipedia.

There are many other standards and guidelines for IT security. A few of these are Open Source Security Testing Methodology Manual (OSSTMM), ISO/IEC 27002 (which replaced ISO 17799), and the Information Technology Infrastructure Library (ITIL) (see www.itlibrary.org for more information).

# Summary

Security management concepts and principles are inherent elements in a security policy and in solution deployment. They define the basic parameters needed for a secure environment. They also define the goals and objectives that both policy designers and system implementers must achieve in order to create a secure solution. It is important for real-world security professionals as well as CISSP exam students to understand these items thoroughly.

The primary goals and objectives of security are contained within the CIA Triad: confidentiality, integrity, and availability. These three principles are considered the most important within the realm of security. Their importance to an organization depends on the organization's security goals and requirements and on how much of a threat to security exists in its environment.

The first principle from the CIA Triad is confidentiality, the principle that objects are not disclosed to unauthorized subjects. Security mechanisms that offer confidentiality offer a high level of assurance that data, objects, or resources are not exposed to unauthorized subjects. If a threat exists against confidentiality, there is the possibility that unauthorized disclosure could take place.

The second principle from the CIA Triad is integrity, the principle that objects retain their veracity and are intentionally modified by only authorized subjects. Security mechanisms that offer integrity offer a high level of assurance that the data, objects, and resources are unaltered from their original protected state. This includes alterations occurring while the object is in storage, in transit, or in process. Maintaining integrity means the object itself is not altered and the operating system and programming entities that manage and manipulate the object are not compromised.

The third principle from the CIA Triad is availability, the principle that authorized subjects are granted timely and uninterrupted access to objects. Security mechanisms that offer availability offer a high level of assurance that the data, objects, and resources are accessible by authorized subjects. Availability includes efficient uninterrupted access to objects and prevention of denial-of-service attacks. It also implies that the supporting infrastructure is functional and allows authorized users to gain authorized access.

Other security-related concepts, principles, and tenets that should be considered and addressed when designing a security policy and deploying a security solution are privacy, identification, authentication, authorization, accountability, nonrepudiation, and auditing.

Other aspects of security solution concepts and principles are the elements of protection mechanisms: layering, abstraction, data hiding, and encryption. These are common characteristics of security controls, and although not all security controls must have them, many controls use these mechanisms to protect confidentiality, integrity, and availability.

The control or management of change is an important aspect of security management practices. When a secure environment is changed, loopholes, overlaps, missing objects, and oversights can lead to new vulnerabilities. You can, however, maintain security by systematically managing change. This typically involves extensive logging, auditing, and monitoring of activities related to security controls and security mechanisms. The resulting data is then used to identify agents of change, whether objects, subjects, programs, communication pathways, or even the network itself.

Data classification is the primary means by which data is protected based on its secrecy, sensitivity, or confidentiality. Because some data items need more security than others, it is inefficient to treat all data the same when designing and implementing a security system. If everything is secured at a low security level, sensitive data is easily accessible, but securing everything at a high security level is too expensive and restricts access to unclassified, noncritical data. Data classification is used to determine how much effort, money, and resources are allocated to protect the data and control access to it.

# Exam Essentials

**Understand the CIA Triad elements of confidentiality, integrity, and availability.** Confidentiality is the principle that objects are not disclosed to unauthorized subjects. Integrity is the principle that objects retain their veracity and are intentionally modified by only authorized subjects. Availability is the principle that authorized subjects are granted timely and uninterrupted access to objects. Know why these are important, the mechanisms that support them, the attacks that focus on each, and the effective countermeasures.

**Know how privacy fits into the realm of IT security.** Know the multiple meanings/ definitions of privacy, why it is important to protect, and the issues surrounding it, especially in a work environment.

**Be able to explain how identification works.** Identification is the process by which a subject professes an identity and accountability is initiated. A subject must provide an identity to a system to start the process of authentication, authorization, and accountability.

**Understand the process of authentication.** The process of verifying or testing that a claimed identity is valid is authentication. Authentication requires information from the subject that must exactly correspond to the identity indicated.

**Know how authorization fits into a security plan.** Once a subject is authenticated, its access must be authorized. The process of authorization ensures that the requested activity or object access is possible given the rights and privileges assigned to the authenticated identity.

**Be able to explain the auditing process.** Auditing, or monitoring, is the programmatic means by which subjects are held accountable for their actions while authenticated on a system. Auditing is also the process by which unauthorized or abnormal activities are detected on a system. Auditing is needed to detect malicious actions by subjects, attempted intrusions, and system failures and to reconstruct events, provide evidence for prosecution, and produce problem reports and analysis.

**Understand the importance of accountability.** An organization's security policy can be properly enforced only if accountability is maintained. In other words, security can be maintained only if subjects are held accountable for their actions. Effective accountability relies upon the capability to prove a subject's identity and track their activities.

**Be able to explain nonrepudiation.**   Nonrepudiation ensures that the subject of an activity or event cannot deny that the event occurred. It prevents a subject from claiming not to have sent a message, not to have performed an action, or not to have been the cause of an event.

**Know how layering simplifies security.**   Layering is simply the use of multiple controls in series. Using a multilayered solution allows for numerous controls to guard against threats.

**Be able to explain the concept of abstraction.**   Abstraction is used to collect similar elements into groups, classes, or roles that are assigned security controls, restrictions, or permissions as a collective. It adds efficiency to carrying out a security plan.

**Understand data hiding.**   Data hiding is exactly what it sounds like: preventing data from being discovered or accessed by a subject. It is often a key element in security controls as well as in programming.

**Understand the need for encryption.**   Encryption is the art and science of hiding the meaning or intent of a communication from unintended recipients. It can take many forms and be applied to every type of electronic communication, including text, audio, and video files, as well as programs themselves. Encryption is an important element in security controls, especially in regard to the transmission of data between systems.

**Be able to explain the concepts of change control and change management.**   Change in a secure environment can introduce loopholes, overlaps, missing objects, and oversights that can lead to new vulnerabilities. The only way to maintain security in the face of change is to systematically manage change.

**Know why and how data is classified.**   Data is classified to simplify the process of assigning security controls to groups of objects rather than to individual objects. The two common classification schemes are government/military and commercial business/private sector. Know the five levels of government/military classification and the four levels of commercial business/private sector classification.

**Understand the importance of declassification.**   Declassification is required once an asset no longer warrants the protection of its currently assigned classification or sensitivity level.

**Know the basics of CobiT.**   Control Objectives for Information and Related Technology (CobiT) is a security concept infrastructure used to organize the complex security solutions of companies.

# Written Lab

1. Discuss and describe the CIA Triad.
2. What are the requirements to hold a person accountable for the actions of their user account?
3. Describe the benefits of change control management.
4. What are the seven major steps or phases in the implementation of a classification scheme?

# Answers to Written Lab

1.  The CIA Triad is the combination of confidentiality, integrity, and availability. This term is used to indicate the three key components of a security solution.

2.  The requirements of accountability are identification, authentication, authorization, and auditing. Each of these components needs to be legally supportable to truly hold someone accountable for their actions.

3.  The benefits of change control management include the prevention of unwanted security reduction because of uncontrolled change, the documentation and tracking of all alterations in the environment, standardization, conforming with security policy, and the ability to roll back changes in the event of an unwanted or unexpected outcome.

4.  (1) Identify the custodian, and define their responsibilities. (2) Specify the evaluation criteria of how the information will be classified and labeled. (3) Classify and label each resource. Although the owner conducts this step, a supervisor should review it. (4) Document any exceptions to the classification policy that are discovered, and integrate them into the evaluation criteria. (5) Select the security controls that will be applied to each classification level to provide the necessary level of protection. (6) Specify the procedures for declassifying resources and the procedures for transferring custody of a resource to an external entity. (7) Create an enterprise-wide awareness program to instruct all personnel about the classification system.

# Review Questions

1. Which of the following contains the primary goals and objectives of security?

   A. A network's border perimeter

   B. The CIA Triad

   C. A stand-alone system

   D. The Internet

2. Vulnerabilities and risks are evaluated based on their threats against which of the following?

   A. One or more of the CIA Triad principles

   B. Data usefulness

   C. Due care

   D. Extent of liability

3. Which of the following is a principle of the CIA Triad that means authorized subjects are granted timely and uninterrupted access to objects?

   A. Identification

   B. Availability

   C. Encryption

   D. Layering

4. Which of the following is not considered a violation of confidentiality?

   A. Stealing passwords

   B. Eavesdropping

   C. Hardware destruction

   D. Social engineering

5. Which of the following is not true?

   A. Violations of confidentiality include human error.

   B. Violations of confidentiality include management oversight.

   C. Violations of confidentiality are limited to direct intentional attacks.

   D. Violations of confidentiality can occur when a transmission is not properly encrypted.

6. Confidentiality is dependent upon which of the following?

   A. Accountability

   B. Availability

   C. Nonrepudiation

   D. Integrity

7. If a security mechanism offers availability, then it offers a high level of assurance that the data, objects, and resources are _____ by authorized subjects.

   **A.** Controlled

   **B.** Audited

   **C.** Accessible

   **D.** Repudiated

8. Which of the following describes the freedom from being observed, monitored, or examined without consent or knowledge?

   **A.** Integrity

   **B.** Privacy

   **C.** Authentication

   **D.** Accountability

9. All but which of the following items require awareness for all individuals affected?

   **A.** Restricting personal email

   **B.** Recording phone conversations

   **C.** Gathering information about surfing habits

   **D.** The backup mechanism used to retain email messages

10. Which of the following is typically not used as an identification factor?

    **A.** Username

    **B.** Smart card swipe

    **C.** Fingerprint scan

    **D.** A challenge/response token device

11. What ensures that the subject of an activity or event cannot deny that the event occurred?

    **A.** CIA Triad

    **B.** Abstraction

    **C.** Nonrepudiation

    **D.** Hash totals

12. Which of the following is the most important and distinctive concept in relation to layered security?

    **A.** Multiple

    **B.** Series

    **C.** Parallel

    **D.** Filter

13. Which of the following is not considered an example of data hiding?

   A. Preventing an authorized reader of an object from deleting that object

   B. Keeping a database from being accessed by unauthorized visitors

   C. Restricting a subject at a lower classification level from accessing data at a higher classification level

   D. Preventing an application from accessing hardware directly

14. What is the primary goal of change management?

   A. Maintaining documentation

   B. Keeping users informed of changes

   C. Allowing rollback of failed changes

   D. Preventing security compromises

15. What is the primary objective of data classification schemes?

   A. To control access to objects for authorized subjects

   B. To formalize and stratify the process of securing data based on assigned labels of importance and sensitivity

   C. To establish a transaction trail for auditing accountability

   D. To manipulate access controls to provide for the most efficient means to grant or restrict functionality

16. Which of the following is typically not a characteristic considered when classifying data?

   A. Value

   B. Size of object

   C. Useful lifetime

   D. National security implications

17. What are the two common data classification schemes?

   A. Military and private sector

   B. Personal and government

   C. Private sector and unrestricted sector

   D. Classified and unclassified

18. Which of the following is the lowest military data classification for classified data?

   A. Sensitive

   B. Secret

   C. Sensitive but unclassified

   D. Private

**19.** Which commercial business/private sector data classification is used to control information about individuals within an organization?

    **A.**  Confidential

    **B.**  Private

    **C.**  Sensitive

    **D.**  Proprietary

**20.** Data classifications are used to focus security controls over all but which of the following?

    **A.**  Storage

    **B.**  Processing

    **C.**  Layering

    **D.**  Transfer

# Answers to Review Questions

1. B. The primary goals and objectives of security are confidentiality, integrity, and availability, commonly referred to as the *CIA Triad*.

2. A. Vulnerabilities and risks are evaluated based on their threats against one or more of the CIA Triad principles.

3. B. Availability means that authorized subjects are granted timely and uninterrupted access to objects.

4. C. Hardware destruction is a violation of availability and possibly integrity. Violations of confidentiality include capturing network traffic, stealing password files, social engineering, port scanning, shoulder surfing, eavesdropping, and sniffing.

5. C. Violations of confidentiality are not limited to direct intentional attacks. Many instances of unauthorized disclosure of sensitive or confidential information are due to human error, oversight, or ineptitude.

6. D. Without integrity, confidentiality cannot be maintained.

7. C. Accessibility of data, objects, and resources is the goal of availability. If a security mechanism offers availability, then it is highly likely that the data, objects, and resources are accessible by authorized subjects.

8. B. Privacy is freedom from being observed, monitored, or examined without consent or knowledge.

9. D. Users should be aware that email messages are retained, but the backup mechanism used to perform this operation does not need to be disclosed to them.

10. D. A challenge/response token device is almost exclusively used as an authentication factor, not an identification factor.

11. C. Nonrepudiation ensures that the subject of an activity or event cannot deny that the event occurred.

12. B. Layering is the deployment of multiple security mechanisms in a series. When security restrictions are performed in a series, they are performed one after the other in a linear fashion. Therefore, a single failure of a security control does not render the entire solution ineffective.

13. A. Preventing an authorized reader of an object from deleting that object is just an access control, not data hiding. If you can read an object, it is not hidden from you.

14. D. The prevention of security compromises is the primary goal of change management.

15. B. The primary objective of data classification schemes is to formalize and stratify the process of securing data based on assigned labels of importance and sensitivity.

16. B.  Size is not a criterion for establishing data classification. When classifying an object, you should take value, lifetime, and security implications into consideration.

17. A.  Military (or government) and private sector (or commercial business) are the two common data classification schemes.

18. B.  Of the options listed, secret is the lowest classified military data classification.

19. B.  The commercial business/private sector data classification of private is used to protect information about individuals.

20. C.  Layering is a core aspect of security mechanisms, but it is not a focus of data classifications.

# Chapter

# 6

# Asset Value, Policies, and Roles

## THE CISSP EXAM TOPICS COVERED IN THIS CHAPTER INCLUDE:

✓ **Information Security Governance and Risk Management**

- Understand and align security function to goals, mission, and objectives of the organization

- Understand and apply security governance

  - Organizational processes; define security roles and responsibilities; legislative and regulatory compliance; privacy requirements compliance; control frameworks; due care; due diligence

- Develop and implement security policy

  - Security policies; standards/baselines; procedures; guidelines; documentation

- Define and implement information classification and ownership

- Ensure security in contractual agreements and procurement processes

- Understand and apply risk management concepts

  - Identify threats and vulnerabilities; risk assessment/ analysis; risk assignment/acceptance; countermeasure selection

- Evaluate personnel security

  - Background checks and employment candidate screening; employment agreements and policies; employee termination processes; vendor, consultant and contractor controls

- Develop and manage security education, training, and awareness
- Develop and implement information system security strategies
- Support certification and accreditation efforts
- Assess the completeness and effectiveness of the security program
- Manage the security function
  - Budget; metrics; resources

✓ **Legal, Regulations, Investigations and Compliance**

- Understand compliance requirements and procedures
  - Regulatory environment; audits; reporting

✓ **Operations Security**

- Understand the following security concepts
  - Need-to-know/least privilege; separation of duties and responsibilities; monitor special privileges (e.g., operators, administrators); job rotation; marking, handling, storing, and destroying of sensitive information and media; record retention

The Information Security Governance and Risk domain of the Common Body of Knowledge (CBK) for the CISSP certification exam deals with hiring practices, security roles, formalizing security structure, risk management, awareness training, and management planning.

Because of the complexity and importance of hardware and software controls, security management for employees is often overlooked in overall security planning. This chapter explores the human side of security, from establishing secure hiring practices and job descriptions to developing an employee infrastructure. Additionally, we look at how employee training, management, and termination practices are considered an integral part of creating a secure environment. Finally, we examine how to assess and manage security risks.

# Employment Policies and Practices

Humans are the weakest element in any security solution. No matter what physical or logical controls are deployed, humans can discover ways to avoid them, circumvent or subvert them, or disable them. Thus, it is important to take into account the humanity of your users when designing and deploying security solutions for your environment. To understand and apply security governance, you must address the weakest link in your security chain—namely people.

Issues, problems, and compromises related to humans occur at all stages of a security solution development. This is because humans are involved throughout the development, deployment, and ongoing administration of any solution. Therefore, you must evaluate the effect users, designers, programmers, developers, managers, and implementers have on the process.

Hiring new staff typically involves several distinct steps: creating a job description, setting a classification for the job, screening candidates, and hiring and training the one best suited for the job. Without a *job description*, there is no consensus on what type of individual should be hired. Personnel should be added to an organization because there is a need for their specific skills and experience. Any job description for any position within an organization should address relevant security issues. You must consider items such as whether the position requires the handling of sensitive material or access to classified information. In effect, the job description defines the roles to which an employee needs to be assigned to perform their work tasks. The job description should define the type and extent of access the position requires on the secured network. Once these issues have been resolved, assigning a security classification to the job description is fairly standard.

### The Importance of Job Descriptions

Job descriptions are important to the design and support of a security solution. However, many organizations either have overlooked this or have allowed job descriptions to become stale and out-of-sync with reality. Try to track down your job description. Do you even have one? If so, when was it last updated? Does it accurately reflect your job? Does it describe the type of security access you need to perform the prescribed job responsibilities?

Important elements in constructing job descriptions that are in line with organizational processes include separation of duties, job responsibilities, and job rotation.

**Separation of duties**   Separation of duties is the security concept in which critical, significant, and sensitive work tasks are divided among several individual administrators or high-level operators. This prevents any one person from having the ability to undermine or subvert vital security mechanisms. Think of separation of duties as the application of the principle of least privilege to administrators. Separation of duties is also a protection against *collusion*, which is the occurrence of negative activity undertaken by two or more people, often for the purposes of fraud, theft, or espionage.

**Job responsibilities**   Job responsibilities are the specific work tasks an employee is required to perform on a regular basis. Depending on their responsibilities, employees require access to various objects, resources, and services. On a secured network, users must be granted access privileges for those elements related to their work tasks. To maintain the greatest security, access should be assigned according to the principle of least privilege. The principle of least privilege states that in a secured environment, users should be granted the minimum amount of access necessary for them to complete their required work tasks or job responsibilities. True application of this principle requires low-level granular access control over all resources and functions.

**Job rotation**   Job rotation, or rotating employees among numerous job positions, is simply a means by which an organization improves its overall security. Job rotation serves two functions. First, it provides a type of knowledge redundancy. When multiple employees are each capable of performing the work tasks required by several job positions, the organization is less likely to experience serious downtime or loss in productivity if an illness or other incident keeps one or more employees out of work for an extended period of time.

Second, moving personnel around reduces the risk of fraud, data modification, theft, sabotage, and misuse of information. The longer a person works in a specific position, the more likely they are to be assigned additional work tasks and thus expand their privileges and access. As a person becomes increasingly familiar with their work tasks, they may abuse their privileges for personal gain or malice. If misuse or abuse is committed by one employee, it will be easier to detect by another employee who knows the job position and work responsibilities. Therefore, job rotation also provides a form of peer auditing and protects against collusion. Job rotation is also known as cross-training.

When multiple people work together to perpetrate a crime, it's called *collusion*. The likelihood that a co-worker will be willing to collaborate on an illegal or abusive scheme is reduced because of the higher risk of detection provided by the combination of separation of duties, restricted job responsibilities, and job rotation. Collusion and other privilege abuses can be reduced through strict monitoring of special privileges, such as those of an administrator, backup operator, user manager, and others.

Job descriptions are not used exclusively for the hiring process; they should be maintained throughout the life of the organization. Only through detailed job descriptions can a comparison be made between what a person should be responsible for and what they actually are responsible for. It is a managerial task to ensure that job descriptions overlap as little as possible and that one worker's responsibilities do not drift or encroach on those of another's. Likewise, managers should audit privilege assignments to ensure that workers do not obtain access that is not strictly required for them to accomplish their work tasks.

## Screening and Background Checks

Screening candidates for a specific position is based on the sensitivity and classification defined by the job description. The sensitivity and classification of a specific position is dependent upon the level of harm that could be caused by accidental or intentional violations of security by a person in the position. Thus, the thoroughness of the screening process should reflect the security of the position to be filled.

Background checks and security clearances are essential elements in proving that a candidate is adequate, qualified, and trustworthy for a secured position. Background checks include obtaining a candidate's work and educational history; checking references; interviewing colleagues, neighbors, and friends; checking police and government records for arrests or illegal activities; verifying identity through fingerprints, driver's license, and birth certificate; and holding a personal interview. This process could also include a polygraph test, drug testing, and personality testing/evaluation.

Performing online background checks and reviewing the social networking accounts of applicants has become standard practice for many organizations. If a potential employee has posted inappropriate materials to their photo sharing site, social networking biographies, or public instant messaging services, then they are not as attractive a candidate as those who did not. Our actions in the public eye become permanent when those actions are recorded in text, photo, or video and then posted online. A general picture of a person's attitude, intelligence, loyalty, common sense, diligence, honesty, respect, consistency, and adherence to social norms and/or corporate culture can be gleaned quickly by viewing a person's online identity.

## Creating Employment Agreements

When a new employee is hired, they should sign an employment agreement. Such a document outlines the rules and restrictions of the organization, the security policy, the acceptable use and activities policies, details of the job description, violations and consequences, and the length of time the position is to be filled by the employee. Many of these items may be separate documents. In such a case, the employment agreement is used to verify that the employment candidate has read and understood the associated documentation for their prospective job position.

In addition to employment agreements, there may be other security-related documentation that must be addressed. One common document is a *nondisclosure agreement* (NDA). An NDA is used to protect the confidential information within an organization from being disclosed by a former employee. When a person signs an NDA, they agree not to disclose any information that is defined as confidential to anyone outside the organization. Violations of an NDA are often met with strict penalties.

---

 **Real World Scenario**

### NCA: The NDA's Evil Twin

The NDA has a common companion contract known as the *noncompete agreement* (NCA). The noncompete agreement attempts to prevent an employee with special knowledge of secrets from one organization from working in a competing organization in order to prevent that second organization from benefiting from the worker's special knowledge of secrets. NCAs are also used to prevent workers from jumping from one company to the next just because of salary increases or other incentives. Often NCAs have a time limit, such as six months, one year, or even three years. The goal is to allow the original company to maintain its competitive edge by keeping its human resources working for its benefit rather than against it.

Many companies require new hires to sign NCAs. However, fully enforcing an NCA in court is often a difficult battle. The court recognizes the need for a worker to be able to work using the skills and knowledge they have in order to provide for themselves and their families. If the NCA would prevent reasonable income, the courts often invalidate the NCA or prevent its consequences from being realized.

Even if an NCA is not always enforceable in court, however, that does not mean it doesn't have benefits to the original company:

- First, the threat of a lawsuit because of NCA violations is often sufficient incentive to prevent a worker from violating the terms of secrecy when they happen to move to a new company.

- Second, if a worker does violate the terms of the NCA, then even without specifically defined consequences being levied by court restrictions, the time and effort, not to mention the cost, of battling the issue in court is a deterrent.

Did you sign an NCA when you were hired? If so, do you know the terms and the potential consequences if you break that NCA?

Throughout the employment lifetime of personnel, managers should regularly audit the job descriptions, work tasks, privileges, and so on for every staff member. It is common for work tasks and privileges to drift over time. This can cause some tasks to be overlooked and others to be performed multiple times. Drifting can also result in security violations. Regularly reviewing the boundaries defined by each job description in relation to what is actually occurring aids in keeping security violations to a minimum. A key part of this review process is mandatory vacations. In many secured environments, mandatory vacations of one to two weeks are used to audit and verify the work tasks and privileges of employees. This removes the employee from the work environment and places a different worker in their position. This often results in easy detection of abuse, fraud, or negligence.

## Employee Termination

When an employee must be terminated, there are numerous issues that must be addressed. A termination procedure policy is essential to maintaining a secure environment even in the face of a disgruntled employee who must be removed from the organization. The reactions of terminated employees can range from calm, understanding acceptance to violent, destructive rage. A sensible procedure for handling terminations must be designed and implemented to reduce incidents.

The termination of an employee should be handled in a private and respectful manner. However, this does not mean that precautions should not be taken. Terminations should take place with at least one witness, preferably a higher-level manager and/or a security guard. Once the employee has been informed of their release, they should be escorted off the premises and not allowed to return to their work area without an escort for any reason. Before the employee is released, all organization-specific identification, access, or security badges as well as cards, keys, and access tokens should be collected. Generally, the best time to terminate an employee is at the end of their shift midweek.

When possible, an exit interview should be performed. However, this typically depends upon the mental state of the employee upon release and numerous other factors. If an exit interview is unfeasible immediately upon termination, it should be conducted as soon as possible. The primary purpose of the exit interview is to review the liabilities and restrictions placed on the former employee based on the employment agreement, nondisclosure agreement, and any other security-related documentation.

The following list includes some other issues that should be handled as soon as possible:

- Make sure the employee returns any organizational equipment or supplies from their vehicle or home.

- Remove or disable the employee's network user account.

- Notify human resources to issue a final paycheck, pay any unused vacation time, and terminate benefit coverage.

- Arrange for a member of the security department to accompany the released employee while they gather their personal belongings from the work area.

- Inform all security personnel and anyone else who watches or monitors any entrance point to ensure that the ex-employee does not attempt to reenter the building without an escort.

In most cases, you should disable or remove an employee's system access at the same time or just before they are notified of being terminated. This is especially true if that employee is capable of accessing confidential data or has the expertise or access to alter or damage data or services. Failing to restrict released employees' activities can leave your organization open to a wide range of vulnerabilities, including theft and destruction of both physical property and logical data.

 **Real World Scenario**

**Firing: Not Just a Pink Slip Anymore**

Firing an employee has become a complex process. Gone are the days of placing a pink slip in an employee's mail slot. In most IT-centric organizations, termination can create a situation in which the employee or the organization is at risk of being harmed or causing harm. That's why you need a well-designed exit interview process.

However, just having the process isn't enough. It has to be followed correctly every time. Unfortunately, there are many historical occurrences where this has not happened. You might even have heard of some fiasco caused by a botched termination procedure. Common examples include performing any of the following before the employee is actually informed of their termination:

- The IT department requesting the return of a notebook

- Disabling a network account

- Blocking a person's PIN or smart card for building entrance

- Revoking a parking pass

- Distributing a company reorganization chart

- Positioning a new employee in the cubicle

- Allowing layoff information to be leaked to the media

It should go without saying that in order for the exit interview and safe termination processes to function properly, they must be implemented in the correct order and at the correct time (that is, at the start of the exit interview), as in the following example:

- Inform the person that they are relieved of their job.

- Request the return of all access badges, keys, and company equipment.

- Disable the person's electronic access to all aspects of the organization.

- Remind the person about the NDA obligations.

- Escort the person off the premises.

# Security Roles

A security role is the part an individual plays in the overall scheme of security implementation and administration within an organization. Security roles are not necessarily prescribed in job descriptions because they are not always distinct or static. Familiarity with security roles will help in establishing a communications and support structure within an organization. This structure will enable the deployment and enforcement of the security policy. The following six roles are presented in the logical order in which they appear in a secured environment:

**Senior manager**    The organizational owner (senior manager) role is assigned to the person who is ultimately responsible for the security maintained by an organization and who should be most concerned about the protection of its assets. The senior manager must sign off on all policy issues. In fact, all activities must be approved by and signed off on by the senior manager before they can be carried out. There is no effective security policy if the senior manager does not authorize and support it. The senior manager's endorsement of the security policy indicates the accepted ownership of the implemented security within the organization. The senior manager is the person who will be held liable for the overall success or failure of a security solution and is responsible for exercising due care and due diligence in establishing security for an organization. Even though senior managers are ultimately responsible for security, they rarely implement security solutions. In most cases, that responsibility is delegated to security professionals within the organization.

**Security professional**    The security professional, information security (InfoSec) officer or computer incident response team (CIRT) role is assigned to a trained and experienced network, systems, and security engineer who is responsible for following the directives mandated by senior management. The security professional has the functional responsibility for security, including writing the security policy and implementing it. The role of security professional can be labeled as an IS/IT function role. The security professional role is often filled by a team that is responsible for designing and implementing security solutions based on the approved security policy. Security professionals are not decision makers; they are implementers. All decisions must be left to the senior manager.

**Data owner**    The data owner role is assigned to the person who is responsible for classifying information for placement and protection within the security solution. The data owner is typically a high-level manager who is ultimately responsible for data protection. However, the data owner usually delegates the responsibility of the actual data management tasks to a data custodian.

**Data custodian**    The data custodian role is assigned to the user who is responsible for the tasks of implementing the prescribed protection defined by the security policy and *senior management*. The data custodian performs all activities necessary to provide adequate protection for the CIA Triad (confidentiality, integrity, and availability) of data and to fulfill the requirements and responsibilities delegated from upper management. These activities can include performing and testing backups, validating data integrity, deploying security solutions, and managing data storage based on classification.

**User**   The user (end user or operator) role is assigned to any person who has access to the secured system. A user's access is tied to their work tasks and is limited so they have enough access to perform the tasks necessary for their job position (the principle of least privilege). Users are responsible for understanding and upholding the security policy of an organization by following prescribed operational procedures and operating within defined security parameters.

**Auditor**   Another role is that of an auditor. An auditor is responsible for testing and verifying that the security policy is properly implemented and the derived security solutions are adequate. The auditor role may be assigned to a security professional or a trained user. The auditor produces compliance and effectiveness reports that are reviewed by the senior manager. Issues discovered through these reports are transformed into new directives assigned by the senior manager to security professionals or data custodians. However, the auditor is listed as the last or final role since the auditor needs a source of activity (that is, users or operators working in an environment) to audit or monitor.

All of these roles serve an important function within a secured environment. They are useful for identifying liability and responsibility as well as for identifying the hierarchical management and delegation scheme.

# Security Management Planning

Security management planning ensures proper creation, implementation, and enforcement of a security policy. The most effective way to tackle security management planning is using a top-down approach. Upper, or senior, management is responsible for initiating and defining policies for the organization. Security policies provide direction for the lower levels of the organization's hierarchy. It is the responsibility of middle management to flesh out the security policy into standards, baselines, guidelines, and procedures. The operational managers or security professionals must then implement the configurations prescribed in the security management documentation. Finally, the end users must comply with all the security policies of the organization.

The opposite of the top-down approach is the bottom-up approach. In a bottom-up approach environment, the IT staff makes security decisions directly without input from senior management. The bottom-up approach is rarely utilized in organizations and is considered problematic in the IT industry.

Security management is a responsibility of upper management, not of the IT staff, and is considered a business operations issue rather than an IT administration issue. The team or department responsible for security within an organization should be autonomous from all other departments. The InfoSec team should be led by a designated chief security officer

(CSO) who must report directly to senior management. Placing the autonomy of the CSO and his team outside the typical hierarchical structure in an organization can improve security management across the entire organization. It also helps to avoid cross-department and internal political issues.

Elements of security management planning include defining security roles; prescribing how security will be managed, who will be responsible for security, and how security will be tested for effectiveness; developing security policies; performing risk analysis; and requiring security education for employees. These responsibilities are guided through the development of management plans.

The best security plan is useless without one key factor: approval by senior management. Without senior management's approval of and commitment to the security policy, the policy will not succeed. It is the responsibility of the policy development team to educate senior management sufficiently so it understands the risks, liabilities, and exposures that remain even after security measures prescribed in the policy are deployed. Developing and implementing a security policy is evidence of due care and due diligence on the part of senior management. If a company does not practice due care and due diligence, managers can be held liable for negligence and held accountable for both asset and financial losses.

A security management planning team should develop three types of plans:

**Strategic plan**   A strategic plan is a long-term plan that is fairly stable. It defines the organization's goals, mission, and objectives. It's useful for about five years if it is maintained and updated annually. The strategic plan also serves as the planning horizon. Long-term goals and visions for the future are discussed in a strategic plan. A strategic plan should include a risk assessment.

**Tactical plan**   The tactical plan is a midterm plan developed to provide more details on accomplishing the goals set forth in the strategic plan. A tactical plan is typically useful for about a year and often prescribes and schedules the tasks necessary to accomplish organizational goals. Some examples of tactical plans include project plans, acquisition plans, hiring plans, budget plans, maintenance plans, support plans, and system development plans.

**Operational plan**   An operational plan is a short-term, highly detailed plan based on the strategic and tactical plans. It is valid or useful only for a short time. Operational plans must be updated often (such as monthly or quarterly) to retain compliance with tactical plans. Operational plans are detailed plans that spell out how to accomplish the various goals of the organization. They include resource allotments, budgetary requirements, staffing assignments, scheduling, and step-by-step or implementation procedures. Operational plans include details on how the implementation processes are in compliance with the organization's security policy. Examples of operational plans include training plans, system deployment plans, and product design plans.

Security is a continuous process. Thus, the activity of security management planning may have a definitive initiation point, but its tasks and work are never fully accomplished or complete. Effective security plans focus attention on specific and achievable objectives, anticipate change and potential problems, and serve as a basis for decision making for the entire organization. Security documentation should be concrete, well defined, and clearly stated. For a security plan to be effective, it must be developed, maintained, and actually used.

# Policies, Standards, Baselines, Guidelines, and Procedures

For most organizations, maintaining security is an essential part of ongoing business. If their security were seriously compromised, many organizations would fail. To reduce the likelihood of a security failure, the process of implementing security has been somewhat formalized. This formalization has greatly reduced the chaos and complexity of designing and implementing security solutions for IT infrastructures. The formalization of security solutions takes the form of a hierarchical organization of documentation. Each level focuses on a specific type or category of information and issues.

## Security Policies

The top tier of the formalization is known as a *security policy*. A security policy is a document that defines the scope of security needed by the organization and discusses the assets that need protection and the extent to which security solutions should go in order to provide the necessary protection. The security policy is an overview or generalization of an organization's security needs. It defines the main security objectives and outlines the security framework of an organization. The security policy also identifies the major functional areas of data processing and clarifies and defines all relevant terminology. It should clearly define why security is important and what assets are valuable. It is a strategic plan for implementing security. It should broadly outline the security goals and practices that should be employed to protect the organization's vital interests. The document discusses the importance of security to every aspect of daily business operation and the importance of the support of the senior staff for the implementation of security. The security policy is used to assign responsibilities, define roles, specify audit requirements, outline enforcement processes, indicate compliance requirements, and define acceptable risk levels. This document is often used as the proof that senior management has exercised due care in protecting itself against intrusion, attack, and disaster. Security policies are compulsory.

Many organizations employ several types of security policies to define or outline their overall security strategy. An organizational security policy focuses on issues relevant to every aspect of an organization. An issue-specific security policy focuses on a specific network service, department, function, or other aspect that is distinct from the organization as a whole. A system-specific security policy focuses on individual systems or types of systems and prescribes approved hardware and software, outlines methods for locking down a system, and even mandates firewall or other specific security controls.

In addition to these focused types of security policies, there are three overall categories of security policies: regulatory, advisory, and informative. A *regulatory* policy is required whenever industry or legal standards are applicable to your organization. This policy discusses the regulations that must be followed and outlines the procedures that should be used to elicit compliance. An *advisory* policy discusses behaviors and activities that are acceptable and defines consequences of violations. It explains the senior management's desires for security and compliance within an organization. Most policies are advisory. An *informative* policy is designed to provide information or knowledge about a specific subject, such as company goals, mission statements, or how the organization interacts with partners and customers. An informative policy provides support, research, or background information relevant to the specific elements of the overall policy.

From the security policies flow many other documents or subelements necessary for a complete security solution. Policies are broad overviews, whereas standards, baselines, guidelines, and procedures include more specific, detailed information on the actual security solution. Standards are the next level below security policies.

---

### Security Policies and Individuals

As a rule of thumb, security policies (as well as standards, guidelines, and procedures) should not address specific individuals. Instead of assigning tasks and responsibilities to a person, the policy should define tasks and responsibilities to fit a role. That role is a function of administrative control or personnel management. Thus, a security policy does not define who is to do what but rather defines what must be done by the various roles within the security infrastructure. Then these defined security roles are assigned to individuals as a job description or an assigned work task.

---

### Acceptable Use Policy

An *acceptable use policy* is a commonly produced document that exists as part of the overall security documentation infrastructure. The acceptable use policy is specifically designed to assign security roles within the organization as well as ensure the responsibilities tied to those roles. This policy defines a level of acceptable performance and expectation of behavior and activity. Failure to comply with the policy may result in job action warnings, penalties, or termination.

## Security Standards, Baselines, and Guidelines

Once the main security policies are set, then the remaining security documentation can be crafted under the guidance of those policies. Standards define compulsory requirements for the homogenous use of hardware, software, technology, and security controls. They provide a course of action by which technology and procedures are uniformly implemented throughout an organization. Standards are tactical documents that define steps or methods to accomplish the goals and overall direction defined by security policies.

At the next level are baselines. A baseline defines a minimum level of security that every system throughout the organization must meet. All systems not complying with the baseline should be taken out of production until they can be brought up to the baseline. The baseline establishes a common foundational secure state upon which all additional and more stringent security measures can be built. Baselines are usually system specific and often refer to an industry or government standard, like the Trusted Computer System Evaluation Criteria (TCSEC) or Information Technology Security Evaluation and Criteria (ITSEC). For example, most military organizations require that all systems support the TCSEC C2 security level at a minimum.

Guidelines are the next element of the formalized security policy structure. A guideline offers recommendations on how standards and baselines are implemented and serves as operational guides for both security professionals and users. Guidelines are flexible so they can be customized for each unique system or condition and can be used in the creation of new procedures. They state which security mechanisms should be deployed instead of prescribing a specific product or control and detailing configuration settings. They outline methodologies, include suggested actions, and are not compulsory.

## Security Procedures

Procedures are the final element of the formalized security policy structure. A procedure is a detailed, step-by-step how-to document that describes the exact actions necessary to implement a specific security mechanism, control, or solution. A procedure could discuss the entire system deployment operation or focus on a single product or aspect, such as deploying a firewall or updating virus definitions. In most cases, procedures are system and software specific. They must be updated as the hardware and software of a system evolve. The purpose of a procedure is to ensure the integrity of business processes. If everything is accomplished by following a detailed procedure, then all activities should be in compliance with policies, standards, and guidelines. Procedures help ensure standardization of security across all systems.

All too often, policies, standards, baselines, guidelines, and procedures are developed only as an afterthought at the urging of a consultant or auditor. If these documents are not used and updated, the administration of a secured environment will be unable to use them as guides. And without the planning, design, structure, and oversight provided by these documents, no environment will remain secure or represent proper diligent due care.

It is also common practice to develop a single document containing aspects of all these elements. This should be avoided. Each of these structures must exist as a separate entity because each performs a different specialized function. At the top of the formalization security policy documentation structure there are fewer documents because they contain general broad discussions of overview and goals. There are more documents further down the formalization structure (in other words, guidelines and procedures) because they contain details specific to a limited number of systems, networks, divisions, and areas.

Keeping these documents as separate entities provides several benefits:

- Not all users need to know the security standards, baselines, guidelines, and procedures for all security classification levels.

- When changes occur, it is easier to update and redistribute only the affected material rather than updating a monolithic policy and redistributing it throughout the organization.

Crafting the totality of security policy and all supporting documentation can be a daunting task. Many organizations struggle just to define the foundational parameters of their security, much less detail every single aspect of their day-to-day activities. However, in theory, a detailed and complete security policy supports real-world security in a directed, efficient, and specific manner. Once the security policy documentation is reasonably complete, it can be used to guide decisions, train new users, respond to problems, and predict trends for future expansion. A security policy should not be an afterthought but a key part of establishing an organization.

# Risk Management

Security is aimed at preventing loss or disclosure of data while sustaining authorized access. The possibility that something could happen to damage, destroy, or disclose data or other resource is known as *risk*.

Managing risk is therefore an element of sustaining a secure environment. Risk management is a detailed process of identifying factors that could damage or disclose data, evaluating those factors in light of data value and countermeasure cost, and implementing cost-effective solutions for mitigating or reducing risk. The overall process of risk management is used to develop and implement information security strategies. The goal of these strategies is to reduce risk and to support the mission of the organization.

The primary goal of risk management is to reduce risk to an acceptable level. What that level actually is depends upon the organization, the value of its assets, the size of its budget, and many other factors. What is deemed acceptable risk to one organization may be a completely unreasonably high level of risk to another. It is impossible to design and deploy a totally risk-free environment; however, significant risk reduction is possible, often with little effort. Risks to an IT infrastructure are not all computer based. In fact, many risks come from noncomputer sources. It is important to consider all possible risks when performing risk evaluation for an organization. Failing to properly evaluate and respond to all forms of risk, a company remains vulnerable. Keep in mind that IT security, commonly referred to as *logical* or *technical* security, can provide protection only against logical or technical attacks. To protect IT against physical attacks, physical protections must be erected.

The process by which the goals of risk management are achieved is known as *risk analysis*. It includes analyzing an environment for risks, evaluating each risk as to its likelihood of occurring and the cost of the damage it would cause if it did occur, assessing the cost of various countermeasures for each risk, and creating a cost/benefit report for safeguards to present to upper management. In addition to these risk-focused activities, risk management also requires evaluation, assessment, and the assignment of value for all assets within the organization. Without proper asset valuations, it is not possible to prioritize and compare risks with possible losses.

## Risk Terminology

Risk management employs a vast terminology that must be clearly understood, especially for the CISSP exam. This section defines and discusses all the important risk-related terminology:

**Asset**   An asset is anything within an environment that should be protected. It can be a computer file, a network service, a system resource, a process, a program, a product, an IT infrastructure, a database, a hardware device, furniture, product recipes/formulas, personnel, software, facilities, and so on. If an organization places any value on an item under its control and deems that item important enough to protect, it is labeled an asset for the purposes of risk management and analysis. The loss or disclosure of an asset could result in an overall security compromise, loss of productivity, reduction in profits, additional expenditures, discontinuation of the organization, and numerous intangible consequences.

**Asset valuation**   Asset valuation is a dollar value assigned to an asset based on actual cost and nonmonetary expenses. These can include costs to develop, maintain, administer, advertise, support, repair, and replace an asset; they can also include more elusive values, such as public confidence, industry support, productivity enhancement, knowledge equity, and ownership benefits. Asset valuation is discussed in detail later in this chapter.

**Threats**   Any potential occurrence that may cause an undesirable or unwanted outcome for an organization or for a specific asset is a threat. Threats are any action or inaction that could cause damage, destruction, alteration, loss, or disclosure of assets or that could block access to or prevent maintenance of assets. Threats can be large or small and result in large or small consequences. They can be intentional or accidental. They can originate from people, organizations, hardware, networks, structures, or nature. Threat agents intentionally exploit vulnerabilities. Threat agents are usually people, but they could also be programs, hardware, or systems. Threat events are accidental and intentional exploitations of vulnerabilities. Threat events can also be natural or manmade. Threat events include fire, earthquake, flood, system failure, human error (due to a lack of training or ignorance), and power outages.

**Vulnerability**   The weakness in an asset or the absence or the weakness of a safeguard or countermeasure is a vulnerability.

In other words, a vulnerability is a flaw, loophole, oversight, error, limitation, frailty, or susceptibility in the IT infrastructure or any other aspect of an organization. If a vulnerability is exploited, loss or damage to assets can occur.

**Exposure**   Exposure is being susceptible to asset loss because of a threat; there is the possibility that a vulnerability can or will be exploited by a threat agent or event. Exposure doesn't mean that a realized threat (an event that results in loss) is actually occurring (the exposure to a realized threat is called *experienced exposure*). It just means that if there is a vulnerability and a threat that can exploit it, there is the possibility that a threat event, or potential exposure, can occur.

**Risk**   Risk is the possibility or likelihood that a threat will exploit a vulnerability to cause harm to an asset. It is an assessment of probability, possibility, or chance. The more likely it is that a threat event will occur, the greater the risk. Every instance of exposure is a risk. When written as a formula, risk can be defined as risk = threat * vulnerability. Thus, reducing either the threat agent or the vulnerability directly results in a reduction in risk.

When a risk is realized, a threat agent or a threat event has taken advantage of a vulnerability and caused harm to or disclosure of one or more assets. The whole purpose of security is to prevent risks from becoming realized by removing vulnerabilities and blocking threat agents and threat events from jeopardizing assets. As a risk management tool, security is the implementation of safeguards.

**Safeguards**   A safeguard, or *countermeasure*, is anything that removes or reduces a vulnerability or protects against one or more specific threats. A safeguard can be installing a software patch, making a configuration change, hiring security guards, altering the infrastructure, modifying processes, improving the security policy, training personnel more effectively, electrifying a perimeter fence, installing lights, and so on. It is any action or product that reduces risk through the elimination or lessening of a threat or a vulnerability anywhere within an organization. Safeguards are the only means by which risk is mitigated or removed. It is important to remember that a safeguard, security control, or countermeasure need not be the purchase of a new product; reconfiguring existing elements or even removing elements from the infrastructure are also valid safeguards.

**Attack**   An attack is the exploitation of a vulnerability by a threat agent. In other words, an attack is any intentional attempt to exploit a vulnerability of an organization's security infrastructure to cause damage, loss, or disclosure of assets. An attack can also be viewed as any violation or failure to adhere to an organization's security policy.

**Breach**   A breach is the occurrence of a security mechanism being bypassed or thwarted by a threat agent. When a breach is combined with an attack, a penetration, or intrusion, can result. A penetration is the condition in which a threat agent has gained access to an organization's infrastructure through the circumvention of security controls and is able to directly imperil assets.

The elements asset, threat, vulnerability, exposure, risk, and safeguard are related, as shown in Figure 6.1. Threats exploit vulnerabilities, which results in exposure. Exposure is risk, and risk is mitigated by safeguards. Safeguards protect assets that are endangered by threats.

**FIGURE 6.1**  The elements of risk

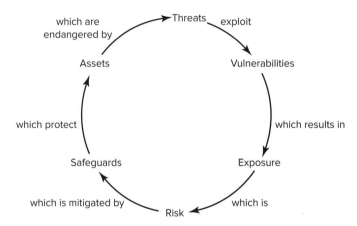

# Risk Assessment Methodologies

Risk management/analysis is primarily an exercise for upper management. It is their responsibility to initiate and support risk analysis and assessment by defining the scope and purpose of the endeavor. The actual processes of performing risk analysis are often delegated to security professionals or an evaluation team. However, all risk assessments, results, decisions, and outcomes must be understood and approved by upper management as an element in providing prudent due care.

All IT systems have risk. There is no way to eliminate 100 percent of all risks. Instead, upper management must decide which risks are acceptable and which are not. Determining which risks are acceptable requires detailed and complex asset and risk assessments.

## Risk Analysis

*Risk analysis* is performed to provide upper management with the details necessary to decide which risks should be mitigated, which should be transferred, and which should be accepted. The result is a cost/benefit comparison between the expected cost of asset loss and the cost of deploying safeguards against threats and vulnerabilities. Risk analysis identifies risks, quantifies the impact of threats, and aids in budgeting for security. Risk analysis helps integrate the needs and objectives of the security policy with the organization's business goals and intentions. The risk analysis/risk assessment is a "point in time" metric. Threats and vulnerabilities constantly change, and the risk assessment need to be redone periodically.

The first step in risk analysis is to appraise the value of an organization's assets. If an asset has no value, then there is no need to provide protection for it. A primary goal of risk analysis is to ensure that only cost-effective safeguards are deployed. It makes no sense to spend $100,000 protecting an asset that is worth only $1,000. The value of an asset directly affects and guides the level of safeguards and security deployed to protect it. As a rule, the annual costs of safeguards should not exceed the expected annual cost of asset loss.

## Asset Valuation

When the cost of an asset is evaluated, there are many aspects to consider. The goal of *asset evaluation* is to assign a specific dollar value to it that encompasses tangible costs as well as intangible ones. Determining an exact value is often difficult if not impossible, but nevertheless, a specific value must be established. (Note that the discussion of qualitative vs. quantitative risk analysis in the next section may clarify this issue.) Improperly assigning value to assets can result in failing to properly protect an asset or implementing financially infeasible safeguards. The following list includes some of the issues that contribute to the valuation of assets:

- Purchase cost

- Development cost

- Administrative or management cost

- Maintenance or upkeep cost

- Cost in acquiring asset

- Cost to protect or sustain asset

- Value to owners and users

- Value to competitors

- Intellectual property or equity value

- Market valuation (sustainable price)

- Replacement cost

- Productivity enhancement or degradation

- Operational costs of asset presence and loss

- Liability of asset loss

- Usefulness

Assigning or determining the value of assets to an organization can fulfill numerous requirements. It serves as the foundation for performing a cost/benefit analysis of asset protection through safeguard deployment. It serves as a means for selecting or evaluating safeguards and countermeasures. It provides values for insurance purposes and establishes an overall net worth or net value for the organization. It helps senior management understand exactly what is at risk within the organization. Understanding the value of assets also helps to prevent negligence of due care and encourages compliance with legal requirements, industry regulations, and internal security policies.

After asset valuation, threats must be identified and examined. This involves creating an exhaustive list of all possible threats for the organization and its IT infrastructure. The list should include threat agents as well as threat events. It is important to keep in mind that threats can come from anywhere. Threats to IT are not limited to IT sources. When compiling a list of threats, be sure to consider the following:

- Viruses
- Cascade errors and dependency faults
- Criminal activities by authorized users
- Movement (vibrations, jarring, etc.)
- Intentional attacks
- Reorganization
- Authorized user illness or epidemics
- Hackers
- User errors
- Natural disasters (earthquakes, floods, fire, volcanoes, hurricanes, tornadoes, tsunamis, and so on)
- Physical damage (crushing, projectiles, cable severing, and so on)
- Misuse of data, resources, or services
- Changes or compromises to data classification or security policies
- Government, political, or military intrusions or restrictions
- Processing errors, buffer overflows
- Personnel privilege abuse
- Temperature extremes
- Energy anomalies (static, EM pulses, radio frequencies [RFs], power loss, power surges, and so on)
- Loss of data
- Information warfare
- Bankruptcy or alteration/interruption of business activity
- Coding/programming errors
- Intruders (physical and logical)
- Environmental factors (presence of gases, liquids, organisms, and so on)
- Equipment failure
- Physical theft
- Social engineering

In most cases, a team rather than a single individual should perform risk assessment and analysis. Also, the team members should be from various departments within the organization. It is not usually a requirement that all team members be security professionals or even network/system administrators. The diversity of the team based on the demographics of the organization will help to exhaustively identify and address all possible threats and risks.

---

**The Consultant Calvary**

Risk assessment is a highly involved, detailed, complex, and lengthy process. Often risk analysis cannot be properly handled by existing employees because of the size, scope, or liability of the risk; thus, many organizations bring in risk management consultants to perform this work. This provides a high level of expertise, does not bog down employees, and can prove to be a more reliable measurement of real-world risk. But even risk management consultants do not perform risk assessment and analysis on paper only; they typically employ complex and expensive risk assessment software. This software streamlines the overall task, provides more reliable results, and produces standardized reports that are acceptable to insurance companies, boards of directors, and so on.

---

Once you develop a list of threats, you must individually evaluate each threat and its related risk. There are two risk assessment methodologies: quantitative and qualitative. *Quantitative* risk analysis assigns real dollar figures to the loss of an asset. *Qualitative* risk analysis assigns subjective and intangible values to the loss of an asset. Both methods are necessary for a complete risk analysis.

## Quantitative Risk Analysis

The quantitative method results in concrete probability percentages. That means it creates a report that has dollar figures for levels of risk, potential loss, cost of countermeasures, and value of safeguards. This report is usually fairly easy to understand, especially for anyone with knowledge of spreadsheets and budget reports. Think of quantitative analysis as the act of assigning a quantity to risk, in other words, placing a dollar figure on each asset and threat. However, a purely quantitative analysis is not possible; not all elements and aspects of the analysis can be quantified because some are qualitative, subjective, and some are intangible. The process of quantitative risk analysis starts with asset valuation and threat identification. Next, you estimate the potential and frequency of each risk. This information is then used to calculate various cost functions that are used to evaluate safeguards.

The six major steps or phases in quantitative risk analysis are as follows:

1. Inventory assets, and assign a value (AV).
2. Research each asset, and produce a list of all possible threats of each individual asset. For each listed threat, calculate the exposure factor (EF) and single loss expectancy (SLE).
3. Perform a threat analysis to calculate the likelihood of each threat being realized within a single year, that is, the annualized rate of occurrence (ARO).
4. Derive the overall loss potential per threat by calculating the annualized loss expectancy (ALE).

5.  Research countermeasures for each threat, and then calculate the changes to ARO and ALE based on an applied countermeasure.

6.  Perform a cost/benefit analysis of each countermeasure for each threat for each asset. Select the most appropriate response to each threat.

## Cost Functions

The cost functions associated with quantitative risk analysis include exposure factor, single loss expectancy, annualized rate of occurrence, and annualized loss expectancy:

**Exposure factor**   The EF represents the percentage of loss that an organization would experience if a specific asset were violated by a realized risk. The EF can also be called the *loss potential*. In most cases, a realized risk does not result in the total loss of an asset. The EF simply indicates the expected overall asset value loss because of a single realized risk. The EF is usually small for assets that are easily replaceable, such as hardware. It can be very large for assets that are irreplaceable or proprietary, such as product designs or a database of customers. The EF is expressed as a percentage.

**Single loss expectancy**   The EF is needed to calculate the SLE. The SLE is the cost associated with a single realized risk against a specific asset. It indicates the exact amount of loss an organization would experience if an asset were harmed by a specific threat occurring. The SLE is calculated using the formula SLE = asset value (AV) * exposure factor (EF) (or SLE = AV * EF). The SLE is expressed in a dollar value. For example, if an asset is valued at $200,000 and it has an EF of 45 percent for a specific threat, then the SLE of the threat for that asset is $90,000.

**Annualized rate of occurrence**   The ARO is the expected frequency with which a specific threat or risk will occur (that is, become realized) within a single year. The ARO can range from a value of 0.0 (zero), indicating that the threat or risk will never be realized, to a very large number, indicating the threat or risk occurs often. Calculating the ARO can be complicated. It can be derived from historical records, statistical analysis, or guesswork. ARO calculation is also known as *probability determination*. The ARO for some threats or risks is calculated by multiplying the likelihood of a single occurrence by the number of users who could initiate the threat. For example, the ARO of an earthquake in Tulsa may be .00001, whereas the ARO of an email virus in an office in Tulsa may be 10,000,000.

**Annualized loss expectancy**   The ALE is the possible yearly cost of all instances of a specific realized threat against a specific asset. The ALE is calculated using the formula ALE = single loss expectancy (SLE) * annualized rate of occurrence (ARO), or ALE = SLE * ARO. For example, if the SLE of an asset is $90,000 and the ARO for a specific threat (such as total power loss) is .5, then the ALE is $45,000. On the other hand, if the ARO for a specific threat (such as compromised user account) were 15, then the ALE would be $1,350,000.

## Threat/Risk Calculations

The task of calculating EF, SLE, ARO, and ALE for every asset and every threat/risk is a daunting one. Fortunately, quantitative risk assessment software tools can simplify and automate much of this process. These tools produce an asset inventory with valuations and then, using predefined AROs along with some customizing options (that is, industry, geography, IT components, and so on), produce risk analysis reports.

### Calculating Annualized Loss Expectancy with a Safeguard

In addition to determining the annual cost of the safeguard, you must calculate the ALE for the asset if the safeguard is implemented. This requires a new EF and ARO specific to the safeguard. In most cases, the EF to an asset remains the same even with an applied safeguard. The EF is the amount of loss incurred if the risk becomes realized. In other words, if the safeguard fails, how much damage does the asset receive? Think about it this way: If you have on body armor but the body armor fails to prevent a bullet from piercing your heart, you are still experiencing the same damage that would have occurred without the presence of the body armor. Thus, if the safeguard fails, the loss on the asset is usually the same as when there is no safeguard. However, some safeguards *do* reduce the resultant damage even when they fail to fully stop an attack. Body armor is usually this type of defense because it will absorb a significant amount of energy from a bullet and thus cause less damage to the body.

Even if the EF remains the same, a safeguard changes the ARO. In fact, the whole point of a safeguard is to reduce the ARO. In other words, a safeguard should reduce the number of times an attack is successful in causing damage to an asset. The best of all possible safeguards would reduce the ARO to zero. Although there are some perfect safeguards, most are not. Thus, many safeguards have an applied ARO that is smaller (you hope much smaller) than the nonsafeguarded ARO, but it is not often zero. With the new ARO (and possible new EF), a new ALE with safeguard application is computed.

With the pre-safeguard ALE and the post-safeguard ALE calculated, there is yet one more valued needed to perform a cost/benefit analysis. This additional value is the annual cost of the safeguard.

### Calculating Safeguard Costs

For each specific risk, you must evaluate one or more safeguards, or countermeasures, on a cost/benefit basis. To perform this evaluation, you must first compile a list of safeguards for each threat. Then you assign each safeguard a deployment value. In fact, you must measure the deployment value or the cost of the safeguard against the value of the protected asset. The value of the protected asset therefore determines the maximum expenditures for protection mechanisms. Security should be cost effective, and thus it is not prudent to spend more (in terms of cash or resources) protecting an asset than its value to the organization. If the cost of the countermeasure is greater than the value of the asset (that is, the cost of the risk), then you should accept the risk.

Numerous factors are involved in calculating the value of a countermeasure:

- Cost of purchase, development, and licensing
- Cost of implementation and customization
- Cost of annual operation, maintenance, administration, and so on
- Cost of annual repairs and upgrades
- Productivity improvement or loss
- Changes to environment
- Cost of testing and evaluation

Once you know the potential cost of a safeguard, it is then possible to evaluate the benefit of that safeguard if applied to an infrastructure. As mentioned earlier, the annual costs of safeguards should not exceed the expected annual cost of asset loss.

## Calculating Safeguard Cost/Benefit

One of the final computations in this process is the cost/benefit calculation to determine whether a safeguard actually improves security without costing too much. To make the determination of whether the safeguard is financially equitable, use the following formula:

ALE before safeguard – ALE after implementing the safeguard – annual cost of safeguard = value of the safeguard to the company

If the result is negative, the safeguard is not a financially responsible choice. If the result is positive, then that value is the annual savings your organization can reap by deploying the safeguard.

The annual savings or loss from a safeguard should not be the only consideration when evaluating safeguards. You should also consider the issues of legal responsibility and prudent due care. In some cases, it makes more sense to lose money in the deployment of a safeguard than to risk legal liability in the event of an asset disclosure or loss.

In review, to perform the cost/benefit analysis of a safeguard, you must calculate the following three elements:

- The pre-countermeasure ALE for an asset-and-threat pairing
- The post-countermeasure ALE for an asset-and-threat pairing
- The ACS

With those elements, you can finally obtain a value for the cost/benefit formula for this specific safeguard against a specific risk against a specific asset:

(pre-countermeasure ALE – post-countermeasure ALE) – ACS

Or, even more simply:

(ALE1 – ALE2) – ACS

The countermeasure with the greatest resulting value from this cost/benefit formula makes the most economic sense to deploy against the specific asset-and-threat pairing.

Table 6.1 illustrates the various formulas associated with quantitative risk analysis.

**TABLE 6.1**   Quantitative risk analysis formulas

| Concept | Formula |
| --- | --- |
| Exposure factor (EF) | % |
| Single loss expectancy (SLE) | SLE = AV * EF |
| Annualized rate of occurrence (ARO) | # / year |
| Annualized loss expectancy (ALE) | ALE = SLE * ARO<br>or<br>ALE = AV * EF * ARO |
| Annual cost of the safeguard (ACS) | $ / year |
| Value or benefit of a safeguard | (ALE1 – ALE2) – ACS |

### Yikes, So Much Math!

Yes, quantitative risk analysis involves a lot of math. If you have math questions on the exam, at least it will be basic multiplication. Most likely, you will be asked definition, application, and concept synthesis questions on the CISSP exam. This means you need to know the definition of the equations/formulas and values, what they mean, why they are important, and how they are used to benefit an organization. The concepts you must know are AV, EF, SLE, ARO, ALE, and the cost/benefit formula.

It is important to realize that with all the calculations used in the quantitative risk assessment process, the end values are used for prioritization and selection. The values themselves do not truly reflect real-world loss or costs due to security breaches. This should be obvious because of the level of guesswork, statistical analysis, and probability predictions required in the process.

Once you have calculated a cost/benefit for each safeguard for each risk that affects each asset, you must then sort these values. In most cases, the cost/benefit with the highest value is the best safeguard to implement for that specific risk against a specific asset. But as all things in the real world, this is only one part of the decision-making process. Although very important and often the primary guiding factor, it is not the sole element of data. Other items include actual cost, security budget, compatibility with existing systems, skill/knowledge base of IT staff, and availability of product as well as political issues, partnerships, market trends, fads, marketing, contracts, and favoritism. As part of senior management or even the IT staff, is it your responsibility to either obtain or use all available data and information to make the best security decision for your organization.

Most organizations have a limited and all-too-finite budget to work with. Thus, obtaining the best security for the cost is an essential part of security management. To effectively manage the security function, you must assess the budget, the benefit and performance metrics, and the necessary resources of each security control. Only after a thorough evaluation can you determine which controls are essential and beneficial not only to security, but also your bottom line.

## Qualitative Risk Analysis

Qualitative risk analysis is more scenario based than it is calculator based. Rather than assigning exact dollar figures to possible losses, you rank threats on a scale to evaluate their risks, costs, and effects. The process of performing qualitative risk analysis involves judgment, intuition, and experience. You can use many techniques to perform qualitative risk analysis:

- Brainstorming
- Delphi technique
- Storyboarding
- Focus groups
- Surveys
- Questionnaires
- Checklists
- One-on-one meetings
- Interviews

Determining which mechanism to employ is based on the culture of the organization and the types of risks and assets involved. It is common for several methods to be employed simultaneously and their results compared and contrasted in the final risk analysis report to upper management.

### Scenarios

The basic process for all these mechanisms involves the creation of scenarios. A *scenario* is a written description of a single major threat. The description focuses on how a threat would be instigated and what effects its occurrence could have on the organization, the IT infrastructure, and specific assets. Generally, the scenarios are limited to one page of text to keep them manageable. For each scenario, one or more safeguards that would completely or partially protect against the major threat discussed in the scenario are described. The analysis participants then assign a threat level to the scenario, a loss potential, and the advantages of each safeguard. These assignments can be grossly simple, such as using High, Medium, and Low or a basic number scale of 1 to 10, or they can be detailed essay responses. The responses from all participants are then compiled into a single report that is presented to upper management. For examples of reference ratings and levels, please see Tables 3-6 and 3-7 in NIST SP 800-30 (http://csrc.nist.gov/publications/nistpubs/800-30/sp800-30.pdf).

The usefulness and validity of a qualitative risk analysis improves as the number and diversity of the participants in the evaluation increases. Whenever possible, include one or more people from each level of the organizational hierarchy, from upper management to end user. It is also important to include a cross section from each major department, division, office, or branch.

## Delphi Technique

The *Delphi technique* is probably the only mechanism on this list that is not immediately recognizable and understood. The Delphi technique is simply an anonymous feedback-and-response process. Its primary purpose is to elicit honest and uninfluenced responses from all participants. The participants are usually gathered into a single meeting room. To each request for feedback, each participant writes down their response on paper anonymously. The results are compiled and presented to the group for evaluation. The process is repeated until a consensus is reached.

Both the quantitative and qualitative risk analysis mechanisms offer useful results. However, each technique involves a unique method of evaluating the same set of assets and risks. Prudent due care requires that both methods be employed. Table 6.2 describes the benefits and disadvantages of these two systems.

**TABLE 6.2**    Comparison of quantitative and qualitative risk analysis

| Characteristic | Qualitative | Quantitative |
|---|---|---|
| Employs complex functions | No | Yes |
| Uses cost/benefit analysis | No | Yes |
| Results in specific values | No | Yes |
| Requires guesswork | Yes | No |
| Supports automation | No | Yes |
| Involves a high volume of information | No | Yes |
| Is objective | No | Yes |
| Uses opinions | Yes | No |
| Requires significant time and effort | No | Yes |
| Offers useful and meaningful results | Yes | Yes |

# Handling Risk

The results of risk analysis are many:

- Complete and detailed valuation of all assets
- An exhaustive list of all threats and risks, rate of occurrence, and extent of loss if realized
- A list of threat-specific safeguards and countermeasures that identifies their effectiveness and ALE
- A cost/benefit analysis of each safeguard

This information is essential for management to make educated, intelligent decisions about safeguard implementation and security policy alterations.

Once the risk analysis is complete, management must address each specific risk. There are four possible responses to risk:

- Reduce or mitigate
- Assign or transfer
- Accept
- Reject or ignore

*Reducing risk*, or risk mitigation, is the implementation of safeguards and countermeasures to eliminate vulnerabilities or block threats. Picking the most cost-effective or beneficial countermeasure is part of risk management, but it is not an element of risk assessment. In fact, countermeasure selection is a post-risk-assessment or -risk-analysis activity. Another potential variation of risk mitigation is risk avoidance. The risk is avoided by eliminating the risk cause. A simple example is removing the FTP protocol from a server to avoid FTP attacks, and a larger example is to move to an inland location to avoid the risks from hurricanes.

*Assigning risk*, or transferring risk, is the placement of the cost of loss a risk represents onto another entity or organization. Purchasing insurance and outsourcing are common forms of assigning or transferring risk.

*Accepting risk* is the valuation by management of the cost/benefit analysis of possible safeguards and the determination that the cost of the countermeasure greatly outweighs the possible cost of loss due to a risk. It also means that management has agreed to accept the consequences and the loss if the risk is realized. In most cases, accepting risk requires a clearly written statement that indicates why a safeguard was not implemented, who is responsible for the decision, and who will be responsible for the loss if the risk is realized, usually in the form of a "sign-off" letter. An organization's decision to accept risk is based on its risk tolerance. Risk tolerance is the ability of an organization to absorb the losses associated with realized risks.

A final but unacceptable possible response to risk is to *reject risk* or ignore risk. Denying that a risk exists or hoping that it will never be realized are not valid prudent due-care responses to risk.

Once countermeasures are implemented, the risk that remains is known as *residual risk*. Residual risk comprises any threats to specific assets against which upper management chooses not to implement a safeguard. In other words, residual risk is the risk that management has chosen to accept rather than mitigate. In most cases, the presence of residual risk indicates that the cost/benefit analysis showed that the available safeguards were not cost-effective deterrents.

Total risk is the amount of risk an organization would face if no safeguards were implemented. A formula for total risk is threats * vulnerabilities * asset value = total risk. (Note that the * here does not imply multiplication, but a combination function; this is not a true mathematical formula.) The difference between total risk and residual risk is known as the *controls gap*. The controls gap is the amount of risk that is reduced by implementing safeguards. A formula for residual risk is total risk – controls gap = residual risk.

As with risk management in general, handling risk is not a one-time process. Instead, security must be continually maintained and reaffirmed. In fact, repeating the risk assessment and analysis process is a mechanism to assess the completeness and effectiveness of the security program over time. Additionally, it helps locate deficiencies and areas where change has occurred. Because security changes over time, reassessing on a periodic basis is essential to maintaining reasonable security.

Selecting a countermeasure within the realm of risk management relies heavily on the cost/benefit analysis results. However, you should consider several other factors:

- The cost of the countermeasure should be less than the value of asset.

- The cost of the countermeasure should be less than the benefit of the countermeasure.

- The result of the applied countermeasure should make the cost of an attack greater for the perpetrator than the derived benefit from an attack.

- The countermeasure should provide a solution to a real and identified problem. (Don't install countermeasures just because they are available, are advertised, or sound cool.)

- The benefit of the countermeasure should not be dependent upon its secrecy. This means that "security through obscurity" is not a viable countermeasure and that any viable countermeasure can withstand public disclosure and scrutiny.

- The benefit of the countermeasure should be testable and verifiable.

- The countermeasure should provide consistent and uniform protection across all users, systems, protocols, and so on.

- The countermeasure should have few or no dependencies to reduce cascade failures.

- The countermeasure should require minimal human intervention after initial deployment and configuration.

- The countermeasure should be tamperproof.

- The countermeasure should have overrides accessible to privileged operators only.

- The countermeasure should provide fail-safe and/or fail-secure options.

# Security Awareness Training

The successful implementation of a security solution requires changes in user behavior. These changes primarily consist of alterations in normal work activities to comply with the standards, guidelines, and procedures mandated by the security policy. Behavior modification involves some level of learning on the part of the user. There are three commonly recognized learning levels: awareness, training, and education.

A prerequisite to actual security training is *awareness*. The goal of creating awareness is to bring security into the forefront and make it a recognized entity for users. Awareness establishes a common baseline or foundation of security understanding across the entire organization. Awareness is not exclusively created through a classroom type of exercise but also through the work environment. There are many tools that can be used to create awareness, such as posters, notices, newsletter articles, screen savers, T-shirts, rally speeches by managers, announcements, presentations, mouse pads, office supplies, and memos as well as the traditional instructor-led training courses. Awareness focuses on key or basic topics and issues related to security that all employees, no matter which position or classification they have, must understand and comprehend.

Awareness is a tool to establish a minimum standard common denominator or foundation of security understanding. All personnel should be fully aware of their security responsibilities and liabilities. They should be trained to know what to do and what not to do.

The issues that users need to be aware of include avoiding waste, fraud, and unauthorized activities. All members of an organization, from senior management to temporary interns, need the same level of awareness. The awareness program in an organization should be tied in with its security policy, incident-handling plan, and disaster recovery procedures. For an awareness-building program to be effective, it must be fresh, creative, and updated often. The awareness program should also be tied to an understanding of how the corporate culture will affect and impact security for individuals as well as the organization as a whole. If employees do not see enforcement of security policies and standards, especially at the awareness level, then they may not feel obligated to abide by them.

*Training* is teaching employees to perform their work tasks and to comply with the security policy. All new employees require some level of training so they will be able to comply with all standards, guidelines, and procedures mandated by the security policy. New users need to know how to use the IT infrastructure, where data is stored, and how and why resources are classified. Many organizations choose to train new employees before they are granted access to the network, whereas others will grant new users limited access until their training in their specific job position is complete. Training is an ongoing activity that must be sustained throughout the lifetime of the organization for every employee. It is considered an administrative security control.

Awareness and training are often provided in-house. That means these teaching tools are created and deployed by and within the organization itself. However, the next level of knowledge distribution is usually obtained from an external third-party source.

*Education* is a more detailed endeavor in which students/users learn much more than they actually need to know to perform their work tasks. Education is most often associated with users pursuing certification or seeking job promotion. It is typically a requirement for personnel seeking security professional positions. A security professional requires extensive knowledge of security and the local environment for the entire organization and not just their specific work tasks.

# Summary

When planning a security solution, it's important to consider how humans are the weakest element. Regardless of the physical or logical controls deployed, humans can discover ways to avoid them, circumvent or subvert them, or disable them. Thus, it is important to take users into account when designing and deploying security solutions for your environment. The aspects of secure hiring practices, roles, policies, standards, guidelines, procedures, risk management, awareness training, and management planning all contribute to protecting assets. The use of these security structures provides some protection from the threat humans present against your security solutions.

Secure hiring practices require detailed job descriptions. Job descriptions are used as a guide for selecting candidates and properly evaluating them for a position. Maintaining security through job descriptions includes the use of separation of duties, job responsibilities, and job rotation.

A termination policy is needed to protect an organization and its existing employees. The termination procedure should include witnesses, return of company property, disabling of network access, an exit interview, and an escort from the property.

Security roles determine who is responsible for the security of an organization's assets. Those assigned the senior management role are ultimately responsible and liable for any asset loss, and they are the ones who define security policy. Security professionals are responsible for implementing security policy, and users are responsible for complying with the security policy. The person assigned the data owner role is responsible for classifying information, and a data custodian is responsible for maintaining the secure environment and backing up data. An auditor is responsible for making sure a secure environment is properly protecting assets.

A formalized security policy structure consists of policies, standards, baselines, guidelines, and procedures. These individual documents are essential elements to the design and implementation of security in any environment.

The process of identifying, evaluating, and preventing or reducing risks is known as risk management. The primary goal of risk management is to reduce risk to an acceptable level. Determining this level depends upon the organization, the value of its assets, and the size of its budget. Although it is impossible to design and deploy a completely risk-free environment, it is possible to significantly reduce risk with little effort. Risk analysis is the process by which risk management is achieved and includes analyzing an environment for risks, evaluating each risk as to its likelihood of occurring and the cost of the resulting damage, assessing the cost of various countermeasures for each risk, and creating a cost/benefit report for safeguards to present to upper management.

To successfully implement a security solution, user behavior must change. Such changes primarily consist of alterations in normal work activities to comply with the standards, guidelines, and procedures mandated by the security policy. Behavior modification involves some level of learning on the part of the user. There are three commonly recognized learning levels: awareness, training, and education.

An important aspect of security management planning is the proper implementation of a security policy. To be effective, the approach to security management must be a top-down approach. The responsibility of initiating and defining a security policy lies with upper or senior management. Security policies provide direction for the lower levels of the organization's hierarchy. Middle management is responsible for fleshing out the security policy into standards, baselines, guidelines, and procedures. It is the responsibility of the operational managers or security professionals to implement the configurations prescribed in the security management documentation. Finally, the end users' responsibility is to comply with all security policies of the organization.

Security management planning includes defining security roles, developing security policies, performing risk analysis, and requiring security education for employees. These responsibilities are guided by the developments of management plans. The security management team should develop strategic, tactical, and operational plans.

# Exam Essentials

**Understand the security implications of hiring new employees.**   To properly plan for security, you must have standards in place for job descriptions, job classification, work tasks, job responsibilities, preventing collusion, candidate screening, background checks, security clearances, employment agreements, and nondisclosure agreements. By deploying such mechanisms, you ensure that new hires are aware of the required security standards, thus protecting your organization's assets.

**Be able to explain separation of duties.**   Separation of duties is the security concept of dividing critical, significant, sensitive work tasks among several individuals. By separating duties in this manner, you ensure that no one person can compromise system security.

**Understand the principle of least privilege.**   The principle of least privilege states that, in a secured environment, users should be granted the minimum amount of access necessary for them to complete their required work tasks or job responsibilities. By limiting user access only to those items that they need to complete their work tasks, you limit the vulnerability of sensitive information.

**Know why job rotation and mandatory vacations are necessary.**   Job rotation serves two functions. It provides a type of knowledge redundancy, and moving personnel around reduces the risk of fraud, data modification, theft, sabotage, and misuse of information. Mandatory vacations of one to two weeks are used to audit and verify the work tasks and privileges of employees. This often results in easy detection of abuse, fraud, or negligence.

**Be able to explain proper termination policies.**   A termination policy defines the procedure for terminating employees. It should include items such as always having a witness, disabling the employee's network access, and performing an exit interview. A termination policy should also include escorting the terminated employee off the premises and requiring the return of security tokens and badges and company property.

**Understand key security roles.**   The primary security roles are senior manager, organizational owner, upper management, security professional, user, data owner, data custodian, and auditor. By creating a security role hierarchy, you limit risk overall.

**Understand security management planning.**   Security management is based on three types of plans: strategic, tactical, and operational. A strategic plan is a long-term plan that is fairly stable. It defines the organization's goals, mission, and objectives. The tactical plan is a midterm plan developed to provide more details on accomplishing the goals set forth in the strategic plan. Operational plans are short-term and highly detailed plans based on the strategic and tactical plans.

**Know the elements of a formalized security policy structure.**   To create a comprehensive security plan, you need the following items in place: security policy, standards, baselines, guidelines, and procedures. Such documentation clearly states security requirements and creates due diligence on the part of the responsible parties.

**Be able to define overall risk management.**   The process of identifying factors that could damage or disclose data, evaluating those factors in light of data value and countermeasure cost, and implementing cost-effective solutions for mitigating or reducing risk is known as risk management. By performing risk management, you lay the foundation for reducing risk overall.

**Understand risk analysis and the key elements involved.**   Risk analysis is the process by which upper management is provided with details to make decisions about which risks are to be mitigated, which should be transferred, and which should be accepted. To fully evaluate risks and subsequently take the proper precautions, you must analyze the following: assets, asset valuation, threats, vulnerability, exposure, risk, realized risk, safeguards, countermeasures, attacks, and breaches.

**Know how to evaluate threats.**   Threats can originate from numerous sources, including IT, humans, and nature. Threat assessment should be performed as a team effort to provide the widest range of perspective. By fully evaluating risks from all angles, you reduce your system's vulnerability.

**Understand quantitative risk analysis.**   Quantitative risk analysis focuses on hard values and percentages. A complete quantitative analysis is not possible because of intangible aspects of risk. The process involves asset valuation and threat identification and then determining a threat's potential frequency and the resulting damage; the result is a cost/benefit analysis of safeguards.

**Be able to explain the concept of an exposure factor (EF).**   An exposure factor is an element of quantitative risk analysis that represents the percentage of loss that an organization would experience if a specific asset were violated by a realized risk. By calculating exposure factors, you are able to implement a sound risk management policy.

**Know what single loss expectancy (SLE) is and how to calculate it.**   SLE is an element of quantitative risk analysis that represents the cost associated with a single realized risk against a specific asset. The formula is SLE = asset value (AV) * exposure factor (EF).

**Understand annualized rate of occurrence (ARO).**   ARO is an element of quantitative risk analysis that represents the expected frequency with which a specific threat or risk will occur (in other words, become realized) within a single year. Understanding AROs further enables you to calculate the risk and take proper precautions.

**Know what annualized loss expectancy (ALE) is and how to calculate it.**   ALE is an element of quantitative risk analysis that represents the possible yearly cost of all instances of a specific realized threat against a specific asset. The formula is ALE = single loss expectancy (SLE) * annualized rate of occurrence (ARO).

**Know the formula for safeguard evaluation.**   In addition to determining the annual cost of a safeguard, you must calculate the ALE for the asset if the safeguard is implemented. To do so, use the formula ALE before safeguard – ALE after implementing the safeguard – annual cost of safeguard = value of the safeguard to the company [(ALE1 – ALE2) – ACS].

**Understand qualitative risk analysis.**   Qualitative risk analysis is based more on scenarios than calculations. Exact dollar figures are not assigned to possible losses; instead, threats are ranked on a scale to evaluate their risks, costs, and effects. Such an analysis assists those responsible in creating proper risk management policies.

**Understand the Delphi technique.**   The Delphi technique is simply an anonymous feedback-and-response process used to arrive at a consensus. Such a consensus gives the responsible parties the opportunity to properly evaluate risks and implement solutions.

**Know the options for handling risk.**   Reducing risk, or risk mitigation, is the implementation of safeguards and countermeasures. Assigning risk or transferring a risk places the cost of loss a risk represents onto another entity or organization. Purchasing insurance is one form of assigning or transferring risk. Accepting risk means the management has evaluated the cost/benefit analysis of possible safeguards and has determined that the cost of the countermeasure greatly outweighs the possible cost of loss due to a risk. It also means that management has agreed to accept the consequences and the loss if the risk is realized.

**Be able to explain total risk, residual risk, and controls gap.**   Total risk is the amount of risk an organization would face if no safeguards were implemented. To calculate total risk, use the formula threats * vulnerabilities * asset value = total risk. Residual risk is the risk that management has chosen to accept rather than mitigate. The difference between total risk and residual risk is the controls gap, which is the amount of risk that is reduced by implementing safeguards. To calculate residual risk, use the following formula: total risk – controls gap = residual risk.

**Know how to implement security awareness training.** Before actual training can take place, awareness of security as a recognized entity must be created for users. Once this is accomplished, training, or teaching employees to perform their work tasks and to comply with the security policy, can begin. All new employees require some level of training so they will be able to comply with all standards, guidelines, and procedures mandated by the security policy. Education is a more detailed endeavor in which students/users learn much more than they actually need to know to perform their work tasks. Education is most often associated with users pursuing certification or seeking job promotion.

# Written Lab

1. Name six different administrative controls used to secure personnel.

2. Name the six primary security roles as defined by ISC2 for CISSP.

3. What are the four components of a complete organizational security policy and their basic purpose?

4. What are the basic formulas used in quantitative risk assessment?

# Answers to Written Lab

1.  Possible answers include job descriptions, principle of least privilege, separation of duties, job responsibilities, job rotation/cross-training, performance reviews, background checks, job action warnings, awareness training, job training, exit interviews/terminations, nondisclosure agreements, noncompete agreements, employment agreement, privacy declaration, and acceptable use policies.

2.  The six security roles are senior management, IT/security staff, owner, custodian, operator/user, and auditor.

3.  The four components of a security policy are policies, standards, guidelines, and procedures. Policies are broad security statements. Standards are definitions of hardware and software security compliance. Guidelines are used when there is not an appropriate procedure. Procedures are detailed step-by-step instructions for performing work tasks in a secure manner.

4.  $SLE = AV * EF$. $ARO = \# / yr$. $ALE = SLE * ARO$. Cost/benefit $= (ALE1 - ALE2) - ACS$.

# Review Questions

1. Which of the following is the weakest element in any security solution?

    **A.** Software products

    **B.** Internet connections

    **C.** Security policies

    **D.** Humans

2. When seeking to hire new employees, what is the first step?

    **A.** Create a job description.

    **B.** Set position classification.

    **C.** Screen candidates.

    **D.** Request résumés.

3. What is the primary purpose of an exit interview?

    **A.** To return the exiting employee's personal belongings

    **B.** To review the nondisclosure agreement

    **C.** To evaluate the exiting employee's performance

    **D.** To cancel the exiting employee's network access accounts

4. When an employee is to be terminated, which of the following should be done?

    **A.** Inform the employee a few hours before they are officially terminated.

    **B.** Disable the employee's network access just as they are informed of the termination.

    **C.** Send out a broadcast email informing everyone that a specific employee is to be terminated.

    **D.** Wait until you and the employee are the only people remaining in the building before announcing the termination.

5. Who is liable for failing to perform prudent due care?

    **A.** Security professionals

    **B.** Data custodian

    **C.** Auditor

    **D.** Senior management

**6.** Which of the following is a document that defines the scope of security needed by an organization, lists the assets that need protection, and discusses the extent to which security solutions should go to provide the necessary protection?

 **A.** Security policy

 **B.** Standard

 **C.** Guideline

 **D.** Procedure

**7.** Which of the following policies is required when industry or legal standards are applicable to your organization?

 **A.** Advisory

 **B.** Regulatory

 **C.** Baseline

 **D.** Informative

**8.** Which of the following is not an element of the risk analysis process?

 **A.** Analyzing an environment for risks

 **B.** Creating a cost/benefit report for safeguards to present to upper management

 **C.** Selecting appropriate safeguards and implementing them

 **D.** Evaluating each risk as to its likelihood of occurring and cost of the resulting damage

**9.** Which of the following would not be considered an asset in a risk analysis?

 **A.** A development process

 **B.** An IT infrastructure

 **C.** A proprietary system resource

 **D.** Users' personal files

**10.** Which of the following represents accidental or intentional exploitations of vulnerabilities?

 **A.** Threat events

 **B.** Risks

 **C.** Threat agents

 **D.** Breaches

**11.** When a safeguard or a countermeasure is not present or is not sufficient, what remains?

 **A.** Vulnerability

 **B.** Exposure

 **C.** Risk

 **D.** Penetration

12. Which of the following is not a valid definition for risk?

   **A.** An assessment of probability, possibility, or chance

   **B.** Anything that removes a vulnerability or protects against one or more specific threats

   **C.** Risk = threat * vulnerability

   **D.** Every instance of exposure

13. When evaluating safeguards, what is the rule that should be followed in most cases?

   **A.** The expected annual cost of asset loss should not exceed the annual costs of safeguards.

   **B.** The annual costs of safeguards should equal the value of the asset.

   **C.** The annual costs of safeguards should not exceed the expected annual cost of asset loss.

   **D.** The annual costs of safeguards should not exceed 10 percent of the security budget.

14. How is single loss expectancy (SLE) calculated?

   **A.** Threat + vulnerability

   **B.** Asset value ($) * exposure factor

   **C.** Annualized rate of occurrence * vulnerability

   **D.** Annualized rate of occurrence * asset value * exposure factor

15. How is the value of a safeguard to a company calculated?

   **A.** ALE before safeguard – ALE after implementing the safeguard – annual cost of safeguard

   **B.** ALE before safeguard * ARO of safeguard

   **C.** ALE after implementing safeguard + annual cost of safeguard – controls gap

   **D.** Total risk – controls gap

16. What security control is directly focused on preventing collusion?

   **A.** Principle of least privilege

   **B.** Job descriptions

   **C.** Separation of duties

   **D.** Qualitative risk analysis

17. Which security role is responsible for assigning the sensitivity label to objects?

   **A.** Users

   **B.** Data owner

   **C.** Senior management

   **D.** Data custodian

**18.** When you are attempting to install a new security mechanism and there is not a detailed step-by-step guide on how to implement that specific product, which element of the security policy should you turn to?

   **A.** Policies

   **B.** Procedures

   **C.** Standards

   **D.** Guidelines

**19.** While performing a risk analysis, you identify a threat of fire and a vulnerability because there are no fire extinguishers. Based on this information, which of the following is a possible risk?

   **A.** Virus infection

   **B.** Damage to equipment

   **C.** System malfunction

   **D.** Unauthorized access to confidential information

**20.** You've performed a basic quantitative risk analysis on a specific threat/vulnerability/risk relation. You select a possible countermeasure. When performing the calculations again, which of the following factors will change?

   **A.** Exposure factor

   **B.** Single loss expectancy

   **C.** Asset value

   **D.** Annualized rate of occurrence

# Answers to Review Questions

1. D. Regardless of the specifics of a security solution, humans are the weakest element.

2. A. The first step in hiring new employees is to create a job description. Without a job description, there is no consensus on what type of individual needs to be found and hired.

3. B. The primary purpose of an exit interview is to review the nondisclosure agreement (NDA).

4. B. You should remove or disable the employee's network user account immediately before or at the same time they are informed of their termination.

5. D. Senior management is liable for failing to perform prudent due care.

6. A. The document that defines the scope of an organization's security requirements is a security policy. The policy lists the assets to be protected and discusses the extent to which security solutions should go to provide the necessary protection.

7. B. A regulatory policy is required when industry or legal standards are applicable to your organization. This policy discusses the rules that must be followed and outlines the procedures that should be used to elicit compliance.

8. C. Risk analysis includes analyzing an environment for risks, evaluating each risk as to its likelihood of occurring and the cost of the damage it would cause, assessing the cost of various countermeasures for each risk, and creating a cost/benefit report for safeguards to present to upper management. Selecting safeguards is a task of upper management based on the results of risk analysis. It is a task that falls under risk management, but it is not part of the risk analysis process.

9. D. The personal files of users are not assets of the organization and thus not considered in a risk analysis.

10. A. Threat events are accidental or intentional exploitations of vulnerabilities.

11. A. A vulnerability is the absence or weakness of a safeguard or countermeasure.

12. B. Anything that removes a vulnerability or protects against one or more specific threats is considered a safeguard or a countermeasure, not a risk.

13. C. The annual costs of safeguards should not exceed the expected annual cost of asset loss.

14. B. SLE is calculated using the formula SLE = asset value ($) * exposure factor (SLE = AV * EF).

15. A. The value of a safeguard to an organization is calculated by ALE before safeguard – ALE after implementing the safeguard – annual cost of safeguard [(ALE1 – ALE2) – ACS].

16. C. The likelihood that a co-worker will be willing to collaborate on an illegal or abusive scheme is reduced because of the higher risk of detection created by the combination of separation of duties, restricted job responsibilities, and job rotation.

**17.**  B.  The data owner is responsible for assigning the sensitivity label to new objects and resources.

**18.**  D.  If no detailed step-by-step instructions or procedures exist, then turn to the guidelines for general principles to follow for the installation.

**19.**  B.  The threat of a fire and the vulnerability of a lack of fire extinguishers lead to the risk of damage to equipment.

**20.**  D.  A countermeasure directly affects the annualized rate of occurrence, primarily because the countermeasure is designed to prevent the occurrence of the risk, thus reducing its frequency per year.

# Chapter 7

# Data and Application Security Issues

---

## THE CISSP EXAM TOPICS COVERED IN THIS CHAPTER INCLUDE:

✓ **Application Development Security**

- Understand and apply security in the system life cycle

  - Systems Development Life Cycle (SDLC); maturity models; operation and maintenance; change management

- Understand the application environment and security controls

  - Security of the application environment; security issues of programming languages; security issues in source code (e.g., buffer overflow); configuration management

- Assess the effectiveness of application security

  - Auditing and logging; Corrective actions

✓ **Operations Security**

- Understand configuration management concepts (e.g., versioning, baselining)

All too often, security administrators are unaware of system vulnerabilities caused by applications with security flaws (either intentional or unintentional). Security professionals often have a background in system administration and don't have an in-depth understanding of the application development process and therefore of application security. This can be a critical oversight. As you will learn in Chapter 14, "Auditing and Monitoring," organization insiders (in other words, employees, contractors, and trusted visitors) are the most likely candidates to commit computer crimes. Security administrators must be aware of all threats to ensure that adequate checks and balances exist to protect against a malicious insider or application vulnerability.

In this chapter, we examine some of the common threats that applications pose to both traditional and distributed computing environments. Next, we explore how to protect data. Finally, we take a look at some of the systems development controls that can help ensure the accuracy, reliability, and integrity of internal application development processes.

# Application Issues

As technology marches on, application environments are becoming much more complex than they were in the days of simple stand-alone DOS systems running precompiled code. To understand the application environment and security controls, you need to evaluate the variety of different situations that software will encounter. Organizations are now faced with challenges that arise from connecting their systems to networks of all shapes and sizes (from the office LAN to the global Internet) as well as from distributed computing environments. These challenges come in the form of malicious code, denial-of-service attacks, application attacks, and other security risks. In the following sections, we'll take a brief look at a few of these issues.

## Local/Nondistributed Environment

In a traditional, nondistributed computing environment, individual computer systems store and execute programs to perform functions for the local user. These functions generally involve networked applications that provide access to remote resources, such as web servers and remote file servers, as well as perform other interactive networked activities, such as the transmission and reception of electronic mail. The key characteristic of a nondistributed system is that all user-executed code is stored on the local machine (or on a file system accessible to that machine, such as a file server on the machine's LAN) and executed using processors on that machine.

The threats that face local/nondistributed computing environments are some of the more common malicious code objects that you are most likely already familiar with, at least in passing. The following sections contain brief descriptions of those objects from an application security standpoint. We cover them in greater detail in Chapter 8, "Malicious Code and Application Attacks."

## Viruses

*Viruses* are the oldest form of malicious code objects that plague cyberspace. Once they are in a system, they attach themselves to legitimate operating system and user files and applications and usually perform some sort of undesirable action, ranging from the somewhat innocuous display of an annoying message on the screen to the more malicious destruction of the entire local file system.

Before the advent of networked computing, viruses spread from system to system through infected media. For example, suppose a user's hard drive is infected with a virus. That user might then format a floppy disk and inadvertently transfer the virus to it along with some data files. When the user inserts the disk into another system and reads the data, that system would also become infected with the virus. The virus might then get spread to several other users, who go on to share it with even more users in an exponential fashion.

 **WARNING**    Macro viruses were among the most insidious viruses out there. They're extremely easy to write and took advantage of some of the advanced features of modern productivity applications to significantly broaden their reach. Today, office applications are set by default to disable the use of macros that haven't been digitally signed by a trusted author.

In this day and age, more and more computers are connected to some type of network and have at least an indirect connection to the Internet. This greatly increases the number of mechanisms that can transport viruses from system to system and expands the potential magnitude of these infections to epidemic proportions. After all, an email macro virus that can automatically propagate itself to every contact in your address book can inflict far more widespread damage than a boot sector virus that requires the sharing of physical storage media to transmit infection. The majority of viruses today are designed to create large botnets. While they historically were designed to cause damage to the infected machine, and many still do this today, most viruses lie hidden as zombies or clones waiting for direction from the botnet controllers. These topics are covered in more detail in Chapter 8.

## Trojan Horses

During the Trojan War, the Greek military used a false horse filled with soldiers to gain access to the fortified city of Troy. The Trojans fell prey to this deception because they believed the horse to be a generous gift and were unaware of its insidious cargo. Modern computer users face a similar threat from today's electronic version of the Trojan horse. A *Trojan horse* is a malicious code object that appears to be a benevolent program—such as a game or simple utility. When a user executes the application, it performs the "cover" functions, as advertised; however, electronic Trojan horses also carry a secret payload. While the computer user is using the cover program, the Trojan horse performs some sort of malicious action—such as opening a security hole in the system for hackers to exploit, tampering with data, or installing keystroke-monitoring software.

## Logic Bombs

*Logic bombs* are malicious code objects that lie dormant until events occur that satisfy one or more logical conditions. At that time, they spring into action, delivering their malicious payload to unsuspecting computer users. They are often planted by disgruntled employees or other individuals who want to harm an organization but for one reason or another want to delay the malicious activity for a period. Many simple logic bombs operate based solely upon the system date or time. For example, an employee who was terminated might set a logic bomb to destroy critical business data on the first anniversary of their termination. Other logic bombs operate using more complex criteria. For example, a programmer who fears termination might plant a logic bomb that alters payroll information after the programmer's account is locked out of the system.

## Worms

*Worms* are an interesting type of malicious code that greatly resemble viruses, with one major distinction. Like viruses, worms spread from system to system bearing some type of malicious payload. However, whereas viruses require some type of user action to propagate, worms are self-replicating. They remain resident in memory and exploit one or more networking vulnerabilities to spread from system to system under their own power. Obviously, this allows for much greater propagation and can result in a denial-of-service attack against entire networks. Indeed, the famous Internet Worm launched by Robert Tappan Morris in November 1988 (we present the technical details of this worm in Chapter 8) actually crippled the entire Internet for several days.

# Distributed Environment

The previous sections discussed how the advent of networked computing facilitated the rapid spread of malicious code objects between computing systems. The following sections examine how distributed computing (an offshoot of networked computing) introduces a variety of new malicious code threats that information system security practitioners must understand and protect their systems against.

Essentially, distributed computing allows a single user to harness the computing power of one or more remote systems to achieve a single goal. A common example of this is the client/server interaction that takes place when a computer user browses the World

Wide Web. The client uses a web browser, such as Microsoft Internet Explorer or Mozilla Firefox, to request information from a remote server. The remote server's web hosting software then receives and processes the request. In many cases, the web server fulfills the request by retrieving an HTML file from the local file system and transmitting it to the remote client. In the case of dynamically generated web pages, that request might involve generating custom content tailored to the needs of the individual user (real-time account information is a good example of this). In effect, the web user is causing remote server(s) to perform actions on their behalf.

## Agents

*Agents* (also known as *bots*) are intelligent code objects that perform actions on behalf of a user. Agents typically take initial instructions from the user and then carry on their activity in an unattended manner for a predetermined period of time, until certain conditions are met, or for an indefinite period.

The most common type of intelligent agent in use today is the *web bot*. These agents continuously crawl a variety of websites retrieving and processing data on behalf of the user. For example, a user interested in finding a low airfare between two cities might use an intelligent agent to scour a variety of airline and travel websites and continuously check fare prices. Whenever the agent detects a fare lower than previous fares, it might send the user an email message, text message, or other notification of the cheaper travel opportunity. More adventurous bot programmers might even provide the agent with credit card information and instruct it to actually order a ticket when the fare reaches a certain level.

 **Real World Scenario**

### Stop Orders as User Agents

If you invest in the stock market, you're probably familiar with another type of user agent: stop orders. These allow investors to place predefined orders instructing their broker (or, more realistically, their broker's computer system) to make trades on the investor's behalf when certain conditions occur.

Stop orders may be used to limit an investor's loss on a stock. Suppose you buy shares of Acme Corporation at $30 and wish to ensure that you don't lose more than 50 percent of your initial investment. You might place a stop loss order at $15, which instructs your broker to sell your stock at the current market price if the share price ever falls below $15.

Similarly, you can use stop orders to lock in profits. In the previous example, the investor might target a 20 percent profit by placing a stop order to execute whenever the stock price exceeds $36.

The popularity of online auctions has created another market for intelligent agents: auction *sniping*. Agents using this strategy log into an auction website seconds before an auction closes to place a last-minute bid on behalf of a buyer. Buyers use sniping in an attempt to ward off last-minute bidding wars.

Although agents can be useful computing objects, they also introduce a variety of new security concerns that must be addressed. For example, what if a hacker programs an agent to continuously probe a network for security holes and report vulnerable systems in real time? How about a malicious individual who uses a number of agents to flood a website with bogus requests, thereby mounting a denial-of-service attack against that site? Or perhaps a commercially available agent accepts credit card information from a user and then transmits it to a hacker at the same time that it places a legitimate purchase.

## Applets

Recall that agents are code objects sent from a user's system to query and process data stored on remote systems. *Applets* perform the opposite function; these code objects are sent from a server to a client to perform some action. In fact, applets are actually self-contained miniature programs that execute independently of the server that sent them.

Imagine a web server that offers a variety of financial tools to web users. One of these tools might be a mortgage calculator that processes a user's financial information and provides a monthly mortgage payment based upon the loan's principal and term and the borrower's credit information. Instead of processing this data and returning the results to the client system, the remote web server might send to the local system an applet that enables it to perform those calculations itself. This provides a number of benefits to both the remote server and the end user:

- The processing burden is shifted to the client, freeing up resources on the web server to process requests from more users.

- The client is able to produce data using local resources rather than waiting for a response from the remote server. In many cases, this results in a quicker response to changes in the input data.

- In a properly programmed applet, the web server does not receive any data provided to the applet as input, therefore maintaining the security and privacy of the user's financial data.

However, just as with agents, applets introduce a number of security concerns. They allow a remote system to send code to the local system for execution. Security administrators must take steps to ensure that code sent to systems on their network is safe and properly screened for malicious activity. Also, unless the code is analyzed line by line, the end user can never be certain that the applet doesn't contain a Trojan horse component. For example, the mortgage calculator might indeed transmit sensitive financial information to the web server without the end user's knowledge or consent.

The following sections explore two common applet types: Java applets and ActiveX controls.

## Java Applets

Java is a platform-independent programming language developed by Sun Microsystems. Most programming languages use compilers that produce applications custom-tailored to run under a specific operating system. This requires the use of multiple compilers to produce different versions of a single application for each platform it must support. Java overcomes this limitation by inserting the Java Virtual Machine (JVM) into the picture. Each system that runs Java code downloads the version of the JVM supported by its operating system. The JVM then takes the Java code and translates it into a format executable by that specific system. The great benefit of this arrangement is that code can be shared between operating systems without modification. Java applets are simply short Java programs transmitted over the Internet to perform operations on a remote system.

Security was of paramount concern during the design of the Java platform, and Sun's development team created the "sandbox" concept to place privilege restrictions on Java code. The sandbox isolates Java code objects from the rest of the operating system and enforces strict rules about the resources those objects can access. For example, the sandbox would prohibit a Java applet from retrieving information from areas of memory not specifically allocated to it, preventing the applet from stealing that information.

## ActiveX Controls

ActiveX controls are Microsoft's answer to Sun's Java applets. They operate in a similar fashion, but they are implemented using any one of a variety of languages, including Visual Basic, C, C++, and Java. There are two key distinctions between Java applets and ActiveX controls. First, ActiveX controls use proprietary Microsoft technology and, therefore, can execute only on systems running Microsoft browsers. Second, ActiveX controls are not subject to the sandbox restrictions placed on Java applets. They have full access to the Windows operating environment and can perform a number of privileged actions. Therefore, you must take special precautions when deciding which ActiveX controls to download and execute. Some security administrators have taken the somewhat harsh position of prohibiting the download of any ActiveX content from all but a select handful of trusted sites.

# Object Request Brokers

To facilitate the growing trend toward distributed computing, the Object Management Group (OMG) set out to develop a common standard for developers around the world. Their work, known as the Common Object Request Broker Architecture (CORBA), has resulted in an international standard (sanctioned by the International Organization for Standardization) for distributed computing. It defines the sequence of interactions between client and server shown in Figure 7.1.

**FIGURE 7.1**  CORBA

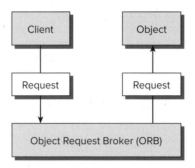

In this model, clients do not need specific knowledge of a server's location or technical details to interact with it. They simply pass their request for a particular object to a local Object Request Broker (ORB) using a well-defined interface. These interfaces are created using the OMG's Interface Definition Language (IDL). The ORB, in turn, invokes the appropriate object, keeping the implementation details transparent to the original client.

Object Request Brokers (ORBs) are an offshoot of object-oriented programming, a topic discussed later in this chapter.

The discussion of CORBA and ORBs presented here is, by necessity, an oversimplification designed to provide security professionals with an overview of the process. CORBA extends well beyond the model presented in Figure 7.1 to facilitate ORB-to-ORB interaction, load balancing, fault tolerance, and a number of other features. If you're interested in learning more about CORBA, the OMG has an excellent tutorial on its website at www.omg.org/gettingstarted/corbafaq.htm.

## Microsoft Component Models

The driving force behind OMG's efforts to implement CORBA was the desire to create a common standard that enabled non-vendor-specific interaction. However, as such things often go, Microsoft decided to develop its own proprietary standards for object management: COM and DCOM.

The Component Object Model (COM) is Microsoft's standard architecture for the use of components within a process or between processes running on the same system. It works across the range of Microsoft products, from development environments to the

Office productivity suite. In fact, Office's object linking and embedding (OLE) model that allows users to create documents that utilize components from different applications uses the COM architecture.

Although COM is restricted to local system interactions, the Distributed Component Object Model (DCOM) extends the concept to cover distributed computing environments. It replaces COM's interprocess communications capability with an ability to interact with the network stack and invoke objects located on remote systems.

 Although DCOM and CORBA are competing component architectures, Microsoft and OMG agreed to allow some interoperability between ORBs utilizing different models.

Microsoft created the .NET Framework as a replacement to DCOM. The .NET Framework provides a Common Language Infrastructure (CLI) as the core foundation for all compiled languages. .NET developers may use Visual Basic .NET, C#, J#, or any of a number of other languages that provide .NET support.

# Databases and Data Warehousing

Almost every modern organization maintains some sort of database that contains information critical to operations—be it customer contact information, order-tracking data, human resource and benefits information, or sensitive trade secrets. It's likely that many of these databases contain personal information that users hold secret, such as credit card usage activity, travel habits, grocery store purchases, and telephone records. Because of the growing reliance on database systems, information security professionals must ensure that adequate security controls exist to protect them against unauthorized access, tampering, or destruction of data.

In the following sections, we'll discuss database management system (DBMS) architecture, the various types of DBMSs, and their features. Then we'll discuss database security features, polyinstantiation, ODBS, aggregation, inference, and data mining. They're loaded sections, so pay attention.

## Database Management System (DBMS) Architecture

Although there are a variety of database management system (DBMS) architectures available today, the vast majority of contemporary systems implement a technology known as relational database management systems (RDBMSs). For this reason, the following sections focus primarily on relational databases. However, first we'll discuss two other important DBMS architectures: hierarchical and distributed.

## Hierarchical and Distributed Databases

A hierarchical data model combines records and fields that are related in a logical tree structure. This results in a "one-to-many" data model, where each node may have zero, one, or many children but only one parent. An example of a hierarchical data model appears in Figure 7.2.

**FIGURE 7.2**   Hierarchical data model

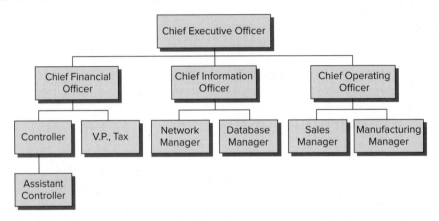

The hierarchical model in Figure 7.2 is a corporate organization chart. Notice that the "one-to-many" data model holds true in this example. Each employee has only one manager (the "one" in "one-to-many"), but each manager may have one or more (the "many") employees. Other examples of hierarchical data models include the NCAA March Madness bracket system and the hierarchical distribution of Domain Name System (DNS) records used on the Internet. Hierarchical databases store data in this type of hierarchical fashion and are useful for specialized applications that fit the model. For example, biologists might use a hierarchical database to store data on specimens according to the kingdom/phylum/class/order/family/genus/species hierarchical model used in that field.

The distributed data model has data stored in more than one database, but those databases are logically connected. The user perceives the database as a single entity, even though it comprises numerous parts interconnected over a network. Each field can have numerous children as well as numerous parents. Thus, the data mapping relationship for distributed databases is many-to-many.

## Relational Databases

A relational database consists of flat two-dimensional tables made up of rows and columns. In fact, each table looks very similar to a spreadsheet file. The row and column structure provides for one-to-one data mapping relationships. The main building block of the relational database is the table (also known as a *relation*). Each table contains a set of related records. For example, a sales database might contain the following tables:

- Customers table that contains contact information for all the organization's clients
- Sales Reps table that contains identity information on the organization's sales force
- Orders table that contains records of orders placed by each customer

---

### Object-Oriented Programming and Databases

Object-relational databases combine relational databases with the power of object-oriented programming. True object-oriented databases (OODBs) benefit from ease of code reuse, ease of troubleshooting analysis, and reduced overall maintenance. OODBs are also better suited for supporting complex applications involving multimedia, CAD, video, graphics, and expert systems than other types of databases.

---

Each of these tables contains a number of attributes, or *fields*. Each attribute corresponds to a column in the table. For example, the Customers table might contain columns for the company name, address, city, state, zip code, and telephone number. Each customer would have its own record, or *tuple*, represented by a row in the table. The number of rows in the relation is referred to as *cardinality*, and the number of columns is the *degree*. The *domain* of a relation is the set of allowable values that the attribute can take. Figure 7.3 shows an example of a Customers table from a relational database.

**FIGURE 7.3**  Customers table from a relational database

| Company ID | Company Name | Address | City | State | ZIP Code | Telephone | Sales Rep |
|---|---|---|---|---|---|---|---|
| 1 | Acme Widgets | 234 Main Street | Columbia | MD | 21046 | (301) 555-1212 | 14 |
| 2 | Abrams Consulting | 1024 Sample Street | Miami | FL | 33131 | (305) 555-1995 | 14 |
| 3 | Dome Widgets | 913 Sorin Street | South Bend | IN | 46556 | (574) 555-5863 | 26 |

In this example, the table has a cardinality of three (corresponding to the three rows in the table) and a degree of eight (corresponding to the eight columns). It's common for the cardinality of a table to change during the course of normal business, such as when a sales rep adds new customers. The degree of a table normally does not change frequently and usually requires database administrator intervention.

To remember the concept of cardinality, think of a deck of cards on a desk, with each card (the first four letters of this term) being a row. To remember the concept of degree, think of a wall thermometer as a column (in other words, the temperature in degrees as measured on a thermometer).

Relationships between the tables are defined to identify related records. In this example, a relationship exists between the Customers table and the Sales Reps table because each customer is assigned a sales representative and because each sales representative is assigned to one or more customers. This relationship is reflected by the Sales Rep column in the Customer table, shown in Figure 7.3. The values in this column refer to a Sales Rep ID field contained in the Sales Rep table (not shown). Additionally, a relationship would probably exist between the Customers table and the Orders table because each order must be associated with a customer and each customer is associated with one or more product orders. The Orders table (not shown) would likely contain a Customer field that contained one of the Customer ID values shown in Figure 7.3.

Records are identified using a variety of keys. Quite simply, keys are a subset of the fields of a table used to uniquely identify records. They are also used to join tables together when you wish to cross-reference information. You should be familiar with three types of keys:

**Candidate keys**   Subsets of attributes that can be used to uniquely identify any record in a table. No two records in the same table will ever contain the same values for all attributes composing a candidate key. Each table may have one or more candidate keys, which are chosen from column headings.

**Primary keys**   Selected from the set of candidate keys for a table to be used to uniquely identify the records in a table. Each table has only one primary key, selected by the database designer from the set of candidate keys. The RDBMS enforces the uniqueness of primary keys by disallowing the insertion of multiple records with the same primary key. In the Customers table shown in Figure 7.3, the Customer ID would likely be the primary key.

**Foreign keys**   Used to enforce relationships between two tables, also known as *referential integrity*. Referential integrity ensures that if one table contains a foreign key, it corresponds to a still-existing primary key in the other table in the relationship. It makes certain that no record/tuple/row contains a reference to a primary key of a nonexistent record/tuple/row. In the example described earlier, the Sales Rep field shown in Figure 7.3 is a foreign key referencing the primary key of the Sales Reps table.

All relational databases use a standard language, the Structured Query Language (SQL), to provide users with a consistent interface for the storage, retrieval, and modification of data and for administrative control of the DBMS. Each DBMS vendor implements a slightly different version of SQL (like Microsoft's Transact-SQL and Oracle's PL/SQL), but all support a core feature set. SQL's primary security feature is its granularity of authorization. This means that SQL allows you to set permissions at a very fine level of detail. You can limit user access by the table, row, column, or even the individual cell in some cases.

### Database Normalization

Database developers strive to create well-organized and efficient databases. To assist with this effort, they've defined several levels of database organization known as *normal forms*. The process of bringing a database table into compliance with normal forms is known as *normalization*.

Although a number of normal forms exist, the three most common are first normal form (1NF), second normal form (2NF), and third normal form (3NF). Each of these forms adds requirements to reduce redundancy in the tables, eliminating misplaced data and performing a number of other housekeeping tasks. The normal forms are cumulative; in other words, to be in 2NF, a table must first be 1NF compliant. Before making a table 3NF compliant, it must first be in 2NF.

The details of normalizing a database table are beyond the scope of the CISSP exam, but several web resources can help you understand the requirements of the normal forms in greater detail. For example, refer to the article "Database Normalization" at http://databases.about.com/od/specificproducts/a/normalization.htm. You can also read the book *SQL Server 2008 for Dummies* (Wiley, 2008) for an introduction to database design.

SQL provides the complete functionality necessary for administrators, developers, and end users to interact with the database. In fact, the graphical database interfaces popular today merely wrap some extra bells and whistles around a standard SQL interface to the DBMS. SQL itself is divided into two distinct components: the Data Definition Language (DDL), which allows for the creation and modification of the database's structure (known as the *schema*), and the Data Manipulation Language (DML), which allows users to interact with the data contained within that schema.

## Database Transactions

Relational databases support the explicit and implicit use of transactions to ensure data integrity. Each transaction is a discrete set of SQL instructions that will either succeed or fail as a group. It's not possible for one part of a transaction to succeed while another part fails. Consider the example of a transfer between two accounts at a bank. You might use the following SQL code to first add $250 to account 1001 and then subtract $250 from account 2002:

```
BEGIN TRANSACTION

UPDATE accounts
SET balance = balance + 250
```

```
WHERE account_number = 1001;

UPDATE accounts
SET balance = balance - 250
WHERE account_number = 2002

END TRANSACTION
```

Imagine a case where these two statements were not executed as part of a transaction but were instead executed separately. If the database failed during the moment between completion of the first transaction and completion of the second transaction, $250 would have been added to account 1001, but there would be no corresponding deduction from account 2002. The $250 would have appeared out of thin air! Flipping the order of the two statements wouldn't help—this would cause $250 to disappear into thin air if interrupted! This simple example underscores the importance of transaction-oriented processing.

When a transaction successfully completes, it is said to be committed to the database and cannot be undone. Transaction committing may be explicit, using SQL's COMMIT command, or it can be implicit if the end of the transaction is successfully reached. If a transaction must be aborted, it can be rolled back explicitly using the ROLLBACK command or implicitly if there is a hardware or software failure. When a transaction is rolled back, the database restores itself to the condition it was in before the transaction began.

All database transactions have four required characteristics: atomicity, consistency, isolation, and durability. Together, these attributes are known as the *ACID model*, which is a critical concept in the development of database management systems. Let's take a brief look at each of these requirements:

**Atomicity**   Database transactions must be atomic—that is, they must be an "all-or-nothing" affair. If any part of the transaction fails, the entire transaction must be rolled back as if it never occurred.

**Consistency**   All transactions must begin operating in an environment that is consistent with all of the database's rules (for example, all records have a unique primary key). When the transaction is complete, the database must again be consistent with the rules, regardless of whether those rules were violated during the processing of the transaction itself. No other transaction should ever be able to utilize any inconsistent data that might be generated during the execution of another transaction.

**Isolation**   The isolation principle requires that transactions operate separately from each other. If a database receives two SQL transactions that modify the same data, one transaction must be completed in its entirety before the other transaction is allowed to modify the same data. This prevents one transaction from working with invalid data generated as an intermediate step by another transaction.

**Durability**   Database transactions must be durable. That is, once they are committed to the database, they must be preserved. Databases ensure durability through the use of backup mechanisms, such as transaction logs.

In the following sections, we'll discuss a variety of specific security issues of concern to database developers and administrators.

# Security for Multilevel Databases

As you learned in Chapter 5, "Security Management Concepts and Principles," many organizations use data classification schemes to enforce access control restrictions based upon the security labels assigned to data objects and individual users. When mandated by an organization's security policy, this classification concept must also be extended to the organization's databases.

Multilevel security databases contain information at a number of different classification levels. They must verify the labels assigned to users and, in response to user requests, provide only information that's appropriate. However, this concept becomes somewhat more complicated when considering security for a database.

When multilevel security is required, it's essential that administrators and developers strive to keep data with different security requirements separate. Mixing data with different classification levels and/or need-to-know requirements is known as *database contamination* and is a significant security challenge. Often, administrators will deploy a trusted front end to add multilevel security to a legacy or insecure DBMS.

 **Real World Scenario**

## Restricting Access with Views

Another way to implement multilevel security in a database is through the use of database views. Views are simply SQL statements that present data to the user as if they were tables themselves. They may be used to collate data from multiple tables, aggregate individual records, or restrict a user's access to a limited subset of database attributes and/or records.

Views are stored in the database as SQL commands rather than as tables of data. This dramatically reduces the space requirements of the database and allows views to violate the rules of normalization that apply to tables. However, retrieving data from a complex view can take significantly longer than retrieving it from a table because the DBMS may need to perform calculations to determine the value of certain attributes for each record.

Because views are so flexible, many database administrators use them as a security tool—allowing users to interact only with limited views rather than with the raw tables of data underlying them.

## Concurrency

*Concurrency*, or edit control, is a preventative security mechanism that endeavors to make certain that the information stored in the database is always correct or at least has its integrity and availability protected. This feature can be employed whether the database is multilevel or single level. Concurrency uses a "lock" feature to allow one user to make changes but deny other users access to view or make changes to data elements at the same time. Then, after the changes have been made, an "unlock" feature restores the ability of other users to access the data they need. In some instances, administrators will use concurrency with auditing mechanisms to track document and/or field changes. When this recorded data is reviewed, concurrency becomes a detective control.

## Other Security Mechanisms

Administrators can deploy several other security mechanisms when using a DBMS. These features are relatively easy to implement and are common in the industry. The mechanisms related to semantic integrity, for instance, are common security features of a DBMS. Semantic integrity ensures that user actions don't violate any structural rules. It also checks that all stored data types are within valid domain ranges, ensures that only logical values exist, and confirms that the system complies with any and all uniqueness constraints.

Administrators may employ time and date stamps to maintain data integrity and availability. Time and date stamps often appear in distributed database systems. When a time stamp is placed on all change transactions and those changes are distributed or replicated to the other database members, all changes are applied to all members, but they are implemented in correct chronological order.

Another common security feature of DBMS is that objects can be controlled granularly within the database; this can also improve security control. Content-dependent access control is an example of granular object control. Content-dependent access control focuses on control based upon the contents or payload of the object being accessed. Since decisions must be made on an object-by-object basis, content-dependent control increases processing overhead. Another form of granular control is *cell suppression*. Cell suppression is the concept of hiding or imposing more security restrictions on individual database fields or cells.

Context-dependent access control is often discussed alongside content-dependent access control because of the similarity of their names. Context-dependent access control evaluates the big picture to make its access control decisions. The key factor in context-dependent access control is how each object or packet or field relates to the overall activity or communication. Any single element may look innocuous by itself, but in a larger context that element may be revealed to be benign or malign.

Administrators may employ database partitioning to subvert aggregation, inferencing, and contamination vulnerabilities, which are discussed later in this chapter. Database partitioning is the process of splitting a single database into multiple parts, each with a unique and distinct security level or type of content.

*Polyinstantiation* occurs when two or more rows in the same relational database table appear to have identical primary key elements but contain different data for use at differing classification levels. It is often used as a defense against some types of inference attacks (we'll discuss inference in just a moment).

Consider a database table containing the location of various naval ships on patrol. Normally, this database contains the exact position of each ship stored at the secret classification level. However, one particular ship, the USS *UpToNoGood*, is on an undercover mission to a top-secret location. Military commanders do not want anyone to know that the ship deviated from its normal patrol. If the database administrators simply change the classification of the *UpToNoGood*'s location to top secret, a user with a secret clearance would know that something unusual was going on when they couldn't query the location of the ship. However, if polyinstantiation is used, two records could be inserted into the table. The first one, classified at the top-secret level, would reflect the true location of the ship and be available only to users with the appropriate top-secret security clearance. The second record, classified at the secret level, would indicate that the ship was on routine patrol and would be returned to users with a secret clearance.

Finally, administrators can insert false or misleading data into a DBMS in order to redirect or thwart information confidentiality attacks. This is a concept known as noise and perturbation. You must be extremely careful when using this technique to ensure that noise inserted into the database does not affect business operations.

# ODBC

Open Database Connectivity (ODBC) is a database feature that allows applications to communicate with different types of databases without having to be directly programmed for interaction with each type. ODBC acts as a proxy between applications and back-end database drivers, giving application programmers greater freedom in creating solutions without having to worry about the back-end database system. Figure 7.4 illustrates the relationship between ODBC and a back-end database system.

**FIGURE 7.4**    ODBC as the interface between applications and a back-end database system

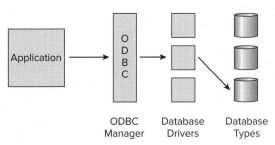

# Aggregation

SQL provides a number of functions that combine records from one or more tables to produce potentially useful information. This process is called *aggregation*. Aggregation is not without its security vulnerabilities. Aggregation attacks are used to collect numerous low-level security items or low-value items and combine them together to create something of a higher security level or value. Some of the functions, known as the *aggregate functions*, are listed here:

COUNT( )   Returns the number of records that meet specified criteria

MIN( )   Returns the record with the smallest value for the specified attribute or combination of attributes

MAX( )   Returns the record with the largest value for the specified attribute or combination of attributes

SUM( )   Returns the summation of the values of the specified attribute or combination of attributes across all affected records

AVG( )   Returns the average value of the specified attribute or combination of attributes across all affected records

These functions, although extremely useful, also pose a risk to the security of information in a database. For example, suppose a low-level military records clerk is responsible for updating records of personnel and equipment as they are transferred from base to base. As part of his duties, this clerk may be granted the database permissions necessary to query and update personnel tables.

The military might not consider an individual transfer request (in other words, Sergeant Jones is being moved from Base X to Base Y) to be classified information. The records clerk has access to that information, as he needs it to process Sergeant Jones's transfer. However, with access to aggregate functions, the records clerk might be able to count the number of troops assigned to each military base around the world. These force levels are often closely guarded military secrets, but the low-ranking records clerk was able to deduce them by using aggregate functions across a large number of unclassified records.

---

**Inference**

The database security issues posed by inference attacks are very similar to those posed by the threat of data aggregation. As with aggregation, inference attacks involve the combination of several pieces of nonsensitive information used to gain access to information that should be classified at a higher level. However, inference makes use of the human mind's deductive capacity rather than the raw mathematical ability of modern database platforms.

A commonly cited example of an inference attack is that of the accounting clerk at a large corporation who is allowed to retrieve the total amount the company spends on salaries for use in a top-level report but is not allowed to access the salaries of individual employees. The accounting clerk often has to prepare those reports with effective dates in the past and so is allowed to access the total salary amounts for any day in the past year. Say, for example, that this clerk must also know the hiring and termination dates of various employees and has access to this information. This opens the door for an inference attack. If an employee was the only person hired on a specific date, the accounting clerk can now retrieve the total salary amount on that date and the day before and deduce the salary of that particular employee—sensitive information that the user would not be permitted to access directly.

As with aggregation, the best defense against inference attacks is to maintain constant vigilance over the permissions granted to individual users. Furthermore, intentional blurring of data may be used to prevent the inference of sensitive information. For example, if the accounting clerk were able to retrieve only salary information rounded to the nearest million, they would probably not be able to gain any useful information about individual employees. Finally, you can use database partitioning (discussed earlier in this chapter) to help subvert these attacks.

For this reason, it's especially important for database security administrators to strictly control access to aggregate functions and adequately assess the potential information they may reveal to unauthorized individuals.

## Data Mining

Many organizations use large databases, known as *data warehouses*, to store large amounts of information from a variety of databases for use with specialized analysis techniques. These data warehouses often contain detailed historical information not normally stored in production databases because of storage limitations or data security concerns.

A *data dictionary* is commonly used for storing critical information about data, including usage, type, sources, relationships, and formats. DBMS software reads the data dictionary to determine access rights for users attempting to access data.

*Data mining* techniques allow analysts to comb through these data warehouses and look for potential correlated information amid the historical data. For example, an analyst might discover that the demand for lightbulbs always increases in the winter months and then use this information when planning pricing and promotion strategies. Data mining techniques result in the development of data models that may be used to predict future activity.

The activity of data mining produces metadata. Metadata is data about data or information about data. Metadata is not exclusively the result of data mining operations;

other functions or services can produce metadata as well. Think of metadata from a data mining operation as a concentration of data. It can also be a superset, a subset, or a representation of a larger data set. Metadata can be the important, significant, relevant, abnormal, or aberrant elements from a data set.

One common security example of metadata is that of a security incident report. A incident report is the metadata extracted from a data warehouse of audit logs through the use of a security auditing data mining tool. In most cases, metadata is of a greater value or sensitivity (due to disclosure) than the bulk of data in the warehouse. Thus, metadata is stored in a more secure container known as the *data mart*.

 You may also hear data mining referred to as Knowledge Discovery in Databases (KDD). It is closely related to the fields of machine learning and artificial intelligence.

Data warehouses and data mining are significant to security professionals for two reasons. First, as previously mentioned, data warehouses contain large amounts of potentially sensitive information vulnerable to aggregation and inference attacks, and security practitioners must ensure that adequate access controls and other security measures are in place to safeguard this data. Second, data mining can actually be used as a security tool when it's used to develop baselines for statistical anomaly–based intrusion detection systems (see Chapter 2, "Attacks and Monitoring," for more information on the various types and functionality of intrusion detection systems).

---

 **Real World Scenario**

**Data Mining for Anomaly Detection**

With several colleagues, Mike Chapple, one of this book's authors, recently published a paper titled "Authentication Anomaly Detection" that explored the usefulness of data mining techniques to explore authentication logs from a virtual private network (VPN). In the study, they used *expectation maximization (EM)* clustering, a data mining technique, to develop models of normal user behavior based upon a user's affiliation with the organization, the distance between the data center and their physical location, the day of the week, the hour of the day, and other attributes.

After developing the models through data mining, they applied them to future activity and identified user connection attempts that didn't look "normal," as defined by the model. Using this approach, they identified several unauthorized uses of the VPN.

# Data/Information Storage

Database management systems have helped harness the power of data and gain some modicum of control over who can access it and the actions they can perform on it. However, security professionals must keep in mind that DBMS security covers access to information through only the traditional "front-door" channels. Data is also processed through a computer's storage resources—both memory and physical media. Precautions must be in place to ensure that these basic resources are protected against security vulnerabilities as well. After all, you would never incur a lot of time and expense to secure the front door of your home and then leave the back door wide open, would you?

## Types of Storage

Modern computing systems use several types of storage to maintain system and user data. The systems strike a balance between the various storage types to satisfy an organization's computing requirements. There are several common storage types:

**Primary (or "real") memory**  Consists of the main memory resources directly available to a system's CPU. Primary memory normally consists of volatile random access memory (RAM) and is usually the most high-performance storage resource available to a system.

**Secondary storage**  Consists of more inexpensive, nonvolatile storage resources available to a system for long-term use. Typical secondary storage resources include magnetic and optical media, such as tapes, disks, hard drives, flash drives, and CD/DVD storage.

**Virtual memory**  Allows a system to simulate additional primary memory resources through the use of secondary storage. For example, a system low on expensive RAM might make a portion of the hard disk available for direct CPU addressing.

**Virtual storage**  Allows a system to simulate secondary storage resources through the use of primary storage. The most common example of virtual storage is the *RAM disk* that presents itself to the operating system as a secondary storage device but is actually implemented in volatile RAM. This provides an extremely fast file system for use in various applications but provides no recovery capability.

**Random access storage**  Allows the operating system to request contents from any point within the media. RAM and hard drives are examples of random access storage resources.

**Sequential access storage**  Requires scanning through the entire media from the beginning to reach a specific address. A magnetic tape is a common example of a sequential access storage resource.

**Volatile storage**  Loses its contents when power is removed from the resource. RAM is the most common type of volatile storage resource.

**Nonvolatile storage**  Does not depend upon the presence of power to maintain its contents. Magnetic/optical media and nonvolatile RAM (NVRAM) are typical examples of nonvolatile storage resources.

## Storage Threats

Information security professionals should be aware of two main threats posed against data storage systems. First, the threat of illegitimate access to storage resources exists no matter what type of storage is in use. If administrators do not implement adequate file system access controls, an intruder might stumble across sensitive data simply by browsing the file system. In more sensitive environments, administrators should also protect against attacks that involve bypassing operating system controls and directly accessing the physical storage media to retrieve data. This is best accomplished through the use of an encrypted file system, which is accessible only through the primary operating system. Furthermore, systems that operate in a multilevel security environment should provide adequate controls to ensure that shared memory and storage resources provide fail-safe controls so that data from one classification level is not readable at a lower classification level.

Covert channel attacks pose the second primary threat against data storage resources. Covert storage channels allow the transmission of sensitive data between classification levels through the direct or indirect manipulation of shared storage media. This may be as simple as writing sensitive data to an inadvertently shared portion of memory or physical storage. More complex covert storage channels might be used to manipulate the amount of free space available on a disk or the size of a file to covertly convey information between security levels. For more information on covert channel analysis, see Chapter 12, "Principles of Security Models."

# Knowledge-Based Systems

Since the advent of computing, engineers and scientists have worked toward developing systems capable of performing routine actions that would bore a human and consume a significant amount of time. The majority of the achievements in this area focused on relieving the burden of computationally intensive tasks. However, researchers have also made giant strides toward developing systems that have an "artificial intelligence" that can simulate (to some extent) the purely human power of reasoning.

The following sections examine two types of knowledge-based artificial intelligence systems: expert systems and neural networks. We'll also take a look at their potential applications to computer security problems.

## Expert Systems

Expert systems seek to embody the accumulated knowledge of experts on a particular subject and apply it in a consistent fashion to future decisions. Several studies have shown that expert systems, when properly developed and implemented, often make better decisions than some of their human counterparts when faced with routine decisions.

Every expert system has two main components. The knowledge base contains the rules known by an expert system. The knowledge base seeks to codify the knowledge of human experts in a series of "if/then" statements. Let's consider a simple expert system designed to help homeowners decide whether they should evacuate an area when a hurricane threatens. The knowledge base might contain the following statements (these statements are for example only):

- If the hurricane is a Category 4 storm or higher, then flood waters normally reach a height of 20 feet above sea level.

- If the hurricane has winds in excess of 120 miles per hour (mph), then wood-frame structures will fail.

- If it is late in the hurricane season, then hurricanes tend to get stronger as they approach the coast.

In an actual expert system, the knowledge base would contain hundreds or thousands of assertions such as those just listed.

The second major component of an expert system—the inference engine—analyzes information in the knowledge base to arrive at the appropriate decision. The expert system user utilizes some sort of user interface to provide the inference engine with details about the current situation, and the inference engine uses a combination of logical reasoning and fuzzy logic techniques to draw a conclusion based upon past experience. Continuing with the hurricane example, a user might inform the expert system that a Category 4 hurricane is approaching the coast with wind speeds averaging 140 mph. The inference engine would then analyze information in the knowledge base and make an evacuation recommendation based upon that past knowledge.

Expert systems are not infallible—they're only as good as the data in the knowledge base and the decision-making algorithms implemented in the inference engine. However, they have one major advantage in stressful situations—their decisions do not involve judgment clouded by emotion. Expert systems can play an important role in analyzing situations such as emergency events, stock trading, and other scenarios in which emotional investment sometimes gets in the way of a logical decision. For this reason, many lending institutions now utilize expert systems to make credit decisions instead of relying upon loan officers who might say to themselves, "Well, Jim hasn't paid his bills on time, but he seems like a perfectly nice guy."

## Fuzzy Logic

As previously mentioned, inference engines commonly use a technique known as *fuzzy logic*. This technique is designed to more closely approximate human thought patterns than the rigid mathematics of set theory or algebraic approaches that utilize "black-and-white" categorizations of data. Fuzzy logic replaces them with blurred boundaries, allowing the algorithm to think in the "shades of gray" that dominate human thought. Fuzzy logic as used by an expert system has four steps or phases: fuzzification, inference, composition, and defuzzification.

For example, consider the task of determining whether a website is undergoing a denial-of-service attack. Traditional mathematical techniques may create basic rules, such as "If we have more than 1,000 connections per second, we are under attack." Fuzzy logic, on the other hand, might define a blurred boundary, saying that 1,000 connections per second represents an 80 percent chance of an attack, while 10,000 connections per second represents a 95 percent chance and 100 connections per second represents a 5 percent chance. The interpretation of these probabilities is left to the analyst.

## Neural Networks

In neural networks, chains of computational units are used in an attempt to imitate the biological reasoning process of the human mind. In an expert system, a series of rules is stored in a knowledge base, whereas in a neural network, a long chain of computational decisions that feed into each other and eventually sum to produce the desired output is set up.

Keep in mind that no neural network designed to date comes close to having the reasoning power of the human mind. Nevertheless, neural networks show great potential to advance the artificial intelligence field beyond its current state. Benefits of neural networks include linearity, input-output mapping, and adaptivity. These benefits are evident in the implementations of neural networks for voice recognition, face recognition, weather prediction, and the exploration of models of thinking and consciousness.

Typical neural networks involve many layers of summation, each of which requires weighting information to reflect the relative importance of the calculation in the overall decision-making process. These weights must be custom-tailored for each type of decision the neural network is expected to make. This is accomplished through the use of a training period during which the network is provided with inputs for which the proper decision is known. The algorithm then works backward from these decisions to determine the proper weights for each node in the computational chain. This activity is known as the *Delta rule* or *learning rule*. Through the use of the Delta rule, neural networks are able to learn from experience.

## Decision Support Systems

A *decision support system (DSS)* is a knowledge-based application that analyzes business data and presents it in such a way as to make business decisions easier for users. It is considered more of an informational application than an operational application. Often a DSS is employed by knowledge workers (such as help desk or customer support personnel) and by sales services (such as phone operators). This type of application may present information in a graphical manner to link concepts and content and guide the script of the operator. Often a DSS is backed by an expert system controlling a database.

## Security Applications

Both expert systems and neural networks have great applications in the field of computer security. One of the major advantages offered by these systems is their capability to rapidly make consistent decisions. One of the major problems in computer security is the inability of system administrators to consistently and thoroughly analyze massive amounts of log and audit trail data to look for anomalies. It seems like a match made in heaven!

One successful application of this technology to the computer security arena is the Next-Generation Intrusion Detection Expert System (NIDES) developed by Philip Porras and his team at the Information and Computing Sciences System Design Laboratory of SRI International. This system provides an inference engine and knowledge base that draws information from a variety of audit logs across a network and provides notification to security administrators when the activity of an individual user varies from their standard usage profile.

# Systems Development Controls

Many organizations use custom-developed hardware and software systems to achieve flexible operational goals. As you will learn in Chapter 8 and Chapter 12, these custom solutions can present great security vulnerabilities as a result of malicious and/or careless developers who create trap doors, buffer-overflow vulnerabilities, or other weaknesses that can leave a system open to exploitation by malicious individuals.

To protect against these vulnerabilities, it's vital to introduce security concerns into the entire systems development life cycle. An organized, methodical process helps ensure that solutions meet functional requirements as well as security guidelines. The following sections explore the spectrum of systems development activities with an eye toward security concerns that should be foremost on the mind of any information security professional engaged in solutions development.

## Software Development

Security should be a consideration at every stage of a system's development, including the software development process. Programmers should strive to build security into every application they develop, with greater levels of security provided to critical applications and those that process sensitive information. It's extremely important to consider the security implications of a software development project from the early stages because it's much easier to build security into a system than it is to add security onto an existing system.

### Assurance

To ensure that the security control mechanisms built into a new application properly implement the security policy throughout the life cycle of the system, administrators use *assurance procedures*. Assurance procedures are simply formalized processes by which trust is built into the life cycle of a system. The Trusted Computer System Evaluation Criteria (TCSEC) Orange Book refers to this process as *life cycle assurance*. We'll discuss this further in Chapter 13, "Administrative Management."

## Avoiding System Failure

No matter how advanced your development team, your systems will likely fail at some point in time. You should plan for this type of failure when you put the software and hardware controls in place, ensuring that the system will respond appropriately. You can employ many methods to avoid failure, including using limit checks and creating fail-safe or fail-open procedures. Let's talk about these in more detail.

### Limit Checks

Environmental controls and hardware devices cannot prevent problems created by poor program coding. It is important to have proper software development and coding practices to ensure that security is a priority during product development. Limit checks are a technique for managing data types, data formats, and data length when accepting input from a user or another application. Limit checks ensure that data does not fall outside the range of allowable values. For example, when creating a database that contains the age of individuals, a limit check might restrict the possible values so that they must be greater than 0 and less than 130. Depending on the application, you may also need to include sequence checks to ensure that data input is properly ordered. Limit checks are a form of input validation—checking to ensure that user input meets the requirements of the application.

In most organizations, security professionals come from a system administration background and don't have professional experience in software development. If your background doesn't include this type of experience, don't let that stop you from learning about it and educating your organization's developers on the importance of secure coding.

### Fail-Secure and Fail-Open

In spite of the best efforts of programmers, product designers, and project managers, developed applications will be used in unexpected ways. Some of these conditions will cause failures. Since failures are unpredictable, programmers should design into their code a general sense of how to respond to and handle failures.

There are two basic choices when planning for system failure, fail-secure (also called fail-safe) or fail-open:

- The *fail-secure failure state* puts the system into a high level of security (and possibly even disables it entirely) until an administrator can diagnose the problem and restore the system to normal operation.

- The *fail-open state* allows users to bypass failed security controls, erring on the side of permissiveness.

In the vast majority of environments, fail-secure is the appropriate failure state because it prevents unauthorized access to information and resources.

Software should revert to a fail-secure condition. This may mean closing just the application or possibly stopping the operation of the entire host system. An example of such failure response is seen in the Windows OS with the appearance of the infamous Blue Screen of Death (BSOD), indicating the occurrence of a STOP error. A STOP error occurs when an undesirable activity occurs in spite of the OS's efforts to prevent it. This could include an application gaining direct access to hardware, an attempt to bypass a security access check, or one process interfering with the memory space of another. Once one of these conditions occurs, the environment is no longer trustworthy. So, rather than continuing to support an unreliable and insecure operating environment, the OS initiates a STOP error as its fail-secure response.

Once a fail-secure operation occurs, the programmer should consider the activities that occur afterward. The options are to remain in a fail-secure state or to automatically reboot the system. The former option requires an administrator to manually reboot the system and oversee the process. This action can be enforced by using a boot password. The latter option does not require human intervention for the system to restore itself to a functioning state, but it has its own unique issues. First, it is subject to initial program load (IPL) vulnerabilities (for more information on IPL, review Chapter 14). Second, it must restrict the system to reboot into a nonprivileged state. In other words, the system should not reboot and perform an automatic logon; instead, it should prompt the user for authorized access credentials.

**WARNING**
In limited circumstances, it may be appropriate to implement a fail-open failure state. This is sometimes appropriate for lower-layer components of a multilayered security system. Fail-open systems should be used with extreme caution. Before deploying a system using this failure mode, clearly validate the business requirement for this move. If it is justified, ensure that adequate alternative controls are in place to protect the organization's resources should the system fail. It's extremely rare that you'd want all your security controls to utilize a fail-open approach.

Even when security is properly designed and embedded in software, that security is often disabled in order to support easier installation. Thus, it is common for the IT administrator to have the responsibility of turning on and configuring security to match the needs of their specific environment. Maintaining security is often a trade-off with user-friendliness and functionality, as you can see from Figure 7.5. Additionally, as you add or increase security, you will also increase costs, increase administrative overhead, and reduce productivity/throughput.

**FIGURE 7.5** Security vs. user-friendliness vs. functionality

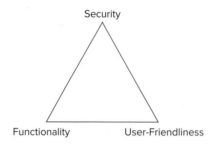

## Programming Languages

As you probably know, software developers use programming languages to develop software code. You might not know that several types of languages can be used simultaneously by the same system. This section takes a brief look at the different types of programming languages and the security implications of each.

Computers understand binary code. They speak a language of 1s and 0s, and that's it! The instructions that a computer follows consist of a long series of binary digits in a language known as *machine language*. Each CPU chipset has its own machine language, and it's virtually impossible for a human being to decipher anything but the simplest machine language code without the assistance of specialized software. Assembly language is a higher-level alternative that uses mnemonics to represent the basic instruction set of a CPU but still requires hardware-specific knowledge of a relatively obscure language. It also requires a large amount of tedious programming; a task as simple as adding two numbers together could take five or six lines of assembly code!

Programmers don't want to write their code in either machine language or assembly language. They prefer to use high-level languages, such as C++, Java, and Visual Basic. These languages allow programmers to write instructions that better approximate human communication, decrease the length of time needed to craft an application, possibly decrease the number of programmers needed on a project, and also allow some portability between different operating systems and hardware platforms. Once programmers are ready to execute their programs, two options are available to them, depending upon the language they've chosen.

Some languages (such as C++, Java, and FORTRAN) are compiled languages. When using a compiled language, the programmer uses a tool known as a *compiler* to convert the higher-level language into an executable file designed for use on a specific operating system. This executable is then distributed to end users who may use it as they see fit. Generally speaking, it's not possible to view or modify the software instructions in an executable file.

Other languages (such as JavaScript and VBScript) are interpreted languages. When these languages are used, the programmer distributes the source code, which contains instructions in the higher-level language. End users then use an interpreter to execute that source code on their system. They're able to view the original instructions written by the programmer.

Each approach has security advantages and disadvantages. Compiled code is generally less prone to manipulation by a third party. However, it's also easier for a malicious (or unskilled) programmer to embed back doors and other security flaws in the code and escape detection because the original instructions can't be viewed by the end user. Interpreted code, however, is less prone to the insertion of malicious code by the original programmer because the end user may view the code and check it for accuracy. On the other hand, everyone who touches the software has the ability to modify the programmer's original instructions and possibly embed malicious code in the interpreted software.

---

### Generational Languages

For the CISSP exam, you should also be familiar with the programming language generations, which are defined as follows:

- *First-generation languages* (1GL) include all machine languages.

- *Second-generation languages* (2GL) include all assembly languages.

- *Third-generation languages* (3GL) include all compiled languages.

- *Fourth-generation languages* (4GL) attempt to approximate natural languages and include SQL which is used by databases.

- *Fifth-generation languages* (5GL) allow programmers to create code using visual interfaces.

---

## Object-Oriented Programming

Many modern programming languages, such as C++, Java, and the .NET languages, support the concept of object-oriented programming (OOP). Older programming styles, such as functional programming, focused on the flow of the program itself and attempted to model the desired behavior as a series of steps. Object-oriented programming focuses on the objects involved in an interaction. You can think of it as a group of objects that can be requested to perform certain operations or exhibit certain behaviors. Objects work together to provide a system's functionality or capabilities. OOP has the potential to be more reliable and able to reduce the propagation of program change errors. As a type of programming method, it is better suited to modeling or mimicking the real world. For example, a banking program might have three object classes that correspond to accounts, account holders, and employees. When a new account is added to the system, a new instance, or copy, of the appropriate object is created to contain the details of that account.

Each object in the OOP model has methods that correspond to specific actions that can be taken on the object. For example, the account object can have methods to add funds, deduct funds, close the account, and transfer ownership.

Objects can also be subclasses of other objects and inherit methods from their parent class. For example, the account object may have subclasses that correspond to specific types of accounts, such as savings, checking, mortgages, and auto loans. The subclasses can use all the methods of the parent class and have additional class-specific methods. For example, the checking object might have a method called write_check(), whereas the other subclasses do not.

---

### Computer-Aided Software Engineering (CASE)

The advent of object-oriented programming has reinvigorated a movement toward applying traditional engineering design principles to the software engineering field. One part of that movement has been toward the use of computer-aided software engineering (CASE) tools to help developers, managers, and customers interact through the various stages of the software development life cycle.

One popular CASE tool, Middle CASE, is used in the design and analysis phase of software engineering to help create screen and report layouts.

---

From a security point of view, object-oriented programming provides a black-box approach to abstraction. Users need to know the details of an object's interface (generally the inputs, outputs, and actions that correspond to each of the object's methods) but don't necessarily need to know the inner workings of the object to use it effectively. To provide the desired characteristics of object-oriented systems, the objects are encapsulated (self-contained), and they can be accessed only through specific messages (in other words, input). Objects can also exhibit the substitution property, which allows different objects providing compatible operations to be substituted for each other.

Here is a list of common object-oriented programming terms you might come across in your work:

**Message**   A message is a communication to or input of an object.

**Method**   A method is internal code that defines the actions an object performs in response to a message.

**Behavior**   The results or output exhibited by an object is a behavior. Behaviors are the results of a message being processed through a method.

**Class**   A collection of the common methods from a set of objects that defines the behavior of those objects is a class.

**Instance**   Objects are instances of or examples of classes that contain their method.

**Inheritance**   Inheritance occurs when methods from a class (parent or superclass) are inherited by another subclass (child).

**Delegation**   Delegation is the forwarding of a request by an object to another object or delegate. An object delegates if it does not have a method to handle the message.

**Polymorphism**   A polymorphism is the characteristic of an object that allows it to respond with different behaviors to the same message or method because of changes in external conditions.

**Cohesiveness**   An object is highly cohesive if it can perform a task with little or no help from others. Highly cohesive objects are not as dependent upon other objects as objects that are less cohesive. Highly cohesive objects are often better. Objects that have high cohesion perform tasks alone and have low coupling.

**Coupling**   Coupling is the level of interaction between objects. Lower coupling means less interaction. Lower coupling provides better software design because objects are more independent. Lower coupling is easier to troubleshoot and update. Objects that have low cohesion require lots of assistance from other objects to perform tasks and have high coupling.

## Systems Development Life Cycle

Security is most effective if it is planned and managed throughout the life cycle of a system or application. Administrators employ project management to keep a development project on target and moving toward the goal of a completed product. Often project management is structured using life cycle models to direct the development process. Using formalized life cycle models helps ensure good coding practices and the embedding of security in every stage of product development.

All systems development processes should have several activities in common. Although they may not necessarily share the same names, these core activities are essential to the development of sound, secure systems:

- Conceptual definition
- Functional requirements determination
- Protection specifications development
- Design review
- Code review walk-through
- System test review
- Maintenance

The section "Life Cycle Models" later in this chapter examines two life cycle models and shows how these activities are applied in real-world software engineering environments.

It's important to note at this point that the terminology used in systems development life cycles varies from model to model and from publication to publication. Don't spend too much time worrying about the exact terms used in this book or any of the other literature you may come across. When taking the CISSP examination, it's much more important that you have an understanding of how the process works and the fundamental principles underlying the development of secure systems.

## Conceptual Definition

The conceptual definition phase of systems development involves creating the basic concept statement for a system. Simply put, it's a simple statement agreed upon by all interested stakeholders (the developers, customers, and management) that states the purpose of the project as well as the general system requirements. The conceptual definition is a very high-level statement of purpose and should not be longer than one or two paragraphs. If you were reading a detailed summary of the project, you might expect to see the concept statement as an abstract or introduction that enables an outsider to gain a top-level understanding of the project in a short period of time.

It's very helpful to refer to the concept statement at all phases of the systems development process. Often, the intricate details of the development process tend to obscure the overarching goal of the project. Simply reading the concept statement periodically can assist in refocusing a team of developers.

## Functional Requirements Determination

Once all stakeholders have agreed upon the concept statement, it's time for the development team to sit down and begin the functional requirements process. In this phase, specific system functionalities are listed, and developers begin to think about how the parts of the system should interoperate to meet the functional requirements. The deliverable from this phase of development is a functional requirements document that lists the specific system requirements.

As with the concept statement, it's important to ensure that all stakeholders agree on the functional requirements document before work progresses to the next level. When it's finally completed, the document shouldn't be simply placed on a shelf to gather dust—the entire development team should constantly refer to this document during all phases to ensure that the project is on track. In the final stages of testing and evaluation, the project managers should use this document as a checklist to ensure that all functional requirements are met.

## Protection Specifications Development

Security-conscious organizations also ensure that adequate protections are designed into every system from the earliest stages of development. It's often very useful to have a protection specifications development phase in your life cycle model. This phase takes place soon after the development of functional requirements and often continues as the design and design review phases progress.

During the development of protection specifications, it's important to analyze the system from a number of security perspectives. First, adequate access controls must be designed into every system to ensure that only authorized users are allowed to access the system and that they are not permitted to exceed their level of authorization. Second, the system must maintain the confidentiality of vital data through the use of appropriate encryption and data protection technologies. Next, the system should provide both an audit trail to enforce individual accountability and a detective mechanism for illegitimate activity. Finally, depending upon the criticality of the system, availability and fault-tolerance issues should be addressed as corrective actions.

Keep in mind that designing security into a system is not a one-shot process and it must be done proactively. All too often, systems are designed without security planning, and then developers attempt to retrofit the system with appropriate security mechanisms. Unfortunately, these mechanisms are an afterthought and do not fully integrate with the system's design, which leaves gaping security vulnerabilities. Also, the security requirements should be revisited each time a significant change is made to the design specification. If a major component of the system changes, it's very likely that the security requirements will change as well.

## Design Review

Once the functional and protection specifications are complete, let the system designers do their thing! In this often-lengthy process, the designers determine exactly how the various parts of the system will interoperate and how the modular system structure will be laid out. Also, during this phase, the design management team commonly sets specific tasks for various teams and lays out initial timelines for the completion of coding milestones.

After the design team completes the formal design documents, a review meeting with the stakeholders should be held to ensure that everyone is in agreement that the process is still on track for the successful development of a system with the desired functionality.

## Code Review Walk-Through

Once the stakeholders have given the software design their blessing, it's time for the software developers to start writing code. Project managers should schedule several code review walk-though meetings at various milestones throughout the coding process. These technical meetings usually involve only development personnel who sit down with a copy of the code for a specific module and walk through it, looking for problems in logical flow or other design/security flaws. The meetings play an instrumental role in ensuring that the code produced by the various development teams performs according to specification.

## System Test Review

After many code reviews and a lot of long nights, there will come a point at which a developer puts in that final semicolon and declares the system complete. As any seasoned software engineer knows, the system is never complete. Now it's time to begin the system test review phase. Initially, most organizations perform the initial system tests using development personnel to seek out any obvious errors. Once this phase is complete, a series of beta test deployments takes place to ensure that customers agree that the system meets all functional requirements and performs according to the original specification. As with any critical development process, it's important that you maintain a copy of the written system test plan and test results for future review.

## Maintenance

Once a system is operational, a variety of maintenance tasks are necessary to ensure continued operation in the face of changing operational, data processing, storage, and environmental requirements. It's essential that you have a skilled support team in place to handle any routine or unexpected maintenance. It's also important that any changes to the code be handled through a formalized change request/control process, as described in Chapter 5.

# Life Cycle Models

One of the major complaints you'll hear from practitioners of the more established engineering disciplines (such as civil, mechanical, and electrical engineering) is that software engineering is not an engineering discipline at all. In fact, they contend, it's simply a combination of chaotic processes that somehow manage to scrape out workable solutions from time to time. Indeed, some of the "software engineering" that takes place in today's development environments is nothing but bootstrap coding held together by "duct tape and chicken wire."

However, the adoption of more formalized life cycle management processes is seen in mainstream software engineering as the industry matures. After all, it's hardly fair to compare the processes of an age-old discipline such as civil engineering to those of an industry that's barely a few decades old. In the 1970s and 1980s, pioneers like Winston Royce and Barry Boehm proposed several software development life cycle (SDLC) models to help guide the practice toward formalized processes. In 1991, the Software Engineering Institute introduced the Capability Maturity Model, which described the process organizations undertake as they move toward incorporating solid engineering principles into their software development processes. In the following sections, we'll take a look at the work produced by these studies. Having a management model in place should improve the resultant products. However, if the SDLC methodology is inadequate, the project may fail to meet business and user needs. Thus, it is important to verify that the SDLC model is properly implemented and is appropriate for your environment. Furthermore, one of the initial steps of implementing an SDLC should include management approval.

## Waterfall Model

Originally developed by Winston Royce in 1970, the waterfall model seeks to view the systems development life cycle as a series of iterative activities. As shown in Figure 7.6, the traditional waterfall model has seven stages of development. As each stage is completed, the project moves into the next phase. As illustrated by the backward arrows, the modern waterfall model does allow development to return to the previous phase to correct defects discovered during the subsequent phase. This is often known as the *feedback loop characteristic* of the waterfall model.

**FIGURE 7.6**   The waterfall life cycle model

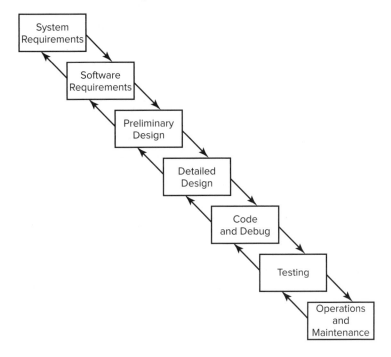

The waterfall model was one of the first comprehensive attempts to model the software development process while taking into account the necessity of returning to previous phases to correct system faults. However, one of the major criticisms of this model is that it allows the developers to step back only one phase in the process. It does not make provisions for the discovery of errors at a later phase in the development cycle.

The waterfall model was improved by adding validation and verification steps to each phase. Verification evaluates the product against specifications, while validation evaluates how well the product satisfies real-world requirements. The improved model was labeled the *modified waterfall model*. However, it did not gain widespread use before the spiral model dominated the project management scene.

## Spiral Model

In 1988, Barry Boehm of TRW proposed an alternative life cycle model that allows for multiple iterations of a waterfall-style process. Figure 7.7 illustrates this model. Because the spiral model encapsulates a number of iterations of another model (the waterfall model), it is known as a *metamodel*, or a "model of models."

**FIGURE 7.7**   The spiral life cycle model

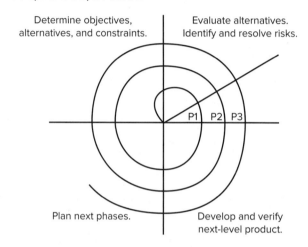

Determine objectives, alternatives, and constraints.

Evaluate alternatives. Identify and resolve risks.

P1   P2   P3

Plan next phases.

Develop and verify next-level product.

Notice that each "loop" of the spiral results in the development of a new system prototype (represented by P1, P2, and P3 in the illustration). Theoretically, system developers would apply the entire waterfall process to the development of each prototype, thereby incrementally working toward a mature system that incorporates all the functional requirements in a fully validated fashion. Boehm's spiral model provides a solution to the major criticism of the waterfall model—it allows developers to return to the planning stages as changing technical demands and customer requirements necessitate the evolution of a system.

## Agile Software Development

More recently, the agile model of software development has gained popularity within the software engineering community. Beginning in the mid-1990s, developers began to embrace approaches to software development that eschewed the rigid models of the past in favor of approaches that placed an emphasis on the needs of the customer and on quickly developing new functionality that meets those needs in an iterative fashion.

Seventeen pioneers of the agile development approach got together in 2001 and produced a document, titled the "Agile Manifesto," that states the core philosophy of the agile approach:

"We are uncovering better ways of developing software by doing it and helping others do it. Through this work we have come to value:

**Individuals and interactions** over processes and tools

**Working software** over comprehensive documentation

**Customer collaboration** over contract negotiation

**Responding to change** over following a plan

"That is, while there is value in the items on the right, we value the items on the left more."

The Agile Manifesto, available at `http://agilemanifesto.org/`, also defines 12 principles that underlie the philosophy:

1. Our highest priority is to satisfy the customer through early and continuous delivery of valuable software.

2. Welcome changing requirements, even late in development. Agile processes harness change for the customer's competitive advantage.

3. Deliver working software frequently, from a couple of weeks to a couple of months, with a preference to the shorter timescale.

4. Business people and developers must work together daily throughout the project.

5. Build projects around motivated individuals. Give them the environment and support they need, and trust them to get the job done.

6. The most efficient and effective method of conveying information to and within a development team is face-to-face conversation.

7. Working software is the primary measure of progress.

8. Agile processes promote sustainable development. The sponsors, developers, and users should be able to maintain a constant pace indefinitely.

9. Continuous attention to technical excellence and good design enhances agility.

10. Simplicity—the art of maximizing the amount of work not done—is essential.

11. The best architectures, requirements, and designs emerge from self-organizing teams.

12. At regular intervals, the team reflects on how to become more effective, then tunes and adjusts its behavior accordingly.

The agile development approach is quickly gaining momentum in the software community and has many variants, including Scrum, Agile Unified Process (AUP), the Dynamic Systems Development Model (DSDM), and Extreme Programming (XP).

## Software Capability Maturity Model

The Software Engineering Institute (SEI) at Carnegie Mellon University introduced the Capability Maturity Model for Software also known as the Software Capability Maturity Model (abbreviated as SW-CMM, CMM, or SCMM), which contends that all organizations engaged in software development move through a variety of maturity phases in sequential fashion. The SW-CMM describes the principles and practices underlying software process maturity. It is intended to help software organizations improve the maturity and quality of their software processes by implementing an evolutionary path from ad hoc, chaotic processes to mature, disciplined software processes. The idea behind the SW-CMM is that the quality of software depends on the quality of its development process.

The stages of the SW-CMM are as follows:

**Level 1: Initial**    In this phase, you'll often find hard-working people charging ahead in a disorganized fashion. There is usually little or no defined software development process.

**Level 2: Repeatable**    In this phase, basic life cycle management processes are introduced. Reuse of code in an organized fashion begins to enter the picture, and repeatable results are expected from similar projects. SEI defines the key process areas for this level as Requirements Management, Software Project Planning, Software Project Tracking and Oversight, Software Subcontract Management, Software Quality Assurance, and Software Configuration Management.

**Level 3: Defined**    In this phase, software developers operate according to a set of formal, documented software development processes. All development projects take place within the constraints of the new standardized management model. SEI defines the key process areas for this level as Organization Process Focus, Organization Process Definition, Training Program, Integrated Software Management, Software Product Engineering, Intergroup Coordination, and Peer Reviews.

**Level 4: Managed**    In this phase, management of the software process proceeds to the next level. Quantitative measures are utilized to gain a detailed understanding of the development process. SEI defines the key process areas for this level as Quantitative Process Management and Software Quality Management.

**Level 5: Optimizing**    In the optimized organization, a process of continuous improvement occurs. Sophisticated software development processes are in place that ensure that feedback from one phase reaches to the previous phase to improve future results. SEI defines the key process areas for this level as Defect Prevention, Technology Change Management, and Process Change Management.

For more information on the Capability Maturity Model for Software, visit the Software Engineering Institute's website at www.sei.cmu.edu.

## IDEAL Model

The Software Engineering Institute also developed the IDEAL model for software development, which implements many of the SW-CMM attributes. The IDEAL model, illustrated in Figure 7.8, has five phases:

**I: Initiating**    In the initiating phase of the IDEAL model, the business reasons behind the change are outlined, support is built for the initiative, and the appropriate infrastructure is put in place.

**D: Diagnosing**   During the diagnosing phase, engineers analyze the current state of the organization and make general recommendations for change.

**E: Establishing**   In the establishing phase, the organization takes the general recommendations from the diagnosing phase and develops a specific plan of action that helps achieve those changes.

**A: Acting**   In the acting phase, it's time to stop "talking the talk" and "walk the walk." The organization develops solutions and then tests, refines, and implements them.

**L: Learning**   As with any quality improvement process, the organization must continuously analyze its efforts to determine whether it has achieved the desired goals and, when necessary, propose new actions to put the organization back on course.

**FIGURE 7.8**   The IDEAL model

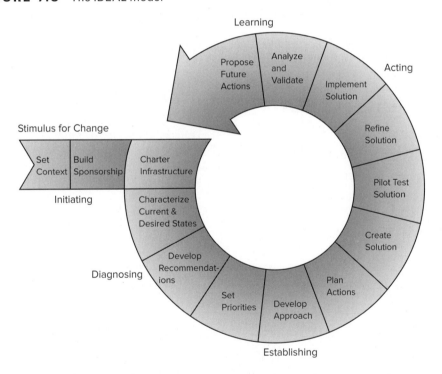

---

**SW-CMM and IDEAL Model Memorization**

To help you remember the initial letters of each of the 10 level names of the SW-CMM and IDEAL models (II DR ED AM LO), imagine yourself sitting on the couch in a psychiatrist's office saying, "I . . . I, Dr. Ed, am lo(w)." If you can remember that phrase, then you can extract the 10 initial letters of the level names. If you write the letters out into two columns, you can reconstruct the level names in order of the two systems. The left column is the IDEAL model, and the right represents the levels of the SW-CMM.

| | |
|---|---|
| Initiating | Initiating |
| Diagnosing | Repeatable |
| Establishing | Defined |
| Acting | Managed |
| Learning | Optimized |

---

## Gantt Charts and PERT

A Gantt chart is a type of bar chart that shows the interrelationships over time between projects and schedules. It provides a graphical illustration of a schedule that helps to plan, coordinate, and track specific tasks in a project. Figure 7.9 shows an example of a Gantt chart.

**FIGURE 7.9**  A Gantt chart

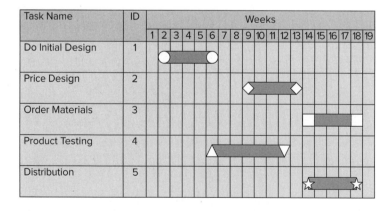

Program Evaluation Review Technique (PERT) is a project-scheduling tool used to judge the size of a software product in development and calculate the standard deviation (SD) for risk assessment. PERT relates the estimated lowest possible size, the most likely size, and the highest possible size of each component. PERT is used to direct improvements to project management and software coding in order to produce more efficient software. As the capabilities of programming and management improve, the actual produced size of software should be smaller.

## Change Control and Configuration Management

Once software has been released into a production environment, users will inevitably request the addition of new features, correction of bugs, and other modifications to the code. Just as the organization developed a regimented process for developing software, they must also put a procedure in place to manage changes in an organized fashion.

 **Real World Scenario**

### Change Control as a Security Tool

Change control plays an important role when monitoring systems in the controlled environment of a data center. One of the authors recently worked with an organization that used change control as an essential component of its efforts to detect unauthorized changes to computing systems.

In Chapter 8, you'll learn how tools for monitoring file integrity, such as Tripwire, allow you to monitor a system for changes. This organization used Tripwire to monitor hundreds of production servers. However, the organization quickly found itself overwhelmed by file modification alerts resulting from normal activity. The author worked with them to tune the Tripwire-monitoring policies and integrate them with change control. Now all Tripwire alerts go to a centralized monitoring center where administrators correlate them with approved changes. System administrators receive an alert only if the security team identifies a change that does not appear to correlate with an approved change request.

This approach greatly reduced the time spent by administrators reviewing file integrity reports and improved the usefulness of the tool to security administrators.

The change control process has three basic components:

**Request control**   The request control process provides an organized framework within which users can request modifications, managers can conduct cost/benefit analysis, and developers can prioritize tasks.

**Change control**   The change control process is used by developers to re-create the situation encountered by the user and analyze the appropriate changes to remedy the situation. It also provides an organized framework within which multiple developers can create and test a solution prior to rolling it out into a production environment. Change control includes conforming to quality control restrictions, developing tools for update or change deployment, properly documenting any coded changes, and restricting the effects of new code to minimize diminishment of security.

**Release control**   Once the changes are finalized, they must be approved for release through the release control procedure. An essential step of the release control process is to double-check and ensure that any code inserted as a programming aid during the change process (such as debugging code and/or back doors) is removed before releasing the new software to production. Release control should also include acceptance testing to ensure that any alterations to end user work tasks are understood and functional.

In addition to the change control process, security administrators should be aware of the importance of configuration management. This process is used to control the version(s) of software used throughout an organization and formally track and control changes to the software configuration. It has four main components:

**Configuration identification**   During the configuration identification process, administrators document the configuration of covered software products throughout the organization.

**Configuration control**   The configuration control process ensures that changes to software versions are made in accordance with the change control and configuration management policies. Updates can be made only from authorized distributions in accordance with those policies.

**Configuration status accounting**   Formalized procedures are used to keep track of all authorized changes that take place.

**Configuration Audit**   A periodic configuration audit should be conducted to ensure that the actual production environment is consistent with the accounting records and that no unauthorized configuration changes have taken place.

Together, change control and configuration management techniques form an important part of the software engineer's arsenal and protect the organization from development-related security issues.

## Software Testing

As part of the development process, your organization should thoroughly test any software before distributing it internally (or releasing it to market). The best time to address testing is as the modules are designed. In other words, the mechanisms you use to test a product and the data sets you use to explore that product should be designed in parallel with the product itself. Your programming team should develop special test suites of data that exercise all paths of the software to the fullest extent possible and know the correct resulting outputs beforehand. This extensive test suite process is known as a *reasonableness check*. Furthermore, while conducting stress tests, you should check how the product handles normal and valid input data, incorrect types, out-of-range values, and other bounds and/or conditions. Live workloads provide the best stress testing possible. However, you should not use live or actual field data for testing, especially in the early development stages, since a flaw or error could result in the violation of integrity or confidentiality of the test data.

When testing software, you should apply the same rules of separation of duties that you do for other aspects of your organization. In other words, you should assign the testing of your software to someone other than the programmer(s) who developed the code to avoid a conflict of interest and assure a more successful finished product. When a third party tests your software, you have a greater likelihood of receiving an objective and nonbiased examination. The third-party test allows for a broader and more thorough test and prevents the bias and inclinations of the programmers from affecting the results of the test.

You can utilize three testing methods or ideologies for software testing:

**White-box testing**   White-box testing examines the internal logical structures of a program and steps through the code line by line, analyzing the program for potential errors.

**Black-box testing**   Black-box testing examines the program from a user perspective by providing a wide variety of input scenarios and inspecting the output. Black-box testers do not have access to the internal code. Final acceptance testing that occurs prior to system delivery is a common example of black-box testing.

**Gray-box testing**   Gray-box testing combines the two approaches and is a popular approach to software validation. In this approach, testers approach the software from a user perspective, analyzing inputs and outputs. They also have access to the source code and use it to help design their tests. They do not, however, analyze the inner workings of the program during their testing.

Proper software test implementation is a key element in the project development process. Many of the common mistakes and oversights often found in commercial and in-house software can be eliminated. Keep the test plan and results as part of the system's permanent documentation.

# Security Control Architecture

All secure systems implement some sort of security control architecture. At the hardware and operating system levels, controls should ensure enforcement of basic security principles. The following sections examine several basic control principles that should be enforced in a secure computing environment.

## Process Isolation

*Process isolation* is one of the fundamental security procedures put into place during system design. Process isolation mechanisms (whether part of the operating system or part of the hardware itself) ensure that each process has its own isolated memory space for storage of data and the actual executing application code itself. This guarantees that processes cannot access each other's reserved memory areas and protects against confidentiality violations or intentional/unintentional modification of data by an unauthorized process. *Hardware segmentation* is a technique that implements process isolation at the hardware level by enforcing memory access constraints.

## Protection Rings

The ring-oriented protection scheme provides for several modes of system operation, thereby facilitating secure operation by restricting processes to running in the appropriate security ring. Figure 7.10 shows the four-layer ring protection scheme supported by Intel microprocessors.

**FIGURE 7.10** Ring protection scheme

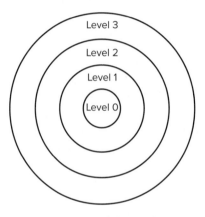

In this scheme, each of the rings has a separate and distinct function:

**Level 0** Represents the ring where the operating system itself resides. This ring contains the security kernel—the core set of operating system services that handles all user/application requests for access to system resources. The kernel also implements the reference monitor, an operating system component that validates all user requests for access to resources against an access control scheme. Processes running at Level 0 are often said to be running in supervisory mode, also called *privileged mode*. Level 0 processes have full control of all system resources, so it's essential to ensure that they are fully verified and validated before implementation.

**Levels 1 and 2** Contain device drivers and other operating system services that provide higher-level interfaces to system resources. However, in practice, most operating systems do not implement either one of these layers.

**Level 3**   Represents the security layer where user applications and processes reside. This layer is commonly referred to as *user mode*, or *protected mode*, and applications running here are not permitted direct access to system resources. In fact, when an application running in protected mode attempts to access an unauthorized resource, a General Protection Fault (GPF) occurs.

> The security kernel and reference monitor are extremely important computer security topics that must be understood by any information security practitioner. These topics commonly appear on the CISSP exam.

The reference monitor component (present at Level 0) is an extremely important element of any operating system offering multilevel secure services. This concept was first formally described in the Department of Defense Trusted Computer System Evaluation Criteria (commonly referred to as the Orange Book because of the color of its cover). The DoD set forth the following three requirements for an operational reference monitor:

- It must be tamperproof.
- It must always be invoked when a program or user requests access to resources.
- It must be small enough to be subject to analysis and tests, the completeness of which can be assured.

## Abstraction

*Abstraction* is a valuable tool drawn from the object-oriented software development model that can be extrapolated to apply to the design of all types of information systems. In effect, abstraction states that a thorough understanding of a system's operational details is not often necessary to perform day-to-day activities. For example, a system developer might need to know that a certain procedure, when invoked, writes information to disk, but it's not necessary for the developer to understand the underlying principles that enable the data to be written to disk or the exact format that the disk procedures use to store and retrieve data. The process of developing increasingly sophisticated objects that draw upon the abstracted methods of lower-level objects is known as *encapsulation*. The deliberate concealment of lower levels of functionality from higher-level processes is known as *data hiding* or *information hiding*.

## Security Modes

In a secure environment, information systems are configured to process information in one of four security modes. These modes are set out by the Department of Defense in CSC-STD-003-85 (the "light yellow book") as follows:

- Systems running in **compartmented security mode** may process two or more types of compartmented information. All system users must have an appropriate clearance to access all information processed by the system but do not necessarily have a need to know all of the information in the system. Compartments are subcategories or compartments within the different classification levels, and extreme care is taken to preserve the information within the different compartments. The system may be classified at the secret level but contain five different compartments, all classified secret. If a user has the need to know about only two of the five different compartments to do their job, that user can access the system but can access only the two compartments.

- Systems running in **dedicated security mode** are authorized to process only a specific classification level at a time, and all system users must have clearance and a need to know that information.

- Systems running in **multilevel security mode** are authorized to process information at more than one level of security even when all system users do not have appropriate clearances or a need to know for all information processed by the system.

- Systems running in **system-high security mode** are authorized to process only information that all system users are cleared to read and have a valid need to know. These systems are not trusted to maintain separation between security levels, and all information processed by these systems must be handled as if it were classified at the same level as the most highly classified information processed by the system.

## Service-Level Agreements

Using service-level agreements (SLAs) is an increasingly popular way to ensure that organizations providing services to internal and/or external customers maintain an appropriate level of service agreed upon by both the service provider and the vendor. It's a wise move to put SLAs in place for any data circuits, applications, information processing systems, databases, or other critical components that are vital to your organization's continued viability. The following issues are commonly addressed in SLAs:

- System uptime (as a percentage of overall operating time)

- Maximum consecutive downtime (in seconds/minutes/and so on)

- Peak load

- Average load

- Responsibility for diagnostics

- Failover time (if redundancy is in place)

Service-level agreements also often commonly include financial and other contractual remedies that kick in if the agreement is not maintained. For example, if a critical circuit is down for more than 15 minutes, the service provider might agree to waive all charges on that circuit for one week.

# Summary

Data is quickly becoming the most valuable resource many organizations possess. Therefore, it's critical that information security practitioners understand the necessity of safeguarding the data itself and the systems and applications that assist in the processing of that data. Protections against malicious code, database vulnerabilities, and system/application development flaws must be implemented in every technology-aware organization.

Malicious code objects pose a threat to the computing resources of organizations. In the nondistributed environment, such threats include viruses, logic bombs, Trojan horses, and worms. Chapter 8 delves more deeply into specific types of malicious code objects as well as other attacks commonly used by hackers. We'll also explore some effective defense mechanisms to safeguard your network against their insidious effects.

By this point, you no doubt recognize the importance of placing adequate access controls and audit trails on these valuable information resources. Database security is a rapidly growing field; if databases play a major role in your security duties, take the time to sit down with database administrators, courses, and textbooks and learn the underlying theory. It's a valuable investment.

Finally, there are various controls that can be put into place during the system and application development process to ensure that the end product of these processes is compatible with operation in a secure environment. Such controls include process isolation, hardware segmentation abstraction, and contractual arrangements, such as service level agreements (SLA). Security should always be introduced in the early planning phases of any development project and continually monitored throughout the design, development, deployment, and maintenance phases of production.

# Exam Essentials

**Understand the application threats present in a local/nondistributed environment.** Describe the functioning of viruses, worms, Trojan horses, and logic bombs. Understand the impact each type of threat may have on a system and the methods they use to propagate.

**Understand the application threats unique to distributed computing environments.** Know the basic functioning of agents and the impact they may have on computer/network security. Understand the functionality behind Java applets and ActiveX controls and be able to determine the appropriate security controls for a given computing environment.

**Explain the basic architecture of a relational database management system (RDBMS).** Know the structure of relational databases. Be able to explain the function of tables (relations), rows (records/tuples), and columns (fields/attributes). Know how relationships are defined between tables.

**Understand the various types of keys used to identify information stored in a database.** You should be familiar with the basic types of keys. Understand that each table has one or more candidate keys that are chosen from a column heading in a database and that uniquely identify rows within a table. The database designer selects one candidate key as the primary key for the table. Foreign keys are used to enforce referential integrity between tables participating in a relationship.

**Recognize the various common forms of DBMS safeguards.** The common DBMS safeguards include concurrency, edit control, semantic integrity mechanisms, use of time and date stamps, granular control of objects, content-dependent access control, context-dependent access control, cell suppression, database partitioning, noise, perturbation, and polyinstantiation.

**Explain the database security threats posed by aggregation and inference.** Aggregation utilizes specialized database functions to draw conclusions about a large amount of data based on individual records. Access to these functions should be restricted if aggregate information is considered more sensitive than the individual records. Inference occurs when database users can deduce sensitive facts from less-sensitive information.

**Know the various types of storage.** Explain the differences between primary memory and virtual memory, secondary storage and virtual storage, random access storage and sequential access storage, and volatile storage and nonvolatile storage.

**Explain how expert systems function.** Expert systems consist of two main components: a knowledge base that contains a series of "if/then" rules and an inference engine that uses that information to draw conclusions about other data.

**Describe the functioning of neural networks.** Neural networks simulate the functioning of the human mind to a limited extent by arranging a series of layered calculations to solve problems. Neural networks require extensive training on a particular problem before they are able to offer solutions.

**Understand the models of systems development.** Know that the waterfall model describes a sequential development process that results in the development of a finished product. Developers may step back only one phase in the process if errors are discovered. The spiral model uses several iterations of the waterfall model to produce a number of fully specified and tested prototypes. Agile development models place an emphasis on the needs of the customer and quickly developing new functionality that meets those needs in an iterative fashion.

**Describe software development maturity models.** Know that maturity models help software organizations improve the maturity and quality of their software processes by implementing an evolutionary path from ad hoc, chaotic processes to mature, disciplined software processes. Describe the SW-CMM and IDEAL models.

**Understand the importance of change and configuration management** Know the three basic components of change control—request control, change control, and release control—and how they contribute to security. Explain how configuration management controls the versions of software used in an organization.

**Explain the ring protection scheme.**   Understand the four rings of the ring protection scheme and the activities that typically occur within each ring. Know that most operating systems only implement Level 0 (privileged or supervisory mode) and Level 3 (protected or user mode).

**Describe the function of the security kernel and reference monitor.**   The security kernel is the core set of operating system services that handles user requests for access to system resources. The reference monitor is a portion of the security kernel that validates user requests against the system's access control mechanisms.

**Understand the importance of testing.**   Software testing should be designed as part of the development process. Testing should be used as a management tool to improve the design, development, and production processes.

**Understand the four security modes approved by the Department of Defense.**   Know the differences between compartmented security mode, dedicated security mode, multilevel security mode, and system-high security mode. Understand the different types of classified information that can be processed in each mode and the types of users that can access each system.

# Written Lab

1.  How does a worm travel from system to system?

2.  Describe three benefits of using applets instead of server-side code for web applications.

3.  What are the three requirements for an operational reference monitor in a secure computing system?

4.  What operating systems are capable of processing ActiveX controls posted on a website?

5.  What type of key is selected by the database developer to uniquely identify data within a relational database table?

6.  What database security technique appears to permit the insertion of multiple rows sharing the same uniquely identifying information?

7.  What type of storage is commonly referred to as a RAM disk?

8.  How far backward does the waterfall model allow developers to travel when a development flaw is discovered?

# Answers to Written Lab

1.  Worms travel from system to system under their own power by exploiting flaws in networking software.

2.  The processing burden is shifted from the server to the client, allowing the web server to handle a greater number of simultaneous requests. The client uses local resources to process the data, usually resulting in a quicker response. The privacy of client data is protected because information does not need to be transmitted to the web server.

3.  It must be tamperproof, it must always be invoked, and it must be small enough to be subject to analysis and tests, the completeness of which can be assured.

4.  Microsoft Windows platforms only.

5.  Primary key.

6.  Polyinstantiation.

7.  Virtual storage.

8.  One phase.

# Review Questions

1. Which one of the following malicious code objects might be inserted in an application by a disgruntled software developer with the purpose of destroying system data after the developer's account has been deleted (presumably following their termination)?

   **A.** Virus

   **B.** Worm

   **C.** Trojan horse

   **D.** Logic bomb

2. What term is used to describe code objects that act on behalf of a user while operating in an unattended manner?

   **A.** Agent

   **B.** Worm

   **C.** Applet

   **D.** Browser

3. Which form of DBMS primarily supports the establishment of treelike relationships?

   **A.** Relational

   **B.** Hierarchical

   **C.** Mandatory

   **D.** Distributed

4. Which of the following characteristics can be used to differentiate worms from viruses?

   **A.** Worms infect a system by overwriting data in the master boot record of a storage device.

   **B.** Worms always spread from system to system without user intervention.

   **C.** Worms always carry a malicious payload that impacts infected systems.

   **D.** All of the above.

5. What programming language(s) can be used to develop ActiveX controls for use on an Internet site?

   **A.** Visual Basic

   **B.** C

   **C.** Java

   **D.** All of the above

**6.** What form of access control is concerned with the data stored by a field rather than any other issue?

   **A.** Content-dependent

   **B.** Context-dependent

   **C.** Semantic integrity mechanisms

   **D.** Perturbation

**7.** Which one of the following key types is used to enforce referential integrity between database tables?

   **A.** Candidate key

   **B.** Primary key

   **C.** Foreign key

   **D.** Super key

**8.** Richard believes that a database user is misusing his privileges to gain information about the company's overall business trends by issuing queries that combine data from a large number of records. What process is the database user taking advantage of?

   **A.** Inference

   **B.** Contamination

   **C.** Polyinstantiation

   **D.** Aggregation

**9.** What database technique can be used to prevent unauthorized users from determining classified information by noticing the absence of information normally available to them?

   **A.** Inference

   **B.** Manipulation

   **C.** Polyinstantiation

   **D.** Aggregation

**10.** Which one of the following terms cannot be used to describe the main RAM of a typical computer system?

   **A.** Volatile

   **B.** Sequential access

   **C.** Real memory

   **D.** Primary memory

11. What type of information is used to form the basis of an expert system's decision-making process?

    **A.** A series of weighted layered computations

    **B.** Combined input from a number of human experts, weighted according to past performance

    **C.** A series of "if/then" rules codified in a knowledge base

    **D.** A biological decision-making process that simulates the reasoning process used by the human mind

12. Which one of the following intrusion detection systems makes use of an expert to detect anomalous user activity?

    **A.** PIX

    **B.** IDIOT

    **C.** AAFID

    **D.** NIDES

13. Which of the following acts as a proxy between two different systems to support interaction and simplify the work of programmers?

    **A.** SDLC

    **B.** ODBC

    **C.** DSS

    **D.** Abstraction

14. Which software development life cycle model allows for multiple iterations of the development process, resulting in multiple prototypes, each produced according to a complete design and testing process?

    **A.** Software Capability Maturity Model

    **B.** Waterfall model

    **C.** Development cycle

    **D.** Spiral model

15. In systems utilizing a ring protection scheme, at what level does the security kernel reside?

    **A.** Level 0

    **B.** Level 1

    **C.** Level 2

    **D.** Level 3

16. Which database security risk occurs when data from a higher classification level is mixed with data from a lower classification level?

   A. Aggregation

   B. Inference

   C. Contamination

   D. Polyinstantiation

17. Machine language is an example of a _____-generation language.

   A. First

   B. Second

   C. Third

   D. Fifth

18. Which one of the following is not part of the change control process?

   A. Request control

   B. Release control

   C. Configuration audit

   D. Change control

19. What transaction management principle ensures that two transactions do not interfere with each other as they operate on the same data?

   A. Atomicity

   B. Consistency

   C. Isolation

   D. Durability

20. Which subset of the Structured Query Language is used to create and modify the database schema?

   A. Data Definition Language

   B. Data Structure Language

   C. Database Schema Language

   D. Database Manipulation Language

# Answers to Review Questions

1. D. Logic bombs are malicious code objects programmed to lie dormant until certain logical conditions, such as a certain date, time, system event, or other criteria, are met. At that time, they spring into action, triggering their malicious payload.

2. A. Intelligent agents are code objects programmed to perform certain operations on behalf of a user in their absence. They are also often referred to as *bots*.

3. B. A hierarchical DBMS supports one-to-many relationships, often expressed in a tree structure.

4. B. The major difference between viruses and worms is that worms are self-replicating, whereas viruses require user intervention to spread from system to system. Infection of the master boot record is a characteristic of a subclass of viruses known as *MBR viruses*. Both viruses and worms are capable of carrying malicious payloads.

5. D. Microsoft's ActiveX technology supports a number of programming languages, including Visual Basic, C, C++, and Java. On the other hand, only the Java language can be used to write Java applets.

6. A. Content-dependent access control is focused on the internal data of each field.

7. C. Foreign keys are used to enforce referential integrity constraints between tables that participate in a relationship.

8. D. In this case, the process the database user is taking advantage of is aggregation. Aggregation attacks involve the use of specialized database functions to combine information from a large number of database records to reveal information that may be more sensitive than the information in individual records would reveal.

9. C. Polyinstantiation allows the insertion of multiple records that appear to have the same primary key values into a database at different classification levels.

10. B. Random access memory (RAM) allows for the direct addressing of any point within the resource. A sequential access storage medium, such as a magnetic tape, requires scanning through the entire media from the beginning to reach a specific address.

11. C. Expert systems utilize a knowledge base consisting of a series of "if/then" statements to form decisions based upon the previous experience of human experts.

12. D. The Next-Generation Intrusion Detection Expert System (NIDES) is an expert system–based intrusion detection system. PIX is a firewall, and IDIOT and AAFID are intrusion detection systems that do not utilize expert systems.

13. B. ODBC acts as a proxy between applications and the back-end DBMS.

14. D. The spiral model allows developers to repeat iterations of another life cycle model (such as the waterfall model) to produce a number of fully tested prototypes.

**15.** A. The security kernel and reference monitor reside at Level 0 in the ring protection scheme, where they have unrestricted access to all system resources.

**16.** C. Contamination is the mixing of data from a higher classification level and/or need-to-know requirement with data from a lower classification level and/or need-to-know requirement.

**17.** A. Machine languages are considered first-generation languages.

**18.** C. Configuration audit is part of the configuration management process rather than the change control process.

**19.** C. The isolation principle states that two transactions operating on the same data must be temporarily separated from each other such that one does not interfere with the other.

**20.** A. The Data Definition Language (DDL) is used to make modifications to a relational database's schema.

# Chapter

# 8

# Malicious Code and Application Attacks

## THE CISSP EXAM TOPICS COVERED IN THIS CHAPTER INCLUDE:

✓ **Operations Security**

- Prevent or respond to attacks (e.g., malicious code, zero-day exploit, denial of service)

- Implement and support patch and vulnerability management

✓ **Application Development Security**

- Understand the application environment and security controls

  - Security of the application environment; security issues of programming languages; security issues in source code (e.g., buffer overflow)

In previous chapters, you learned about many general security principles and the policy and procedure mechanisms that help security practitioners develop adequate protection against malicious individuals. This chapter takes an in-depth look at some of the specific threats faced on a daily basis by administrators in the field.

This material is not only critical for the CISSP exam, but it's also some of the most basic information a computer security professional must understand to effectively practice their trade. We'll begin this chapter by looking at the risks posed by malicious code objects—viruses, worms, logic bombs, and Trojan horses. We'll then take a look at some of the other security exploits used by someone attempting to gain unauthorized access to a system or to prevent legitimate users from gaining such access.

# Malicious Code

Malicious code objects include a broad range of programmed computer security threats that exploit various network, operating system, software, and physical security vulnerabilities to spread malicious payloads to computer systems. Some malicious code objects, such as computer viruses and Trojan horses, depend upon irresponsible computer use by humans in order to spread from system to system with any success. Other objects, such as worms, spread rapidly among vulnerable systems under their own power.

All computer security practitioners must be familiar with the risks posed by the various types of malicious code objects so they can develop adequate countermeasures to protect the systems under their care as well as implement appropriate responses if their systems are compromised.

## Sources

Where does malicious code come from? In the early days of computer security, malicious code writers were extremely skilled (albeit misguided) software developers who took pride in carefully crafting innovative malicious code techniques. Indeed, they actually served a somewhat useful function by exposing security holes in popular software packages and operating systems, raising the security awareness of the computing community. For an example of this type of code writer, see the sidebar "RTM and the Internet Worm" later in this chapter.

Modern times have given rise to the *script kiddie*—the malicious individual who doesn't understand the technology behind security vulnerabilities but downloads ready-to-use software (or scripts) from the Internet and uses them to launch attacks against remote systems. This trend gave birth to a new breed of virus creation software that allows anyone with a minimal level of technical expertise to create a virus and unleash it upon the Internet. This is reflected in the large number of viruses documented by antivirus experts to date. The amateur malicious code developers are usually just experimenting with the new tool they downloaded or attempting to cause problems for one or two enemies. Unfortunately, the malware sometimes spread rapidly and cause problems for Internet users in general. In addition, the tools used by script kiddies are freely available to those with more sinister criminal intent. Indeed, many in law enforcement believe that international organized crime syndicates may now play a role in malware proliferation. These criminals, located in countries with weak law enforcement mechanisms, use malware to steal the money and identities of people from around the world, especially residents of the United States.

# Viruses

The computer virus is perhaps the earliest form of malicious code to plague security administrators. Indeed, viruses are so prevalent nowadays that major outbreaks receive attention from the mass media and provoke mild hysteria among average computer users. According to Symantec, one of the major antivirus software vendors, there were over 1.1 million strains of viruses roaming the global network in 2008. Hundreds of thousands of variations of these viruses strike unsuspecting computer users each day. Many carry malicious payloads that cause damage ranging in scope from displaying a profane message on the screen all the way to causing complete destruction of all data stored on the local hard drive.

As with biological viruses, computer viruses have two main functions—propagation and destruction. Miscreants who create viruses carefully design code to implement these functions in new and innovative methods that they hope escape detection and bypass increasingly sophisticated antivirus technology. It's fair to say that an arms race has developed between virus writers and antivirus technicians, each hoping to develop technology one step ahead of the other. The propagation function defines how the virus will spread from system to system, infecting each machine it leaves in its wake. A virus's payload delivers the destructive power by implementing whatever malicious activity the virus writer had in mind. This could be anything that negatively impacts the confidentiality, integrity, or availability of systems or data.

## Virus Propagation Techniques

By definition, a virus must contain technology that enables it to spread from system to system, aided by unsuspecting computer users seeking to share data by exchanging disks, sharing networked resources, sending electronic mail, or using some other means. Once they've "touched" a new system, they use one of several propagation techniques to infect the new victim and expand their reach. In the following sections, we'll look at three common propagation techniques: master boot record infection, file infection, and macro infection.

### Master Boot Record Viruses

The *master boot record virus* (or *MBR virus*) is one of the earliest known forms of virus infection. These viruses attack the MBR, the portion of bootable media (such as a hard drive, floppy disk, or CD/DVD) that the computer uses to load the operating system during the boot process. Because the MBR is extremely small (usually 512 bytes), it can't contain all the code required to implement the virus's propagation and destructive functions. To bypass this space limitation, MBR viruses store the majority of their code on another portion of the storage media. When the system reads the infected MBR, the virus instructs it to read and execute the code stored in this alternate location, thereby loading the entire virus into memory and potentially triggering the delivery of the virus's payload.

---

**The Boot Sector and the Master Boot Record**

You'll often see the terms *boot sector* and *master boot record* used interchangeably to describe the portion of a storage device used to load the operating system and the types of viruses that attack that process. This is not technically correct. The MBR is a single disk sector, normally the first sector of the media that is read in the initial stages of the boot process. The MBR determines which media partition contains the operating system and then directs the system to read that partition's boot sector to load the operating system.

Viruses can attack both the MBR and the boot sector, with substantially similar results. MBR viruses act by redirecting the system to an infected boot sector, which loads the virus into memory before loading the operating system from the legitimate boot sector. Boot sector viruses actually infect the legitimate boot sector and are loaded into memory during the operating system load process.

---

Most MBR viruses are spread between systems through the use of infected media inadvertently shared between users. If the infected media is in the drive during the boot process, the target system reads the infected MBR, and the virus loads into memory, infects the MBR on the target system's hard drive, and spreads its infection to yet another machine.

### File Infector Viruses

Many viruses infect different types of executable files and trigger when the operating system attempts to execute them. For Windows-based systems, the names of these files end with .exe and .com extensions. The propagation routines of file infector viruses may slightly alter the code of an executable program, therefore implanting the technology the virus needs to replicate and damage the system. In some cases, the virus might actually replace the entire file with an infected version. Standard file infector viruses that do not use cloaking techniques such as stealth or encryption (see the section "Virus Technologies" later in this chapter) are often easily detected by comparing file characteristics (such as size and modification date) before and after infection or by comparing hash values. The section "Antivirus Mechanisms" provides technical details behind these techniques.

A variation of the file infector virus is the companion virus. These viruses are self-contained executable files that escape detection by using a filename similar to, but slightly different from, a legitimate operating system file. They rely on the default filename extensions that Windows-based operating systems append to commands when executing program files (.com, .exe, and .bat, in that order). For example, if you had a program on your hard disk named GAME.EXE, a companion virus might use the name GAME.COM. If you then open a Command tool and simply type GAME, the operating system would execute the virus file, GAME.COM, instead of the file you actually intended to execute, GAME.EXE. This is a very good reason to avoid shortcuts and fully specify the name of the file you want to execute.

### Macro Viruses

Many common software applications implement some sort of scripting functionality to assist with the automation of repetitive tasks. These functionalities often use simple, yet powerful, programming languages such as Visual Basic for Applications (VBA). Although macros do indeed offer great productivity-enhancing opportunities to computer users, they also expose systems to yet another avenue of infection—*macro viruses*.

Macro viruses first appeared on the scene in the mid-1990s, utilizing crude technologies to infect documents created in the popular Microsoft Word environment. Although they were relatively unsophisticated, these viruses spread rapidly because the antivirus community didn't anticipate them, and therefore, antivirus applications didn't provide any defense against them. Macro viruses quickly became more and more commonplace, and vendors rushed to modify their antivirus platforms to scan application documents for malicious macros. In 1999, the Melissa virus spread through the use of a Word document that exploited a security vulnerability in Microsoft Outlook to replicate. The infamous I Love You virus quickly followed on its heels, exploiting similar vulnerabilities in early 2000.

**WARNING**     Macro viruses proliferate because of the ease of writing code in the scripting languages (such as VBA) utilized by modern productivity applications.

Although the vast majority of macro viruses infect documents created by applications belonging to the Microsoft Office suite (including Word, Excel, PowerPoint, Access, and Outlook), users of other applications are not immune. Viruses exist that infect Lotus Notes, WordPerfect, and more. Macro viruses are the primary reason that modern office productivity software disables unsigned macros by default.

## Platforms

Just as most macro viruses infect systems running the popular Microsoft Office suite of applications, most computer viruses are designed to disrupt activity on systems running versions of the world's most popular operating system—Microsoft Windows. It's estimated that less than 1 percent of the viruses "in the wild" today are designed to impact other operating systems, such as Unix and Mac OS.

The main reason for this is that there really is no "Unix" operating system. Rather, there is a series of many similar operating systems that implement the same functions in a similar fashion and that are independently designed by a large number of developers. Large-scale corporate efforts, such as Sun's Solaris and SCO Unix, compete with the myriad of freely available versions of the Linux operating system developed by the public at large. The sheer number of Unix versions and the fact that they are developed on entirely different kernels (the core code of an operating system) make it difficult to write a virus that would impact a large portion of Unix systems.

That said, Macintosh and Unix users should not rest on their laurels. The fact that there are only a few viruses out there that pose a risk to their systems does not mean that one of those viruses couldn't affect their systems at any moment. Anyone responsible for the security of a computer system should implement adequate antivirus mechanisms to ensure the continued safety of their resources.

## Antivirus Mechanisms

Almost every desktop computer in service today runs some sort of antivirus software package. Popular desktop titles include McAfee VirusScan and Norton AntiVirus, but a plethora of other products on the market offer protection for anything from a single system to an entire enterprise; other packages are designed to protect against specific common types of virus invasion vectors, such as inbound email.

The vast majority of these packages utilize a method known as *signature-based detection* to identify potential virus infections on a system. Essentially, an antivirus package maintains an extremely large database that contains the telltale characteristics of all known viruses. Depending upon the antivirus package and configuration settings, it scans storage media periodically, checking for any files that contain data matching those criteria. If any are detected, the antivirus package takes one of the following actions:

- If the software can eradicate the virus, it disinfects the affected files and restores the machine to a safe condition.

- If the software recognizes the virus but doesn't know how to disinfect the files, it may quarantine the files until the user or an administrator can examine them manually.

- If security settings/policies do not provide for quarantine or the files exceed a predefined danger threshold, the antivirus package may delete the infected files in an attempt to preserve system integrity.

When using a signature-based antivirus package, it's essential to remember that the package is only as effective as the virus definition file upon which it's based. If you don't frequently update your virus definitions (usually requiring an annual subscription fee), your antivirus software will not be able to detect newly created viruses. With thousands of viruses appearing on the Internet each year, an outdated definition file will quickly render your defenses ineffective.

Many antivirus packages also use heuristic-based mechanisms to detect potential malware infections. These methods analyze the behavior of software, looking for the telltale signs of virus activity, such as attempts to elevate privilege level, cover their electronic tracks, and alter unrelated or operating system files.

Most of the modern antivirus software products are able to detect and remove a wide variety of types of malicious code and then clean the system. In other words, antivirus solutions are rarely limited to just viruses. These tools are often able to provide protection against worms, Trojan horses, logic bombs, rootkits, spyware, and various other forms of email- or web-borne code. In the event that you suspect new malicious code is sweeping the Internet, your best course of action is to contact your antivirus software vendor to inquire about your state of protection against the new threat. Don't wait until the next scheduled or automated signature dictionary update. Furthermore, never accept the word of any third party about protection status offered by an antivirus solution. Always contact the vendor directly. Most responsible antivirus vendors will send alerts to their customers as soon as new, substantial threats are identified, so be sure to register for such notifications as well.

Other security packages, such as the popular Tripwire data integrity assurance package, also provide a secondary antivirus functionality. Tripwire is designed to alert administrators of unauthorized file modifications. It's often used to detect web server defacements and similar attacks, but it also may provide some warning of virus infections if critical system executable files, such as COMMAND.COM, are modified unexpectedly. These systems work by maintaining a database of hash values for all files stored on the system (see Chapter 9, "Cryptography and Symmetric Key Algorithms," for a full discussion of the hash functions used to create these values). These archived hash values are then compared to current computed values to detect any files that were modified between the two periods. At the most basic level, a hash is a number used to summarize the contents of a file. As long as the file stays the same, the hash will stay the same. If the file is modified, even slightly, the hash will change dramatically, indicating that the file has been modified. Unless the action seems explainable, such as happening after the installation of new software, application of an operating system patch, or similar change, sudden changes in executable files may be a sign of malware infection.

## Virus Technologies

As virus detection and eradication technology rises to meet new threats programmed by malicious developers, new kinds of viruses designed to defeat those systems emerge. The following sections examine four specific types of viruses that use sneaky techniques in an attempt to escape detection—multipartite viruses, stealth viruses, polymorphic viruses, and encrypted viruses.

### Multipartite Viruses

*Multipartite viruses* use more than one propagation technique in an attempt to penetrate systems that defend against only one method or the other. For example, the Marzia virus discovered in 1993 infects critical .COM and .EXE files, most notably the COMMAND.COM system file, by adding 2,048 bytes of malicious code to each file. This characteristic qualifies it as a file infector virus. In addition, two hours after it infects a system, it writes malicious code to the system's master boot record, qualifying it as a boot sector virus.

### Stealth Viruses

*Stealth viruses* hide themselves by actually tampering with the operating system to fool antivirus packages into thinking that everything is functioning normally. For example, a stealth boot sector virus might overwrite the system's master boot record with malicious code but then also modify the operating system's file access functionality to cover its tracks. When the antivirus package requests a copy of the MBR, the modified operating system code provides it with exactly what the antivirus package expects to see—a clean version of the MBR free of any virus signatures. However, when the system boots, it reads the infected MBR and loads the virus into memory.

### Polymorphic Viruses

*Polymorphic viruses* actually modify their own code as they travel from system to system. The virus's propagation and destruction techniques remain the same, but the signature of the virus is somewhat different each time it infects a new system. It is the hope of polymorphic virus creators that this constantly changing signature will render signature-based antivirus packages useless. However, antivirus vendors have "cracked the code" of many polymorphism techniques, so current versions of antivirus software are able to detect known polymorphic viruses. The only concern that remains is that it takes vendors longer to generate the necessary signature files to stop a polymorphic virus in its tracks, resulting in a lengthened period that the virus can run free on the Internet.

### Encrypted Viruses

*Encrypted viruses* use cryptographic techniques, such as those described in Chapter 9, to avoid detection. In their outward appearance, they are actually quite similar to polymorphic viruses—each infected system has a virus with a different signature. However, they do not generate these modified signatures by changing their code; instead, they alter the way they are stored on the disk. Encrypted viruses use a very short segment of code, known as the *virus decryption routine*, which contains the cryptographic information necessary to load and decrypt the main virus code stored elsewhere on the disk. Each infection utilizes a different cryptographic key, causing the main code to appear completely different on each system. However, the virus decryption routines often contain telltale signatures that render them vulnerable to updated antivirus software packages.

## Hoaxes

No discussion of viruses is complete without mentioning the nuisance and wasted resources caused by virus *hoaxes*. Almost every email user has, at one time or another, received a message forwarded by a friend or relative that warns of the latest virus threat roaming the Internet. Invariably, this purported "virus" is the most destructive virus ever unleashed, and no antivirus package is able to detect and/or eradicate it. One famous example of such a hoax is the Good Times virus warning that first surfaced on the Internet in 1994 and still circulates today.

For more information on this topic, the renowned virus hoax expert Rob Rosenberger maintains a website that contains a comprehensive repository of virus hoaxes. You can find it at www.vmyths.com.

## Logic Bombs

As you learned in Chapter 7, "Data and Application Security Issues," *logic bombs* are malicious code objects that infect a system and lie dormant until they are triggered by the occurrence of one or more conditions such as time, program launch, website logon, and so on. The vast majority of logic bombs are programmed into custom-built applications by software developers seeking to ensure that their work is destroyed if they unexpectedly leave the company. The previous chapter provided several examples of this type of logic bomb.

However, it's important to remember that, like any malicious code object, logic bombs come in many shapes and sizes. Indeed, many viruses and Trojan horses contain a logic bomb component. The famous Michelangelo virus caused a media frenzy when it was discovered in 1991 because of the logic bomb trigger it contained. The virus infected a system's master boot record through the sharing of infected floppy disks and then hid itself until March 6—the birthday of the famous Italian artist Michelangelo Buonarroti. On that date, it sprung into action, reformatting the hard drives of infected systems and destroying all the data they contain.

## Trojan Horses

System administrators constantly warn computer users not to download and install software from the Internet unless they are absolutely sure it comes from a trusted source. In fact, many companies strictly prohibit the installation of any software not prescreened by the IT department. These policies serve to minimize the risk that an organization's network will be compromised by a *Trojan horse*—a software program that appears benevolent but carries a malicious, behind-the-scenes payload that has the potential to wreak havoc on a system or network.

Trojans differ very widely in functionality. Some will destroy all the data stored on a system in an attempt to cause a large amount of damage in as short a time frame as possible. Some are fairly innocuous. For example, a series of Trojans appeared on the Internet in mid-2002 that claimed to provide PC users with the ability to run games designed for the Microsoft Xbox gaming system on their computers. When users ran the program, it simply didn't work. However, it also inserted a value into the Windows Registry that caused a specific web page to open each time the computer booted. The Trojan creators hoped to cash in on the advertising revenue generated by the large number of page views their website received from the Xbox Trojan horses. Unfortunately for them, antivirus experts quickly discovered their true intentions, and the website was shut down.

One category of Trojan that has recently made a significant impact on the security community is rogue antivirus software. This software tricks the user into installing it by claiming to be an antivirus package, often under the guise of a pop-up ad that mimics the look and feel of a security warning. Once the user installs the software, it either steals personal information or prompts the user for payment to "update" the rogue antivirus. The "update" simply disables the Trojan!

 **Real World Scenario**

**Botnets**

A few years ago, one of the authors of this book visited an organization that suspected it had a security problem, but the organization didn't have the expertise to diagnose or resolve the issue. The major symptom was network slowness. A few basic tests found that none of the systems on the company's network ran basic antivirus software, and some of them were infected with a Trojan horse.

Why did this cause network slowness? Well, the Trojan horse made all the infected systems members of a *botnet*, a collection of computers (sometimes thousands or even millions!) across the Internet under the control of an attacker known as the *botmaster*.

The botmaster of this particular botnet used the systems on their network as part of a denial-of-service attack against a website that he didn't like for one reason or another. He instructed all the systems in his botnet to retrieve the same web page, over and over again, in hopes that the website would fail under the heavy load. With close to 30 infected systems on the organization's network, the botnet's attack was consuming almost all its bandwidth!

The solution was simple: Antivirus software was installed on the systems and it removed the Trojan horse. Network speeds returned to normal quickly.

## Worms

*Worms* pose a significant risk to network security. They contain the same destructive potential as other malicious code objects with an added twist—they propagate themselves without requiring any human intervention.

The worm called Internet Worm was the first major computer security incident to occur on the Internet. Since that time, hundreds of new worms (with thousands of variant strains) have unleashed their destructive power on the Internet.

The Code Red worm received a good deal of media attention in the summer of 2001 when it rapidly spread among web servers running unpatched versions of Microsoft's

Internet Information Server (IIS). Code Red performed three malicious actions on the systems it penetrated:

- It randomly selected hundreds of IP addresses and then probed those hosts to see whether they were running a vulnerable version of IIS. Any systems it found were quickly compromised. This greatly magnified Code Red's reach because each host it infected sought many new targets.

- It defaced HTML pages on the local web server, replacing normal content with the following text:

```
Welcome to http://www.worm.com!
Hacked By Chinese!
```

- It planted a logic bomb that would initiate a denial-of-service attack against the IP address 198.137.240.91, which at that time belonged to the web server hosting the White House's home page. Quick-thinking government web administrators changed the White House's IP address before the attack actually began.

The destructive power of Internet Worm, Code Red, and their many variants poses an extreme risk to the modern Internet. System administrators simply must ensure that they apply appropriate security patches to their Internet-connected systems as software vendors release them. As a case in point, a security fix for an IIS vulnerability exploited by Code Red was available from Microsoft for more than a month before the worm attacked the Internet. Had security administrators applied it promptly, Code Red would have been a miserable failure.

---

### RTM and the Internet Worm

In November 1988, a young computer science student named Robert Tappan Morris brought the fledgling Internet to its knees with a few lines of computer code. He released a malicious worm he claimed to have created as an experiment onto the Internet. It spread quickly and crashed a large number of systems.

This worm spread by exploiting four specific security holes in the Unix operating system.

**Sendmail debug mode**  Then-current versions of the popular Sendmail software package used to route electronic mail messages across the Internet contained a security vulnerability. This vulnerability allowed the worm to spread itself by sending a specially crafted email message that contained the worm's code to the Sendmail program on a remote system. When the remote system processed the message, it became infected.

**Password attack**  The worm also used a dictionary attack to attempt to gain access to remote systems by utilizing the username and password of a valid system user (you'll learn more about dictionary attacks later in this chapter).

**Finger vulnerability** Finger, a popular Internet utility, allowed users to determine who was logged on to a remote system. Then-current versions of the finger software contained a buffer-overflow vulnerability that allowed the worm to spread (you'll find a detailed discussion of buffer overflows later in this chapter). The finger program has since been removed from most Internet-connected systems.

**Trust relationships** After the worm infected a system, it analyzed any existing trust relationships with other systems on the network and attempted to spread itself to those systems through the trusted path.

This multipronged approach made Internet Worm extremely dangerous. Fortunately, the (then-small) computer security community quickly put together a crack team of investigators who disarmed the worm and patched the affected systems. Their efforts were facilitated by several inefficient routines in the worm's code that limited the rate of its spread.

Because of the lack of experience among law enforcement authorities and the court system in dealing with computer crimes, Morris received only a slap on the wrist for his transgression. He was sentenced to three years' probation, 400 hours of community service, and a $10,000 fine under the Computer Fraud and Abuse Act of 1986. Ironically, Morris's father, Robert Morris, was serving as the director of the National Security Agency's National Computer Security Center (NCSC) at the time of the incident.

## Spyware and Adware

Two other types of unwanted software interfere with the way you normally use your computer. *Spyware* monitors your actions and transmits important details to a remote system that spies on your activity. For example, spyware might wait for you to log into a banking website and then transmit your username and password to the creator of the spyware. Alternatively, it might wait for you to enter your credit card number on an e-commerce site and transmit it to a fraudster to resell on the black market.

*Adware*, while quite similar to spyware in form, has a different purpose. It uses a variety of techniques to display advertisements on infected computers. The simplest forms of adware display pop-up ads on your screen while you surf the Web. More nefarious versions may monitor your shopping behavior and redirect you to competitor websites.

## Active Content

The increasing demand of web users for more and more dynamic content on the sites they visit has created a dilemma for web administrators. Delivering this dynamic content requires the use of web applications that can place an enormous computational burden on the server, and the increased demand for them requires a commitment of a large number of resources.

In an effort to solve this problem, software developers created the concept of *active content*, web programs that are downloaded to users' own computers for execution rather than consuming server-side resources. These programs, utilizing technologies such as Java applets and ActiveX controls, greatly reduce the load on the server and client waiting time. Most web browsers allow users to choose to have the active content automatically downloaded, installed, and executed from trusted sites. Additionally, developers have the ability to digitally sign active content to identify the author, and users can configure their browsers to run only signed content from trusted sources, reducing the risk of running active content.

Unfortunately, this technology can pose a major threat to client systems. Unsuspecting users may download active content from an untrusted source and allow it to execute on their systems, creating a significant security vulnerability. This vulnerability led to the creation of a whole new type of malicious code—the *hostile applet*. Like other forms of malware, hostile applets have a variety of intentions, from causing a denial-of-service attack that merely consumes system resources to more insidious goals, such as theft of data.

# Countermeasures

The primary means of defense against malicious code is the use of antivirus-filtering software. These packages are primarily signature-based systems, designed to detect known viruses running on a system. It's wise to consider implementing antivirus filters in at least three key areas, described next.

With current antivirus software, removal is often possible within hours after new malicious code is discovered. *Removal* removes the malicious code but does not repair the damage caused by it. Cleaning capabilities are usually made available within a few days after new malicious code is discovered. *Cleaning* not only removes the code, it also repairs any damage it causes.

**Client systems**   Every workstation on a network should have updated antivirus software searching the local file system for malicious code.

**Server systems**   Servers should have similar protections. This is even more critical than protecting client systems because a single virus on a common server could quickly spread throughout an entire network.

**Content filters**   The majority of viruses today are exchanged over email. It's a wise move to implement on your network content filtering that scans inbound and outbound electronic mail and web traffic for signs of malicious code.

Remember, most antivirus filters are signature based. Therefore, they're only as good as the most recent update to their virus definition files. It's critical that you update these files frequently, especially when a new piece of high-profile malicious code appears on the Internet.

Signature-based filters rely upon the descriptions of known viruses provided by software developers. Therefore, there is a period of time between when any given virus first appears "in the wild" and when updated filters are made available. This problem has two solutions that are commonly used today:

- Integrity checking software, such as Tripwire (an open source version is available at www.tripwire.org), scans your file system for unexpected modifications and reports to you periodically.

- Access controls should be strictly maintained and enforced to limit the ability of malicious code to damage your data and spread on your network.

Two additional techniques can specifically prevent systems from being infected by malicious code embedded in active content:

- Java's sandbox provides applets with an isolated environment in which they can run safely without gaining access to critical system resources.

- ActiveX control signing utilizes a system of digital signatures to ensure that the code originates from a trusted source. It is up to the end user to determine whether the authenticated source should be trusted.

For an in-depth explanation of digital signature technology, see Chapter 10, "PKI and Cryptographic Applications."

Many forms of malicious code take advantage of "zero day" vulnerabilities, security flaws discovered by hackers that have not been thoroughly addressed by the security community. There are two main reasons systems are affected by these vulnerabilities. First, it may be the result of the necessary delay between the discovery of a new type of malicious code and the issuance of patches and antivirus updates. Second, it may be due to slowness in applying updates on the part of system administrators. The existence of zero-day vulnerabilities makes it critical that you have a strong patch management program in your organization that ensures the prompt application of critical security updates. Additionally, you may wish to use a vulnerability scanner to scan your systems on a regular basis for known security issues.

# Password Attacks

One of the simplest techniques attackers use to gain illegitimate access to a system is to learn the username and password of an authorized system user. Once they've gained access as a regular user, they have a foothold into the system. At that point, they can use other techniques, including automated rootkit packages, to gain increased levels of access to the system (see the section "Rootkits" later in this chapter). They may also use the compromised system as a jumping-off point for attacks on other, more attractive targets on the same network.

The following sections examine three methods attackers use to learn the passwords of legitimate users and access a system: password-guessing attacks, dictionary attacks, and social-engineering attacks. Many of these attacks rely upon weak password storage mechanisms. For example, many Unix operating systems store encrypted versions of a user's password in the /etc/passwd file.

## Password Guessing

In the most basic type of password attack, attackers simply attempt to guess a user's password. No matter how much security education users receive, they often use extremely weak passwords. If attackers are able to obtain a list of authorized system users, they can often quickly figure out the correct usernames. (On most networks, usernames consist of the first initial of the user's first name followed by a portion of their last name.) With this information, they can begin making some educated guesses about the user's password. The most commonly used password is some form of the user's last name, first name, or username. For example, the user *mchapple* might use the weak password *elppahcm* because it's easy to remember. Unfortunately, it's also easy to guess.

If that attempt fails, attackers turn to widely available lists of the most common passwords on the Internet. Some of these are shown in the sidebar "Most Common Passwords."

---

### Most Common Passwords

Attackers often use the Internet to distribute lists of commonly used passwords based on data gathered during system compromises. Many of these are no great surprise. Here are just a very few of the 815 passwords contained in an attacker list retrieved from the Internet:

| | | |
|---|---|---|
| Password | computer | work |
| Secret | football | office |
| sex | hello | online |
| money | morning | terminal |
| love | ibm | internet |

Along with these common words, the password list contained more than 300 first names, 70 percent of which were female names.

---

Finally, a little knowledge about a person can provide extremely good clues about their password. Many people use the name of a spouse, child, family pet, relative, or favorite entertainer. Common passwords also include birthdays, anniversaries, Social Security numbers, phone numbers, and (believe it or not!) ATM PINs.

## Dictionary Attacks

As mentioned previously, many Unix systems store encrypted versions of user passwords in an /etc/passwd file accessible to all system users. To provide some level of security, the file doesn't contain the actual user passwords; it contains an encrypted value obtained from a one-way encryption function (see Chapter 9 for a discussion of encryption functions). When a user attempts to log on to the system, access verification routines use the same encryption function to encrypt the password entered by the user and then compare it with the encrypted version of the actual password stored in the /etc/passwd file. If the values match, the user is allowed access.

Password attackers use automated tools like the Crack program to run automated dictionary attacks that exploit a simple vulnerability in this mechanism. They take a large dictionary file that contains thousands of words and then run the encryption function against all those words to obtain their encrypted equivalents. Crack then searches the password file for any encrypted values for which there is a match in the encrypted dictionary. When a match is found, it reports the username and password (in plain text), and the attacker gains access to the system.

### Password Crackers

Crack is just one password cracking program. There are many others available on the Internet that use a variety of attack techniques. These include Cain & Abel, John the Ripper, L0phtcrack, Pwdump, and RainbowCrack. Each tool specializes in different operating systems and password types.

It sounds like simple security mechanisms and education would prevent users from using passwords that are easily guessed by Crack, but the tool is surprisingly effective at compromising live systems. As new versions of Crack are released, more advanced features are introduced to defeat common techniques used by users to defeat password complexity rules. Some of these are included in the following list:

- Rearranging the letters of a dictionary word

- Appending a number to a dictionary word

- Replacing each occurrence of the letter O in a dictionary word with the number 0 (or the letter l with the number 1)

- Combining two dictionary words in some form

## Social Engineering

*Social engineering* is one of the most effective tools attackers use to gain access to a system. In its most basic form, a social-engineering attack consists of simply calling the user and asking for their password, posing as a technical support representative or other authority figure who needs the information immediately. Fortunately, most contemporary computer users are aware of these scams, and the effectiveness of directly asking a user for a password is somewhat diminished today. Instead, these attacks rely upon phishing emails that prompt users to log in to a fake site using their actual username and password, which are then captured by the attacker and used to log into the actual site. Phishing attacks often target financial services websites, where user credentials can be used to quickly transfer cash. In addition to tricking users into giving up their passwords, phishing attacks are often used to get users to install malware or provide other sensitive personal information.

However, social engineering still poses a significant threat to the security of passwords (and networks in general). Attackers can often obtain sensitive personal information by "chatting up" computer users, office gossips, and administrative personnel. This information can provide excellent ammunition when mounting a password-guessing attack. Furthermore, attackers can sometimes obtain sensitive network topography or configuration data that is useful when planning other types of electronic attacks against an organization.

## Countermeasures

The cornerstone of any security program is education. Security personnel should continually remind users of the importance of choosing a secure password and keeping it secret. Users should receive training when they first enter an organization, and they should receive periodic refresher training, even if it's just an email from the administrator reminding them of the threats.

Provide users with the knowledge they need to create secure passwords. Tell them about the techniques attackers use when guessing passwords, and give them advice on how to create a strong password. One of the most effective techniques is to use a mnemonic device such as thinking of an easy-to-remember sentence and creating a password out of the first letter of each word. For example, "My son Richard likes to eat four pies" would become MsRlte4p—an extremely strong password.

One of the most common mistakes made by overzealous security administrators is to create a series of strong passwords and then assign them to users (who are then prevented from changing their password). At first glance, this seems to be a sound security policy. However, the first thing a user will do when they receive a password like 1mf0A8flt is write it down on a sticky note and put it under their computer keyboard. Whoops! Security just went out the window (or under the keyboard)!

If your network includes Unix operating systems that implement the /etc/passwd file, consider using some other access verification mechanism to increase security. One popular technique available in many versions of Unix and Linux is the use of a shadow password file, /etc/shadow. This file contains the true encrypted passwords of each user, but it is not accessible to anyone but the administrator. The publicly accessible /etc/passwd file then simply contains a list of usernames without the data necessary to mount a dictionary attack.

# Denial-of-Service Attacks

As you learned in Chapter 2, malicious individuals often use denial-of-service (DoS) attacks in an attempt to prevent legitimate users from accessing resources. This is often a "last-ditch" effort when an attacker realizes that they can't penetrate a system—"If I can't have it, then nobody can." In the following sections, we'll take a look at five specific denial-of-service attacks and the mechanisms they use to disable computing systems. In some of these attacks, a brute-force attack is used, simply overwhelming a targeted system with so many requests that it can't possibly sort out the legitimate ones from those that are part of the attack. Others include elegantly crafted commands that cause vulnerable systems to crash or hang indefinitely.

## SYN Flood

Recall from Chapter 2 that the TCP/IP protocol utilizes a three-way handshaking process to set up connections between two hosts. In a typical connection, the originating host sends a single packet with the SYN flag enabled, attempting to open one side of the communications channel. The destination host receives this packet and sends a reply with the ACK flag enabled (confirming that the first side of the channel is open) and the SYN flag enabled (attempting to open the reverse channel). Finally, the originating host transmits a packet with the ACK flag enabled, confirming that the reverse channel is open and the connection is established. If, for some reason, the process is not completed, the communicating hosts leave the connection in a half-open state for a predetermined period of time before aborting the attempt. Figure 8.1 illustrates the standard handshaking process.

**FIGURE 8.1**    Standard TCP/IP three-way handshaking

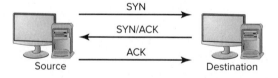

In a SYN flood attack, attackers use special software that sends a large number of fake packets with the SYN flag set to the targeted system. The victim then reserves space in memory for the connection and attempts to send the standard SYN/ACK reply but never hears back from the originator. This process repeats hundreds or even thousands of times, and the targeted computer eventually becomes overwhelmed and runs out of available resources for the half-opened connections. At that time, it either crashes or simply ignores all inbound connection requests because it can't possibly handle any more half-open connections. This prevents everyone—both attackers and legitimate users—from connecting to the machine and results in an extremely effective denial-of-service attack. Figure 8.2 shows the SYN flood modified handshaking process.

**FIGURE 8.2**    SYN flood modified handshaking process

The SYN flood attack crippled many computing systems in the late 1990s and the year 2000. Web servers were especially vulnerable to this type of attack. Fortunately, modern firewalls contain specialized technology designed to prevent successful SYN flood attacks in the future. For example, Checkpoint Software's popular Firewall-1 package contains the SYNDefender functionality that acts as a proxy for SYN requests and shelters the destination system from any barrage of requests.

## Distributed DoS Toolkits

*Distributed denial-of-service (DDoS)* attacks allow attackers to harness the power of many third-party systems to attack the ultimate target. In many DDoS attacks, an attacker will first use some other technique to compromise a large number of systems. They then install software on those compromised systems that enables them to participate in the main attack, effectively enlisting those machines into an army of attackers known as a botnet.

Trinoo and the Tribal Flood Network (TFN) are two commonly used DDoS toolkits. Attackers compromise third-party systems and install Trinoo/TFN clients that lie dormant waiting for instructions to begin an attack. When the attacker is satisfied that enough clients are lying in wait, they use a Trinoo/TFN master server to "wake up" the clients and initiate a coordinated attack against a single destination system or network from many directions. The current versions of Trinoo and TFN allow the master server to initiate many common DoS attacks, including SYN floods and smurf attacks, from the third-party client machines.

Distributed denial-of-service attacks using these toolkits pose extreme risks to Internet-connected systems and are very difficult to defend against. In February 2000, attackers launched a week-long DDoS campaign against a number of high-profile websites, including those of Yahoo!, CNN, and Amazon.com. The attacks rendered these sites virtually inaccessible to legitimate users for an extended period of time. In fact, many security practitioners consider DDoS attacks the single greatest threat facing the Internet today.

# Smurf

The *smurf* attack takes the distributed denial-of-service attack to the next level by harnessing the power of many unwitting third-party hosts to attack a system. Attacks that are like smurf and are amplified using third-party networks are known as *distributed reflective denial-of-service (DRDoS)* attacks.

The smurf DRDoS attack in particular exploits a vulnerability in the implementation of the Internet Control Message Protocol (ICMP) ping functionality. The intended use of ping allows users to send single "Are you there?" packets to other systems. If the system is alive and responding, it returns a single "Yes, I am" packet. It offers an efficient way to check network connectivity and diagnose potential networking issues. The typical exchange involves only two packets traversing the network and consumes minimal computer/network resources.

In a smurf attack, the originating system creates a false ping packet that appears to be from the target of the attack. The destination of the packet is the broadcast address of the third-party network. Therefore, each machine on the third-party network receives a copy of the ping request. According to the request they received, the originator is the victim system, and each machine on the network sends a "Yes, I'm alive" packet to the victim. The originator repeats this process by rapidly sending a large number of these requests through different intermediary networks, and the victim quickly becomes overwhelmed by the number of requests. Figure 8.3 illustrates the smurf attack data flow.

**FIGURE 8.3**    Smurf attack data flow

Hacker

Third-Party Network A

Third-Party Network B

Third-Party Network C

Victim

The prevention of smurf attacks depends upon the use of responsible filtering rules by networks across the entire Internet. System administrators should set rules at the router and/or firewall that prohibit inbound ping packets sent to a broadcast address (or perhaps even prohibit inbound pings entirely!). Furthermore, administrators should use *egress filtering*—a technique that prohibits systems on a network from transmitting packets with IP addresses that do not belong to the network. This prevents a network from being utilized by malicious individuals seeking to initiate a smurf attack or any type of masquerading attack aimed at a remote network (see the section "Masquerading Attacks" for more information on this topic).

**Fraggle**

*Fraggle* is another distributed reflective denial-of-service (DRDoS) attack that works in a manner similar to that of smurf attacks. However, rather than using ICMP packets, fraggle attacks take advantage of the uncommonly used chargen and echo User Datagram Protocol (UDP) services. An easy way to prevent fraggle attacks on your network is to disable these services. It's more than likely that you'll never have a legitimate use for them.

## DNS Amplification Attacks

Another type of distributed denial-of-service attack seen in recent years is the *DNS amplification* attack. The DNS amplification mechanism is similar to that of a smurf attack: An attacker tricks unwitting participants into sending unwanted traffic to a third party, flooding that third party's network connection.

The two attacks differ in their implementation. While smurf attacks take advantage of broadcast network addresses, DNS amplification attacks leverage recursive DNS queries. Attackers simply locate some of the many DNS servers on the Internet that will perform recursive name resolution on behalf of any client. They then spoof DNS queries to that address using the source address of their intended target. The attacker intentionally crafts these queries to elicit a voluminous response from the DNS server. DNS leverages UDP packets. Unlike TCP, UDP is a connectionless protocol, so it is not necessary for the attacker to actually establish a TCP session with the server, allowing the attacker to successfully impersonate the victim system.

Go check your DNS servers to ensure that you're not an unwitting participant in DNS amplification attacks. You'll rest easier knowing that you're not only preserving your valuable bandwidth but that you're acting as a responsible Net citizen.

Using DNS amplification attacks, malicious individuals can quickly bring a victim to its knees by amplifying a relatively small amount of network traffic (in the form of DNS queries) into a barrage of unwanted traffic (in the form of DNS responses).

## Teardrop

The *teardrop* attack is a member of a subclass of DoS attacks known as *fragmentation attacks* that exploit vulnerabilities in the fragment reassembly functionality of the TCP/IP protocol stack. System administrators can configure the maximum size allowed for TCP/IP packets that traverse each network that carries them. They usually choose this value based upon the available hardware, quality of service, and typical network traffic parameters to maximize network efficiency and throughput.

When a network receives a packet larger than its maximum allowable packet size, it breaks it up into two or more fragments. These fragments are each assigned a size (corresponding to the length of the fragment) and an offset (corresponding to the starting location of the fragment). For example, if a packet is 250 bytes long and the maximum packet size for the network is 100 bytes, it will require fragmentation. In a correctly functioning TCP/IP stack, the packet would be broken up into three fragments, as shown in Figure 8.4.

**FIGURE 8.4**   Standard packet fragmentation

In the teardrop attack, attackers use software that sends out packet fragments that don't conform to the protocol specification. Specifically, they send two or more overlapping fragments, illustrated in Figure 8.5. The malicious individual might send out fragment 1, a perfectly normal packet fragment of length 100. Under normal conditions, this fragment would be followed by a second fragment with offset 100 (correlating to the length of the first fragment). However, in the teardrop attack, the attacker sends a second fragment with an offset value that is too low, placing the second fragment right in the middle of the first fragment. When the receiving system attempts to reassemble the fragmented packet, it doesn't know how to properly handle the overlapping fragments and freezes or crashes.

**FIGURE 8.5** Teardrop attack

As with many of the attacks described in this book, the teardrop attack is a well-known exploit, and most operating system vendors have released security patches that prevent this type of attack from crippling updated systems. However, attacks like teardrop continue to cause damage on a daily basis because of neglectful system administrators who fail to apply appropriate patches, leaving their systems vulnerable to attack.

## Land

The *land* denial-of-service attack causes many older operating systems (such as Windows NT 4, Windows 95, and SunOS 4.1.4) to freeze and behave in an unpredictable manner. It works by creating an artificial TCP packet that has the SYN flag set. The attacker sets the destination IP address to the address of the victim machine and sets the destination port to an open port on that machine. Next, the attacker sets the source IP address and source port to the same values as the destination IP address and port. When the targeted host receives this unusual packet, the operating system doesn't know how to process it and freezes, crashes, or behaves in an unusual manner as a result.

## DNS Poisoning

Another DoS attack, *DNS poisoning*, works without ever touching the targeted host. Instead, it exploits vulnerabilities in the Domain Name System (DNS) protocol and attempts to redirect traffic to an alternative server without the targeted victim's knowledge.

Consider an example—suppose an attacker wants to redirect all legitimate traffic headed for www.whitehouse.gov to an alternative site, say www.youvebeenhacked.com.

We can assume that the White House site, as a frequent target of attackers, is highly secure. Instead of attempting to directly penetrate that site, the attacker might try to insert false data into the DNS that provides the IP address of www.youvebeenhacked.com when users query for the IP address of www.whitehouse.gov.

How could this happen? When you create a domain name, you use one of several domain name registrars that serve as central clearinghouses for DNS registrations. If an attacker is able to gain access to your registrar account (or the registrar's infrastructure itself), they might be able to alter your DNS records without your knowledge. In the early days of DNS, authentication was weak, and users could change DNS information by simply sending an unauthenticated email message. Fortunately, registrars have since implemented more secure authentication techniques that use cryptographic technology to verify user identities. *DNS poisoning* attacks use more advanced techniques to exploit weaknesses in DNS technology to redirect users to unexpected sites.

> DNS authentication techniques will protect you only if you use them! Ensure that you've enabled all the security features offered by your registrar. Also, when an administrator leaves your organization, remember to change the passwords for any accounts used to manage DNS information. DNS poisoning is an easy way for a disgruntled former employee to get revenge!

## Ping of Death

The final denial-of-service attack we'll examine in this chapter is the infamous *ping-of-death* attack that plagued systems in the mid-1990s. This exploit is actually quite simple. According to the ICMP specification, the largest permissible ICMP packet is 65,536 bytes. However, many early operating system developers simply relied upon the assumption that the protocol stacks of sending machines would never exceed this value and did not build in error-handling routines to monitor for packets that exceeded this maximum.

Attackers seeking to exploit the ping-of-death vulnerability simply used a packet generation program to create a ping packet destined for the victim host with a size of at least 65,537 bytes. If the victim's operating system didn't check the length of the packet and attempted to process it, unpredictable results would occur. Some operating systems hung or crashed.

After this exploit was discovered, operating system manufacturers quickly updated their ICMP algorithms to prevent future occurrences. However, machines running older versions of certain operating systems may still be vulnerable to this attack. Some notable versions include Windows 3.11 and Mac OS 7, along with unpatched versions of Windows 95, Windows NT 4, and Solaris 2.4–2.5.1. If you're running any of those operating systems on your network, update them to the appropriate patch level or version to protect yourself against this exploit.

# Application Attacks

In Chapter 7, you learned about the importance of utilizing solid software engineering processes when developing operating systems and applications. In the following sections, you'll take a brief look at some of the specific techniques attackers use to exploit vulnerabilities left behind by sloppy coding practices.

## Buffer Overflows

*Buffer overflow* vulnerabilities exist when a developer does not properly validate user input to ensure that it is of an appropriate size and therefore it can "overflow" a data structure to affect other data stored in the computer's memory. For example, if a web form has a field that ties to a back-end variable that allows 10 characters but the form processor does not verify the length of the input, the operating system may try to simply write data past the end of the memory space reserved for that variable, potentially corrupting other data stored in memory. In the worst case, that data can be used to overwrite system commands, allowing an attacker to exploit the buffer overflow vulnerability to execute arbitrary commands on the server.

When creating software, developers must pay special attention to variables that allow user input. Many programming languages do not enforce size limits on variables intrinsically—they rely on the programmer to perform this bounds checking in the code. This is an inherent vulnerability because many programmers feel parameter checking is an unnecessary burden that slows down the development process. As a security practitioner, it's your responsibility to ensure that developers in your organization are aware of the risks posed by buffer-overflow vulnerabilities and that they take appropriate measures to protect their code against this type of attack.

Any time a program variable allows user input, the programmer should take steps to ensure that each of the following conditions is met:

- The user can't enter a value longer than the size of any buffer that will hold it (for example, a 10-letter word into a 5-letter string variable).

- The user can't enter an invalid value for the variable types that will hold it (for example, a letter into a numeric variable).

- The user can't enter a value that will cause the program to operate outside of its specified parameters (for example, answer a "yes" or "no" question with "maybe").

Failure to perform simple checks to make sure these conditions are met can result in a buffer-overflow vulnerability that may cause the system to crash or even allow the user to execute shell commands and gain access to the system. Buffer-overflow vulnerabilities are especially prevalent in code developed rapidly for the Web using CGI or other languages that allow unskilled programmers to quickly create interactive web pages. Most buffer overflow vulnerabilities are mitigated with patches provided by software and operating system vendors, magnifying the importance of keeping systems and software up-to-date.

## Time-of-Check-to-Time-of-Use

The *time-of-check-to-time-of-use (TOCTTOU or TOC/TOU)* issue is a timing vulnerability that occurs when a program checks access permissions too far in advance of a resource request. For example, if an operating system builds a comprehensive list of access permissions for a user upon logon and then consults that list throughout the logon session, a TOCTTOU vulnerability exists. If the system administrator revokes a particular permission, that restriction would not be applied to the user until the next time they log on. If the user is logged on when the access revocation takes place, they will have access to the resource indefinitely. The user simply needs to leave the session open for days, and the new restrictions will never be applied.

## Trap Doors

*Trap doors* (or *back doors*) are undocumented command sequences that allow software developers to bypass normal access restrictions. They are often used during the development and debugging process to speed up the workflow and avoid forcing developers to continuously authenticate to the system. Occasionally, developers leave these trap doors in the system after it reaches a production state, either by accident or so they can "take a peek" at their system when it is processing sensitive data to which they should not have access.

Obviously, the undocumented nature of trap doors makes them a significant threat to the security of any system that contains them, especially when they are undocumented and forgotten. If a developer leaves the firm, they could later use the trap door to access the system and retrieve confidential information or participate in industrial sabotage.

## Rootkits

*Rootkits* are specialized software packages that have only one purpose—to allow attackers to gain expanded access to a system. Rootkits are freely available on the Internet and exploit known vulnerabilities in various operating systems. Attackers often obtain access to a standard system user account through the use of a password attack or social engineering and then use a rootkit to increase their access to the root (or administrator) level.

Administrators can take one simple precaution to protect their systems against the vast majority of rootkit attacks, and it's nothing new. Administrators must keep themselves informed about new security patches released for operating systems used in their environment and apply these corrective measures consistently. This straightforward step will fortify a network against almost all rootkit attacks as well as a large number of other potential vulnerabilities.

# Web Application Security

The Web allows you to purchase airline tickets, check your email, pay your bills, and purchase stocks all from the comfort of your living room. Almost every business today operates a website, and many allow you to conduct sensitive transactions through that site.

Along with the convenience benefits of web applications comes a series of new vulnerabilities that may expose web-enabled organizations to security risks. In the next several sections, we'll cover two common web application attacks.

# Cross-Site Scripting (XSS)

*Cross-site scripting (XSS)* attacks occur when web applications contain some type of *reflected input*. For example, consider a simple web application that contains a single text box asking a user to enter their name. When the user clicks Submit, the web application loads a new page that says, "Hello, *name*."

Under normal circumstances, this web application functions as designed. However, a malicious individual could take advantage of this web application to trick an unsuspecting third party. As you may know, you can embed scripts in web pages by using the HTML <SCRIPT> and </SCRIPT> tags. Suppose that, instead of entering **Mike** in the Name field, you enter the following text:

```
Mike<SCRIPT>alert('hello')</SCRIPT>
```

When the web application "reflects" this input in the form of a web page, your browser processes it as it would any other web page: It displays the text portions of the web page and executes the script portions. In this case, the script simply opens a pop-up window that says "Hello" in it. However, you could be more malicious and include a more sophisticated script that asks the user to provide a password and transmits it to a malicious third party.

At this point, you're probably asking yourself how anyone would fall victim to this type of attack. After all, you're not going to attack yourself by embedding scripts in the input that you provide to a web application that performs reflection. The key to this attack is that it's possible to embed form input in a link. A malicious individual could create a web page with a link titled "Check your account at First Bank" and encode form input in the link. When the user visits the link, the web page appears to be an authentic First Bank website (because it is!) with the proper address in the toolbar and a valid SSL certificate. However, the website would then execute the script included in the input by the malicious user, but it would appear to be part of the valid web page.

What's the answer to cross-site scripting? When you create web applications that allow any type of user input, you must be sure to perform *input validation*. At the most basic level, you should never allow a user to include the <SCRIPT> tag in a reflected input field. However, this doesn't solve the problem completely; there are many clever alternatives available to an industrious web application attacker. The best solution is to determine the type of input that you *will* allow and then validate the input to ensure that it matches that pattern. For example, if you have a text box that allows users to enter their age, you should accept between only one and three digits as input. Your application should reject any other input as invalid.

# SQL Injection

*SQL injection* attacks are even riskier than XSS attacks from an organization's perspective. As with XSS attacks, SQL injection attacks use unexpected input to a web application.

However, instead of using this input to attempt to fool a user, SQL injection attacks use it to gain unauthorized access to an underlying database.

## Dynamic Web Applications

In the early days of the Web, all web pages were *static*, or unchanging. Webmasters created web pages containing information and placed them on a web server, where users could retrieve them using their web browsers. The Web quickly outgrew this model because users wanted the ability to access customized information based upon their individual needs. For example, visitors to a bank website aren't interested only in static pages containing information about the bank's locations, hours, and services. They also want to retrieve *dynamic* content containing information about their personal accounts. Obviously, the webmaster can't possibly create pages on the web server for each individual user with that user's personal account information. At a large bank, that would require maintaining millions of pages with up-to-the-minute information. That's where dynamic web applications come into play.

Web applications take advantage of a database to create content on-demand when the user makes a request. In the banking example, the user logs into the web application, providing an account number and password. The web application then retrieves current account information from the bank's database and uses it to instantly create a web page containing the user's current account information. If that user returns an hour later, the web server would repeat the process, obtaining updated account information from the database. Figure 8.6 illustrates this model.

**FIGURE 8.6** Typical database-driven website architecture

What does this mean to you as a security professional? Web applications add complexity to our traditional security model. As shown in Figure 8.6, the web server, as a publicly accessible server, belongs in a separate network zone from other servers, commonly referred to as a DMZ. The database server, on the other hand, is not meant for public access, so it belongs on the internal network. The web application needs access to the database, so the firewall administrator must create a rule allowing access from the web server to the database server. This rule creates a potential path for Internet users to gain access to the database server. (For more on firewalls and DMZs, see Chapter 3.)

If the web application functions properly, it will allow only authorized requests to the database. However, if there is a flaw in the web application, it may allow individuals to tamper with the database in an unexpected and unauthorized fashion through the use of SQL injection attacks.

## SQL Injection Attacks

SQL injection attacks allow a malicious individual to directly perform SQL transactions against the underlying database, in violation of the isolation model shown in Figure 8.6.

For more on databases and SQL, see Chapter 7.

In the example used earlier, a bank customer might enter an account number to gain access to a dynamic web application that retrieves current account details. The web application must use a SQL query to obtain that information, perhaps of the following form, where <number> is the account number provided by the user on the web form:

```
SELECT *
FROM transactions
WHERE account_number = '<number>'
```

There's one more important fact you need to know: Databases will process multiple SQL statements at the same time, provided that you end each one with a semicolon.

If the web application doesn't perform proper input validation, the user may be able to insert their own SQL code into the statement executed by the web server. For example, if the user's account number is 145249, he could enter the following:

```
145249'; DELETE * FROM transactions WHERE 'a' = 'a
```

The web application would then obediently plug this in to the <number> field in the earlier SQL statement, resulting in the following:

```
SELECT *
FROM transactions
WHERE account_number ='145249'; DELETE * FROM transactions WHERE 'a' = 'a'
```

Reformatting that command slightly, you get the following:

```
SELECT *
FROM transactions
WHERE account_number ='145249';
DELETE *
FROM transactions
WHERE 'a' = 'a'
```

This is a valid SQL transaction containing two statements. The first one retrieves the requested information from the database. The second statement deletes all the records stored in the database. Whoops!

### Protecting against SQL Injection

You can use two techniques to protect your web applications against SQL injection attacks:

**Perform input validation**   As described earlier in this chapter when talking about cross-site scripting, input validation allows you to limit the types of data a user provides in a form. In the case of the SQL injection example we provided in the previous section, removing the single quote characters (') from the input would prevent the successful use of this attack.

**Limit account privileges**   The database account used by the web server should have the smallest set of privileges possible. If the web application needs only to retrieve data, it should have that ability only. In the example, the DELETE command would fail if the account had SELECT privileges only.

# Reconnaissance Attacks

As with any attacking force, attackers require solid intelligence to effectively focus their efforts against the targets most likely to yield the best results. To assist with this targeting, attacker-tool developers have created a number of automated tools that perform network reconnaissance. In the following sections, we'll cover three of those automated techniques—IP probes, port scans, and vulnerability scans—and then explain how these techniques can be supplemented by the more physically intensive dumpster-diving technique.

## IP Probes

*IP probes* (also called *IP sweeps* or *ping sweeps*) are often the first type of network reconnaissance carried out against a targeted network. With this technique, automated tools simply attempt to ping each address in a range. Systems that respond to the ping request are logged for further analysis. Addresses that do not produce a response are assumed to be unused and are ignored.

**Nmap**

Nmap is one of the most common tools used to perform both IP probes and port scans. It's available for free download from www.nmap.org.

IP probes are extremely prevalent on the Internet today. Indeed, if you configure a system with a public IP address and connect it to the Internet, you'll probably receive at least one IP probe within hours of booting up. The widespread use of this technique makes a strong case for disabling ping functionality by disabling ICMP, at least for users external to a network.

## Port Scans

After an attacker performs an IP probe, they are left with a list of active systems on a given network. The next task is to select one or more systems to target with additional attacks. Often, attackers have a type of target in mind; web servers, file servers, and other servers supporting critical operations are prime targets.

To narrow down their search, attackers use *port scan* software to probe all the active systems on a network and determine what public services are running on each machine. For example, if the attacker wants to target a web server, they might run a port scan to locate any systems with a service running on port 80, the default port for HTTP services.

## Vulnerability Scans

The third technique is the *vulnerability scan*. Once the attacker determines a specific system to target, they need to discover a specific vulnerability in that system that can be exploited to gain the desired access permissions. A variety of tools available on the Internet assist with this task. Two of the more popular ones are the Nessus and Saint vulnerability scanners. These packages contain a database of known vulnerabilities and probe targeted systems to locate security flaws. They then produce very attractive reports that detail every vulnerability detected. From that point, it's simply a matter of locating a script that exploits a specific vulnerability and launching an attack against the victim.

It's important to note that vulnerability scanners are highly automated tools. They can be used to launch an attack against a specific system, but it's just as likely that an attacker would use a series of IP probes, port scans, and vulnerability scans to narrow down a list of potential victims. However, chances are an intruder will run a vulnerability scanner against an entire network to probe for any weakness that could be exploited.

Once again, simply updating operating systems to the most recent security patch level can repair almost every weakness reported by a vulnerability scanner. Furthermore, wise system administrators learn to think like the enemy—they download and run these vulnerability scanners against their own networks (with the permission of upper management) to see what security holes might be pointed out to a potential attacker. This allows them to quickly focus their resources on fortifying the weakest points on their networks.

## Dumpster Diving

Every organization generates trash—often significant amounts on a daily basis. Have you ever taken the time to sort through your trash to see the sensitivity of the materials that hit the recycle bin? Give it a try—the results may frighten you. When you're analyzing the work papers thrown away each day, look at them from an attacker's perspective. What type of intelligence could you glean from them that might help you launch an attack? Is there sensitive data about network configurations or installed software versions? A list of employees' birthdays from a particular department that might be used in a social-engineering attack? A policy manual that contains detailed procedures on the creation of new accounts? Discarded floppy disks or other storage media?

Don't underestimate the value of even trivial corporate documents to a social engineer. Kevin Mitnick, a famous social engineer, once admitted to using company newsletters as a key component of his attacks. He skipped right to the section containing a listing of new hires, recognizing that these individuals were perfect victims: all too eager to please someone calling from the "top floor" requesting sensitive information.

Dumpster diving is one of the oldest attacker tools in the book, and it's still used today. The best defense against these attacks is quite simple—make them more difficult. Purchase shredders for key departments, and encourage employees to use them. Keep the trash locked up in a secure area until the garbage collectors arrive. A little common sense goes a long way in this area.

# Masquerading Attacks

One of the easiest ways to gain access to resources you're not otherwise entitled to use is to impersonate someone who does have the appropriate access permissions. In the offline world, teenagers often borrow the driver's license of an older sibling to purchase alcohol, and the same type of thing happens in the computer security world. Attackers borrow the identities of legitimate users and systems to gain the trust of third parties. In the following sections, we'll take a look at two common masquerading attacks—IP spoofing and session hijacking.

## IP Spoofing

In an *IP spoofing* attack, the malicious individual simply reconfigures their system so that it has the IP address of a trusted system and then attempts to gain access to other external resources. This is surprisingly effective on many networks that don't have adequate filters installed to prevent this type of traffic from occurring. System administrators should configure filters at the perimeter of each network to ensure that packets meet at least the following criteria:

- Packets with internal source IP addresses don't enter the network from the outside.

- Packets with external source IP addresses don't exit the network from the inside.

- Packets with private IP addresses don't pass through the router in either direction (unless specifically allowed as part of an intranet configuration).

These three simple filtering rules can eliminate the vast majority of IP spoofing attacks and greatly enhance the security of a network.

## Session Hijacking

Session hijacking attacks occur when a malicious individual intercepts part of the communication between an authorized user and a resource and then uses a hijacking technique to take over the session and assume the identity of the authorized user. The following list includes some common techniques:

- Capturing details of the authentication between a client and server and using those details to assume the client's identity

- Tricking the client into thinking the attacker's system is the server, acting as the middleman as the client sets up a legitimate connection with the server, and then disconnecting the client

- Accessing a web application using the cookie data of a user who did not properly close the connection

All of these techniques can have disastrous results for the end user and must be addressed with both administrative controls (such as antireplay authentication techniques) and application controls (such as expiring cookies within a reasonable period of time).

# Decoy Techniques

Attackers aren't the only ones with tricks up their sleeves—security administrators have also mastered sleight-of-hand tricks and use them to lure attackers into a sense of false security. After they've had the opportunity to observe attackers and trace their actions back to the source, they take action to protect their networks from future attacks. In the following sections, we'll examine two such techniques used by creative system administrators: honeypots and pseudoflaws.

## Honeypots

Administrators often create *honeypots* that appear to be extremely lucrative attacker targets. They may contain files that appear to be sensitive and/or valuable or run false services (like a web server) that appear to be critical to an organization's operations. In reality, these systems are nothing but decoys set up to lure attackers away from truly critical resources and allow administrators to monitor and trace their activities.

## Pseudoflaws

*Pseudoflaws* are false vulnerabilities or apparent loopholes intentionally implanted in a system in an attempt to detect attackers. They are often used on honeypot systems and on critical resources to emulate well-known operating system vulnerabilities. Attackers seeking to exploit a known flaw might stumble across a pseudoflaw and think that they have successfully penetrated a system. More sophisticated pseudoflaw mechanisms actually simulate the penetration and convince the attacker that they have gained additional access privileges to a system. However, while the attacker is exploring the bounds of these newfound rights, monitoring and alerting mechanisms trigger in the background to alert administrators to the threat and increase the defensive posture surrounding critical network resources.

# Summary

Throughout history, criminals have always been extremely creative. No matter what security mechanisms have been put in place to deter them, criminals have found methods to bypass them and reach their ultimate goals. This is no less true in the realm of computer security than in any other aspect of criminal psychology. Attackers use a number of automated tools to perform network reconnaissance so they can focus their efforts on the targets most likely to yield the best results. Examples include IP probes, port scans, malicious code, password attacks, denial-of-service attacks, application attacks, reconnaissance attacks, masquerading attacks, and decoy techniques.

By no means was this a comprehensive look at all possible hacking methods—that would be an impossible task. New tools and techniques appear in the hacking subculture almost on a daily basis. However, you should now have a good feeling for the types of weapons attackers have at their disposal as well as some of the best defense mechanisms security administrators can use to fortify their protected systems and networks against attacker intrusions.

Remember the following key actions you can take to increase your security posture:

- Use strong passwords.

- Update operating systems and applications with security patches as they are released by vendors.

- Use commonsense filtering techniques to ensure that traffic on your network is what it appears to be.

Pay particular attention to the technical details of the attacks presented in this chapter. Be familiar with the technology underlying each attack, and be prepared to identify them in a multiple-choice format. Just as important, understand the countermeasures system administrators can apply to prevent each one of those attacks from occurring on protected networks.

# Exam Essentials

**Understand the propagation techniques used by viruses.**   Viruses use three main propagation techniques—file infection, boot sector infection, and macro infection—to penetrate systems and spread their malicious payloads.

**Know how antivirus software packages detect known viruses.**   Most antivirus programs use signature-based detection algorithms to look for telltale patterns of known viruses. This makes it essential to periodically update virus definition files in order to maintain protection against newly authored viruses as they emerge.

**Be able to explain the techniques viruses use to escape detection.**   Viruses use polymorphism and encryption to avoid leaving behind signature footprints. Multipartite viruses use more than one propagation technique to infiltrate systems. Stealth viruses alter operating systems to trick antivirus packages into thinking everything is normal.

**Understand the basic principles behind logic bombs, Trojan horses, and worms.**   Logic bombs remain dormant until one or more conditions are met. At that time, they trigger their malicious payload. Trojan horses penetrate systems by masquerading as a benevolent program while unleashing their payload in the background. Worms spread from system to system under their own power, potentially consuming massive amounts of resources.

**Be familiar with common password attacks, and understand how to develop strong passwords.**   Attackers attempting to gain access to a system use straightforward guessing in combination with dictionary attacks and social-engineering techniques to learn user passwords. System administrators should implement security education programs and operating system controls to ensure that users choose strong passwords.

**Understand common denial-of-service attacks and appropriate countermeasures.**   Attackers use standard denial-of-service attacks like SYN flooding, teardrop fragmentation attacks, and the ping of death to cripple targeted systems. They also harness the power of the global computing grid through the use of smurf attacks and other distributed denial-of-service attacks.

**Be familiar with the various types of application attacks attackers use to exploit poorly written software.**   Buffer-overflow vulnerabilities are one of the greatest threats to modern computing. Attackers also exploit trap doors, time-of-check-to-time-of-use vulnerabilities, and rootkits to gain illegitimate access to a system. Malicious individuals may also use cross-site scripting and SQL injection to exploit vulnerable web applications.

**Know the network reconnaissance techniques used by attackers preparing to attack a network.**   Before launching an attack, attackers use IP sweeps to search out active hosts on a network. These hosts are then subjected to port scans and other vulnerability probes to locate weak spots that might be attacked in an attempt to compromise the network.

**Understand decoy techniques used by system administrators seeking to lure attackers into a trap.** System administrators use honeypot systems that appear to be lucrative, easy-to-hit targets for attackers in attempts to draw them away from critical systems and track their activities. These systems might contain pseudoflaws—apparent vulnerabilities that don't really exist—in an attempt to lull malicious individuals into a false sense of security.

# Written Lab

1. What is the major difference between a virus and a worm?

2. Explain the four propagation methods used by Robert Tappan Morris's Internet Worm.

3. Describe how the normal TCP/IP handshaking process works and how the SYN flood attack exploits this process to cause a denial of service.

4. What are the actions an antivirus software package might take when it discovers an infected file?

5. Explain how a data integrity assurance package like Tripwire provides some secondary virus detection capabilities.

# Answers to Written Lab

1. Viruses and worms both travel from system to system attempting to deliver their malicious payloads to as many machines as possible. However, viruses require some sort of human intervention, such as sharing a file, network resource, or email message, to propagate. Worms, on the other hand, seek out vulnerabilities and spread from system to system under their own power, thereby greatly magnifying their reproductive capability, especially in a well-connected network.

2. The Internet Worm used four propagation techniques. First, it exploited a bug in the Sendmail utility that allowed the worm to spread itself by sending a specially crafted email message that contained its code to the Sendmail program on a remote system. Second, it used a dictionary-based password attack to attempt to gain access to remote systems by utilizing the username and password of a valid system user. Third, it exploited a buffer-overflow vulnerability in the finger program to infect systems. Finally, it analyzed any existing trust relationships with other systems on the network and attempted to spread itself to those systems through the trusted path.

3. In a typical connection, the originating host sends a single packet with the SYN flag enabled, attempting to open one side of the communications channel. The destination host receives this packet and sends a reply with the ACK flag enabled (confirming that the first side of the channel is open) and the SYN flag enabled (attempting to open the reverse channel). Finally, the originating host transmits a packet with the ACK flag enabled, confirming that the reverse channel is open and the connection is established. In a SYN flood attack, attackers use special software that sends a large number of fake packets with the SYN flag set to the targeted system. The victim then reserves space in memory for the connection and attempts to send the standard SYN/ACK reply but never hears back from the originator. This process repeats hundreds or even thousands of times, and the targeted computer eventually becomes overwhelmed and runs out of available memory for the half-opened connections.

4. If possible, it may try to disinfect the file, removing the virus's malicious code. If that fails, it might either quarantine the file for manual review or automatically delete it to prevent further infection.

5. Data integrity assurance packages like Tripwire compute hash values for each file stored on a protected system. If a file infector virus strikes the system, this would result in a change in the affected file's hash value and would, therefore, trigger a file integrity alert.

# Review Questions

1. What is the size of the master boot record on a system installed with a typical configuration?

   A. 256 bytes

   B. 512 bytes

   C. 1,024 bytes

   D. 2,048 bytes

2. How many steps take place in the standard TCP/IP handshaking process?

   A. One

   B. Two

   C. Three

   D. Four

3. Which one of the following types of attacks relies upon the difference between the timing of two events?

   A. Smurf

   B. TOCTTOU

   C. Land

   D. Fraggle

4. What propagation technique does the Good Times virus use to spread infection?

   A. File infection

   B. Boot sector infection

   C. Macro infection

   D. None of the above

5. What advanced virus technique modifies the malicious code of a virus on each system it infects?

   A. Polymorphism

   B. Stealth

   C. Encryption

   D. Multipartitism

6. Which one of the following files might be modified or created by a companion virus?

   A. COMMAND.EXE

   B. CONFIG.SYS

   C. AUTOEXEC.BAT

   D. WIN32.DLL

7. What is the best defensive action that system administrators can take against the threat posed by new malicious code objects that exploit known software vulnerabilities?

   **A.** Update antivirus definitions monthly.

   **B.** Install antiworm filters on the proxy server.

   **C.** Apply security patches as they are released.

   **D.** Prohibit Internet use on the corporate network.

8. Which one of the following passwords is least likely to be compromised during a dictionary attack?

   **A.** *mike*

   **B.** *elppa*

   **C.** *dayorange*

   **D.** *dlayna*

9. What file is instrumental in preventing dictionary attacks against Unix systems?

   **A.** `/etc/passwd`

   **B.** `/etc/shadow`

   **C.** `/etc/security`

   **D.** `/etc/pwlog`

10. Which one of the following tools can be used to launch a distributed denial-of-service attack against a system or network?

    **A.** Satan

    **B.** Saint

    **C.** Trinoo

    **D.** Nmap

11. Which one of the following network attacks takes advantages of weaknesses in the fragment reassembly functionality of the TCP/IP protocol stack?

    **A.** Teardrop

    **B.** Smurf

    **C.** Ping of death

    **D.** SYN flood

12. What type of reconnaissance attack provides attackers with useful information about the services running on a system?

    **A.** Session hijacking

    **B.** Port scan

    **C.** Dumpster diving

    **D.** IP sweep

13. What condition is necessary on a web page for it to be used in a cross-site scripting attack?

    **A.** Reflected input

    **B.** Database-driven content

    **C.** .NET technology

    **D.** CGI scripts

14. What type of virus utilizes more than one propagation technique to maximize the number of penetrated systems?

    **A.** Stealth virus

    **B.** Companion virus

    **C.** Polymorphic virus

    **D.** Multipartite virus

15. What is the most effective defense against cross-site scripting attacks?

    **A.** Limiting account privileges

    **B.** Input validation

    **C.** User authentication

    **D.** Encryption

16. Jim recently downloaded an application from a website that ran within his browser and caused his system to crash by consuming all available resources. Jim was most likely the victim of what type of malicious code?

    **A.** Virus

    **B.** Worm

    **C.** Trojan horse

    **D.** Hostile applet

17. Alan is the security administrator for a public network. In an attempt to detect hacking attempts, he installed a program on his production servers that imitates a well-known operating system vulnerability and reports exploitation attempts to the administrator. What is this type of technique called?

    **A.** Honeypot

    **B.** Pseudoflaw

    **C.** Firewall

    **D.** Bear trap

18. What technology does the Java language use to minimize the threat posed by applets?

    **A.** Confidentiality

    **B.** Encryption

    **C.** Stealth

    **D.** Sandbox

19. Renee is the security administrator for a research network. She's attempting to convince her boss that they should disable two unused services—chargen and echo. What attack is the network more vulnerable to with these services running?

    A. Smurf

    B. Land

    C. Fraggle

    D. Ping of death

20. Which one of the following attacks uses a TCP packet with the SYN flag set and identical source/destination IP addresses and ports?

    A. Smurf

    B. Land

    C. Fraggle

    D. Ping of death

# Answers to Review Questions

1. B. The master boot record is a single sector of a floppy disk or hard drive. Each sector is normally 512 bytes. The MBR contains only enough information to direct the proper loading of the operating system.

2. C. The TCP/IP handshake consists of three phases: SYN, SYN/ACK, and ACK. Attacks like the SYN flood abuse this process by taking advantage of weaknesses in the handshaking protocol to mount a denial-of-service attack.

3. B. The time-of-check-to-time-of-use (TOCTTOU) attack relies upon the timing of the execution of two events.

4. D. The Good Times virus is a famous hoax that does not actually exist.

5. A. In an attempt to avoid detection by signature-based antivirus software packages, polymorphic viruses modify their own code each time they infect a system.

6. A. Companion viruses are self-contained executable files with filenames similar to those of existing system/program files but with a modified extension. The virus file is executed when an unsuspecting user types the filename without the extension at the command prompt.

7. C. The vast majority of new malicious code objects exploit known vulnerabilities that were already addressed by software manufacturers. The best action administrators can take against new threats is to maintain the patch level of their systems.

8. D. Except option D, the choices are forms of common words that might be found during a dictionary attack. *mike* is a name and would be easily detected. *elppa* is simply *apple* spelled backwards, and *dayorange* combines two dictionary words. Crack and other utilities can easily see through these "sneaky" techniques. *dlayna* is simply a random string of characters that a dictionary attack would not uncover.

9. B. Shadow password files move encrypted password information from the publicly readable `/etc/passwd` file to the protected `/etc/shadow` file.

10. C. Trinoo and the Tribal Flood Network (TFN) are the two most commonly used distributed denial-of-service (DDoS) attack toolkits. The other three tools mentioned are reconnaissance techniques used to map networks and scan for known vulnerabilities.

11. A. The teardrop attack uses overlapping packet fragments to confuse a target system and cause the system to reboot or crash.

12. B. Port scans reveal the ports associated with services running on a machine and available to the public.

13. A. Cross-site scripting attacks are successful only against web applications that include reflected input.

14. D. Multipartite viruses use two or more propagation techniques (for example, file infection and boot sector infection) to maximize their reach.

15. B. Input validation prevents cross-site scripting attacks by limiting user input to a predefined range. This prevents the attacker from including the HTML <SCRIPT> tag in the input.

16. D. Hostile applets are a type of malicious code that users download from a remote website and run within their browsers. These applets, written using technologies like ActiveX and Java, may then perform a variety of malicious actions.

17. B. Alan has implemented pseudoflaws in his production systems. Honeypots often use pseudoflaws, but they are not the technology used in this case because honeypots are stand-alone systems dedicated to detecting attackers.

18. D. The Java sandbox isolates applets and allows them to run within a protected environment, limiting the effect they may have on the rest of the system.

19 C. The fraggle attack utilizes the uncommonly used UDP services chargen and echo to implement a denial-of-service attack.

20. B. The land attack uses a TCP packet constructed with the SYN flag set and identical source and destination sockets. It causes older operating systems to behave in an unpredictable manner.

# Chapter 9

# Cryptography and Symmetric Key Algorithms

---

## THE CISSP EXAM TOPICS COVERED IN THIS CHAPTER INCLUDE:

✓ **Cryptography**

- Understand the application and use of cryptography

  - Data at rest (e.g., hard drive); data in transit (e.g., "on the wire")

- Understand encryption concepts

  - Foundational concepts; symmetric cryptography; asymmetric cryptography; hybrid cryptography; message digests; hashing

Cryptography provides added levels of security to data during processing, storage, and communications. Over the years, mathematicians and computer scientists have developed a series of increasingly complex algorithms designed to ensure confidentiality, integrity, authentication, and nonrepudiation. While cryptographers spent time developing strong encryption algorithms, hackers and governments alike devoted significant resources to undermining them. This led to an "arms race" in cryptography and resulted in the development of the extremely sophisticated algorithms in use today. This chapter looks at the history of cryptography, the basics of cryptographic communications, and the fundamental principles of private key cryptosystems. The next chapter continues the discussion of cryptography by examining public key cryptosystems and the various techniques attackers use to defeat cryptography.

# Historical Milestones in Cryptography

Since the beginning of mankind, human beings have devised various systems of written communication, ranging from ancient hieroglyphics written on cave walls to CD/DVDs stuffed with encyclopedias full of information in modern English. As long as mankind has been communicating, we've used secretive means to hide the true meaning of those communications from the uninitiated. Ancient societies used a complex system of secret symbols to represent safe places to stay during times of war. Modern civilizations use a variety of codes and ciphers to facilitate private communication between individuals and groups. In the following sections, you'll look at the evolution of modern cryptography and several famous attempts to covertly intercept and decipher encrypted communications.

## Caesar Cipher

One of the earliest known cipher systems was used by Julius Caesar to communicate with Cicero in Rome while he was conquering Europe. Caesar knew that there were several risks when sending messages—one of the messengers might be an enemy spy or might be ambushed while en route to the deployed forces. For that reason, Caesar developed a cryptographic system now known as the *Caesar cipher*. The system is extremely simple. To encrypt a message, you simply shift each letter of the alphabet three places to the right. For example, *A* would become *D*, and *B* would become *E*. If you reach the end of the alphabet during this process, you simply wrap around to the beginning so that

X becomes *A*, *Y* becomes *B*, and *Z* becomes C. For this reason, the Caesar cipher also became known as the ROT3 (or Rotate 3) cipher. The Caesar cipher is a substitution cipher that is monoalphabetic; it's also known as a C3 cipher.

While the Caesar cipher uses a shift of 3, the more general shift cipher uses the same algorithm to shift any number of characters desired by the user. For example, the ROT12 cipher would turn an *A* into an *M*, a *B* into an *N*, and so on.

Here's an example of the Caesar cipher in action. The first line contains the original sentence, and the second line shows what the sentence looks like when it is encrypted using the Caesar cipher:

```
THE DIE HAS BEEN CAST
WKH GLH KDV EHHQ FDVW
```

To decrypt the message, you simply shift each letter three places to the left.

Although the Caesar cipher is easy to use, it's also easy to crack. It's vulnerable to a type of attack known as frequency analysis. As you may know, the most common letters in the English language are *E, T, A, O, N, R, I, S,* and *H*. An attacker seeking to break a Caesar-style cipher merely needs to find the most common letters in the encrypted text and experiment with substitutions of these common letters to help determine the pattern.

## American Civil War

Between the time of Caesar and the early years of the United States, scientists and mathematicians made significant advances beyond the early ciphers used by ancient civilizations. During the American Civil War, Union and Confederate troops both used relatively advanced cryptographic systems to secretly communicate along the front lines because each side was tapping into the telegraph lines to spy on the other side. These systems used complex combinations of word substitutions and transposition (see the section "Ciphers" for more details) to attempt to defeat enemy decryption efforts. Another system used widely during the Civil War was a series of flag signals developed by army doctor Albert Myer.

Photos of many of the items discussed in this chapter are available online at www.nsa.gov/about/cryptologic_heritage/museum.

## Ultra vs. Enigma

Americans weren't the only ones who expended significant resources in the pursuit of superior code-making machines. Prior to World War II, the German military-industrial complex adapted a commercial code machine nicknamed Enigma for government use. This machine used a series of three to six rotors to implement an extremely complicated substitution cipher. The only possible way to decrypt the message with contemporary technology was to use a similar machine with the same rotor settings used by the transmitting device. The Germans recognized the importance of safeguarding these devices and made it extremely difficult for the Allies to acquire one.

The Allied forces began a top-secret effort known by the code name Ultra to attack the Enigma codes. Eventually, their efforts paid off when the Polish military successfully reconstructed an Enigma prototype and shared their findings with British and American cryptology experts. The Allies successfully broke the Enigma code in 1940, and historians credit this triumph as playing a significant role in the eventual defeat of the Axis powers.

The Japanese used a similar machine, known as the Japanese Purple Machine, during World War II. A significant American attack on this cryptosystem resulted in breaking the Japanese code prior to the end of the war. The Americans were aided by the fact that Japanese communicators used very formal message formats that resulted in a large amount of similar text in multiple messages, easing the cryptanalytic effort.

# Cryptographic Basics

The study of any science must begin with a discussion of some of the fundamental principles upon which it is built. The following sections lay this foundation with a review of the goals of cryptography, an overview of the basic concepts of cryptographic technology, and a look at the major mathematical principles utilized by cryptographic systems.

## Goals of Cryptography

Security practitioners utilize cryptographic systems to meet four fundamental goals: confidentiality, integrity, authentication, and nonrepudiation. Achieving each of these goals requires the satisfaction of a number of design requirements, and not all cryptosystems are intended to achieve all four goals. In the following sections, we'll examine each goal in detail and give a brief description of the technical requirements necessary to achieve it.

### Confidentiality

*Confidentiality* ensures that data remains private while at rest, such as when stored on a disk, or in motion, such as during transmission between two or more parties. This is perhaps the most widely cited goal of cryptosystems—the facilitation of secret communications between individuals and groups. Two main types of cryptosystems enforce confidentiality. Symmetric key cryptosystems use a shared secret key available to all users of the cryptosystem. Asymmetric cryptosystems utilize individual combinations of public and private keys for each user of the system. Both of these concepts are explored in the section "Modern Cryptography" later in this chapter.

When developing a cryptographic system for the purpose of providing confidentiality, you must think about two different types of data: data at rest and data in motion. Data at rest, or stored data, is that which resides in a permanent location awaiting access. Examples of data at rest include data stored on hard drives, backup tapes, USB devices, and other storage media. Data in motion, or data "on the wire," is data being transmitted across a network between two systems. Data in motion might be traveling on a corporate network, a wireless network, or the public Internet. Both data in motion and data at rest pose different types of confidentiality risks that cryptography can protect against. For example, data in motion may be susceptible to eavesdropping attacks, while data at rest is more susceptible to the theft of physical devices.

## Integrity

*Integrity* ensures that a message is not altered while in transit. If integrity mechanisms are in place, the recipient of a message can be certain that the message received is identical to the message that was sent. This protects against all forms of alteration: intentional alteration by a third party attempting to insert false information and unintentional alteration by faults in the transmission process. Message integrity is enforced through the use of digitally signed message digests created upon transmission of a message. The recipient of the message simply verifies that the message's digest and signature is valid, ensuring that the message was not altered in transit. Integrity can be enforced by both public and secret key cryptosystems. This concept is discussed in detail in the section "Digital Signatures" in Chapter 10, "PKI and Cryptographic Applications." The use of cryptographic hash functions to protect file integrity was discussed in Chapter 8.

## Authentication

*Authentication* verifies the claimed identity of system users and is a major function of cryptosystems. For example, suppose that Jim wants to establish a communications session with Bob and they are both participants in a shared secret communications system. Jim might use a challenge-response authentication technique to ensure that Bob is who he claims to be.

Figure 9.1 shows how this challenge-response protocol might work in action. In this example, the shared-secret code used by Jim and Bob is quite simple—the letters of each word are simply reversed. Bob first contacts Jim and identifies himself. Jim then sends a challenge message to Bob, asking him to encrypt a short message using the secret code known only to Jim and Bob. Bob replies with the encrypted message. After Jim verifies that the encrypted message is correct, he trusts that Bob himself is truly on the other end of the connection.

**FIGURE 9.1**   Challenge-response authentication protocol

"Hi, I'm Bob!"

"Prove it. Encrypt 'apple.'"

"elppa"

"Hi Bob, good to talk to you again."

## Nonrepudiation

*Nonrepudiation* provides assurance to the recipient that the message was actually originated by the sender and not someone masquerading as the sender. It prevents the sender from claiming that they never sent the message in the first place (also known as *repudiating* the message). Secret key, or symmetric key, cryptosystems (such as the ROT3 cipher) do not provide this guarantee of nonrepudiation. If Jim and Bob participate in a secret key communication system, they can both produce the same encrypted message using their shared secret key. Nonrepudiation is offered only by public key, or asymmetric, cryptosystems, a topic discussed in greater detail in Chapter 10.

## Cryptography Concepts

As with any science, you must be familiar with certain terminology before studying cryptography. Let's take a look at a few of the key terms used to describe codes and ciphers. Before a message is put into a coded form, it is known as a *plain-text* message and is represented by the letter *P* when encryption functions are described. The sender of a message uses a cryptographic algorithm to *encrypt* the plain-text message and produce a *cipher-text* message, represented by the letter *C*. This message is transmitted by some physical or electronic means to the recipient. The recipient then uses a predetermined algorithm to decrypt the cipher-text message and retrieve the plain-text version.

All cryptographic algorithms rely upon keys to maintain their security. For the most part, a key is nothing more than a number. It's usually a very large binary number, but a number nonetheless. Every algorithm has a specific *key space*. The key space is the range of values that are valid for use as a key for a specific algorithm. A key space is defined by its bit size. Bit size is nothing more than the number of binary bits (0s and 1s) in the key. The key space is the range between the key that has all 0s and the key that has all 1s. Or to state it another way, the key space is the range of numbers from 0 to $2^n$, where n is the bit size of the key. So, a 128-bit key can have a value from 0 to $2^{128}$ (which is roughly $3.40282367 * 10^{38}$, that is, a very big number!). Even though a key is just a number, it is a very important number. In fact, if the algorithm is known, then all the security you gain from cryptography rests on your ability to keep the keys used private.

---

### The Kerchoff Principle

All cryptography is based upon the idea of an *algorithm*. An algorithm is a set of rules, usually mathematical, that dictates how enciphering and deciphering processes are to take place. Most algorithms are dictated by the Kerchoff principle, a concept that makes algorithms known and public, allowing anyone to examine and test them. Specifically, the Kerchoff principle (also known as Kerchoff's assumption) is that all algorithms should be public but all keys should remain private.

A large number of cryptographers adhere to this principle, but not all of them do. In fact, a significant group adheres to the opposite view and believes better overall security can be maintained by keeping both the algorithm and the key private. Kerchoff's adherents retort that the opposite approach includes the dubious practice of "security through obscurity" and believe that public exposure produces more activity and exposes more weaknesses more readily, leading to the abandonment of insufficiently strong algorithms and quicker adoption of suitable ones.

---

As you'll learn in this chapter and the next, different types of algorithms require different types of keys. In private key (or secret key) cryptosystems, all participants use a single shared key. In public key cryptosystems, each participant has their own pair of keys. Cryptographic keys are sometimes referred to as *cryptovariables*.

The art of creating and implementing secret codes and ciphers is known as *cryptography*. This practice is paralleled by the art of *cryptanalysis*—the study of methods to defeat codes and ciphers. Together, cryptography and cryptanalysis are commonly referred to as *cryptology*. Specific implementations of a code or cipher in hardware and software are known as *cryptosystems*. Federal Information Processing Standards–140 (FIPS-140), "Security Requirements for Cryptographic Modules," defines the hardware and software requirements for cryptographic modules that the federal government uses.

Be sure to understand the meanings of the terms in this section before continuing your study of this chapter and the following chapter. They are essential to understanding the technical details of the cryptographic algorithms presented in the following sections.

## Cryptographic Mathematics

Cryptography is no different from most computer science disciplines in that it finds its foundations in the science of mathematics. To fully understand cryptography, you must first understand the basics of binary mathematics and the logical operations used to manipulate binary values. The following sections present a brief look at some of the most fundamental concepts with which you should be familiar.

## Binary Mathematics

*Binary mathematics* defines the rules used for the bits and bytes that form the nervous system of any computer. You're most likely familiar with the decimal system. It is a base 10 system in which an integer from 0 to 9 is used in each place and each place value is a multiple of 10. It's likely that our reliance upon the decimal system has biological origins— human beings have 10 fingers that can be used to count.

Binary math can be very confusing at first, but it's well worth the investment of time to learn how the various logical operations work, specifically logical functions. More important, you need to understand these concepts to truly understand the inner workings of cryptographic algorithms.

Similarly, the computer's reliance upon the binary system has electrical origins. In an electrical circuit, there are only two possible states—on (representing the presence of electrical current) and off (representing the absence of electrical current). All computation performed by an electrical device must be expressed in these terms, giving rise to the use of binary computation in modern electronics. In general, computer scientists refer to the on condition as a *true* value and the off condition as a *false* value.

## Logical Operations

The binary mathematics of cryptography utilizes a variety of logical functions to manipulate data. We'll take a brief look at several of these operations.

### AND

The AND operation (represented by the ∧ symbol) checks to see whether two values are both true. The truth table that follows illustrates all four possible outputs for the AND function. Remember, the AND function takes only two variables as input. In binary math, there are only two possible values for each of these variables, leading to four possible inputs to the AND function. It's this finite number of possibilities that makes it extremely easy for computers to implement logical functions in hardware. Notice in the following truth table that only one combination of inputs (where both inputs are true) produces an output value of true:

| X | Y | X ∧ Y |
|---|---|-------|
| 0 | 0 | 0 |
| 0 | 1 | 0 |
| 1 | 0 | 0 |
| 1 | 1 | 1 |

Logical operations are often performed on entire binary words rather than single values. Take a look at the following example:

```
X:   0 1 1 0 1 1 0 0
Y:   1 0 1 0 0 1 1 1
```
---
```
X ∧ Y:   0 0 1 0 0 1 0 0
```

Notice that the AND function is computed by comparing the values of X and Y in each column. The output value is true only in columns where both X and Y are true.

## OR

The OR operation (represented by the ∨ symbol) checks to see whether at least one of the input values is true. Refer to the following truth table for all possible values of the OR function. Notice that the only time the OR function returns a false value is when both of the input values are false:

| X | Y | X ∨ Y |
|---|---|-------|
| 0 | 0 | 0 |
| 0 | 1 | 1 |
| 1 | 0 | 1 |
| 1 | 1 | 1 |

We'll use the same example we used in the previous section to show you what the output would be if X and Y were fed into the OR function rather than the AND function:

```
X:   0 1 1 0 1 1 0 0
Y:   1 0 1 0 0 1 1 1
```
---
```
X ∨ Y:   1 1 1 0 1 1 1 1
```

## NOT

The NOT operation (represented by the ~ or ! symbol) simply reverses the value of an input variable. This function operates on only one variable at a time. Here's the truth table for the NOT function:

| X | ~X |
|---|----|
| 0 | 1 |
| 1 | 0 |

In this example, you take the value of X from the previous examples and run the NOT function against it:

```
X:      0 1 1 0 1 1 0 0
```
---
```
~X:     1 0 0 1 0 0 1 1
```

## Exclusive OR

The final logical function you'll examine in this chapter is perhaps the most important and most commonly used in cryptographic applications—the exclusive OR (XOR) function. It's referred to in mathematical literature as the XOR function and is commonly represented by the ⊕ symbol. The XOR function returns a true value when only one of the input values is true. If both values are false or both values are true, the output of the XOR function is false. Here is the truth table for the XOR operation:

| X | Y | X ⊕ Y |
|---|---|-------|
| 0 | 0 | 0 |
| 0 | 1 | 1 |
| 1 | 0 | 1 |
| 1 | 1 | 0 |

The following operation shows the X and Y values when they are used as input to the XOR function:

```
X:      0 1 1 0 1 1 0 0
Y:      1 0 1 0 0 1 1 1
```
---
```
X ⊕ Y:  1 1 0 0 1 0 1 1
```

## Modulo Function

The *modulo* function is extremely important in the field of cryptography. Think back to the early days when you first learned division. At that time, you weren't familiar with decimal numbers and compensated by showing a remainder value each time you performed a division operation. Computers don't naturally understand the decimal system either, and these remainder values play a critical role when computers perform many mathematical functions. The modulo function is, quite simply, the remainder value left over after a division operation is performed.

The modulo function is just as important to cryptography as the logical operations are. Be sure you're familiar with its functionality and can perform simple modular math.

The modulo function is usually represented in equations by the abbreviation *mod*, although it's also sometimes represented by the % operator. Here are several inputs and outputs for the modulo function:

```
 8 mod 6 = 2
 6 mod 8 = 6
10 mod 3 = 1
10 mod 2 = 0
32 mod 8 = 0
```

We'll revisit this function in Chapter 10 when we explore the RSA public key encryption algorithm (named after Rivest, Shamir, and Adleman, its inventors).

## One-Way Functions

A *one-way function* is a mathematical operation that easily produces output values for each possible combination of inputs but makes it impossible to retrieve the input values. Public key cryptosystems are all based upon some sort of one-way function. In practice, however, it's never been proven that any specific known function is truly one way. Cryptographers rely upon functions that they suspect may be one way, but it's theoretically possible that they might be broken by future cryptanalysts.

Here's an example. Imagine you have a function that multiplies three numbers together. If you restrict the input values to single-digit numbers, it's a relatively straightforward matter to reverse-engineer this function and determine the possible input values by looking at the numerical output. For example, the output value 15 was created by using the input values 1, 3, and 5. However, suppose you restrict the input values to five-digit prime numbers. It's still quite simple to obtain an output value by using a computer or a good calculator, but reverse-engineering is not quite so simple. Can you figure out what three prime numbers were used to obtain the output value 10,718,488,075,259? Not so simple, eh? (That number is the product of the prime numbers 17,093, 22,441, and 27,943.) There are actually 8,363 five-digit prime numbers, so this problem might be attacked using a computer and a brute-force algorithm, but there's no easy way to figure it out in your head, that's for sure!

## Confusion and Diffusion

Cryptographic algorithms rely upon two basic operations to obscure plain-text messages—confusion and diffusion. *Confusion* occurs when the relationship between the plain text and the key is so complicated that an attacker can't merely continue altering the plain text and analyzing the resulting cipher text to determine the key. *Diffusion* occurs when a change in the plain text results in multiple changes spread throughout the cipher text.

## Nonce

Cryptography often gains strength by adding randomness to the encryption process. One method by which this is accomplished is through the use of a *nonce*. A nonce is a random number generator. It acts as a placeholder variable in mathematical functions. When the function is executed, the nonce is replaced with a random number generated at the moment of processing for one-time use. The nonce produces a unique number each time it is used. One of the more recognizable examples of a nonce is an initialization vector (IV), a random bit string that is the same length as the block size and is XORed with the message. IVs are used to create unique cipher text every time the same message is encrypted using the same key.

## Zero-Knowledge Proof

One of the benefits of cryptography is found in the mechanism to prove your knowledge of a fact to a third party without revealing the fact itself to that third party. This is often done with passwords and other secret authenticators.

The classic example of a *zero-knowledge proof* involves two individuals: Peggy and Victor. Peggy knows the password to a secret door located inside a circular cave, as shown in Figure 9.2. Victor would like to buy the password from Peggy, but he wants Peggy to prove that she knows the password before paying her for it. Peggy doesn't want to tell Victor the password for fear that he won't pay later. The zero-knowledge proof can solve their dilemma.

**FIGURE 9.2**   The magic door (illustration by Dake)

Victor can stand at the entrance to the cave and watch Peggy depart down the path. Peggy then reaches the door and opens it using the password. She then passes through the door and returns via path 2. Victor saw her leave down path 1 and return via path 2, proving that she must know the correct password to open the door.

## Split Knowledge

When the information or privilege required to perform an operation is divided among multiple users, no single person has sufficient privileges to compromise the security of an environment. This separation of duties and two-person control contained in a single solution is called *split knowledge*. Split knowledge is mentioned in Chapter 13, "Administrative Management," but it makes most sense as it relates to cryptography.

The best example of split knowledge is seen in the concept of *key escrow* when the security practice of M of N Control is enforced (we'll explain M of N Control in a second). Using key escrow cryptographic keys, digital signatures, and even digital certificates can be stored or backed up in a special database called the *key escrow database*. In the event a user loses or damages their key, that key can be extracted from the backup. However, if only a single key escrow recovery agent exists, there is opportunity for fraud and abuse of this privilege. M of N Control requires that a minimum number of agents (M) out of the total number of agents (N) work together to perform high-security tasks. So, implementing three of eight controls would require three people out of the eight with the assigned work task of key escrow recovery agent to work together to pull a single key out of the key escrow database (thereby also illustrating that M is always less than or equal to N).

## Work Function

You can measure the strength of a cryptography system by measuring the effort in terms of cost and/or time using a work function or work factor. Usually the time and effort required to perform a complete brute-force attack against an encryption system is what the work function represents. The security and protection offered by a cryptosystem is directly proportional to the value of the work function/factor. The size of the work function should be matched against the relative value of the protected asset. The work function need be only slightly greater than the time value of that asset. In other words, all security, including cryptography, should be cost effective and cost efficient. Spend no more effort to protect an asset than it warrants, but be sure to provide sufficient protection. Thus, if information loses its value over time, the work function needs to be only large enough to ensure protection until the value of the data is gone.

# Ciphers

Cipher systems have long been used by individuals and governments interested in preserving the confidentiality of their communications. In the following sections, we'll cover the definition of a cipher and explore several common cipher types that form the basis of modern ciphers. It's important to remember that these concepts seem somewhat basic, but when used in combination, they can be formidable opponents and cause cryptanalysts many hours of frustration.

## Codes vs. Ciphers

People often use the words *code* and *cipher* interchangeably, but technically, they aren't interchangeable. There are important distinctions between the two concepts. *Codes*, which are cryptographic systems of symbols that represent words or phrases, are sometime secret, but they are not necessarily meant to provide confidentiality. A common example of a code is the "10 system" of communications used by law enforcement agencies. Under this system, the sentence "I received your communication and understand the contents" is represented by the code phrase "10-4." This code is commonly known by the public, but it does provide for ease of communication. Some codes are secret. They may use mathematical functions or a secret dictionary to convey confidential messages by representing words, phrases, or sentences. For example, a spy might transmit the sentence "The eagle has landed" to report the arrival of an enemy aircraft.

*Ciphers*, on the other hand, are always meant to hide the true meaning of a message. They use a variety of techniques to alter and/or rearrange the characters or bits of a message to achieve confidentiality. Ciphers convert messages from plain text to cipher text on a bit basis (that is, a single digit of a binary code), character basis (that is, a single character of an ASCII message), or block basis (this is, a fixed-length segment of a message, usually expressed in number of bits). The following sections cover several common ciphers in use today.

An easy way to keep the difference between codes and ciphers straight is to remember that codes work on words and phrases whereas ciphers work on individual characters and bits.

## Transposition Ciphers

*Transposition ciphers* use an encryption algorithm to rearrange the letters of a plain-text message, forming the cipher-text message. The decryption algorithm simply reverses the encryption transformation to retrieve the original message.

In the challenge-response protocol example in Figure 9.1, a simple transposition cipher was used to reverse the letters of the message so that *apple* became *elppa*. Transposition ciphers can be much more complicated than this. For example, you can use a keyword to perform a columnar transposition. In this example, we're attempting to encrypt the message "The fighters will strike the enemy bases at noon" using the secret key *attacker*. Our first step is to take the letters of the keyword and number them in alphabetical order. The first appearance of the letter *A* receives the value 1; the second appearance is numbered 2. The next letter in sequence, *C*, is numbered 3, and so on. This results in the following sequence:

```
A T T A C K E R
1 7 8 2 3 5 4 6
```

Next, the letters of the message are written in order underneath the letters of the keyword:

```
A T T A C K E R
1 7 8 2 3 5 4 6
T H E F I G H T
E R S W I L L S
T R I K E T H E
E N E M Y B A S
E S A T N O O N
```

Finally, the sender enciphers the message by reading down each column; the order in which the columns are read corresponds to the numbers assigned in the first step. This produces the following cipher text:

```
T E T E E F W K M T I I E Y N H L H A O G L T B O T S E S
  N H R R N S E S I E A
```

On the other end, the recipient reconstructs the eight-column matrix using the cipher text and the same keyword and then simply reads the plain-text message across the rows.

## Substitution Ciphers

*Substitution ciphers* use the encryption algorithm to replace each character or bit of the plain-text message with a different character. The Caesar cipher discussed in the beginning of this chapter is a good example of a substitution cipher. Now that you've learned a little bit about cryptographic math, we'll take another look at the Caesar cipher. Recall that we simply shifted each letter three places to the right in the message to generate the cipher text. However, we ran into a problem when we got to the end of the alphabet and ran out of letters. We solved this by wrapping around to the beginning of the alphabet so that the plain-text character Z became the cipher-text character C.

You can express the ROT3 cipher in mathematical terms by converting each letter to its decimal equivalent (where *A* is 0 and *Z* is 25). You can then add three to each plain-text letter to determine the cipher text. You account for the wrap-around by using the modulo function discussed in the section "Cryptographic Mathematics." The final encryption function for the Caesar cipher is then this:

```
C = (P + 3) mod 26
```

The corresponding decryption function is as follows:

```
P = (C - 3) mod 26
```

As with transposition ciphers, there are many substitution ciphers that are more sophisticated than the examples provided in this chapter. Polyalphabetic substitution ciphers use multiple alphabets in the same message to hinder decryption efforts. One of the most notable examples of a polyalphabetic substitution cipher system is the Vigenere cipher. The Vigenere cipher uses a single encryption/decryption chart as shown here:

```
A B C D E F G H I J K L M N O P Q R S T U V W X Y Z
A B C D E F G H I J K L M N O P Q R S T U V W X Y Z
B C D E F G H I J K L M N O P Q R S T U V W X Y Z A
C D E F G H I J K L M N O P Q R S T U V W X Y Z A B
D E F G H I J K L M N O P Q R S T U V W X Y Z A B C
E F G H I J K L M N O P Q R S T U V W X Y Z A B C D
F G H I J K L M N O P Q R S T U V W X Y Z A B C D E
G H I J K L M N O P Q R S T U V W X Y Z A B C D E F
H I J K L M N O P Q R S T U V W X Y Z A B C D E F G
I J K L M N O P Q R S T U V W X Y Z A B C D E F G H
J K L M N O P Q R S T U V W X Y Z A B C D E F G H I
K L M N O P Q R S T U V W X Y Z A B C D E F G H I J
L M N O P Q R S T U V W X Y Z A B C D E F G H I J K
M N O P Q R S T U V W X Y Z A B C D E F G H I J K L
N O P Q R S T U V W X Y Z A B C D E F G H I J K L M
O P Q R S T U V W X Y Z A B C D E F G H I J K L M N
P Q R S T U V W X Y Z A B C D E F G H I J K L M N O
Q R S T U V W X Y Z A B C D E F G H I J K L M N O P
R S T U V W X Y Z A B C D E F G H I J K L M N O P Q
S T U V W X Y Z A B C D E F G H I J K L M N O P Q R
T U V W X Y Z A B C D E F G H I J K L M N O P Q R S
U V W X Y Z A B C D E F G H I J K L M N O P Q R S T
V W X Y Z A B C D E F G H I J K L M N O P Q R S T U
W X Y Z A B C D E F G H I J K L M N O P Q R S T U V
X Y Z A B C D E F G H I J K L M N O P Q R S T U V W
Y Z A B C D E F G H I J K L M N O P Q R S T U V W X
Z A B C D E F G H I J K L M N O P Q R S T U V W X Y
```

Notice that the chart is simply the alphabet written repeatedly (26 times) under the master heading, shifting by one letter each time. You need a key to use the Vigenere system. For example, the key could be *secret*. Then, you would perform the following encryption process:

1. Write out the plain text.

2. Underneath, write out the encryption key, repeating the key as many times as needed to establish a line of text that is the same length as the plain text.

3. Convert each letter position from plain text to cipher text.

   a. Locate the column headed by the first plain-text character (a).

   b. Next, locate the row headed by the first key word character (s).

   **c.**   Finally, locate where these two items intersect, and write down the letter that appears there (*s*). This is the cipher-text for that letter position.

**4.**   Repeat steps 1 through 3 for each letter in the plain-text version.

| | |
|---|---|
| Plain text: | a t t a c k a t d a w n |
| Key word: | s e c r e t s e c r e t |
| Cipher text: | s x v r g d s x f r a g |

While polyalphabetic substitution protects against direct frequency analysis, it is vulnerable to a second-order form of frequency analysis called *period analysis*, which is an examination of frequency based upon the repeated use of the key.

## One-Time Pads

A *one-time pad* is an extremely powerful type of substitution cipher. One-time pads use a different substitution alphabet for each letter of the plain-text message. They can be represented by the following encryption function, where *K* is the encryption key for the letter represented by *C*:

C = (P + K) mod 26

Usually, one-time pads are written as a very long series of numbers to be plugged into the function.

One-time pads are also known as *Vernam ciphers*, after the name of their inventor — Gilbert Sandford Vernam of AT&T.

The great advantage of one-time pads is that, when used properly, they are an unbreakable encryption scheme. There is no repeating pattern of alphabetic substitution, rendering cryptanalytic efforts useless. However, several requirements must be met to ensure the integrity of the algorithm:

- The encryption key must be randomly generated. Using a phrase or a passage from a book would introduce the possibility of cryptanalysts breaking the code.

- The one-time pad must be physically protected against disclosure. If the enemy has a copy of the pad, they can easily decrypt the enciphered messages.

You may be thinking at this point that the Caesar cipher, Vigenere cipher, and one-time pad sound very similar. They are! The only difference is the key length. The Caesar shift cipher uses a key of length one, the Vigenere cipher uses a longer key (usually a word or sentence), and the one-time pad uses a key that is as long as the message itself.

- Each one-time pad must be used only once. If pads are reused, cryptanalysts can compare similarities in multiple messages encrypted with the same pad and possibly determine the key values used.

- The key must be at least as long as the message to be encrypted. This is because each key element is used to encode only one character of the message.

> These one-time pad security requirements are essential knowledge for any network security professional. All too often, people attempt to implement a one-time pad cryptosystem but fail to meet one or more of these fundamental requirements. Read on for an example of how an entire Soviet code system was broken because of carelessness in this area.

If any one of these requirements is not met, the impenetrable nature of the one-time pad instantly breaks down. In fact, one of the major intelligence successes of the United States resulted when cryptanalysts broke a top-secret Soviet cryptosystem that relied upon the use of one-time pads. In this project, code-named VENONA, a pattern in the way the Soviets generated the key values used in their pads was discovered. The existence of this pattern violated the first requirement of a one-time pad cryptosystem: The keys must be randomly generated without the use of any recurring pattern. The entire VENONA project was recently declassified and is publicly available on the National Security Agency website at www.nsa.gov/about/_"les/cryptologic_heritage/publications/coldwar/venona_story.pdf.

One-time pads have been used throughout history to protect extremely sensitive communications. The major obstacle to their widespread use is the difficulty of generating, distributing, and safeguarding the lengthy keys required. One-time pads can realistically be used only for short messages, because of key lengths.

## Running Key Ciphers

Many cryptographic vulnerabilities surround the limited length of the cryptographic key. As you learned in the previous section, one-time pads avoid these vulnerabilities by using separate alphabets for each cryptographic transformation during encryption and decryption. However, one-time pads are awkward to implement because they require the physical exchange of pads.

One common solution to this dilemma is the use of a *running key cipher* (also known as a *book cipher*). In this cipher, the encryption key is as long as the message itself and is often chosen from a common book. For example, the sender and recipient might agree in advance to use the text of a chapter from *Moby Dick*, beginning with the third paragraph, as the key. They would both simply use as many consecutive characters as necessary to perform the encryption and decryption operations.

Let's look at an example. Suppose you wanted to encrypt the message "Richard will deliver the secret package to Matthew at the bus station tomorrow" using the key just described. This message is 66 characters in length, so you'd use the first 66 characters of the running key: "With much interest I sat watching him. Savage though he was, and hideously marred." Any algorithm could then be used to encrypt the plain-text message using this key. Let's look at the example of modulo 26 addition, which converts each letter to a decimal equivalent, then adds the plain text to the key, and then performs a modulo 26 operation to yield the cipher text. If you assign the letter *A* the value 0 and the letter *Z* the value 25, you have the following encryption operation for the first two words of the cipher text:

| Plain text | R | I | C | H | A | R | D | W | I | L | L |
|---|---|---|---|---|---|---|---|---|---|---|---|
| Key | W | I | T | H | M | U | C | H | I | N | T |
| Numeric plain text | 17 | 8 | 2 | 7 | 0 | 17 | 3 | 22 | 8 | 11 | 11 |
| Numeric key | 22 | 8 | 19 | 7 | 12 | 20 | 2 | 7 | 8 | 13 | 19 |
| Numeric cipher text | 13 | 16 | 21 | 14 | 12 | 11 | 5 | 3 | 16 | 24 | 4 |
| Cipher text | N | Q | V | O | M | L | F | D | Q | Y | E |

When the recipient receives the cipher text, they use the same key and then subtract the key from the cipher text, perform a modulo 26 operation, and then convert the resulting plain text back to alphabetic characters.

## Block Ciphers

*Block ciphers* operate on "chunks," or blocks, of a message and apply the encryption algorithm to an entire message block at the same time. The transposition ciphers are examples of block ciphers. The simple algorithm used in the challenge-response algorithm takes an entire word and reverses its letters. The more complicated columnar transposition cipher works on an entire message (or a piece of a message) and encrypts it using the transposition algorithm and a secret keyword. Most modern encryption algorithms implement some type of block cipher.

## Stream Ciphers

*Stream ciphers* are ciphers that operate on each character or bit of a message (or data stream) one character/bit at a time. The Caesar cipher is an example of a stream cipher. The one-time pad is also a stream cipher because the algorithm operates on each letter of the plain-text message independently. Stream ciphers can also function as a type of block cipher. In such operations there is a buffer that fills up to real-time data that is then encrypted as a block and transmitted to the recipient.

# Modern Cryptography

Modern cryptosystems utilize computationally complex algorithms and long cryptographic keys to meet the cryptographic goals of confidentiality, integrity, authentication, and nonrepudiation. The following sections cover the roles cryptographic keys play in the world of data security and examine three types of algorithms commonly used today: symmetric encryption algorithms, asymmetric encryption algorithms, and hashing algorithms.

## Cryptographic Keys

In the early days of security, one of the predominant principles was "security through obscurity." Security professionals thought the best way to keep an encryption algorithm secure was to hide the details of the algorithm from outsiders. Old cryptosystems required communicating parties to keep the algorithm used to encrypt and decrypt messages secret from third parties. Any disclosure of the algorithm could lead to compromise of the entire system by an adversary.

Modern cryptosystems do not rely upon the secrecy of their algorithms. In fact, the algorithms for most cryptographic systems are widely available for public review in the accompanying literature and on the Internet. This actually improves the security of algorithms by opening them to public scrutiny. Widespread analysis of algorithms by the computer security community allows practitioners to discover and correct potential security vulnerabilities and ensure that the algorithms they use to protect their communications are as secure as possible.

Instead of relying upon secret algorithms, modern cryptosystems rely upon the secrecy of one or more cryptographic keys used to personalize the algorithm for specific users or groups of users. Recall from the discussion of transposition ciphers that a keyword is used with the columnar transposition to guide the encryption and decryption efforts. The algorithm used to perform columnar transposition is well known — you just read the details of it in this book! However, columnar transposition can be used to securely communicate between parties as long as a keyword that would not be guessed by an outsider is chosen. As long as the security of this keyword is maintained, it doesn't matter that third parties know the details of the algorithm. (Note, however, that columnar transposition possesses several inherent weaknesses that make it vulnerable to cryptanalysis and therefore make it an inadequate technology for use in modern secure communication.)

In the discussion of one-time pads earlier in this chapter, you learned that the main strength of the one-time pad algorithm is derived from the fact that it uses an extremely long key. In fact, for that algorithm, the key is at least as long as the message itself. Most modern cryptosystems do not use keys quite that long, but the length of the key is still an extremely important factor in determining the strength of the cryptosystem and the likelihood that the encryption will not be compromised through cryptanalytic techniques.

The rapid increase in computing power allows you to use increasingly long keys in your cryptographic efforts. However, this same computing power is also in the hands of cryptanalysts attempting to defeat the algorithms you use. Therefore, it's essential that you outpace adversaries by using sufficiently long keys that will defeat contemporary cryptanalysis efforts. Additionally, if you are concerned that your data remains safe from cryptanalysis some time into the future, you must strive to use keys that will outpace the projected increase in cryptanalytic capability during the entire time period the data must be kept safe.

Several decades ago, when the Data Encryption Standard was created, a 56-bit key was considered sufficient to maintain the security of any data. However, there is now widespread agreement that the 56-bit DES algorithm is no longer secure because of advances in cryptanalysis techniques and supercomputing power. Modern cryptographic systems use at least a 128-bit key to protect data against prying eyes. Remember, the length of the key directly relates to the work function of the cryptosystem: the longer the key, the harder it is to break the cryptosystem.

## Symmetric Key Algorithms

Symmetric key algorithms rely upon a "shared secret" encryption key that is distributed to all members who participate in the communications. This key is used by all parties to both encrypt and decrypt messages, so the sender and the receiver both possess a copy of the shared key. The same key on both ends of the communication is used to encrypt and decrypt messages. When large-sized keys are used, symmetric encryption is very difficult to break. It is primarily employed to perform bulk encryption and provides only for the security service of confidentiality. Symmetric key cryptography can also be called *secret key cryptography* and *private key cryptography*. Figure 9.3 illustrates the symmetric key encryption and decryption processes.

The use of the term *private key* can be tricky because it is part of three different terms that have two different meanings. The term *private key* always means the private key from the key pair of public key cryptography (aka asymmetric). However, both *private key cryptography* and *shared private key* refer to symmetric cryptography. The meaning of the word *private* is stretched to mean when two people share a secret that they keep confidential instead of its true meaning that only a single person has a secret that's kept confidential. Be sure to keep these confusing terms straight in your studies.

**FIGURE 9.3**  Symmetric key cryptography

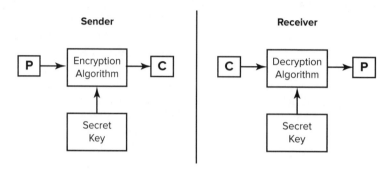

Symmetric key cryptography has several weaknesses:

**Key distribution is a major problem.**   Parties must have a secure method of exchanging the secret key before establishing communications with the symmetric key protocol. If a secure electronic channel is not available, an offline key distribution method must often be used (that is, out-of-band exchange).

**Symmetric key cryptography does not implement nonrepudiation.**   Because any communicating party can encrypt and decrypt messages with the shared secret key, there is no way to prove where a given message originated.

**The algorithm is not scalable.**   It is extremely difficult for large groups to communicate using symmetric key cryptography. Secure private communication between individuals in the group could be achieved only if each possible combination of users shared a private key.

**Keys must be regenerated often.**   Each time a participant leaves the group, all keys that involved that participant must be discarded.

The major strength of symmetric key cryptography is the great speed at which it can operate. Symmetric keying is very fast, often 1,000 to 10,000 times faster than asymmetric. By nature of the mathematics involved, symmetric key cryptography also naturally lends itself to hardware implementations, creating the opportunity for even higher-speed operations.

The section "Symmetric Cryptography" later in this chapter provides a detailed look at the major secret key algorithms in use today.

## Asymmetric Key Algorithms

*Asymmetric key algorithms*, also known as *public key algorithms*, provide a solution to the weaknesses of symmetric key encryption. In these systems, each user has two keys: a public key, which is shared with all users, and a private key, which is kept secret and known only to the user. But here's a twist: opposite and related keys must be used in tandem to encrypt and decrypt. In other words, if the public key encrypts a message, then only the private key can decrypt it, and vice versa.

Figure 9.4 shows the algorithm used to encrypt and decrypt messages in a public key cryptosystem. Consider this example: If Alice wants to send a message to Bob using public key cryptography, she creates the message and then encrypts it using Bob's public key. The only possible way to decrypt this cipher text is to use Bob's private key, and the only user with access to that key is Bob. Therefore, Alice can't even decrypt the message herself after she encrypts it. If Bob wants to send a reply to Alice, he simply encrypts the message using Alice's public key, and then Alice reads the message by decrypting it with her private key.

**FIGURE 9.4**   Asymmetric key cryptography

 **Real World Scenario**

**Key Requirements**

In a class one of the authors of this book taught recently, a student wanted to see an illustration of the scalability issue associated with symmetric encryption algorithms. The fact that symmetric cryptosystems require each pair of potential communicators to have a shared private key makes the algorithm nonscalable. The total number of keys required to completely connect n parties using symmetric cryptography is given by the following formula:

$$\text{Number of Keys} = \frac{n*(n-1)}{2}$$

Now, this might not sound so bad (and it's not for small systems), but consider the figures below. Obviously, the larger the population, the less likely a symmetric cryptosystem will be suitable to meet its needs.

| Number of Participants | Number of Symmetric Keys Required | Number of Asymmetric Keys Required |
| --- | --- | --- |
| 2 | 1 | 4 |
| 3 | 3 | 6 |
| 4 | 6 | 8 |
| 5 | 10 | 10 |
| 10 | 45 | 20 |
| 100 | 4,950 | 200 |
| 1,000 | 499,500 | 2,000 |
| 10,000 | 49,995,000 | 20,000 |

Asymmetric key algorithms also provide support for digital signature technology. Basically, if Bob wants to assure other users that a message with his name on it was actually sent by him, he first creates a message digest by using a hashing algorithm (you'll find more on hashing algorithms in the next section). Bob then encrypts that digest using his private key. Any user who wants to verify the signature simply decrypts the message digest using Bob's public key and then verifies that the decrypted message digest is accurate. Chapter 10 explains this process in greater detail.

The following is a list of the major strengths of asymmetric key cryptography:

**The addition of new users requires the generation of only one public-private key pair.**   This same key pair is used to communicate with all users of the asymmetric cryptosystem. This makes the algorithm extremely scalable.

**Users can be removed far more easily from asymmetric systems.**   Asymmetric algorithms provide a key revocation mechanism that allows a key to be canceled, effectively removing a user from the system.

**Key regeneration is required only when a user's private key is compromised.**   If a user leaves the community, the system administrator simply needs to invalidate that user's keys. No other keys are compromised and therefore key regeneration is not required for any other user.

**Asymmetric key encryption can provide integrity, authentication, and nonrepudiation.**   If a user does not share their private key with other individuals, a message signed by that user can be shown to be accurate and from a specific source and cannot be later repudiated.

**Key distribution is a simple process.**   Users who want to participate in the system simply make their public key available to anyone with whom they want to communicate. There is no method by which the private key can be derived from the public key.

**No preexisting communication link needs to exist.**   Two individuals can begin communicating securely from the moment they start communicating. Asymmetric cryptography does not require a preexisting relationship to provide a secure mechanism for data exchange.

The major weakness of public key cryptography is its slow speed of operation. For this reason, many applications that require the secure transmission of large amounts of data use public key cryptography to establish a connection and then exchange a symmetric secret key. The remainder of the session then uses symmetric cryptography. Table 9.1 compares the symmetric and asymmetric cryptography systems. Close examination of this table reveals that a weakness in one system is matched by a strength in the other.

 Chapter 10 provides technical details on modern public key encryption algorithms and some of their applications.

**TABLE 9.1**   Comparison of symmetric and asymmetric cryptography systems

| Symmetric | Asymmetric |
| --- | --- |
| Single shared key | Key pair sets |
| Out-of-band exchange | In-band exchange |
| Not scalable | Scalable |
| Fast | Slow |
| Bulk encryption | Small blocks of data, digital signatures, digital envelopes, digital certificates |
| Confidentiality | Confidentiality, integrity, authenticity, nonrepudiation |

# Hashing Algorithms

In the previous section, you learned that public key cryptosystems can provide digital signature capability when used in conjunction with a message digest. Message digests are summaries of a message's content (not unlike a file checksum) produced by a hashing algorithm. It's extremely difficult, if not impossible, to derive a message from an ideal hash function, and it's very unlikely that two messages will produce the same hash value.

The following are some of the more common hashing algorithms in use today:

- Message Digest 2 (MD2)
- Message Digest 5 (MD5)
- Secure Hash Algorithm (SHA-0, SHA-1, and SHA-2)
- Hashed Message Authentication Code (HMAC)

Chapter 10 provides details on these contemporary hashing algorithms and explains how they are used to provide digital signature capability, which helps meet the cryptographic goals of integrity and nonrepudiation.

# Symmetric Cryptography

You've learned the basic concepts underlying symmetric key cryptography, asymmetric key cryptography, and hashing functions. In the following sections, we'll take an in-depth look at several common symmetric cryptosystems: the Data Encryption Standard (DES), Triple DES (3DES), International Data Encryption Algorithm (IDEA), Blowfish, Skipjack, and the Advanced Encryption Standard (AES).

## Data Encryption Standard

The U.S. government published the Data Encryption Standard in 1977 as a proposed standard cryptosystem for all government communications. Indeed, many government entities continue to use DES for cryptographic applications today, even though it was superseded by the Advanced Encryption Standard in December 2001. DES is a 64-bit block cipher that has five modes of operation: Electronic Codebook (ECB) mode, Cipher Block Chaining (CBC) mode, Cipher Feedback (CFB) mode, Output Feedback (OFB) mode, and Counter (CTR) mode. These modes are explained in the following sections. All of the DES modes operate on 64 bits of plain text at a time to generate 64-bit blocks of cipher text. The key used by DES is 56 bits long.

DES utilizes a long series of exclusive OR (XOR) operations to generate the cipher text. This process is repeated 16 times for each encryption/decryption operation. Each repetition is commonly referred to as a *round* of encryption, explaining the statement that DES performs 16 rounds of encryption.

As mentioned, DES uses a 56-bit key to drive the encryption and decryption process. However, you may read in some literature that DES uses a 64-bit key. This is not an inconsistency — there's a perfectly logical explanation. The DES specification calls for a 64-bit key. However, of those 64 bits, only 56 actually contain keying information. The remaining 8 bits are supposed to contain parity information to ensure that the other 56 bits are accurate. In practice, however, those parity bits are rarely used. You should commit the 56-bit figure to memory.

## Electronic Codebook Mode

Electronic Codebook (ECB) mode is the simplest mode to understand and the least secure. Each time the algorithm processes a 64-bit block, it simply encrypts the block using the chosen secret key. This means that if the algorithm encounters the same block multiple times, it will produce the same encrypted block. If an enemy were eavesdropping on the communications, they could simply build a "code book" of all the possible encrypted values. After a sufficient number of blocks were gathered, cryptanalytic techniques could be used to decipher some of the blocks and break the encryption scheme.

This vulnerability makes it impractical to use ECB mode on all but the shortest transmissions. In everyday use, ECB is used only for exchanging small amounts of data, such as keys and parameters used to initiate other DES modes as well as the cells in a database.

## Cipher Block Chaining Mode

In Cipher Block Chaining (CBC) mode, each block of unencrypted text is XORed with the block of cipher text immediately preceding it before it is encrypted using the DES algorithm. The decryption process simply decrypts the cipher text and reverses the XOR operation. CBC implements an IV and XORs it with the first block of the message, producing a unique output every time the operation is performed. The IV must be sent to the recipient, perhaps by tacking the IV onto the front of the completed cipher text in plain form or by protecting it with ECB mode encryption using the same key used for the message. One important consideration when using CBC mode is that errors propagate — if one block is corrupted during transmission, it becomes impossible to decrypt that block and the next block as well.

## Cipher Feedback Mode

Cipher Feedback (CFB) mode is the streaming cipher version of CBC. In other words, CFB operates against data produced in real time. However, instead of breaking a message into blocks, it uses memory buffers of the same block size. As the buffer becomes full, it is encrypted and then sent to the recipient(s). Then the system waits for the next buffer to be filled as the new data is generated before it is in turn encrypted and then transmitted. Other than the change from preexisting data to real-time data, CFB operates in the same fashion as CBC. It uses an IV and it uses chaining.

CBC and CFB are best suited for authentication encryption.

## Output Feedback Mode

In Output Feedback (OFB) mode, DES operates in almost the same fashion as it does in CFB mode. However, instead of XORing an encrypted version of the previous preceding block of cipher text, DES XORs the plain text with a seed value. For the first encrypted block, an initialization vector is used to create the seed value. Future seed values are derived by running the DES algorithm on the previous preceding seed value. The major advantages of OFB mode are that there is no chaining function and transmission errors do not propagate to affect the decryption of future blocks.

## Counter Mode

DES run in Counter (CTR) mode uses a stream cipher similar to that used in CFB and OFB modes. However, instead of creating the seed value for each encryption/decryption operation from the results of the previous seed values, it uses a simple counter that increments for each operation. As with OFB mode, errors do not propagate in CTR mode.

CTR mode allows you to break an encryption or decryption operation into multiple independent steps. This makes CTR mode well suited for use in parallel computing.

## Triple DES

As mentioned in previous sections, the Data Encryption Standard's 56-bit key is no longer considered adequate in the face of modern cryptanalytic techniques and supercomputing power. However, an adapted version of DES, Triple DES, uses the same algorithm to produce a more secure encryption.

There are four versions of 3DES. The first simply encrypts the plain text three times, using three different keys: $K_1$, $K_2$, and $K_3$. It is known as DES-EEE3 mode (the $E$s indicate that there are three encryption operations, whereas the numeral 3 indicates that three different keys are used). DES-EEE3 can be expressed using the following notation, where $E(K,P)$ represents the encryption of plain-text $P$ with key $K$:

$E(K_1,E(K_2,E(K_3,P)))$

DES-EEE3 has an effective key length of 168 bits.

The second variant (DES-EDE3) also uses three keys but replaces the second encryption operation with a decryption operation:

$E(K_1,D(K_2,E(K_3,P)))$

The third version of 3DES (DES-EEE2) uses only two keys, $K_1$ and $K_2$, as follows:

$E(K_1,E(K_2,E(K_1,P)))$

The fourth variant of 3DES (DES-EDE2) also uses two keys but uses a decryption operation in the middle:

$E(K_1,D(K_2,E(K_1,P)))$

Both the third and fourth variants have an effective key length of 112 bits.

Technically, there is a fifth variant of 3DES, DES-EDE1, which uses only one cryptographic key. However, it results in the same algorithm (and strength) as standard DES and is provided only for backward compatibility purposes.

These four variants of 3DES were developed over the years because several cryptologists put forth theories that one variant was more secure than the others. However, the current belief is that all modes are equally secure.

Take some time to understand the variants of 3DES. Sit down with a pencil and paper and be sure you understand the way each variant uses two or three keys to achieve stronger encryption.

This discussion begs an obvious question — what happened to Double DES (2DES)? You'll read in Chapter 10 that Double DES was tried but quickly abandoned when it was proven that an attack existed that rendered 2DES no more secure than standard DES.

## International Data Encryption Algorithm

The International Data Encryption Algorithm (IDEA) block cipher was developed in response to complaints about the insufficient key length of the DES algorithm. Like DES, IDEA operates on 64-bit blocks of plain/cipher text. However, it begins its operation with a 128-bit key. This key is broken up in a series of operations into 52 16-bit subkeys. The subkeys then act on the input text using a combination of XOR and modulus operations to produce the encrypted/decrypted version of the input message. IDEA is capable of operating in the same five modes utilized by DES: ECB, CBC, CFB, OFB, and CTR.

All of this material on key length block size and the number of rounds of encryption may seem dreadfully boring; however, it's important material, so be sure to brush up on it while preparing for the exam.

The IDEA algorithm is patented by its Swiss developers. However, they have granted an unlimited license to anyone who wants to use IDEA for noncommercial purposes. One popular implementation of IDEA is found in Phil Zimmerman's popular Pretty Good Privacy (PGP) secure email package. Chapter 10 covers PGP in further detail.

## Blowfish

Bruce Schneier's Blowfish block cipher is another alternative to DES and IDEA. Like its predecessors, Blowfish operates on 64-bit blocks of text. However, it extends IDEA's key strength even further by allowing the use of variable-length keys ranging from a relatively insecure 32 bits to an extremely strong 448 bits. Obviously, the longer keys will result in a corresponding increase in encryption/decryption time. However, time trials have established Blowfish as a much faster algorithm than both IDEA and DES. Also, Mr. Schneier released Blowfish for public use with no license required. Blowfish encryption is built into a number of commercial software products and operating systems. There are also a number of Blowfish libraries available for software developers.

## Skipjack

The Skipjack algorithm was approved for use by the U.S. government in Federal Information Processing Standard (FIPS) 185, the Escrowed Encryption Standard (EES). Like many block ciphers, Skipjack operates on 64-bit blocks of text. It uses an 80-bit key and supports the same four modes of operation supported by DES. Skipjack was quickly embraced by the U.S. government and provides the cryptographic routines supporting the Clipper and Capstone high-speed encryption chips designed for mainstream commercial use.

However, Skipjack has an added twist — it supports the escrow of encryption keys. Two government agencies, the National Institute of Standards and Technology (NIST) and the Department of the Treasury, hold a portion of the information required to reconstruct a Skipjack key. When law enforcement authorities obtain legal authorization, they contact the two agencies, obtain the pieces of the key, and are able to decrypt communications between the affected parties.

Skipjack and the Clipper chip have not been embraced by the cryptographic community at large because of its mistrust of the escrow procedures in place within the U.S. government. In fact, it's unlikely that any key escrow arrangement will succeed given the proliferation of inexpensive, powerful encryption technology on the Internet and the fact that Skipjack's 80-bit key is relatively insecure.

---

### Rivest Cipher 5 (RC5)

Rivest Cipher 5, or RC5, is a symmetric algorithm patented by Rivest, Shamir, and Adleman (RSA) Data Security, the people who developed the RSA asymmetric algorithm. RC5 is a block cipher of variable block sizes (32, 64, or 128 bits) that uses key sizes between 0 (zero) length and 2,048 bits.

---

## Advanced Encryption Standard

In October 2000, the National Institute of Standards and Technology (NIST) announced that the Rijndael (pronounced "rhine-doll") block cipher had been chosen as the replacement for DES. In December of that same year, the secretary of commerce approved FIPS 197, which mandated the use of AES/Rijndael for the encryption of all sensitive but unclassified data by the U.S. government.

The AES cipher allows the use of three key strengths: 128 bits, 192 bits, and 256 bits. The original specification for AES called for the processing of 128-bit blocks, but Rijndael exceeded this specification, allowing cryptographers to use a block size equal to the key length. The number of encryption rounds depends upon the key length chosen:

- 128-bit keys require 9 rounds of encryption.
- 192-bit keys require 11 rounds of encryption.
- 256-bit keys require 13 rounds of encryption.

---

### Twofish

The Twofish algorithm developed by Bruce Schneier (also the creator of Blowfish) was another one of the AES finalists. Like Rijndael, Twofish is a block cipher. It operates on 128-bit blocks of data and is capable of using cryptographic keys up to 256 bits in length.

Twofish utilizes two techniques not found in other algorithms. Prewhitening involves XORing the plain text with a separate subkey before the first round of encryption. Postwhitening uses a similar operation after the 16th round of encryption.

---

Two of the other AES finalists were MARS and SERPENT.

The AES algorithm uses three layers of transformations to encrypt/decrypt blocks of message text:

- Linear mix transform
- Nonlinear transform
- Key addition transform

The total number of round key bits needed is equal to the following:

Block length * (number of rounds + 1)

For example, with a block length of 128 bits and 13 rounds of encryption, 1,792 round key bits are needed.

AES is just one of the many symmetric encryption algorithms you need to be familiar with. Table 9.2 lists several common and well-known symmetric encryption algorithms along with their block size and key size.

**TABLE 9.2**  Symmetric memorization chart

| Name | Block Size | Key Size |
| --- | --- | --- |
| Data Encryption Standard (DES) | 64 | 56 |
| Triple DES (3DES) | 64 | 168 |
| Advanced Encryption Standard (AES), Rijndael | Variable | 128, 192, 256 |
| Twofish | 128 | 1–256 |
| Blowfish (often used in SSH) | Variable | 1–448 |
| IDEA (used in PGP) | 64 | 128 |
| Rivest Cipher 5 (RC5), based on RSA | 32, 64, 128 | 0–2048 |
| Rivest Cipher 4 (RC4), based on RSA | Streaming | 128 |
| Rivest Cipher 2 (RC2), based on RSA | 64 | 128 |
| Skipjack | 64 | 80 |

# Key Distribution

As previously mentioned, one of the major problems underlying symmetric encryption algorithms is the secure distribution of the secret keys required to operate the algorithms. In the following sections, we'll examine the three main methods used to exchange secret keys securely: offline distribution, public key encryption, and the Diffie-Hellman key exchange algorithm.

## Offline Distribution

The most technically simple method involves the physical exchange of key material. One party provides the other party with a sheet of paper or piece of storage media containing the secret key. In many hardware encryption devices, this key material comes in the form of an electronic device that resembles an actual key that is inserted into the encryption device. If participants recognize each other's voice, they might use the (tedious) process of reading keying material over the telephone. However, each one of these methods has its own inherent flaws. If keying material is sent through the mail, it might be intercepted. Telephones can be wiretapped. Papers containing keys might be inadvertently thrown in the trash or lost.

## Public Key Encryption

Many communicators want to obtain the speed benefits of secret key encryption without the hassles of key distribution. For this reason, many people use public key encryption to set up an initial communications link. Once the link is successfully established and the parties are satisfied as to each other's identity, they exchange a secret key over the secure public key link. They then switch communications from the public key algorithm to the secret key algorithm and enjoy the increased processing speed. In general, secret key encryption is thousands of times faster than public key encryption.

## Diffie-Hellman

In some cases, neither public key encryption nor offline distribution is sufficient. Two parties might need to communicate with each other, but they have no physical means to exchange key material, and there is no public key infrastructure in place to facilitate the exchange of secret keys. In situations like this, key exchange algorithms like the Diffie-Hellman algorithm prove to be extremely useful mechanisms.

 The Diffie-Hellman algorithm represented a major advance in the state of cryptographic science when it was released in 1976. It's still in use today.

The Diffie-Hellman algorithm works as follows:

1. The communicating parties (we'll call them Richard and Sue) agree on two large numbers: $p$ (which is a prime number) and $g$ (which is an integer) such that $1 < g < p$.

2. Richard chooses a random large integer $r$ and performs the following calculation:

   $R = g^r \bmod p$

3. Sue chooses a random large integer $s$ and performs the following calculation:

   $S = g^s \bmod p$

4. Richard sends $R$ to Sue and Sue sends $S$ to Richard.

5. Richard then performs the following calculation:

   $K = S^r \bmod p$

6. Sue then performs the following calculation:

   $K = R^s \bmod p$

At this point, Richard and Sue both have the same value, $K$, and can use this for secret key communication between the two parties.

 Secure RPC (SRPC) employs Diffie-Hellman for key exchange.

## Key Escrow

Cryptography is a powerful tool. Like most tools, it can be used for a number of beneficent purposes, but it can also be used with malicious intent. To gain a handle on the explosive growth of cryptographic technologies, governments around the world have floated ideas to implement key escrow systems. These systems allow the government, under limited circumstances such as a court order, to obtain the cryptographic key used for a particular communication from a central storage facility.

There are two major approaches to key escrow that have been proposed over the past decade:

- In the Fair Cryptosystems escrow approach, the secret keys used in a communication are divided into two or more pieces, each of which is given to an independent third party. Each of these pieces is useless on its own but may be recombined to obtain the secret key. When the government obtains legal authority to access a particular key, it provides evidence of the court order to each of the third parties and then reassembles the secret key.

- The Escrowed Encryption Standard takes a different approach by providing the government with a technological means to decrypt cipher text. This standard is the basis behind the Skipjack algorithm discussed earlier in this chapter.

It's highly unlikely that government regulators will ever overcome the legal and privacy hurdles necessary to implement key escrow on a widespread basis. The technology is certainly available, but the general public will likely never accept the potential government intrusiveness it facilitates.

# Summary

Cryptographers and cryptanalysts are in a never-ending race to develop more secure cryptosystems and advanced cryptanalytic techniques designed to circumvent those systems. Cryptography dates back as early as Caesar and has been an ongoing study for many years. In this chapter, you learned some of the fundamental concepts underlying the field of cryptography, gained a basic understanding of the terminology used by cryptographers, and looked at some historical codes and ciphers used in the early days of cryptography. This chapter also examined the similarities and differences between symmetric key cryptography (where communicating parties use the same key) and asymmetric key cryptography (where each communicator has a pair of public and private keys).

We wrapped up the chapter by analyzing some of the symmetric algorithms currently available and their strengths and weaknesses as well as some solutions to the key exchange dilemma that plagues secret key cryptographers. The next chapter expands this discussion to cover contemporary public key cryptographic algorithms. Additionally, some of the common cryptanalytic techniques used to defeat both types of cryptosystems will be explored.

# Exam Essentials

**Understand the role confidentiality plays in cryptosystems.**   Confidentiality is one of the major goals of cryptography. It protects the secrecy of data both while it is at rest and in transit. Confidentiality can be assured by both symmetric and asymmetric cryptosystems.

**Understand the role integrity plays in cryptosystems.**   Integrity provides the recipient of a message with the assurance that data was not altered (intentionally or unintentionally) between the time it was created and the time it was accessed. Integrity can be assured by both symmetric and asymmetric cryptosystems.

**Understand the importance of providing nonrepudiation capability in cryptosystems.** Nonrepudiation provides undeniable proof that the sender of a message actually authored it. It prevents the sender from subsequently denying that they sent the original message. Nonrepudiation is possible only with asymmetric cryptosystems.

**Know how cryptosystems can be used to achieve authentication goals.**   Authentication provides assurances as to the identity of a user. One possible scheme that uses authentication is the challenge-response protocol, in which the remote user is asked to encrypt a message using a key known only to the communicating parties. Authentication can be achieved with both symmetric and asymmetric cryptosystems.

**Be familiar with the basic terminology of cryptography.**   When a sender wants to transmit a private message to a recipient, the sender takes the plain-text (unencrypted) message and encrypts it using an algorithm and a key. This produces a cipher-text message that is transmitted to the recipient. The recipient then uses a similar algorithm and key to decrypt the cipher text and re-create the original plain-text message for viewing.

**Be able to explain how the binary system works and know the basic logical and mathematical functions used in cryptographic applications.**   Binary mathematics uses only the numbers 0 and 1 to represent false and true states, respectively. You use logical operations such as AND, OR, NOT, and XOR on these values to perform computational functions. The modulo function returns the remainder of integer division and is critical in implementing several cryptographic algorithms. Public key cryptography relies upon the use of one-way functions that are difficult to reverse.

**Understand the difference between a code and a cipher and explain the basic types of ciphers.**   Codes are cryptographic systems of symbols that operate on words or phrases and are sometimes secret but don't always provide confidentiality. Ciphers, however, are always meant to hide the true meaning of a message. Know how the following types of ciphers work: transposition ciphers, substitution ciphers (including one-time pads), stream ciphers, and block ciphers.

**Know the requirements for successful use of a one-time pad.**    For a one-time pad to be successful, the key must be generated randomly without any known pattern. The key must be at least as long as the message to be encrypted. The pads must be protected against physical disclosure and each pad must be used only one time and then discarded.

**Understand what an initialization vector (IV) is.**    An initialization vector (IV) is a random bit string (a nonce) that is the same length as the block size that is XORed with the message. IVs are used to create unique cipher-text every time the same message is encrypted with the same key.

**Understand the concept of zero knowledge proof.**    Zero knowledge proof is a communication concept. A specific type of information is exchanged but no real data is transferred, as with digital signatures and digital certificates.

**Understand split knowledge.**    Split knowledge means that the information or privilege required to perform an operation is divided among multiple users. This ensures that no single person has sufficient privileges to compromise the security of the environment. M of N Control is an example of split knowledge.

**Understand work function (work factor).**    Work function, or work factor, is a way to measure the strength of a cryptography system by measuring the effort in terms of cost and/or time to decrypt messages. Usually the time and effort required to perform a complete brute-force attack against an encryption system is what a work function rating represents. The security and protection offered by a cryptosystem is directly proportional to the value of its work function/factor.

**Understand the importance of key security.**    Cryptographic keys provide the necessary element of secrecy to a cryptosystem. Modern cryptosystems utilize keys that are at least 128 bits long to provide adequate security. It's generally agreed that the 56-bit key of the Data Encryption Standard (DES) is no longer sufficiently long enough to provide security.

**Know the differences between symmetric and asymmetric cryptosystems.**    Symmetric key cryptosystems (or secret key cryptosystems) rely upon the use of a shared secret key. They are much faster than asymmetric algorithms, but they lack support for scalability, easy key distribution, and nonrepudiation. Asymmetric cryptosystems use public-private key pairs for communication between parties but operate much more slowly than symmetric algorithms.

**Be able to explain the basic operational modes of the Data Encryption Standard (DES) and Triple DES (3DES).**    The Data Encryption Standard operates in four modes: Electronic Codebook (ECB) mode, Cipher Block Chaining (CBC) mode, Cipher Feedback (CFB) mode, and Output Feedback (OFB) mode. ECB mode is considered the least secure and is used only for short messages. 3DES uses three iterations of DES with two or three different keys to increase the effective key strength to 112 bits.

**Know the Advanced Encryption Standard (AES).**   The Advanced Encryption Standard (AES) utilizes the Rijndael algorithm and is the U.S. government standard for the secure exchange of sensitive but unclassified data. AES uses key lengths and block sizes of 128, 192, and 256 bits to achieve a much higher level of security than that provided by the older DES algorithm.

# Written Lab

1.  What is the major hurdle preventing the widespread adoption of one-time pad cryptosystems to ensure data confidentiality?
2.  Encrypt the message "I will pass the CISSP exam and become certified next month" using columnar transposition with the keyword SECURE.
3.  Decrypt the message "F R Q J U D W X O D W L R Q V B R X J R W L W" using the Caesar ROT3 substitution cipher.

# Answers to Written Lab

1.  The major obstacle to the widespread adoption of one-time pad cryptosystems is the difficulty in creating and distributing the very lengthy keys that the algorithm depends on.

2.  The first step in encrypting this message requires the assignment of numeric column values to the letters of the secret keyword:

    ```
    S E C U R E
    5 2 1 6 4 3
    ```

    Next, the letters of the message are written in order underneath the letters of the keyword:

    ```
    S E C U R E
    5 2 1 6 4 3
    I W I L L P
    A S S T H E
    C I S S P E
    X A M A N D
    B E C O M E
    C E R T I F
    I E D N E X
    T M O N T H
    ```

    Finally, the sender enciphers the message by reading down each column; the order in which the columns are read corresponds to the numbers assigned in the first step. This produces the following cipher text:

    ```
    I S S M C R D O W S I A E E E M P E E D E F X H L H P N
      M I E T I A C X B C I T L T S A O T N N
    ```

3.  This message is decrypted by using the following function:

    ```
    P = (C - 3) mod 26
    C: F R Q J U D W X O D W L R Q V B R X J R W L W
    P: C O N G R A T U L A T I O N S Y O U G O T I T
    ```

    And the hidden message is "Congratulations You Got It." Congratulations, you got it!

# Review Questions

1. Which one of the following is not a goal of cryptographic systems?

   **A.** Nonrepudiation

   **B.** Confidentiality

   **C.** Availability

   **D.** Integrity

2. John recently received an electronic mail message from Bill. What cryptographic goal would need to be met to convince John that Bill was actually the sender of the message?

   **A.** Nonrepudiation

   **B.** Confidentiality

   **C.** Availability

   **D.** Integrity

3. What is the length of the cryptographic key used in the Data Encryption Standard (DES) cryptosystem?

   **A.** 56 bits

   **B.** 128 bits

   **C.** 192 bits

   **D.** 256 bits

4. What type of cipher relies upon changing the location of characters within a message to achieve confidentiality?

   **A.** Stream cipher

   **B.** Transposition cipher

   **C.** Block cipher

   **D.** Substitution cipher

5. Which one of the following is not a possible key length for the Advanced Encryption Standard Rijndael cipher?

   **A.** 56 bits

   **B.** 128 bits

   **C.** 192 bits

   **D.** 256 bits

6. Which one of the following is a cryptographic goal that cannot be achieved by a secret key cryptosystem?

   **A.** Nonrepudiation

   **B.** Confidentiality

   **C.** Availability

   **D.** Integrity

7. When correctly implemented, what is the only cryptosystem known to be unbreakable?

   **A.** Transposition cipher

   **B.** Substitution cipher

   **C.** Advanced Encryption Standard

   **D.** One-time pad

8. What is the output value of the mathematical function 16 mod 3?

   **A.** 0

   **B.** 1

   **C.** 3

   **D.** 5

9. In the 1940s, a team of cryptanalysts from the United States successfully broke a Soviet code based upon a one-time pad in a project known as VENONA. What rule did the Soviets break that caused this failure?

   **A.** Key values must be random.

   **B.** Key values must be the same length as the message.

   **C.** Key values must be used only once.

   **D.** Key values must be protected from physical disclosure.

10. Which one of the following cipher types operates on large pieces of a message rather than individual characters or bits of a message?

    **A.** Stream cipher

    **B.** Caesar cipher

    **C.** Block cipher

    **D.** ROT3 cipher

11. What is the minimum number of cryptographic keys required for secure two-way communications in symmetric key cryptography?

    **A.** One

    **B.** Two

    **C.** Three

    **D.** Four

12. What is the minimum number of cryptographic keys required for secure two-way communications in asymmetric key cryptography?

   A. One

   B. Two

   C. Three

   D. Four

13. Which one of the following Data Encryption Standard (DES) operating modes can be used for large messages with the assurance that an error early in the encryption/decryption process won't spoil results throughout the communication?

   A. Cipher Block Chaining (CBC)

   B. Electronic Codebook (ECB)

   C. Cipher Feedback (CFB)

   D. Output Feedback (OFB)

14. What encryption algorithm is used by the Clipper chip, which supports the Escrowed Encryption Standard sponsored by the U.S. government?

   A. Data Encryption Standard (DES)

   B. Advanced Encryption Standard (AES)

   C. Skipjack

   D. IDEA

15. What is the minimum number of cryptographic keys required to achieve a higher level of security than DES with the Triple DES algorithm?

   A. 1

   B. 2

   C. 3

   D. 4

16. What approach to key escrow divides the secret key into several pieces that are distributed to independent third parties?

   A. Fair Cryptosystems

   B. Key Escrow Standard

   C. Escrowed Encryption Standard

   D. Fair Escrow

17. What kind of attack makes the Caesar cipher virtually unusable?

   A. Meet-in-the-middle attack

   B. Escrow attack

   C. Frequency attack

   D. Transposition attack

18. What type of cryptosystem commonly makes use of a passage from a well-known book for the encryption key?

   **A.** Vernam cipher

   **B.** Running key cipher

   **C.** Skipjack cipher

   **D.** Twofish cipher

19. Which AES finalist makes use of prewhitening and postwhitening techniques?

   **A.** Rijndael

   **B.** Twofish

   **C.** Blowfish

   **D.** Skipjack

20. Matthew and Richard want to communicate using symmetric cryptography but do not have a prearranged secret key. What algorithm might they use to resolve this situation?

   **A.** DES

   **B.** AES

   **C.** Diffie-Hellman

   **D.** Skipjack

# Answers to Review Questions

1.  C. The four goals of cryptographic systems are confidentiality, integrity, authentication, and nonrepudiation.

2.  A. Nonrepudiation prevents the sender of a message from later denying that they sent it.

3.  A. DES uses a 56-bit key. This is considered one of the major weaknesses of this cryptosystem.

4.  B. Transposition ciphers use a variety of techniques to reorder the characters within a message.

5.  A. The Rijndael cipher allows users to select a key length of 128, 192, or 256 bits, depending upon the specific security requirements of the application.

6.  A. Nonrepudiation requires the use of a public key cryptosystem to prevent users from falsely denying that they originated a message.

7.  D. Assuming that it is used properly, the one-time pad is the only known cryptosystem that is not vulnerable to attacks.

8.  B. Option B is correct because 16 divided by 3 equals 5, with a remainder value of 1.

9.  A. The cryptanalysts from the United States discovered a pattern in the method the Soviets used to generate their one-time pads. After this pattern was discovered, much of the code was eventually broken.

10. C. Block ciphers operate on message "chunks" rather than on individual characters or bits. The other ciphers mentioned are all types of stream ciphers that operate on individual bits or characters of a message.

11. A. Symmetric key cryptography uses a shared secret key. All communicating parties utilize the same key for communication in any direction.

12. D. In asymmetric (public key) cryptography, each communicating party must have a pair of public and private keys. Therefore, two-way communication between parties requires a total of four cryptographic keys (a public and private key for each user).

13. D. Output Feedback (OFB) mode does not allow early errors to interfere with future encryption/decryption. Cipher Block Chaining and Cipher Feedback modes will carry errors throughout the entire encryption/decryption process. Electronic Codebook (ECB) operation is not suitable for large amounts of data.

14. C. The Skipjack algorithm implemented the key escrow standard supported by the U.S. government.

**15.** B.  To achieve added security over DES, 3DES must use at least two cryptographic keys.

**16.** A.  The Fair Cryptosystems approach would have independent third parties each store a portion of the secret key and then provide them to the government upon presentation of a valid court order.

**17.** C.  The Caesar cipher (and other simple substitution ciphers) is vulnerable to frequency attacks that analyze the rate at which specific letters appear in the cipher text.

**18.** B.  Running key (or "book") ciphers often use a passage from a commonly available book as the encryption key.

**19.** B.  The Twofish algorithm, developed by Bruce Schneier, uses prewhitening and postwhitening.

**20.** C.  The Diffie-Hellman algorithm allows for the secure exchange of symmetric keys over an insecure medium.

# Chapter 10

# PKI and Cryptographic Applications

---

## THE CISSP EXAM TOPICS COVERED IN THIS CHAPTER INCLUDE:

✓ **Cryptography**

- Understand the application and use of cryptography

    - Data at rest (e.g., hard drive); data in transit (e.g., "on the wire")

- Understand encryption concepts

    - Foundational concepts; symmetric cryptography; asymmetric cryptography; hybrid cryptography; message digests; hashing

- Understand key management process

    - Creation/distribution; storage/destruction; recovery; key escrow

- Understand digital signatures

- Understand methods of cryptanalytic attacks

    - Chosen plain-text; social engineering for key discovery; brute force; cipher-text only; known plaintext; frequency analysis; chosen cipher-text; implementation attacks

- Employ cryptography in network security

- Use cryptography to maintain e-mail security

- Understand Public Key Infrastructure (PKI)

- Understand certificate related issues

- Understand information hiding alternatives (e.g., steganography, watermarking)

In Chapter 9, we introduced basic cryptography concepts and explored a variety of private key cryptosystems. These symmetric cryptosystems offer fast, secure communication but introduce the substantial challenge of key exchange between previously unrelated parties. This chapter explores the world of asymmetric (or public key) cryptography and the public key infrastructure (PKI) that supports worldwide secure communication between parties that don't necessarily know each other prior to the communication. We'll also explore several practical applications of cryptography: securing electronic mail, web communications, electronic commerce, and networking. The chapter concludes with an examination of a variety of attacks malicious individuals might use to compromise weak cryptosystems.

# Asymmetric Cryptography

The section "Modern Cryptography" in Chapter 9 introduced the basic principles behind both private (symmetric) and public (asymmetric) key cryptography. You learned that symmetric key cryptosystems require both communicating parties to have the same shared secret key, creating the problem of secure key distribution. You also learned that asymmetric cryptosystems avoid this hurdle by using pairs of public and private keys to facilitate secure communication without the overhead of complex key distribution systems. The security of these systems relies upon the difficulty of reversing a one-way function.

In the following sections, we'll explore the concepts of public key cryptography in greater detail and look at three of the more common public key cryptosystems in use today: RSA, El Gamal, and the elliptic curve cryptosystem.

## Public and Private Keys

Recall from Chapter 9 that *public key cryptosystems* rely on pairs of keys assigned to each user of the cryptosystem. Every user maintains both a public key and a private key. As the names imply, public key cryptosystem users make their public keys freely available to anyone with whom they want to communicate. The mere possession of the public key by third parties does not introduce any weaknesses into the cryptosystem. The *private key*, on the other hand, is reserved for the sole use of the individual. It is never shared with any other cryptosystem user.

Normal communication between public key cryptosystem users is quite straightforward. Figure 10.1 shows the general process.

**FIGURE 10.1**   Asymmetric key cryptography

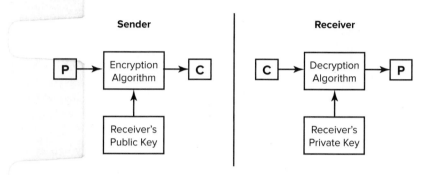

Notice that the process does not require the sharing of private keys. The sender encrypts the plain-text message (P) with the recipient's public key to create the cipher-text message (C). When the recipient opens the cipher-text message, they decrypt it using their private key to re-create the original plain-text message. Once the sender encrypts the message with the recipient's public key, no user (including the sender) can decrypt that message without knowing the recipient's private key (the second half of the public-private key pair used to generate the message). This is the beauty of public key cryptography—public keys can be freely shared using unsecured communications and then used to create secure communications channels between users previously unknown to each other.

You also learned in the previous chapter that public key cryptography entails a higher degree of computational complexity. Keys used within public key systems must be longer than those used in private key systems to produce cryptosystems of equivalent strengths.

# RSA

The most famous public key cryptosystem is named after its creators. In 1977, Ronald Rivest, Adi Shamir, and Leonard Adleman proposed the *RSA* public key algorithm that remains a worldwide standard today. They patented their algorithm and formed a commercial venture known as RSA Security to develop mainstream implementations of their security technology. Today, the RSA algorithm forms the security backbone of a large number of well-known security infrastructures produced by companies like Microsoft, Nokia, and Cisco.

The RSA algorithm depends upon the computational difficulty inherent in factoring large prime numbers. Each user of the cryptosystem generates a pair of public and private keys using the algorithm described in the following steps:

1. Choose two large prime numbers (approximately 200 digits each), labeled p and q.
2. Compute the product of those two numbers, $n = p * q$.

3.   Select a number, e, that satisfies the following two requirements:

   **a.**   e is less than n.

   **b.**   e and (n − 1)(q − 1) are relatively prime—that is, the two numbers have no common factors other than 1.

4.   Find a number, d, such that (ed − 1) mod (p − 1)(q − 1) = 0.

5.   Distribute e and n as the public key to all cryptosystem users. Keep d secret as the private key.

   If Alice wants to send an encrypted message to Bob, she generates the cipher text (C) from the plain text (P) using the following formula (where e is Bob's public key and n is the product of p and q created during the key generation process):

$C = P^e \bmod n$

   When Bob receives the message, he performs the following calculation to retrieve the plain-text message:

$P = C^d \bmod n$

---

### Merkle-Hellman Knapsack

Another early asymmetric algorithm, the Merkle-Hellman Knapsack algorithm, was developed the year after RSA was publicized. Like RSA, it's based upon the difficulty of performing factoring operations, but it relies upon a component of set theory known as *super-increasing sets* rather than on large prime numbers. Merkle-Hellman was proven ineffective when it was broken in 1984.

---

### Importance of Key Length

The length of the cryptographic key is perhaps the most important security parameter that can be set at the discretion of the security administrator. It's important to understand the capabilities of your encryption algorithm and choose a key length that provides an appropriate level of protection. This judgment can be made by weighing the difficulty of defeating a given key length (measured in the amount of processing time required to defeat the cryptosystem) against the importance of the data.

Generally speaking, the more critical your data, the stronger the key you use to protect it should be. Timeliness of the data is also an important consideration. You must take into account the rapid growth of computing power—the famous Moore's law states that computing power doubles approximately every 18 months. If it takes current computers one year of processing time to break your code, it will take only three months if the attempt is made with contemporary technology three years down the road. If you expect that your data will still be sensitive at that time, you should choose a much longer cryptographic key that will remain secure well into the future.

The strengths of various key lengths also vary greatly according to the cryptosystem you're using. According to a white paper published by Certicom, a provider of wireless security solutions, the key lengths shown in the following table for three asymmetric cryptosystems all provide equal protection:

| Cryptosystem | Key Length |
|---|---|
| RSA | 1,088 bits |
| DSA | 1,024 bits |
| Elliptic curve | 160 bits |

# El Gamal

In Chapter 9, you learned how the Diffie-Hellman algorithm uses large integers and modular arithmetic to facilitate the secure exchange of secret keys over insecure communications channels. In 1985, Dr. T. El Gamal published an article describing how the mathematical principles behind the Diffie-Hellman key exchange algorithm could be extended to support an entire public key cryptosystem used for encrypting and decrypting messages.

At the time of its release, one of the major advantages of El Gamal over the RSA algorithm was that it was released into the public domain. Dr. El Gamal did not obtain a patent on his extension of Diffie-Hellman, and it is freely available for use, unlike the then-patented RSA technology. RSA released its algorithm into the public domain in 2000.

However, El Gamal also has a major disadvantage—the algorithm doubles the length of any message it encrypts. This presents a major hardship when encrypting long messages or data that will be transmitted over a narrow bandwidth communications circuit.

# Elliptic Curve

Also in 1985, two mathematicians, Neil Koblitz from the University of Washington and Victor Miller from International Business Machines (IBM), independently proposed the application of *elliptic curve cryptography* theory to develop secure cryptographic systems.

The mathematical concepts behind elliptic curve cryptography are quite complex and well beyond the scope of this book. However, you should be generally familiar with the elliptic curve algorithm and its potential applications when preparing for the CISSP exam. If you are interested in learning the detailed mathematics behind elliptic curve cryptosystems, an excellent tutorial exists at www.certicom.com//index.php/ecc-tutorial.

Any elliptic curve can be defined by the following equation:

$y^2 = x^3 + ax + b$

In this equation, x, y, a, and b are all real numbers. Each elliptic curve has a corresponding *elliptic curve group* made up of the points on the elliptic curve along with the point O, located at infinity. Two points within the same elliptic curve group (P and Q) can be added together with an elliptic curve addition algorithm. This operation is expressed, quite simply, as follows:

$P + Q$

This problem can be extended to involve multiplication by assuming that Q is a multiple of P, meaning the following:

$Q = xP$

Computer scientists and mathematicians believe that it is extremely hard to find x, even if P and Q are already known. This difficult problem, known as the elliptic curve discrete logarithm problem, forms the basis of elliptic curve cryptography. It is widely believed that this problem is harder to solve than both the prime factorization problem that the RSA cryptosystem is based upon and the standard discrete logarithm problem utilized by Diffie-Hellman and El Gamal. This is illustrated by the data shown in the table in the sidebar "Importance of Key Length," which noted that a 1,024-bit RSA key is cryptographically equivalent to a 160-bit elliptic curve cryptosystem key.

# Hash Functions

Later in this chapter, you'll learn how cryptosystems implement digital signatures to provide proof that a message originated from a particular user of the cryptosystem and to ensure that the message was not modified while in transit between the two parties. Before you can completely understand that concept, we must first explain the concept of *hash functions*. This section explores the basics of hash functions and looks at several common hash functions used in modern digital signature algorithms.

Hash functions have a very simple purpose—they take a potentially long message and generate a unique output value derived from the content of the message. This value is commonly referred to as the *message digest*. Message digests can be generated by the sender of a message and transmitted to the recipient along with the full message for two reasons. First, the recipient can use the same hash function to recompute the message digest from the full message. They can then compare the computed message digest to the transmitted one to ensure that the message sent by the originator is the same one received by the recipient. If the message digests do not match, it indicates that the message was somehow modified while in transit. Second, the message digest can be used to implement a digital signature algorithm. This concept is covered in "Digital Signatures" later in this chapter.

The term *message digest* can be used interchangeably with a wide variety of synonyms, including *hash*, *hash value*, *hash total*, *CRC*, *fingerprint*, *checksum*, and *digital ID*.

In most cases, a message digest is 128 bits or larger. However, a single-digit value can be used to perform the function of parity, a low-level or single-digit checksum value used to provide a single individual point of verification. In most cases, the longer the message digest, the more reliable its verification of integrity.

According to RSA Security, there are five basic requirements for a cryptographic hash function:

- The input can be of any length.

- The output has a fixed length.

- The hash function is relatively easy to compute for any input.

- The hash function is one-way (meaning that it is extremely hard to determine the input when provided with the output). One-way functions and their usefulness in cryptography are described in Chapter 9.

- The hash function is collision free (meaning that it is extremely hard to find two messages that produce the same hash value).

In the following sections, we'll look at four common hashing algorithms: SHA, MD2, MD4, and MD5. HMAC is also discussed later in this chapter.

There are numerous hashing algorithms not addressed in this exam. In addition to SHA, MD2, MD4, MD5, and HMAC, you should recognize HAVAL. Hash of Variable Length (HAVAL) is a modification of MD5. HAVAL uses 1,024-bit blocks and produces hash values of 128, 160, 192, 224, and 256 bits.

# SHA

The Secure Hash Algorithm (SHA) and its successor, SHA-1, are government standard hash functions developed by the National Institute of Standards and Technology (NIST) and are specified in an official government publication—the Secure Hash Standard (SHS), also known as Federal Information Processing Standard (FIPS) 180.

SHA-1 takes an input of virtually any length (in reality, there is an upper bound of approximately 2,097,152 terabytes on the algorithm) and produces a 160-bit message digest. The SHA-1 algorithm processes a message in 512-bit blocks. Therefore, if the message length is not a multiple of 512, the SHA algorithm pads the message with additional data until the length reaches the next highest multiple of 512. Recent cryptanalytic attacks demonstrated that there are weaknesses in the SHA-1 algorithm. This led to the creation of SHA-2, which has four variants:

- SHA-224 produces a 224-bit message digest using a 512-bit block size.
- SHA-256 produces a 256-bit message digest using a 512-bit block size.
- SHA-512 produces a 512-bit message digest using a 1,024-bit block size.
- SHA-384 uses a truncated version of the SHA-512 hash to produce a 384-bit digest using a 1,024-bit block size.

 Although it might seem trivial, take the time to memorize the size of the message digests produced by each one of the hash algorithms described in this chapter.

The cryptographic community generally considers the SHA-2 algorithms secure, but they theoretically suffer from the same weakness as the SHA-1 algorithm. In 2007, the federal government announced a competition to create SHA-3 and expect to announce a winner in 2012.

## MD2

The Message Digest 2 (MD2) hash algorithm was developed by Ronald Rivest (the same Rivest of Rivest, Shamir, and Adleman fame) in 1989 to provide a secure hash function for 8-bit processors. MD2 pads the message so that its length is a multiple of 16 bytes. It then computes a 16-byte checksum and appends it to the end of the message. A 128-bit message digest is then generated by using the entire original message along with the appended checksum.

Cryptanalytic attacks exist against the MD2 algorithm. Specifically, Nathalie Rogier and Pascal Chauvaud discovered that if the checksum is not appended to the message before digest computation, collisions may occur. Frederic Mueller later proved that MD2 is not a one-way function. Therefore, it should no longer be used.

## MD4

In 1990, Rivest enhanced his message digest algorithm to support 32-bit processors and increase the level of security. This enhanced algorithm is known as *MD4*. It first pads the message to ensure that the message length is 64 bits smaller than a multiple of 512 bits. For example, a 16-bit message would be padded with 432 additional bits of data to make it 448 bits, which is 64 bits smaller than a 512-bit message.

The MD4 algorithm then processes 512-bit blocks of the message in three rounds of computation. The final output is a 128-bit message digest.

 The MD2, MD4, and MD5 algorithms are no longer accepted as suitable hashing functions. However, the details of the algorithms may still appear on the CISSP exam.

Several mathematicians have published papers documenting flaws in the full version of MD4 as well as improperly implemented versions of MD4. In particular, Hans Dobbertin published a paper in 1996 outlining how a modern PC could be used to find collisions for MD4 message digests in less than one minute. For this reason, MD4 is no longer considered to be a secure hashing algorithm, and its use should be avoided if at all possible.

# MD5

In 1991, Rivest released the next version of his message digest algorithm, which he called *MD5*. It also processes 512-bit blocks of the message, but it uses four distinct rounds of computation to produce a digest of the same length as the MD2 and MD4 algorithms (128 bits). MD5 has the same padding requirements as MD4—the message length must be 64 bits less than a multiple of 512 bits.

MD5 implements additional security features that reduce the speed of message digest production significantly. Unfortunately, recent cryptanalytic attacks demonstrated that the MD5 protocol is subject to collisions, making it not a one-way function. Specifically, Arjen Lenstra and others demonstrated in 2005 that it is possible to create two digital certificates from different public keys that have the same MD5 hash.

Table 10.1 lists well-known hashing algorithms and their resultant hash value lengths in bits. Earmark this page for memorization.

**TABLE 10.1**   Hash algorithm memorization chart

| Name | Hash Value Length |
| --- | --- |
| Secure Hash Algorithm (SHA-1) | 160 |
| SHA-224 | 224 |
| SHA-256 | 256 |
| SHA-384 | 384 |
| SHA-512 | 512 |
| Message Digest 5 (MD5) | 128 |
| Message Digest 4 (MD4) | 128 |
| Message Digest 2 (MD2) | 128 |
| Hash Message Authenticating Code (HMAC) | Variable |
| Hash of Variable Length (HAVAL)—an MD5 variant | 128, 160, 192, 224, and 256 bits |

# Digital Signatures

Once you have chosen a cryptographically sound hashing algorithm, you can use it to implement a *digital signature* system. Digital signature infrastructures have two distinct goals:

- Digitally signed messages assure the recipient that the message truly came from the claimed sender, and they enforce nonrepudiation (that is, they preclude the sender from later claiming that the message is a forgery).

- Digitally signed messages assure the recipient that the message was not altered while in transit between the sender and recipient. This protects against both malicious modification (a third party wanting to alter the meaning of the message) and unintentional modification (because of faults in the communications process, such as electrical interference).

Digital signature algorithms rely upon a combination of the two major concepts already covered in this chapter—public key cryptography and hashing functions. If Alice wants to digitally sign a message she's sending to Bob, she performs the following actions:

1. Alice generates a message digest of the original plain-text message using one of the cryptographically sound hashing algorithms, such as SHA-512.

2. Alice then encrypts only the message digest using her private key. This encrypted message digest is the digital signature.

3. Alice appends the signed message digest to the plain-text message.

4. Alice transmits the appended message to Bob.

> **NOTE**  Digital signatures are used for more than just messages. Software vendors often use digital signature technology to authenticate code distributions that you download from the Internet, such as applets and software patches.

When Bob receives the digitally signed message, he reverses the procedure, as follows:

1. Bob decrypts the digital signature using Alice's public key.

2. Bob uses the same hashing function to create a message digest of the full plain-text message received from Alice.

3. Bob then compares the decrypted message digest he received from Alice with the message digest he computed himself. If the two digests match, he can be assured that the message he received was sent by Alice. If they do not match, either the message was not sent by Alice or the message was modified while in transit.

Note that the digital signature process does not provide any privacy in and of itself. It only ensures that the cryptographic goals of integrity, authentication, and nonrepudiation are met. However, if Alice wanted to ensure the privacy of her message to Bob, she would add a step to the message creation process. After appending the signed message digest to the plain-text message, Alice could encrypt the entire message with Bob's public key. When Bob received the message, he would decrypt it with his own private key before following the steps just outlined.

## HMAC

The Hashed Message Authentication Code (HMAC) algorithm implements a partial digital signature—it guarantees the integrity of a message during transmission, but it does not provide for nonrepudiation.

 **Real World Scenario**

### Which Key Should I Use?

If you're new to public key cryptography, selecting the correct key for various applications can be quite confusing. Encryption, decryption, message signing, and signature verification all use the same algorithm with different key inputs. Here are a few simple rules to help keep these concepts straight in your mind when preparing for the CISSP exam:

- If you want to encrypt a message, use the recipient's public key.

- If you want to decrypt a message sent to you, use your private key.

- If you want to digitally sign a message you are sending to someone else, use your private key.

- If you want to verify the signature on a message sent by someone else, use the sender's public key.

These four rules are the core principles of public key cryptography and digital signatures. If you understand each of them, you're off to a great start!

HMAC can be combined with any standard message digest generation algorithm, such as SHA-2. It can be combined with these algorithms by using a shared secret key. Therefore, only communicating parties who know the key can generate or verify the digital signature. If the recipient decrypts the message digest but cannot successfully compare it to a message digest generated from the plain-text message, the message was altered in transit.

Because HMAC relies on a shared secret key, it does not provide any nonrepudiation functionality (as previously mentioned). However, it operates in a more efficient manner than the digital signature standard described in the following section and may be suitable for applications in which symmetric key cryptography is appropriate. In short, it represents a halfway point between unencrypted use of a message digest algorithm and computationally expensive digital signature algorithms based upon public key cryptography.

## Digital Signature Standard

The National Institute of Standards and Technology specifies the digital signature algorithms acceptable for federal government use in Federal Information Processing Standard (FIPS) 186-3, also known as the Digital Signature Standard (DSS). This document specifies that all federally approved digital signature algorithms must use the SHA-1 or SHA-2 hashing functions.

DSS also specifies the encryption algorithms that can be used to support a digital signature infrastructure. There are three currently approved standard encryption algorithms:

- The Digital Signature Algorithm (DSA) as specified in FIPS 186-3
- The Rivest, Shamir, Adleman (RSA) algorithm as specified in ANSI X9.31
- The Elliptic Curve DSA (ECDSA) as specified in ANSI X9.62

Two other digital signature algorithms you should recognize, at least by name, are Schnorr's signature algorithm and Nybergrueppel's signature algorithm.

# Public Key Infrastructure

The major strength of public key encryption is its ability to facilitate communication between parties previously unknown to each other. This is made possible by the *public key infrastructure (PKI)* hierarchy of trust relationships. PKI combines asymmetric cryptography with symmetric cryptography along with hashing and digital certificates. Thus, it is also called hybrid cryptography. In the following sections, you'll learn the basic components of the public key infrastructure and the cryptographic concepts that make global secure communications possible. You'll learn the composition of a digital certificate, the role of certificate authorities, and the process used to generate and destroy certificates.

## Certificates

Digital *certificates* provide communicating parties with the assurance that the people they are communicating with truly are who they claim to be. Digital certificates are essentially endorsed copies of an individual's public key. When users verify that a certificate was signed by a trusted CA, they know that the public key is legitimate.

Digital certificates contain specific identifying information, and their construction is governed by an international standard—X.509. Certificates that conform to X.509 contain the following data:

- Version of X.509 to which the certificate conforms

- Serial number (from the certificate creator)

- Signature algorithm identifier (specifies the technique used by the certificate authority to digitally sign the contents of the certificate)

- Issuer name (identification of the certificate authority that issued the certificate)

- Validity period (specifies the dates and times—a starting date and time and an ending date and time—during which the certificate is valid)

- Subject's name (contains the distinguished name, or DN, of the entity that owns the public key contained in the certificate)

- Subject's public key (the meat of the certificate—the actual public key the certificate owner used to set up secure communications)

The current version of X.509 (version 3) supports certificate extensions—customized variables containing data inserted into the certificate by the certificate authority to support tracking of certificates or various applications.

 If you're interested in building your own X.509 certificates or just want to explore the inner workings of the public key infrastructure, you can purchase the complete official X.509 standard from the International Telecommunications Union. It's part of the Open Systems Interconnection (OSI) series of communication standards and can be purchased electronically on the ITU website at www.itu.int.

X.509 has not been officially accepted as a standard, and implementations can vary from vendor to vendor. However, both Microsoft and Mozilla have adopted X.509 as their de facto standard for Secure Sockets Layer (SSL) communication between their web clients and servers. SSL is covered in greater detail in the section "Applied Cryptography" later in this chapter.

## Certificate Authorities

*Certificate authorities (CAs)* are the glue that binds the public key infrastructure together. These neutral organizations offer notarization services for digital certificates. To obtain a digital certificate from a reputable CA, you must prove your identify to the satisfaction of the CA. The following list includes the major CAs:

- VeriSign

- Thawte

- Geotrust

- Comodo Limited
- Starfield Technologies
- GoDaddy
- DigiCert
- Network Solutions, LLC
- Entrust.net

Nothing is preventing any organization from simply setting up shop as a CA. However, the certificates issued by a CA are only as good as the trust placed in the organization that issued them. This is an important item to consider when receiving a digital certificate from a third party. If you don't recognize and trust the name of the CA that issued the certificate, you shouldn't place any trust in the certificate at all. PKI relies upon a hierarchy of trust relationships. If you configure your browser to trust a CA, it will automatically trust all of the digital certificates issued by that CA. Browser developers preconfigure browsers to trust the major CAs to avoid placing this burden on users.

*Registration authorities (RAs)* assist CAs with the burden of verifying users' identities prior to issuing digital certificates. They do not directly issue certificates themselves, but they play an important role in the certification process, allowing CAs to remotely validate user identities.

 **Real World Scenario**

**Certificate Path Validation**

You may have heard of *certificate path validation (CPV)* in your studies of certificate authorities. CPV means that each certificate in a certificate path from the original start or root of trust down to the server or client in question is valid and legitimate. CPV can be important if you need to verify that every link between "trusted" endpoints remains current, valid, and trustworthy. This issue arises from time to time when intermediary systems' certificates expire or are replaced; this can break the chain of trust or the verification path. By forcing a reverification of all stages of trust, you can reestablish all trust links and prove that the assumed trust remains assured.

# Certificate Generation and Destruction

The technical concepts behind the public key infrastructure are relatively simple. In the following sections, we'll cover the processes used by certificate authorities to create, validate, and revoke client certificates.

## Enrollment

When you want to obtain a digital certificate, you must first prove your identity to the CA in some manner; this process is called *enrollment*. As mentioned in the previous section, this sometimes involves physically appearing before an agent of the certification authority with the appropriate identification documents. Some certificate authorities provide other means of verification, including the use of credit report data and identity verification by trusted community leaders.

Once you've satisfied the certificate authority regarding your identity, you provide them with your public key. The CA next creates an X.509 digital certificate containing your identifying information and a copy of your public key. The CA then digitally signs the certificate using the CA's private key and provides you with a copy of your signed digital certificate. You may then safely distribute this certificate to anyone with whom you want to communicate securely.

## Verification

When you receive a digital certificate from someone with whom you want to communicate, you *verify* the certificate by checking the CA's digital signature using the CA's public key. Next, you must check and ensure that the certificate was not published on a *certificate revocation list (CRL)*. At this point, you may assume that the public key listed in the certificate is authentic, provided that it satisfies the following requirements:

- The digital signature of the CA is authentic.
- You trust the CA.
- The certificate is not listed on a CRL.
- The certificate actually contains the data you are trusting.

The last point is a subtle but extremely important item. Before you trust an identifying piece of information about someone, be sure that it is actually contained within the certificate. If a certificate contains the email address (`billjones@foo.com`) but not the individual's name, you can be certain only that the public key contained therein is associated with that email address. The CA is not making any assertions about the actual identity of the `billjones@foo.com` email account. However, if the certificate contains the name Bill Jones along with an address and telephone number, the CA is vouching for that information as well.

Digital certificate verification algorithms are built in to a number of popular web browsing and email clients, so you won't often need to get involved in the particulars of the process. However, it's important to have a solid understanding of the technical details taking place behind the scenes to make appropriate security judgments for your organization.

## Revocation

Occasionally, a certificate authority needs to *revoke* a certificate. This might occur for one of the following reasons:

- The certificate was compromised (for example, the certificate owner accidentally gave away the private key).
- The certificate was erroneously issued (for example, the CA mistakenly issued a certificate without proper verification).

- The details of the certificate changed (for example, the subject's name changed).

- The security association changed (for example, the subject is no longer employed by the organization sponsoring the certificate).

Revocation request grace period is the maximum response time within which a CA will perform any requested revocation. This is defined in the *certificate practice statement (CPS)*. The CPS states the practices a CA employs when issuing or managing certificates.

You can use two techniques to verify the authenticity of certificates and identify revoked certificates:

**Certificate revocation lists**   Certificate revocation lists (CRLs) are maintained by the various certification authorities and contain the serial numbers of certificates that have been issued by a CA that have been revoked along with the date and time the revocation went into effect. The major disadvantage to certificate revocation lists is that they must be downloaded and cross-referenced periodically, introducing a period of latency between the time a certificate is revoked and the time end users are notified of the revocation. However, CRLs remain the most common method of checking certificate status in use today.

**Online Certificate Status Protocol (OCSP)**   This protocol eliminates the latency inherent in the use of certificate revocation lists by providing a means for real-time certificate verification. When a client receives a certificate, it sends an OCSP request to the CA's OCSP server. The server then responds with a status of valid, invalid, or unknown.

## Key Management

When working within the public key infrastructure, it's important that you comply with several best practice requirements to maintain the security of your communications.

First, choose your encryption system wisely. As you learned earlier, "security through obscurity" is not an appropriate approach. Choose an encryption system with an algorithm in the public domain that has been thoroughly vetted by industry experts. Be wary of systems that use a "black-box" approach and maintain that the secrecy of their algorithm is critical to the integrity of the cryptosystem.

You must also select your keys in an appropriate manner. Use a key length that balances your security requirements with performance considerations. Also, ensure that your key is truly random. Any patterns within the key increase the likelihood that an attacker will be able to break your encryption and degrade the security of your cryptosystem.

When using public key encryption, keep your private key secret! Do not, under any circumstances, allow anyone else to gain access to your private key. Remember, allowing someone access even once permanently compromises all communications that take place (past, present, or future) using that key and allows the third party to successfully impersonate you.

Retire keys when they've served a useful life. Many organizations have mandatory key rotation requirements to protect against undetected key compromise. If you don't have a formal policy that you must follow, select an appropriate interval based upon the frequency with which you use your key. You might want to change your key pair every few months, if practical.

Back up your key! If you lose the file containing your private key because of data corruption, disaster, or other circumstances, you'll certainly want to have a backup available. You may want to either create your own backup or use a key escrow service that maintains the backup for you. In either case, ensure that the backup is handled in a secure manner. After all, it's just as important as your primary key file!

# Applied Cryptography

Up to this point, you've learned a great deal about the foundations of cryptography, the inner workings of various cryptographic algorithms, and the use of the public key infrastructure to distribute identity credentials using digital certificates. You should now feel comfortable with the basics of cryptography and prepared to move on to higher-level applications of this technology to solve everyday communications problems. In the following sections, we'll examine the use of cryptography to secure data at rest, such as that stored on portable devices, as well as to data in transit, using techniques that include secure electronic mail, web communications services, electronic commerce, and networking.

## Portable Devices

The now ubiquitous nature of notebook computers, netbooks, smartphones, PDAs, and other small portable computing devices brings new risks to the world of computing. Those devices often contain highly sensitive information that, if lost or stolen, could cause serious harm to an organization and its customers, employees, and affiliates. For this reason, many organizations turn to encryption to protect the data on these devices in the event they are misplaced.

Current versions of popular operating systems now include disk encryption capabilities that make it easy to apply and manage encryption on portable devices. For example, Microsoft Windows includes the BitLocker and Encrypting File System (EFS) technologies, Mac OS X includes FileVault encryption, and the TrueCrypt open-source package allows the encryption of disks on Linux, Windows, and Mac systems. There is also a wide variety of commercial tools available that provide added features and management capability.

 Don't forget about smartphones when developing your portable device encryption policy. BlackBerries, iPhones, and other devices all include enterprise-level functionality that supports encryption of data stored on the phone.

# Electronic Mail

We have mentioned several times that security should be cost effective. When it comes to electronic mail, simplicity is the most cost-effective option, but sometimes cryptography functions provide specific security services that you can't avoid using. Since ensuring security is also cost effective, here are some simple rules about encrypting email:

- If you need confidentiality when sending an email message, then encrypt the message.
- If your message must maintain integrity, then you must hash the message.
- If your message needs authentication, integrity and/or nonrepudiation, then you should digitally sign the message.
- If your message requires confidentiality, integrity, authentication, and nonrepudiation, then you should encrypt and digitally sign the message.

It is always the responsibility of the sender to ensure that proper mechanisms are in place to ensure that the security (that is, confidentiality, integrity, authenticity, and nonrepudiation) and privacy of a message or transmission are maintained.

One of the most demanded applications of cryptography is encrypting and signing electronic mail messages. Until recently, encrypted email required the use of complex, awkward software that in turn required manual intervention and complicated key exchange procedures. An increased emphasis on security in recent years resulted in the implementation of strong encryption technology in mainstream electronic mail packages. Next, we'll look at some of the secure electronic mail standards in widespread use today.

## Pretty Good Privacy

Phil Zimmerman's Pretty Good Privacy (PGP) secure email system appeared on the computer security scene in 1991. It combines the CA hierarchy described earlier in this chapter with the "web of trust" concept—that is, you must become trusted by one or more PGP users to begin using the system. You then accept their judgment regarding the validity of additional users and, by extension, trust a multilevel "web" of users descending from your initial trust judgments. PGP initially encountered a number of hurdles to widespread use. The most difficult obstruction was the U.S. government export regulations, which treated encryption technology as munitions and prohibited the distribution of strong encryption technology outside the United States. Fortunately, this restriction has since been repealed, and PGP may be freely distributed to most countries.

PGP is available in two versions. The commercial version uses RSA for key exchange, IDEA for encryption/decryption, and MD5 for message digest production. The freeware version uses Diffie-Hellman key exchange, the Carlisle Adams/Stafford Tavares (CAST) 128-bit encryption/decryption algorithm, and the SHA-1 hashing function.

## Privacy Enhanced Mail

The Privacy Enhanced Mail (PEM) standard addresses implementation guidelines for secure electronic mail in a variety of Internet Request for Comments (RFC) documents. RFC 1421 outlines an architecture that provides the following services:

- Disclosure protection
- Originator authenticity
- Message integrity
- Nonrepudiation (if asymmetric cryptography is used)

However, the same RFC also notes that PEM is not intended to provide the following services:

- Access control
- Traffic flow confidentiality
- Address list accuracy
- Routing control
- Assurance of message receipt and nondeniability of receipt
- Automatic association of acknowledgments with the messages to which they refer
- Replay protection

Security administrators who desire any of the services just listed should implement additional controls over and above those provided by a PEM-compliant electronic mail system. An important distinction between PEM and PGP is that PEM uses a CA-managed hierarchy of digital certificates, whereas PGP relies upon the "web of trust" between system users.

## MOSS

Another Request for Comments document, RFC 1848, specifies the MIME Object Security Services (MOSS), yet another standard for secure electronic mail, designed to supersede Privacy Enhanced Mail. Like PGP, MOSS does not require the use of digital certificates and provides easy associations between certificates and email addresses. It also allows the secure exchange of attachments to email messages. However, MOSS does not provide any interoperability with PGP or PEM.

## S/MIME

The Secure Multipurpose Internet Mail Extensions (S/MIME) protocol has emerged as a likely standard for future encrypted electronic mail efforts. S/MIME utilizes the RSA encryption algorithm and has received the backing of major industry players, including RSA Security. S/MIME has already been incorporated in a large number of commercial products, including these:

- Microsoft Outlook and Outlook Express
- Netscape Communicator
- Lotus Notes
- VeriSign Digital ID
- Eudora WorldSecure

S/MIME relies upon the use of X.509 certificates for exchanging cryptographic keys. The public keys contained in these certificates are used for digital signatures and for the exchange of symmetric keys used for longer communications sessions. RSA is the only public key cryptographic protocol supported by S/MIME. The protocol supports the following symmetric encryption algorithms:

- DES
- 3DES
- RC2

The strong industry support for the S/MIME standard makes it likely that S/MIME will be widely adopted and approved as an Internet standard for secure electronic mail by the Internet Engineering Task Force (IETF) in the near future.

# Web

Although secure electronic mail is still in its early days, secure web browsing has achieved widespread acceptance in recent years. This is mainly because of the strong movement toward electronic commerce and the desire of both e-commerce vendors and consumers to securely exchange financial information (such as credit card information) over the Web. We'll look at the two technologies that are responsible for the small lock icon at the bottom of web browsers—Secure Sockets Layer (SSL) and Secure HTTP (S-HTTP).

## Secure Sockets Layer/Transport Layer Security

Secure Sockets Layer (SSL) was developed by Netscape to provide client/server encryption for web traffic. Hypertext Transfer Protocol over Secure Sockets Layer (HTTPS) uses port 443 to negotiate encrypted communications sessions between web servers and browser clients. Although SSL originated as a standard for Netscape browsers, Microsoft also adopted it as a security standard for its popular Internet Explorer browser. The incorporation of SSL into both of these products made it the de facto Internet standard.

SSL relies upon the exchange of server digital certificates to negotiate RSA encryption/ decryption parameters between the browser and the web server. SSL's goal is to create secure communications channels that remain open for an entire web browsing session.

SSL relies upon a combination of symmetric and asymmetric cryptography. When a user accesses a website, the browser retrieves the web server's certificate and extracts the server's public key from it. The browser then creates a random symmetric key, uses the server's public key to encrypt it, and then sends the encrypted symmetric key to the server. The server then decrypts the symmetric key using its own private key, and the two systems exchange all future messages using the symmetric encryption key. This approach allows SSL to leverage the advanced functionality of asymmetric cryptography while encrypting and decrypting the vast majority of the data exchanged using the faster symmetric algorithm.

SSL forms the basis for a newer security standard, the Transport Layer Security (TLS) protocol, specified in RFC 2246. TLS is slowly surpassing SSL in popularity. SSL and TLS both support server authentication (mandatory) and client authentication (optional).

 Be certain to know the differences between HTTP over SSL (HTTPS) and Secure HTTP (S-HTTP).

## Secure HTTP

Secure HTTP (S-HTTP) is the second major protocol used to provide security on the World Wide Web. S-HTTP is not nearly as popular as SSL/TLS, but it has two major differences:

- S-HTTP secures individual messages between a client and server rather than creating a secure communications channel as SSL does.

- S-HTTP supports two-way authentication between a client and a server rather than the server-only authentication supported by SSL.

## Steganography

*Steganography* is the art of using cryptographic techniques to embed secret messages within another message. Steganographic algorithms work by making alterations to the least significant bits of the many bits that make up image files. The changes are so minor that there is no appreciable effect on the viewed image. This technique allows communicating parties to hide messages in plain sight—such as embedding a secret message within an illustration on an otherwise innocent web page.

Steganographers often embed their secret messages within images or WAV files. These files are often so large that the secret message would easily be missed by even the most observant inspector. Steganography techniques are often used for illegal or questionable activities, such as espionage and child pornography. However, they can also be used for legitimate purposes, such as adding digital watermarks to documents to protect intellectual property. The process of digital watermarking hides information within a file that is known only to the file's creator. If someone later creates an unauthorized copy of the content, the watermark can be used to detect the copy and (if uniquely watermarked files are provided to each original recipient) trace the offending copy back to the source.

## E-commerce

As mentioned in the previous section, the rapid growth of electronic commerce led to the widespread adoption of SSL and HTTPS as standards for securely exchanging information through web browsers. Recently, industry experts have recognized the added security necessary for electronic transactions. In this section, we'll explore the Secure Electronic Transaction protocol designed to add this enhanced security.

The Secure Electronic Transaction (SET) standard was originally developed jointly by Visa and MasterCard—the two largest providers of credit cards in the United States—as a means for securing e-commerce transactions. When they outlined the business case for SET, the two vendors identified the following seven requirements:

- Provide confidentiality of payment information and enable confidentiality of order information transmitted along with the payment information.

- Ensure the integrity of all transmitted data.

- Provide authentication that a cardholder is a legitimate user of a branded payment card account.

- Provide authentication that a merchant can accept branded payment card transactions through its relationship with an acquiring financial institution.

- Ensure the use of the best security practices and system design techniques to protect all legitimate parties in an electronic commerce transaction.

- Create a protocol that neither depends on transport security mechanisms nor prevents their use.

- Facilitate and encourage interoperability among software and network providers.

 SET is no longer used by anyone, anywhere. However, questions about it still pop up on the CISSP exam from time to time.

SET utilizes a combination of RSA public key cryptography and DES private key cryptography in conjunction with digital certificates to secure electronic transactions. The original SET standard was published in 1997.

---

**MONDEX**

The MONDEX payment system, owned by MasterCard, uses cryptographic technology to allow electronic commerce users to store value on smart chips in proprietary payment cards. The value can then be instantly transferred to a vendor at the point of purchase.

---

# Networking

The final application of cryptography we'll explore in this chapter is the use of cryptographic algorithms to provide secure networking services. In the following sections, we'll take a brief look at two methods used to secure communications circuits as well as IPSec and the ISAKMP protocol. We'll also look at some of the security issues surrounding wireless networking.

## Circuit Encryption

Security administrators use two types of encryption techniques to protect data traveling over networks—link encryption and end-to-end encryption.

*Link encryption* protects entire communications circuits by creating a secure tunnel between two points using either a hardware solution or a software solution that encrypts all traffic entering one end of the tunnel and decrypts all traffic entering the other end of the tunnel. For example, a company with two offices connected via a data circuit might use link encryption to protect against attackers monitoring at a point in between the two offices.

*End-to-end encryption* protects communications between two parties (for example, a client and a server) and is performed independently of link encryption. An example of end-to-end encryption would be the use of Privacy Enhanced Mail to pass a message between a sender and a receiver. This protects against an intruder who might be monitoring traffic on the secure side of an encrypted link or traffic sent over an unencrypted link.

The critical difference between link and end-to-end encryption is that in link encryption, all the data, including the header, trailer, address, and routing data, is also encrypted. Therefore, each packet has to be decrypted at each hop so it can be properly routed to the next hop and then reencrypted before it can be sent along its way, which slows the routing. End-to-end encryption does not encrypt the header, trailer, address, and routing data, so it moves faster from point to point but is more susceptible to sniffers and eavesdroppers. When encryption happens at the higher OSI layers, it is usually end-to-end encryption, and if encryption is done at the lower layers of the OSI model, it is usually link encryption.

Secure Shell (SSH) is a good example of an end-to-end encryption technique. This suite of programs provides encrypted alternatives to common Internet applications such as FTP, Telnet, and rlogin. There are actually two versions of SSH. SSH1 (which is now considered insecure) supports the DES, 3DES, IDEA, and Blowfish algorithms. SSH2 drops support for DES and IDEA but adds support for several other algorithms.

## IPSec

Various security architectures are in use today, each one designed to address security issues in different environments. One such architecture that supports secure communications is the Internet Protocol Security (IPSec) standard. IPSec is a standard architecture set forth by the Internet Engineering Task Force (IETF) for setting up a secure channel to exchange information between two entities. The two entities could be two systems, two routers, two gateways, or any combination of entities. Although generally used to connect two networks, IPSec can be used to connect individual computers, such as a server and a workstation or a pair of workstations (sender and receiver, perhaps). IPSec does not dictate all implementation details but is an open, modular framework that allows many manufacturers and software developers to develop IPSec solutions that work well with products from other vendors.

IPSec uses public key cryptography to provide encryption, access control, nonrepudiation, and message authentication, all using IP protocols. The primary use of IPSec is for virtual private networks (VPNs), so IPSec operates in either transport or tunnel mode. IPSec is commonly paired with the Layer 2 Tunneling Protocol (L2TP) as L2TP/IPSec.

The IP Security (IPSec) protocol provides a complete infrastructure for secured network communications. IPSec has gained widespread acceptance and is now offered in a number of commercial operating systems out of the box. IPSec relies upon security associations, and there are two main components:

- The Authentication Header (AH) provides assurances of message integrity and non-repudiation. AH also provides authentication and access control and prevents replay attacks.

- The Encapsulating Security Payload (ESP) provides confidentiality and integrity of packet contents. It provides encryption and limited authentication and prevents replay attacks.

> ESP also provides some limited authentication, but not to the degree of the AH. Though ESP is sometimes used without AH, it's rare to see AH used without ESP.

IPSec provides for two discrete modes of operation. When IPSec is used in *transport mode*, only the packet payload is encrypted. This mode is designed for peer-to-peer communication. When it's used in *tunnel mode*, the entire packet, including the header, is encrypted. This mode is designed for gateway-to-gateway communication.

> IPSec is an extremely important concept in modern computer security. Be certain that you're familiar with the component protocols and modes of IPSec operation.

At runtime, you set up an IPSec session by creating a *security association (SA)*. The SA represents the communication session and records any configuration and status information about the connection. The SA represents a simplex connection. If you want a two-way channel, you need two SAs, one for each direction. Also, if you want to support a bidirectional channel using both AH and ESP, you will need to set up four SAs. Some of IPSec's greatest strengths come from being able to filter or manage communications on a per-SA basis so that clients or gateways between which security associations exist can be rigorously managed in terms of what kinds of protocols or services can use an IPSec connection. Also, without a valid security association defined, pairs of users or gateways cannot establish IPSec links.

Further details of the IPSec algorithm are provided in Chapter 3, "ISO Model, Protocols, Network Security, and Network Infrastructure."

## ISAKMP

The Internet Security Association and Key Management Protocol (ISAKMP) provides background security support services for IPSec by negotiating, establishing, modifying, and deleting security associations. As you learned in the previous section, IPSec relies upon a system of security associations (SAs). These SAs are managed through the use of ISAKMP. There are four basic requirements for ISAKMP, as set forth in Internet RFC 2408:

- Authenticate communicating peers.

- Create and manage security associations.

- Provide key generation mechanisms.

- Protect against threats (for example, replay and denial-of-service attacks).

## Wireless Networking

The widespread rapid adoption of wireless networks poses a tremendous security risk. Many traditional networks do not implement encryption for routine communications between hosts on the local network and rely upon the assumption that it would be too difficult for an attacker to gain physical access to the network wire inside a secure location to eavesdrop on the network. However, wireless networks transmit data through the air, leaving them extremely vulnerable to interception.

### Wired Equivalent Privacy

The security community responded with the introduction of Wired Equivalent Privacy (WEP), which provides 40-, 64-, and 128-bit encryption options to protect communications within the wireless LAN. WEP is described in IEEE 802.11 as an optional component of the wireless networking standard.

**WARNING**     Recent cryptanalysis attacks have demonstrated that significant flaws exist in the WEP algorithm, making it possible to completely undermine the security of a WEP-protected network within seconds. You should never use WEP encryption to protect a wireless network. In fact, the use of WEP encryption on a store network was the root cause behind the TJX security breach that was widely publicized in 2007. Again, you should *never* use WEP encryption on a wireless network.

### WiFi Protected Access

WiFi Protected Access (WPA) improves upon WEP encryption by implementing the Temporal Key Integrity Protocol (TKIP), eliminating the cryptographic weaknesses that undermined WEP. A further improvement to the technique, dubbed WPA-2, replaces TKIP with AES cryptography. Both are secure algorithms appropriate for use on modern wireless networks.

**WARNING**    Remember that WPA does not provide an end-to-end security solution. It encrypts traffic only between a mobile computer and the nearest wireless access point. Once the traffic hits the wired network, it's in the clear again.

Another commonly used wireless security standard, IEEE 802.1x, provides a flexible framework for authentication and key management in wired and wireless networks. To use 802.1x, the client runs a piece of software known as the *supplicant*. The supplicant communicates with the authentication server. After successful authentication, the network switch or wireless access point allows the client to access the network. WPA was designed to interact with 802.1x authentication servers.

# Cryptographic Attacks

As with any security mechanism, malicious individuals have found a number of attacks to defeat cryptosystems. It's important that you, as a security administrator, understand the threats posed by various cryptographic attacks to minimize the risks posed to your systems:

**Analytic attack**    This is an algebraic manipulation that attempts to reduce the complexity of the algorithm. Analytic attacks focus on the logic of the algorithm itself.

**Implementation attack**    This is a type of attack that exploits weaknesses in the implementation of a cryptography system. It focuses on exploiting the software code, not just errors and flaws but the methodology employed to program the encryption system.

**Statistical attack**    A statistical attack exploits statistical weaknesses in a cryptosystem, such as inability to produce random numbers and floating-point errors. Statistical attacks attempt to find a vulnerability in the hardware or operating system hosting the cryptography application.

**Brute force**    Brute-force attacks are quite straightforward. Such an attack attempts every possible valid combination for a key or password. They involve using massive amounts of processing power to methodically guess the key used to secure cryptographic communications. For a nonflawed protocol, the average amount of time required to discover the key through a brute-force attack is directly proportional to the length of the key. A brute-force attack will always be successful given enough time. Every additional bit of key length doubles the time to perform a brute-force attack because the number of potential keys doubles.

**Frequency analysis**    In many cases, the only information you have at your disposal is the encrypted cipher-text message, a scenario known as the "cipher-text only attack." In this case, one technique that proves helpful against simple ciphers is frequency analysis— counting the number of times each letter appears in the cipher text. Using your knowledge that the letters E, T, O, A, I, and N are the most common in the English language, you can then test several hypotheses:

- If these letters are also the most common in the cipher text, the cipher was likely a transposition cipher, which rearranged the characters of the plain text without altering them.

- If other letters are the most common in the cipher text, the cipher is probably some form of substitution cipher that replaced the plain-text characters.

This is a simple overview of frequency analysis, and many sophisticated variations on this technique can be used against polyalphabetic ciphers and other sophisticated cryptosystems.

**Known plain text**   In the known plain-text attack, the attacker has a copy of the encrypted message along with the plain-text message used to generate the cipher text (the copy). This knowledge greatly assists the attacker in breaking weaker codes. For example, imagine the ease with which you could break the Caesar cipher described in Chapter 9 if you had both a plain-text copy and a cipher-text copy of the same message.

**Chosen cipher text**   In a chosen cipher-text attack, the attacker has the ability to decrypt chosen portions of the cipher-text message and use the decrypted portion of the message to discover the key.

**Chosen plain text**   In a chosen plain-text attack, the attacker has the ability to encrypt plain-text messages of their choosing and can then analyze the cipher-text output of the encryption algorithm.

**Meet in the middle**   Attackers might use a meet-in-the-middle attack to defeat encryption algorithms that use two rounds of encryption. This attack is the reason that Double DES (2DES) was quickly discarded as a viable enhancement to the DES encryption in favor of Triple DES (3DES). In the meet-in-the-middle attack, the attacker uses a known plain-text message. The plain text is then encrypted using every possible key (k1), while the equivalent cipher text is decrypted using all possible keys (k2). When a match is found, the corresponding pair (k1, k2) represents both portions of the double encryption. This type of attack generally takes only double the time necessary to break a single round of encryption (or $2^n$ rather than the anticipated $2^n * 2^n$), offering minimal added protection.

**Man in the middle**   In the man-in-the-middle attack, a malicious individual sits between two communicating parties and intercepts all communications (including the setup of the cryptographic session). The attacker responds to the originator's initialization requests and sets up a secure session with the originator. The attacker then establishes a second secure session with the intended recipient using a different key and posing as the originator. The attacker can then "sit in the middle" of the communication and read all traffic as it passes between the two parties.

Be careful not to confuse the meet-in-the-middle attack with the man-in-the-middle attack. They may have similar names but are quite different!

**Birthday**    The birthday attack, also known as a *collision attack* or *reverse hash matching* (see the discussion of brute-force and dictionary attacks in Chapter 2), seeks to find flaws in the one-to-one nature of hashing functions. In this attack, the malicious individual seeks to substitute in a digitally signed communication a different message that produces the same message digest, thereby maintaining the validity of the original digital signature.

 Don't forget that social engineering techniques can also be used in cryptanalysis. If you're able to obtain a decryption key by simply asking the sender for it, that's much easier than attempting to crack the cryptosystem!

**Replay**    The replay attack is used against cryptographic algorithms that don't incorporate temporal protections. In this attack, the malicious individual intercepts an encrypted message between two parties (often a request for authentication) and then later "replays" the captured message to open a new session. This attack can be defeated by incorporating a time stamp and expiration period into each message.

# Summary

Public key encryption provides an extremely flexible infrastructure, facilitating simple, secure communication between parties that do not necessarily know each other prior to initiating the communication. It also provides the framework for the digital signing of messages to ensure nonrepudiation and message integrity. This chapter explored public key encryption, which is made possible by the public key infrastructure (PKI) hierarchy of trust relationships. We also described some popular cryptographic algorithms, such as link encryption and end-to-end encryption. Finally, we introduced you to the public key infrastructure, which uses certificate authorities (CAs) to generate digital certificates containing the public keys of system users and digital signatures, which rely upon a combination of public key cryptography and hashing functions.

We also looked at some of the common applications of cryptographic technology in solving everyday problems. You learned how cryptography can be used to secure electronic mail (using PGP, PEM, MOSS, and S/MIME), web communications (using SSL and S-HTTP), electronic commerce (using SET), and both peer-to-peer and gateway-to-gateway networking (using IPSec and ISAKMP) as well as wireless communications (using WPA).

Finally, we covered some of the more common attacks used by malicious individuals attempting to interfere with or intercept encrypted communications between two parties. Such attacks include birthday, cryptanalytic, replay, brute-force, known plain-text, chosen plain-text, chosen cipher-text, meet-in-the-middle, man-in-the-middle, and birthday attacks. It's important for you to understand these attacks in order to provide adequate security against them.

# Exam Essentials

**Understand the key types used in asymmetric cryptography.** Public keys are freely shared among communicating parties, whereas private keys are kept secret. To encrypt a message, use the recipient's public key. To decrypt a message, use your own private key. To sign a message, use your own private key. To validate a signature, use the sender's public key.

**Be familiar with the three major public key cryptosystems.** RSA is the most famous public key cryptosystem; it was developed by Rivest, Shamir, and Adleman in 1977. It depends upon the difficulty of factoring the product of prime numbers. El Gamal is an extension of the Diffie-Hellman key exchange algorithm that depends upon modular arithmetic. The elliptic curve algorithm depends upon the elliptic curve discrete logarithm problem and provides more security than other algorithms when both are used with keys of the same length.

**Know the fundamental requirements of a hash function.** Good hash functions have five requirements. They must allow input of any length, provide fixed-length output, make it relatively easy to compute the hash function for any input, provide one-way functionality, and be collision free.

**Be familiar with the four major hashing algorithms.** The successors to the Secure Hash Algorithm (SHA), SHA-1 and SHA-2, make up the government standard message digest function. SHA-1 produces a 160-bit message digest while SHA-2 supports variable lengths, ranging up to 512 bits.

**Understand how digital signatures are generated and verified.** To digitally sign a message, first use a hashing function to generate a message digest. Then encrypt the digest with your private key. To verify the digital signature on a message, decrypt the signature with the sender's public key and then compare the message digest to one you generate yourself. If they match, the message is authentic.

**Know the components of the Digital Signature Standard (DSS).** The Digital Signature Standard uses the SHA-1 message digest function along with one of three encryption algorithms: the Digital Signature Algorithm (DSA); the Rivest, Shamir, Adleman (RSA) algorithm; or the Elliptic Curve DSA (ECDSA) algorithm.

**Understand the public key infrastructure (PKI).** In the public key infrastructure, certificate authorities (CAs) generate digital certificates containing the public keys of system users. Users then distribute these certificates to people with whom they want to communicate. Certificate recipients verify a certificate using the CA's public key.

**Know the common applications of cryptography to secure electronic mail.** The emerging standard for encrypted messages is the S/MIME protocol. Other popular email security protocols include Phil Zimmerman's Pretty Good Privacy (PGP), Privacy Enhanced Mail (PEM), and MIME Object Security Services (MOSS).

**Know the common applications of cryptography to secure web activity.**   The de facto standard for secure web traffic is the use of HTTP over Secure Sockets Layer (SSL), otherwise known as HTTPS. Secure HTTP (S-HTTP) also plays an important role in protecting individual messages. Most web browsers support both standards.

**Know the common applications of cryptography to secure networking.**   The IPSec protocol standard provides a common framework for encrypting network traffic and is built in to a number of common operating systems. In IPSec transport mode, packet contents are encrypted for peer-to-peer communication. In tunnel mode, the entire packet, including header information, is encrypted for gateway-to-gateway communications.

**Describe IPSec.**   IPSec is a security architecture framework that supports secure communication over IP. IPSec establishes a secure channel in either transport mode or tunnel mode. It can be used to establish direct communication between computers or to set up a VPN between networks. IPSec uses two protocols: Authentication Header (AH) and Encapsulating Security Payload (ESP).

**Explain common cryptographic attacks.**   Brute-force attacks are attempts to randomly find the correct cryptographic key. Known plain-text, chosen cipher-text, and chosen plain-text attacks require the attacker to have some extra information in addition to the cipher text. The meet-in-the-middle attack exploits protocols that use two rounds of encryption. The man-in-the-middle attack fools both parties into communicating with the attacker instead of directly with each other. The birthday attack is an attempt to find collisions in hash functions. The replay attack is an attempt to reuse authentication requests.

# Written Lab

1.   Explain the process Bob should use if he wants to send a confidential message to Alice using asymmetric cryptography.

2.   Explain the process Alice would use to decrypt the message Bob sent in question 1.

3.   Explain the process Bob should use to digitally sign a message to Alice.

4.   Explain the process Alice should use to verify the digital signature on the message from Bob in question 3.

# Answers to Written Lab

1. Bob should encrypt the message using Alice's public key and then transmit the encrypted message to Alice.

2. Alice should decrypt the message using her private key.

3. Bob should generate a message digest from the plain-text message using a hash function. He should then encrypt the message digest using his own private key to create the digital signature. Finally, he should append the digital signature to the message and transmit it to Alice.

4. Alice should decrypt the digital signature in Bob's message using Bob's public key. She should then create a message digest from the plain-text message using the same hashing algorithm Bob used to create the digital signature. She should then compare the two message digests. If they are identical, the signature is authentic.

# Review Questions

1. In the RSA public key cryptosystem, which one of the following numbers will always be largest?

   **A.** e

   **B.** n

   **C.** p

   **D.** q

2. Which cryptographic algorithm forms the basis of the El Gamal cryptosystem?

   **A.** RSA

   **B.** Diffie-Hellman

   **C.** 3DES

   **D.** IDEA

3. If Richard wants to send an encrypted message to Sue using a public key cryptosystem, which key does he use to encrypt the message?

   **A.** Richard's public key

   **B.** Richard's private key

   **C.** Sue's public key

   **D.** Sue's private key

4. If a 2,048-bit plain-text message were encrypted with the El Gamal public key cryptosystem, how long would the resulting cipher-text message be?

   **A.** 1,024 bits

   **B.** 2,048 bits

   **C.** 4,096 bits

   **D.** 8,192 bits

5. Acme Widgets currently uses a 1,024-bit RSA encryption standard companywide. The company plans to convert from RSA to an elliptic curve cryptosystem. If it wants to maintain the same cryptographic strength, what ECC key length should it use?

   **A.** 160 bits

   **B.** 512 bits

   **C.** 1,024 bits

   **D.** 2,048 bits

**6.** John wants to produce a message digest of a 2,048-byte message he plans to send to Mary. If he uses the SHA-1 hashing algorithm, what size will the message digest for this particular message be?

   **A.** 160 bits

   **B.** 512 bits

   **C.** 1,024 bits

   **D.** 2,048 bits

**7.** Which one of the following technologies is considered flawed and should no longer be used?

   **A.** SHA-2

   **B.** PGP

   **C.** WEP

   **D.** SSL

**8.** What encryption technique does WPA use to protect wireless communications?

   **A.** TKIP

   **B.** DES

   **C.** 3DES

   **D.** AES

**9.** Richard received an encrypted message sent to him from Sue. Which key should he use to decrypt the message?

   **A.** Richard's public key

   **B.** Richard's private key

   **C.** Sue's public key

   **D.** Sue's private key

**10.** Richard wants to digitally sign a message he's sending to Sue so that Sue can be sure the message came from him without modification while in transit. Which key should he use to encrypt the message digest?

   **A.** Richard's public key

   **B.** Richard's private key

   **C.** Sue's public key

   **D.** Sue's private key

**11.** Which one of the following algorithms is not supported by the Digital Signature Standard?

   **A.** Digital Signature Algorithm

   **B.** RSA

   **C.** El Gamal DSA

   **D.** Elliptic Curve DSA

**12.** Which International Telecommunications Union (ITU) standard governs the creation and endorsement of digital certificates for secure electronic communication?

   **A.** X.500

   **B.** X.509

   **C.** X.900

   **D.** X.905

**13.** What cryptosystem provides the encryption/decryption technology for the commercial version of Phil Zimmerman's Pretty Good Privacy secure email system?

   **A.** ROT13

   **B.** IDEA

   **C.** ECC

   **D.** El Gamal

**14.** What TCP/IP communications port is utilized by Secure Sockets Layer traffic?

   **A.** 80

   **B.** 220

   **C.** 443

   **D.** 559

**15.** What type of cryptographic attack rendered Double DES (2DES) no more effective than standard DES encryption?

   **A.** Birthday attack

   **B.** Chosen cipher-text attack

   **C.** Meet-in-the-middle attack

   **D.** Man-in-the-middle attack

**16.** Which of the following security systems was created to support the use of stored-value payment cards?

   **A.** SET

   **B.** IPSec

   **C.** MONDEX

   **D.** PGP

**17.** Which of the following links would be protected by WPA encryption?

   **A.** Firewall to firewall

   **B.** Router to firewall

   **C.** Client to wireless access point

   **D.** Wireless access point to router

18. What is the major disadvantage of using certificate revocation lists?

    A. Key management

    B. Latency

    C. Record keeping

    D. Vulnerability to brute force attacks

19. Which one of the following encryption algorithms is now considered insecure?

    A. El Gamal

    B. RSA

    C. Skipjack

    D. Merkle-Hellman Knapsack

20. What does IPSec define?

    A. All possible security classifications for a specific configuration

    B. A framework for setting up a secure communication channel

    C. The valid transition states in the Biba model

    D. TCSEC security categories

# Answers to Review Questions

1. B. The number n is generated as the product of the two large prime numbers p and q. Therefore, n must always be greater than both p and q. Furthermore, it is an algorithm constraint that e must be chosen such that e is smaller than n. Therefore, in RSA cryptography n is always the largest of the four variables shown in the options to this question.

2. B. The El Gamal cryptosystem extends the functionality of the Diffie-Hellman key exchange protocol to support the encryption and decryption of messages.

3. C. Richard must encrypt the message using Sue's public key so that Sue can decrypt it using her private key. If he encrypted the message with his own public key, the recipient would need to know Richard's private key to decrypt the message. If he encrypted it with his own private key, any user could decrypt the message using Richard's freely available public key. Richard could not encrypt the message using Sue's private key because he does not have access to it. If he did, any user could decrypt it using Sue's freely available public key.

4. C. The major disadvantage of the El Gamal cryptosystem is that it doubles the length of any message it encrypts. Therefore, a 2,048-bit plain-text message would yield a 4,096-bit cipher-text message when El Gamal is used for the encryption process.

5. A. The elliptic curve cryptosystem requires significantly shorter keys to achieve encryption that would be the same strength as encryption achieved with the RSA encryption algorithm. A 1,024-bit RSA key is cryptographically equivalent to a 160-bit elliptic curve cryptosystem key.

6. A. The SHA-1 hashing algorithm always produces a 160-bit message digest, regardless of the size of the input message. In fact, this fixed-length output is a requirement of any secure hashing algorithm.

7. C. The WEP algorithm has documented flaws that make it trivial to break. It should never be used to protect wireless networks.

8. A. WiFi Protected Access (WPA) uses the Temporal Key Integrity Protocol (TKIP) to protect wireless communications. WPA-2 uses AES encryption.

9. B. Sue would have encrypted the message using Richard's public key. Therefore, Richard needs to use the complementary key in the key pair, his private key, to decrypt the message.

10. B. Richard should encrypt the message digest with his own private key. When Sue receives the message, she will decrypt the digest with Richard's public key and then compute the digest herself. If the two digests match, she can be assured that the message truly originated from Richard.

11. C. The Digital Signature Standard allows federal government use of the Digital Signature Algorithm, RSA, or the Elliptic Curve DSA in conjunction with the SHA-1 hashing function to produce secure digital signatures.

12. B. X.509 governs digital certificates and the public key infrastructure (PKI). It defines the appropriate content for a digital certificate and the processes used by certificate authorities to generate and revoke certificates.

**13.** B. Pretty Good Privacy uses a "web of trust" system of digital signature verification. The encryption technology is based upon the IDEA private key cryptosystem.

**14.** C. Secure Sockets Layer utilizes TCP port 443 for encrypted client/server communications.

**15.** C. The meet-in-the-middle attack demonstrated that it took relatively the same amount of computation power to defeat 2DES as it does to defeat standard DES. This led to the adoption of Triple DES (3DES) as a standard for government communication.

**16.** C. The MONDEX payment system, owned by MasterCard, provides the cryptographic technology necessary to support stored-value payment cards.

**17.** C. The WiFi Protected Access protocol encrypts traffic passing between a mobile client and the wireless access point. It does not provide end-to-end encryption.

**18.** B. Certificate revocation lists (CRLs) introduce an inherent latency to the certificate expiration process due to the time lag between CRL distributions.

**19.** D. The Merkle-Hellman Knapsack algorithm, which relies upon the difficulty of factoring super-increasing sets, has been broken by cryptanalysts.

**20.** B. IPSec is a security protocol that defines a framework for setting up a secure channel to exchange information between two entities.

# Chapter

# 11

# Principles
# of Computer Design

---

## THE CISSP EXAM TOPICS COVERED
## IN THIS CHAPTER INCLUDE:

✓ **Security Architecture and Design**

- Understand the fundamental concepts of security models (e.g., confidentiality; integrity; and multi-level models)

- Understand security capabilities of information systems (e.g., memory protection; virtualization, trusted platform module)

- Understand the vulnerabilities of security architecture

  - System (e.g., covert channels; states attacks; emanations); technology and process integration (e.g., single point of failure, service oriented architecture)

- Understand application and system vulnerabilities and threats

  - Web-based (e.g., XML, SAML); client-based (e.g., applets); server-based (e.g., data flow control); database security (e.g., inference, aggregation, data mining)

In previous chapters of this book, we've covered basic security principles and the protective mechanisms put in place to prevent violation of them. We've also examined some of the specific types of attacks used by malicious individuals seeking to circumvent those protective mechanisms. Until this point, when discussing preventative measures, we have focused on policy measures and the software that runs on a system. However, security professionals must also pay careful attention to the system itself and ensure that their higher-level protective controls are not built upon a shaky foundation. After all, the most secure firewall configuration in the world won't do a bit of good if the computer it runs on has a fundamental security flaw that allows malicious individuals to simply bypass the firewall completely.

In this chapter, we'll cover those underlying security concerns by conducting a brief survey of a field known as *computer architecture*: the physical design of computers from various components. We'll examine each of the major physical components of a computing system—hardware and firmware—looking at each from a security perspective. Obviously, the detailed analysis of a system's hardware components is not always a luxury available to you because of resource and time constraints. However, all security professionals should have at least a basic understanding of these concepts in case they encounter a security incident that reaches down to the system design level.

The federal government takes an active interest in the design and specification of the computer systems used to process classified national security information. Government security agencies have designed elaborate controls, such as the TEMPEST program used to protect against unwanted electromagnetic emanations and the Orange Book (TCSEC) security levels that define acceptable parameters for secure systems.

This chapter also introduces two key concepts: security models and security modes, both of which tie into computer architectures and system designs. A security model defines basic approaches to security that sit at the core of any security policy implementation. Security models address such basic questions as these: What basic entities or operations need security? What is a security principle? What is an access control list? Security modes represent ways in which systems can operate, depending on various elements such as the sensitivity or security classification of the data involved, the clearance level of the user involved, and the type of data operations requested. A security mode describes the conditions under which a system runs. Four such modes are recognized: dedicated security, system high security, compartmented security, and multilevel security modes, all covered in detail in this chapter.

Chapter 12, "Principles of Security Models," examines how security models and security modes condition system behavior and capabilities and explores security controls and the criteria used to evaluate compliance with them.

# Computer Architecture

*Computer architecture* is an engineering discipline concerned with the design and construction of computing systems at a logical level. Many college-level computer engineering and computer science programs find it difficult to cover all the basic principles of computer architecture in a single semester, so this material is often divided into two one-semester courses for undergraduates. Computer architecture courses delve into the design of central processing unit (CPU) components, memory devices, device communications, and similar topics at the bit level, defining processing paths for individual logic devices that make simple "0 or 1" decisions. Most security professionals do not need that level of knowledge, which is well beyond the scope of this book and the CISSP exam. However, if you will be involved in the security aspects of the design of computing systems at this level, you would be well advised to conduct a more thorough study of this field.

The more complex a system, the less assurance it provides. More complexity means more areas for vulnerabilities exist and more areas must be secured against threats. More vulnerabilities and more threats mean that the subsequent security provided by the system is less trustworthy.

## Hardware

Any computing professional is familiar with the concept of hardware. As in the construction industry, hardware is the physical "stuff" that makes up a computer. The term *hardware* encompasses any tangible part of a computer that you can actually reach out and touch, from the keyboard and monitor to its CPU(s), storage media, and memory chips. Take careful note that although the physical portion of a storage device (such as a hard disk or SIMM) may be considered hardware, the contents of those devices—the collections of 0s and 1s that make up the software and data stored within them—may not. After all, you can't reach inside the computer and pull out a handful of bits and bytes!

### Processor

The central processing unit (CPU), generally called the *processor*, is the computer's nerve center—it is the chip, or chips in a multiprocessor system, that governs all major operations and either directly performs or coordinates the complex symphony of calculations that allows a computer to perform its intended tasks. Surprisingly, the CPU is actually capable of performing only a limited set of computational and logical operations, despite the complexity of the tasks it allows the computer to perform. It is the responsibility of the operating system and compilers to translate high-level programming languages used to design software into simple assembly language instructions that a CPU understands. This limited range of functionality is intentional—it allows a CPU to perform computational and logical operations at blazing speeds, often measured in units known as MIPS (which stands for "million instructions per second").

To give you an idea of the magnitude of the progress in computing technology over the years, consider this: The original Intel 8086 processor introduced in 1978 operated at a rate of 0.33 MIPS (that's 330,000 calculations per second). A reasonably current 3.33 GHz Intel Core 2 Extreme processor introduced in 2007 operates at a blazing speed of 57,000 MIPS (57 gigaFLOPS, which stands for "floating operations per second"), or 57,000,000,000 calculations per second. That's almost 200,000 times as fast as the original from 1978! Also, the PS3 gaming system with its GPU and seven CPUs combined operates as 2 teraFLOPS (or 2,000,000 MIPS). Note that MIPS and FLOPS are roughly equivalent, but the latter is useful for comparisons across different CPU architecture, while the former is not.

## Execution Types

As computer processing power increased, users demanded more advanced features to enable these systems to process information at greater rates and to manage multiple functions simultaneously. Computer engineers devised several methods to meet these demands.

At first blush, the terms *multitasking, multiprocessing, multiprogramming,* and *multithreading* may seem nearly identical. However, they describe very different ways of approaching the "doing two things at once" problem. We strongly advise that you take the time to review the distinctions between these terms until you feel comfortable with them.

**Multitasking**   In computing, multitasking means handling two or more tasks simultaneously. In reality, most systems do not truly multitask; they rely upon the operating system to simulate multitasking by carefully structuring the sequence of commands sent to the CPU for execution. After all, when your processor is humming along at 57,000 MIPS, it's hard to tell that it's switching between tasks rather than actually working on two tasks at once. However, you can assume that a multitasking system is able to juggle more than one task or process at any given time.

**Multiprocessing**   In a multiprocessing environment, a multiprocessor computing system (that is, one with more than one CPU) harnesses the power of more than one processor to complete the execution of a single application. For example, a database server might run on a system that contains three processors. If the database application receives a number of separate queries simultaneously, it might send each query to a separate processor for execution.

Two types of multiprocessing are most common in modern systems with multiple CPUs. The scenario just described, where a single computer contains more than one processor controlled by a single operating system, is called *symmetric multiprocessing (SMP)*. In SMP, processors share not only a common operating system but also a common data bus and memory resources. In this type of arrangement, systems may use a large number of processors. Fortunately, this type of computing power is more than sufficient to drive most systems.

Some computationally intensive operations, such as those that support the research of scientists and mathematicians, require more processing power than a single operating system can deliver. Such operations may be best served by a technology known as *massively parallel processing (MPP)*. MPP systems house hundreds or even thousands of processors, each of which has its own operating system and memory/bus resources. When the software that coordinates the entire system's activities and schedules them for processing encounters a computationally intensive task, it assigns responsibility for the task to a single processor. This processor in turn breaks the task up into manageable parts and distributes them to other processors for execution. Those processors return their results to the coordinating processor where they are assembled and returned to the requesting application. MPP systems are extremely powerful (not to mention extremely expensive!) and are the focus of a good deal of computing research.

Both types of multiprocessing provide unique advantages and are suitable for different types of situations. SMP systems are adept at processing simple operations at extremely high rates, whereas MPP systems are uniquely suited for processing very large, complex, computationally intensive tasks that lend themselves to decomposition and distribution into a number of subordinate parts.

### Next-Generation Multiprocessing

Until the release of dual-core and quad-core processors, the only way to create a multiprocessing system was to place two or more CPUs onto the motherboard. However, today we have several options of multicore CPUs so that with a single CPU chip on the motherboard, there are two or four (or more!) execution paths. This truly allows single CPU multiprocessing because it allows two (or more) calculations to occur simultaneously. Do you have a multicore CPU in the desktop or notebook computer you use?

**Multiprogramming**    Multiprogramming is similar to multitasking. It involves the pseudosimultaneous execution of two tasks on a single processor coordinated by the operating system as a way to increase operational efficiency. For the most part, multiprogramming is a way to batch or serialize multiple processes so that when one process stops to wait on a peripheral, its state is saved and the next process in line begins to process. The first program does not return to processing until all other processes in the batch have had their chance to execute and they in turn stop for a peripheral. For any single program, this methodology causes significant delays in completing a task. However, across all processes in the batch, the total time to complete all tasks is reduced.

Multiprogramming is considered a relatively obsolete technology and is rarely found in use today except in legacy systems. There are two main differences between multiprogramming and multitasking:

- Multiprogramming usually takes place on large-scale systems, such as mainframes, whereas multitasking takes place on PC operating systems, such as Windows and Linux.

- Multitasking is normally coordinated by the operating system, whereas multiprogramming requires specially written software that coordinates its own activities and execution through the operating system.

**Multithreading**   Multithreading permits multiple concurrent tasks to be performed within a single process. Unlike multitasking, where multiple tasks occupy multiple processes, multithreading permits multiple tasks to operate within a single process. A thread is a self-contained sequence of instructions that can execute in parallel with other threads that are part of the same parent process. Multithreading is often used in applications where frequent context switching between multiple active processes consumes excessive overhead and reduces efficiency. In multithreading, switching between threads incurs far less overhead and is therefore more efficient. In modern Windows implementations, for example, the overhead involved in switching from one thread to another within a single process is on the order of 40 to 50 instructions, with no substantial memory transfers needed. By contrast, switching from one process to another involves 1,000 instructions or more and requires substantial memory transfers as well.

A good example of multithreading occurs when multiple documents are opened at the same time in a word processing program. In that situation, you do not actually run multiple instances of the word processor—this would place far too great a demand on the system. Instead, each document is treated as a single thread within a single word processor process, and the software chooses which thread it works on at any given moment.

Symmetric multiprocessing systems actually use threading at the operating system level. As in the word processing example just described, the operating system also contains a number of threads that control the tasks assigned to it. In a single-processor system, the OS sends one thread at a time to the processor for execution. SMP systems send one thread to each available processor for simultaneous execution.

## Processing Types

Many high-security systems control the processing of information assigned to various security levels, such as the classification levels of unclassified, sensitive, confidential, secret, and top secret the U.S. government assigns to information related to national defense. Computers must be designed so that they do not—ideally, so that they cannot—inadvertently disclose information to unauthorized recipients.

Computer architects and security policy administrators have attacked this problem at the processor level in two different ways. One is through a policy mechanism, whereas the other is through a hardware solution. The following list explores each of those options:

**Single state**   Single state systems require the use of policy mechanisms to manage information at different levels. In this type of arrangement, security administrators approve a processor and system to handle only one security level at a time. For example, a system might be labeled to handle only secret information. All users of that system must then be approved to handle information at the secret level. This shifts the burden of protecting the information being processed on a system away from the hardware and operating system and onto the administrators who control access to the system.

**Multistate**   Multistate systems are capable of implementing a much higher level of security. These systems are certified to handle multiple security levels simultaneously by using specialized security mechanisms such as those described in the next section, "Protection Mechanisms." These mechanisms are designed to prevent information from crossing between security levels. One user might be using a multistate system to process secret information, while another user is processing top secret information at the same time. Technical mechanisms prevent information from crossing between the two users and thereby crossing between security levels.

In actual practice, multistate systems are relatively uncommon owing to the expense of implementing the necessary technical mechanisms. This expense is sometimes justified; however, when you're dealing with a very expensive resource, such as a massively parallel system, the cost of obtaining multiple systems far exceeds the cost of implementing the additional security controls necessary to enable multistate operation on a single such system.

## Protection Mechanisms

If a computer isn't running, it's an inert lump of plastic, silicon, and metal doing nothing. When a computer is running, it operates a runtime environment that represents the combination of the operating system and whatever applications may be active. When running, the computer also has the capability to access files and other data as the user's security permissions allow. Within that runtime environment it's necessary to integrate security information and controls to protect the integrity of the operating system itself, to manage which users are allowed to access specific data items, to authorize or deny operations requested against such data, and so forth. The ways in which running computers implement and handle security at runtime may be broadly described as a collection of protection mechanisms. What follows are descriptions of various protection mechanisms such as protection rings, operational states, and security modes.

Because the ways in which computers implement and use protection mechanisms are so important to maintaining and controlling security, you should understand how all three mechanisms covered here—rings, operational states, and security modes—are defined and how they behave. Don't be surprised to see exam questions about specifics in all three areas because this is such important stuff!

**Protection rings**    The ring protection scheme is an oldie but a goodie. It dates all the way back to work on the Multics operating system. This experimental operating system was designed and built between 1963 and1969 through the collaboration of Bell Laboratories, MIT, and General Electric. Though it did see commercial use in implementations from Honeywell, Multics has left two enduring legacies in the computing world. First, it inspired the creation of a simpler, less intricate operating system called Unix (a play on the word *multics*), and second, it introduced the idea of protection rings to operating system design.

From a security standpoint, protection rings organize code and components in an operating system (as well as applications, utilities, or other code that runs under the operating system's control) into concentric rings, as shown in Figure 11.1. The deeper inside the circle you go, the higher the privilege level associated with the code that occupies a specific ring. Though the original Multics implementation allowed up to seven rings (numbered 0 through 6), most modern operating systems use a four-ring model (numbered 0 through 3).

**FIGURE 11.1**    In the commonly used four-ring model, protection rings segregate the operating system into kernel, components, and drivers in rings 0 through 2 and applications and programs run at ring 3.

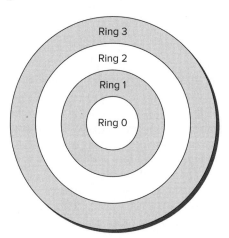

Ring 0: OS Kernel/Memory (Resident Components)
Ring 1: Other OS Components
Ring 2: Drivers, Protocols, etc.
Ring 3: User-Level Programs and Applications

Rings 0–2 run in supervisory or privileged mode.
Ring 3 runs in user mode.

As the innermost ring, 0 has the highest level of privilege and can basically access any resource, file, or memory location. The part of an operating system that always remains resident in memory (so that it can run on demand at any time) is called the *kernel*. It occupies ring 0 and can preempt code running at any other ring. The remaining parts of the operating system— those that come and go as various tasks are requested, operations performed, processes switched, and so forth—occupy ring 1. Ring 2 is also somewhat privileged in that it's where I/O drivers and system utilities reside; these are able to access peripheral devices, special files, and so forth, that applications and other programs cannot themselves access directly. Those applications and programs occupy the outermost ring, ring 3.

The essence of the ring model lies in priority, privilege, and memory segmentation. Any process that wants to execute must get in line (a pending process queue). The process associated with the lowest ring number always runs before processes associated with higher-numbered rings. Processes in lower-numbered rings can access more resources and interact with the operating system more directly than those in higher-numbered rings. Those processes that run in higher-numbered rings must generally ask a handler or a driver in a lower-numbered ring for services they need; this is sometimes called a *mediated-access model*. In its strictest implementation, each ring has its own associated memory segment. Thus, any request from a process in a higher-numbered ring for an address in a lower-numbered ring must call on a helper process in the ring associated with that address. In practice, many modern operating systems break memory into only two segments: one for system-level access (rings 0 through 2), often called *kernel mode* or *privileged mode*, and one for user-level programs and applications (ring 3), often called *user mode*.

From a security standpoint, the ring model enables an operating system to protect and insulate itself from users and applications. It also permits the enforcement of strict boundaries between highly privileged operating system components (such as the kernel) and less-privileged parts of the operating system (such as other parts of the operating system, plus drivers and utilities). Within this model, direct access to specific resources is possible only within certain rings; likewise, certain operations (such as process switching, termination, and scheduling) are allowed only within certain rings.

The ring that a process occupies determines its access level to system resources (and determines what kinds of resources it must request from processes in lower-numbered, more-privileged rings). Processes may access objects directly only if they reside within their own ring or within some ring outside its current boundaries (in numerical terms, for example, this means a process at ring 1 can access its own resources directly, plus any associated with rings 2 and 3, but it can't access any resources associated only with ring 0). The mechanism whereby mediated access occurs—that is, the driver or handler request mentioned previously—is usually known as a *system call* and usually involves invocation of a specific system or programming interface designed to pass the request to an inner ring for service. Before any such request can be honored, however, the called ring must check to make sure that the calling process has the right credentials and authorization to access the data and to perform the operation(s) involved in satisfying the request.

**Process states**   Also known as *operating states*, process states are various forms of execution in which a process may run. Where the operating system is concerned, it can be in one of two modes at any given moment: operating in a privileged, all-access mode known as *supervisor state* or operating in what's called the *problem state* associated with user mode, where privileges are low and all access requests must be checked against credentials for authorization before they are granted or denied. The latter is called the problem state not because problems are guaranteed to occur but because the unprivileged nature of user access means that problems can occur and the system must take appropriate measures to protect security, integrity, and confidentiality.

Processes line up for execution in an operating system in a processing queue, where they will be scheduled to run as a processor becomes available. Because many operating systems allow processes to consume processor time only in fixed increments or chunks, when a new process is created, it enters the processing queue for the first time; should a process consume its entire chunk of processing time (called a *time slice*) without completing, it returns to the processing queue for another time slice the next time its turn comes around. Also, the process scheduler usually selects the highest-priority process for execution, so reaching the front of the line doesn't always guarantee access to the CPU (because a process may be preempted at the last instant by another process with higher priority).

According to whether a process is running, it can operate in one of several states:

**Ready**   In the ready state, a process is ready to resume or begin processing as soon as it is scheduled for execution. If the CPU is available when the process reaches this state, it will transition directly into the running state; otherwise, it sits in the ready state until its turn comes up. This means the process has all the memory and other resources it needs to begin executing immediately.

**Waiting**   Waiting can also be understood as "waiting for a resource"—that is, the process is ready for continued execution but is waiting for a device or access request (an interrupt of some kind) to be serviced before it can continue processing (for example, a database application that asks to read records from a file must wait for that file to be located and opened and for the right set of records to be found). There are some references that label this state as a blocked state, as in the process is blocked from further execution until an external event occurs.

**Running**   The running process executes on the CPU and keeps going until it finishes, its time slice expires, or it blocks for some reason (usually because it has generated an interrupt for access to a device or the network and is waiting for that interrupt to be serviced). If the time slice ends and the process isn't completed, it returns to the ready state (and queue); if the process blocks while waiting for a resource to become available, it goes into the waiting state (and queue).

The running state is also often called the *problem state*. However, don't associate the word *problem* with an error. Instead, think of the problem state as you would think of a math problem being solved to obtain the answer. But keep in mind that it is called the problem state because it is possible for problems or errors to occur, just as you could do a math problem incorrectly. The problem state is separated from the supervisory state so that in the event of an error, it does not easily affect the stability of the overall system, just the process that experienced the error.

**Supervisory**   The supervisory state is used when the process must perform an action that requires privileges that are greater than the problem state's set of privileges, including modifying system configuration, installing device drivers, or modifying security settings. Basically, any function not occurring in the user mode (ring 3) or problem state takes place in the supervisory mode.

**Stopped**   When a process finishes or must be terminated (because an error occurs, a required resource is not available, or a resource request can't be met), it goes into a stopped state. At this point, the operating system can recover all memory and other resources allocated to the process and reuse them for other processes as needed.

Figure 11.2 shows a diagram of how these various states relate to one another. New processes always transition into the ready state. From there, ready processes always transition into the running state. While running, a process can transition into the stopped state if it completes or is terminated, return to the ready state for another time slice, or transition to the waiting state until its pending resource request is met. When the operating system decides which process to run next, it checks the waiting queue and the ready queue and takes the highest-priority job that's ready to run (so that only waiting jobs whose pending requests have been serviced, or are ready to service, are eligible in this consideration). A special part of the kernel, called the *program executive* or the *process scheduler*, is always around (waiting in memory) so that when a process state transition must occur, it can step in and handle the mechanics involved.

In Figure 11.2, the process scheduler manages the processes awaiting execution in the ready and waiting states and decides what happens to running processes when they transition into another state (ready, waiting, or stopped).

**FIGURE 11.2**   The process scheduler

**Security modes**   The U.S. government has designated four approved security modes for systems that process classified information. These are described next. In Chapter 5, "Security Management Concepts and Principles," we reviewed the classification system used by the federal government and the concepts of security clearances and access approval. The only new term in this context is *need to know*, which refers to an access authorization scheme in which a subject's right to access an object takes into consideration not just a privilege level but also the relevance of the data involved in the role the subject plays (or the job they perform). This indicates that the subject requires access to the object to perform their job properly or to fill some specific role. Those with no need to know may not access the object, no matter what level of privilege they hold. If you need a refresher on those concepts, please review them in Chapter 5 before proceeding.

Three specific elements must exist before the security modes themselves can be deployed:

- A hierarchical MAC environment
- Total physical control over which subjects can access the computer console
- Total physical control over which subjects can enter into the same room as the computer console

You will rarely, if ever, encounter the following modes outside of the world of government agencies and contractors. However, you may discover this terminology in other contexts, so you'd be well advised to commit the terms to memory.

**Dedicated mode**   Dedicated mode systems are essentially equivalent to the single state system described in the section "Processing Types" earlier in this chapter. Three requirements exist for users of dedicated systems:

- Each user must have a security clearance that permits access to all information processed by the system.
- Each user must have access approval for all information processed by the system.
- Each user must have a valid need to know for all information processed by the system.

In the definitions of each of these modes, we use "all information processed by the system" for brevity. The official definition is more comprehensive and uses "all information processed, stored, transferred, or accessed." If you want to explore the source, search for *Department of Defense 8510.1-M DoD Information Technology Security Certification and Accreditation Process (DITSCAP) Manual*.

**System high mode**   System high mode systems have slightly different requirements that must be met by users:

- Each user must have a valid security clearance that permits access to all information processed by the system.

- Each user must have access approval for all information processed by the system.
- Each user must have a valid need to know for some information processed by the system, but not necessarily all information processed by the system.

Note that the major difference between the dedicated mode and the system high mode is that all users do not necessarily have a need to know for all information processed on a system high mode computing device. Thus, although the same user could access both a dedicated mode system and a system high mode system, that user could access all data on the former but be restricted from some of the data on the latter.

**Compartmented mode**     Compartmented mode systems weaken these requirements one step further:

- Each user must have a valid security clearance that permits access to all information processed by the system.
- Each user must have access approval for any information they will have access to on the system.
- Each user must have a valid need to know for all information they will have access to on the system.

Notice that the major difference between compartmented mode systems and system high mode systems is that users of a compartmented mode system do not necessarily have access approval for all the information on the system. However, as with system high and dedicated systems, all users of the system must still have appropriate security clearances. In a special implementation of this mode called *compartmented mode workstations (CMWs)*, users with the necessary clearances can process multiple compartments of data at the same time.

CMWs require that two forms of security labels be placed on objects: sensitivity levels and information labels. Sensitivity levels describe the levels at which objects must be protected. These are common among all four of the modes. Information labels prevent data overclassification and associate additional information with the objects, which assists in proper and accurate data labeling not related to access control.

**Multilevel mode**     The government's definition of multilevel mode systems pretty much parallels the technical definition given in the previous section. However, for consistency, we'll express it in terms of clearance, access approval, and need to know:

- Some users do not have a valid security clearance for all information processed by the system. Thus, access is controlled by whether the subject's clearance level dominates the object's sensitivity label.
- Each user must have access approval for all information they will have access to on the system.
- Each user must have a valid need to know for all information they will have access to on the system.

As you look through the requirements for the various modes of operation approved by the federal government, you'll notice that the administrative requirements for controlling the types of users that access a system decrease as you move from dedicated systems down to multilevel systems. However, this does not decrease the importance of limiting individual access so that users can obtain only the information they are legitimately entitled to access. As discussed in the previous section, it's simply a matter of shifting the burden of enforcing these requirements from administrative personnel—who physically limit access to a computer—to the hardware and software—which control what information can be accessed by each user of a multiuser system.

    Multilevel security mode can also be called the *controlled security mode*.

Table 11.1 summarizes and compares these four security modes according to security clearances required, need to know, and the ability to process data from multiple clearance levels (abbreviated PDMCL). When comparing all four security modes, it is generally understood that the multilevel mode is exposed to the highest level of risk.

**TABLE 11.1**    Comparing security modes

| Mode | Clearance | Need to Know | PDMCL |
| --- | --- | --- | --- |
| Dedicated | Same | None | None |
| System high | Same | Yes | None |
| Compartmented | Same | Yes | Yes |
| Multilevel | Different | Yes | Yes |

Clearance is **Same** if all users must have the same security clearances, **Different** if otherwise.

Need to Know is **None** if it does not apply and is not used or if it is used but all users have the need to know all data present on the system, **Yes** if access is limited by need-to-know restrictions.

Applies if and when CMW implementations are used (**Yes**); otherwise, PDMCL is **None**.

## Operating Modes

Modern processors and operating systems are designed to support multiuser environments in which individual computer users might not be granted access to all components of a system or all the information stored on it. For that reason, the processor itself supports two modes of operation, user mode and privileged mode.

**User**   User mode is the basic mode used by the CPU when executing user applications. In this mode, the CPU allows the execution of only a portion of its full instruction set. This is designed to protect users from accidentally damaging the system through the execution of poorly designed code or the unintentional misuse of that code. It also protects the system and its data from a malicious user who might try to execute instructions designed to circumvent the security measures put in place by the operating system or who might mistakenly perform actions that could result in unauthorized access or damage to the system or valuable information assets.

Often processes within user mode are executed within a controlled environment called a *virtual machine (VM)* or a *virtual subsystem machine*. A virtual machine is a simulated environment created by the OS to provide a safe and efficient place for programs to execute. Each VM is isolated from all other VMs, and each VM has its own assigned memory address space that can be used by the hosted application. It is the responsibility of the elements in privileged mode (aka kernel mode) to create and support the VMs and prevent the processes in one VM from interfering with the processes in other VMs.

**Privileged**   CPUs also support privileged mode, which is designed to give the operating system access to the full range of instructions supported by the CPU. This mode goes by a number of names, and the exact terminology varies according to the CPU manufacturer. Some of the more common monikers are included in the following list:

- Privileged mode
- Supervisory mode
- System mode
- Kernel mode

No matter which term you use, the basic concept remains the same—this mode grants a wide range of permissions to the process executing on the CPU. For this reason, well-designed operating systems do not let any user applications execute in privileged mode. Only those processes that are components of the operating system itself are allowed to execute in this mode, for both security and system integrity purposes.

Don't confuse processor modes with any type of user access permissions. The fact that the high-level processor mode is sometimes called *privileged* or *supervisory* mode has no relationship to the role of a user. All user applications, including those of system administrators, run in user mode. When system administrators use system tools to make configuration changes to the system, those tools also run in user mode. When a user application needs to perform a privileged action, it passes that request to the operating system using a system call, which evaluates it and either rejects the request or approves it and executes it using a privileged mode process outside the user's control.

# Memory

The second major hardware component of a system is *memory*, the storage bank for information that the computer needs to keep readily available. There are many different kinds of memory, each suitable for different purposes, and we'll take a look at each in the sections that follow.

## Read-Only Memory

*Read-only memory (ROM)* works like the name implies—it's memory the PC can read but can't change (no writing allowed). The contents of a standard ROM chip are burned in at the factory, and the end user simply cannot alter it. ROM chips often contain "bootstrap" information that computers use to start up prior to loading an operating system from disk. This includes the familiar power-on self-test (POST) series of diagnostics that run each time you boot a PC.

ROM's primary advantage is that it can't be modified. There is no chance that user or administrator error will accidentally wipe out or modify the contents of such a chip. This attribute makes ROM extremely desirable for orchestrating a computer's innermost workings. There is a type of ROM that may be altered by administrators to some extent. It is known as programmable read-only memory (PROM) and it and its several subtypes are described next:

**Programmable read-only memory (PROM)**    A basic programmable read-only memory (PROM) chip is similar to a ROM chip in functionality, but with one exception. During the manufacturing process, a PROM chip's contents aren't "burned in" at the factory as with standard ROM chips. Instead, a PROM incorporates special functionality that allows an end user to burn in the chip's contents later. However, the burning process has a similar outcome—once data is written to a PROM chip, no further changes are possible. After it's burned it, a PROM chip essentially functions like a ROM chip.

PROM chips provide software developers with an opportunity to store information permanently on a high-speed, customized memory chip. PROMs are commonly used for hardware applications where some custom functionality is necessary but seldom changes once programmed.

**Erasable programmable read-only memory (EPROM)**    Combine the relatively high cost of PROM chips and software developers' inevitable desires to tinker with their code once it's written and you have the rationale that led to the development of erasable PROM (EPROM). These chips have a small window that, when illuminated with a special ultraviolet light, causes the contents of the chip to be erased. After this process is complete, end users can burn new information into the EPROM as if it had never been programmed before.

**Electronically erasable programmable read-only memory (EEPROM)**    Although it's better than no erase function at all, EPROM erasure is pretty cumbersome. It requires the physical removal of the chip from the computer and exposure to a special kind of ultraviolet light. A more flexible, friendly alternative is electronically erasable PROM (EEPROM), which uses electric voltages delivered to the pins of the chip to force erasure. EEPROM chips can be erased without removing them from the computer, which makes them much more attractive than standard PROM or EPROM chips. One well-known type of EEPROM is the flash memory chips often used in modern computers, PDAs, MP3 players, and digital cameras to store files, data, music, and images.

## Random Access Memory

Random access memory (RAM) is readable and writable memory that contains information a computer uses during processing. RAM retains its contents only when power is continuously supplied to it. Unlike with ROM, when a computer is powered off, all data stored in RAM disappears. For this reason, RAM is useful only for temporary storage. Critical data should never be stored solely in RAM; a backup copy should always be kept on another storage device to prevent its disappearance in the event of a sudden loss of electrical power. The following are types of RAM:

**Real memory** Real memory (also known as *main memory* or *primary memory*) is typically the largest RAM storage resource available to a computer. It is normally composed of a number of dynamic RAM chips and, therefore, must be refreshed by the CPU on a periodic basis (see the sidebar "Dynamic vs. Static RAM" for more information on this subject).

**Cache RAM** Computer systems contain a number of caches that improve performance by taking data from slower devices and temporarily storing it in faster devices when repeated use is likely; this is cache RAM. The processor normally contains an onboard cache of extremely fast memory used to hold data on which it will operate. This on-chip, or level 1, cache, is often backed up by a static RAM cache on a separate chip, called a *level 2 cache*, which holds data from the computer's main bank of real memory. Likewise, real memory often contains a cache of information stored on magnetic media. This chain continues down through the memory/storage hierarchy to enable computers to improve performance by keeping data that's likely to be used next closer at hand (be it for CPU instructions, data fetches, file access, or what have you).

Many peripherals also include onboard caches to reduce the storage burden they place on the CPU and operating system. For example, many higher-end printers include large RAM caches so that the operating system can quickly spool an entire job to the printer. After that, the processor can forget about the print job; it won't be forced to wait for the printer to actually produce the requested output, spoon-feeding it chunks of data one at a time. The printer can preprocess information from its onboard cache, thereby freeing the CPU and operating system to work on other tasks.

 **Real World Scenario**

**Dynamic vs. Static RAM**

There are two main types of RAM: dynamic RAM and static RAM. Most computers contain a combination of both types and use them for different purposes.

To store data, dynamic RAM uses a series of capacitors, tiny electrical devices that hold a charge. These capacitors either hold a charge (representing a 1 bit in memory) or do not hold a charge (representing a 0 bit). However, because capacitors naturally lose their charges over time, the CPU must spend time refreshing the contents of dynamic RAM to ensure that 1 bits don't unintentionally change to 0 bits, thereby altering memory contents.

Static RAM uses more sophisticated technology—a logical device known as a *flip-flop*, which to all intents and purposes is simply an on/off switch that must be moved from one position to another to change a 0 to 1 or vice versa. More important, static memory maintains its contents unaltered so long as power is supplied and imposes no CPU overhead for periodic refresh operations.

That said, dynamic RAM is cheaper than static RAM because capacitors are cheaper than flip-flops. However, static RAM runs much faster than dynamic RAM. This creates a trade-off for system designers, who combine static and dynamic RAM modules to strike the right balance of cost vs. performance.

### Registers

The CPU also includes a limited amount of onboard memory, known as *registers*, that provide it with directly accessible memory locations that the brain of the CPU, the arithmetic-logical unit (or ALU), uses when performing calculations or processing instructions. In fact, any data that the ALU is to manipulate must be loaded into a register unless it is directly supplied as part of the instruction. The main advantage of this type of memory is that it is part of the ALU itself and, therefore, operates in lockstep with the CPU at typical CPU speeds.

### Memory Addressing

When utilizing memory resources, the processor must have some means of referring to various locations in memory. The solution to this problem is known as *addressing*, and there are several different addressing schemes used in various circumstances. The following are five of the more common addressing schemes:

**Register addressing**   As you learned in the previous section, registers are small memory locations directly in the CPU. When the CPU needs information from one of its registers to complete an operation, it uses a register address (for example, "register 1") to access its contents.

**Immediate addressing**   Immediate addressing is not a memory addressing scheme per se but rather a way of referring to data that is supplied to the CPU as part of an instruction. For example, the CPU might process the command "Add 2 to the value in register 1." This command uses two addressing schemes. The first is immediate addressing—the CPU is being told to add the value 2 and does not need to retrieve that value from a memory location—it's supplied as part of the command. The second is register addressing; it's instructed to retrieve the value from register 1.

**Direct addressing**   In direct addressing, the CPU is provided with an actual address of the memory location to access. The address must be located on the same *memory page* as the instruction being executed. Direct addressing is more flexible than immediate addressing since the contents of the memory location can be changed more readily than reprogramming the immediate addressing's hard-coded data.

**Indirect addressing**   Indirect addressing uses a scheme similar to direct addressing. However, the memory address supplied to the CPU as part of the instruction doesn't contain the actual value that the CPU is to use as an operand. Instead, the memory address contains another memory address (perhaps located on a different page). The CPU reads the indirect address to learn the address where the desired data resides and then retrieves the actual operand from that address.

**Base+offset addressing**   Base+offset addressing uses a value stored in one of the CPU's registers as the base location from which to begin counting. The CPU then adds the offset supplied with the instruction to that base address and retrieves the operand from that computed memory location.

## Secondary Memory

*Secondary memory* is a term commonly used to refer to magnetic/optical media or other storage devices that contain data not immediately available to the CPU. For the CPU to access data in secondary memory, the data must first be read by the operating system and stored in real memory. However, secondary memory is much more inexpensive than primary memory and can be used to store massive amounts of information. In this context, hard disks, floppy drives, and optical media such as CDs and DVDs can all function as secondary memory.

Virtual memory is a special type of secondary memory that the operating system manages to make look and act just like real memory. The most common type of virtual memory is the pagefile that most operating systems manage as part of their memory management functions. This specially formatted file contains data previously stored in memory but not recently used. When the operating system needs to access addresses stored in the pagefile, it checks to see whether the page is memory-resident (in which case it can access it immediately) or whether it has been swapped to disk, in which case it reads the data from disk back into real memory (this process is called *paging*).

Using virtual memory is an inexpensive way to make a computer operate as if it had more real memory than is physically installed. Its major drawback is that the paging operations that occur when data is exchanged between primary and secondary memory are relatively slow (memory functions in microseconds, disk systems in milliseconds; usually, this means four orders of magnitude difference!) and consume significant computer overhead, slowing down the entire system.

## Memory Security Issues

Memory stores and processes your data—some of which may be extremely sensitive. It's essential that you understand the various types of memory and know how they store and retain data. Any memory devices that may retain sensitive data should be purged before they are allowed to leave your organization for any reason. This is especially true for secondary memory and ROM/PROM/EPROM/EEPROM devices designed to retain data even after the power is turned off.

However, memory data retention issues are not limited to those types of memory designed to retain data. Remember that static and dynamic RAM chips store data through the use of capacitors and flip-flops (see the sidebar "Dynamic vs. Static RAM"). It is technically possible that those electrical components could retain some of their charge for a limited period of time after power is turned off. A technically sophisticated individual could theoretically take electrical measurements of those components and retrieve portions of the data stored on such devices. However, this requires a good deal of technical expertise and is not a likely threat unless you have adversaries with mind-bogglingly deep pockets.

The greatest security threat posed by RAM chips is a simple one. They are highly pilferable and are quite often stolen. After all, who checks to see how much memory is in their computer at the start of each day? Someone could easily remove a single memory module from each of a large number of systems and walk out the door with a small bag containing valuable chips. Today, this threat is diminishing as the price of memory chips continues to fall ($20 for 1 GB DDR2 DIMM RAM as we write).

One of the most important security issues surrounding memory is controlling who may access data stored in memory while a computer is in use. This is primarily the responsibility of the operating system and is the main memory security issue underlying the various processing modes described in previous sections in this chapter. In the section "Security Protection Mechanisms" later in this chapter, you'll learn how the principle of process isolation can be used to ensure that processes don't have access to read or write to memory spaces not allocated to them. If you're operating in a multilevel security environment, it's especially important to ensure that adequate protections are in place to prevent the unwanted leakage of memory contents between security levels, through either direct memory access or covert channels (a full discussion of covert channels appears in Chapter 12).

## Storage

Data storage devices make up the third class of computer system components we'll discuss. These devices are used to store information that may be used by a computer any time after it's written. We'll first examine a few common terms that relate to storage devices and then cover some of the security issues related to data storage.

### Primary vs. Secondary

The concepts of primary and secondary storage can be somewhat confusing, especially when compared to primary and secondary memory. There's an easy way to keep it straight—they're the same thing! *Primary memory*, also known as *primary storage*, is the RAM that a computer uses to keep necessary information readily available to the CPU while the computer is running. *Secondary memory* (or *secondary storage*) includes all the familiar long-term storage devices that you use every day. Secondary storage consists of magnetic and optical media such as hard drives, floppy disks, magnetic tapes, compact discs (CDs), digital video disks (DVDs), flash memory cards, and the like.

## Volatile vs. Nonvolatile

You're already familiar with the concept of volatility from our discussion of memory, although you may not have heard it described using that term before. The volatility of a storage device is simply a measure of how likely it is to lose its data when power is turned off. Devices designed to retain their data (such as magnetic media) are classified as *nonvolatile*, whereas devices such as static or dynamic RAM modules, which are designed to lose their data, are classified as *volatile*. Recall from the discussion in the previous section that sophisticated technology may sometimes be able to extract data from volatile memory after power is removed, so the lines between the two may sometimes be blurry.

## Random vs. Sequential

Storage devices may be accessed in one of two fashions. *Random access storage* devices allow an operating system to read (and sometimes write) immediately from any point within the device by using some type of addressing system. Almost all primary storage devices are random access devices. You can use a memory address to access information stored at any point within a RAM chip without reading the data that is physically stored before it. Most secondary storage devices are also random access. For example, hard drives use a movable head system that allows you to move directly to any point on the disk without spinning past all the data stored on previous tracks; likewise, CD and DVD devices use an optical scanner that can position itself anywhere on the platter surface.

*Sequential storage* devices, on the other hand, do not provide this flexibility. They require that you read (or speed past) all the data physically stored prior to the desired location. A common example of a sequential storage device is a magnetic tape drive. To provide access to data stored in the middle of a tape, the tape drive must physically scan through the entire tape (even if it's not necessarily processing the data that it passes in fast-forward mode) until it reaches the desired point.

Obviously, sequential storage devices operate much slower than random access storage devices. However, here again you're faced with a cost/benefit decision. Many sequential storage devices can hold massive amounts of data on relatively inexpensive media. This property makes tape drives uniquely suited for backup tasks associated with a disaster recovery/business continuity plan (see Chapter 15, "Business Continuity Planning," and Chapter 16, "Disaster Recovery Planning"). In a backup situation, you often have extremely large amounts of data that need to be stored, and you infrequently need to access that stored information. The situation just begs for a sequential storage device!

## Storage Media Security

We discussed the security problems that surround primary storage devices in the previous section. There are three main concerns when it comes to the security of secondary storage devices; all of them mirror concerns raised for primary storage devices:

- Data may remain on secondary storage devices even after it has been erased. This condition is known as *data remanence*. Most technically savvy computer users know that utilities are available that can retrieve files from a disk even after they have been deleted. It's also technically possible to retrieve data from a disk that has been reformatted (commonly called *purging*). If you truly want to remove data from a secondary storage device, you must use a specialized utility designed to destroy all traces of data on the device or damage or destroy it beyond possible repair (commonly called *sanitizing*).

- Secondary storage devices are also prone to theft. Economic loss is not the major factor (after all, how much does a CD-R disc or even a hard drive cost?), but the loss of confidential information poses great risks. If someone copies your trade secrets onto a removable media disc and walks out the door with it, it's worth a lot more than the cost of the disc itself.

- Access to data stored on secondary storage devices is one of the most critical issues facing computer security professionals. For hard disks, data can often be protected through a combination of operating system access controls. Removable media pose a greater challenge, so securing them often requires encryption technologies.

## Input and Output Devices

Input and output devices are often seen as basic, primitive peripherals and usually don't receive much attention until they stop working properly. However, even these basic devices can present security risks to a system. Security professionals should be aware of these risks and ensure that appropriate controls are in place to mitigate them. The next four sections examine some of the risks posed by specific input and output devices.

### Monitors

Monitors seem fairly innocuous. After all, they simply display the data presented by the operating system. When you turn them off, the data disappears from the screen and can't be recovered. However, technology from a program known as TEMPEST can compromise the security of data displayed on a monitor.

TEMPEST is a technology that allows the electronic emanations that every monitor produces (known as *Van Eck radiation*) to be read from a distance (known as *Van Eck phreaking*) and even from another location. The technology is also used to protect against such activity. Various demonstrations have shown that you can easily read the screens of monitors inside an office building using gear housed in a van parked outside on the street. Unfortunately, the protective controls required to prevent Van Eck radiation (lots and lots of copper!) are expensive to implement and cumbersome to use. Generally, CRT monitors are more prone to radiate significantly, while LCD monitors leak much less (some claim not enough to reveal critical data). It is arguable that the biggest risk with any monitor is still shoulder surfing or telephoto lenses on cameras.

### Printers

Printers also may represent a security risk, albeit a simpler one. Depending upon the physical security controls used at your organization, it may be much easier to walk out with sensitive information in printed form than to walk out with a floppy disk or other magnetic media. Also, if printers are shared, users may forget to retrieve their sensitive printouts, leaving them vulnerable to prying eyes. These are all issues that are best addressed by an organization's security policy.

### Keyboards/Mice

Keyboards, mice, and similar input devices are not immune to security vulnerabilities either. All of these devices are vulnerable to TEMPEST monitoring. Also, keyboards are vulnerable to less-sophisticated bugging. A simple device can be placed inside a keyboard or along its connection cable to intercept all the keystrokes that take place and transmit them to a remote receiver using a radio signal. This has the same effect as TEMPEST monitoring but can be done with much less-expensive gear. Additionally, if your keyboard and mouse are wireless, including Bluetooth, their radio signals can be intercepted as well.

### Modems

With the advent of ubiquitous broadband and wireless connectivity, modems are becoming a scarce legacy computer component. However, it is still common for a modem to be part of the hardware configuration in existing desktop and notebook systems. Whether common or not, the presence of a modem on a user system is often one of the greatest woes of a security administrator. Modems allow users to create uncontrolled access points into your network. In the worst case, if improperly configured, they can create extremely serious security vulnerabilities that allow an outsider to bypass all your perimeter protection mechanisms and directly access your network resources. At best, they create an alternate egress channel that insiders can use to funnel data outside your organization.

You should seriously consider an outright ban on modems in your organization's security policy unless you truly need them for business reasons. In those cases, security officials should know the physical and logical locations of all modems on the network, ensure that they are correctly configured, and make certain that appropriate protective measures are in place to prevent their illegitimate use.

# Input/Output Structures

Certain computer activities related to general input/output (I/O) operations, rather than individual devices, also have security implications. Some familiarity with manual input/output device configuration is required to integrate legacy peripheral devices (those that do not autoconfigure or support Plug and Play, or PnP, setup) in modern PCs as well. Three types of operations that require manual configuration on legacy devices are involved here:

**Memory-mapped I/O**    For many kinds of devices, memory-mapped I/O is a technique used to manage input/output. That is, a part of the address space that the CPU manages functions to provide access to some kind of device through a series of mapped memory addresses or locations. Thus, by reading mapped memory locations, you're actually reading the input from the corresponding device (which is automatically copied to those memory locations at the system level when the device signals that input is available). Likewise, by writing to those mapped memory locations, you're actually sending output to that device (automatically handled by copying from those memory locations to the device at the system level when the CPU signals that the output is available).

From a configuration standpoint, it's important to make sure that only one device maps into a specific memory address range and that the address range is used for no other purpose than to handle device I/O. From a security standpoint, access to mapped memory locations should be mediated by the operating system and subject to proper authorization and access controls.

**Interrupt (IRQ)** Interrupt (IRQ) is an abbreviation for *interrupt request* line, a technique for assigning specific signal lines to specific devices through a special interrupt controller. When a device wants to supply input to the CPU, it sends a signal on its assigned IRQ (which usually falls in a range of 0 to 16 on older PCs for two cascaded 8-line interrupt controllers and 0 to 23 on newer ones with three cascaded 8-line interrupt controllers). Where newer PnP-compatible devices may actually share a single interrupt (IRQ number), older legacy devices must generally have exclusive use of a unique IRQ number (a well-known pathology called *interrupt conflict* occurs when two or more devices are assigned the same IRQ number and is best recognized by an inability to access all affected devices). From a configuration standpoint, finding unused IRQ numbers that will work with legacy devices can be a sometimes trying exercise. From a security standpoint, only the operating system should be able to mediate access to IRQs at a sufficiently high level of privilege to prevent tampering or accidental misconfiguration.

**Direct Memory Access (DMA)** Direct Memory Access (DMA) works as a channel with two signal lines, where one line is a DMA request (DMQ) line and the other is a DMA acknowledgment (DACK) line. Devices that can exchange data directly with real memory (RAM) without requiring assistance from the CPU use DMA to manage such access. Using its DRQ line, a device signals the CPU that it wants to make direct access (which may be read or write or some combination of the two) to another device, usually real memory. The CPU authorizes access and then allows the access to proceed independently while blocking other access to the memory locations involved. When the access is complete, the device uses the DACK line to signal that the CPU may once again permit access to previously blocked memory locations. This is faster than requiring the CPU to mediate such access and permits the CPU to move on to other tasks while the memory access is underway. DMA is used most commonly to permit disk drives, optical drives, display cards, and multimedia cards to manage large-scale data transfers to and from real memory. From a configuration standpoint, it's important to manage DMA addresses to keep device addresses unique and to make sure such addresses are used only for DMA signaling. From a security standpoint, only the operating system should be able to mediate DMA assignment and the use of DMA to access I/O devices.

If you understand common IRQ assignments, how memory-mapped I/O and DMA work, and related security concerns, you know enough to tackle the CISSP exam. If not, some additional reading may be warranted. In that case, PC Guide's excellent overview of system memory (`www.pcguide.com/ref/ram/`) should tell you everything you need to know.

## Firmware

*Firmware* (also known as *microcode* in some circles) is a term used to describe software that is stored in a ROM chip. This type of software is changed infrequently (actually, never, if it's stored on a true ROM chip as opposed to an EPROM/EEPROM) and often drives the basic operation of a computing device.

## BIOS

The Basic Input/Output System (BIOS) contains the operating-system-independent primitive instructions that a computer needs to start up and load the operating system from disk. The BIOS is contained in a firmware device that is accessed immediately by the computer at boot time. In most computers, the BIOS is stored on an EEPROM chip to facilitate version updates. The process of updating the BIOS is known as "flashing the BIOS."

## Device Firmware

Many hardware devices, such as printers and modems, also need some limited processing power to complete their tasks while minimizing the burden placed on the operating system itself. In many cases, these "mini" operating systems are entirely contained in firmware chips onboard the devices they serve. As with a computer's BIOS, device firmware is frequently stored on an EEPROM device so it can be updated as necessary.

## Security Capabilities of Information Systems

The security capabilities of information systems include memory protection, virtualization, and trusted platform module. Memory protection is discussed elsewhere in this book with the topics of isolation, virtual memory, segmentation, memory management, and protection rings.

Virtualization technology is used to host one or more operating systems within the memory of a single host computer. This mechanism allows virtually any OS to operate on any hardware. It also allows multiple OSes to work simultaneously on the same hardware. Common examples include VMWare, Microsoft's Virtual PC, Microsoft Virtual Server 2005, Hyper-V with Windows Server 2008, and Apple's Bootcamp.

Virtualization has several benefits, such as being able to launch individual instances of servers or services as needed, real-time scalability, and being able to run the exact needed OS version for the needed application. Virtualized servers and services are indistinguishable from traditional servers and services from a user's perspective. Additionally, recovery from damaged, crashed, or corrupted virtual systems is often quick, simply consisting of replacing the virtual system's main hard drive file with a clean backup version and then relaunching it.

The Trusted Platform Module (TPM) is both a specification for a cryptoprocessor and the chip in a mainboard supporting the functions of cryptography. A TPM chip is used to store and process cryptographic keys for the purposes of a hardware supported/implemented hard-drive encryption system. Generally, a hardware implementation, rather than a software-only implementation of hard-drive encryption, is considered to be more secure.

When TPM-based whole-disk encryption is in use, the user/operator must supply a password or physical USB token device to the computer to authenticate and allow the TPM chip to release the hard-drive encryption keys into memory. While this seems similar to a software implementation, the key difference is that if the hard drive is removed from its original system, it cannot be decrypted. Only with the original TPM chip can an encryption be decrypted and accessed. With software-only hard-drive encryption, the hard drive can be moved to a different computer without any access or use limitations.

# Security Protection Mechanisms

The need for security mechanisms within an operating system comes down to one simple fact: software is not trusted. Third-party software is inherently untrustworthy, no matter who or where it comes from. This is not to say that all software is evil. Instead, this is a protection stance—since all third-party software is written by someone other than the OS creator, that software might cause problems. Thus, treating all non-OS software as potentially damaging allows the OS to prevent many disastrous occurrences through the use of software management protection mechanisms. The OS must employ protection mechanisms to keep the computing environment stable and to keep processes isolated from each other. Without these efforts, the security of data could never be reliable or even possible.

Computer system designers should adhere to a number of common protection mechanisms when designing secure systems. These principles are specific instances of the more general security rules that govern safe computing practices. In the following sections, we'll divide the discussion into two areas: technical mechanisms and policy mechanisms.

## Technical Mechanisms

Technical mechanisms are the controls that system designers can build right into their systems. We'll look at five: layering, abstraction, data hiding, process isolation, and hardware segmentation.

### Layering

By *layering* processes, you implement a structure similar to the ring model used for operating modes (and discussed earlier in this chapter) and apply it to each operating system process. It puts the most-sensitive functions of a process at the core, surrounded by a series of increasingly larger concentric circles with correspondingly lower sensitivity levels (using a slightly different approach, this is also sometimes explained in terms of upper and lower layers, where security and privilege decrease when climbing up from lower to upper layers). In discussions of OS architectures, the protected ring concept is common, and it is not exclusive. There are other ways of representing the same basic ideas with levels rather than rings. In such a system, the highest level is the most privileged, while the lowest level is the least privileged.

## Levels Instead of Rings

When discussing a multilayer or multilevel system, often many of the same features and restrictions of the protecting ring concept apply. Think about a high-rise apartment building. The low-rent apartments are often found in the lower floors. As you reach the middle floors, the apartments are often larger and offer better views. Finally, the top floor (or floors) is the most lavish and expensive (often deemed the *penthouse*). Usually, if you are living in a low-rent apartment in the building, you are unable to ride the elevators any higher than the highest floor of the low-rent apartments. If you are a middle-floor apartment resident, you can ride the elevators everywhere except to the penthouse floor(s). And if you are a penthouse resident, you can ride the elevators anywhere you want to go. You may also find this floor restriction system in office buildings and hotels.

The top of a layered or multilevel system is the same as the center ring of a protection ring scheme. Likewise, the bottom of a layered or multilevel system is the same as the outer ring of a protection ring scheme. A *level* is usually the same thing as a *layer*, which is often the same thing as a *ring* (at least in terms of protection and access concepts). Also, a level, layer, or ring may be called a *domain* (that is, a collection of objects with a singular characteristic).

Communication between layers takes place only through the use of well-defined, specific interfaces to provide necessary security. All inbound requests from outer (less-sensitive) layers are subject to stringent authentication and authorization checks before they're allowed to proceed (or denied, if they fail such checks). As you'll understand more completely later in this chapter, using layering for security is similar to using security domains and lattice-based security models in that security and access controls over certain subjects and objects are associated with specific layers and privileges and access increases as one moves from outer to inner layers.

In fact, separate layers can communicate only with one another through specific interfaces designed to maintain a system's security and integrity. Even though less-secure outer layers depend on services and data from more-secure inner layers, they know only how to interface with those layers and are not privy to those inner layers' internal structure, characteristics, or other details. To maintain layer integrity, inner layers neither know about nor depend on outer layers. No matter what kind of security relationship may exist between any pair of layers, neither can tamper with the other (so that each layer is protected from tampering by any other layer). Finally, outer layers cannot violate or override any security policy enforced by an inner layer.

## Abstraction

*Abstraction* is one of the fundamental principles behind the field known as *object-oriented programming*. It is the "black-box" doctrine that says that users of an object (or operating system component) don't necessarily need to know the details of how the object works; they need to know just the proper syntax for using the object and the type of data that will be returned as a result (that is, how to send input and receive output). This is very much what's involved in mediated access to data or services, such as when user mode applications use system calls to request administrator mode services or data (and where such requests may be granted or denied depending on the requester's credentials and permissions) rather than obtaining direct, unmediated access.

Another way in which abstraction applies to security is in the introduction of object groups, sometimes called *classes*, where access controls and operation rights are assigned to groups of objects rather than on a per-object basis. This approach allows security administrators to define and name groups easily (often related to job roles or responsibilities) and helps make the administration of rights and privileges easier (adding an object to a class confers rights and privileges rather than having to manage rights and privileges for each object separately).

## Data Hiding

*Data hiding* is an important characteristic in multilevel secure systems. It ensures that data existing at one level of security is not visible to processes running at different security levels. Chapter 7, "Data and Application Security Issues," covers a number of data hiding techniques used to prevent users from deducing even the very existence of a piece of information. The key concept behind data hiding is a desire to make sure those who have no need to know the details involved in accessing and processing data at one level have no way to learn or observe those details covertly or illicitly. From a security perspective, data hiding relies on placing objects in security containers that are different from those that subjects occupy to hide object details from those with no need to know about them.

## Process Isolation

*Process isolation* requires that the operating system provide separate memory spaces for each process's instructions and data. It also requires that the operating system enforce those boundaries, preventing one process from reading or writing data that belongs to another process. There are two major advantages to using this technique:

- It prevents unauthorized data access. Process isolation is one of the fundamental requirements in a multilevel security mode system.

- It protects the integrity of processes. Without such controls, a poorly designed process could go haywire and write data to memory spaces allocated to other processes, causing the entire system to become unstable rather than affecting only the execution of the errant process. In a more malicious vein, processes could attempt (and perhaps even succeed at) reading or writing to memory spaces outside their scope, intruding upon or attacking other processes.

Many modern operating systems address the need for process isolation by implementing so-called virtual machines on a per-user or per-process basis. A virtual machine presents a user or process with a processing environment—including memory, address space, and other key system resources and services—that allows that user or process to behave as though they have sole, exclusive access to the entire computer. This allows each user or process to operate independently without requiring it to take cognizance of other users or processes that might actually be active simultaneously on the same machine. As part of the mediated access to the system that the operating system provides, it maps virtual resources and access in user mode so that they use supervisory mode calls to access corresponding real resources. This not only makes things easier for programmers, it also protects individual users and processes from one another.

## Hardware Segmentation

*Hardware segmentation* is similar to process isolation in purpose—it prevents the access of information that belongs to a different process/security level. The main difference is that hardware segmentation enforces these requirements through the use of physical hardware controls rather than the logical process isolation controls imposed by an operating system. Such implementations are rare, and they are generally restricted to national security implementations where the extra cost and complexity is offset by the sensitivity of the information involved and the risks inherent in unauthorized access or disclosure.

# Security Policy and Computer Architecture

Just as security policy guides the day-to-day security operations, processes, and procedures in organizations, it has an important role to play when designing and implementing systems. This is equally true whether a system is entirely hardware based, entirely software based, or a combination of both. In this case, the role of a security policy is to inform and guide the design, development, implementation, testing, and maintenance of some particular system. Thus, this kind of security policy tightly targets a single implementation effort. (Although it may be adapted from other, similar efforts, it should reflect the target as accurately and completely as possible.)

For system developers, a security policy is best encountered in the form of a document that defines a set of rules, practices, and procedures that describe how the system should manage, protect, and distribute sensitive information. Security policies that prevent information flow from higher security levels to lower security levels are called multilevel security policies. As a system is developed, the security policy should be designed, built, implemented, and tested as it relates to all applicable system components or elements, including any or all of the following: physical hardware components, firmware, software, and how the organization interacts with and uses the system. The overall point is that security needs be considered for the entire life of the project. When security is applied only at the end, it typically fails.

# Policy Mechanisms

As with any security program, policy mechanisms should also be put into place. These mechanisms are extensions of basic computer security doctrine, but the applications described in this section are specific to the field of computer architecture and design.

## Principle of Least Privilege

In Chapter 1, "Accountability and Access Control," you learned about the general security *principle of least privilege* and how it applies to users of computing systems. This principle is also important to the design of computers and operating systems, especially when applied to system modes. When designing operating system processes, you should always ensure that they run in user mode whenever possible. The greater the number of processes that execute in privileged mode, the higher the number of potential vulnerabilities that a malicious individual could exploit to gain supervisory access to the system. In general, it's better to use APIs to ask for supervisory mode services or to pass control to trusted, well-protected supervisory mode processes as they're needed from within user mode applications than it is to elevate such programs or processes to supervisory mode altogether.

## Separation of Privilege

The principle of *separation of privilege* builds upon the principle of least privilege. It requires the use of granular access permissions, that is, different permissions for each type of privileged operation. This allows designers to assign some processes rights to perform certain supervisory functions without granting them unrestricted access to the system. It also allows individual requests for services or access to resources to be inspected, checked against access controls, and granted or denied based on the identity of the user making the requests or on the basis of groups to which the user belongs or security roles that the user occupies.

Think of separation of duties as the application of the principle of least privilege to administrators. In most moderate to large organizations, there are many administrators, each with different assigned tasks. Thus, there are usually few or no individual administrators with complete and total need for access across the entire environment or infrastructure. For example, a user administrator has no need for privileges that enable reconfiguring network routing, formatting storage devices, or performing backup functions.

Separation of duties is also a tool used to prevent conflicts of interest in the assignment of access privileges and work tasks. For example, those persons responsible for programming code should not be tasked to test and implement that code. Likewise, those who work in accounts payable should not also have accounts receivable responsibilities. There are many such job or task conflicts that can be securely managed through the proper implementation of separation of duties.

## Accountability

*Accountability* is an essential component in any security design. Many high-security systems contain physical devices (such as paper-and-pen visitor logs and nonmodifiable audit trails) that enforce individual accountability for privileged functionality. In general, however, such capabilities rely on a system's ability to monitor activity on and interactions with a system's resources and configuration data and to protect resulting logs from unwanted access or alteration so that they provide an accurate and reliable record of activity and interaction that documents every user's (including administrators or other trusted individuals with high levels of privilege) history on that system. In addition to the need for reliable auditing and monitoring systems to support accountability, there must be a resilient authorization system and an impeccable authentication system.

# Distributed Architecture

As computing has evolved from a host/terminal model (where users could be physically distributed but all functions, activity, data, and resources resided on a single centralized system) to a client/server model (where users operate independent fully functional desktop computers but also access services and resources on networked servers), security controls and concepts have had to evolve to follow suit. This means that clients have computing and storage capabilities and, typically, that multiple servers do likewise. Thus, security must be addressed everywhere instead of at a single centralized host. From a security standpoint, this means that because processing and storage are distributed on multiple clients and servers, all those computers must be properly secured and protected. It also means that the network links between clients and servers (and in some cases, these links may not be purely local) must also be secured and protected.

## Vulnerabilities

Distributed architectures are prone to vulnerabilities unthinkable in monolithic host/terminal systems. Desktop systems can contain sensitive information that may be at some risk of being exposed and must therefore be protected. Individual users may lack general security savvy or awareness, and therefore the underlying architecture has to compensate for those deficiencies. Desktop PCs, workstations, and laptops can provide avenues of access into critical information systems elsewhere in a distributed environment because users require access to networked servers and services to do their jobs. By permitting user machines to access a network and its distributed resources, organizations must also recognize that those user machines can become threats if they are misused or compromised.

Communications equipment can also provide unwanted points of entry into a distributed environment. For example, modems attached to a desktop machine that's also attached to an organization's network can make that network vulnerable to dial-in attacks. Likewise, users who download data from the Internet increase the risk of infecting their own and other systems with malicious code, Trojan horses, and so forth. Desktops, laptops, and workstations—and associated disks or other storage devices—may not be secure from physical intrusion or theft. Finally, when data resides only on client machines, it may not be secured with a proper backup (it's often the case that while servers are backed up routinely, the same is not true for client computers).

There is a wide variety of application and system vulnerabilities and threats, and the range is constantly expanding. Vulnerabilities occur in database infrastructures (such as inferencing, aggregation, and data mining), server-based attacks (such as data flow control, denial of service, and data poisoning), client-based attacks (such as malicious applets, cookie manipulations, and click-spoofing), and web-based attacks (such as XML exploitation, SQL injection, and SAML abuses). All of these issues, except for XML exploitation and SAML abuses, are covered elsewhere in this book.

XML exploitation is a form of programming attack that is used to either falsify information being sent to a visitor or cause their system to give up information without authorization. One area of growing concern in regard to XML attacks is Security Association Markup Language (SAML). SAML abuses are often focused on web-based authentication. SAML is an XML-based convention for communication authentication and authorization details between security domains, often over Web protocols. SAML is often used to provide a web-based SSO solution. If an attacker can falsify SAML communications or steal a visitor's access token, they may be able to bypass authentication and gain unauthorized access to a site.

## Safeguards

You should see that the foregoing litany of potential vulnerabilities in distributed architectures means that such environments require numerous safeguards to implement appropriate security and to ensure that such vulnerabilities are eliminated, mitigated, or remedied. Clients must be subjected to policies that impose safeguards on their contents and their users' activities. These include the following:

- Email must be screened so that it cannot become a vector for infection by malicious software; email should also be subject to policies that govern appropriate use and limit potential liability.

- Download/upload policies must be created so that incoming and outgoing data is screened and suspect materials blocked.

- Systems must be subject to robust access controls, which may include multifactor authentication and/or biometrics to restrict access to desktops and to prevent unauthorized access to servers and services.

- Graphical user interface mechanisms and database management systems should be installed, and their use required, to restrict and manage access to critical information.

- File encryption may be appropriate for files and data stored on client machines (indeed, drive-level encryption is a good idea for laptops and other mobile computing gear that is subject to loss or theft outside an organization's premises).

- It's essential to separate and isolate processes that run in user and supervisory modes so that unauthorized and unwanted access to high-privilege processes and capabilities is prevented.

- Protection domains should be created so that compromise of a client won't automatically compromise an entire network.

- Disks and other sensitive materials should be clearly labeled as to their security classification or organizational sensitivity; procedural processes and system controls should combine to help protect sensitive materials from unwanted or unauthorized access.

- Files on desktop machines should be backed up, as well as files on servers—ideally, using some form of centralized backup utility that works with client agent software to identify and capture files from clients stored in a secure backup storage archive.

- Desktop users need regular security awareness training to maintain proper security awareness; they also need to be notified about potential threats and instructed on how to deal with them appropriately.

- Desktop computers and their storage media require protection against environmental hazards (temperature, humidity, power loss/fluctuation, and so forth).

- Desktop computers should be included in disaster recovery and business continuity planning because they're potentially as important (if not more important) to getting their users back to work as other systems and services within an organization.

- Developers of custom software built in and for distributed environments also need to take security into account, including using formal methods for development and deployment, such as code libraries, change control mechanisms, configuration management, and patch and update deployment.

In general, safeguarding distributed environments means understanding the vulnerabilities to which they're subject and applying appropriate safeguards. These can (and do) range from technology solutions and controls to policies and procedures that manage risk and seek to limit or avoid losses, damage, unwanted disclosure, and so on.

# Summary

Designing secure computing systems is a complex task, and many security engineers have dedicated their entire careers to understanding the innermost workings of information systems and ensuring that they support the core security functions required to safely operate in the current environment. Many security professionals don't necessarily require an in-depth knowledge of these principles, but they should have at least a broad understanding of the basic fundamentals that drive the process to enhance security within their own organizations.

Such understanding begins with an investigation of hardware, software, and firmware and how those pieces fit into the security puzzle. It's important to understand the principles of common computer and network organizations, architectures, and designs, including addressing (both physical and symbolic), the difference between address space and memory space, and machine types (real, virtual, multistate, multitasking, multiprogramming, multiprocessing, multiprocessor, and multiuser).

Additionally, a security professional must have a solid understanding of operating states (single state, multistate), operating modes (user, supervisor, privileged), storage types (primary, secondary, real, virtual, volatile, nonvolatile, random, sequential), and protection mechanisms (layering, abstraction, data hiding, process isolation, hardware segmentation, principle of least privilege, separation of privilege, accountability).

# Exam Essentials

**Be able to explain the differences between multitasking, multithreading, multiprocessing, and multiprogramming.**   Multitasking is the simultaneous execution of more than one application on a computer and is managed by the operating system. Multithreading permits multiple concurrent tasks to be performed within a single process. Multiprocessing is the use of more than one processor to increase computing power. Multiprogramming is similar to multitasking but takes place on mainframe systems and requires specific programming.

**Understand the differences between single state processors and multistate processors.** Single state processors are capable of operating at only one security level at a time, whereas multistate processors can simultaneously operate at multiple security levels.

**Describe the four security modes approved by the federal government for processing classified information.**   Dedicated systems require that all users have appropriate clearance, access permissions, and need to know for all information stored on the system. System high mode removes the need-to-know requirement. Compartmented mode removes the need-to-know requirement and the access permission requirement. Multilevel mode removes all three requirements.

**Explain the two layered operating modes used by most modern processors.**   User applications operate in a limited instruction set environment known as user mode. The operating system performs controlled operations in privileged mode, also known as system mode, kernel mode, and supervisory mode.

**Describe the different types of memory used by a computer.**   ROM is nonvolatile and can't be written to by the end user. PROM chips allow the end user to write data once. EPROM chips may be erased through the use of ultraviolet light and then rewritten. EEPROM chips may be erased with electrical current and then rewritten. RAM chips are volatile and lose their contents when the computer is powered off.

**Know the security issues surrounding memory components.**   Three main security issues surround memory components: the fact that data may remain on the chip after power is removed, the fact that memory chips are highly pilferable, and the control of access to memory in a multiuser system.

**Describe the different characteristics of storage devices used by computers.**   Primary storage is the same as memory. Secondary storage consists of magnetic and optical media that must be first read into primary memory before the CPU can use the data. Random access storage devices can be read at any point, whereas sequential access devices require scanning through all the data physically stored before the desired location.

**Know the security issues surrounding secondary storage devices.**   There are three main security issues surrounding secondary storage devices: Removable media can be used to steal data, access controls and encryption must be applied to protect data, and data can remain on the media even after file deletion or media formatting.

**Understand security risks that input and output devices can pose.**   Input/output devices can be subject to eavesdropping and tapping, used to smuggle data out of an organization, or used to create unauthorized, insecure points of entry into an organization's systems and networks. Be prepared to recognize and mitigate such vulnerabilities.

**Understand I/O addresses, configuration, and setup.**   Working with legacy PC devices requires some understanding of IRQs, DMA, and memory-mapped I/O. Be prepared to recognize and work around potential address conflicts and misconfigurations and to integrate legacy devices with Plug and Play (PnP) counterparts.

**Know the purpose of firmware.**   Firmware is software stored on a ROM chip. At the computer level, it contains the basic instructions needed to start a computer. Firmware is also used to provide operating instructions in peripheral devices such as printers.

**Be able to describe process isolation, layering, abstraction, data hiding, and hardware segmentation.**   Process isolation ensures that individual processes can access only their own data. Layering creates different realms of security within a process and limits communication between them. Abstraction creates "black-box" interfaces for programmers to use without requiring knowledge of an algorithm's or devices inner workings. Data hiding prevents information from being read from a different security level. Hardware segmentation enforces process isolation with physical controls.

**Understand how a security policy drives system design, implementation, testing, and deployment.**   The role of a security policy is to inform and guide the design, development, implementation, testing, and maintenance of some particular system.

**Understand how the principle of least privilege, separation of privilege, and accountability apply to computer architecture.**   The principle of least privilege ensures that only a minimum number of processes are authorized to run in supervisory mode. Separation of privilege increases the granularity of secure operations. Accountability ensures that an audit trail exists to trace operations back to their source.

# Written Lab

1.   What are the terms used to describe the various computer mechanisms that allow multiple simultaneous activities?

2.   What are the four security modes for systems processing classified information?

3.   Name the three pairs of aspects or features used to describe storage.

4.   Name some vulnerabilities found in distributed architectures.

# Answers to Written Lab

1. The terms used to describe the various computer mechanisms that allow multiple simultaneous activities are *multitasking, multiprocessing, multiprogramming, multithreading,* and *multistate processing.*

2. The four security modes are dedicated, system high, compartmented, and multilevel.

3. The three pairs of aspects or features used to describe storage are primary vs. secondary, volatile vs. nonvolatile, and random vs. sequential.

4. Some vulnerabilities found in distributed architecture include sensitive data found on desktops/terminals/notebooks, lack of security understanding among users, greater risk of physical component theft, compromise of a client leading to the compromise of the whole network, greater risk from malware because of user-installed software and removable media, and data on clients less likely to be included in backups.

# Review Questions

1.  Many PC operating systems provide functionality that enables them to support the simultaneous execution of multiple applications on single-processor systems. What term is used to describe this capability?

    A.  Multiprogramming

    B.  Multithreading

    C.  Multitasking

    D.  Multiprocessing

2.  Which one of the following devices is most susceptible to TEMPEST monitoring of its emanations?

    A.  Floppy drive

    B.  CRT Monitor

    C.  CD

    D.  Keyboard

3.  You have three applications running on a single-core single processor system that supports multitasking. One of those applications is a word processing program that is managing two threads simultaneously. The other two applications are using only one thread of execution. How many application threads are running on the processor at any given time?

    A.  1

    B.  2

    C.  3

    D.  4

4.  What type of federal government computing system requires that all individuals accessing the system have a need to know all of the information processed by that system?

    A.  Dedicated

    B.  System high

    C.  Compartmented

    D.  Multilevel

5.  What term describes the processor mode used to run the system tools used by administrators seeking to make configuration changes to a machine?

    A.  User mode

    B.  Supervisory mode

    C.  Kernel mode

    D.  Privileged mode

6.   What type of memory chip allows the end user to write information to the memory only
     one time and then preserves that information indefinitely without the possibility of erasure?

     **A.**   ROM

     **B.**   PROM

     **C.**   EPROM

     **D.**   EEPROM

7.   Which type of memory chip can be erased only when it is removed from the computer and
     exposed to a special type of ultraviolet light?

     **A.**   ROM

     **B.**   PROM

     **C.**   EPROM

     **D.**   EEPROM

8.   Which one of the following types of memory might retain information after being removed
     from a computer and, therefore, represent a security risk?

     **A.**   Static RAM

     **B.**   Dynamic RAM

     **C.**   Secondary memory

     **D.**   Real memory

9.   Why do operating systems need security mechanisms?

     **A.**   Humans are perfect.

     **B.**   Software is not trusted.

     **C.**   Technology is always improving.

     **D.**   Hardware is faulty.

10.  What type of electrical component serves as the primary building block for dynamic
     RAM chips?

     **A.**   Capacitor

     **B.**   Resistor

     **C.**   Flip-flop

     **D.**   Transistor

11.  Which one of the following storage devices is most likely to require encryption technology
     in order to maintain data security in a networked environment?

     **A.**   Hard disk

     **B.**   Backup tape

     **C.**   Removable drives

     **D.**   RAM

12. In which of the following security modes can you be assured that all users have access permissions for all information processed by the system but will not necessarily need to know of all that information?

   **A.** Dedicated

   **B.** System high

   **C.** Compartmented

   **D.** Multilevel

13. Which one of the following security modes does not require that all users have a security clearance for the highest level of information processed by the system?

   **A.** Dedicated

   **B.** System high

   **C.** Compartmented

   **D.** Multilevel

14. What type of memory device is usually used to contain a computer's motherboard BIOS?

   **A.** PROM

   **B.** EEPROM

   **C.** ROM

   **D.** EPROM

15. What type of memory is directly available to the CPU and is often part of the CPU?

   **A.** RAM

   **B.** ROM

   **C.** Register memory

   **D.** Virtual memory

16. In what type of addressing scheme is the data actually supplied to the CPU as an argument to the instruction?

   **A.** Direct addressing

   **B.** Immediate addressing

   **C.** Base+offset addressing

   **D.** Indirect addressing

17. What type of addressing scheme supplies the CPU with a location that contains the memory address of the actual operand?

   **A.** Direct addressing

   **B.** Immediate addressing

   **C.** Base+offset addressing

   **D.** Indirect addressing

18. What security principle helps prevent users from accessing memory spaces assigned to applications being run by other users?

    **A.** Separation of privilege

    **B.** Layering

    **C.** Process isolation

    **D.** Least privilege

19. Which security principle mandates that only a minimum number of operating system processes should run in supervisory mode?

    **A.** Abstraction

    **B.** Layering

    **C.** Data hiding

    **D.** Least privilege

20. Which security principle takes the concept of process isolation and implements it using physical controls?

    **A.** Hardware segmentation

    **B.** Data hiding

    **C.** Layering

    **D.** Abstraction

# Answers to Review Questions

1.  C. Multitasking is processing more than one task at the same time. In most cases, multi-tasking is actually simulated by the operating system even when not supported by the processor.

2.  B. Although all electronic devices emit some unwanted emanations, CRT monitors are the devices most susceptible to this threat (at least from this list of options).

3.  A. A single-processor system can operate on only one thread at a time. There would be a total of four application threads (ignoring any threads created by the operating system), but the operating system would be responsible for deciding which single thread is running on the processor at any given time.

4.  A. In a dedicated system, all users must have a valid security clearance for the highest level of information processed by the system, they must have access approval for all information processed by the system, and they must have a valid need to know of all information processed by the system.

5.  A. All user applications, regardless of the security permissions assigned to the user, execute in user mode. Supervisory mode, kernel mode, and privileged mode are all terms that describe the mode used by the processor to execute instructions that originate from the operating system.

6.  B. Programmable read-only memory (PROM) chips may be written once by the end user but may never be erased. The contents of ROM chips are burned in at the factory, and the end user is not allowed to write data. EPROM and EEPROM chips both make provisions for the end user to somehow erase the contents of the memory device and rewrite new data to the chip.

7.  C. EPROMs may be erased through exposure to high-intensity ultraviolet light. ROM and PROM chips do not provide erasure functionality. EEPROM chips may be erased through the application of electrical currents to the chip pins and do not require removal from the computer prior to erasure.

8.  C. *Secondary memory* is a term used to describe magnetic and optical media. These devices will retain their contents after being removed from the computer and may be later read by another user.

9.  B. The need for security mechanisms within an operating system is because software is not trusted.

10. A. Dynamic RAM chips are built from a large number of capacitors, each of which holds a single electrical charge. These capacitors must be continually refreshed by the CPU in order to retain their contents. The data stored in the chip is lost when power is removed.

11. C. Removable drives are easily taken out of their authorized physical location, and it is often not possible to apply operating system access controls to them. Therefore, encryption is often the only security measure short of physical security that can be afforded to them. Backup tapes are most often well controlled through physical security measures. Hard disks and RAM chips are often secured through operating system access controls.

12. B. In system high mode, all users have appropriate clearances and access permissions for all information processed by the system but need to know only some of the information processed by that system.

13. D. In a multilevel security mode system, there is no requirement that all users have appropriate clearances to access all the information processed by the system.

14. B. BIOS and device firmware are often stored on EEPROM chips in order to facilitate future firmware updates.

15. C. Registers are small memory locations that are located directly on the CPU chip itself. The data stored within them is directly available to the CPU and can be accessed extremely quickly.

16. B. In immediate addressing, the CPU does not need to actually retrieve any data from memory. The data is contained in the instruction itself and can be immediately processed.

17. D. In indirect addressing, the location provided to the CPU contains a memory address. The CPU retrieves the operand by reading it from the memory address provided (which is why it's called *indirect*).

18. C. Process isolation provides separate memory spaces to each process running on a system. This prevents processes from overwriting each other's data and ensures that a process can't read data from another process.

19. D. The principle of least privilege states that only processes that absolutely need kernel-level access should run in supervisory mode. The remaining processes should run in user mode to reduce the number of potential security vulnerabilities.

20. A. Hardware segmentation achieves the same objectives as process isolation but takes them to a higher level by implementing them with physical controls in hardware.

# Chapter 12

# Principles of Security Models

## THE CISSP EXAM TOPICS COVERED IN THIS CHAPTER INCLUDE:

✓ **Information Security Governance and Risk Management**

- Support certification and accreditation efforts
- Assess the completeness and effectiveness of the security program

✓ **Security Architecture and Design**

- Understand the fundamental concepts of security models (e.g., confidentiality; integrity; and multi-level models)
- Understand the components of information systems security evaluation models
  - Product evaluation models (e.g., common criteria); industry and international security implementation guidelines (e.g., PCI-DSS, ISO)
- Understand security capabilities of information systems (e.g., memory protection; virtualization, trusted platform module)
- Understand the vulnerabilities of security architecture
  - System (e.g., covert channels; states attacks; emanations); technology and process integration (e.g., single point of failure, service oriented architecture)
- Understand application and system vulnerabilities and threats
  - Web-based (e.g., XML, SAML); client-based (e.g., applets); server-based (e.g., data flow control); database security (e.g., inference, aggregation, data mining)
- Understand countermeasure principles (e.g., defense in depth)

Increasing the security level of information systems is a challenging task for any organization. Ideally, security is something that is planned and integrated from the very inception of a system's architecture and considered at each stage of its development, testing, deployment, and day-to-day use. The first step in this endeavor is to evaluate an organization's current levels of security exposure by carefully examining its information systems and checking for vulnerability to threats or attack. Next, you must decide what steps to take to remedy any such exposures as may be discovered during the examination process. Making decisions about which solutions will work well can be the most difficult part of the process when seeking to secure information systems properly. If this is not to become a constant case of discovering vulnerabilities and applying relevant security patches or fixes—as is so common with systems such as Windows, Unix, and Linux today—the level of security consciousness and attention during initial system design and implementation must be substantially increased.

Understanding the philosophy behind security solutions helps to limit your search for the best security controls for a specific situation and for specific security needs. In this chapter, we discuss security models, including state machine, Bell-LaPadula, Biba, Clark-Wilson, information flow, noninterference, Take-Grant, access control matrix, and Brewer and Nash. This chapter also includes discussions of Common Criteria and other methods that governments and corporations alike use to evaluate information systems from a security perspective, with particular emphasis on U.S. Department of Defense and international security evaluation criteria. We finish off this chapter by discussing commonly encountered design flaws and other security-related issues that can make information systems susceptible to attack.

The process of determining how secure a system is can be difficult and time-consuming. Organizations need methods to evaluate given systems, to assign general security ratings, and to determine whether a system meets a security policy's requirements. Further, any such security rating should be general enough to enable meaningful comparison among multiple systems along with their relative levels of security. The following sections describe the process involved in evaluating a computer system's level of security. We begin by introducing and explaining basic concepts and terminology used to describe information system security concepts and talk about secure computing, secure perimeters, security and access monitors, and kernel code. We turn to security models to explain how access and security controls can be implemented. We also briefly explain how system security may be categorized as either open or closed; describe a set of standard security techniques used to ensure confidentiality, integrity, and availability of data; discuss security controls; and introduce a standard suite of secure networking protocols.

# Security Models

In information security, models provide a way to formalize security policies. Such models can be abstract or intuitive (some are decidedly mathematical), but all are intended to provide an explicit set of rules that a computer can follow to implement the fundamental security concepts, processes, and procedures that make up a security policy. These models offer a way to deepen your understanding of how a computer operating system should be designed and developed to support a specific security policy.

A security model provides a way for designers to map abstract statements into a security policy that prescribes the algorithms and data structures necessary to build hardware and software. Thus, a security model gives software designers something against which to measure their design and implementation. That model, of course, must support each part of the security policy. In this way, developers can be sure their security implementation supports the security policy.

---

### Tokens, Capabilities, and Labels

Several different methods are used to describe the necessary security attributes for an object. A security *token* is a separate object that is associated with a resource and describes its security attributes. This token can communicate security information about an object prior to requesting access to the actual object. In other implementations, various lists are used to store security information about multiple objects. A *capabilities list* maintains a row of security attributes for each controlled object. Although not as flexible as the token approach, capabilities lists generally offer quicker lookups when a subject requests access to an object. A third common type of attribute storage is called a *security label*, which is generally a permanent part of the object to which it's attached. Once a security label is set, it usually cannot be altered. This permanence provides another safeguard against tampering that neither tokens nor capabilities lists provide.

---

You'll explore several security models in the following sections; all of them can shed light on how security enters into computer architectures and operating system design:

- Trusted computing base
- State machine model
- Information flow model
- Noninterference model
- Take-Grant model

- Access control matrix
- Bell-LaPadula
- Biba
- Clark-Wilson
- Brewer and Nash model (also known as Chinese Wall)

Although it is understood that no system can be totally secure, it is possible to design and build reasonably secure systems. In fact, if a secured system complies with a specific set of security criteria, it can be said to exhibit a level of trust. Therefore, trust can be built into a system and then evaluated, certified, and accredited. But before we can discuss each security model, we have to establish a foundation upon which most security models are built. This foundation is the TCB.

# Trusted Computing Base (TCB)

An old U.S. Department of Defense standard known colloquially as the Orange Book (DoD Standard 5200.28, covered in more detail later in this chapter in the section "Rainbow Series") describes a *trusted computing base (TCB)* as a combination of hardware, software, and controls that work together to form a trusted base to enforce your security policy. The TCB is a subset in a complete information system. It should be as small as possible so that a detailed analysis can reasonably ensure that the system meets design specifications and requirements. The TCB is the only portion of that system that can be trusted to adhere to and enforce the security policy. It is not necessary that every component of a system be trusted. But any time you consider a system from a security standpoint, your evaluation should include all trusted components that define that system's TCB.

In general, TCB components in a system are responsible for controlling access to the system. The TCB must provide methods to access resources both inside and outside the TCB itself. TCB components commonly restrict the activities of components outside the TCB. It is the responsibility of TCB components to ensure that a system behaves properly in all cases and that it adheres to the security policy under all circumstances.

## Security Perimeter

The *security perimeter* of your system is an imaginary boundary that separates the TCB from the rest of the system. For the TCB to communicate with the rest of the system, it must create secure channels, also called *trusted paths*. A trusted path is a channel established with strict standards to allow necessary communication to occur without exposing the TCB to security vulnerabilities. A trusted path also protects system users (sometimes known as *subjects*) from compromise as a result of a TCB interchange. As you learn more about formal security guidelines and evaluation criteria later in this chapter, you'll also learn that trusted paths are required in systems that seek to deliver high levels of security to their users. According to the TCSEC guidelines described later in this chapter, trusted paths are required in B2 and higher systems.

## Reference Monitors and Kernels

When the time comes to implement a secure system, it's essential to develop some part of the TCB to enforce access controls on system assets and resources (sometimes known as *objects*). The part of the TCB that validates access to every resource prior to granting access requests is called the *reference monitor*. The reference monitor stands between every subject and object, verifying that a requesting subject's credentials meet the object's access requirements before any requests are allowed to proceed. If such access requirements aren't met, access requests are turned down. The reference monitor may be a conceptual part of the TCB; it doesn't need to be an actual, stand-alone, or independent working system component.

The collection of components in the TCB that work together to implement reference monitor functions is called the *security kernel*. The reference monitor is a concept or theory that is put into practice via the implementation of a security kernel in software and hardware. The purpose of the security kernel is to launch appropriate components to enforce reference monitor functionality and resist all known attacks. The security kernel uses a trusted path to communicate with subjects. It also mediates all resource access requests, granting only those requests that match the appropriate access rules in use for a system.

The reference monitor requires descriptive information about each resource that it protects. Such information normally includes its classification and designation. When a subject requests access to an object, the reference monitor consults the object's descriptive information to discern whether access should be granted or denied (see the sidebar "Tokens, Capabilities, and Labels" for more information on how this works).

# State Machine Model

The *state machine model* describes a system that is always secure no matter what state it is in. It's based on the computer science definition of a finite state machine (FSM). An FSM combines an external input with an internal machine state to model all kinds of complex systems, including parsers, decoders, and interpreters. Given an input and a state, an FSM transitions to another state and may create an output. Mathematically, the next state is a function of the current state and the input next state (i.e. the next state = F(input, current state). Likewise, the output is also a function of the input and the current state output (i.e. the output = F(input, current state).

Many security models are based on the secure state concept. According to the state machine model, a *state* is a snapshot of a system at a specific moment in time. If all aspects of a state meet the requirements of the security policy, that state is considered secure. A transition occurs when accepting input or producing output. A transition always results in a new state (also called a *state transition*). All state transitions must be evaluated. If each possible state transition results in another secure state, the system can be called a *secure state machine*. A secure state machine model system always boots into a secure state, maintains a secure state across all transitions, and allows subjects to access resources only in a secure manner compliant with the security policy. The secure state machine model is the basis for many other security models.

## Information Flow Model

The *information flow model* focuses on the flow of information. Information flow models are based on a state machine model. The Bell-LaPadula and Biba models, which we will discuss in detail later in this chapter, are both information flow models. Bell-LaPadula is concerned with preventing information from flowing from a high security level to a low security level. Biba is concerned with preventing information from flowing from a low security level to a high security level. Information flow models don't necessarily deal with only the direction of information flow; they can also address the type of flow.

Information flow models are designed to prevent unauthorized, insecure, or restricted information flow. Information flow can be between subjects and objects at the same classification level as well as between subjects and objects at different classification levels. An information flow model allows all authorized information flows, whether within the same classification level or between classification levels. It prevents all unauthorized information flows, whether within the same classification level or between classification levels.

Another interesting perspective on the information flow model is that it is used to establish a relationship between two versions or states of the same object when those two versions or states exist at different points in time. Thus, information flow dictates the transformation of an object from one state at one point in time to another state at another point in time. The information flow model also addresses covert channels by specifically excluding all nondefined flow pathways.

## Noninterference Model

The *noninterference model* is loosely based on the information flow model. However, instead of being concerned about the flow of information, the noninterference model is concerned with how the actions of a subject at a higher security level affect the system state or actions of a subject at a lower security level. Basically, the actions of subject A (high) should not affect the actions of subject B (low) or even be noticed by subject B. The real concern is to prevent the actions of subject A at a high level of security classification from affecting the system state at a lower level. If this occurs, subject B may be placed into an insecure state or be able to deduce or infer information about a higher level of classification. This is a type of information leakage and implicitly creates a covert channel. Thus, the noninterference model can be imposed to provide a form of protection against damage caused by malicious programs such as Trojan horses.

> ### ⊕ Real World Scenario
>
> #### Composition Theories
>
> Some other models that fall into the information flow category build on the notion of how inputs and outputs between multiple systems relate to one another—which follows how information flows between systems rather than within an individual system. These are called *composition theories* because they explain how outputs from one system relate to inputs to another system. There are three recognized types of composition theories:
>
> - *Cascading*: Input for one system comes from the output of another system.
>
> - *Feedback*: One system provides input to another system, which reciprocates by reversing those roles (so that system A first provides input for system B and then system B provides input to system A).
>
> - *Hookup*: One system sends input to another system but also sends input to external entities.

## Take-Grant Model

The *Take-Grant model* employs a directed graph to dictate how rights can be passed from one subject to another or from a subject to an object. Simply put, a subject with the grant right can grant another subject or another object any other right they possess. Likewise, a subject with the take right can take a right from another subject.

## Access Control Matrix

An *access control matrix* is a table of subjects and objects that indicates the actions or functions that each subject can perform on each object. Each column of the matrix is an access control list (ACL). Each row of the matrix is a *capabilities list*. An ACL is tied to the object; it lists valid actions each subject can perform. A capability list is tied to the subject; it lists valid actions that can be taken on each object. From an administration perspective, using only capability lists for access control is a management nightmare. A capability list method of access control can be accomplished by storing on each subject a list of rights the subject has for every object. This effectively gives each user a key ring of accesses and rights to objects within the security domain. To remove access to a particular object, every user (subject) that has access to it must be individually manipulated. Thus, managing access on each user account is much more difficult than managing access on each object (in other words, via ACLs).

Implementing an access control matrix model usually involves constructing an environment that can create and manage lists of subjects and objects and a function that can return the type associated with whatever object is supplied to that function as input (this is important because an object's type determines what kinds of operations may be applied to it).

The access control matrix shown in Table 12.1 is for a discretionary access control system. A mandatory or rule-based matrix can be constructed simply by replacing the subject names with classifications or roles. Access control matrixes are used by systems to quickly determine whether the requested action by a subject for an object is authorized.

**TABLE 12.1**    An access control matrix

**Objects (Categorized by Type)**

| Subjects | Document File | Printer | Network Folder Share |
|----------|---------------|---------|----------------------|
| Bob | Read | No Access | No Access |
| Mary | No Access | No Access | Read |
| Amanda | Read, Write | Print | No Access |
| Mark | Read, Write | Print | Read, Write |
| Kathryn | Read, Write | Print, Manage Print Queue | Read, Write, Execute |
| Colin | Read, Write, Change Permissions | Print, Manage Print Queue, Change Permissions | Read, Write, Execute, Change Permissions |

# Bell-LaPadula Model

The U.S. Department of Defense (DoD) developed the *Bell-LaPadula model* in the 1970s to address concerns about protecting classified information. The DoD manages multiple levels of classified resources, and the Bell-LaPadula model was derived from the DoD's multilevel security policies. The classifications the DoD uses are numerous; however, discussions of classifications within the CISSP CBK are usually limited to unclassified, sensitive but unclassified, confidential, secret, and top secret. The multilevel security policy states that a subject with any level of clearance can access resources at or below its clearance level. However, within the higher clearance levels, access is granted only on a need-to-know basis. In other words, access to a specific object is granted to the classified levels only if a specific work task requires such access. For example, any person with a secret security clearance can access secret, confidential, sensitive but unclassified, and unclassified documents but not top-secret documents. Also, to access a document within the secret level, the person seeking access must also have a need to know for that document.

By design, the Bell-LaPadula model prevents the leaking or transfer of classified information to less-secure clearance levels. This is accomplished by blocking lower-classified subjects from accessing higher-classified objects. With these restrictions, the Bell-LaPadula model is focused on maintaining the confidentiality of objects. Thus, the complexities involved in ensuring the confidentiality of documents are addressed in the Bell-LaPadula model. However, Bell-LaPadula does not address the aspects of integrity or availability for objects. Bell-LaPadula is also the first mathematical model of a multilevel security policy.

 **Real World Scenario**

### Lattice-Based Access Control

This general category for nondiscretionary access controls was introduced in Chapter 1. Here's a quick refresher on the subject (which drives the underpinnings for most access control security models): Subjects under lattice-based access controls are assigned positions in a lattice. These positions fall between defined security labels or classifications. Subjects can access only those objects that fall into the range between the least upper bound (the nearest security label or classification higher than their lattice position) and the highest lower bound (the nearest security label or classification lower than their lattice position) of the labels or classifications for their lattice position. Thus, a subject that falls between the private and sensitive labels in a commercial scheme that reads bottom up as public, sensitive, private, proprietary, and confidential can access only private and sensitive data but not public, proprietary, or confidential data. Lattice-based access controls also fit into the general category of information flow models and deal primarily with confidentiality (that's the reason for the connection to Bell-LaPadula).

This model is built on a state machine concept and the information flow model. It also employs mandatory access controls and the lattice concept. The lattice tiers are the *classification levels* used by the security policy of the organization. The state machine supports multiple states with explicit transitions between any two states; this concept is used because the correctness of the machine, and guarantees of document confidentiality, can be proven mathematically. There are three basic properties of this state machine:

- The *Simple Security Property* states that a subject may not read information at a higher sensitivity level (no read up).

- The * *(star) Security Property* states that a subject may not write information to an object at a lower sensitivity level (no write down). This is also known as the *confinement property*.

- The *Discretionary Security Property* states that the system uses an access matrix to enforce discretionary access control.

These two rules define the states into which the system can transition. No other transitions are allowed. All states accessible through these two rules are secure states. Thus, Bell-LaPadula–modeled systems offer state machine model security (see Figure 12.1).

**FIGURE 12.1**   The Bell-LaPadula model

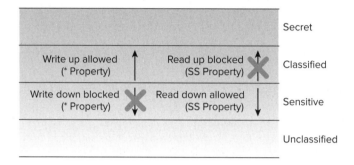

An exception in the Bell-LaPadula model states that a "trusted subject" is not constrained by the * Property. A trusted subject is defined as "a subject that is guaranteed not to consummate a security-breaching information transfer even if it is possible." This means that a trusted subject is allowed to violate the * Property and perform a write down.

The Bell-LaPadula properties are in place to protect data confidentiality. A subject cannot read an object that is classified at a higher level than the subject is cleared for. Because objects at one level have data that is more sensitive or secret than data in objects at a lower level, a subject cannot write data from one level to an object at a lower level (with the exception of a trusted subject). That action would be similar to pasting a top-secret memo into an unclassified document file. The third property enforces a subject's need to know in order to access an object.

The Bell-LaPadula model addresses only the confidentiality of data. It does not address its integrity or availability. Because it was designed in the 1970s, it does not support many operations that are common today, such as file sharing and networking. It also assumes secure transitions between security layers and does not address covert channels (covered later in this chapter). Bell-LaPadula does handle confidentiality well, so it is often used in combination with other models that provide mechanisms to handle integrity and availability.

# Biba Model

For many nonmilitary organizations, integrity is more important than confidentiality. Out of this need, several integrity-focused security models were developed, such those developed by Biba and Clark-Wilson. The *Biba model* was designed after the Bell-LaPadula model. Where the Bell-LaPadula model addresses confidentiality, the Biba model addresses integrity. The Biba model is also built on a state machine concept. In fact, Biba appears to be pretty similar to the Bell-LaPadula model, except inverted. Both use states and transitions. Both have basic properties. The biggest difference is their primary focus: Biba primarily protects data integrity. Here are the basic properties of the Biba model state machine:

- The *Simple Integrity Property* states that a subject cannot read an object at a lower integrity level (no read down).

- The * *(star) Integrity Property* states that a subject cannot modify an object at a higher integrity level (no write up).

In both the Biba and Bell-LaPadula models, there are two primary properties. However, they may also be labeled as axioms, principles, or rules. What you should focus on is the simple and star designations. Take note that simple is always about reading, and star is always about writing. Also, in both cases of simple and star, they are rules that define what cannot or should not be done. In most cases, what is not prevented or disallowed is supported or allowed.

Figure 12.2 illustrates these Biba model axioms.

**FIGURE 12.2**  The Biba model

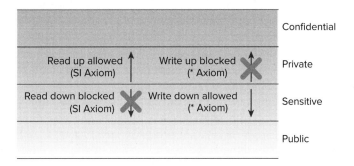

When you compare Biba to Bell-LaPadula, you will notice that they look like they are opposite. That's because they focus on different areas of security. Where Bell-LaPadula model ensures data confidentiality, Biba ensures data integrity.

Biba was designed to address three integrity issues:

- Prevent modification of objects by unauthorized subjects.

- Prevent unauthorized modification of objects by authorized subjects.

- Protect internal and external object consistency.

As with Bell-LaPadula, Biba requires that all subjects and objects have a classification label. Thus, data integrity protection is dependent upon data classification.

Consider the Biba properties. The second property of the Biba model is pretty straightforward. A subject cannot write to an object at a higher integrity level. That makes sense. What about the first property? Why can't a subject read an object at a lower integrity level? The answer takes a little thought. Think of integrity levels as being like the purity level of air. You would not want to pump air from the smoking section into the clean room environment. The same applies to data. When integrity is important, you do not want unvalidated data read into validated documents. The potential for data contamination is too great to permit such access.

Critiques of the Biba model reveal a few drawbacks:

- It addresses only integrity, not confidentiality or availability.

- It focuses on protecting objects from external threats; it assumes that internal threats are handled programmatically.

- It does not address access control management, and it doesn't provide a way to assign or change an object's or subject's classification level.

- It does not prevent covert channels.

Because the Biba model focuses on data integrity, it is a more common choice for commercial security models than the Bell-LaPadula model. Most commercial organizations are more concerned with the integrity of their data than its confidentiality.

## Clark-Wilson Model

Although the Biba model works in commercial applications, another model was designed in 1987 specifically for the commercial environment. The *Clark-Wilson model* uses a multifaceted approach to enforcing data integrity. Instead of defining a formal state machine, the Clark-Wilson model defines each data item and allows modifications through only a small set of programs.

The Clark-Wilson model does not require the use of a lattice structure; rather, it uses a three-part relationship of subject/program/object (or subject/transaction/object) known as a *triple* or an *access control triple*. Subjects do not have direct access to objects. Objects can be accessed only through programs. Through the use of two principles—well-formed transactions and separation of duties—the Clark-Wilson model provides an effective means to protect integrity.

Well-formed transactions take the form of programs. A subject is able to access objects only by using a program. Each program has specific limitations on what it can and cannot do to an object. This effectively limits the subject's capabilities. If the programs are properly designed, then the triple relationship provides a means to protect the integrity of the object.

Clark-Wilson defines the following items and procedures:

- A constrained data item (CDI) is any data item whose integrity is protected by the security model.

- An unconstrained data item (UDI) is any data item that is not controlled by the security model. Any data that is to be input and hasn't been validated or any output would be considered an unconstrained data item.

- An integrity verification procedure (IVP) is a procedure that scans data items and confirms their integrity.
- Transformation procedures (TPs) are the only procedures that are allowed to modify a CDI. The limited access to CDIs through TPs forms the backbone of the Clark-Wilson integrity model. (We wonder whether this is where TPS reports come from . . .)

The Clark-Wilson model uses security labels to grant access to objects, but only through transformation procedures and a *restricted interface model*. A restricted interface model uses classification-based restrictions to offer only subject-specific authorized information and functions. One subject at one classification level will see one set of data and have access to one set of functions, whereas another subject at a different classification level will see a different set of data and have access to a different set of functions. Through these mechanisms, the Clark-Wilson model ensures that data is protected from unauthorized changes from any user. In effect, the Clark-Wilson model enforces separation of duties. The Clark-Wilson design makes it a very good model for commercial applications.

## Brewer and Nash Model (aka Chinese Wall)

This model was created to permit access controls to change dynamically based on a user's previous activity (making it a kind of state machine model as well). This model applies to a single integrated database; it seeks to create security domains that are sensitive to the notion of conflict of interest (for example, someone who works at Company C who has access to proprietary data for Company A should not also be allowed access to similar data for Company B if those two companies compete with one another). This model is known as the *Chinese Wall* because it creates a class of data that defines which security domains are potentially in conflict and prevents any subject with access to one domain that belongs to a specific conflict class from accessing any other domain that belongs to the same conflict class. Metaphorically, this puts a wall around all other information in any conflict class and explains the terminology. Thus, this model also uses the principle of data isolation within each conflict class to keep users out of potential conflict-of-interest situations (for example, management of company datasets). Because company relationships change all the time, this explains the importance of dynamic update to members of and definitions for conflict classes.

# Objects and Subjects

Controlling access to any resource in a secure system involves two entities. The *subject* of the access is the user or process that makes a request to access a resource. Access can mean reading from or writing to a resource. The *object* of an access is the resource a user or process wants to access. Keep in mind that the subject and object refer to some specific access request, so the same resource can serve as a subject and an object in different access requests.

For example, process A may ask for data from process B. To satisfy process A's request, process B must ask for data from process C. In this example, process B is the object of the first request and the subject of the second request:

| First request | process A (subject) | process B (object) |
| Second request | process B (subject) | process C (object) |

## Closed and Open Systems

Systems are designed and built according to one of two differing philosophies: closed and open systems. A *closed system* is designed to work well with a narrow range of other systems, generally all from the same manufacturer. The standards for closed systems are often proprietary and not normally disclosed. *Open systems*, on the other hand, are designed using agreed-upon industry standards. Open systems are much easier to integrate with systems from different manufacturers that support the same standards.

Closed systems are harder to integrate with unlike systems, but they can be more secure. A closed system often comprises proprietary hardware and software that does not incorporate industry standards. This lack of integration ease means that attacks on many generic system components either will not work or must be customized to be successful. In many cases, attacking a closed system is harder than launching an attack on an open system. Many software and hardware components with known vulnerabilities may not exist on a closed system. In addition to the lack of known vulnerable components on a closed system, it is often necessary to possess more in-depth knowledge of the specific target system to launch a successful attack.

Open systems are generally far easier to integrate with other open systems. It is easy, for example, to create a LAN with a Microsoft Windows 2003 machine, a Linux machine, and a Macintosh machine. Although all three computers use different operating systems and represent at least two different hardware architectures, each supports industry standards and makes it easy for networked (or other) communications to occur. This ease comes at a price, however. Because standard communications components are incorporated into each of these three open systems, there are far more entry points and methods for launching attacks. In general, their openness makes them more vulnerable to attack, and their widespread availability makes it possible for attackers to find (and even to practice on) plenty of potential targets. Also, open systems are more popular than closed systems and attract more attention. An attacker who develops basic attacking skills will find more targets on open systems than on closed ones. This larger "market" of potential targets usually means that there is more emphasis on targeting open systems. Inarguably, there's a greater body of shared experience and knowledge on how to attack open systems than there is for closed systems.

There is also a distinction between open-source and closed-source systems. An open-source solution is one where the source code and other internal logic is exposed to the public. A closed-source solution is one where the source code and other internal logic is hidden from the public. Open-source solutions often depend upon public inspection and review to improve the product over time. Closed-source solutions are more dependent on the vendor/programmer to revise the product over time. Both open-source and closed-source solutions can be paid or free as well.

Also, the term "commercial" typically implies closed source.

# Techniques for Ensuring Confidentiality, Integrity, and Availability

To guarantee the confidentiality, integrity, and availability of data, you must ensure that all components that have access to data are secure and well behaved. Software designers use different techniques to ensure that programs do only what is required and nothing more. Suppose a program writes to and reads from an area of memory that is being used by another program. The first program could potentially violate all three security tenets: confidentiality, integrity, and availability. If an affected program is processing sensitive or secret data, that data's confidentiality is no longer guaranteed. If that data is overwritten or altered in an unpredictable way (a common problem when multiple readers and writers inadvertently access the same shared data), there is no guarantee of integrity. And, if data modification results in corruption or outright loss, it could become unavailable for future use. Although the concepts we discuss in the following sections all relate to software programs, they are also commonly used in all areas of security. For example, physical confinement guarantees that all physical access to hardware is controlled.

## Confinement

Software designers use process confinement to restrict the actions of a program. Simply put, process *confinement* allows a process to read from and write to only certain memory locations and resources. The operating system, or some other security component, disallows illegal read/write requests. If a process attempts to initiate an action beyond its granted authority, that action will be denied. In addition, further actions, such as logging the violation attempt, may be taken. Systems that must comply with higher security ratings most likely record all violations and respond in some tangible way. Generally, the offending process is terminated.

## Bounds

Each process that runs on a system is assigned an authority level. The authority level tells the operating system what the process can do. In simple systems, there may be only two authority levels: user and kernel. The authority level tells the operating system how to set the bounds for a process. The *bounds* of a process consist of limits set on the memory addresses and resources it can access. The bounds state the area within which a process is confined. In most systems, these bounds segment logical areas of memory for each process to use. It is the responsibility of the operating system to enforce these logical bounds and to disallow access to other processes. More secure systems may require physically bounded processes. Physical bounds require each bounded process to run in an area of memory that is physically separated from other bounded processes, not just logically bounded in the same memory space. Physically bounded memory can be very expensive, but it's also more secure than logical bounds.

## Isolation

When a process is confined through enforcing access bounds, that process runs in *isolation*. Process isolation ensures that any behavior will affect only the memory and resources associated with the isolated process. These three concepts (confinement, bounds, and isolation) make designing secure programs and operating systems more difficult, but they also make it possible to implement more secure systems.

## Controls

We introduced the concept of security controls in Chapter 1, "Accountability and Access Control." To ensure the security of a system, you need to allow subjects to access only authorized objects. A *control* uses access rules to limit the access by a subject to an object. Access rules state which objects are valid for each subject. Further, an object might be valid for one type of access and be invalid for another type of access. One common control is for file access. A file can be protected from modification by making it read-only for most users but read-write for a small set of users who have the authority to modify it.

Recall from Chapter 1 that there are both mandatory and discretionary access controls, often called MAC and DAC, respectively. With mandatory controls, static attributes of the subject and the object are considered to determine the permissibility of an access. Each subject possesses attributes that define its clearance, or authority, to access resources. Each object possesses attributes that define its classification. Different types of security methods classify resources in different ways. For example, subject A is granted access to object B if the security system can find a rule that allows a subject with subject A's clearance to access an object with object B's classification. This is called *rule-based access control*. The predefined rules state which subjects can access which objects.

Discretionary controls differ from mandatory controls in that the subject has some ability to define the objects to access. Within limits, discretionary access controls allow the subject to define a list of objects to access as needed. This access control list serves as a dynamic access rule set that the subject can modify. The constraints imposed on the modifications often relate to the subject's identity. Based on the identity, the subject may be allowed to add or modify the rules that define access to objects.

Both mandatory and discretionary access controls limit the access to objects by subjects. The primary goals of controls are to ensure the confidentiality and integrity of data by disallowing unauthorized access by authorized or unauthorized subjects.

## Trust and Assurance

Proper security concepts, controls, and mechanisms must be integrated before and during the design and architectural period in order to produce a reliably secure product. Security issues should not be added on as an afterthought; this causes oversights, increased costs, and less reliability. Once security is integrated into the design, it must be engineered, implemented, tested, audited, evaluated, certified, and finally accredited.

A *trusted system* is one in which all protection mechanisms work together to process sensitive data for many types of users while maintaining a stable and secure computing environment. *Assurance* is simply defined as the degree of confidence in satisfaction of security needs. Assurance must be continually maintained, updated, and reverified. This is true whether the trusted system experiences a known change or a significant amount of time has passed. In either case, change has occurred at some level. Change is often the antithesis of security; it often diminishes security. So, whenever change occurs, the system needs to be reevaluated to verify that the level of security it provided previously is still intact. Assurance varies from one system to another and must be established on individual systems. However, there are grades or levels of assurance that can be placed across numerous systems of the same type, systems that support the same services, or systems that are deployed in the same geographic location.

# Understanding System Security Evaluation

Those who purchase information systems for certain kinds of applications—think, for example, about national security agencies where sensitive information may be extremely valuable (or dangerous in the wrong hands) or central banks or securities traders where certain data may be worth billions of dollars—often want to understand their security strengths and weaknesses. Such buyers are often willing to consider only systems that have been subjected to formal evaluation processes in advance and received some kind of security rating so that they know what they're buying (and, usually, also what steps they must take to keep such systems as secure as possible).

When formal evaluations are undertaken, systems are usually subjected to a two-step process. In the first step, a system is tested and a technical evaluation is performed to make sure that the system's security capabilities meet criteria laid out for its intended use. In the second step, the system is subjected to a formal comparison of its design and security criteria and its actual capabilities and performance, and individuals responsible for the security and veracity of such systems must decide whether to adopt them, reject them, or make some changes to their criteria and try again. Very often, in fact, trusted third parties (such as CyberTrust, well known for its security testing laboratories) are hired to perform such evaluations; the most important result from such testing is their "seal of approval" that the system meets all essential criteria. Regardless of whether the evaluations are conducted inside an organization or out of house, the adopting organization must decide to accept or reject the proposed systems. An organization's management must take formal responsibility if and when systems are adopted and be willing to accept any risks associated with its deployment and use.

The three main product evaluation models or classification criteria models addressed here are TCSEC, ITSEC, and Common Criteria. You should be aware that TCSEC was repealed and replaced by the Common Criteria (as well as many other DoD directives). It is still included here as a historical reference and as an example of static-based assessment criteria to offset the benefits of dynamic (although subjective) assessment criteria.

## Rainbow Series

Since the 1980s, governments, agencies, institutions, and business organizations of all kinds have had to face the risks involved in adopting and using information systems. This led to a historical series of information security standards that attempted to specify minimum acceptable security criteria for various categories of use. Such categories were important as purchasers attempted to obtain and deploy systems that would protect and preserve their contents or that would meet various mandated security requirements (such as those that contractors must routinely meet to conduct business with the government). The first such set of standards resulted in the creation of the Trusted Computer System Evaluation Criteria (TCSEC) in the 1980s, as the U.S. Department of Defense (DoD) worked to develop and impose security standards for the systems it purchased and used. In turn, this led to a whole series of such publications through the mid-1990s. Since these publications were routinely identified by the color of their covers, they are known collectively as the *rainbow series*.

Following in the DoD's footsteps, other governments or standards bodies created computer security standards that built and improved on the rainbow series elements. Significant standards in this group include a European model called the Information Technology Security Evaluation Criteria (ITSEC), which was developed in 1990 and used through 1998. Eventually TCSEC and ITSEC were replaced with the so-called Common Criteria, adopted by the United States, Canada, France, Germany, and the United Kingdom in 1998 but more formally known as the "Arrangement on the Recognition of Common Criteria Certificates in the Field of IT Security." Both of these standards will be discussed in later sections as well.

When governments or other security-conscious agencies evaluate information systems, they make use of various standard evaluation criteria. In 1985, the National Computer Security Center (NCSC) developed the TCSEC, usually called the Orange Book because of the color of this publication's covers. The TCSEC established guidelines to be used when evaluating a stand-alone computer from the security perspective. These guidelines address basic security functionality and allow evaluators to measure and rate a system's functionality and trustworthiness. In the TSCEC, in fact, functionality and security assurance are combined and not separated as they are in security criteria developed later. TCSEC guidelines were designed to be used when evaluating vendor products or by vendors to ensure that they build all necessary functionality and security assurance into new products.

Next, we'll take a look at some of the details in the Orange Book itself and then talk about some of the other important elements in the rainbow series.

## TCSEC Classes and Required Functionality

TCSEC combines the functionality and assurance rating of the confidentiality protection offered by a system into four major categories. These categories are then subdivided into additional subcategories identified with numbers, such as C1 and C2. Furthermore, TCSEC's categories are assigned through the evaluation of a target system. Applicable systems are stand-alone systems that are not networked. TCSEC defines the following major categories:

**Category A**   Verified protection

**Category B**   Mandatory protection

**Category C**   Discretionary protection

**Category D**   Minimal protection

Category D is reserved for systems that have been evaluated but do not meet requirements to belong to any other category. In this scheme, category A systems have the highest level of security, and category D represents systems with the lowest level of security. The sections that follow include brief discussions of categories A through C along with numeric suffixes that represent any applicable subcategories.

### Discretionary Protection (Categories C1, C2)

Discretionary protection systems provide basic access control. Systems in this category do provide some security controls but are lacking in more sophisticated and stringent controls that address specific needs for secure systems. C1 and C2 systems provide basic controls and complete documentation for system installation and configuration.

**Discretionary security protection (C1)**   A discretionary security protection system controls access by user IDs and/or groups. Although there are some controls in place that limit object access, systems in this category provide only weak protection.

**Controlled access protection (C2)**   Controlled access protection systems are stronger than C1 systems. Users must be identified individually to gain access to objects. C2 systems must also enforce media cleansing. With media cleansing, any media that is reused by another user must first be thoroughly cleansed so that no remnant of the previous data remains available for inspection or use. Additionally, strict logon procedures must be enforced that restrict access for invalid or unauthorized users.

### Mandatory Protection (Categories B1, B2, B3)

Mandatory protection systems provide more security controls than category D or C systems. More granularity of control is mandated, so security administrators can apply specific controls that allow only very limited sets of subject/object access. This category of systems is based on the Bell-LaPadula model. Mandatory access is based on security labels.

**Labeled security (B1)** In a labeled security system, each subject and each object has a security label. A B1 system grants access by matching up the subject and object labels and comparing their permission compatibility. B1 systems support sufficient security to house classified data.

**Structured protection (B2)** In addition to the requirement for security labels (as in B1 systems), B2 systems must ensure that no covert channels exist. Operator and administrator functions are separated, and process isolation is maintained. B2 systems are sufficient for classified data that requires more security functionality than a B1 system can deliver.

**Security domains (B3)** Security domain systems provide more secure functionality by further increasing the separation and isolation of unrelated processes. Administration functions are clearly defined and separate from functions available to other users. The focus of B3 systems shifts to simplicity to reduce any exposure to vulnerabilities in unused or extra code. The secure state of B3 systems must also be addressed during the initial boot process. B3 systems are difficult to attack successfully and provide sufficient secure controls for very sensitive or secret data.

### Verified Protection (Category A1)

Verified protection systems are similar to B3 systems in the structure and controls they employ. The difference is in the development cycle. Each phase of the development cycle is controlled using formal methods. Each phase of the design is documented, evaluated, and verified before the next step is taken. This forces extreme security consciousness during all steps of development and deployment and is the only way to formally guarantee strong system security.

A verified design system starts with a design document that states how the resulting system will satisfy the security policy. From there, each development step is evaluated in the context of the security policy. Functionality is crucial, but assurance becomes more important than in lower security categories. A1 systems represent the top level of security and are designed to handle top-secret data. Every step is documented and verified, from the design all the way through to delivery and installation.

## Other Colors in the Rainbow Series

Altogether, there are nearly 30 titles in the collection of DoD documents that either add to or further elaborate on the Orange Book. Although the colors don't necessarily mean anything, they're used to describe publications in this series. Other important elements in this collection of documents include the following (for a more complete list, please consult Table 12.2):

**Red Book** Because the Orange Book applies only to stand-alone computers not attached to a network and so many systems were used on networks (even in the 1980s), the Red Book was developed to interpret the TCSEC in a networking context. In fact, the official title of the Red Book is the *Trusted Network Interpretation (TNI)*, so it could be considered an interpretation of the Orange Book with a bent on networking. Quickly, the Red Book became more relevant and important to system buyers and builders than the Orange Book. The following list includes a few other functions of the Red Book:

- Rates confidentiality and integrity
- Addresses communications integrity
- Addresses denial of service protection
- Addresses compromise (in other words, intrusion) protection and prevention
- Is restricted to a limited class of networks that are labeled as "centralized networks with a single accreditation authority"
- Uses only four rating levels: None, C1 (Minimum), C2 (Fair), and B2 (Good)

**Green Book** The Green Book, or the *Department of Defense Password Management Guidelines*, provides password creation and management guidelines; it's important for those who configure and manage trusted systems.

**TABLE 12.2** Important rainbow series elements

| Publication Number | Title | Book Name |
|---|---|---|
| 5200.28-STD | *DoD Trusted Computer System Evaluation Criteria* | Orange Book |
| CSC-STD-002-85 | *DoD Password Management Guidelines* | Green Book |
| CSC-STD-003-85 | *Guidance for Applying TCSEC in Specific Environments* | Yellow Book |
| NCSC-TG-001 | *A Guide to Understanding Audit in Trusted Systems* | Tan Book |
| NCSC-TG-002 | *Trusted Product Evaluation: A Guide for Vendors* | Bright Blue Book |
| NCSC-TG-002-85 | *PC Security Considerations* | Light Blue Book |
| NCSC-TG-003 | *A Guide to Understanding Discretionary Access Controls in Trusted Systems* | Neon Orange Book |
| NCSC-TG-005 | *Trusted Network Interpretation* | Red Book |

**TABLE 12.2** Important rainbow series elements *(continued)*

| Publication Number | Title | Book Name |
|---|---|---|
| NCSC-TG-004 | *Glossary of Computer Security Terms* | Aqua Book |
| NCSC-TG-006 | *A Guide to Understanding Configuration Management in Trusted Systems* | Amber Book |
| NCSC-TG-007 | *A Guide to Understanding Design Documentation in Trusted Systems* | Burgundy Book |
| NCSC-TG-008 | *A Guide to Understanding Trusted Distribution in Trusted Systems* | Lavender Book |
| NCSC-TG-009 | *Computer Security Subsystem Interpretation of the TCSEC* | Venice Blue Book |

For more information, please consult http://csrc.nist.gov/publications/secpubs/rainbow/; download links are available.

Given all the time and effort that went into formulating the TCSEC, it's not unreasonable to wonder why evaluation criteria have evolved to newer, more advanced standards. The relentless march of time and technology aside, these are the major critiques of TCSEC and help to explain why newer standards are now in use worldwide:

- Although the TCSEC puts considerable emphasis on controlling user access to information, it doesn't exercise control over what users do with information once access is granted. This can be a problem in military and commercial applications alike.

- Given the origins of evaluation standards at the U.S. Department of Defense, it's understandable that the TCSEC focuses its concerns entirely on confidentiality, which assumes that controlling how users access data means that concerns about data accuracy or integrity are irrelevant. This doesn't work in commercial environments where concerns about data accuracy and integrity can be more important than concerns about confidentiality.

- Outside the evaluation standards' own emphasis on access controls, the TCSEC does not carefully address the kinds of personnel, physical, and procedural policy matters or safeguards that must be exercised to fully implement security policy. They don't deal much with how such matters can impact system security either.

- The Orange Book, per se, doesn't deal with networking issues (though the Red Book, developed later in 1987, does).

To some extent, these criticisms reflect the unique security concerns of the military, which developed the TCSEC. Then, too, the prevailing computing tools and technologies widely available at the time (networking was really just getting started in 1985) had an impact as well. Certainly, an increasingly sophisticated and holistic view of security within organizations helps to explain why and where the TCSEC also fell short, procedurally and policy-wise. But because ITSEC has been largely superseded by the Common Criteria, coverage in the next section explains ITSEC as a step along the way toward the Common Criteria (covered in the section after that).

## ITSEC Classes and Required Assurance and Functionality

The ITSEC represents an initial attempt to create security evaluation criteria in Europe. It was developed as an alternative to the TCSEC guidelines. The ITSEC guidelines evaluate the functionality and assurance of a system using separate ratings for each category. In this context, a system's functionality is a measurement of the system's utility value for users. The functionality rating of a system states how well the system performs all necessary functions based on its design and intended purpose. The assurance rating represents the degree of confidence that the system will work properly in a consistent manner.

ITSEC refers to any system being evaluated as a target of evaluation (TOE). All ratings are expressed as TOE ratings in two categories. ITSEC uses two scales to rate functionality and assurance. The functionality of a system is rated from F-D through F-B3 (there is no F-A1). The assurance of a system is rated from E0 through E6. Most ITSEC ratings generally correspond with TCSEC ratings (for example, a TCSEC C1 system corresponds to an ITSEC F-C1, E1 system). See Table 12.4 (at the end of the next section) for a comparison of TCSEC, ITSEC, and Common Criteria ratings.

> There are some instances where the F ratings of ITSEC are defined using F1 through F5 rather than reusing the labels from TCSEC. These alternate labels are F1 = F-C1, F2 = F-C2, F3 = F-B1, F4 = F-B2, and F5 = F-B3. There is no numbered F rating for F-D, but there are a few cases where F0 is used. This is a fairly ridiculous label because if there are no functions to rate, there is no need for a rating label.

Differences between TCSEC and ITSEC are many and varied. Following are some of the most important differences between the two standards:

- Although the TCSEC concentrates almost exclusively on confidentiality, ITSEC addresses concerns about the loss of integrity and availability in addition to confidentiality, thereby covering all three elements so important to maintaining complete information security.

- ITSEC does not rely on the notion of a TCB, and it doesn't require that a system's security components be isolated within a TCB.

- Unlike TCSEC, which required any changed systems to be reevaluated anew—be it for operating system upgrades, patches, or fixes; application upgrades or changes; and so forth—ITSEC includes coverage for maintaining targets of evaluation after such changes occur without requiring a new formal evaluation.

For more information on ITSEC (now largely supplanted by the Common Criteria, covered in the next section), please visit the official ITSEC website at www.cesg.gov.uk/products_services/iacs/cc_and_itsec/index.shtml or view the original ITSEC specification at www.ssi.gouv.fr/site_documents/ITSEC/ITSEC-uk.pdf.

# Common Criteria

The Common Criteria represent a more or less global effort that involves everybody who worked on TCSEC and ITSEC as well as other global players. Ultimately, it results in the ability to purchase CC-evaluated products (where CC, of course, stands for Common Criteria). The Common Criteria define various levels of testing and confirmation of systems' security capabilities, and the number of the level indicates what kind of testing and confirmation has been performed. Nevertheless, it's wise to observe that even the highest CC ratings do not equate to a guarantee that such systems are completely secure or that they are entirely devoid of vulnerabilities or susceptibility to exploit.

## Recognition of Common Criteria

Caveats and disclaimers aside, a document titled "Arrangement on the Recognition of Common Criteria Certificates in the Field of IT Security" was signed by representatives from government organizations in Canada, France, Germany, the United Kingdom, and the United States in 1998, making it an international standard. This document was converted by ISO into an official standard, namely, ISO 15408, Evaluation Criteria for Information Technology Security. The objectives of the CC guidelines are as follows:

- To add to buyer's confidence in the security of evaluated, rated IT products.

- To eliminate duplicate evaluations (among other things, this means that if one country, agency, or validation organization follows the CC in rating specific systems and configurations, others elsewhere need not repeat this work).

- To keep making security evaluations and the certification process more cost effective and efficient.

- To make sure evaluations of IT products adhere to high and consistent standards.

- To promote evaluation and increase availability of evaluated, rated IT products.

- To evaluate the functionality (in other words, what the system does) and assurance (in other words, how much can you trust the system) of the TOE.

Common Criteria documentation is available online at www.niap-ccevs.org/cc-scheme/. Visit it to get information on the current version of the CC guidelines and guidance on using the CC along with lots of other useful, relevant information.

The Common Criteria process is based on two key elements: protection profiles and security targets. *Protection profiles (PPs)* specify the security requirements and protections of a product that is to be evaluated (the TOE), which are considered the security desires or the "I want" from a customer. *Security targets (STs)* specify the claims of security from the vendor that are built into a TOE. STs are considered the implemented security measures or the "I will provide" from the vendor. In addition to offering security targets, vendors may also offer packages of additional security features. A *package* is an intermediate grouping of security requirement components that can be added or removed from a TOE (like the option packages when purchasing a new vehicle).

The PP is compared to various STs from the selected vendor's TOEs. The closest or best match is what the client purchases. The client initially selects a vendor based on published or marketed evaluation assurance levels, or EALs (see the next section for more details on EALs), for currently available systems. Using common criteria to choose a vendor allows clients to request exactly what they need for security rather than having to use static fixed security levels. It also allows vendors more flexibility on what they design and create. A well-defined set of common criteria supports subjectivity and versatility, and it automatically adapts to changing technology and threat conditions. Furthermore, the EALs provide a method for comparing vendor systems that is more standardized (like the old TCSEC).

## Structure of the Common Criteria

The CC guidelines are divided into three topical areas, as follows:

**Part 1**   Introduction and General Model describes the general concepts and underlying model used to evaluate IT security and what's involved in specifying targets of evaluation. It's useful introductory and explanatory material for those unfamiliar with the workings of the security evaluation process or who need help reading and interpreting evaluation results.

**Part 2**   Security Functional Requirements describes various functional requirements in terms of security audits, communications security, cryptographic support for security, user data protection, identification and authentication, security management, TOE security functions (TSFs), resource utilization, system access, and trusted paths. Covers the complete range of security functions as envisioned in the CC evaluation process, with additional appendices (called *annexes*) to explain each functional area.

**Part 3**   Security Assurance covers assurance requirements for TOEs in the areas of configuration management, delivery and operation, development, guidance documents, and life cycle support plus assurance tests and vulnerability assessments. Covers the complete range of security assurance checks and protects profiles as envisioned in the CC evaluation process, with information on evaluation assurance levels that describe how systems are designed, checked, and tested.

Most important of all the information that appears in these various CC documents (worth at least a cursory read-through) are the evaluation assurance levels commonly known as EALs. Table 12.3 summarizes EALs 1 through 7.

**TABLE 12.3** CC evaluation assurance levels

| Level | Assurance Level | Description |
|---|---|---|
| EAL1 | Functionally tested | Applies when some confidence in correct operation is required but where threats to security are not serious. This is of value when independent assurance that due care has been exercised in protecting personal information. |
| EAL2 | Structurally tested | Applies when delivery of design information and test results are in keeping with good commercial practices. This is of value when developers or users require low to moderate levels of independently assured security. IT is especially relevant when evaluating legacy systems. |
| EAL3 | Methodically tested and checked | Applies when security engineering begins at the design stage and is carried through without substantial subsequent alteration. This is of value when developers or users require a moderate level of independently assured security, including thorough investigation of TOE and its development. |
| EAL4 | Methodically designed, tested, and reviewed | Applies when rigorous, positive security engineering and good commercial development practices are used. This does not require substantial specialist knowledge, skills, or resources. It involves independent testing of all TOE security functions. |
| EAL5 | Semi-formally designed and tested | Uses rigorous security engineering and commercial development practices, including specialist security engineering techniques, for semi-formal testing. This applies when developers or users require a high level of independently assured security in a planned development approach, followed by rigorous development. |
| EAL6 | Semi-formally verified, designed, and tested | Uses direct, rigorous security engineering techniques at all phases of design, development, and testing to produce a premium TOE. This applies when TOEs for high-risk situations are needed, where the value of protected assets justifies additional cost. Extensive testing reduces risks of penetration, probability of cover channels, and vulnerability to attack. |
| EAL7 | Formally verified, designed, and tested | Used only for highest-risk situations or where high-value assets are involved. This is limited to TOEs where tightly focused security functionality is subject to extensive formal analysis and testing. |

For a complete description of EALs, consult the CC documents hosted at www.niap-ccevs.org/cc_docs/ and view the latest revision's Part 3.

Though the CC guidelines are flexible and accommodating enough to capture most security needs and requirements, they are by no means perfect. As with other evaluation criteria, the CC guidelines do nothing to make sure that how users act on data is also secure. The CC guidelines also do not address administrative issues outside the specific purview of security. As with other evaluation criteria, the CC guidelines do not include evaluation of security *in situ*—that is, they do not address controls related to personnel, organizational practices and procedures, or physical security. Likewise, controls over electromagnetic emissions are not addressed, nor are the criteria for rating the strength of cryptographic algorithms explicitly laid out. Nevertheless, the CC guidelines represent some of the best techniques whereby systems may be rated for security. To conclude this discussion of security evaluation standards, Table 12.4 summarizes how various ratings from the TCSEC, ITSEC, and the CC can be compared.

**TABLE 12.4** Comparing security evaluation standards

| TCSEC | ITSEC | CC | Designation |
|-------|-------|-----|-------------|
| D | F-D+E0 | EAL0, EAL1 | Minimal/no protection |
| C1 | F-C1+E1 | EAL2 | Discretionary security mechanisms |
| C2 | F-C2+E2 | EAL3 | Controlled access protection |
| B1 | F-B1+E3 | EAL4 | Labeled security protection |
| B2 | F-B2+E4 | EAL5 | Structured security protection |
| B3 | F-B3+E5 | EAL6 | Security domains |
| A1 | F-B3+E6 | EAL7 | Verified security design |

# Industry and International Security Implementation Guidelines

In addition to overall security assess models, such as Common Criteria, there are many other more specific or focused security standards for various aspects of storage, communication, transactions, and the like. Two of these standards you should be familiar with are Payment Card Industry – Data Security Standard (PCI-DSS) and International Organization for Standardization (ISO).

PCI-DSS is a collection of requirements for improving the security of electronic payment transactions. These standards were defined by the PCI Security Standards Council members, who are primarily credit card banks and financial institutions. The PCI-DSS defines requirements for security management, policies, procedures, network architecture, software design, and other critical protective measures. For more information on PCI-DSS, please visit the website at www.pcisecuritystandards.org.

ISO is a worldwide standards-setting group of representatives from various national standards organizations. ISO defines standards for industrial and commercial equipment, software, protocols, and management, among others. It issues six main products: International Standards, Technical Reports, Technical Specifications, Publicly Available Specifications, Technical Corrigenda, and Guides. ISO standards are widely accepted across many industries, and have even been adopted as requirements or laws by various governments. For more information on ISO, please visit the website at www.iso.org.

## Certification and Accreditation

Organizations that require secure systems need one or more methods to evaluate how well a system meets their security requirements. The formal evaluation process is divided into two phases, called *certification* and *accreditation*. The actual steps required in each phase depend on the evaluation criteria an organization chooses. A CISSP candidate must understand the need for each phase and the criteria commonly used to evaluate systems. The two evaluation phases are discussed in the next two sections, and then we present various evaluation criteria and considerations you must address when assessing the security of a system. Certification and accreditation processes are used to assess the effectiveness of application security as well as operating system and hardware security.

The process of evaluation provides a way to assess how well a system measures up to a desired level of security. Because each system's security level depends on many factors, all of them must be taken into account during the evaluation. Even though a system is initially described as secure, the installation process, physical environment, and general configuration details all contribute to its true general security. Two identical systems could be assessed at different levels of security because of configuration or installation differences.

The terms *certification*, *accreditation*, and *maintenance* as used in the following sections are official terms used by the defense establishment, and you should be familiar with them.

Certification and accreditation are additional steps in the software and IT systems development process normally required from defense contractors and others working in a military environment. The official definitions of these terms as used by the U.S. government are from Department of Defense Instruction 5200.40, Enclosure 2.

## Certification

The first phase in a total evaluation process is *certification*. Certification is the comprehensive evaluation of the technical and nontechnical security features of an IT system and other safeguards made in support of the accreditation process to establish the extent to which a particular design and implementation meets a set of specified security requirements.

System certification is the technical evaluation of each part of a computer system to assess its concordance with security standards. First, you must choose evaluation criteria (we will present criteria alternatives in later sections). Once you select criteria to use, you analyze each system component to determine whether it satisfies the desired security goals. The certification analysis includes testing the system's hardware, software, and configuration. All controls are evaluated during this phase, including administrative, technical, and physical controls.

After you assess the entire system, you can evaluate the results to determine the security level the system supports in its current environment. The environment of a system is a critical part of the certification analysis, so a system can be more or less secure depending on its surroundings. The manner in which you connect a secure system to a network can change its security standing. Likewise, the physical security surrounding a system can affect the overall security rating. You must consider all factors when certifying a system.

You complete the certification phase when you have evaluated all factors and determined the level of security for the system. Remember that the certification is valid only for a system in a specific environment and configuration. Any changes could invalidate the certification. Once you have certified a security rating for a specific configuration, you are ready to seek acceptance of the system. Management accepts the certified security configuration of a system through the accreditation process.

## Accreditation

In the certification phase, you test and document the security capabilities of a system in a specific configuration. With this information in hand, the management of an organization compares the capabilities of a system to the needs of the organization. It is imperative that the security policy clearly states the requirements of a security system. Management reviews the certification information and decides whether the system satisfies the security needs of the organization. If management decides the certification of the system satisfies their needs, the system is *accredited*. Accreditation is the formal declaration by the Designated Approving Authority (DAA) that an IT system is approved to operate in a particular security mode using a prescribed set of safeguards at an acceptable level of risk. Once accreditation is performed, management can formally accept the adequacy of the overall security performance of an evaluated system.

 Certification and accreditation do seem similar, and thus it is often a challenge to really understand them. One perspective you might consider is that certification is often an internal verification of security, and the results of that verification are trusted only by your organization. Accreditation is often performed by a third-party testing service, and the results are trusted by everyone in the world who trusts the specific testing group involved.

The process of certification and accreditation is often an iterative process. In the accreditation phase, it is not uncommon to request changes to the configuration or additional controls to address security concerns. Remember that whenever you change the configuration, you must recertify the new configuration. Likewise, you need to recertify the system when a specific time period elapses. Your security policy should specify what conditions require recertification. A sound policy would list the amount of time a certification is valid along with any changes that would require you to restart the certification and accreditation process.

## Certification and Accreditation Systems

Two government standards are currently in place for the certification and accreditation of computing systems: the DoD standard is the Defense Information Technology Security Certification and Accreditation Process (DITSCAP), and the standard for all U.S. government executive branch departments, agencies, and their contractors and consultants is the National Information Assurance Certification and Accreditation Process (NIACAP). Both of these processes are divided into four phases:

**Phase 1: Definition**   Involves the assignment of appropriate project personnel; documentation of the mission need; and registration, negotiation, and creation of a System Security Authorization Agreement (SSAA) that guides the entire certification and accreditation process

**Phase 2: Verification**   Includes refinement of the SSAA, systems development activities, and a certification analysis

**Phase 3: Validation**   Includes further refinement of the SSAA, certification evaluation of the integrated system, development of a recommendation to the DAA, and the DAA's accreditation decision

**Phase 4: Post Accreditation**   Includes maintenance of the SSAA, system operation, change management, and compliance validation

These phases are adapted from Department of Defense Instruction 5200.40, Enclosure 3. DoDI 5200.40, which defines Department of Defense Information Technology Security Certification and Accreditation Process (DITSCAP) and was created on December 30, 1997, was replaced by the Interim DIACAP on July 6, 2006. DoDI 8510.bb defines the DoD Information Assurance Certification and Accreditation Process (DIACAP). DIACAP is a five-step certification and accreditation process that covers the entire system life cycle from mission and information assurance requirements development to disposal.

The NIACAP process, administered by the Information Systems Security Organization of the National Security Agency, outlines three different types of accreditation that may be granted. The definitions of these types of accreditation (from National Security Telecommunications and Information Systems Security Instruction 1000) are as follows:

- For a system accreditation, a major application or general support system is evaluated.

- For a site accreditation, the applications and systems at a specific, self-contained location are evaluated.

- For a type accreditation, an application or system that is distributed to a number of different locations is evaluated.

# Common Flaws and Security Issues

No security architecture is complete and totally secure. Every computer system has weaknesses and vulnerabilities. The goal of security models and architectures is to address as many known weaknesses as possible. Due to this fact, corrective actions must be taken to resolve security issues. The following sections present some of the more common security issues that affect computer systems. You should understand each of the issues and how they can degrade the overall security of your system. Some issues and flaws overlap one another and are used in creative ways to attack systems. Although the following discussion covers the most common flaws, the list is not exhaustive. Attackers are very clever.

## Covert Channels

A *covert channel* is a method that is used to pass information over a path that is not normally used for communication. Because the path is not normally used for communication, it may not be protected by the system's normal security controls. Using a covert channel provides a means to violate, bypass, or circumvent a security policy undetected. As you might imagine, a covert channel is the opposite of an *overt channel*. An overt channel is a known, expected, authorized, designed, monitored, and controlled method of communication.

There are two basic types of covert channels:

**Covert timing channel**   Conveys information by altering the performance of a system component or modifying a resource's timing in a predictable manner. Using a covert timing channel is generally a more sophisticated method to covertly pass data and is very difficult to detect.

**Covert storage channel**   Conveys information by writing data to a common storage area where another process can read it. Be diligent for any process that writes to any area of memory that another process can read.

Both types of covert channels rely on the use of communication techniques to exchange information with otherwise unauthorized subjects. Because the nature of the covert channel is that it is unusual and outside the normal data transfer environment, detecting it can be difficult. The best defense is to implement auditing and analyze log files for any covert channel activity.

The lowest level of security that addresses covert channels is B2 (F-B2+E4 for ITSEC, EAL5 for CC). All levels at or above level B2 must contain controls that detect and prohibit covert channels.

# Attacks Based on Design or Coding Flaws and Security Issues

Certain attacks may result from poor design techniques, questionable implementation practices and procedures, or poor or inadequate testing. Some attacks may result from deliberate design decisions when special points of entry built into code to circumvent access controls, login, or other security checks often added to code while under development are not removed when that code is put into production. For what we hope are obvious reasons, such points of egress are properly called *back doors* because they avoid security measures by design (they're covered later in this chapter in "Maintenance Hooks and Privileged Programs"). Extensive testing and code review are required to uncover such covert means of access, which are incredibly easy to remove during final phases of development but can be incredibly difficult to detect during the testing and maintenance phases.

Although functionality testing is commonplace for commercial code and applications, separate testing for security issues has been gaining attention and credibility only in the past few years, courtesy of widely publicized virus and worm attacks, SQL injection attacks, cross-site scripting attacks, and occasional defacements of or disruptions to widely used public sites online. In the sections that follow, we cover common sources of attack or security vulnerability that can be attributed to failures in design, implementation, prerelease code cleanup, or out-and-out coding mistakes. Although they're avoidable, finding and fixing such flaws requires rigorous security-conscious design from the beginning of a development project and extra time and effort spent in testing and analysis. Although this helps to explain the often-lamentable state of software security, it does not excuse it!

## Initialization and Failure States

When an unprepared system crashes and subsequently recovers, two opportunities to compromise its security controls may arise during that process. Many systems unload security controls as part of their shutdown procedures. *Trusted recovery* ensures that all controls remain intact in the event of a crash. During a trusted recovery, the system ensures that there are no opportunities for access to occur when security controls are disabled. Even the recovery phase runs with all controls intact.

For example, suppose a system crashes while a database transaction is being written to disk for a database classified as top secret. An unprotected system might allow an unauthorized user to access that temporary data before it gets written to disk. A system that supports trusted recovery ensures that no data confidentiality violations occur, even during the crash. This process requires careful planning and detailed procedures for handling system failures. Although automated recovery procedures may make up a portion of the entire recovery, manual intervention may still be required. Obviously, if such manual action is needed, appropriate identification and authentication for personnel performing recovery is likewise essential.

## Input and Parameter Checking

One of the most notorious security violations is a buffer overflow. This violation occurs when programmers fail to validate input data sufficiently, particularly when they do not impose a limit on the amount of data their software will accept as input. Because such data is usually stored in an input buffer, when the normal maximum size of the buffer is exceeded, the extra data is called *overflow*. Thus, the type of attack that results when someone attempts to supply malicious instructions or code as part of program input is called a *buffer overflow*. Unfortunately, in many systems such overflow data is often executed directly by the system under attack at a high level of privilege or at whatever level of privilege attaches to the process accepting such input. For nearly all types of operating systems, including Windows, Unix, Linux, and others, buffer overflows expose some of the most glaring and profound opportunities for compromise and attack of any kind of known security vulnerability.

The party responsible for a buffer overflow vulnerability is always the programmer who wrote the nonsanitized code. Due diligence from programmers can eradicate buffer overflows completely, but only if programmers check all input and parameters before storing them in any data structure (and limit how much data can be proffered as input). Proper data validation is the only way to do away with buffer overflows. Otherwise, discovery of buffer overflows leads to a familiar pattern of critical security updates that must be applied to affected systems to close the point of attack.

---

### Checking Code for Buffer Overflows

In early 2002, Bill Gates acted in his traditional role as the archetypal Microsoft spokesperson when he announced something he called the "Trustworthy Computing Initiative," a series of design philosophy changes intended to beef up the often questionable standing of Microsoft's operating systems and applications when viewed from a security perspective. As discussion on this subject continued through 2002 and 2003, the topic of buffer overflows occurred repeatedly (more often, in fact, than Microsoft security bulletins reported security flaws related to this kind of problem, which is among the most serious yet most frequently reported types of programming errors with security implications). As is the case for many other development organizations and also for the builders of software development environments (the software tools that developers use to create other software), increased awareness of buffer overflow exploits has caused changes at many stages during the development process:

- Designers must specify bounds for input data or state acceptable input values and set hard limits on how much data will be accepted, parsed, and handled when input is solicited.

- Developers must follow such limitations when building code that solicits, accepts, and handles input.

- Testers must check to make sure that buffer overflows can't occur and attempt to circumvent or bypass security settings when testing input handling code.

In his book *Secrets & Lies*, noted information security expert Bruce Schneier makes a great case that security testing is in fact quite different from standard testing activities like unit testing, module testing, acceptance testing, and quality assurance checks (see the glossary) that software companies have routinely performed as part of the development process for years and years. What's not yet clear at Microsoft (and at other development companies as well, to be as fair to the colossus of Redmond as possible) is whether this change in design and test philosophy equates to the right kind of rigor necessary to foil all buffer overflows (some of the most serious security holes that Microsoft reports clearly invoke "buffer overruns" or identify the cause of the vulnerability as an "unchecked buffer").

## Maintenance Hooks and Privileged Programs

*Maintenance hooks* are entry points into a system that are known only by the developer of the system. Such entry points are also called *back doors*. Although the existence of maintenance hooks is a clear violation of security policy, they still pop up in many systems. The original purpose of back doors was to provide guaranteed access to the system for maintenance reasons or if regular access was inadvertently disabled. The problem is that this type of access bypasses all security controls and provides free access to anyone who knows that the back doors exist. It is imperative that you explicitly prohibit such entry points and monitor your audit logs to uncover any activity that may indicate unauthorized administrator access.

Another common system vulnerability is the practice of executing a program whose security level is elevated during execution. Such programs must be carefully written and tested so they do not allow any exit and/or entry points that would leave a subject with a higher security rating. Ensure that all programs that operate at a high security level are accessible only to appropriate users and that they are hardened against misuse.

## Incremental Attacks

Some forms of attack occur in slow, gradual increments rather than through obvious or recognizable attempts to compromise system security or integrity. Two such forms of attack are data diddling and the salami attack. *Data diddling* occurs when an attacker gains access to a system and makes small, random, or incremental changes to data during storage, processing, input, output, or transaction rather than obviously altering file contents or damaging or deleting entire files. Such changes can be difficult to detect unless files and data are protected by encryption or unless some kind of integrity check (such as a checksum or message digest) is routinely performed and applied each time a file is read or written. Encrypted file systems, file-level encryption techniques, or some form of file monitoring (which includes integrity checks like those performed by applications such as Tripwire) usually offer adequate guarantees that no data diddling is underway. Data diddling is often considered an attack performed more often by insiders rather than outsiders (in other words, external intruders). It should be obvious that since data diddling is an attack that alters data, it is considered an active attack.

The *salami attack* is more mythical by all published reports. The name of the attack refers to a systematic whittling at assets in accounts or other records with financial value, where very small amounts are deducted from balances regularly and routinely. Metaphorically, the attack may be explained as stealing a very thin slice from a salami each time it's put on the slicing machine when it's being accessed by a paying customer. In reality, though no documented examples of such an attack are available, most security experts concede that salami attacks are possible, especially when organizational insiders could be involved. Only by proper separation of duties and proper control over code can organizations completely prevent or eliminate such an attack. Setting financial transaction monitors to track very small transfers of funds or other items of value should help to detect such activity; regular employee notification of the practice should help to discourage attempts at such attacks.

If you want an entertaining method of learning about the salami attack or the salami technique, view the movies *Office Space*, *Sneakers*, and *Superman III*.

## Programming

We have already mentioned the biggest flaw in programming. The buffer overflow comes from the programmer failing to check or sanitize the format and/or the size of input data. There are other potential flaws with programs. Any program that does not handle any exception gracefully is in danger of exiting in an unstable state. It is possible to cleverly crash a program after it has increased its security level to carry out a normal task. If an attacker is successful in crashing the program at the right time, they can attain the higher security level and cause damage to the confidentiality, integrity, and availability of your system.

All programs that are executed directly or indirectly must be fully tested to comply with your security model. Make sure you have the latest version of any software installed, and be aware of any known security vulnerabilities. Because each security model, and each security policy, is different, you must ensure that the software you execute does not exceed the authority you allow. Writing secure code is difficult, but it's certainly possible. Make sure all programs you use are designed to address security concerns.

## Timing, State Changes, and Communication Disconnects

Computer systems perform tasks with rigid precision. Computers excel at repeatable tasks. Attackers can develop attacks based on the predictability of task execution. The common sequence of events for an algorithm is to check that a resource is available and then access it if you are permitted. The *time of check (TOC)* is the time at which the subject checks on the status of the object. There may be several decisions to make before returning to the object to access it. When the decision is made to access the object, the procedure accesses it at the *time of use (TOU)*. The difference between the TOC and the TOU is sometimes large enough for an attacker to replace the original object with another object that suits their own needs. *Time-of-check-to-time-of-use* (TOCTTOU) attacks are often called *race conditions* because the attacker is racing with the legitimate process to replace the object before it is used.

A classic example of a TOCTTOU attack is replacing a data file after its identity has been verified but before data is read. By replacing one authentic data file with another file of the attacker's choosing and design, an attacker can potentially direct the actions of a program in many ways. Of course, the attacker would have to have in-depth knowledge of the program and system under attack.

Likewise, attackers can attempt to take action between two known states when the state of a resource or the entire system changes. Communication disconnects also provide small windows that an attacker might seek to exploit. Any time a status check of a resource precedes action on the resource, a window of opportunity exists for a potential attack in the brief interval between check and action. These attacks must be addressed in your security policy and in your security model. TOC/TOU attacks, race condition exploits, and communication disconnects are known as state attacks because they attack timing, data flow control, and transition between one system state to another.

## Technology and Process Integration

It is important to evaluate and understand the vulnerabilities in system architectures, especially in regard to technology and process integration. As multiple technologies and complex processes are intertwined in the act of crafting new and unique business functions, new issues and security problems often surface. As systems are integrated, attention should be paid to potential single points of failure as well as to emergent weaknesses in service-oriented architecture (SOA). An SOA constructs new applications or functions out of existing but separate and distinct software services. The resulting application is often new; thus, its security issues are unknown, untested, and unprotected. All new deployments, especially new applications or functions, need to be thoroughly vetted before allowing them to go live into a production network or the public Internet.

## Electromagnetic Radiation

Simply because of the kinds of electronic components from which they're built, many computer hardware devices emit electromagnetic (EM) radiation during normal operation. The process of communicating with other machines or peripheral equipment creates emanations that can be intercepted. It's even possible to re-create keyboard input or monitor output by intercepting and processing electromagnetic radiation from the keyboard and computer monitor. You can also detect and read network packets passively (that is, without actually tapping into the cable) as they pass along a network segment. These emanation leaks can cause serious security issues but are generally easy to address.

The easiest way to eliminate electromagnetic radiation interception is to reduce emanation through cable shielding or conduit and block unauthorized personnel and devices from getting too close to equipment or cabling by applying physical security controls. By reducing the signal strength and increasing the physical buffer around sensitive equipment, you can dramatically reduce the risk of signal interception.

As discussed previously, several TEMPEST technologies could provide protection against EM radiation eavesdropping. These include Faraday cages, jamming or noise generators, and control zones. A *Faraday cage* is a special enclosure that acts as an EM capacitor. It often resembles a copper-wire-mesh box. When a Faraday cage is in use, no EM signals can enter or leave the area enclosed. *Jamming or noise generators* use the idea that it is difficult or impossible to retrieve a signal when there is too much interference. Thus, by broadcasting your own interference, you can prevent unwanted EM interception. The only issue with this concept is that you have to ensure that the interference won't affect the normal operations of your devices. One way to ensure that is to use *control zones*, which are Faraday cages used to block purposely broadcast interference. For example, if you wanted to use wireless networking within a few rooms of your office but not allow it anywhere else, you could enclose those rooms in a single Faraday cage and then plant several noise generators outside the control zone. This would allow normal wireless networking within the designated rooms but completely prevent normal use and eavesdropping anywhere outside those designated areas.

# Summary

Secure systems are not just assembled. They are designed to support security. Systems that must be secure are judged for their ability to support and enforce the security policy. This process of evaluating the effectiveness of a computer system is certification. The certification process is the technical evaluation of a system's ability to meet its design goals. Once a system has satisfactorily passed the technical evaluation, the management of an organization begins the formal acceptance of the system. The formal acceptance process is accreditation.

The entire certification and accreditation process depends on standard evaluation criteria. Several criteria exist for evaluating computer security systems. The earliest criteria,

TCSEC, was developed by the U.S. Department of Defense. TCSEC, also called the Orange Book, provides criteria to evaluate the functionality and assurance of a system's security components. ITSEC is an alternative to the TCSEC guidelines and is used more often in European countries. Regardless of which criteria you use, the evaluation process includes reviewing each security control for compliance with the security policy. The better a system enforces the good behavior of subjects' access to objects, the higher the security rating.

When security systems are designed, it is often helpful to create a security model to represent the methods the system will use to implement the security policy. We discussed several security models in this chapter. The Bell-LaPadula model supports data confidentiality only. It was designed for the military and satisfies military concerns. The Biba model and the Clark-Wilson model address the integrity of data and do so in different ways. These two security models are appropriate for commercial applications.

All of this understanding must culminate into an effective system security implementation in terms of preventive, detective, and corrective controls. That's why you must also know the access control models and their functions. This includes the state machine model, Bell-LaPadula, Biba, Clark-Wilson, the information flow model, the noninterference model, the Take-Grant model, the access control matrix model, and the Brewer and Nash model.

No matter how sophisticated a security model is, flaws exist that attackers can exploit. Some flaws, such as buffer overflows and maintenance hooks, are introduced by programmers, whereas others, such as covert channels, are architectural design issues. It is important to understand the impact of such issues and modify the security architecture when appropriate to compensate.

# Exam Essentials

**Know details about each of the access control models.** Know the access control models and their functions. The state machine model ensures that all instances of subjects accessing objects are secure. The information flow model is designed to prevent unauthorized, insecure, or restricted information flow. The noninterference model prevents the actions of one subject from affecting the system state or actions of another subject. The Take-Grant model dictates how rights can be passed from one subject to another or from a subject to an object. An access control matrix is a table of subjects and objects that indicates the actions or functions that each subject can perform on each object. Bell-LaPadula subjects have a clearance level that allows them to access only those objects with the corresponding classification levels. This enforces confidentiality. Biba prevents subjects with lower security levels from writing to objects at higher security levels. Clark-Wilson is an integrity model that relies on auditing to ensure that unauthorized subjects cannot access objects and that authorized users access objects properly. Biba and Clark-Wilson enforce integrity.

**Know the definitions of certification and accreditation.**   Certification is the technical evaluation of each part of a computer system to assess its concordance with security standards. Accreditation is the process of formal acceptance of a certified configuration from a designated authority.

**Be able to describe open and closed systems.**   Open systems are designed using industry standards and are usually easy to integrate with other open systems. Closed systems are generally proprietary hardware and/or software. Their specifications are not normally published, and they are usually harder to integrate with other systems.

**Know what confinement, bounds, and isolation are.**   Confinement restricts a process to reading from and writing to certain memory locations. Bounds are the limits of memory a process cannot exceed when reading or writing. Isolation is the mode a process runs in when it is confined through the use of memory bounds.

**Be able to define *object* and *subject* in terms of access.**   The subject of an access is the user or process that makes a request to access a resource. The object of an access request is the resource a user or process wants to access.

**Know how security controls work and what they do.**   Security controls use access rules to limit the access by a subject to an object.

**Be able to list the classes of TCSEC, ITSEC, and the Common Criteria.**   The classes of TCSEC include verified protection, mandatory protection, discretionary protection, and minimal protection. Table 12.4 covers and compares equivalent and applicable rankings for TCSEC, ITSEC, and the CC (remember that functionality ratings from F7 to F10 in ITSEC have no corresponding ratings in TCSEC).

**Define a trusted computing base (TCB).**   A TCB is the combination of hardware, software, and controls that form a trusted base that enforces the security policy.

**Be able to explain what a security perimeter is.**   A security perimeter is the imaginary boundary that separates the TCB from the rest of the system. TCB components communicate with non-TCB components using trusted paths.

**Know what the reference monitor and the security kernel are.**   The reference monitor is the logical part of the TCB that confirms whether a subject has the right to use a resource prior to granting access. The security kernel is the collection of the TCB components that implement the functionality of the reference monitor.

**Be able to explain what covert channels are.**   A covert channel is any method that is used to pass information but that is not normally used for information.

**Understand what buffer overflows and input checking are.**   A buffer overflow occurs when the programmer fails to check the size of input data prior to writing the data into a specific memory location. In fact, any failure to validate input data could result in a security violation.

**Describe common flaws to security architectures.**   In addition to buffer overflows, programmers can leave back doors and privileged programs on a system after it is deployed. Even well-written systems can be susceptible to time-of-check-to-time-of-use (TOCTTOU) attacks. Any state change could be a potential window of opportunity for an attacker to compromise a system.

# Written Lab

1.  Name at least seven security models.
2.  Describe the primary components of TCB.
3.  What are the two rules or principles of the Bell-LaPadula security model? Also, what are the two rules of Biba?
4.  What is the difference between open and closed systems and open and closed source?

# Answers to Written Lab

1.  Security models include state machine, information flow, noninterference, Take-Grant, access control matrix, Bell-LaPadula, Biba, Clark-Wilson, and Brewer and Nash (aka Chinese Wall).

2.  The primary components of the TCB are the hardware and software elements used to enforce the security policy (these elements are called the TCB), the security perimeter distinguishing and separating TCB components from non-TCB components, and the reference monitor that serves as an access control device across the security perimeter.

3.  The two rules of Bell-LaPadula are the simple rule of no read up and the star rule of no write down. The two rules of Biba are the simple rule of no read down and the star rule of no write up.

4.  An open system is one with published APIs that allow third parties to develop products to interact with it. A closed system is one that is proprietary with no third-party product support. Open source is a coding stance that allows others to view the source code of a program. Closed source is an opposing coding stance that keeps source code confidential.

# Review Questions

1. What is system certification?

    **A.** Formal acceptance of a stated system configuration

    **B.** A technical evaluation of each part of a computer system to assess its compliance with security standards

    **C.** A functional evaluation of the manufacturer's goals for each hardware and software component to meet integration standards

    **D.** A manufacturer's certificate stating that all components were installed and configured correctly

2. What is system accreditation?

    **A.** Formal acceptance of a stated system configuration

    **B.** A functional evaluation of the manufacturer's goals for each hardware and software component to meet integration standards

    **C.** Acceptance of test results that prove the computer system enforces the security policy

    **D.** The process to specify secure communication between machines

3. What is a closed system?

    **A.** A system designed around final, or closed, standards

    **B.** A system that includes industry standards

    **C.** A proprietary system that uses unpublished protocols

    **D.** Any machine that does not run Windows

4. Which best describes a confined or constrained process?

    **A.** A process that can run only for a limited time

    **B.** A process that can run only during certain times of the day

    **C.** A process that can access only certain memory locations

    **D.** A process that controls access to an object

5. What is an access object?

    **A.** A resource that a user or process wants to access

    **B.** A user or process that wants to access a resource

    **C.** A list of valid access rules

    **D.** The sequence of valid access types

6.  What is a security control?
    A.  A security component that stores attributes that describe an object
    B.  A document that lists all data classification types
    C.  A list of valid access rules
    D.  A mechanism that limits access to an object

7.  For what type of information system security accreditation are the applications and systems at a specific, self-contained location evaluated?
    A.  System accreditation
    B.  Site accreditation
    C.  Application accreditation
    D.  Type accreditation

8.  How many major categories do the TCSEC criteria define?
    A.  Two
    B.  Three
    C.  Four
    D.  Five

9.  What is a trusted computing base (TCB)?
    A.  Hosts on your network that support secure transmissions
    B.  The operating system kernel and device drivers
    C.  The combination of hardware, software, and controls that work together to enforce a security policy
    D.  The software and controls that certify a security policy

10. What is a security perimeter? (Choose all that apply.)
    A.  The boundary of the physically secure area surrounding your system
    B.  The imaginary boundary that separates the TCB from the rest of the system
    C.  The network where your firewall resides
    D.  Any connections to your computer system

11. What part of the TCB concept validates access to every resource prior to granting the requested access?
    A.  TCB partition
    B.  Trusted library
    C.  Reference monitor
    D.  Security kernel

**12.** What is the best definition of a security model?

    **A.** A security model states policies an organization must follow.

    **B.** A security model provides a framework to implement a security policy.

    **C.** A security model is a technical evaluation of each part of a computer system to assess its concordance with security standards.

    **D.** A security model is the process of formal acceptance of a certified configuration.

**13.** Which security models are built on a state machine model?

    **A.** Bell-LaPadula and Take-Grant

    **B.** Biba and Clark-Wilson

    **C.** Clark-Wilson and Bell-LaPadula

    **D.** Bell-LaPadula and Biba

**14.** Which security model addresses data confidentiality?

    **A.** Bell-LaPadula

    **B.** Biba

    **C.** Clark-Wilson

    **D.** Brewer and Nash

**15.** Which Bell-LaPadula property keeps lower-level subjects from accessing objects with a higher security level?

    **A.** * (star) Security Property

    **B.** No write up property

    **C.** No read up property

    **D.** No read down property

**16.** What is a covert channel?

    **A.** A method that is used to pass information and that is not normally used for communication

    **B.** Any communication used to transmit secret or top-secret data

    **C.** A trusted path between the TCB and the rest of the system

    **D.** Any channel that crosses the security perimeter

**17.** What term describes an entry point that only the developer knows about into a system?

    **A.** Maintenance hook

    **B.** Covert channel

    **C.** Buffer overflow

    **D.** Trusted path

**18.** What is the time of check?

**A.** The length of time it takes a subject to check the status of an object

**B.** The time at which the subject checks on the status of the object

**C.** The time at which a subject accesses an object

**D.** The time between checking and accessing an object

**19.** How can electromagnetic radiation be used to compromise a system?

**A.** Electromagnetic radiation can be concentrated to disrupt computer operation.

**B.** Electromagnetic radiation makes some protocols inoperable.

**C.** Electromagnetic radiation can be intercepted.

**D.** Electromagnetic radiation is necessary for some communication protocol protection schemes to work.

**20.** What is the most common programmer-generated security flaw?

**A.** TOCTTOU vulnerability

**B.** Buffer overflow

**C.** Inadequate control checks

**D.** Improper logon authentication

# Answers to Review Questions

1.  B. A system certification is a technical evaluation. Option A describes system accreditation. Options C and D refer to manufacturer standards, not implementation standards.

2.  A. Accreditation is the formal acceptance process. Option B is not an appropriate answer because it addresses manufacturer standards. Options C and D are incorrect because there is no way to prove that a configuration enforces a security policy and accreditation does not entail secure communication specification.

3.  C. A closed system is one that uses largely proprietary or unpublished protocols and standards. Options A and D do not describe any particular systems, and Option B describes an open system.

4.  C. A constrained process is one that can access only certain memory locations. Options A, B, and D do not describe a constrained process.

5.  A. An object is a resource a user or process want to access. Option A describes an access object.

6.  D. A control limits access to an object to protect it from misuse by unauthorized users.

7.  B. The applications and systems at a specific, self-contained location are evaluated for DITSCAP and NIACAP site accreditation.

8.  C. TCSEC defines four major categories: category A is verified protection, category B is mandatory protection, category C is discretionary protection, and category D is minimal protection.

9.  C. The TCB is the combination of hardware, software, and controls that work together to enforce a security policy.

10.  A, B. Although the most correct answer in the context of this chapter is option B, option A is also a correct answer in the context of physical security.

11.  C. Option D, the security kernel, is the collection of TCB components that work together to implement the reference monitor functions. In other words, the security kernel is the implementation of the reference monitor concept. Options A and B are not valid TCB concept components.

12.  B. Option B is the only option that correctly defines a security model. Options A, C, and D define part of a security policy and the certification and accreditation process.

13.  D. The Bell-LaPadula and Biba models are built on the state machine model.

14.  A. Only the Bell-LaPadula model addresses data confidentiality. The Biba and Clark-Wilson models address data integrity. The Brewer and Nash model prevents conflicts of interest.

15.  C. The no read up property, also called the Simple Security Policy, prohibits subjects from reading a higher security level object.

**16.** A.  A covert channel is any method that is used to secretly pass data and that is not normally used for communication. All the other options describe normal communication channels.

**17.** A.  An entry point that only the developer knows about into a system is a maintenance hook, or back door.

**18.** B.  Option B defines the time of check (TOC), which is the time at which a subject verifies the status of an object.

**19.** C.  If a receiver is in close enough proximity to an electromagnetic radiation source, it can be intercepted.

**20.** B.  By far, the buffer overflow is the most common, and most avoidable, programmer-generated vulnerability.

# Chapter

# 13

# Administrative Management

## THE CISSP EXAM TOPICS COVERED IN THIS CHAPTER INCLUDE:

✓ **Operations Security**

- Understand the following security concepts

  - Need-to-know/least privilege; separation of duties and responsibilities; monitor special privileges (e.g., operators, administrators); job rotation; marking, handling, storing, and destroying of sensitive information and media; record retention

- Employ resource protection

  - Media management; asset management; personnel privacy and safety

- Understand configuration management concepts (e.g., versioning, baselining)

All companies must take into account any issues that can make day-to-day operations susceptible to breaches in security. *Personnel management* is a form of administrative control, or administrative management, and is an important factor in maintaining operations security. Clearly defined personnel management practices must be included in your security policy and subsequent formal security structure documentation (including all necessary relevant standards, guidelines, and procedures).

Operations security topics are related to personnel management because personnel management can directly affect security and daily operations. They are included in the Operations Security domain of the Common Body of Knowledge (CBK) for the CISSP certification exam, which deals with topics and issues related to maintaining an established and secure IT environment. Operations security concerns itself with maintaining an IT infrastructure after it has been designed and deployed: That means using hardware controls, media controls, and subject (user) controls designed to protect against asset threats.

This domain is discussed in this chapter and further in the following chapter (Chapter 14, "Auditing and Monitoring"). Be sure to read and study both chapters to ensure your understanding of the essential anti-malware and operations material.

# Operations Security Concepts

The primary purpose for operations security is to safeguard information assets that reside in a system on a day-to-day basis, to identify and safeguard any vulnerabilities that might be present in the system, and to prevent any exploitation of threats. Administrators sometimes call the relationship between assets, vulnerabilities, and threats an *operations security triple*. The trick in the arena then becomes how best to tackle the operations security triple.

The Operations Security domain is a broad collection of many concepts that are both distinct and interrelated, including antivirus or antimalware management, operational assurance, backup maintenance, changes in location, privileges, trusted recovery, configuration and change management control, due care and due diligence, privacy, security, and operations controls.

The following sections highlight these important day-to-day issues that affect company operations by discussing them as they relate to maintaining security.

# Antivirus Management

Viruses represent the most common type of security breach in the IT world. Any communications pathway can and will be exploited as a delivery mechanism for a virus or other malicious code (more generically called malware). Viruses proliferate via email (the most common means), websites, shared documents, and even occasionally within tainted commercial software. In 2001, Microsoft was dealt a blow when the FunLove virus infected security hotfix files on partner and premier support sites, and in 2007, Windows Vista Home Premium came preinstalled on a batch of notebooks accompanied by a 13-year-old boot sector virus named Stoned.Angelina—and these are just two examples that targeted a high-profile vendor. Antivirus management is the design, deployment, and maintenance of an antivirus solution for your IT environment.

If users are allowed to install and execute software without restriction, then the IT infrastructure becomes absolutely vulnerable to virus infections. To provide a more virus-free environment, make sure that software changes, installations, and upgrades are rigidly controlled. Users should be able to install and execute only company-approved and vendor-distributed software. All new software should be thoroughly tested and scanned before it is deployed or distributed on a production network. Even commercial software has become an inadvertent carrier of viruses, worms, and other malware, which happened again to Microsoft in 2002 when it accidentally distributed the Nimda worm to South Korea as it distributed Korean-language versions of Visual Studio .NET.

Users should be trained in safe computing best practices, especially those granted Internet access or who use any form of email. In areas where technical controls cannot prevent virus infections, users must be trained to prevent them through safe completion of their daily duties. User awareness training must include information about handling attachments or downloads from unknown senders and unrequested attachments of any kind. Users should be told never to test an executable by executing it directly. All instances of suspect software should be reported immediately to a security administrator.

Antivirus software should be deployed at multiple levels on a network. All traffic—including internal, inbound, and outbound—should be scanned for viruses. A virus-scanning tool should be present on all border connection points, on all servers, and on all clients. Installing products from different vendors in each of these three arenas can provide a more thorough and foolproof scanning gauntlet.

Try to avoid installing more than one virus-scanning tool on any single system. Though defense in depth is often merited and in many cases warranted, doubling-up antivirus applications can cause unrecoverable system failure in some cases and often consumes excessive memory and CPU cycles.

Seek to maintain 100 percent virus-free servers and 100 percent virus-free backups. To accomplish the former, you must scan every bit of data before it is allowed into or onto a server for processing or storage. To accomplish the latter, you must scan every bit of data before writing it onto backup media. Maintaining virus-free systems and backups enables efficient, timely recovery from a virus infection.

In addition to using a multilevel or *concentric circle* antivirus strategy, you must routinely maintain all elements that implement the strategy. A concentric circle strategy basically consists of multiple layers of antivirus scanning throughout the environment to ensure that all current data and backups remain free from viruses. Regular updates to virus signature and definitions databases should be automated. However, you should distribute updates only after verifying that the are benign. It is possible for virus lists or engine updates to crash some systems. Many organizations employ the following strategy: (1) install AV software on all systems including desktops and servers, (2) install specialized AV software on email systems, and (3) perform content filtering in the firewall (or a special content-filtering appliance).

Maintain constant vigilance by tracking notification newsletters, mailing lists, RSS feeds, and vendor sites. Whenever a new virus epidemic breaks out, take appropriate action: Shut down or tightly restrict access to email or the Internet (if at all possible or practical) until a workable solution/repair/inoculation becomes available.

---

### Multiple Defenses

*Defense in depth* is a common security strategy used to provide a protective multilayer barrier against various forms of attack. It's reasonable to assume that there is greater difficulty in passing bad traffic or data through a network heavily fortified by a firewall, an IDS, and a diligent administration staff than one with a firewall alone. Why shouldn't you double up your defenses?

Jonas is an IT administrator for a fledgling Class C network where Kelly is employed as a data entry specialist. Kelly receives emails that contain all sorts of multimedia attachments as part of her daily duties, which also explains why she receives a ton of spam, spyware, and Trojan horses (among other unwanted and unsolicited items).

Jonas explains to Kelly that she needs more than just a virus scanner to prevent unwanted intrusion or inclusion of undesirable software. What might he suggest Kelly do to create a defense-in-depth strategy on her desktop? At a minimum, added antispyware coverage appears warranted, and it will also be useful to route Kelly's incoming email through a third-party spam-screening/filtering service (like those from companies such as Spam Arrest, MailWasher, and so forth).

---

## Operational Assurance and Life Cycle Assurance

*Assurance* is the degree of confidence you can place in the satisfaction of security needs for a computer, network, solution, and so on. It is based on how well a specific system complies with stated security needs and how well it supports the security services it provides.

Assurance was discussed in Chapter 12, "Principles of Security Models," but there is another element of assurance that applies to the Operation Security domain.

The Trusted Computer System Evaluation Criteria (TCSEC) guidelines are used to assign a level of assurance to systems. TCSEC, or the Orange Book, also defines two additional types or levels of assurance: operational assurance and life cycle assurance. As you are aware, TCSEC was replaced by the Common Criteria in October 2002. It is, however, important to be aware of TCSEC-related material simply as a means to convey concepts and theories about security evaluation. Thus, you don't need to know the complete details of these two assurance levels, but you should be familiar with a few specific issues.

Operational assurance focuses on basic features and architecture of systems that lend themselves to supporting security. There are five requirements or elements that apply to operational assurance:

- System architecture. (We discuss system architecture in Chapter 7, "Data and Application Security Issues" in the sections on distributed environments, object request brokers, Microsoft component models, DBMS architecture, and other applications.)

- System integrity. (For more information, see the section "Protection Mechanisms" in Chapter 11, and also see Chapter 12.)

- Covert channel analysis. (For more information, see Chapter 12.)

- Trusted facility management. (Check out Chapter 19, "Physical Security Requirements," for information about trusted facility management.)

- Trusted recovery. (We cover this subject later in this chapter.)

Life cycle assurance focuses on the controls and standards that are necessary to design, build, and maintain a system. The following items represent the four requirements or elements for life cycle assurance:

- Security testing

- Design specification and testing

- Configuration management

- Trusted distribution

## Backup Maintenance

Backing up critical information is essential to maintaining the availability and integrity of data. Systems fail for various reasons, such as hardware failure, physical damage, software corruption, or malicious destruction from intrusions and attacks. Providing ready access to a reliable backup is the best form of assurance that data on an affected system is not permanently lost. Without a backup, it is often impossible to restore data to its pre-disaster state. A backup can be considered reliable only if it is periodically tested and routinely maintained. Testing involves restoring files from backup media, then checking their integrity to ensure that they're readable and correct.

Backups are an essential part of maintaining operations security and are discussed further in Chapter 16, "Disaster Recovery Planning."

## Changes in Workstation/Location

You can use changes in a user's workstation or in their physical location within an organization to improve or maintain security. Similar to job rotation, changing a user's workstation prevents a user from altering the system or installing unapproved software because the next person to use the system is likely to discover it.

Having nonpermanent workstations encourages users to keep all materials stored on network servers where it can be easily protected, overseen, and audited. It also discourages storing personal information on the system as a whole. A periodic change in the physical location of a user's workspace can also deter collusion because employees are less likely to be able to convince colleagues with whom they're not familiar to perform unauthorized or illegal activities.

### Preventing Bad Behavior

Preventive controls are crucial in the workplace, especially where sensitive data is involved. You can always instruct employees not to act on information in an illicit or illegal manner, but you cannot be sure they will always follow through. A preventive control can help you steer employees into behaving correctly and at the very least hold them accountable if they do misbehave on the system.

Lindsey is responsible for processing large volumes of privileged client information as part of her job description. Periodically, her activities and access to certain information changes, but her role and responsibility remains constant. Michael, a system administrator who oversees workstation and responsibility rotation, cannot seem to adequately explain why her contact with sensitive information dictates this rotation cycle.

How might you approach the subject and explain to Lindsey that she isn't being punished for any of her actions and that this is a necessary and vital security function? You might point out the exposure that could result from unintended disclosure, set up two accounts (one for everyday, routine office work and the other for handling client data only), and point out that a judicious separation of roles protects everybody and makes her own job both safer and easier. In particular, you might point out how rotation prevents Lindsey and those around her from falling into predictable, everyday habits or behaviors that might create opportunities to compromise security. Change not only does a body good, but it also helps prevent falling into ruts that could pose potential security problems.

Also consider controlling portable installation media at every critical junction on the network, wherever there is a user with a PC serving as a potential vector for viral outbreak. Removable media devices are relatively cheap, generously capacious, and easily portable, which makes them a perfect vehicle to transmit digital disease and pestilence. Create *choke points* to deliberately restrict or obstruct use of removable media on specified workstations where there's no removable storage, then require users to work on such machines to create a better barrier against viral attack.

Removable storage media and drives vary widely among computing environments and include USB-based flash drives, memory cards and memory card readers, floppy drives and Zip disks (where applicable), CD/DVD drives, and self-contained storage units generally known as *external storage drives* (network attached, USB attached, eSATA or FireWire attached, and otherwise).

## Need to Know and the Principle of Least Privilege

Need to know and the principle of least privilege are two standard axioms in high-security environments. A user must have a need to know to gain access to data or resources. Even if that user has an equal or greater security classification than the requested information, without a need to know, they are denied access. A *need to know* is the requirement to have access to, knowledge about, or possession of data or a resource to perform specific work tasks. The *principle of least privilege* is the notion that, in a secure environment, users should be granted the least amount of access possible to be able to complete their work tasks.

### Periodic Reviews of User Account Management

Many administrators utilize periodic reviews of user account management to revisit and maintain processes and procedures employed by the administrative staff in supporting users. Such reviews should include examining how well the principle of least privilege is enforced, whether inactive accounts are still in use, whether out-of-use accounts have been disabled or deleted, and whether or not all current practices are approved by management and consistent with current security policies.

Reviewing user account management typically does not address whether some specific password conforms to stated company password policy. That issue is addressed by enrollment tools, password policies, and periodic penetration testing or ethical hacking.

It is also important to note that the actions involved in adding, removing, and managing user account settings fall under the purview of the account administrators or operations administrators, not that of a security administrator. However, it is the responsibility of security administrators to set clearances for users in a mandatory access control (MAC) environment.

# Privileged Operations Functions

*Privileged operations functions* are activities that require special access or privileges to be performed within a secured IT environment. In most cases, these functions are restricted to administrators and system operators. Maintaining privileged control over these functions is essential to sustain the system's security. Many of these functions could be easily exploited to violate confidentiality, integrity, or availability of a system's assets.

The following list includes some examples of privileged operations functions:

- Using operating system control commands
- Configuring interfaces
- Accessing audit logs
- Managing user accounts
- Configuring security mechanism controls
- Running script/task automation tools
- Backing up and restoring the system
- Controlling communication
- Using database recovery tools and log files
- Controlling system reboots

Managing privileged access is an important part of keeping security under control. In addition to restricting privileged operations functions, you should employ separation of duties. Separation of duties ensures that no single person has total control over a system's or environment's security mechanisms. This is necessary to ensure that no single person can compromise the system as a whole. It can also be called a form of *split knowledge*. In deployment, separation of duties is enforced by dividing the top- and mid-level administrative capabilities and functions among multiple trusted users.

Further control and restriction of privileged capabilities can be implemented by using two-person controls and rotation of duties. *Two-person control* is the configuration of privileged activities so that they require two administrators to work together to complete a task. The necessity of two operators also confers the benefits of peer review and reduced likelihood of collusion and fraud. *Rotation of duties* is the security control that involves switching several privileged security or operational roles among several users on a regular basis.

For example, if an organization has divided its administrative activities into six distinct roles or job descriptions, then six or seven people need to be cross-trained for those roles. Each person could work in a specific role for two to three months, and then everyone in the group would switch or rotate into another role. When the organization employs more than the necessary minimum number of trained administrators, each rotation leaves out one person, who can take some vacation time or serve as a fill-in if needed. Using rotation of duties as a security control provides for peer review, reduces collusion and fraud, and enables cross-training. Cross-training makes your environment less dependent on any single individual.

## Trusted Recovery

For a secured system, *trusted recovery* means recovering securely from operation failures or system crashes. The purpose of trusted recovery is to provide assurance that after a failure or crash, the rebooted system is no less secure than it was before that failure or crash occurred.

You must address two elements of the recovery process to implement a trusted solution. The first element is failure preparation. In most cases, this simply means deployment of a reliable backup solution that keeps a current backup of all data. A reliable backup solution also implies that there is a means by which data on the backup media can be restored in a protected and efficient manner. The second element is the process of system recovery. The system should be forced to reboot into a single-user nonprivileged state. This means that the system should reboot so that a normal user account can be used to log in and that the system does not grant unauthorized access to users. System recovery also includes the restoration of all affected files and services actively in use on the system at the time of the failure or crash. Any missing or damaged files are restored, any changes to classification labels corrected, and settings on all security critical files are then verified.

Trusted recovery is a security mechanism discussed in the Common Criteria. The Common Criteria define three types or hierarchical levels of trusted recovery:

**Manual recovery**   An administrator is required to manually perform the actions necessary to implement a secured or trusted recovery after a failure or system crash.

**Automated recovery**   The system itself is able to perform trusted recovery activities to restore a system, but only against a single failure.

**Automated recovery without undue loss**   The system is able to perform trusted recovery activities to restore itself. This level of trusted recovery allows for additional steps to provide verification and protection of classified objects. The additional protection mechanisms may include restoring corrupted files, rebuilding data from transaction logs, and verifying the integrity of key system and security components.

What happens when a systems suffers from an uncontrolled trusted computing base (TCB, the processing platforms on which secure processing normally occurs) or media failure? Such failures may compromise the stability and security of the environment, and the only possible response is to terminate the current environment and re-create the environment through rebooting. Related to trusted recovery, an emergency system restart is the feature of a security system that forces an immediate reboot once the system goes down.

# Configuration and Change Management Control

Once a system has been properly secured, it is important to keep that security intact. Change in a secure environment can introduce loopholes, overlaps, missing objects, and oversights that can lead to new vulnerabilities. The only way to maintain security in the face of change is to manage change systematically. Typically, this involves extensive logging, auditing, and monitoring of activities related to security controls and mechanisms. The resulting data is then used to identify agents of change, whether objects, subjects, programs, communication pathways, or even the network itself. The means to provide this function is to deploy *configuration management* control or change management control. Such mechanisms ensure that any alterations or changes to a system do not result in diminished security.

Changes can create unintended side effects causing outages if not properly controlled and managed. For example, suppose an administrator makes a change to one system with the intention of resolving a problem, but that change then affects operability of other systems. This directly affects the *A* in the CIA triad, availability. Change management processes give various IT experts an opportunity to review proposed changes for unintended side effects before they are implemented and lets them check their work in controlled circumstances before propagating changes into production environments.

Configuration/change management controls provide a process by which all system changes are tracked, audited, controlled, identified, and approved. It requires that all system changes undergo a rigorous testing procedure before being deployed in the production environment. It also requires documentation of any changes to user work tasks and training for any affected users. Configuration/change management controls should minimize the effect on security from any alteration to the system. They often provide a means to roll back a change if it is found to cause a negative or unwanted effect on the system or on security.

Five steps or phases are involved in configuration/change management control:

1.  Applying to introduce a change
2.  Cataloging the intended change
3.  Scheduling the change
4.  Implementing the change
5.  Reporting the change to the appropriate parties

When a configuration/change management control solution is enforced, it creates complete documentation for all changes to a system. This provides a trail of information if the change needs to be reversed. It also provides a road map or procedure to follow if the same change is implemented on other systems. When a change is properly documented, such documentation assists administrators in minimizing the negative effects of the change throughout the environment.

## Controlling Change

Unauthorized changes (possibly by unauthorized parties) to configurations, installations, or operations necessitate change management controls. Software publishers, hardware vendors, and other involved parties can be adversely affected by unverified or undesirable changes to important system parameters or properties.

A given attack may involve downgrading software to some known vulnerable state or changing critical system properties to introduce a new vulnerability. Attackers may even assert themselves through email correspondence as official representatives to encourage unsuspecting administrators to install trapdoors on their networks.

What sort of integrity checks, preventive measures, and change control might you include to prevent such attacks from succeeding against your network? To begin with, a formal change control mechanism will help document and track valid changes and immediately identify bogus ones as unscheduled and therefore unauthorized. Regular integrity checks like those from programs such as Tripwire can help flag unexpected or unauthorized changes and make it easy to reverse or repair them. Stronger access controls may very well block unauthorized changes from occurring as well.

Configuration/change management control is a mandatory element for some security assurance requirements (SARs) in the ISO Common Criteria, but it's recommended for all situations. Ultimately, change management improves the security of an environment by protecting implemented security from unintentional, tangential, or malicious diminishments. Those in charge of change management should oversee alterations to every aspect of a system, including hardware configuration and system and application software. It should be included in their design, development, testing, evaluation, implementation, distribution, evolution, growth, operation, and application of modifications.

Change management requires a detailed inventory of every component and configuration. It also requires the collection and maintenance of complete documentation for every system component (including hardware and software) and for everything from configuration settings to security features. This process, called versioning, is the act of using a labeling/numbering system to differentiate between different software sets and configurations across multiple machines or at different points in time on a single machine. Versioning is used to keep track of changes over time to deployed software. Versioning can also be tied in with baselining. The first deployed version of a software set and its configuration can be defined as the baseline. Each subsequent modified version on other systems or on the original system will be assigned unique versioning labels. This process of versioning and baselining provides a form of change documentation and a control tracking system.

Another aspect of configuration and change management control is the management of patches, updates, and service packs. The installation of improvement modules from software and hardware vendors is another form of change that must be controlled. Patch management, vulnerability management, and even update management are additional areas of change that must be audited, reviewed, tested, and approved before they may be applied to production equipment.

## Standards of Due Care and Due Diligence

*Due care* means using reasonable care to protect the interests of an organization. *Due diligence* is practicing those activities that maintain due care. For example, due care means developing a formalized security structure containing a security policy, standards, baselines, guidelines, and procedures. Due diligence means continued application of this security structure onto the IT infrastructure for an organization. Operational security is the ongoing maintenance of continued due care and due diligence by all responsible parties within an organization.

In today's business environment, prudence is mandatory: Showing due care and due diligence is the only way to disprove negligence should any losses occur. Likewise, senior management must show due care and due diligence to reduce their culpability and liability if a loss is experienced. Otherwise, senior management could be responsible for monetary damages up to $10 million or twice the gain of the offender for nonperformance of due diligence in accordance with the U.S. Federal Sentencing Guidelines of 1991.

## Privacy and Protection

*Privacy* means protecting personal information from disclosure to any unauthorized individual or entity. In today's online world, the line between public and private information is often blurry. For example, is information about your web-surfing habits private or public? Can that information be gathered legally without your consent? And can the gathering organization sell that information for a profit that you don't share in? In addition, your personal information includes more than information about your online habits; it also includes who you are (name, address, phone, race, religion, age, and so on), your health and medical records, your financial records, and even your criminal or legal records. In general such information falls under the heading of personally identifiable information, aka PII, as described in the NIST publication *Guide to Protecting the Confidentiality of Personally Identifiable Information (PII)* available online at http://csrc.nist.gov/publications/nistpubs/800-122/sp800-122.pdf.

Dealing with privacy is a requirement for any organization that has employees. Thus, privacy is a central issue for all organizations. Protection of privacy should be a core mission or goal set forth in the security policy for any organization. Personnel privacy issues are discussed at greater length in Chapter 17, "Law and Investigations."

# Legal Requirements

Every organization operates within a certain industry and country. Both of these entities impose legal requirements, restrictions, and regulations on the practices of organizations that fall within their realm. These *legal requirements* can apply to licensed use of software, hiring restrictions, handling of sensitive materials, and compliance with safety regulations.

Complying with all applicable legal requirements is a key part of sustaining security. The legal requirements for an industry and a country (and often also a state and city) must be considered a baseline or foundation upon which the remainder of the security infrastructure is built.

# Illegal Activities

*Illegal activities* are actions that violate some legal restriction, regulation, or requirement. They include fraud, misappropriation, unauthorized disclosure, theft, destruction, espionage, entrapment, and so on. A secure environment should provide mechanisms to hinder illegal activities and provide a means to track them and assign accountability to individuals perpetrating any such offenses.

Preventive control mechanisms include identification and authentication, access control, separation of duties, job rotation, mandatory vacations, background screening, awareness training, least privilege, and many more. Detective mechanisms include auditing, intrusion detection systems, and more.

# Record Retention

*Record retention* is an organizational policy that defines what information is maintained and for how long. In most cases, the records in question are audit trails of user activity. This may include file and resource access, logon patterns, email, and the use of privileges. Note that in some legal jurisdictions, users must also be informed that their activities are being tracked.

Depending upon your industry and your relationship with the government, you may need to retain records for three years, seven years, or indefinitely. In most cases, a separate backup mechanism is used to create archived copies of sensitive audit trails and accountability information. This allows the main data backup system to periodically reuse its media without violating the requirement to retain audit trails and the like.

If data about individuals is being retained by your organization (such as a conditional employment agreement or a use agreement), those employees and customers need to be aware of what information is being kept. In many cases, notification is a legal requirement; in others, it is simply a courtesy. In either case, it is a good idea to discuss the issue with appropriate legal counsel.

# Sensitive Information and Media

Managing information and media properly—especially in a high-security environment in which sensitive, confidential, or proprietary data is processed—is crucial to the security and stability of an organization. Because the value of the stored data greatly exceeds the cost of the storage media, always purchase media of the highest quality. In addition to media selection, there are several key areas of information and media management that must be addressed: marking, handling, storage, life span, reuse, and destruction. Marking, handling, storing media and observing its life span ensure the viability of data on a storage media. Reuse and destruction focus on destroying the hosted data, not retaining it. Proper marking, handling, storing, and destroying of sensitive information and the media it is housed on is an essential part of maintaining overall organizational security through media management and asset management.

## Marking and Labeling Media

*Marking* media is the simple and obvious activity of clearly and accurately defining its contents. The most important aspect of marking is to indicate the security classification for the data stored on the media so that the media itself can be handled properly. Tapes with unclassified data do not need as much security in their storage and transport as do tapes with classified data. Data labels should be created automatically and stored as part of the backup set on the media.

Additionally, a physical label should be applied to the media and maintained over its entire lifetime. Media used to store classified information should never be reused to store less-sensitive data. Media labels help ensure proper handling of hosted sensitive, classified, or confidential data. All removable media, including tapes, USB drives, floppies, CDs, hard drives, and printouts, should be labeled.

## Handling Media

*Handling* refers to the secured transportation of media from the point of purchase through storage and finally to destruction. Media must be handled in a manner consistent with the classification of the data it hosts. The environment within which media is stored can significantly affect its useful lifetime. For example, warm or dusty environments can damage tape media, shortening its life span. Strong magnetic fields can potentially disturb the contents of magnetic storage drives, physical and chemical delamination can ruin CD or DVD media, and so forth.

Here are some useful guidelines for handling media:

- Keep new media in its original sealed packaging until it's needed to protect it from dust and dirt.

- When opening a media package, take extra caution not to damage the media in any way. This includes avoiding sharp objects and not twisting or flexing the media.

- Avoid exposing the media to temperature extremes; it shouldn't be stored close to heaters, radiators, air conditioners, or other sources of extreme temperatures.

- Do not use media that has been damaged, exposed to abnormal levels of dust and dirt, or dropped.

- Media should be transported from one site to another in a temperature-controlled vehicle.

- Media should be protected from exposure to the outside environment; avoid sunlight, moisture, humidity, heat, and cold. Always transport media in an airtight, waterproof, secured container.

- Media should be acclimated for 24 hours before use.

- Appropriate security should be maintained over media from the point of departure from the backup device to the secured offsite storage facility. Media is vulnerable to damage and theft at any point during transportation.

- Appropriate security should be maintained over media at all other times (including when it's reused) throughout the lifetime of the media until destruction.

- Keep magnetic storage media away from strong magnetic fields and—in the case of sensitive drive electronics—store them in appropriately padded or protective containers.

- Avoid corrosive chemicals or physical abrasion when handling CD and DVD media, and utilize protective sleeves where possible.

- Never utilize adhesive tape (that you intend to later remove) on the printed or data-bearing top side of a CD or DVD.

## Storing Media

Media should be stored only in a secured location in which the temperature and humidity is controlled, and it should not be exposed to magnetic fields, especially tape media. Elevator motors, printers, and CRT monitors all have strong electric fields. The cleanliness of the storage area will directly affect the life span and usefulness of media. Access to the storage facility should be controlled at all times. Physical security is essential to maintaining the confidentiality, integrity, and availability of backup media.

## Managing Media Life Span

All media has a useful life span. Reusable media is subject to a *mean time to failure* (MTTF) that is usually represented in the number of times it can safely be reused. Most tape backup media can be reused 3 to 10 times. When media is reused, it must be properly cleared. *Clearing* is a method of sufficiently deleting data on media for reuse in the same secured environment. *Purging* means erasing the data so the media can be reused in a less-secure environment. Unless absolutely necessary, do not employ media purging. The cost of supplying each classification level with its own media is insignificant compared to the damage that can be caused by unwanted disclosure. If media will neither be archived nor be reused within the same environment, it should be securely destroyed.

Once a backup media has reached its MTTF, it should be destroyed. Securely destroying media that contained confidential and sensitive data is just as important as the storage of such media. When media is destroyed, it should be erased properly to remove magnetized data traces that remain, called *remanence* (for magnetic tape, a device called a degausser may be used to erase its contents, but this is not always sufficient to completely purge such media). Once properly purged, media should be physically destroyed to prevent easy reuse and attempted data gleaning through casual (keyboard attacks) or high-tech (laboratory attacks) means. Physical crushing is often sufficient, but incineration may be necessary.

## Preventing Disclosure via Reused Media

Preventing disclosure of information from backup media is an important aspect of maintaining operational security. Disclosure prevention must occur at numerous instances in the life span of media. It must be addressed upon every reuse in the same secure environment, upon every reuse in a different or less-secure environment, upon removal from service, and upon destruction. Addressing this issue can take many forms, including erasing, clearing, purging, declassification, sanitization, degaussing, and destruction:

**Erasing**   Erasing media is simply performing a delete operation against a file, a selection of files, or the entire media. In most cases, the deletion or removal process removes only the directory or catalog link to the data. The actual data remains on the drive. The data will remain on the drive until it is overwritten by other data or properly removed from the media.

**Clearing**   Clearing, or *overwriting*, is a process of preparing media for reuse and assuring that the cleared data cannot be recovered by any means. When media is cleared, unclassified data is written over specific locations or over the entire media where classified data was stored. Often, the unclassified data is strings of 1s and 0s. The clearing process typically prepares media for reuse in the same secure environment, not for transfer to other environments.

**Purging**   Purging is a more intense form of clearing that prepares media for reuse in less-secure environments. Depending on the classification of the data and the security of the environment, the purging process is repeated 7 to 10 times to provide assurance against data recovery via laboratory attacks.

**Declassification**   Declassification involves any process that clears media for reuse in less-secure environments. In most cases, purging is used to prepare media for declassification, but most of the time, the efforts required to securely declassify media are significantly greater than the cost of new media for a less-secure environment.

**Sanitization**   Sanitization is any number of processes that prepares media for destruction. It ensures that data cannot be recovered by any means from destroyed or discarded media. Sanitization can also be the actual means by which media is destroyed. Media can be sanitized by purging or degaussing without being physically destroyed. Sanitization methods that result in the physical destruction of the media include incineration, crushing, and shredding.

**Degaussing**   Degaussing magnetic media returns it to its original pristine, unused state. It occurs by subjecting the media to strong magnetic fields that return it to the same condition it enjoyed immediately after manufacture. This technique works only for magnetic tape, however; degaussing a hard disk will render it inoperable.

WARNING    Be careful when performing any type of sanitization, clearing, or purging process. It is possible that the human operator or the tool involved in the activity may not properly perform its task of removing data from the media. Software can be flawed, magnets can be faulty, and either can be used improperly. Always verify that the desired result is achieved after performing any sanitization process.

**Destruction**   Destruction is the final stage in the life cycle of backup media. Destruction should occur after proper sanitization or as a means of sanitization. When media destruction takes place, you must ensure that the media cannot be reused or repaired and that data cannot be extracted from the destroyed media by any possible means. Methods of destruction can include incineration, crushing, shredding, and dissolving using caustic or acidic chemicals.

NOTE    When donating or selling used computer equipment, it is usually recommended that you remove and destroy storage devices rather than attempting to purge or sanitize them. If sanitization processes are used, perform a secure erasure with an appropriate number of passes. Better still, take advantage of incineration services for storage media.

## Security Control Types

You can use several methods to classify security controls. A classification may be based on the nature of the control, such as administrative, technical/logical, or physical. It may also be based on the action or objective of the control, such as directive, preventive, detective, corrective, and recovery. Some controls can have multiple action/objective classifications:

**Directive control**   A directive control is a security tool used to guide the security implementation of an organization. Examples of directive controls include security policies, standards, guidelines, procedures, laws, and regulations. The goal or objective of directive controls is to cause or promote a desired result.

**Preventive control**   A preventive control is a security mechanism, tool, or practice that can deter or mitigate undesired actions or events. Preventive controls are designed to stop or reduce the occurrence of various crimes, such as fraud, theft, destruction, embezzlement, espionage, and so on. They are also designed to avert common human failures such as errors, omissions, and oversights. Preventive controls are designed to reduce risk. Although not always the most cost effective, they are preferred over detective or corrective controls from the perspective of maintaining security.

Stopping an unwanted or unauthorized action before it occurs results in a more secure environment than detecting and resolving problems after they do occur. Examples of preventive controls include firewalls, authentication methods, access controls, antivirus software, data classification, separation of duties, job rotation, risk analysis, encryption, warning banners, data validation, prenumbered forms, checks for duplications, and account lockouts.

**Detective control**    A detective control is a security mechanism used to verify the success of directive and preventive controls. Detective controls actively search for both violations of the security policy and actual crimes. They are used to identify attacks and errors so that appropriate action can be taken. Examples of detective controls include audit trails, logs, closed-circuit television (CCTV), intrusion detection systems, penetration testing, password crackers, performance monitoring, and cyclical redundancy checks (CRCs).

**Corrective control**    Corrective controls are instructions, procedures, or guidelines used to mitigate the effects of an unwanted activity, such as attacks and errors. Examples of corrective controls include manuals, procedures, malware cleanup, logging and journaling, incident handling, and fire extinguishers.

**Recovery control**    A recovery control is used to return affected systems back to normal operations after an attack or an error has occurred. Examples of recovery controls include system restoration, backups, rebooting, key escrow, insurance, redundant equipment, fault-tolerant systems, failover, checkpoints, and contingency plans.

## Operations Controls

*Operations controls* are the mechanisms and daily procedures that provide protection for systems. They are typically security controls that must be implemented or performed by people rather than automated by the system. Most operations controls are administrative in nature, but they also include some technical or logical controls.

When possible, operations controls should be invisible or transparent to users. The less a user sees the security controls, the less likely they will think that security is hampering their productivity. Likewise, the less users know about the security of a system, the less likely it is that they will be able to circumvent it.

### Resource Protection

Operations controls for resource protection are designed to provide security for resources in an IT environment. Resources are those hardware, software, and data assets that make up an organization's IT infrastructure. To maintain confidentiality, integrity, and availability of hosted assets, resources must also be protected.

When designing a protection scheme for resources, keep the following aspects or elements of the IT infrastructure in mind:

- Communication hardware/software
- Boundary devices
- Processing equipment
- Password files
- Application program libraries
- Application source code
- Vendor software
- Operating systems
- System utilities
- Directories and address tables
- Proprietary packages
- Main storage
- Removable storage
- Sensitive/critical data
- System logs/audit trails
- Violation reports
- Backup files and media
- Sensitive forms and printouts
- Isolated devices, such as printers and faxes
- Telephone network

## Privileged Entity Controls

Another aspect of operations controls is privileged entity controls. A *privileged entity* is an administrator or system operator who has access to special, higher-order functions and capabilities inaccessible to normal users. Privileged entity access is required for many administrative and control job tasks, such as creating new user accounts, adding new routes to a router table, or altering the configuration of a firewall.

Privileged entity access can include system commands, system control interfaces, system log/audit files, and special control parameters. Access to privileged entity controls should be restricted and audited to prevent the usurping of power by unauthorized users.

## Hardware Controls

*Hardware controls* are another part of operations controls. Hardware controls focus on restricting and managing access to the IT infrastructure hardware. In many cases, periodic maintenance, error/attack repair, and system configuration changes require direct physical access to hardware. An operations control to manage access to hardware is a form of a physical access control. All personnel who are granted access to the physical components of the system must have authorization. It is also a good idea to provide supervision while third parties perform any hardware operations.

Other issues related to hardware controls include managing maintenance accounts and port controls. *Maintenance accounts* are predefined default accounts that are installed on hardware (and in software) with preset and widely known passwords. These accounts should be renamed and a strong password assigned. Many hardware devices have diagnostic or configuration/console ports. They should be accessible only to authorized personnel, and if possible, they should be disabled when not in use for approved maintenance operations.

## Input/Output Controls

*Input and output controls* are mechanisms used to protect the flow of information into and out of a system. These controls also protect applications and resources by preventing invalid, oversized, or malicious input from causing errors or security breaches.

Output controls restrict the data that is revealed to users by restricting content based on subject classification and the security of the communication's connection.

Input and output controls are not limited to technical mechanisms; they can also be physical controls (for example, restrictions against bringing memory flashcards, USB flash drives, printouts, floppy disks, CD-Rs, and so on into or out of secured areas).

## Application Controls

*Application controls* are designed into software applications to minimize and detect operational irregularities. They limit an end user's use of applications so that only particular screens, records, and data are visible and only specific authorized functions enabled. Monitoring and auditing can then focus on particular uses of applications with potential security implications. Application controls are transparent to endpoint applications, so changes are not required to the applications involved.

Some applications include integrity verification controls, much like those employed by database management systems (DBMSs). These controls look for evidence of data manipulation, errors, and omissions. These types of controls are considered application controls (that is, internal controls) rather than software management controls (that is, external controls).

## Media Controls

*Media controls* revisit topics discussed in the section "Sensitive Information and Media" earlier in this chapter. Media controls must encompass the marking, handling, storage, transportation, and destruction of media such as floppies, memory cards, hard drives, backup tapes, CD-Rs, CD-RWs, and so on. A tracking mechanism should be used to record and monitor the location and uses of media. Secured media should never leave the boundaries of the secured environment. Likewise, any media brought into a secured environment should not contain viruses, malicious code, or other unwanted code elements, and that media should never leave the secured environment except after proper sanitization or destruction.

## Administrative Controls

Operations controls include many of the administrative controls that we have already discussed numerous times, such as separation of duties and responsibilities, rotation of duties, least privilege, and so on. However, in addition to these controls, you must consider how the maintenance of hardware and software is performed.

When assessing controls used to manage and sustain hardware and software maintenance, here are key issues to ponder:

- Are program libraries properly restricted and controlled?

- Is version control or configuration management enforced?

- Are all components of a new product properly tested, documented, and approved prior to release to production?

- Are the systems properly hardened? Hardening a system involves removing unnecessary processes, segregating interprocess communications, and reducing executing privileges to increase system security.

# Personnel Controls

No matter how much effort, expense, and expertise you put into physical access control and logical/technical security mechanisms, you will always have to deal with people. In fact, people are both your last line of defense and your worse security management issue. People are vulnerable to a wide range of technical and social attacks, and they can intentionally violate security policy and attempt to circumvent physical and logical/technical security controls. Because of this, you must endeavor to employ only those people who are entirely trustworthy.

Security controls to manage personnel are considered a type of administrative control. These controls and issues should be clearly outlined in your security policy and followed as closely as possible. Failing to employ strong personnel controls may render all other security efforts worthless.

The first type of personnel controls occur in the hiring process. To hire a new employee, you must first know what position needs to be filled. This requires creating a detailed job description. The job description should outline the work tasks and responsibilities for the position, which in turn dictates the access and privileges needed in the environment. Furthermore, the job description defines the knowledge, skill, and experience level required for the position. Only after the job description has been created can you begin screening applicants.

The next step in using personnel controls is selecting the best person for the job. In terms of security, this means the most trustworthy. Often trustworthiness is determined through employment candidate screening, including a thorough background check and reference verification, employment history verification, and education and certificate verification. This process could even include credit checks and FBI background checks.

Once a person has been hired, personnel controls should be deployed to continue to monitor and evaluate their work. Personnel controls monitoring activity should be deployed for all employees, not just new ones. These controls can include access audit and review, validation of security clearances, periodic skills assessment, supervisory employee ratings, and supervisor oversight and review.

Often companies employ a policy of mandatory vacations in one- or two-week increments. Such a tool removes the employee from the environment and allows another cross-trained employee to perform their work tasks during the interim. This activity serves as a form of peer review, providing a means to detect fraud and collusion. At any time, if an employee is found to be in violation of the security policy, they should be properly reprimanded and warned. If an employee continues to commit violations, they should be terminated.

Finally, there are personnel controls that govern the termination process. When an employee is to be fired, an exit interview should be conducted. For the exit interview, the soon-to-be-released employee is brought to a manager's office for a private meeting. This meeting is designed to remove them from their workspace and to minimize the effect of the firing activity on other employees. The meeting usually consists of the employee, a manager, and a security guard. The security guard acts as a witness and as a protection agent. The exit interview should be coordinated with the security administration staff so that just as the exit interview begins, the employee's network and building access is revoked. During an exit interview, the employee is reminded of his legal obligations to comply with any nondisclosure agreements and not to disclose any confidential data. The employee must return all badges, keys, and other company equipment on their person.

Once the exit interview is complete, the security guard escorts the terminated employee out of the facility and possibly even off the grounds. If the ex-employee has any company equipment at home or at some other location, the security guard should accompany the ex-employee to recover those items. The purpose of an exit interview is primarily to reinforce the nondisclosure issue, but it also serves the purpose of removing the ex-employee from the environment, having all access removed and devices returned, and preventing or minimizing any retaliatory activities because of the termination.

In addition to processes used to evaluate personnel security for internal employees, you must consider the temporary and external worker. Your screening process should include procedures focusing on vendor, consultant, and contractor controls as well as part-time staff, temporary workers, interns, and volunteers. Leave no individual with physical or logical access to your organization outside the realm of focused security scrutiny.

# Summary

Many areas of day-to-day operations are susceptible to security breaches. Therefore, all standards, guidelines, and procedures should clearly define personnel management practices. Important aspects of personnel management include antivirus management and operations security.

Personnel management is a form of administrative control or administrative management. You must include clearly defined personnel management practices in your security policy and subsequent formalized security documentation. From a security perspective, personnel management focuses on three main areas: hiring practices, ongoing job performance, and termination procedures.

Operations security consists of controls to maintain security in an office environment from design to deployment. Such controls include hardware, media, and subject (user) controls that are designed to protect against asset threats. Because viruses are the most common form of security breach in the IT world, managing a system's antivirus protection is one of the most important aspects of operations security.

Any communications pathway, such as email, websites, documents, and even commercial software, can and will be exploited as a delivery mechanism for a virus or other malicious code. Antivirus management is the design, deployment, and maintenance of an antivirus solution for your IT environment.

Backing up critical information is a key part of maintaining the availability and integrity of data and an essential part of maintaining operations security. Having a reliable backup is the best form of insurance that the data on the affected system is not permanently lost.

Changes in a user's workstation or their physical location within an organization can be used as a means to improve or maintain security. When a user's workstation is changed, the user is less likely to alter the system or install unapproved software because the next person to use the system would most likely be able to discover it.

The concepts of need to know and the principle of least privilege are two important aspects of a high-security environment. A user must have a need to know to gain access to data or resources. To comply with the principle of least privilege, users should be granted the least amount of access to the secure environment as possible for them to be able to complete their work tasks.

Activities that require special access or privilege to perform within a secured IT environment are considered privileged operations functions. Such functions should be restricted to administrators and system operators.

Due care is performing reasonable care to protect the interest of an organization. Due diligence is practicing the activities that maintain the due care effort. Operational security is the ongoing maintenance of continued due care and due diligence by all responsible parties within an organization.

Another central issue for all organizations is privacy, which means providing protection of personal information from disclosure to any unauthorized individual or entity. The protection of privacy should be a core mission or goal set forth in an organization's security policy.

It's also important that an organization operate within the legal requirements, restrictions, and regulations of its country and industry. Complying with all applicable legal requirements is a key part of sustaining security.

Illegal activities are actions that violate a legal restriction, regulation, or requirement. Fraud, misappropriation, unauthorized disclosure, theft, destruction, espionage, and entrapment are all examples of illegal activities. A secure environment should provide mechanisms to prevent the committal of illegal activities and the means to track illegal activities and maintain accountability from the individuals perpetrating the crimes.

In a high-security environment where sensitive, confidential, and proprietary data is processed, managing information and media properly is crucial to the environment's security and stability.

There are four key areas in information and media management: marking, handling, storage, and destruction. Record retention is the organizational policy that defines what information is maintained and for how long. If your organization retains data about individuals, the employees or customers must be informed about what is being kept and for how long.

The classification of security controls can be based on their nature, such as administrative, technical/logical, or physical. It can also be based on the action or objective of the control, such as directive, preventive, detective, corrective, and recovery.

Operations controls are the mechanisms and daily procedures that provide protection for systems. They are typically security controls that must be implemented or performed by people rather than automated by the system. Most operations controls are administrative in nature, but as you can see from the following list, they also include some technical or logical controls:

- Resource protection

- Privileged-entity controls

- Change control management

- Hardware controls

- Input/output controls

- Media controls

- Administrative controls

- Trusted recovery process

# Exam Essentials

**Understand that personnel management is a form of administrative control, also called administrative management.** You must clearly define personnel management practices in your security policy and subsequent formal security structure documentation. Personnel management focuses on three main areas: hiring practices, ongoing job performance, and termination procedures.

**Understand antivirus management.** Antivirus management includes the design, deployment, and maintenance of an antivirus solution for your IT environment.

**Know how to prevent unrestricted installation of software.** To provide a virus-free environment, you should rigidly control the installation of software. This includes allowing users to install and execute only company-approved and company-distributed software as well as thoroughly testing and scanning all new software before it is distributed on a production network. Even commercial software has become an inadvertent carrier of viruses.

**Understand backup maintenance.**    A key part of maintaining the availability and integrity of data is a reliable backup of critical information. Having a reliable backup is the only form of insurance that the data on a system that has failed or has been damaged or corrupted is not permanently lost.

**Know how changes in workstation or location promote a secure environment.**    Changes in a user's workstation or their physical location within an organization can be used as a means to improve or maintain security. Having a policy of changing users' workstations prevents them from altering the system or installing unapproved software and encourages them to keep all material stored on network servers where it can be easily protected, overseen, and audited.

**Understand the need-to-know concept and the principle of least privilege.**    Need to know and the principle of least privilege are two standard axioms in high-security environments. To gain access to data or resources, a user must have a need to know. If users do not have a need to know, access is denied. The principle of least privilege means that users should be granted only as much access to the secure environment as they need to complete their work tasks and no more.

**Understand privileged operations functions.**    Privileged operations functions are activities that require special access or privileges to be performed within a secured IT environment. For maximum security, such functions should be restricted to administrators and system operators.

**Know the standards of due care and due diligence.**    Due care is using reasonable care to protect the interest of an organization. Due diligence is practicing activities that maintain due care. Senior management must show reasonable due care and due diligence to reduce their culpability and liability when a loss occurs.

**Understand how to maintain privacy.**    Maintaining privacy means protecting personal information from disclosure to any unauthorized individual or entity. In today's online world, the line between public information and private information is often blurry. The protection of privacy should be a core mission or goal set forth in the security policy for an organization.

**Know the legal requirements in your region and field of expertise.**    Every organization operates within a certain industry and country, both of which impose legal requirements, restrictions, and regulations on its practices. Legal requirements can involve licensed use of software, hiring restrictions, handling of sensitive materials, and compliance with safety regulations.

**Understand what constitutes an illegal activity.**    An illegal activity is an action that violates a legal restriction, regulation, or requirement. A secure environment should provide mechanisms to prevent illegal activities from being committed and the means to track illegal activities and maintain accountability from the individuals perpetrating the crimes.

**Know the proper procedure for record retention.**    Record retention is an organizational policy that defines what information is retained and for how long. In most cases, the records in question are audit trails of user activity. This can include file and resource access, logon patterns, email, and the use of privileges.

**Understand the elements of securing sensitive media.**   Managing information and media properly, especially in a high-security environment where sensitive, confidential, and proprietary data is processed, is crucial to the security and stability of an organization. In addition to media selection, there are several key areas of information and media management: marking, handling, storage, life span, reuse, and destruction.

**Know and understand the security control types.**   Several methods are used to classify security controls. A classification may be based on the nature of the control (administrative, technical/logical, or physical) or on the action or objective of the control (directive, preventive, detective, corrective, and recovery).

**Know the importance of control transparency.**   When possible, operations controls should be invisible or transparent to users to prevent users from thinking security is hampering their productivity. Likewise, the less users know about the security of the system, the less likely they will be able to circumvent it.

**Understand how to protect resources.**   The operations controls for resource protection are designed to provide security for the IT environment's resources, including hardware, software, and data assets. To maintain confidentiality, integrity, and availability of the hosted assets, the resources themselves must be protected.

**Be able to explain change and configuration control management.**   Change in a secure environment can introduce loopholes, overlaps, misplaced objects, and oversights that can lead to new vulnerabilities. Therefore, you must systematically manage change by logging, auditing, and monitoring activities related to security controls and security mechanisms. The resulting data is then used to identify agents of change, whether they are objects, subjects, programs, communication pathways, or even the network itself. The goal of change management is to ensure that any change does not lead to reduced or compromised security.

**Understand the trusted recovery process.**   The trusted recovery process ensures that a system is not breached during a crash, failure, or reboot and that every time one of these occurs, the system returns to a secure state.

# Written Lab

1.   Describe the primary form of security breach and relevant security best practices.

2.   Identify and define the difference between need to know and principle of least privilege.

3.   What is workstation rotation, and why is it necessary?

4.   Name at least five common examples of privileged operations functions.

# Answers to Written Lab

1. Computer viruses are a large portion of computer network security breaches, and they are handled through antivirus management practices that include proper screening of new software components; restricted access to software changes, installations, and upgrades/updates; and the utilization of company-approved and vendor-distributed software.

2. A need to know is the requirement to have access to, knowledge about, or possession of data or a resource to perform specific work tasks. The principle of least privilege is granting only the necessary access rights for a user to complete their job tasks.

3. Workstation rotation is the alternation of employee seating assignments as a means to improve or maintain a strong security posture against malicious changes or unauthorized modification to the operation or capability of any given computer. It also discourages storage of personal or private data on an organization's systems.

4. Privileged operations functions include operating system control commands, configuration interfaces, audit log access, account management, and backup and restoration operations.

# Review Questions

1.  Personnel management is a form of what type of control?
    A.  Administrative
    B.  Technical
    C.  Logical
    D.  Physical

2.  What is the most common means of distribution for viruses?
    A.  Unapproved software
    B.  Email
    C.  Websites
    D.  Commercial software

3.  Which of the following causes the vulnerability of being affected by viruses to increase?
    A.  Length of time the system is operating
    B.  The classification level of the primary user
    C.  Installation of software
    D.  Use of roaming profiles

4.  In areas where technical controls cannot be used to prevent virus infections, what should be used to prevent them?
    A.  Security baselines
    B.  Awareness training
    C.  Traffic filtering
    D.  Network design

5.  Which of the following is not true?
    A.  Complying with all applicable legal requirements is a key part of sustaining security.
    B.  It is often possible to disregard legal requirements if complying with regulations would cause a reduction in security.
    C.  The legal requirements of an industry and of a country should be considered the baseline or foundation upon which the remainder of the security infrastructure must be built.
    D.  Industry and governments impose legal requirements, restrictions, and regulations on the practices of an organization.

6.  Which of the following is not an illegal activity that can be performed over a computer network?

    **A.** Theft

    **B.** Destruction of assets

    **C.** Waste of resources

    **D.** Espionage

7.  Who does not need to be informed when records about their activities on a network are being recorded and retained?

    **A.** Administrators

    **B.** Normal users

    **C.** Temporary guest visitors

    **D.** No one

8.  What is the best form of antivirus protection?

    **A.** Multiple solutions on each system

    **B.** A single solution throughout the organization

    **C.** Concentric circles of different solutions

    **D.** One-hundred-percent content filtering at all border gateways

9.  Which of the following is an effective means of preventing and detecting the installation of unapproved software?

    **A.** Workstation change

    **B.** Separation of duties

    **C.** Discretionary access control

    **D.** Job responsibility restrictions

10. What is the requirement to have access to, knowledge about, or possession of data or a resource to perform specific work tasks commonly known as?

    **A.** Principle of least privilege

    **B.** Prudent man theory

    **C.** Need to know

    **D.** Role-based access control

11. Which are activities that require special access to be performed within a secured IT environment?

    **A.** Privileged operations functions

    **B.** Logging and auditing

    **C.** Maintenance responsibilities

    **D.** User account management

12. Which of the following requires that archives of audit logs be kept for long periods of time?

    **A.** Data remanence

    **B.** Record retention

    **C.** Data diddling

    **D.** Data mining

13. What is the most important aspect of marking media?

    **A.** Date labeling

    **B.** Content description

    **C.** Electronic labeling

    **D.** Classification

14. Which operation is performed on media so it can be reused in a less-secure environment?

    **A.** Erasing

    **B.** Clearing

    **C.** Purging

    **D.** Overwriting

15. Sanitization can be unreliable because of which of the following?

    **A.** No media can be fully swept clean of all data remnants.

    **B.** Even fully incinerated media can offer extractable data.

    **C.** The process can be performed improperly.

    **D.** Stored data is physically etched into the media.

16. Which security tool is used to guide the security implementation of an organization?

    **A.** Directive control

    **B.** Preventive control

    **C.** Detective control

    **D.** Corrective control

17. Which security mechanism is used to verify whether the directive and preventive controls have been successful?

    **A.** Directive control

    **B.** Preventive control

    **C.** Detective control

    **D.** Corrective control

**18.** When possible, operations controls should be _____.

    **A.** simple

    **B.** administrative

    **C.** preventive

    **D.** transparent

**19.** What is the primary goal of change management?

    **A.** Personnel safety

    **B.** Allowing rollback of changes

    **C.** Ensuring that changes do not reduce security

    **D.** Auditing privilege access

**20.** What type of trusted recovery process requires the intervention of an administrator?

    **A.** Restricted

    **B.** Manual

    **C.** Automated

    **D.** Controlled

# Answers to Review Questions

1. A. Personnel management is a form of administrative control. Administrative controls also include separation of duties and responsibilities, rotation of duties, least privilege, and so on.

2. B. Email is the most common distribution method for viruses.

3. C. As more software is installed, more vulnerabilities are added to the system, thus adding more avenues of attack for viruses.

4. B. In areas where technical controls cannot prevent virus infections, users should be trained on how to prevent them.

5. B. Laws and regulations must be obeyed and security concerns must be adjusted accordingly.

6. C. Although wasting resources is considered inappropriate activity, it is not actually a crime in most cases.

7. D. Everyone should be informed when records about their activities on a network are being recorded and retained.

8. C. Concentric circles of different solutions are the best form of antivirus protection.

9. A. Workstation change is an effective means of preventing and detecting the presence of unapproved software.

10. C. Need to know is the requirement to have access to, knowledge about, or possession of data or a resource to perform specific work tasks.

11. A. Privileged operations functions are activities that require special access to perform within a secured IT environment. They may include auditing, maintenance, and user account management.

12. B. To use record retention properly, archives of audit logs must be kept for long periods of time.

13. D. Classification is the most important aspect of marking media because it determines the precautions necessary to ensure the security of the hosted content.

14. C. Purging media is erasing media so it can be reused in a less-secure environment. The purging process may need to be repeated numerous times depending on the classification of the data and the security of the environment.

15. C. Sanitization can be unreliable because the purging, degaussing, or other processes can be performed improperly.

16. A. A directive control is a security tool used to guide the security implementation of an organization.

**17.** C. A detective control is a security mechanism used to verify whether the directive and preventive controls have been successful.

**18.** D. When possible, operations controls should be invisible, or transparent, to users. This keeps users from feeling hampered by security and reduces their knowledge of the overall security scheme, thus further restricting the likelihood that users will violate system security deliberately.

**19.** C. The goal of change management is to ensure that any change does not lead to reduced or compromised security.

**20.** B. A manual recovery type of trusted recovery process requires the intervention of an administrator.

# Chapter
# 14

# Auditing and Monitoring

## THE CISSP EXAM TOPICS COVERED IN THIS CHAPTER INCLUDE:

✓ **Access Control**

  ▪ Control access by applying the following concepts/methodology/techniques

    ▪ Policies; types of controls (preventative, detective, corrective, etc.); techniques (e.g., nondiscretionary, discretionary and mandatory); identification and authentication; decentralized/distributed access control techniques; authorization mechanisms; logging and monitoring

  ▪ Assess effectiveness of access controls

The Operations Security domain of the Common Body of Knowledge (CBK) for the CISSP certification exam deals with the activities and efforts directed at maintaining operational security and includes the primary concerns of auditing and monitoring. Auditing and monitoring prompt IT departments to make efforts at detecting intrusions and unauthorized activities, with an emphasis on examining and recording such events. Vigilant administrators must sort through a selection of countermeasures, pore over system-generated log files, and perform penetration testing that helps to identify, detect, limit, restrict, and prevent inappropriate activities, crimes or criminal events, and various other forms of threat.

We discussed the Operations Security domain in some detail in Chapter 13, "Administrative Management," and we will be finishing up coverage on this domain in this chapter. Be sure to read and study the materials from both chapters to ensure complete coverage of the essential operations security material for the CISSP certification exam. Some of the material introduced in this chapter also relates to the Access Control domain of the CBK, more about which you can also learn in Chapter 1 of this book, particularly in regard to security policy and access control techniques.

# Auditing

*Auditing* is a methodical examination or review of an environment to ensure compliance with regulations and to detect abnormalities, unauthorized occurrences, or outright crimes. Secure IT environments rely heavily on auditing. Overall, auditing is the primary type of detective control used in a secure environment.

## Auditing Basics

Auditing encompasses a wide variety of different activities, including the recording of event/occurrence data, examination of data, data reduction, the use of event/occurrence alarm triggers, and log file analysis. These activities are better known as logging, monitoring, examining alerts, event analysis, and even intrusion detection.

*Logging* is the activity of recording information about events or occurrences to a log file or database. *Monitoring* is the activity of manually or programmatically reviewing information logs looking for something specific. *Alarm triggers* are notifications sent to administrators when specific events occur. *Log analysis* is a more detailed and systematic form of monitoring in which the logged information is analyzed in detail for trends and patterns as well as abnormal, unauthorized, illegal, and policy-violating activities. *Intrusion detection* is a specific form of monitoring both recorded information and real-time events to detect unwanted system access.

## Accountability

Auditing and monitoring are required to sustain and enforce accountability. Monitoring is the programmatic means by which subjects are held accountable for their actions while authenticated on a system. Without an electronic account of a subject's actions, it is not possible to correlate IT activities, events, and occurrences with subjects. Monitoring is also the process by which unauthorized or abnormal activities may be detected on a system. Monitoring is needed to detect malicious actions by subjects, attempted or successful intrusions, and system failures and to reconstruct events, provide evidence for prosecution, and create problem reports and analyses.

Auditing and logging are usually native features in an operating system and for most applications and services. Thus, configuring a system to record information about specific types of events is fairly straightforward.

Auditing is also used to monitor the health and performance of a system through recording the activities of subjects and objects as well as core system functions that maintain the operating environment and its security mechanisms. The audit trails created when writing system events to logs can be used to evaluate the health and performance of a system. System crashes can indicate faulty programs, corrupt drivers, or intrusion attempts and many readily identifiable patterns, events, or actions that originate from malicious parties. The event logs leading up to a crash can often be used to discover the reason a system failed. Log files provide an audit trail to re-create the history of an event, intrusion, or system failure step-by-step, moment by moment.

In most cases, when sufficient logging and auditing is enabled to monitor a system, so much data is collected that important details get lost in the noise. The art of data reduction is crucial when working with large volumes of monitoring data. There are numerous tools to search through log files for specific events or ID codes. However, for true automation and even real-time analysis of events, an intrusion detection system (IDS) is required. IDS solutions are discussed in Chapter 2, "Attacks and Monitoring."

## Compliance

Auditing is also commonly used for *compliance testing*, also called *compliance checking*. Verification that a system complies with laws, regulations, baselines, guidelines, standards, and policies is an important part of maintaining security in any environment. Compliance testing ensures that all necessary and required elements of a security solution are properly deployed and functioning as expected. Compliance checks can take many forms, such as vulnerability scans and penetration testing. They can also use log analysis tools to determine whether any vulnerabilities for which countermeasures have been deployed have been attempted or exploited on the system.

Proper auditing seeks to measure the effectiveness of deployed security solutions. Audits can be performed from one of two perspectives: internal or external. Organizational employees from inside the IT environment, who are (and should be) aware of the implemented security solutions, perform internal audits. Independent auditors from outside the IT environment, who are not familiar with the implemented security solutions, perform external audits. Insurance agencies, accounting firms, or even the organization itself can—and often do—hire external auditors to test the validity of security claims.

## Audit Time Frames

The frequency of an IT infrastructure security audit or security review derives from risk, a process formally called *risk analysis*. When performing risk analysis, one determines whether sufficient risk exists to warrant the expense of any possible interruption to business functionality that may be caused by a security audit on a regular or irregular basis. In any case, the frequency of audit reviews should be clearly defined in the security guidelines or standards for an organization. Once defined in the formal security infrastructure, it should be strongly applied and strictly followed. Without regular assessments of the state of security of an IT infrastructure, there is no way to know how secure the environment is until an attack either succeeds or fails. Waiting until the battle to determine whether you will win or lose is a poor business strategy.

As with many other aspects of deploying and maintaining security, security audits and effectiveness reviews are often viewed as key elements in displaying due care. If senior management fails to enforce compliance with regular periodic security reviews, then they will be held accountable and liable for any asset losses that occur because of security breaches or policy violations.

## Audit Trails

*Audit trails* are records created when writing information about events and occurrences into a database or log file. They are used to reconstruct an event, to extract information about an incident, to prove or disprove culpability, and much more. Audit trails allow events to be examined or traced in forward or reverse order. This flexibility helps when tracking down problems, coding errors, performance issues, attacks, intrusions, security breaches, and other policy violations.

Using audit trails is a passive form of detective security control. They serve as a deterrent in the same manner closed-circuit television (CCTV) or security guards do: If attackers know they are being watched and their activities recorded, they are less likely to commit illegal, unauthorized, or malicious activity—at least in theory (in reality, some criminals are too careless or clueless for this to apply in all cases). Audit trails are also essential as evidence in the prosecution of criminals. They can often be used to produce a before-and-after picture of the state of resources, systems, and assets. This in turn helps to determine whether a change or alteration is the result of an action by a user or an action by the OS or software or caused by some other sources (such as hardware failure).

Accountability is maintained for individual subjects through the use of audit trails. When activities and events are recorded while users are online, they can be held accountable for their individual or cooperative actions. This directly promotes good user behavior and compliance within the organization's security policy. Users who are aware that their IT activities are being recorded are less likely to try to circumvent security controls or to perform unauthorized or restricted activities.

Audit trails give system administrators the ability to reconstruct events long after they have occurred. When a security violation is detected, the conditions and system state leading up to the event, during the event, and after the event can be reconstructed through a close examination of the audit trail. This process is largely facilitated and validated through the use of accurate time stamps, which must remain consistent throughout the network environment to correctly and positively identify the correct sequence of events after an intrusion. As such, they must also be kept safe and secure from modification at the hands of a malicious end user or intrusive attacker, who may otherwise modify (and therefore *nullify*) the contents of these files to remove any traces of intrusion and error.

Configuration and audit control can be validated and managed through passive triggering tools such as Tripwire, a file integrity tool designed to observe and report unusual or unauthorized changes to critical system files. Tripwire calculates and stores signatures for file permissions, ownership, and contents.

Audit trails offer details about recorded events. A wide range of information can be recorded in log files, including time, date, system, user, process, and type of error/event. Log files can even capture the memory state or the contents of memory for the applications and services designed to report failure conditions to these global log file repositories. This information can help pinpoint the cause of the event, whether good or bad and intentional or otherwise. Using log files for this purpose is often labeled as *problem identification*. Once a problem is identified, performing problem resolution involves little more than following up on the disclosed information. Audit trails record system failures, OS bugs, and software errors as well as abuses of access, violations of privileges, attempted intrusions, and many forms of attack. Intrusion detection is a specialized form of problem identification through the use of audit trails.

**WARNING**   If auditing records or logs are transmitted across a network from a sentry agent to a collector warehouse, that transmission should be encrypted. Log and audit information should never be allowed on the network in clear text.

Once a security policy violation or a breach occurs, the source of that violation should be determined. If it is possible to track the individuals who perpetrated the activity, they should be reprimanded or terminated (if employees) or prosecuted (if external intruders). In any case where a critical security policy violation or personal information breach has occurred (especially if any loss can be pinpointed), you should seriously consider reporting the incident to your local authorities (in the United States, this may mean notifying the FBI; in Europe, Interpol). If a violation occurs online, particularly where sensitive customer information is involved, report the incident to one or more Internet incident-tracking organizations.

Most countries (and many smaller jurisdictions, including states and cities) have enacted significant regulatory compliance laws to govern security breaches, particularly as they apply to sensitive data retained within information systems. Laws differ from locale to locale, but all seek to protect the privacy of individual records and information, to protect consumer identities, and to establish standards for financial practice and corporate governance. Be sure to consult local authorities for more information on compliance standards and requirements in your area.

 Time-synchronize all systems against a centralized or trusted public time server. This keeps all audit logs in sync so you can perform dependable and secure logging activities.

## Reporting Concepts

The actual formats used by an organization to produce reports from audit trails will vary greatly. However, those reports should all address a few basic or central concepts: the purpose of the audit, the scope of the audit, and the results discovered or revealed by the audit. In addition to these basic concepts, audit reports often include many details specific to the environment, such as time, date, specific systems, and so on. Audit reports can include a wide range of content that focuses on problems, events, and conditions; standards, criteria, and baselines; causes, reasons, impact, and effect; or solutions, recommendations, and safeguards.

### Reporting Format

Audit reports should have a structure or design that is clear, concise, and objective. It is common for an auditor to include opinions or recommendations for response to the content of a report, but its actual findings should be based on fact and evidence from audit trails. Audit reports include sensitive information and should be assigned a classification label and handled appropriately.

Within the hierarchy of the organization, only those people with sufficient privilege, such as the *privileged entities* you learned about in Chapter 13, should have access to audit reports. An audit report may also be prepared in various forms according to the hierarchy of the organization. They should provide only the details relevant to the position of the staff members who have access to them.

For example, senior management does not need to know all the minute details of an audit report. Therefore, the audit report for senior management is much more concise and offers more of an overview or summary of findings. An audit report for an IT manager or a security administrator should be very detailed and include all available information on the events it covers.

## Reporting Time Frames

The frequency of producing audit reports is based on the value of the assets covered and the level of risk involved. The more valuable the assets and the higher the risks, the more often you'll want to produce an audit report. Once an audit report is completed, it should be submitted to its assigned recipients (as defined in security policy documentation) and a signed confirmation of receipt should be filed. When an audit report contains information about serious security violations or performance issues, that report should be escalated to higher levels of management for review, notification, and assignment of a response.

Keep in mind that, in a formal security infrastructure, only higher levels of management have any decision-making power. All entities at the lower end of the structure must follow prescribed procedures and follow instructions to the letter.

# Sampling

*Sampling*, or *data extraction*, is the process of extracting elements from a large collection of data to construct a meaningful representation or summary of the whole. In other words, sampling is a form of data reduction that allows an auditor to quickly elicit important issues or events from an audit trail. There are two forms of sampling: statistical and nonstatistical. An auditing tool using precise mathematical functions to extract meaningful information from a large volume of data performs *statistical sampling*. There is always a risk that sampled data is not an accurate representation of the whole body of data or that it may mislead auditors and managers, and statistical sampling can be used to measure that risk.

*Clipping* is a form of nonstatistical sampling: It selects only error events that exceed a *clipping-level threshold*, a specified cutoff point for the accumulation of such events. *Clipping levels* are widely used in the process of auditing events to establish a baseline of system or user activity that is considered routine activity. If this baseline is exceeded, an alarm is triggered to signal abnormal events. This works especially well when individuals exceed their authority, when there are too many people with unrestricted access, and for serious intrusion patterns.

Clipping levels are often associated with a form of mainframe auditing known as *violation analysis*. In violation analysis, an older form of auditing, the environment is monitored for error occurrences. The baseline for errors is expected and known, and this level of common errors defines the clipping level. Any errors that exceed the clipping level threshold trigger a violation and details about such events are recorded into a violation record for later analysis.

In general, *nonstatistical sampling* can be described as random sampling or sampling at the auditor's discretion. It offers neither assurance of an accurate representation of the whole body of data nor a gauge of the sampling risk. Nonstatistical sampling is less expensive, requires less training, and does not require computer facilities. By focusing only on error events above a threshold, for example, clipping enables direct focus on signs of potential anomaly or trouble.

Both statistical and nonstatistical sampling are accepted as valid mechanisms to create summaries or overviews of large bodies of audit data. However, statistical sampling is more reliable (and mathematically defensible).

# Record Retention

As the term implies, *record retention* involves retaining and maintaining important information. An organization should have a policy that defines what information is maintained and for how long. As it applies to the security infrastructure, in most cases, the records in question are audit trails of user activity, which may include file and resource access, logon patterns, email, and the use of privileges.

## Retention Time Frames

Depending upon your industry and your relationship with the government, you may need to retain records for three or seven years, or perhaps indefinitely. In most cases, a separate backup mechanism is used to create archived copies of sensitive audit trails and accountability information. This permits the main data backup system to periodically reuse its media without violating any requirement to retain audit trails and the like.

If data about individuals is being retained by your organization, employees and customers must be informed about that data (such as in a conditional employment agreement or a use agreement). In many cases, the notification requirement is a legal issue, whereas in others it is a simply a courtesy. In either case, it is a good idea to discuss this issue with a lawyer.

## Media, Destruction, and Security

The media used to store or retain audit trails must be properly maintained. This includes taking secure measures for marking, handling, storing, and destroying media. For details on handling sensitive media, please see the section "Sensitive Information and Media" in Chapter 13, "Administrative Management."

Retained records should be protected against unauthorized and untimely destruction, against alteration, and against hindrances to availability. Many of the same security controls used to protect online resources and assets can be imposed to protect audit logs, audit trails, audit reports, and backup media containing audit information.

Access to audit information should be strictly controlled. Audit information can be used in inference attacks to discover information about higher classifications of data; thus, the audit logs containing records about highly confidential assets should be handled in the same secure manner as the actual assets. In other words, when an audit log is created, you are creating another asset entity with the same security needs as the original audited asset.

As the value of assets and the audit data goes up and risk increases, so does the need for an increase in security and the frequency of backups for the audit information. Audit data should be treated with the same security precautions as all other high-classification data within an IT environment. It should be protected by physical and logical security controls, it should itself be audited, it should be regularly backed up, and the backup media should be stored off site in a controlled facility. The backup media hosting such audit data should be able to protect against loss, destruction, alteration, and unauthorized physical and logical access. The integrity of audit data must be maintained and protected at all times because without it, any and all audit data may be legally impugned and will become useless from a legal and logical standpoint.

## External Auditors

It is often necessary to test or verify the security mechanisms deployed in an environment. The test process is designed to ensure that the requirements dictated by the security policy are followed and that no significant holes or weaknesses exist in deployed security solutions. Many organizations conduct independent audits by hiring outside or external security auditors to check the security of their environments. External audits provide a level of objectivity that an internal audit cannot provide and bring a fresh, outside perspective to your internal policies, practices, and procedures.

An external auditor is given access to the company's security policy and the authorization to inspect every aspect of the IT and physical environment. Thus, the auditor must be a trusted entity. The goal of the audit activity is to obtain a final report that details any findings and suggests countermeasures when appropriate. However, an audit of this type can take a considerable amount of time to complete—weeks or months, in fact. During the course of the audit, the auditor may issue interim reports. An *interim report* is a written or verbal report given to the organization about any observed security weaknesses or policy/procedure mismatches that demand immediate attention. Interim reports are issued whenever a problem or issue is too important to wait until a final audit report is issued.

Once the auditors complete their investigations, an exit conference is held. During that conference, the auditors present and discuss their findings and discuss resolution issues with the affected parties. However, only after the exit conference is over and the auditors have left the premises do they write and submit their final audit report to the organization. This allows the final audit report to remain unaffected by office politics and coercion. After the final audit report is received, internal auditors should determine whether the recommendations in the report should be acted upon. However, it is the responsibility of senior management to select which recommendations to follow and to delegate their implementation to the security team.

# Monitoring

*Monitoring* is a form of auditing that focuses on the active review of audited information or an audited asset. For example, you would audit the activity of failed logons, but you would *monitor* CPU performance. Monitoring is most often used in conjunction with performance, but it can be used in a security context as well. Monitoring can focus on events, subsystems, users, hardware, software, or any other object within the IT environment.

A common implementation of monitoring is known as *illegal software monitoring*. This type of monitoring is used to watch for attempted or successful installation of unapproved software, use of unauthorized software, or unauthorized use of approved software (in other words, attempts to bypass the restrictions of the security classification hierarchy). Monitoring in this fashion reduces the likelihood of a virus or Trojan horse being installed or of software circumventing whatever security controls may be in place.

# Monitoring Tools and Techniques

The actual tools and techniques used to perform monitoring vary greatly between environments and system platforms. However, several common elements appear in most environments. These include warning banners, keystroke monitoring, traffic analysis, and trend analysis as well as other monitoring tools.

## Warning Banners

*Warning banners* serve to inform would-be intruders or those who attempt to violate security policy that their intended activities are restricted and that any further activities will be audited and monitored. A warning banner is basically an electronic equivalent of a "no trespassing" sign. In most situations, wording in banners is important from a legal standpoint because these banners can legally bind users to some permissible set of actions, behaviors, and processes. Be sure to consult with your attorneys about proper wording for your banners.

Only through valid, legally enforceable warnings (in other words, clear explanations that unauthorized access is prohibited and that any such activity will be monitored and recorded) can most intrusions and attacks be prosecuted. Both authorized and unauthorized users should be informed when their activities are being logged. Most authorized users should assume as much, and often their employment agreements include specific statements indicating that all activity on the IT infrastructure may be recorded.

## Keystroke Monitoring

*Keystroke monitoring* is the act of recording the key presses a user performs on a physical keyboard. The act of recording can be visual (such as with a video recorder) or logical/technical (such as with a capturing hardware device or a software program). In most cases, keystroke monitoring is used for malicious purposes. Only in extreme circumstances and highly restricted environments is keystroke monitoring actually employed as a means to audit and analyze the activity of users at the keyboard.

Keystroke monitoring can be extremely useful to track the keystroke-by-keystroke activities of physical intruders in order to learn about the kinds of attacks and methods used to infiltrate a system.

 Companies can and do utilize keystroke monitoring for a few good reasons, but they generally (and legally) must inform employees through acceptable use policies (AUP) and logon banners.

Keystroke monitoring is often compared to wiretapping. There is some debate about whether keystroke monitoring should be restricted and controlled in the same manner as telephone wiretaps. Because there is no legal precedent as yet, many organizations that employ keystroke monitoring notify authorized and unauthorized users of such monitoring through employment agreements, security policies, and warning banners at sign-on or login areas. The software or hardware devices used to perform keystroke monitoring can be described as "keystroke loggers," and the popular name for such programs or devices is *keylogger*.

## Traffic Analysis and Trend Analysis

*Traffic analysis* and *trend analysis* are forms of monitoring that examine the flow of packets rather than actual packet contents. Traffic and trend analysis can be used to infer a lot of information, such as primary communication routes, sources of encrypted traffic, location of primary servers, primary and backup communication pathways, amount of traffic supported by the network, typical direction of traffic flow, frequency of communications, and much more.

These techniques can also sometimes reveal questionable traffic patterns such as when an employee mass-emails a resume to dozens of employers on any given day or when an unscrupulous insider forwards internal information to unauthorized parties via an email attachment. Such events also leave behind distinct signatures that can often be detected through traffic or trend analysis.

## Other Monitoring Tools

Many tools are available to perform monitoring. Some are automated and perform their monitoring activities in real time. Some monitoring tools may be developed in-house as ad hoc tools that focus on a single type of observation. Most monitoring tools are passive in nature, which means they cause no effect on the monitored activity, event, or traffic and make no original transmissions of their own.

A common example of a tool for monitoring physical access is the use of CCTV. CCTV can be configured to automatically record the viewed events onto tape for later review, and personnel who watch for unwanted, unauthorized, or illegal activities in real time can watch it live. This system can work alone or in conjunction with security guards, who themselves can be monitored by the CCTV and held accountable for any negative actions taken under observation.

Failure recognition and response is an important part of monitoring and auditing. Otherwise, what is the point of performing monitoring and auditing activities? On systems that use manual review, failure recognition is the responsibility of the observer or auditor. To recognize a failure, you must understand what is normal and expected. When monitored or audited events stray from a standard baseline, then a failure, breach, intrusion, error, or problem has occurred, and a response must be initiated.

Automated monitoring and auditing systems are usually programmed to recognize failures. Failure recognition can be signature based or knowledge based, driven by a recognizable pattern or sequence or by learning new, presumably abnormal behaviors in light of some baseline of known-good activities. For a discussion of these mechanisms, see the intrusion detection discussion in Chapter 2.

Be recognition manual or automated, the first step in a response is to notify the authority responsible for sustaining security and handling the problem or breach. Often this is a local administrator, a local manager, or a local security professional. The notification usually takes the form of an alarm or warning message. Once notification is made, the responsible personnel (in other words, the administrator, manager, or security professional) or the automated tool can initiate a response. Responsible persons can adapt a standard or predetermined response to specific conditions and the situation on the ground. For this reason, personnel-controlled responses are often the most effective.

Automated tool responses are typically predefined response scripts that are usually much broader in scope than is strictly necessary. Automated tools are excellent for quick and efficient lockdown, but often the countermeasure or response imposed by a tool will significantly affect the ability of the system to support and perform productive work. Whenever an automated tool response is initiated, personnel should be notified so the response can be fine-tuned and the network can be returned to normal as soon as possible.

# Penetration-Testing Techniques

In security terms, a *penetration* occurs when an attack is successful and an intruder is able to breach the perimeter of your environment. A breach can be as small as reading a few bits of data from your network or as big as logging in as a user with unrestricted privileges. One primary goal for security is to prevent penetrations.

A common method to ascertain the strength of your security measures is to perform penetration testing. *Penetration testing* is a vigorous attempt to break into a protected network using any means necessary or available. It is common for organizations to hire external consultants to perform penetration testing so the testers are not privy to confidential elements of the security solution's configuration, network design, and other internal secrets. Because the security apparatus is a black box to unauthorized outsiders who seek to penetrate its defenses, or so the thinking goes, it should be likewise for authorized outsiders who seek to probe and test those defenses and to find and document weaknesses.

In this context, it's important to understand two sets of terms for penetration (and other forms of) testing. A *black box* is literally a device of unknown composition whose internal circuits, makeup, and processing functions are unknown but whose outputs in response to various kinds of inputs can be observed and analyzed. On the other hand, a *white box* is a device whose internal structure or processing is known and understood. This distinction is important in penetration testing, where black-box testing proceeds without making use of any knowledge of how an organization is structured, what kinds of hardware and software it uses, or its security policies, processes, and procedures. White-box testing, on the other hand, seeks to exploit everything known about those things to focus and guide testing efforts. Black-box penetration testing proceeds without using any knowledge about an organization; white-box penetration testing proceeds using all available knowledge to drive its efforts.

## Planning Penetration Testing

Penetration testing is the art and science of evaluating and validating implemented safeguards. It is just another name for launching intrusion attempts and re-creating attacks against a network or entities on that network. The activity in either a real intrusion or a simulated intrusion is the same, but formal penetration testing is performed with prior approval and advance knowledge of senior management by security professionals in a controlled and monitored environment. Malicious users intent on violating the security of your IT environment perform legally punishable intrusion attacks. If an internal user performs an informal test against a security measure without authorization, then it can be viewed as an illegal attack rather than as a penetration test.

 Penetration testing typically includes social engineering attacks, network and system configuration review, and environment vulnerability assessment. Vulnerability analysis or vulnerability assessment is an element or phase within penetration testing where networks or hosts are evaluated or tested to determine whether they are vulnerable to known attacks.

Penetration testing can be performed using automated attack tools (mechanically) or manually (by hand). Automated attack tools range from professional vulnerability scanners to wild, underground attack tools discovered on the Internet. Manual attacks often employ tools and penetration suites such as ISS, Nessus, and Core Impact, but much more onus is placed on the attacker to know the details involved in perpetrating an attack.

It is generally considered unethical and a poor business practice to hire ex-attackers, especially those with criminal records, for any security activity including security assessment, penetration testing, or ethical hacking. Although it's reasonable to argue that few better understand the *intrusion* process, it also stands to reason that criminal intent establishes a lack of credibility and that breaking into a system does not necessarily imply knowledge of how to secure it.

Penetration testing should be performed only with the consent and knowledge of the management staff. Performing unapproved security testing could result in productivity loss, trigger emergency response teams into action, or even cost you your job. However, even with full consent of senior management, your security assessment activities must stop short of actual damage to target systems. Subversion or target destruction is never a valid or ethical activity during a penetration test. Furthermore, demonstrating the effect of flaws, weaknesses, and vulnerabilities should not be included as part of any penetration test. If such evidence is required, it should be performed only on a dedicated and isolated lab system created for the sole purpose of exploit demonstration.

Regularly staged penetration attempts are a good way to gauge the security configurations, mechanisms, and processes deployed by an organization, with reasonably accurate results. Penetration testing may also reveal areas where patches or security settings are insufficient and where new vulnerabilities have developed or become exposed.

## Penetration Testing Teams

Penetration testing teams may have varying levels of knowledge about the environment to be evaluated. Three commonly recognized knowledge levels are zero, partial, and full. Here are brief descriptions:

**Zero-knowledge team**   This group knows nothing about the site except for basic information, such as domain name and company address. An attack by a zero-knowledge team closely resembles a real external attack because all information about the environment must be obtained from scratch. To return to terminology introduced earlier in this chapter, a zero-knowledge team conducts black-box penetration testing.

**Partial-knowledge team**   This team is given an inventory of hardware and software used at the site and possibly network design and configuration details. The team is then able to focus its efforts on attacks and vulnerabilities specific to actual hardware and software in use at the site.

**Full-knowledge team**   These people are completely aware of every aspect of the environment, down to patch and upgrades installed and exact security configurations. To return to terminology introduced earlier in this chapter, a full-knowledge team conducts white-box penetration testing, which explains why partial-knowledge teams are sometimes said to conduct gray-box testing because they operate between the extremes of black (zero knowledge) and white (full knowledge).

The regular security administration staff can be considered a full-knowledge team. Unfortunately, a full-knowledge team is the least preferred type of penetration testing cadre because its members are often biased and likely have blind spots or gaps in their understanding, estimation, or capabilities with certain security subjects. A full-knowledge team knows what has been secured, so it may fail to properly test every possibility by relying on false assumptions, a frequent and inexcusable occurrence in the security realm.

## The Bane of False Assumptions

False assumptions are a hobgoblin to any inexperienced technology professional. Such things can be a source of ceaseless torment for those who are unfortunate enough to make them, particularly in the context of information security.

Francesca implements security patches, bug fixes, and product updates whenever Garrick releases them. She's very efficient and timely about this task because her entire job is at stake along with the integrity of the company. Garrick is usually pretty responsive to security-related problems and issues his probable fixes and likely workarounds as quickly as his fingers can carry him.

What kinds of errors might a focus on speed cause for this dynamic duo? To begin with, it's essential to be as sure as possible that patches, fixes, and updates introduce no new vulnerabilities, or the cure may be worse than the disease. Garrick would be well advised to test his work and to keep in touch with power users and key adopters for potential signs of trouble. Francesca might also want to think about deploying changes in a simulated test environment to look for trouble before inflicting it across an entire operation or enterprise.

Hannah noticed that one of Francesca's latest installments, a security patch from Garrick, exposes sensitive data on the company servers. When Hannah confronted Francesca, she wasn't aware of any such issue but was clearly aware of the latest fix. Since Garrick assumed he found the right solution to a security problem, he implemented it right away and so did Francesca, thinking that code guru Garrick never misses a target. See how two people can easily make a false assumption go terribly awry? Without testing and verification, fixes are as suspect as any other new software that appears on your doorstep.

Conventional wisdom proffers several suggestions on how to conduct penetration testing using teams. A well-known resource, for example, recommends that appropriate personnel be well versed in the flaw hypothesis methodology of penetration testing. Following the flaw hypothesis, general-purpose OSs are assessed using an open-box testing technique.

Team members are required to document and analyze potential flaws in the system—essentially to hypothesize any flaws that may exist. Using a system of probability, team members prioritize the list of potential flaws based on whether flaws exist, the vulnerability and exploitability of such flaws (if they do indeed exist), and the amount of control or compromise those flaws may inflict on the system. This list of priorities then becomes the basis for the team's testing initiative.

## Ethical Hacking

*Ethical hacking* is often used as another name for penetration testing. However, it is not the same as penetration testing. *Ethical hacking* is a security assessment process whereby hacking techniques and tools are employed. When an ethical hacker is engaged as part of your assessment team, it is important to ensure that the person does not have a conflict of interest. This could be a person who also is a provider, reseller, or consultant for security products or add-in or value-add services. An ethical hacker should not exploit discovered vulnerabilities.

Although many argue that ethical hacking is in fact penetration testing, there is a subtle difference in what an ethical hacker will utilize that penetration testers might not, namely, the underground tools that unethical attackers also use.

Writing to, altering, or damaging a target of evaluation is a violation of the concept of ethical hacking and bleeds into the realm of unethical (and often criminal) hacking, which is specifically called *cracking*. The true ethos of any ethical hacker's mind-set is never to alter or observe sensitive processes in an unauthorized security context. Here we make the distinction only once for completeness, but the world at large typically perceives hacking and cracking under the same umbrella of criminal intent or mischief.

## War Dialing

*War dialing* means using a modem to search for a system that accepts inbound connection attempts. A war dialer might be a typical computer with a modem attached and war dialer software running, or it can be a stand-alone device. In either case, war dialers systematically dial phone numbers and listen for computer carrier tones, which can be differentiated from human voices and automated voice message systems. When a computer carrier tone is detected, the war dialer adds this number to a report generated at the end of the search process. A war dialer can search any range of numbers, such as all 10,000 numbers within a specific prefix or all 10,000,000 within a specific area code.

War dialing may be used to locate unauthorized modems that are installed on client systems within an otherwise secured network and that have been inadvertently configured to answer inbound calls. An attacker can guess a relatively small range of phone numbers to scan by learning one or more of an organization's phone numbers.

War dialing as a penetration test method is a useful way to ensure that no unauthorized answering modems are present within an organization. In most cases, you will have a definitive list of the phone numbers controlled by or assigned to your organization. Such a list provides a focused plan of testing for war dialing.

Countermeasures against malicious war dialing include imposing strong remote access security (primarily in the arena of authentication), ensuring that no unauthorized modems are present, and using callback security, protocol restriction, and call logging.

## Sniffing and Eavesdropping

*Sniffing* is a form of network traffic monitoring. Sniffing often involves capture or duplication of network traffic for examination, re-creation, and extraction. It can be used as a penetration test mechanism or as a malicious attack method. Sniffing is often an effective tool for capturing or extracting data from unencrypted network traffic streams. Passwords, usernames, IP addresses, message contents, and much more can be captured using software- or hardware-based sniffers.

Sniffers can capture either only traffic directed to their host system's IP address or all traffic passing over a local network segment. To capture all traffic on a local network segment, the sniffer's NIC must be placed into promiscuous mode. Placing a NIC into promiscuous mode grants the operator the ability to obtain a complete statistical understanding of local network activity.

Many commercial, freeware, and attackware sniffers are available. These include Etherpeek, WinDump, Wireshark, sniffit, and Snmpsniff. Each has its own particular set of strengths, weaknesses, and features, but they all essentially perform the same function.

The primary countermeasure for sniffing attacks is to use encrypted traffic, often carried within encapsulating security protocols and payloads. Sniffing can also be thwarted by preventing unwanted software from being installed; by locking down all unused ports, outlawing hubs, and using switches instead (hubs copy all traffic to all other ports; switches only duplicate traffic from specific ports as a tightly controlled configuration option); and by using an IDS or a vulnerability scanner that is able to detect the telltale signs of a sniffer product in use.

*Eavesdropping* is just another term for sniffing. However, eavesdropping can include more than just capturing and recording network traffic. Eavesdropping also includes recording or listening to audio communications, faxes, radio signals, and so on. In other words, eavesdropping is listening in on, recording, capturing, or otherwise becoming aware of the contents of any form of communication.

## Radiation Monitoring

*Radiation monitoring* is a specific form of sniffing or eavesdropping that involves the detection, capture, and recording of radio frequency signals and other radiated communication methods, including sound and light. Radiation monitoring can be as simple as using a hidden microphone in a room to record voices or as sophisticated as using a camera to record the light reflections in a room to reconstruct the contents of a visual computer display that is otherwise hidden from direct view.

Radiation monitoring also includes tapping of radio frequencies often used by cell phones, wireless network interfaces, two-way radios, radio and television broadcastings, short-wave radios, and CBs. In addition, it includes tapping of a wide range of electrical signal variations that may not directly offer information but can be used in inference attacks. These include changes in electrical usage in an entire computer system, a hard drive, a modem, a network interface, a switch, and a router. Depending on the device, the electromagnetic signals produced by hardware can be captured and used to re-create the data, or at least metadata about the data, and the communication session.

TEMPEST is a standard that defines the study and control of electronic signals produced by various types of electronic hardware, such as computers, televisions, and phones. Its primary goal is to prevent electromagnetic interference (EMI) and radio frequency interference (RFI) radiation from leaving a strictly defined area to eliminate the possibility of external radiation monitoring, eavesdropping, and signal sniffing. TEMPEST defines control zones, which generally consist of rooms or facilities that are enclosed with copper or some other kind of shielding (Faraday cages, TEMPEST tents, and so on) to prevent EMI/RFI from either leaving or entering a facility. Such facilities are surrounded by radiation capturing, stopping, hiding, and disrupting equipment. TEMPEST may use a form of white noise to broadcast an unintelligible worthless signal to mask the presence of a real signal. TEMPEST countermeasures are designed to protect against undetectable passive monitoring of EMI and RFI signals.

## Dumpster Diving

*Dumpster diving* is the act of digging through the refuse, remains, or leftovers from an organization or operation in order to discover or infer confidential information. Dumpster diving is primarily associated with digging through actual garbage. Researching an organization for its useful details, or *information gathering*, includes searching, investigating, and reverse-engineering an organization's website and commercial products and obtaining publicly accessible literature (such as financial statements, brochures, product information, shareholder reports, and so on). Much of what can be determined about an organization is revealed through its paper waste, which is known to turn up viable private or personally identifiable information.

*Scavenging* is a form of information gathering performed electronically. Online scavenging is searching for useful information in the remnants of data left over after processes or tasks are completed or remnants of deleted files. This could include audit trails, log files, memory dumps, variable settings, port mappings, and cached data.

Dumpster diving and scavenging (both are forms of information gathering) can be employed ahead of an informal penetration test to discover how much information about your organization is carelessly discarded or left around after closing a facility. The best countermeasure for dumpster diving and scavenging is to dispose of all garbage securely. This usually means shredding all documentation. Other safeguards include maintaining physical access control.

---

**From Trash to Treasure**

Garbage is often an inadvertent source of information, often played up in movies as a way to obtain private information on a subject or potential target. An investigator may sort through garbage to obtain DNA evidence on a suspect, or a criminal may glean personal details on a targeted victim.

Ian is curious to know what sort of sensitive information is being carelessly discarded by his staff, so he asks Jocelyn to collect all paper waste from the IT department for one week. Ian and Jocelyn discover private letters, internal memos, photo IDs, handwritten passwords, a few doctors' notes, and even some credit and personal identity information. The results are surprising for Ian and unsettling for Jocelyn.

What strategy might you suggest Ian and Jocelyn implement to prevent this information from reaching undesirable parties? Certainly there must be some policy changes and personnel training, but can you think of any physical countermeasures you might use? The most obvious approach requires educating employees to watch what they're throwing out and to require them to dispose of anything sensitive in secure receptacles regularly picked up for shredding or incineration.

---

## Social Engineering

A social engineering attack is an attempt by an attacker to convince an employee to perform an unauthorized activity to subvert the security of an organization. Often the goal of social engineering is to gain access to the IT infrastructure or the physical facility.

*Social engineering* is a skill by which an unknown person gains the trust of someone inside your organization. Adept individuals can convince employees that they are associated with upper management, technical support, the help desk, or anyone of influential status. Once this deception is successful, the victim is often encouraged to make a change to their user account on the system, such as resetting their password. Other attacks include instructing the victim to open specific email attachments, launch an application, or connect to a specific URL. Whatever the actual activity is, the result is usually directed toward opening a back door that the attacker can use to gain access to the network or toward obtaining sensitive information.

Social engineering attacks do not exclusively occur by phone; they can happen in person as well. Malicious individuals often impersonate repair technicians, upper management, or traveling company managers to intimidate or coerce employees into performing activities that violate security. Countermeasures to in-person social engineering attacks include verifying the identity of the intruder/visitor via a secured photograph, contacting their source company, or finding a local manager who recognizes the individual.

Three well-known forms of social engineering attack all share a piscatorial emphasis. *Phishing* is the process of attempting to obtain sensitive information such as usernames, passwords, credit card details, or other personally identifiable information by masquerading as a trustworthy entity (a bank, a service provider, a merchant, for example) in electronic communication (usually emailing). Spearphishing is more targeted form of phishing where the message requesting information appears to originate from a colleague or co-worker at one's own company or organization, often someone in a position of authority. Whaling is a form of phishing that targets specific individuals (by title, industry, from media coverage, and so forth) and sends messages tailored to the needs and interests of those individuals. All take advantage of people's willingness to extend trust to apparently legitimate third parties without applying rules of basic, common-sense information security (the most germane of these principles here is "never open unexpected email attachments" and "never share sensitive information via e-mail").

Social engineering attacks can be used as or in conjunction with penetration tests. These sorts of tests help determine how vulnerable your frontline employees are to individuals adept at lying and how familiar they are with security policy provisions intended to head such things off. For a more detailed discussion of social engineering attacks, see Chapter 4, "Communications Security and Countermeasures."

## Problem Management

Once auditing, monitoring, and penetration testing has occurred, the next step is problem management. *Problem management* is exactly what it sounds like: a formal process or structure for resolving problems. For the most part, problem management is a solution developed in-house to address the various types of issues and problems encountered in your environment. Problem management is typically defined as having three goals or purposes:

- To reduce failures to a manageable level
- To prevent the occurrence or reoccurrence of a problem
- To mitigate the negative impact of problems on computing services and resources

# Inappropriate Activities

*Inappropriate activities* are actions that may take place on a computer or over the IT infrastructure and that may not be actual crimes but are often grounds for internal punishment or termination. Inappropriate activities include creating or viewing inappropriate content, sexual and racial harassment, waste, and abuse.

Inappropriate content can be defined as anything that is not related to or supportive of the work tasks in an organization. It includes but is not limited to pornography, sexually explicit material, entertainment, political data, and violent content. The definition of inappropriate content can be defined by example (by listing types of information deemed inappropriate) or by exclusion (by listing types of information deemed appropriate). Inappropriate content can be defined to include personal email that is not work related.

Keeping inappropriate content to a minimum requires several steps. First, it must be included as an objective in the security policy. Second, staff must have awareness training in regard to inappropriate content. Third, content filtering tools can be deployed to filter data based on source or word content. It is not possible to programmatically block all inappropriate content, but sufficient penalties can be levied against violations along with regular auditing/monitoring to keep its level to a minimum. Also, by defining a clear policy for acceptable use of systems and networks (usually abbreviated AUP for acceptable use policy), you can train users to avoid inappropriate content in the workplace and to stay away from sources of questionable material.

Sexual and racial harassment is a form of inappropriate content or activity on company equipment. Sexual harassment can take many forms, including distribution of images, videos, audio clips, or text information (such as jokes). Sexual and racial harassment controls include awareness training and content filtering.

Waste of resources can have a direct effect on the profitability of an organization. If storage space, computing power, or networking bandwidth capacity is consumed by inappropriate or non-work-related data, the organization is losing money on non-profit-making activities. Some of the more common examples of resource waste include operating a personal business using company equipment, accessing and distributing inappropriate data (pornography, entertainment, music, videos, and so on), or aimlessly surfing the Internet. Just as with inappropriate material, resource waste can be reduced but not eliminated. Some of the primary means to reduce waste include user awareness training, activity monitoring, and content filtering.

Abuse of rights and privileges is the attempt to perform activities or gain access to resources that are restricted or assigned to a higher classification and access level. When access is gained inappropriately, the confidentiality of data is violated and sensitive information can be disclosed. Countermeasures to abuse include strong implementations of access controls and activity logging.

# Indistinct Threats and Countermeasures

Not all problems that an IT infrastructure will face have definitive countermeasures or are even recognizable threats. There are numerous vulnerabilities against which there are no immediate or distinct threats, and against such threats there are few countermeasures. Many of these vulnerabilities lack direct-effect countermeasures, or the deployment of available countermeasures offers little risk reduction.

## Errors and Omissions

One of the most common vulnerabilities that is hardest to protect against is the occurrence of errors and omissions. Errors and omissions occur because humans interact with, program, control, and provide data for IT. There are no direct countermeasures to prevent all errors and omissions. Some safeguards against errors and omissions are input validators and user training. However, these mechanisms offer only a minimal reduction in overall errors and omissions encountered in an IT environment.

## Fraud and Theft

Fraud and theft are criminal activities that can be perpetrated or enabled by using computers. Most of the access controls deployed in a secured environment will reduce fraud and theft, but not every form of such crimes can be predicted and protected against. Both internal authorized users and external unauthorized intruders can exploit your IT infrastructure to perform various types of fraud and theft. Maintaining an intensive auditing and monitoring program and prosecuting all criminal incidents will help reduce fraud and theft.

Theft is an increasing problem in the IT realm that carries the potential for exponential loss, receives lots of publicized attention, and yet remains largely unchecked in many organizations. The simple act of stealing a notebook PC containing private and personal information for hundreds or even thousands of customers, clients, or patients can geometrically expand into a complex problem of identity theft and possible fraud. It happens with alarming regularity and with costly consequences, both in terms of money and in terms of reputation.

*Personally identifiable information* is the uniquely recognizable data about any given person (maiden name, Social Security number, and so on) that is often used to conduct private matters of business. A strong, full-coverage security policy stands up to potential data theft with a proactive approach toward securing it in the first place, both for data in use and *data at rest*, or data that is stored and offline. Any responsible organization will protect private business information equally well against theft, tampering, and fraud.

Protection for personally identifiable information (PII) drives privacy and confidentiality requirements for rules, regulations, and legislation all over the world (especially in North America and the European Union). Be sure to acquaint yourself with the contents of NIST publication 800-122, *Guide to Protecting the Confidentiality of Personally Identifiable Information (PII)*. It is available from the NIST Special Publications (800 Series) download page: http://csrc.nist.gov/publications/PubsSPs.html.

# Collusion

*Collusion* is an agreement among multiple people to perform an unauthorized or illegal action. It is hindered by separation of duties, restricted job responsibilities, audit logging, and job rotation. All of these reduce the likelihood that a co-worker will agree to collaborate on an illegal or abusive scheme because of the higher risk of detection.

However, these safeguards are not primarily directed toward collusion prevention. Reducing collusion is simply a side benefit of these security controls.

---

### Reducing Opportunities for Collusion

Collusion is a real and present danger anywhere highly desirable sensitive information is stored or wherever business transactions occur; collusion is even satirized in the comedy movie *Office Space*.

It depicts three disenfranchised parties—Peter, Michael, and Samir—plotting to commit a crime (embezzlement) against an imaginary company (Initech). Michael creates a virus that will steal fractional portions of electronic money transactions that Peter uploads to the company accounting system. Samir is their conspirator in this operation, which nets hundreds of thousands of dollars in one day.

Although this account is entirely fictional, there are real-world accounts of such crimes resulting in both success and failure. Peter, Michael, and Samir's collusion is not entirely unique, and their story is probably based on some grain of truth from the real world.

How does the separation of duties help to prevent such behavior, and why is auditing so important as a means of ensuring that it doesn't occur anyway? Separation of duties is designed to minimize opportunities for collusion and to maximize requirements and opportunities for reporting of shady or suspect behavior. Careful auditing should reveal that even small amounts of funds are disappearing from accounts and should also ultimately lead auditors to where they are going as well.

---

# Sabotage

Employee *sabotage* can become an issue if an employee is knowledgeable enough about the IT infrastructure of an organization, has sufficient access to manipulate critical aspects of the environment, and has become disgruntled. Employee sabotage occurs most often when an employee suspects they will be terminated without just cause.

This is one important reason terminations should be handled swiftly, including disabling all access to the infrastructure (IT and physical) and escorting the ex-employee off the premises. Safeguards against employee sabotage are intensive auditing, monitoring for abnormal or unauthorized activity, keeping lines of communication open between employees and managers, and properly compensating and recognizing employees for excellence and extra work.

# Loss of Physical and Infrastructure Support

Loss of physical and infrastructure support may occur owing to power outages, natural disasters, communications interruptions, severe weather, loss of a core utility or service, disruption of transportation, strikes, or national emergencies. It may result in IT downtime and invariably reduces productivity and profitability significantly for the duration of the event. It is nearly impossible to predict and protect against events that cause physical and infrastructure support loss.

*Disaster recovery* and *business continuity planning* provide restoration methods when loss events are severe. In most cases, you must wait until the emergency or condition expires and things return to normal.

---

### Unix Details

For the most part, the CISSP exam is product and vendor independent. However, a handful of issues are specific to Unix. If you have worked with Unix or even Linux, most of these items will be simply review. If you have never touched a Unix system, please read this sidebar carefully.

On Unix systems, passwords are stored in a password file. The password file is stored as a shadow file so that it does not appear by default in a directory listing. The shadow setting is similar to the file setting for hidden Windows system files. Although this is an improvement, it is not a valid security mechanism because everyone knows that the password file is set not to display in a directory listing by default and a simple modification of the directory command parameters reveals all hidden or shadowed files.

The most privileged account on a Unix system is known as *root*. Other powerful accounts with similar levels of access are known as *superusers*. It is important to restrict access to these types of user accounts to only those people who absolutely need that level of access to perform their work tasks. The root and superuser accounts on Unix are similar to the administrator account(s) on Windows systems. Whenever possible, restrict root and superuser access to the local console so that these accounts won't work over a network connection.

Two utilities, setuid and setgid, should be closely monitored and their uses logged. These two tools are used to manipulate access to resources. Thus, if they are employed by a nonadministrator or if they are employed by an administrator in an unapproved fashion, it can indicate security policy violations.

Another important command to monitor is the `mount` command, used to map a local drive letter to a shared network drive. This activity may seem like an efficient way to access network resources. However, it also makes malicious code and intruder attacks easier to implement. When the `mount` command is used when it is not authorized, it could indicate an intrusion or an attempt to create a security loophole.

You should also consider monitoring use of the following commands: `systat`, `bootp`, `tftp`, `sunrpc`, `snmp`, `snmp-trap`, and `nfs`.

Finally, Unix systems can be configured to boot into a fixed dedicated security mode where authentication is not required. In that case, anyone accessing the system has complete access to everything at the security level at which the system is currently operating. You can easily determine whether a system has been configured to perform this operation if there is a `/etc/host.equiv` file present. Remove this file to disable this feature.

## Malicious Attackers

*Malicious attackers* are individuals who actively seek to infiltrate your IT infrastructure whether for fame, access, or financial gain. These intrusions or attacks are important threats against which your security policy and your entire security infrastructure is designed to protect. Most safeguards and countermeasures protect against one specific threat or another, but it is not possible to protect against all possible threats that a cracker represents.

Remaining vigilant about security, tracking activity, and implementing intrusion detection systems can provide a reasonable level of protection. Remaining current on security-related subjects (through active forums, mailing lists, and so on) can provide a reasonable level of confidence in your security strategy.

## Espionage

*Espionage* is the malicious act of gathering proprietary, secret, private, sensitive, or confidential information about an organization for the express purpose of disclosing and often selling that data to a competitor or other interested organization (such as a foreign government). Espionage is sometimes committed by internal employees who have become dissatisfied with their jobs or have become compromised in some way. It can also be committed by a mole or plant placed in your organization to steal information for a primary secret employer. Or it can occur far removed from the workplace, perhaps at a convention or an event, perpetrated by someone who specifically targets your employees' mobile assets.

Countermeasures against espionage are to strictly control access to all nonpublic data (both at home and abroad), thoroughly screen new employee candidates, and efficiently track all employee activities.

# Malicious Code

*Malicious code* is any script or program that performs an unwanted, unauthorized, or unknown activity on a computer system. Malicious code can take many forms, including viruses, worms, Trojan horses, documents with destructive macros, and logic bombs. Malicious code exists for every type of computer or computing device.

Monitoring and filtering traffic that enters into and travels within a secured environment (both via network and portable storage devices) is the only effective countermeasure against malicious code.

---

### Education, Policy, and Tools

Malicious software is the stinging bull nettle on a business network and an incessant pest for IT staffers. Alas, users can and will track in malicious software in the most casual and often unwitting ways.

Kim forwards a seemingly harmless interoffice joke through email to Larry's account. Larry opens the document, which actually contains active code segments that perform harmful or destructive actions on his system. Next, Larry reports a host of "performance issues" and "stability problems" with his workstation, which he never complained about before now.

In this scenario, Kim and Larry have little cause to be concerned about their apparently innocuous activities. After all, sharing anecdotes and jokes through company email is a common way to bond and socialize. What's the harm in that, right? The real question is, how can you educate Kim, Larry, and all your other users to be more discreet and discerning in handling shared documents and executables? Can you reasonably prevent malware from coming in on flash drives?

The key is a combination of education, policy, and tools. Anti-malware tools of all types (antivirus, antispyware, antispam, and so forth) should be employed to prevent such materials from crossing the transom onto the network. Education should inform Kim that forwarding non-work materials on the company network is counter to policy and good behavior, and Larry should likewise learn that opening attachments not related to specific work tasks, especially unexpected ones, can lead to all kinds of problems (including those to which he falls prey here). And finally, policy should state terms of acceptable use clearly to prevent unauthorized materials from circulating and from being opened and read.

---

# Traffic and Trend Analysis

The ongoing activities of a network and even a business environment may produce recognizable patterns, which can be deemed normal or abnormal on a circumstantial and situational basis. These patterns are known as *trends* or *traffic patterns*. A specific type of attack called *traffic* or *trend analysis* examines these patterns for what they reveal. What is interesting about these types of examinations or attacks is that they reveal only the patterns of traffic, not the actual content of the traffic. Patterns and trends can reveal operations that occur on a regular basis or that are somehow considered important.

For example, suppose an attacker watches your T1 line and notices that from 3 p.m. to approximately 4:30 p.m. every Friday your organization consumes nearly 80 percent of the capacity of the T1 line. The attacker can infer that the noticeable pattern is a file or data transfer activity that is important because it always occurs at the same time every week. Thus, the attacker can schedule an attack for 2:45 p.m. to take out the T1 or otherwise cause a denial of service to prevent legitimate activity from occurring. Traffic and trend analysis can be used against both encrypted and unencrypted traffic because patterns of traffic rather than contents are examined. Traffic and trend analysis can be used against physical environments and people as well. For example, an observer need only watch a security guard to discover that it takes 12 minutes for him to walk the perimeter of a building and for 8 of those minutes, he is unable to see a section of fence that an intruder could easily climb.

Countermeasures to traffic and trend analysis include performing traffic and trend analysis on your own environment to see what types of information you are inadvertently revealing if anyone happens to be watching. You can alter your common and mission-critical activities so you don't produce easily recognizable patterns. Other countermeasures to traffic and trend analysis are traffic padding, noise, and use of covert channels. You can pad your communication channels through traffic generation tools or broadcasting noise whenever legitimate traffic is not occurring.

# Initial Program Load Vulnerabilities

There is a period of time between the moments when a device is off and when it is fully booted and operational that the system is not fully protected by its security mechanisms. This time period is known as the *initial program load (IPL)*, and it has numerous vulnerabilities. Without physical security, there are no countermeasures for IPL vulnerabilities. Anyone with physical access to a device can easily exploit its weaknesses during its boot-up process. Some IPL vulnerabilities are accessing alternate boot menus, booting to a mobile operating system off a CD or floppy, and accessing the CMOS to alter configuration settings, such as enabling or disabling devices.

---

**Linux Details**

Just as you should be aware of a few Unix issues, you should be aware of a few Linux items as well.

*Salts* are added to Linux passwords (and these days, even to Windows passwords as well) to increase randomness and ensure uniqueness of the stored hash. Think of a salt as a random number appended to the password before hashing.

*Low Water-Mark Mandatory Access Control* (LOMAC) is a loadable kernel module for Linux designed to protect the integrity of processes and data. It is an OS security architecture extension or enhancement that provides flexible support for security policies.

Flask is an OS prototyped in the Fluke research OS. Flask is a security architecture for operating systems that includes flexible support for security policies. Some features of the Fluke prototype were ported into the OSKit (a programmer's toolkit for writing OSs). Many of the Flask architecture features were being incorporated into Security-Enhanced Linux (SE Linux) since it was built using the OSKit. Therefore, Flask led to the Fluke OS, which led to the OSKit. The OSKit was used to write SE Linux, which incorporates flask features.

---

# Summary

Maintaining operations security requires directed efforts in auditing and monitoring. These efforts give rise to detecting attacks and intrusions. This in turn guides the selection of countermeasures, encourages penetration testing, and helps to limit, restrict, and prevent inappropriate activities, crimes, and other threats.

Auditing is a methodical examination or review of an environment to ensure compliance with regulations and to detect abnormalities, unauthorized occurrences, or outright crimes. Secure IT environments rely heavily on auditing. Overall, auditing serves as the primary type of detective control used by a secure environment.

Audit trails are the records created by recording information about events and occurrences into a database or log file, and they can be used to, for example, reconstruct an event, extract information about an incident, and prove or disprove culpability. Audit trails provide a passive form of detective security control and serve as a deterrent in the same manner as CCTV or security guards do. In addition, they can be essential as evidence in the prosecution of criminals.

Record retention is the organizational policy that defines what information is maintained and for how long. In most cases, the records in question are audit trails of user activity, including file and resource access, logon patterns, email, and the use of privileges.

Monitoring is a form of auditing that focuses more on the active review of the audited information or the audited asset. It is most often used in conjunction with performance, but it can be used in a security context as well. The actual tools and techniques used to perform monitoring vary greatly between environments and system platforms, but there are several common forms found in most environments: warning banners, keystroke monitoring, traffic analysis and trend analysis, and other monitoring tools.

Penetration testing is a vigorous attempt to break into a protected network using any means necessary. It is a common method for testing the strength of your security measures. Organizations often hire external consultants to perform penetration testing so that testers are not privy to confidential elements of the security's configuration, network design, and other internal secrets. Penetration testing methods can include war dialing, sniffing, eavesdropping, radiation monitoring, dumpster diving, and social engineering.

Inappropriate activities may take place on a computer or over the IT infrastructure and may not be actual crimes, but they are often grounds for disciplinary action or termination. Inappropriate activities include creating or viewing inappropriate content, sexual and racial harassment, waste, and abuse.

An IT infrastructure can include numerous vulnerabilities against which there is no immediate or distinct threat, and against such threats there are few countermeasures. These types of threats include errors, omissions, fraud, theft, collusion, sabotage, loss of physical and infrastructure support, attackers, espionage, and malicious code. There are, however, steps you can take to lessen the impact of most of these.

# Exam Essentials

**Understand auditing.**   Auditing is a methodical examination or review of an environment to ensure compliance with regulations and to detect abnormalities, unauthorized occurrences, or outright crimes. Secure IT environments rely heavily on auditing. Overall, auditing serves as the primary type of detective control used by a secure environment.

**Know the types or forms of auditing.**   Auditing encompasses a wide variety of different activities, including the recording of event/occurrence data, examination of data, data reduction, the use of event/occurrence alarm triggers, log analysis, and response (some other names for these activities are logging, monitoring, examining alerts, analysis, and even intrusion detection). Be able to explain what each type of auditing activity involves.

**Understand compliance checking.**   Compliance checking (or compliance testing) ensures that all the necessary and required elements of a security solution are properly deployed and functioning as expected. Compliance checks can take many forms, such as vulnerability scans and penetration testing. They can also involve auditing and be performed using log analysis tools to determine whether any vulnerabilities for which countermeasures have been deployed have been realized on the system.

**Understand the need for frequent security audits.**   The frequency of an IT infrastructure security audit or security review is based on risk. You must determine whether sufficient risk exists to warrant the expense and interruption of a security audit on a more or less frequent basis. You should clearly define and adhere to the frequency of audit reviews.

**Understand that auditing is an aspect of due care.**   Security audits and effectiveness reviews are key elements in displaying due care. Senior management must enforce compliance with regular periodic security reviews or they will be held accountable and liable for any asset losses that occur as a result.

**Understand audit trails.**   Audit trails are the records created by recording information about events and occurrences into a database or log file. They are used to reconstruct an event, to extract information about an incident, and to prove or disprove culpability. Using audit trails is a passive form of detective security control, and audit trails are essential evidence in the prosecution of criminals.

**Understand how accountability is maintained.**   Accountability is maintained for individual subjects through the use of audit trails. Activities of users and events caused by the actions of users while online can be recorded so users can be held accountable for their actions. This directly promotes good user behavior and compliance with the organization's security policy.

**Know the basic elements of an audit report.**   Audit reports should all address a few basic or central concepts: the purpose of the audit, the scope of the audit, and the results discovered or revealed by the audit. They often include many other details specific to the environment, such as time, date, and specific systems. Audit reports can include a wide range of content that focuses on problems/events/conditions, standards/criteria/baselines, causes/reasons, impact/effect, or solutions/recommendations/safeguards.

**Understand the need to control access to audit reports.**   Audit reports include sensitive information and should be assigned a classification label and handled appropriately. Only people with sufficient privilege should have access to them. An audit report should also be prepared in various versions according to the hierarchy of the organization, providing only the details relevant to the position of the staff members for which they are prepared.

**Understand sampling.**   Sampling, or data extraction, is the process of extracting elements from a large body of data to construct a meaningful representation or summary of the whole. There are two forms of sampling: statistical and nonstatistical. An auditing tool using precise mathematical functions to extract meaningful information from a large volume of data performs statistical sampling. Statistical sampling is used to measure the risk associated with the sampling process.

**Understand record retention.**   Record retention is the act of retaining and maintaining important information. There should be an organizational policy that defines what information is maintained and for how long. The records in question are usually audit trails of user activity, including file and resource access, logon patterns, email, and the use of privileges. Depending upon your industry and your relationship with the government, you may need to retain records for three years, seven years, or indefinitely.

**Understand monitoring and uses of monitoring tools.**   Monitoring is a form of auditing that focuses more on the active review of the audited information or the audited asset. It's most often used in conjunction with performance, but it can be used in a security context as well. Monitoring can focus on events, subsystems, users, hardware, software, or any other object within the IT environment. Although the actual tools and techniques used to perform monitoring vary greatly between environments and system platforms, several common forms are found in most environments: warning banners, keystroke monitoring, traffic analysis and trend analysis, and other monitoring tools. Be able to list the various monitoring tools and know when and how to use each one.

**Understand failure recognition and response.**   On systems with manual review, the observer or auditor is responsible for failure recognition. To recognize a failure, one must understand what is normal and expected. When monitored or audited events stray from a standard baseline, then a failure, breach, intrusion, error, or problem has occurred, and a response must be initiated.

**Understand what penetration testing is and be able to explain the methods used.** Organizations use penetration testing to evaluate the strength of their security infrastructure. Know that it involves launching intrusion attacks on your network and be able to explain the methods used: war dialing, sniffing and eavesdropping, radiation monitoring, dumpster diving, and social engineering.

**Know what TEMPEST is.**   TEMPEST is a standard for the study and control of electronic signals produced by various types of electronic hardware, such as computers, televisions, phones, and so on. Its primary goal is to prevent EMI and RFI radiation from leaving a strictly defined area so as to eliminate the possibility of external radiation monitoring, eavesdropping, and signal sniffing.

**Know what dumpster diving and scavenging are.**   Dumpster diving and scavenging involve digging through refuse, remains, or leftovers from an organization or operation to discover or infer confidential information. Countermeasures for dumpster diving and scavenging include secure disposal of all garbage. This usually means shredding all documentation and incinerating all shredded material and other waste. Other safeguards include maintaining physical access control and monitoring privilege activity use online.

**Understand social engineering.**   A social engineering attack is an attempt by an attacker to convince an employee to perform an unauthorized activity to subvert the security of an organization. Often the goal of social engineering is to gain access to the IT infrastructure or the physical facility. The only way to protect against social engineering attacks is to thoroughly train users how to respond and interact with communications as well as with unknown personnel.

**Know what inappropriate activities are.**   Inappropriate activities are actions that may take place on a computer or over the IT infrastructure and that may not be actual crimes but are often grounds for internal punishments or termination. Some types of inappropriate activities are creating or viewing inappropriate content, sexual and racial harassment, waste, and abuse.

**Know that errors and omissions can cause security problems.**   One of the most common vulnerabilities and hardest to protect against are errors and omissions. Errors and omissions occur because humans interact with, program, control, and provide data for IT. There are no direct countermeasures to prevent all errors and omissions. Some safeguards against errors and omissions include input validators and user training. However, these mechanisms offer only a minimal reduction in overall errors and omissions encountered in an IT environment.

**Understand fraud and theft.**   Fraud and theft are criminal activities that can be perpetrated using or enabled by computers. Most access controls deployed in a secured environment will reduce fraud and theft, but not every form of these crimes can be predicted and protected against. Both internal authorized users and external unauthorized intruders can exploit your IT infrastructure to perform various forms of fraud and theft. Maintaining an intensive auditing and monitoring program and prosecuting all criminal incidents will help reduce fraud and theft.

**Know what collusion is.**   Collusion is an agreement among multiple persons to perform some unauthorized or illegal action. It is hindered by separation of duties, restricted job responsibilities, audits, and job rotation. All of these reduce the likelihood that a co-worker will agree to collaborate on an illegal or abusive scheme because of the higher risk of detection.

**Understand employee sabotage.**   Employee sabotage can become an issue if an employee is knowledgeable enough about the IT infrastructure of an organization, has sufficient access to manipulate critical aspects of the environment, and has become disgruntled. Safeguards against employee sabotage are intensive auditing, monitoring for abnormal or unauthorized activity, keeping lines of communication open between employees and managers, and properly compensating and recognizing employees for excellence and extra work.

**Know how loss of physical and infrastructure support can cause security problems.**   Loss of physical and infrastructure support comes from power outages, natural disasters, communication interruptions, severe weather, loss of any core utility or service, disruption of transportation, strikes, and national emergencies. It is nearly impossible to predict and protect against events of this kind. Disaster recovery and business continuity planning can provide restoration methods if losses are severe. In most cases, you must wait until the emergency or condition subsides and things return to normal.

**Understand espionage.**   Espionage is the malicious act by an internal employee of gathering proprietary, secret, private, sensitive, or confidential information about an organization for the express purpose of disclosing and often selling that data to a competitor or other interested organization (such as a foreign government). Countermeasures against espionage are to strictly control access to all nonpublic data, thoroughly screen new employee candidates, and efficiently track all employee activities.

# Written Lab

1.   What are audit trails, and why are they important?
2.   How are accountability and auditing interrelated?

# Answers to Written Lab

1.  Auditing is a methodical examination or review of an environment that encompasses a wide variety of different activities to ensure compliance with regulations and to detect abnormalities, unauthorized occurrences, or outright crimes. Audit trails provide the data that supports such examination or review and essentially is what makes auditing and subsequent detection of malfeasance or misbehavior possible.

2.  Accountability is the property that enables activities on a system to be traced to specific entities who then can be held responsible for their actions. Auditing and audit trails provide the means for accountability on information systems where users interact with other users and objects.

# Review Questions

1.  What is a methodical examination or review of an environment to ensure compliance with regulations and to detect abnormalities, unauthorized occurrences, or outright crimes?

    **A.**  Penetration testing

    **B.**  Auditing

    **C.**  Risk analysis

    **D.**  Entrapment

2.  Which of the following is not considered a type of auditing activity?

    **A.**  Recording of event data

    **B.**  Data reduction

    **C.**  Log analysis

    **D.**  Deployment of countermeasures

3.  Monitoring can be used to perform all but which of the following?

    **A.**  Determine validity of software licenses in use.

    **B.**  Detect malicious actions by subjects.

    **C.**  Detect attempted intrusions.

    **D.**  Detect system failures.

4.  What provides data for re-creating the history of an event, intrusion, or system failure step-by-step?

    **A.**  Security policies

    **B.**  Log files

    **C.**  Audit reports

    **D.**  Business continuity planning

5.  What is the frequency of an IT infrastructure security audit or security review based on?

    **A.**  Asset value

    **B.**  Management discretion

    **C.**  Risk

    **D.**  Level of realized threats

6.  Failure to perform which of the following can result in the perception that due care is not being maintained?

    **A.**  Periodic security audits

    **B.**  Deployment of all available safeguards

    **C.**  Performance reviews

    **D.**  Creating audit reports for shareholders

7. Audit trails are considered to be what type of security control?

   **A.** Administrative

   **B.** Passive detective

   **C.** Corrective

   **D.** Physical

8. Which essential element of an audit report is not considered to be a basic concept of the audit?

   **A.** Purpose of the audit

   **B.** Recommendations of the auditor

   **C.** Scope of the audit

   **D.** Results of the audit

9. Why should access to audit reports be controlled and restricted?

   **A.** They contain copies of confidential data stored on the network.

   **B.** They contain information about the vulnerabilities of the system.

   **C.** They are useful only to upper management.

   **D.** They include the details about the configuration of security controls.

10. What are used to inform would-be intruders or those who attempt to violate security policy that their intended activities are restricted and that any further activities will be audited and monitored?

   **A.** Security policies

   **B.** Interoffice memos

   **C.** Warning banners

   **D.** Honeypots

11. Which of the following focuses more on the patterns and trends of data rather than the actual content?

   **A.** Keystroke monitoring

   **B.** Traffic analysis

   **C.** Event logging

   **D.** Security auditing

12. Which of the following activities is not considered a valid form of penetration testing?

   **A.** Denial-of-service attacks

   **B.** Port scanning

   **C.** Distribution of malicious code

   **D.** Packet sniffing

**13.** The act of searching for unauthorized modems is known as _____.

    **A.** scavenging

    **B.** espionage

    **C.** system auditing

    **D.** war dialing

**14.** Which of the following is not a useful countermeasure to war dialing?

    **A.** Restricted and monitored Internet access

    **B.** Imposing strong remote access security

    **C.** Callback security

    **D.** Call logging

**15.** The standard for study and control of electronic signals produced by various types of electronic hardware is known as _____.

    **A.** eavesdropping

    **B.** TEMPEST

    **C.** SESAME

    **D.** wiretapping

**16.** Searching through the refuse, remains, or leftovers from an organization or operation to discover or infer confidential information is known as _____.

    **A.** impersonation

    **B.** dumpster diving

    **C.** social engineering

    **D.** inference

**17.** Which of the following is not an effective countermeasure against inappropriate content being hosted or distributed over a secured network?

    **A.** Activity logging

    **B.** Content filtering

    **C.** Intrusion detection system

    **D.** Penalties and termination for violations

**18.** One of the most common vulnerabilities of an IT infrastructure and hardest to protect against is the occurrence of _____.

    **A.** errors and omissions

    **B.** inference

    **C.** data destruction by malicious code

    **D.** data scavenging

**19.** The willful destruction of assets or elements within the IT infrastructure as a form of revenge or justification for perceived wrongdoing is known as _____.

   **A.** espionage

   **B.** entrapment

   **C.** sabotage

   **D.** permutation

**20.** What is the most common reaction to the loss of physical and infrastructure support?

   **A.** Deploying OS updates

   **B.** Vulnerability scanning

   **C.** Waiting for the event to expire

   **D.** Tightening of access controls

# Answers to Review Questions

1. B. Auditing is a methodical examination or review of an environment to ensure compliance with regulations and to detect abnormalities, unauthorized occurrences, or outright crimes.

2. D. Deployment of countermeasures is not considered a type of auditing activity; rather, it's an active attempt to prevent security problems.

3. A. Monitoring is not used to detect the validity of software licenses in use.

4. B. Log files provide an audit trail for re-creating step-by-step the history of an event, intrusion, or system failure. An audit trail is used to reconstruct an event, to extract information about an incident, to prove or disprove culpability, and to do much more.

5. C. The frequency of an IT infrastructure security audit or security review is based on risk. You must establish the existence of sufficient risk to warrant the expense of and interruption caused by a security audit on a more or less frequent basis.

6. A. Failing to perform periodic security audits can result in the perception that due care is not being maintained. Such audits alert personnel that senior management is practicing due diligence in maintaining system security.

7. B. Audit trails are a passive form of detective security control. Administrative, corrective, and physical security controls are active ways to maintain security.

8. B. Recommendations of the auditor are not considered basic and essential concepts to be included in an audit report. Key elements of an audit report include the purpose, scope, and results of the audit.

9. B. Audit reports should be secured because they contain information about the vulnerabilities of the system. Disclosure of such vulnerabilities to the wrong person could lead to security breaches.

10. C. Warning banners are used to inform would-be intruders or those who attempt to violate the security policy that their intended activities are restricted and that any further activities will be audited and monitored.

11. B. Traffic analysis focuses more on the patterns and trends of data rather than the actual content. Such an analysis offers insight into primary communication routes, sources of encrypted traffic, location of primary servers, primary and backup communication pathways, amount of traffic supported by the network, typical direction of traffic flow, frequency of communications, and much more.

12. C. Distribution of malicious code will almost always result in damage or loss of assets. Thus, it is not an element of penetration testing under any circumstance, even if it's done with the approval of upper management.

13. D. War dialing is the act of searching for unauthorized modems that will accept inbound calls on an otherwise secure network in an attempt to gain access.

**14.** A. Users often install unauthorized modems because of restricted and monitored Internet access. Because war dialing is often used to locate unauthorized modems, restricting and monitoring Internet access wouldn't be an effective countermeasure.

**15.** B. TEMPEST is the standard that defines the study and control of electronic signals produced by various types of electronic hardware.

**16.** B. Dumpster diving is the act of searching through the refuse, remains, or leftovers from an organization or operation to discover or infer confidential information.

**17.** C. An IDS is not a countermeasure against inappropriate content.

**18.** A. One of the most common vulnerabilities and hardest to protect against is the occurrence of errors and omissions.

**19.** C. The willful destruction of assets or elements within the IT infrastructure as a form of revenge or justification for perceived wrongdoing is known as sabotage.

**20.** C. In most cases, you must simply wait until the emergency or condition expires and things return to normal.

# Chapter
# 15

# Business Continuity Planning

---

## THE CISSP EXAM TOPICS COVERED IN THIS CHAPTER INCLUDE:

✓ **Business Continuity and Disaster Recovery Planning**

- Understand business continuity requirements
  - Develop and document project scope and plan
- Conduct business impact analysis
  - Identify and prioritize critical business functions; determine maximum tolerable downtime and other criteria; assess exposure to outages (e.g., local, regional, global); define recovery objectives
- Develop recovery strategy
  - Implement a backup storage strategy (e.g., offsite storage, electronic vaulting, tape rotation); recovery site strategies

✓ **Operations Security**

- Manage incident response
  - Detection; response; reporting; recovery; remediation
- Understand fault tolerance requirements

Despite our best wishes, disasters of one form or another eventually strike every organization. Whether it's a natural disaster such as a hurricane or earthquake or a manmade calamity such as a building fire or burst water pipes, every organization will encounter events that threaten their very existence. Strong organizations have plans and procedures in place to help mitigate the effects a disaster has on their continuing operations and to speed the return to normal operations. Recognizing the importance of planning for business continuity and disaster recovery, the organization (ISC)² designated these two processes as one of the 10 domains of the Common Body of Knowledge for the CISSP program. Knowledge of these fundamental topics will help you prepare for the exam and help you prepare your organization for the unexpected.

In this chapter, we'll explore the concepts behind business continuity planning. Chapter 16, "Disaster Recovery Planning," will continue our discussion.

# Business Continuity Planning

*Business continuity planning (BCP)* involves assessing a variety of risks to organizational processes and creating policies, plans, and procedures to minimize the impact those risks might have on the organization if they were to occur. BCP is used to maintain the continuous operation of a business in the event of an emergency situation. The goal of BCP planners is to implement a combination of policies, procedures, and processes such that a potentially disruptive event has as little impact on the business as possible.

BCP focuses on maintaining business operations with reduced or restricted infrastructure capabilities or resources. As long as the continuity of the organization's ability to perform its mission-critical work tasks is maintained, BCP can be used to manage and restore the environment. If the continuity is broken, then business processes have stopped and the organization is in disaster mode; thus, DRP takes over.

The top priority of BCP and DRP is always *people.* The primary concern is to get people out of harm's way; then you can address IT recovery and restoration issues.

### Business Continuity Planning vs. Disaster Recovery Planning

You should understand the distinction between business continuity planning and disaster recovery planning. One easy way to remember the difference is that BCP comes first, and if the BCP efforts fail, DRP steps in to fill the gap. For example, consider the case of a data center located downstream from a dam. BCP efforts might involve performing preventive maintenance on the dam and reinforcing the data center to protect it from floodwaters.

Despite your best efforts, it's possible that your business continuity efforts will fail. Pressure on the dam might increase to the point that the dam fails and the area beneath it floods. The level of those floodwaters might be too much for the data center reinforcements to handle, causing flooding of the data center and a disruption in business operations. At this point, your business continuity efforts have failed, and it's time to invoke your disaster recovery plan.

We'll discuss disaster recovery planning in Chapter 16. The eventual goal of those efforts is to restore business operations in the primary data center as quickly as possible.

The overall goal of BCP is to provide a quick, calm, and efficient response in the event of an emergency and to enhance a company's ability to recover from a disruptive event promptly. The BCP process, as defined by (ISC)$^2$, has four main steps:

- Project scope and planning
- Business impact assessment
- Continuity planning
- Approval and implementation

The next three sections of this chapter cover each of these phases in detail. The last portion of this chapter will introduce some of the critical elements you should consider when compiling documentation of your organization's business continuity plan.

# Project Scope and Planning

As with any formalized business process, the development of a strong business continuity plan requires the use of a proven methodology. This requires the following:

- Structured analysis of the business's organization from a crisis planning point of view
- The creation of a BCP team with the approval of senior management
- An assessment of the resources available to participate in business continuity activities
- An analysis of the legal and regulatory landscape that governs an organization's response to a catastrophic event

The exact process you use will depend upon the size and nature of your organization and its business. There really isn't a "one-size-fits-all" guide to business continuity project planning. You should consult with project planning professionals within your organization and determine the approach that will work best within your organizational culture.

## Business Organization Analysis

One of the first responsibilities of the individuals responsible for business continuity planning is to perform an analysis of the business organization to identify all departments and individuals who have a stake in the BCP process. Some areas to consider are included in the following list:

- Operational departments that are responsible for the core services the business provides to its clients

- Critical support services, such as the information technology department, plant maintenance department, and other groups responsible for the upkeep of systems that support the operational departments

- Senior executives and other key individuals essential for the ongoing viability of the organization

This identification process is critical for two reasons. First, it provides the groundwork necessary to help identify potential members of the BCP team (see the next section). Second, it provides the foundation for the remainder of the BCP process.

Normally, the business organization analysis is performed by the individuals spearheading the BCP effort. This is acceptable, given that they normally use the output of the analysis to assist with the selection of the remaining BCP team members. However, a thorough review of this analysis should be one of the first tasks assigned to the full BCP team when it is convened. This step is critical because the individuals performing the original analysis may have overlooked critical business functions known to BCP team members that represent other parts of the organization. If the team were to continue without revising the organizational analysis, the entire BCP process may be negatively affected, resulting in the development of a plan that does not fully address the emergency-response needs of the organization as a whole.

Each location of an organization should have its own distinct plan addressing the unique needs of that location. A single plan should not cover multiple geographic locations.

## BCP Team Selection

In many organizations, the IT and/or security departments are given sole responsibility for BCP without obtaining input from other operational and support departments. In fact, those departments may not even know of the plan's existence until disaster strikes or is imminent. This is a critical flaw! The isolated development of a business continuity plan can spell disaster in two ways. First, the plan itself may not take into account knowledge possessed only by the individuals responsible for the day-to-day operation of the business. Second, it keeps operational elements "in the dark" about plan specifics until implementation becomes necessary. This reduces the possibility that operational elements will agree with the provisions of the plan and work effectively to implement it. It also denies organizations the benefits achieved by a structured training and testing program for the plan.

To prevent these events from adversely impacting the BCP process, the individuals responsible for the effort should take special care when selecting the BCP team. The team should include, as a minimum, the following individuals:

- Representatives from each of the organization's departments responsible for the core services performed by the business
- Representatives from the key support departments identified by the organizational analysis
- IT representatives with technical expertise in areas covered by the BCP
- Security representatives with knowledge of the BCP process
- Legal representatives familiar with corporate legal, regulatory, and contractual responsibilities
- Representatives from senior management

WARNING    Select your team carefully! You need to strike a balance between representing different points of view and creating a team with explosive personality differences. Your goal should be to create a group that is as diverse as possible and still operates in harmony.

Each one of the individuals mentioned in the preceding list brings a unique perspective to the BCP process and will have individual biases. For example, the representatives from each of the operational departments will often consider their department the most critical to the organization's continued viability. Although these biases may at first seem divisive, the leader of the BCP effort should embrace them and harness them in a productive manner. If used effectively, the biases will help achieve a healthy balance in the final plan as each representative advocates the needs of their department. On the other hand, if proper leadership isn't provided, these biases may devolve into destructive turf battles that derail the BCP effort and harm the organization as a whole.

NOTE    Take some time to think about the BCP team membership and who would be appropriate for your organization's technical, financial, and political environment. Who would you include?

### Senior Management and BCP

The role of senior management in the BCP process varies widely from organization to organization and depends upon the internal culture of the business, interest in the plan from above, and the legal and regulatory environment in which the business operates. Important roles played by senior management usually include setting priorities, providing staff and financial resources, and arbitrating disputes about the criticality of services.

One of the authors recently completed a BCP consulting engagement with a large nonprofit institution. At the beginning of the engagement, he had a chance to sit down with one of the organization's senior executives to discuss his goals and objectives for their work together. During that meeting, the senior executive asked him, "Is there anything you need from me to complete this engagement?"

He must have expected a perfunctory response because his eyes widened when the response began with, "Well, as a matter of fact. . ." He was then told that his active participation in the process was critical to its success.

When you work on a business continuity plan, you, as the BCP team leader, must seek and obtain as active a role as possible from a senior executive. This conveys the importance of the BCP process to the entire organization and fosters the active participation of individuals who might otherwise write BCP off as a waste of time better spent on operational activities. Furthermore, laws and regulations might require the active participation of those senior leaders in the planning process. If you work for a publicly traded company, you may want to remind executives that the officers and directors of the firm might be found personally liable if a disaster cripples the business and they are found not to have exercised *due diligence* in their contingency planning.

You may also have to convince management that BCP and DRP spending should not be viewed as a discretionary expense. Management's fiduciary responsibilities to the organization's shareholders require them to at least ensure that adequate BCP measures are in place.

In the case of this BCP engagement, the executive acknowledged the importance of his support and agreed to participate. He sent an email to all employees introducing the effort and stating that it had his full backing. He also attended several of the high-level planning sessions and mentioned the effort in an organization-wide "town hall" meeting.

## Resource Requirements

After the team validates the business organization analysis, it should turn to an assessment of the resources required by the BCP effort. This involves the resources required by three distinct BCP phases:

**BCP development**    The BCP team will require some resources to perform the four elements of the BCP process (project scope and planning, business impact assessment, continuity planning, and approval and implementation). It's more than likely that the major resource consumed by this BCP phase will be effort expended by members of the BCP team and the support staff they call upon to assist in the development of the plan.

**BCP testing, training, and maintenance**    The testing, training, and maintenance phases of BCP will require some hardware and software commitments, but once again, the major commitment in this phase will be effort on the part of the employees involved in those activities.

**BCP implementation**    When a disaster strikes and the BCP team deems it necessary to conduct a full-scale implementation of the business continuity plan, this implementation will require significant resources. This includes a large amount of effort (BCP will likely become the focus of a large part, if not all, of the organization) and the utilization of "hard" resources. For this reason, it's important that the team uses its BCP implementation powers judiciously yet decisively.

An effective business continuity plan requires the expenditure of a large amount of corporate resources, ranging all the way from the purchase and deployment of redundant computing facilities to the pencils and paper used by team members scratching out the first drafts of the plan. However, as you saw earlier, personnel are one of the most significant resources consumed by the BCP process. Many security professionals overlook the importance of accounting for labor. However, you can rest assured that senior management will not. Business leaders are keenly aware of the effect that time-consuming side activities have on the operational productivity of their organizations and the real cost of personnel in terms of salary, benefits, and lost opportunities. These concerns become especially paramount when you are requesting the time of senior executives. You should expect that leaders responsible for resource utilization management will put your BCP proposal under a microscope, and you should be prepared to defend the necessity of your plan with coherent, logical arguments that address the business case for BCP.

---

**Explaining the Benefits of BCP**

At a recent conference, one of the authors had the opportunity to discuss business continuity planning with the chief information security officer (CISO) of a health system from a medium-sized U.S. city. The CISO's attitude was shocking. His organization had not conducted a formal BCP process, and he was confident that a "seat-of-the-pants" approach would work fine in the unlikely event of a disaster.

This "seat-of-the-pants" argument is one of the most common arguments against committing resources to BCP. In many organizations, the attitude that the business has always survived and the key leaders will figure something out in the event of a disaster pervades corporate thinking. If you encounter this objection, you might want to point out to management the costs that will be incurred by the business (both direct costs and the indirect cost of lost opportunities) for each day that the business is down. Then ask them to consider how long a "seat-of-the-pants" recovery might take when compared to an orderly, planned continuity of operations.

## Legal and Regulatory Requirements

Many industries may find themselves bound by federal, state, and local laws or regulations that require them to implement various degrees of BCP. We've already discussed one example in this chapter—the officers and directors of publicly traded firms have a fiduciary responsibility to exercise due diligence in the execution of their business continuity duties. In other circumstances, the requirements (and consequences of failure) might be more severe. Emergency services, such as police, fire, and emergency medical operations, have a responsibility to the community to continue operations in the event of a disaster. Indeed, their services become even more critical in an emergency when public safety is threatened. Failure on their part to implement a solid BCP could result in the loss of life and/or property and the decreased confidence of the population in their government.

In many countries, financial institutions, such as banks, brokerages, and the firms that process their data, are governed by strict government and international banking and securities regulations designed to facilitate their continued operation to ensure the viability of the national economy. When pharmaceutical manufacturers must produce products in less-than-optimal circumstances following a disaster, they are required to certify the purity of their products to government regulators. There are countless other examples of industries that are required to continue operating in the event of an emergency by various laws and regulations.

Even if you're not bound by any of these considerations, you might have contractual obligations to your clients that require you to implement sound BCP practices. If your contracts include some type of *service-level agreement (SLA)*, you might find yourself in breach of those contracts if a disaster interrupts your ability to service your clients. Many clients may feel sorry for you and want to continue using your products/services, but their own business requirements might force them to sever the relationship and find new suppliers.

On the flip side of the coin, developing a strong, documented business continuity plan can help your organization win new clients and additional business from existing clients. If you can show your customers the sound procedures you have in place to continue serving them in the event of a disaster, they'll place greater confidence in your firm and might be more likely to choose you as their preferred vendor. Not a bad position to be in!

All of these concerns point to one conclusion—it's essential to include your organization's legal counsel in the BCP process. They are intimately familiar with the legal, regulatory, and contractual obligations that apply to your organization and can help your team implement a plan that meets those requirements while ensuring the continued viability of the organization to the benefit of all—employees, shareholders, suppliers, and customers alike.

> Laws regarding computing systems, business practices, and disaster management change frequently and vary from jurisdiction to jurisdiction. Be sure to keep your attorneys involved throughout the lifetime of your BCP, including the testing and maintenance phases. If you restrict their involvement to a preimplementation review of the plan, you may not become aware of the impact that changing laws and regulations have on your corporate responsibilities.

# Business Impact Assessment

Once your BCP team completes the four stages of preparing to create a business continuity plan, it's time to dive into the heart of the work—the *business impact assessment (BIA)*. The BIA identifies the resources that are critical to an organization's ongoing viability and the threats posed to those resources. It also assesses the likelihood that each threat will actually occur and the impact those occurrences will have on the business. The results of the BIA provide you with quantitative measures that can help you prioritize the commitment of business continuity resources to the various risks your organization faces.

It's important to realize that there are two different types of analyses that business planners use when facing a decision:

**Quantitative decision making** Quantitative decision making involves the use of numbers and formulas to reach a decision. This type of data often expresses options in terms of the dollar value to the business.

**Qualitative decision making** Qualitative decision making takes nonnumerical factors, such as emotions, investor/customer confidence, workforce stability, and other concerns, into account. This type of data often results in categories of prioritization (such as high, medium, and low).

> Quantitative analysis and qualitative analysis both play an important role in the BCP process. However, most people tend to favor one type of analysis over the other. When selecting the individual members of the BCP team, try to achieve a balance between people who prefer each strategy. This will result in the development of a well-rounded BCP and benefit the organization in the long run.

The BIA process described in this chapter approaches the problem from both quantitative and qualitative points of view. However, it's very tempting for a BCP team to "go with the numbers" and perform a quantitative assessment while neglecting the somewhat more difficult qualitative assessment. It's important that the BCP team perform a qualitative analysis of the factors affecting your BCP process. For example, if your business is highly dependent upon a few very important clients, your management team is probably willing to suffer significant short-term financial loss in order to retain those clients in the long term. The BCP team must sit down and discuss (preferably with the involvement of senior management) qualitative concerns to develop a comprehensive approach that satisfies all stakeholders.

## Identify Priorities

The first BIA task facing the BCP team is identifying business priorities. Depending upon your line of business, there will be certain activities that are most essential to your day-to-day operations when disaster strikes. The priority identification task, or *criticality prioritization*, involves creating a comprehensive list of business processes and ranking them in order of importance. Although this task may seem somewhat daunting, it's not as hard as it seems. A great way to divide the workload of this process among the team members is to assign each participant responsibility for drawing up a prioritized list that covers the business functions for which their department is responsible. When the entire BCP team convenes, team members can use those prioritized lists to create a master prioritized list for the entire organization.

   This process helps identify business priorities from a qualitative point of view. Recall that we're describing an attempt to simultaneously develop both qualitative and quantitative BIAs. To begin the quantitative assessment, the BCP team should sit down and draw up a list of organization *assets* and then assign an *asset value (AV)* in monetary terms to each asset. These numbers will be used in the remaining BIA steps to develop a financially based BIA. The second quantitative measure that the team must develop is the *maximum tolerable downtime (MTD)*. The MTD is the maximum length of time a business function can be inoperable without causing irreparable harm to the business. The MTD provides valuable information when you're performing both BCP and DRP planning. Once you have defined your recovery objectives, you can design and plan the procedures necessary to accomplish the recovery tasks. This leads to another metric, the *recovery time objective (RTO)*, for each business function. This is the amount of time in which you think you can feasibly recover the function in the event of a disruption. The goal of the BCP process is to ensure that your RTOs are less than your MTDs, resulting in a situation in which a function should never be unavailable beyond the maximum tolerable downtime.

## Risk Identification

The next phase of the BIA is the identification of risks posed to your organization. Some elements of this organization-specific list may come to mind immediately. The identification of other, more obscure risks might take a little creativity on the part of the BCP team.

*Risks* come in two forms: natural risks and man-made risks. The following list includes some events that pose natural threats:

- Violent storms/hurricanes/tornadoes/blizzards
- Earthquakes
- Mudslides/avalanches
- Volcanic eruptions

Man-made threats include the following events:

- Terrorist acts/wars/civil unrest
- Theft/vandalism
- Fires/explosions
- Prolonged power outages
- Building collapses
- Transportation failures

Remember, these are by no means all-inclusive lists. They merely identify some common risks that many organizations face. You may want to use them as a starting point, but a full listing of risks facing your organization will require input from all members of the BCP team.

The risk identification portion of the process is purely qualitative in nature. At this point in the process, the BCP team should not be concerned about the likelihood that each type of risk will actually materialize or the amount of damage such an occurrence would inflict upon the continued operation of the business. The results of this analysis will drive both the qualitative and quantitative portions of the remaining BIA tasks.

## Likelihood Assessment

The preceding step consisted of the BCP team drawing up a comprehensive list of the events that can be a threat to an organization. You probably recognized that some events are much more likely to happen than others. For example, a business in Southern California is much more likely to face the risk of an earthquake than to face the risk posed by a volcanic eruption. A business based in Hawaii might have the exact opposite likelihood that each risk would occur.

To account for these differences, the next phase of the business impact assessment identifies the likelihood that each risk will occur. To keep calculations consistent, this assessment is usually expressed in terms of an *annualized rate of occurrence (ARO)* that reflects the number of times a business expects to experience a given disaster each year.

The BCP team should sit down and determine an ARO for each risk identified in the previous section. These numbers should be based upon corporate history, professional experience of team members, and advice from experts, such as meteorologists, seismologists, fire prevention professionals, and other consultants, as needed.

In many cases, you may be able to find likelihood assessments for some risks prepared by experts at no cost to you. For example, the U.S. Geological Survey (USGS) developed the earthquake hazard map shown in Figure 15.1. This map illustrates the ARO for earthquakes in various regions of the United States. Similarly, the Federal Emergency Management Agency (FEMA) coordinates the development of detailed flood maps of local communities throughout the United States. These resources are available online and offer a wealth of information to organizations performing a business impact assessment.

**FIGURE 15.1**    Earthquake hazard map of the United States

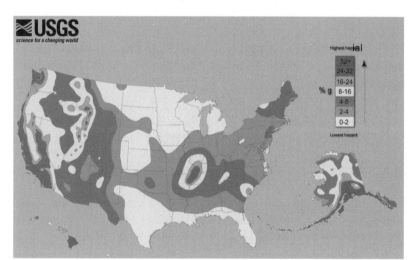

(Source: U.S. Geological Survey)

## Impact Assessment

As you may have surmised based upon its name, the impact assessment is one of the most critical portions of the business impact assessment. In this phase, you analyze the data gathered during risk identification and likelihood assessment and attempt to determine what impact each one of the identified risks would have upon the business if it were to occur.

From a quantitative point of view, we will cover three specific metrics: the exposure factor, the single loss expectancy, and the annualized loss expectancy. Each one of these values is computed for each specific risk/asset combination evaluated during the previous phases.

The *exposure factor (EF)* is the amount of damage that the risk poses to the asset, expressed as a percentage of the asset's value. For example, if the BCP team consults with fire experts and determines that a building fire would cause 70 percent of the building to be destroyed, the exposure factor of the building to fire is 70 percent.

The *single loss expectancy (SLE)* is the monetary loss that is expected each time the risk materializes. You can compute the SLE using the following formula:

SLE = AV × EF

Continuing with the preceding example, if the building is worth $500,000, the single loss expectancy would be 70 percent of $500,000, or $350,000. You can interpret this figure to mean that a single fire in the building would be expected to cause $350,000 worth of damage.

The *annualized loss expectancy (ALE)* is the monetary loss that the business expects to occur as a result of the risk harming the asset over the course of a year. You already have all the data necessary to perform this calculation. The SLE is the amount of damage you expect each time a disaster strikes, and the ARO (from the likelihood analysis) is the number of times you expect a disaster to occur each year. You compute the ALE by simply multiplying those two numbers:

ALE = SLE × ARO

Returning once again to our building example, if fire experts predict that a fire will occur in the building once every 30 years, the ARO is ⅟₃₀, or 0.03. The ALE is then 3 percent of the $350,000 SLE, or $11,667. You can interpret this figure to mean that the business should expect to lose $11,667 each year due to a fire in the building.

Obviously, a fire will not occur each year—this figure represents the average cost over the 30 years between fires. It's not especially useful for budgeting considerations but proves invaluable when attempting to prioritize the assignment of BCP resources to a given risk. These concepts were also covered in Chapter 6, "Asset Value, Policies, and Roles."

Be certain you're familiar with the quantitative formulas contained in this chapter and the concepts of asset value, exposure factor, annualized rate of occurrence, single loss expectancy, and annualized loss expectancy. Know the formulas and be able to work through a scenario.

From a qualitative point of view, you must consider the nonmonetary impact that interruptions might have on your business. For example, you might want to consider the following:

- Loss of goodwill among your client base
- Loss of employees to other jobs after prolonged downtime
- Social/ethical responsibilities to the community
- Negative publicity

It's difficult to put dollar values on items like these in order to include them in the quantitative portion of the impact assessment, but they are equally important. After all, if you decimate your client base, you won't have a business to return to when you're ready to resume operations!

## Resource Prioritization

The final step of the BIA is to prioritize the allocation of business continuity resources to the various risks that you identified and assessed in the preceding tasks of the BIA.

From a quantitative point of view, this process is relatively straightforward. You simply create a list of all the risks you analyzed during the BIA process and sort them in descending order according to the ALE computed during the impact assessment phase. This provides you with a prioritized list of the risks that you should address. Simply select as many items as you're willing and able to address simultaneously from the top of the list and work your way down. Eventually, you'll reach a point at which you've exhausted either the list of risks (unlikely!) or all your available resources (much more likely!).

Recall from the previous section that we also stressed the importance of addressing qualitatively important concerns. In previous sections about the BIA, we treated quantitative and qualitative analysis as mainly separate functions with some overlap in the analysis. Now it's time to merge the two prioritized lists, which is more of an art than a science. You must sit down with the BCP team and representatives from the senior management team and combine the two lists into a single prioritized list. Qualitative concerns may justify elevating or lowering the priority of risks that already exist on the ALE-sorted quantitative list. For example, if you run a fire suppression company, your number-one priority might be the prevention of a fire in your principal place of business despite the fact that an earthquake might cause more physical damage. The potential loss of reputation within the business community resulting from the destruction of a fire suppression company by fire might be too difficult to overcome and result in the eventual collapse of the business, justifying the increased priority.

# Continuity Planning

The first two phases of the BCP process (project scope and planning and the business impact assessment) focus on determining how the BCP process will work and prioritizing the business assets that must be protected against interruption. The next phase of BCP development, continuity planning, focuses on developing and implementing a continuity strategy to minimize the impact realized risks might have on protected assets.

In this section, you'll learn about the subtasks involved in continuity planning:

- Strategy development
- Provisions and processes
- Plan approval
- Plan implementation
- Training and education

# Strategy Development

The strategy development phase bridges the gap between the business impact assessment and the continuity planning phases of BCP development. The BCP team must now take the prioritized list of concerns raised by the quantitative and qualitative resource prioritization exercises and determine which risks will be addressed by the business continuity plan. Fully addressing all the contingencies would require the implementation of provisions and processes that maintain a zero-downtime posture in the face of every possible risk. For obvious reasons, implementing a policy this comprehensive is simply impossible.

The BCP team should look back to the MTD estimates created during the early stages of the BIA and determine which risks are deemed acceptable and which must be mitigated by BCP continuity provisions. Some of these decisions are obvious—the risk of a blizzard striking an operations facility in Egypt is negligible and would be deemed an acceptable risk. The risk of a monsoon in New Delhi is serious enough that it must be mitigated by BCP provisions.

Keep in mind that there are four possible responses to a risk: reduce, assign, accept, and reject. Each may be an acceptable response based upon the circumstances.

Once the BCP team determines which risks require mitigation and the level of resources that will be committed to each mitigation task, they are ready to move on to the provisions and processes phase of continuity planning.

# Provisions and Processes

The provisions and processes phase of continuity planning is the meat of the entire business continuity plan. In this task, the BCP team designs the specific procedures and mechanisms that will mitigate the risks deemed unacceptable during the strategy development stage. Three categories of assets must be protected through BCP provisions and processes: people, buildings/facilities, and infrastructure. In the next three sections, we'll explore some of the techniques you can use to safeguard these categories.

## People

First and foremost, you must ensure that the people within your organization are safe before, during, and after an emergency. Once you've achieved that goal, you must make provisions to allow your employees to conduct both their BCP and operational tasks in as normal a manner as possible given the circumstances.

Don't lose sight of the fact that people are your most valuable asset. The safety of people must always come before the organization's business goals. Make sure that your business continuity plan makes adequate provisions for the security of your employees, customers, suppliers, and any other individuals who may be affected!

People should be provided with all the resources they need to complete their assigned tasks. At the same time, if circumstances dictate that people be present in the workplace for extended periods of time, arrangements must be made for shelter and food. Any continuity plan that requires these provisions should include detailed instructions for the BCP team in the event of a disaster. The organization should maintain stockpiles of provisions sufficient to feed the operational and support teams for an extended period of time in an accessible location. Plans should specify the periodic rotation of those stockpiles to prevent spoilage.

## Buildings and Facilities

Many businesses require specialized facilities in order to carry out their critical operations. These might include standard office facilities, manufacturing plants, operations centers, warehouses, distribution/logistics centers, and repair/maintenance depots, among others. When you perform your BIA, you will identify those facilities that play a critical role in your organization's continued viability. Your continuity plan should address two areas for each critical facility:

**Hardening provisions**   Your BCP should outline mechanisms and procedures that can be put into place to protect your existing facilities against the risks defined in the strategy development phase. This might include steps as simple as patching a leaky roof or as complex as installing reinforced hurricane shutters and fireproof walls.

**Alternate sites**   In the event that it's not feasible to harden a facility against a risk, your BCP should identify alternate sites where business activities can resume immediately (or at least in a period of time that's shorter than the maximum tolerable downtime for all affected critical business functions). Chapter 16, "Disaster Recovery Planning," describes a few of the facility types that might be useful in this stage.

## Infrastructure

Every business depends upon some sort of infrastructure for its critical processes. For many businesses, a critical part of this infrastructure is an IT backbone of communications and computer systems that process orders, manage the supply chain, handle customer interaction, and perform other business functions. This backbone comprises a number of servers, workstations, and critical communications links between sites. The BCP must address how these systems will be protected against risks identified during the strategy development phase. As with buildings and facilities, there are two main methods of providing this protection:

**Physically hardening systems**   You can protect systems against the risks by introducing protective measures such as computer-safe fire suppression systems and uninterruptible power supplies.

**Alternative systems**   You can also protect business functions by introducing redundancy (either redundant components or completely redundant systems/communications links that rely on different facilities).

These same principles apply to whatever infrastructure components serve your critical business processes—transportation systems, electrical power grids, banking and financial systems, water supplies, and so on.

## Plan Approval

Once the BCP team completes the design phase of the BCP document, it's time to gain top-level management endorsement of the plan. If you were fortunate enough to have senior management involvement throughout the development phases of the plan, this should be a relatively straightforward process. On the other hand, if this is your first time approaching management with the BCP document, you should be prepared to provide a lengthy explanation of the plan's purpose and specific provisions.

Senior management approval and buy-in is essential to the success of the overall BCP effort.

If possible, you should attempt to have the plan endorsed by the top executive in your business—the chief executive officer, chairman, president, or similar business leader. This move demonstrates the importance of the plan to the entire organization and showcases the business leader's commitment to business continuity. The signature of such an individual on the plan also gives it much greater weight and credibility in the eyes of other senior managers, who might otherwise brush it off as a necessary but trivial IT initiative.

## Plan Implementation

Once you've received approval from senior management, it's time to dive in and start implementing your plan. The BCP team should get together and develop an implementation schedule that utilizes the resources dedicated to the program to achieve the stated process and provision goals in as prompt a manner as possible given the scope of the modifications and the organizational climate.

After all the resources are fully deployed, the BCP team should supervise the conduct of an appropriate BCP maintenance program to ensure that the plan remains responsive to evolving business needs.

## Training and Education

Training and education are essential elements of the BCP implementation. All personnel who will be involved in the plan (either directly or indirectly) should receive some sort of training on the overall plan and their individual responsibilities. Everyone in the organization should receive at least a plan overview briefing to provide them with the confidence that business leaders have considered the possible risks posed to continued operation of the business and have put a plan in place to mitigate the impact on the organization should business be disrupted. People with direct BCP responsibilities should be trained and evaluated on their specific BCP tasks to ensure that they are able to complete them efficiently when disaster strikes. Furthermore, at least one backup person should be trained for every BCP task to ensure redundancy in the event personnel are injured or cannot reach the workplace during an emergency.

# BCP Documentation

Documentation is a critical step in the business continuity planning process. Committing your BCP methodology to paper provides several important benefits:

- It ensures that BCP personnel have a written continuity document to reference in the event of an emergency, even if senior BCP team members are not present to guide the effort.

- It provides a historical record of the BCP process that will be useful to future personnel seeking to both understand the reasoning behind various procedures and implement necessary changes in the plan.

- It forces the team members to commit their thoughts to paper—a process that often facilitates the identification of flaws in the plan. Having the plan on paper also allows draft documents to be distributed to individuals not on the BCP team for a "sanity check."

In the following sections, we'll explore some of the important components of the written business continuity plan.

## Continuity Planning Goals

First and foremost, the plan should describe the goals of continuity planning as set forth by the BCP team and senior management. These goals should be decided upon at or before the first BCP team meeting and will most likely remain unchanged throughout the life of the BCP.

The most common goal of the BCP is quite simple: to ensure the continuous operation of the business in the face of an emergency situation. Other goals may also be inserted in this section of the document to meet organizational needs. For example, you might have goals that your customer call center experience no more than 15 consecutive minutes of downtime or that your backup servers be able to handle 75 percent of your processing load within 1 hour of activation.

## Statement of Importance

The statement of importance reflects the criticality of the BCP to the organization's continued viability. This document commonly takes the form of a letter to the organization's employees stating the reason that the organization devoted significant resources to the BCP development process and requesting the cooperation of all personnel in the BCP implementation phase. Here's where the importance of senior executive buy-in comes into play. If you can put out this letter under the signature of the CEO or an officer at a similar level, the plan will carry tremendous weight as you attempt to implement changes throughout the organization. If you have the signature of a lower-level manager, you may encounter resistance as you attempt to work with portions of the organization outside of that individual's direct control.

## Statement of Priorities

The statement of priorities flows directly from the identify priorities phase of the business impact assessment. It simply involves listing the functions considered critical to continued business operations in a prioritized order. When listing these priorities, you should also include a statement that they were developed as part of the BCP process and reflect the importance of the functions to continued business operations in the event of an emergency and nothing more. Otherwise, the list of priorities could be used for unintended purposes and result in a political turf battle between competing organizations to the detriment of the business continuity plan.

## Statement of Organizational Responsibility

The statement of organizational responsibility also comes from a senior-level executive and can be incorporated into the same letter as the statement of importance. It basically echoes the sentiment that "business continuity is everyone's responsibility!" The statement of organizational responsibility restates the organization's commitment to business continuity planning and informs the organization's employees, vendors, and affiliates that they are individually expected to do everything they can to assist with the BCP process.

## Statement of Urgency and Timing

The statement of urgency and timing expresses the criticality of implementing the BCP and outlines the implementation timetable decided upon by the BCP team and agreed to by upper management. The wording of this statement will depend upon the actual urgency assigned to the BCP process by the organization's leadership. If the statement itself is included in the same letter as the statement of priorities and statement of organizational responsibility, the timetable should be included as a separate document. Otherwise, the timetable and this statement can be put into the same document.

## Risk Assessment

The risk assessment portion of the BCP documentation essentially recaps the decision-making process undertaken during the business impact assessment. It should include a discussion of all the risks considered during the BIA as well as the quantitative and qualitative analyses performed to assess these risks. For the quantitative analysis, the actual AV, EF, ARO, SLE, and ALE figures should be included. For the qualitative analysis, the thought process behind the risk analysis should be provided to the reader. It's important to note that the risk assessment should be updated on a regular basis because it reflects a point-in-time assessment.

## Risk Acceptance/Mitigation

The risk acceptance/mitigation section of the BCP documentation contains the outcome of the strategy development portion of the BCP process. It should cover each risk identified in the risk analysis portion of the document and outline one of two thought processes:

- For risks that were deemed acceptable, it should outline the reasons the risk was considered acceptable as well as potential future events that might warrant reconsideration of this determination.

- For risks that were deemed unacceptable, it should outline the risk management provisions and processes put into place to reduce the risk to the organization's continued viability.

## Vital Records Program

The BCP documentation should also outline a vital records program for the organization. This document states where critical business records will be stored and the procedures for making and storing backup copies of those records.

## Emergency-Response Guidelines

The emergency-response guidelines outline the organizational and individual responsibilities for immediate response to an emergency situation. This document provides the first employees to detect an emergency with the steps that should be taken to activate provisions of the BCP that do not automatically activate. These guidelines should include the following:

- Immediate response procedures (security and safety procedures, fire suppression procedures, notification of appropriate emergency-response agencies, and so on)

- Whom to notify (executives, BCP team members, and so on)

- Secondary response procedures to take while waiting for the BCP team to assemble

## Maintenance

The BCP documentation and the plan itself must be living documents. Every organization encounters nearly constant change, and this dynamic nature ensures that the business's continuity requirements will also evolve. The BCP team should not be disbanded after the plan is developed but should still meet periodically to discuss the plan and review the results of plan tests to ensure that it continues to meet organizational needs. Obviously, minor changes to the plan do not require conducting the full BCP development process from scratch; they can simply be made at an informal meeting of the BCP team by unanimous consent. However, keep in mind that drastic changes in an organization's mission or resources may require going back to the BCP drawing board and beginning again. All older versions of the BCP should be physically destroyed and replaced by the most current version so that there is never any confusion as to the correct implementation of the BCP. It is also a good practice to include BCP components into job descriptions to ensure that the BCP remains fresh and correctly performed. Including BCP responsibilities in an employee's job description also makes them fair game for the performance review process.

## Testing

The BCP documentation should also outline a formalized testing program to ensure that the plan remains current and that all personnel are adequately trained to perform their duties in the event of an actual disaster. The testing process is actually quite similar to that used for the disaster recovery plan, so we'll reserve the discussion of the specific test types for Chapter 16.

# Summary

Every organization dependent upon technological resources for its survival should have a comprehensive business continuity plan in place to ensure the sustained viability of the organization when unforeseen emergencies take place. There are a number of important concepts that underlie solid business continuity planning (BCP) practices, including project scope and planning, business impact assessment, continuity planning, and approval and implementation. Every organization must have plans and procedures in place to help mitigate the effects a disaster has on continuing operations and to speed the return to normal operations. To determine the risks that your business faces and that require mitigation, you must conduct a business impact assessment from both quantitative and qualitative points of view. You must take the appropriate steps in developing a continuity strategy for your organization and know what to do to weather future disasters.

Finally, you must create the documentation required to ensure that your plan is effectively communicated to present and future BCP team participants. Such documentation must include continuity planning guidelines. The business continuity plan must also contain statements of importance, priorities, organizational responsibility, and urgency and timing. In addition, the documentation should include plans for risk assessment, acceptance, and mitigation; a vital records program; emergency-response guidelines; and plans for maintenance and testing.

The next chapter will take this planning to the next step—developing and implementing a disaster recovery plan. The disaster recovery plan kicks in where the business continuity plan leaves off. When an emergency occurs that interrupts your business in spite of the BCP measures, the disaster recovery plan guides the recovery efforts necessary to restore your business to normal operations as quickly as possible.

# Exam Essentials

**Understand the four steps of the business continuity planning process.**   Business continuity planning (BCP) involves four distinct phases: project scope and planning, business impact assessment, continuity planning, and approval and implementation. Each task contributes to the overall goal of ensuring that business operations continue uninterrupted in the face of an emergency situation.

**Describe how to perform the business organization analysis.**   In the business organization analysis, the individuals responsible for leading the BCP process determine which departments and individuals have a stake in the business continuity plan. This analysis is used as the foundation for BCP team selection and, after validation by the BCP team, is used to guide the next stages of BCP development.

**List the necessary members of the business continuity planning team.**   The BCP team should contain, as a minimum, representatives from each of the operational and support departments; technical experts from the IT department; security personnel with BCP skills; legal representatives familiar with corporate legal, regulatory, and contractual responsibilities; and representatives from senior management. Additional team members depend upon the structure and nature of the organization.

**Know the legal and regulatory requirements that face business continuity planners.**
Business leaders must exercise due diligence to ensure that shareholders' interests are protected in the event disaster strikes. Some industries are also subject to federal, state, and local regulations that mandate specific BCP procedures. Many businesses also have contractual obligations to their clients that must be met, before and after a disaster.

**Explain the steps of the business impact assessment process.**   The five steps of the business impact assessment process are identification of priorities, risk identification, likelihood assessment, impact assessment, and resource prioritization.

**Describe the process used to develop a continuity strategy.**   During the strategy development phase, the BCP team determines which risks will be mitigated. In the provisions and processes phase, mechanisms and procedures that will actually mitigate the risks are designed. The plan must then be approved by senior management and implemented. Personnel must also receive training on their roles in the BCP process.

**Explain the importance of fully documenting an organization's business continuity plan.**   Committing the plan to writing provides the organization with a written record of the procedures to follow when disaster strikes. It prevents the "it's in my head" syndrome and ensures the orderly progress of events in an emergency.

# Written Lab

1. Why is it important to include legal representatives on your BCP team?
2. What is wrong with the "seat-of-the-pants" approach to BCP?
3. What is the different between quantitative and qualitative risk assessment?
4. What critical components should be included in your BCP training plan?
5. What are the four main steps of the BCP process?

# Answers to Written Lab

1.  Many federal, state, and local laws or regulations require businesses to implement BCP provisions. Including legal representation on your BCP team helps ensure that you remain compliant with laws, regulations, and contractual obligations.

2.  The "seat-of-the-pants" approach is an excuse used by individuals who do not want to invest time and money in the proper creation of a BCP. This can lead to catastrophe when a firmly laid plan isn't in place to guide the response during a stressful emergency situation.

3.  Quantitative risk assessment involves using numbers and formulas to make a decision. Qualitative risk assessment includes nonnumeric factors, such as emotions, investor/consumer confidence, and workforce stability.

4.  The BCP training plan should include a plan overview briefing for all employees and specific training for individuals with direct or indirect involvement. In addition, backup personnel should be trained for each key BCP role.

5.  The four steps of the BCP process are project scope and planning, business impact assessment, continuity planning, and approval/implementation.

# Review Questions

1.  What is the first step that individuals responsible for the development of a business continuity plan should perform?

    **A.**  BCP team selection

    **B.**  Business organization analysis

    **C.**  Resource requirements analysis

    **D.**  Legal and regulatory assessmentt

2.  Once the BCP team is selected, what should be the first item placed on the team's agenda?

    **A.**  Business impact assessment

    **B.**  Business organization analysis

    **C.**  Resource requirements analysis

    **D.**  Legal and regulatory assessment

3.  What is the term used to describe the responsibility of a firm's officers and directors to ensure that adequate measures are in place to minimize the effect of a disaster on the organization's continued viability?

    **A.**  Corporate responsibility

    **B.**  Disaster requirement

    **C.**  Due diligence

    **D.**  Going concern responsibility

4.  What will be the major resource consumed by the BCP process during the BCP phase?

    **A.**  Hardware

    **B.**  Software

    **C.**  Processing time

    **D.**  Personnel

5.  What unit of measurement should be used to assign quantitative values to assets in the priority identification phase of the business impact assessment?

    **A.**  Monetary

    **B.**  Utility

    **C.**  Importance

    **D.**  Time

6. Which one of the following BIA terms identifies the amount of money a business expects to lose to a given risk each year?

   A. ARO

   B. SLE

   C. ALE

   D. EF

7. What BIA metric can be used to express the longest time a business function can be unavailable without causing irreparable harm to the organization?

   A. SLE

   B. EF

   C. MTD

   D. ARO

8. You are concerned about the risk that an avalanche poses to your $3 million shipping facility. Based upon expert opinion, you determine that there is a 5 percent chance that an avalanche will occur each year. Experts advise you that an avalanche would completely destroy your building and require you to rebuild on the same land. Ninety percent of the $3 million value of the facility is attributed to the building and 10 percent is attributed to the land itself. What is the single loss expectancy of your shipping facility to avalanches?

   A. $3,000,000

   B. $2,700,000

   C. $270,000

   D. $135,000

9. Referring to the scenario in question 8, what is the annualized loss expectancy?

   A. $3,000,000

   B. $2,700,000

   C. $270,000

   D. $135,000

10. You are concerned about the risk that a hurricane poses to your corporate headquarters in South Florida. The building itself is valued at $15 million. After consulting with the National Weather Service, you determine that there is a 10 percent likelihood that a hurricane will strike over the course of a year. You hired a team of architects and engineers who determined that the average hurricane would destroy approximately 50 percent of the building. What is the annualized loss expectancy (ALE)?

    A. $750,000

    B. $1.5 million

    C. $7.5 million

    D. $15 million

11. Which task of BCP bridges the gap between the business impact assessment and the continuity planning phases?

    **A.** Resource prioritization

    **B.** Likelihood assessment

    **C.** Strategy development

    **D.** Provisions and processes

12. Which resource should you protect first when designing continuity plan provisions and processes?

    **A.** Physical plant

    **B.** Infrastructure

    **C.** Financial

    **D.** People

13. Which one of the following concerns is not suitable for quantitative measurement during the business impact assessment?

    **A.** Loss of a plant

    **B.** Damage to a vehicle

    **C.** Negative publicity

    **D.** Power outage

14. Lighter Than Air Industries expects that it would lose $10 million if a tornado struck its aircraft operations facility. It expects that a tornado might strike the facility once every 100 years. What is the single loss expectancy for this scenario?

    **A.** 0.01

    **B.** $10,000,000

    **C.** $100,000

    **D.** 0.10

15. Referring to the scenario in question 13, what is the annualized loss expectancy?

    **A.** 0.01

    **B.** $10,000,000

    **C.** $100,000

    **D.** 0.10

16. In which business continuity planning task would you actually design procedures and mechanisms to mitigate risks deemed unacceptable by the BCP team?

    **A.** Strategy development

    **B.** Business impact assessment

    **C.** Provisions and processes

    **D.** Resource prioritization

17. What type of mitigation provision is utilized when redundant communications links are installed?

    **A.** Hardening systems

    **B.** Defining systems

    **C.** Reducing systems

    **D.** Alternative systems

18. What type of plan outlines the procedures to follow when a disaster interrupts the normal operations of a business?

    **A.** Business continuity plan

    **B.** Business impact assessment

    **C.** Disaster recovery plan

    **D.** Vulnerability assessment

19. What is the formula used to compute the single loss expectancy for a risk scenario?

    **A.** $SLE = AV \times EF$

    **B.** $SLE = RO \times EF$

    **C.** $SLE = AV \times ARO$

    **D.** $SLE = EF \times ARO$

20. Of the individuals listed, who would provide the best endorsement for a business continuity plan's statement of importance?

    **A.** Vice president of business operations

    **B.** Chief information officer

    **C.** Chief executive officer

    **D.** Business continuity manager

# Answers to Review Questions

1.  B. The business organization analysis helps the initial planners select appropriate BCP team members and then guides the overall BCP process.

2.  B. The first task of the BCP team should be the review and validation of the business organization analysis initially performed by those individuals responsible for spearheading the BCP effort. This ensures that the initial effort, undertaken by a small group of individuals, reflects the beliefs of the entire BCP team.

3.  C. A firm's officers and directors are legally bound to exercise due diligence in conducting their activities. This concept creates a fiduciary responsibility on their part to ensure that adequate business continuity plans are in place.

4.  D. During the planning phase, the most significant resource utilization will be the time dedicated by members of the BCP team to the planning process itself. This represents a significant use of business resources and is another reason that buy-in from senior management is essential.

5.  A. The quantitative portion of the priority identification should assign asset values in monetary units.

6.  C. The annualized loss expectancy (ALE) represents the amount of money a business expects to lose to a given risk each year. This figure is quite useful when performing a quantitative prioritization of business continuity resource allocation.

7.  C. The maximum tolerable downtime (MTD) represents the longest period a business function can be unavailable before causing irreparable harm to the business. This figure is very useful when determining the level of business continuity resources to assign to a particular function.

8.  B. The SLE is the product of the AV and the EF. From the scenario, you know that the AV is $3,000,000 and the EF is 90 percent, based upon that the same land can be used to rebuild the facility. This yields an SLE of $2,700,000.

9.  D. This problem requires you to compute the ALE, which is the product of the SLE and the ARO. From the scenario, you know that the ARO is 0.05 (or 5 percent). From question 8, you know that the SLE is $2,700,000. This yields an SLE of $135,000.

10. A. This problem requires you to compute the ALE, which is the product of the SLE and ARO. From the scenario, you know that the ARO is 0.10 (or 10 percent). From the scenario presented, you know that the SLE is $7.5 million. This yields an SLE of $750,000.

11. C. The strategy development task bridges the gap between business impact assessment and continuity planning by analyzing the prioritized list of risks developed during the BIA and determining which risks will be addressed by the BCP.

**12. D.** The safety of human life must always be the paramount concern in business continuity planning. Be sure that your plan reflects this priority, especially in the written documentation that is disseminated to your organization's employees!

**13. C.** It is very difficult to put a dollar figure on the business lost because of negative publicity. Therefore, this type of concern is better evaluated through a qualitative analysis.

**14. B.** The single loss expectancy (SLE) is the amount of damage that would be caused by a single occurrence of the risk. In this case, the SLE is $10 million, the expected damage from one tornado. The fact that a tornado occurs only once every 100 years is not reflected in the SLE but would be reflected in the annualized loss expectancy (ALE).

**15. C.** The annualized loss expectancy (ALE) is computed by taking the product of the single loss expectancy (SLE), which was $10 million in this scenario, and the annualized rate of occurrence (ARO), which was 0.01 in this example. These figures yield an ALE of $100,000.

**16. C.** In the provisions and processes phase, the BCP team actually designs the procedures and mechanisms to mitigate risks that were deemed unacceptable during the strategy development phase.

**17. D.** This is an example of alternative systems. Redundant communications circuits provide backup links that may be used when the primary circuits are unavailable.

**18. C.** Disaster recovery plans pick up where business continuity plans leave off. After a disaster strikes and the business is interrupted, the disaster recovery plan guides response teams in their efforts to quickly restore business operations to normal levels.

**19. A.** The single loss expectancy (SLE) is computed as the product of the asset value (AV) and the exposure factor (EF). The other formulas displayed here do not accurately reflect this calculation.

**20. C.** You should strive to have the highest-ranking person possible sign the BCP's statement of importance. Of the choices given, the chief executive officer is the highest ranking.

# Chapter 16

# Disaster Recovery Planning

## THE CISSP EXAM TOPICS COVERED IN THIS CHAPTER INCLUDE:

✓ **Business Continuity and Disaster Recovery Planning**

- Understand business continuity requirements
  - Develop and document project scope and plan
- Conduct business impact analysis
  - Identify and prioritize critical business functions; determine maximum tolerable downtime and other criteria; assess exposure to outages (e.g., local, regional, global); define recovery objectives
- Develop recovery strategy
  - Implement a backup storage strategy (e.g., offsite storage, electronic vaulting, tape rotation); recovery site strategies
- Understand disaster recovery process
  - Response; personnel; communications; assessment; restoration
- Provide training
- Test, update, assess and maintain the plan (e.g., version control, distribution)

✓ **Operations Security**

- Manage incident response
  - Detection; response; reporting; recovery; remediation

In the previous chapter, you learned the essential elements of business continuity planning (BCP)—the art of helping your organization avoid business interruption as the result of an emergency or disaster. Recall that a primary BCP principle is risk management; you must assess the likelihood that a vulnerability will be exploited and use that likelihood to determine an appropriate allocation of resources to combat the threat.

Because of this risk management principle, business continuity plans do not seek to prevent every possible disaster from affecting an organization—that is impossible. On the contrary, they are designed to limit the effects of predictable, more likely disasters. Naturally, this leaves an organization vulnerable to interruption from any number of threats—those judged unworthy of mitigation or those not anticipated.

Disaster recovery planning (DRP) steps in where BCP leaves off. When a disaster strikes and a business continuity plan fails to prevent interruption of business activities, the disaster recovery plan kicks in and guides the actions of emergency-response personnel until the end goal is reached, which is to see the business restored to full operating capacity in its primary operations facilities.

While reading this chapter, you may notice many areas of overlap between the BCP and DRP processes. Indeed, our discussion of specific disasters provides information on how to handle them from both BCP and DRP points of view. This illustrates the close linkage between these two sets of activities and processes. In fact, although the (ISC)² CISSP curriculum draws a distinction between these two areas, most organizations simply have a single team and plan to address both business continuity and disaster recovery concerns in an effort to consolidate responsibilities. In many organizations, in fact, the single discipline known as business continuity management (BCM) encompasses BCP, DRP, and incident management under a single umbrella.

# The Nature of Disaster

Disaster recovery planning brings order to the chaos that surrounds the interruption of an organization's normal activities. By its very nature, a *disaster recovery plan* is implemented only when tension is high and cooler heads might not naturally prevail. Picture the circumstances in which you might find it necessary to implement DRP measures—a hurricane destroys your main operations facility, a fire devastates your main processing center, terrorist activity closes off access to a major metropolitan area.

Any event that stops, prevents, or interrupts an organization's ability to perform its work tasks is considered a disaster. The moment that IT becomes unable to support mission-critical processes is the moment DRP kicks in to manage the restoration and recovery procedures.

A disaster recovery plan should be set up so that it can almost run on autopilot. The DRP should also be designed to eliminate decision-making activities during a disaster as much as possible. Essential personnel should be well trained in their duties and responsibilities in the wake of a disaster and also know the steps they need to take to get the organization up and running as soon as possible. We'll begin by analyzing some of the possible disasters that might strike your organization and the particular threats that they pose. Many of these are mentioned in the previous chapter, but we now explore them in further detail.

To plan for natural and unnatural disasters in the workplace, you must first understand their various forms, as explained in the following sections.

# Natural Disasters

*Natural disasters* reflect the occasional fury of our habitat—violent occurrences that result from changes in the earth's surface or atmosphere that are beyond human control. In some cases, such as hurricanes, scientists have developed sophisticated predictive models that provide ample warning before a disaster strikes. Others, such as earthquakes, can cause devastation at a moment's notice. A disaster recovery plan should provide mechanisms for responding to both types of disasters, either with a gradual buildup of response forces or as an immediate reaction to a rapidly emerging crisis.

## Earthquakes

Earthquakes are caused by the shifting of seismic plates and can occur almost anywhere in the world without warning. However, they are far more likely to occur along known fault lines that exist in many areas of the world. A well-known example is the San Andreas fault, which poses a significant risk to portions of the western United States. If you live in a region along a fault line where earthquakes are likely, your DRP should address the procedures your business will implement should a seismic event interrupt your normal activities.

You might be surprised by some of the regions of the world where earthquakes are considered possible. Table 16.1 shows parts of the United States (and U.S. territories) that the Federal Emergency Management Agency (FEMA) considers moderate, high, or very high seismic hazards. Note that the states listed in the table include 82 percent (41) of the 50 states, meaning that the majority of the country has at least a moderate risk of seismic activity.

**TABLE 16.1**   Seismic hazard level by U.S. state or territory

| Moderate Seismic Hazard | High Seismic Hazard | Very High Seismic Hazard |
| --- | --- | --- |
| Alabama | American Samoa | Alaska |
| Colorado | Arizona | California |
| Connecticut | Arkansas | Guam |
| Delaware | Illinois | Hawaii |
| Georgia | Indiana | Idaho |
| Maine | Kentucky | Montana |
| Maryland | Missouri | Nevada |
| Massachusetts | New Mexico | Oregon |
| Mississippi | South Carolina | Puerto Rico |
| New Hampshire | Tennessee | Virgin Islands |
| New Jersey | Utah | Washington |
| New York | | Wyoming |
| North Carolina | | |
| Ohio | | |
| Oklahoma | | |
| Pennsylvania | | |
| Rhode Island | | |
| Texas | | |
| Vermont | | |
| Virginia | | |
| West Virginia | | |

## Floods

Flooding can occur almost anywhere in the world at any time of the year. Some flooding results from the gradual accumulation of rainwater in rivers, lakes, and other bodies of water that then overflow their banks and flood the community. Other floods, known as *flash floods*, strike when a sudden severe storm dumps more rainwater on an area than the ground can absorb in a short period of time. Floods can also occur when dams are breached. Large waves caused by seismic activity, or *tsunamis*, combine the awesome power and weight of water with flooding, as we saw during the December 26, 2004, tsunami disaster in the South Pacific and Indian Oceans. This tsunami amply demonstrated the enormous destructive capabilities of water and the havoc it can wreak on various businesses and economies.

According to government statistics, flooding is responsible for more than $1 billion (that's billion with a *b*!) in damage to businesses and homes each year in the United States. It's important that your DRP make appropriate response plans for the eventuality that a flood may strike your facilities.

**WARNING**    When you evaluate a firm's risk of damage from flooding to develop business continuity and disaster recovery plans, it's also a good idea to check with responsible individuals and ensure that your organization has sufficient insurance in place to protect it from the financial impact of a flood. In the United States, most general business policies do not cover flood damage, and you should investigate obtaining specialized government-backed flood insurance under FEMA's National Flood Insurance Program.

Although flooding is theoretically possible in almost any region of the world, it is much more likely to occur in certain areas. FEMA's National Flood Insurance Program is responsible for completing a flood risk assessment for the entire United States and providing this data to citizens in graphical form. You can view flood maps online at www .esri.com/hazards/. This site also provides valuable information on recorded earthquakes, hurricanes, windstorms, hailstorms, and other natural disasters to help you prepare your organization's risk assessment.

When viewing flood maps, like the one shown in Figure 16.1, you'll find that the two risks often assigned to an area are the "100-year flood plain" and the "500-year flood plain." These evaluations mean that the government estimates chances of flooding in any given year at 1 in 100 or at 1 in 500, respectively. For a more detailed tutorial on reading flood maps, visit www.fema.gov/media/fhm/firm/ot_firm.htm.

**FIGURE 16.1** Flood hazard map for Miami–Dade County, Florida

## Storms

Storms come in many forms and pose diverse risks to a business. Prolonged periods of intense rainfall bring the risk of flash flooding described in the previous section. Hurricanes and tornadoes come with the threat of winds exceeding 100 miles per hour that threaten the structural integrity of buildings and turn everyday objects such as trees, lawn furniture, and even vehicles into deadly missiles. Hailstorms bring a rapid onslaught of destructive ice chunks falling from the sky. Many storms also bring the risk of lightning, which can cause severe damage to sensitive electronic components. For this reason, your business continuity plan should detail appropriate mechanisms to protect against lightning-induced damage, and your disaster recovery plan should provide adequate provisions for power outages and equipment damage that might result from a lightning strike. Never underestimate the damage that a single storm can do.

In 2005, the Category 5 Atlantic hurricane Katrina marked the costliest, deadliest, and strongest hurricane ever to make landfall in the continental United States. It bored a path of destruction from Alabama to Louisiana, destroying everything natural and man-made throughout those areas. The total economic impact stemming from the damage this storm caused is estimated at upward of $100 billion, eliminating a major Gulf Coast highway and impeding commodities exports, not to mention inundating nearly 80 percent of the city of New Orleans.

If you live in an area susceptible to a certain type of severe storm, it's important to regularly monitor weather forecasts from responsible government agencies. For example, disaster recovery specialists in hurricane-prone areas should periodically check the website of the National Weather Service's Tropical Prediction Center (www.nhc.noaa.gov) during hurricane season. This website allows you to monitor Atlantic and Pacific storms that may pose a risk to your region before word about them hits the local news. This lets you begin a gradual response to the storm before time runs out.

## Fires

Fires can start for a variety of reasons, both natural and man made, but both forms can be equally devastating. During the BCP/DRP process, you should evaluate the risk of fire and implement at least basic measures to mitigate that risk and prepare the business for recovery from a catastrophic fire in a critical facility.

Some regions of the world are susceptible to wildfires during the warm season. These fires, once started, spread in somewhat predictable patterns, and fire experts working with meteorologists can produce relatively accurate forecasts of a wildfire's potential path.

As with many other types of large-scale natural disasters, you can obtain valuable information about impending threats on the Web. In the United States, the National Interagency Fire Center posts daily fire updates and forecasts on its website: www.nifc.gov/fire_info/maps.htm. Other countries have similar warning systems in place.

## Other Regional Events

Some regions of the world are prone to localized types of natural disasters. During the BCP/DRP process, your assessment team should analyze all of your organization's operating locations and gauge the impact that such events might have on your business. For example, many parts of the world are subject to volcanic eruptions. If you conduct operations in an area in close proximity to an active or dormant volcano, your DRP should probably address this eventuality. Other localized natural occurrences include monsoons in Asia, tsunamis in the South Pacific, avalanches in mountainous regions, and mudslides in the western United States.

If your business is geographically diverse, it is prudent to include area natives on your planning team. At the very least, make use of local resources such as government emergency preparedness teams, civil defense organizations, and insurance claim offices to help guide your efforts. These organizations possess a wealth of knowledge and are usually more than happy to help you prepare your organization for the unexpected—after all, every organization that successfully weathers a natural disaster is one less organization that requires a portion of their valuable recovery resources after disaster strikes.

# Man-Made Disasters

Our advanced civilization has become increasingly dependent upon complex interactions between technological, logistical, and natural systems. The same complex interactions that make our sophisticated society possible also present a number of potential vulnerabilities from both intentional and unintentional *man-made disasters*. In the following sections, we'll examine a few of the more common disasters to help you analyze your organization's vulnerabilities when preparing a business continuity plan and disaster recovery plan.

## Fires

Earlier in the chapter, we explained how some regions of the world are susceptible to wildfires during the warm season, and these types of fires can be described as natural disasters. Many smaller-scale fires result from human action—be it carelessness, faulty electrical wiring, improper fire protection practices, or other reasons. Studies from the Insurance Information Institute indicate that there are at least 1,000 building fires in the United States *every day*. If such a fire strikes your organization, do you have the proper preventative measures in place to quickly contain it? If the fire destroys your facilities, how quickly does your disaster recovery plan allow you to resume operations elsewhere?

## Acts of Terrorism

Since the terrorist attacks on September 11, 2001, businesses are increasingly concerned about risks posed by terrorist threats. The attacks on September 11 caused many small businesses to fail because they did not have business continuity/disaster recovery plans in place that were adequate to ensure their continued viability. Many larger businesses experienced significant losses that caused severe long-term damage. The Insurance Information Institute issued a study one year after the attacks that estimated the total damage from the attacks in New York City at $40 billion (yes, that's with a *b* again!).

WARNING

General business insurance may not properly cover an organization against acts of terrorism. Prior to the September 11, 2001, attacks, most policies either covered acts of terrorism or didn't mention them explicitly. After suffering such a catastrophic loss, many insurance companies responded by amending policies to exclude losses from terrorist activity. Policy riders and endorsements are sometimes available but often at extremely high cost. If your business continuity or disaster recovery plan includes insurance as a means of financial recovery (as it probably should!), you'd be well advised to check your policies and contact your insurance professionals to ensure that you're still covered.

Terrorist acts pose a unique challenge to DRP teams because of their unpredictable nature. Prior to the September 11, 2001, terrorist attacks in New York and Washington, D.C., few DRP teams considered the threat of an airplane crashing into their corporate headquarters significant enough to merit mitigation. Many companies are now asking themselves a number of new "what if" questions regarding terrorist activity. In general, these questions are healthy because they promote dialog between business elements regarding potential threats. On the other hand, disaster recovery planners must emphasize solid risk-management principles and ensure that resources aren't over-allocated to terrorist threats to the detriment of other DRP/BCP activities that protect against more likely threats.

## Bombings/Explosions

Explosions can result from a variety of man-made occurrences. Explosive gases from leaks might fill a room/building and later ignite and cause a damaging blast. In many areas, bombings are also cause for concern. From a disaster planning perspective, the effects of bombings and explosions are like those caused by a large-scale fire. However, planning to avoid the impact of a bombing is much more difficult and relies on physical security measures we cover in Chapter 19, "Physical Security Requirements."

## Power Outages

Even the most basic disaster recovery plan contains provisions to deal with the threat of a short power outage. Critical business systems are often protected by uninterruptible power supply (UPS) devices to keep them running at least long enough to shut down or long enough to get emergency generators up and working. Even so, could your organization keep operating during a sustained power outage?

After Hurricane Katrina made landfall in 2005, a reported 900,000 people in Mississippi lost power, with another 600,000 in Alabama. Does your business continuity plan include provisions to keep your business viable during such a prolonged period without power? Does your disaster recovery plan make ample preparations for the timely restoration of power even if the commercial power grid remains unavailable?

WARNING Check your UPSs regularly! These critical devices are often overlooked until they become necessary. Many UPSs contain self-testing mechanisms that report problems automatically, but it's still a good idea to subject them to regular testing. Also, be sure to audit the number/type of devices plugged in to each UPS. It's amazing how many people think it's okay to add "just one more system" to a UPS, and you don't want to be surprised when the device can't handle the load during a real power outage!

Today's technology-driven organizations depend increasingly on electric power, so your BCP/DRP team should consider provisioning alternative power sources that can run business systems indefinitely. An adequate backup generator could make a huge difference when the survival of your business is at stake.

## Other Utility and Infrastructure Failures

When planners consider the impact that utility outages may have on their organizations, they naturally think first about the impact of a power outage. However, keep other utilities in mind too. Do any of your critical business systems rely on water, sewers, natural gas, or other utilities? Also consider regional infrastructure such as highways, airports, and railroads. Any of these systems can suffer failures that might not be related to weather or other conditions described in this chapter. Many businesses depend on one or more of these infrastructure elements to move people or materials. Their failure can paralyze your business's ability to continue functioning.

 If you quickly answered no when asked whether you have critical business systems that rely on water, sewers, natural gas, or other utilities, think again. Do you consider people a critical business system? If a major storm knocks out the water supply to your facilities and you need to keep those facilities up and running, can you supply your employees with enough drinking water to meet their needs?

What about your fire protection systems? If any of them are water based, is there a holding tank system in place that contains ample water to extinguish a serious building fire if the public water system is unavailable? Fires often cause serious damage in areas ravaged by storms, earthquakes, and other disasters that might also interrupt the delivery of water.

## Hardware/Software Failures

Like it or not, computer systems fail. Hardware components simply wear out and refuse to continue performing, or they suffer physical damage. Software systems contain bugs or fall prey to improper or unexpected inputs. For this reason, BCP/DRP teams must provide adequate redundancy in their systems. If zero downtime is a mandatory requirement, the best solution is to use fully redundant failover servers in separate locations attached to separate communications links and infrastructures (also designed to operate in a failover mode). If one server is damaged or destroyed, the other will instantly take over the processing load. For more information on this concept, see the section "Remote Mirroring" later in this chapter.

Because of financial constraints, it isn't always feasible to maintain fully redundant systems. In those circumstances, the BCP/DRP team should address how replacement parts can be quickly obtained and installed. As many parts as possible should be kept in a local parts inventory for quick replacement; this is especially true for hard-to-find parts that must otherwise be shipped in. After all, how many organizations could do without telephones for three days while a critical PBX component is en route from an overseas location to be installed on site?

### NYC Blackout

On August 14, 2003, the lights went out in New York City and in large areas of the northeastern and midwestern United States when a series of cascading failures caused the collapse of a major power grid.

Fortunately, security professionals in the New York area were ready. Spurred to action by the September 11, 2001, terrorist attacks, many businesses updated their disaster recovery plans and took steps to ensure their continued operations in the wake of another disaster. This blackout served to test those plans, and many organizations were able to continue operating on alternate power sources or transferred control seamlessly to offsite data-processing centers.

Lessons learned during this blackout offer insight for BCP/DRP teams around the world:

- Ensure that alternate processing sites are far enough away from your main site that they are unlikely to be affected by the same disaster.

- Remember that threats to your organization are both internal and external. Your next disaster may come from a terrorist attack, building fire, or malicious code running loose on your network. Take steps to ensure that your alternate sites are segregated from the main facility to protect against all of these threats.

- Disasters don't usually come with advance warning. If real-time operations are critical to your organization, be sure that your backup sites are ready to assume primary status at a moment's notice.

## Strikes/Picketing

When designing your business continuity and disaster recovery plans, don't forget about the importance of the human factor in emergency planning. One form of man-made disaster that is often overlooked is the possibility of a strike or other labor crisis. If a large number of your employees walk out at the same time, what impact would that have on your business? How long would you be able to sustain operations without the regular full-time employees that staff a certain area? Your BCP and DRP teams should address these concerns, providing alternative plans should a labor crisis occur.

## Theft/Vandalism

In a previous section, we talked about the threat that terrorist activities pose to an organization. Theft and vandalism represent the same kind of threat on a much smaller scale. In most cases, however, there's a far greater chance that your organization will be affected by theft or vandalism than by a terrorist attack. Insurance provides some financial protection against these events (subject to deductibles and limitations of coverage), but acts of this kind can cause serious damage to your business, on both a short-term and long-term basis. Your business continuity and disaster recovery plans should include adequate preventive measures to control the frequency of these occurrences as well as contingency plans to mitigate the effects theft and vandalism have on ongoing operations.

## Offsite Challenges to Security

The constant threat of theft and vandalism is the bane of information security professionals worldwide. Personal identity information, proprietary or trade secrets, and other forms of confidential data are just as interesting to those who create and possess them as they are to direct competitors and other unauthorized parties.

Aaron knows this first-hand working as a security officer for a very prominent and highly visible computing enterprise. His chief responsibility is to keep sensitive information from exposure to various elements and entities. Bethany is one of his more troublesome employees because she's constantly taking her notebook computer off site without properly securing its contents.

Even a casual smash-and-grab theft attempt could put thousands of client contacts and their confidential business dealings at risk of being leaked and possibly sold to malicious parties. Aaron knows the potential dangers, but Bethany just doesn't seem to care.

This poses the question, How might you better inform, train, or advise Bethany so that Aaron does not have to relieve her of her position should her notebook be stolen? Bethany must come to understand and appreciate the importance of keeping sensitive information secure. It may be necessary to emphasize the potential loss and exposure that comes with losing such data to wrongdoers, competitors, or other unauthorized third parties. It may suffice to point out to Bethany that the employee handbook clearly states that employees whose behavior leads to the unauthorized disclosure or loss of information assets are subject to loss of pay or termination. If such behavior recurs after a warning, Bethany should be rebuked and reassigned to a position where she can't expose sensitive or proprietary information, that is, if she's not fired on the spot.

Keep the impact that theft may have on your operations in mind when planning your parts inventory. It's a good idea to keep extra inventory of items with a high pilferage rate, such as RAM chips and laptops. It's also a good idea to keep such materials in secure storage and to require employees to sign such items out whenever they are used.

# Recovery Strategy

When a disaster interrupts your business, your disaster recovery plan should kick in nearly automatically and begin providing support for recovery operations. The disaster recovery plan should be designed so that the first employees on the scene can immediately begin the recovery effort in an organized fashion, even if members of the official DRP team have not yet arrived on site. In the following sections, we'll cover critical subtasks involved in crafting an effective disaster recovery plan that can guide rapid restoration of regular business processes and resumption of activity at the primary business location.

In addition to improving your response capabilities, purchasing insurance can reduce the risk of financial losses. When selecting insurance, be sure to purchase sufficient coverage to enable you to recover from a disaster. Simple value coverage may be insufficient to encompass actual replacement costs. If your property insurance includes an actual cash value (ACV) clause, then your damaged property will be compensated based on the fair market value of the items on the date of loss less all accumulated depreciation since the time of their purchase. The important point here is that unless you have a replacement cost clause in your insurance coverage, your organization is likely to be out of pocket as a result of any losses it might sustain.

Valuable paper insurance coverage provides protection for inscribed, printed, and written documents and manuscripts and other printed business records. However, it does not cover damage to paper money and printed security certificates.

## Business Unit and Functional Priorities

To recover your business operations with the greatest possible efficiency, you must engineer your disaster recovery plan so that those business units with the highest priority are recovered first. You must identify and prioritize critical business functions as well so you can define which functions to restore after a disaster or failure and in what order.

To achieve this goal, the DRP team must first identify those business units and agree on an order of prioritization, and they must do likewise with business functions. (And take note: Not all critical business functions will necessarily be carried out in critical business units, so the final results of this analysis will very probably comprise a superset of critical business units plus other select units.)

If this process sounds familiar, it should! This is very like the prioritization task the BCP team performs during the business impact assessment discussed in the previous chapter. In fact, most organizations will complete a business impact analysis (BIA) as part of their business continuity planning process. This analysis identifies vulnerabilities, develops strategies to minimize risk, and ultimately produces a BIA report that describes the potential risks that an organization faces and identifies critical business units and functions. A BIA also identifies costs related to failures that include loss of cash flow, equipment replacement, salaries paid to clear work backlogs, profit losses, opportunity costs from the inability to attract new business, and so forth. Such failures are assessed in terms of potential impacts on finances, personnel, safety, legal compliance, contract fulfillment, and quality assurance, preferably in monetary terms to make impacts comparable and to set budgetary expectations. With all this BIA information in hand, you should use the resulting documentation as the basis for this prioritization task.

At a minimum, the output from this task should be a simple listing of business units in priority order. However, a more detailed list, broken down into specific business processes listed in order of priority, would be a much more useful deliverable. This business-process-oriented list is more reflective of real-world conditions, but it requires considerable additional effort. It will, however, greatly assist in the recovery effort—after all, not every task performed by the highest-priority business unit will be of the highest priority. You might find that it would be best to restore the highest-priority unit to 50 percent capacity and then move on to lower-priority units to achieve some minimum operating capacity across the organization before attempting a full recovery effort.

By the same token, the same exercise must be completed for critical business processes and functions. Not only can these things involve multiple business units and cross the lines between them, they define the operational elements that must be restored in the wake of a disaster or other business interruption. Here also, the final result should be a checklist of items in priority order, each with its own risk and cost assessment, and a corresponding set of mean time to recovery (MTR) and related recovery objectives and milestones.

## Crisis Management

If a disaster strikes your organization, panic is likely to set in. The best way to combat this is with an organized disaster recovery plan. The individuals in your business who are most likely to first notice an emergency situation (that is, security guards, technical personnel, and so on) should be fully trained in disaster recovery procedures and know the proper notification procedures and immediate response mechanisms.

Many things that normally seem like common sense (such as calling 911 in the event of a fire) may slip the minds of panicked employees seeking to flee an emergency. The best way to combat this is with continuous training on disaster recovery responsibilities. Returning to the fire example, all employees should be trained to activate the fire alarm or contact emergency officials when they spot a fire (after, of course, taking appropriate measures to protect themselves). After all, it's better that the fire department receives 10 different phone calls reporting a fire at your organization than it is for everyone to assume that someone else already took care of it.

Crisis management is a science and an art form. If your training budget permits, investing in crisis training for your key employees is a good idea. This ensures that at least some of your employees know how to handle emergency situations properly and can provide all-important "on-the-scene" leadership to panic-stricken co-workers.

## Emergency Communications

When a disaster strikes, it is important that the organization be able to communicate internally as well as with the outside world. A disaster of any significance is easily noticed, but if an organization is unable to keep the outside world informed of its recovery status, the public is apt to fear the worst and assume that the organization is unable to recover. It is also essential that the organization be able to communicate internally during a disaster so that employees know what is expected of them—whether they are to return to work or report to another location, for instance.

In some cases, the circumstances that brought about the disaster to begin with may have also damaged some or all normal means of communications. A violent storm or an earthquake may have also knocked out telecommunications systems; at that point it's too late to try to figure out other means of communicating both internally and externally.

## Work Group Recovery

When designing a disaster recovery plan, it's important to keep your goal in mind—the restoration of work groups to the point that they can resume their activities in their usual work locations. It's very easy to get sidetracked and think of disaster recovery as purely an IT effort focused on restoring systems and processes to working order.

To facilitate this effort, it's sometimes best to develop separate recovery facilities for different work groups. For example, if you have several subsidiary organizations that are in different locations and that perform tasks similar to the tasks that work groups at your office perform, you may want to consider temporarily relocating those work groups to the other facility and having them communicate electronically and via telephone with other business units until they're ready to return to the main operations facility.

Larger organizations may have difficulty finding recovery facilities capable of handling the entire business operation. This is another example of a circumstance in which independent recovery of different work groups is appropriate.

## Alternate Processing Sites

One of the most important elements of the disaster recovery plan is the selection of alternate processing sites to be used when the primary sites are unavailable. Many options are available when considering recovery facilities, limited only by the creative minds of disaster recovery planners and service providers. In the following sections, we cover several types of sites commonly used in disaster recovery planning: cold sites, warm sites, hot sites, mobile sites, service bureaus, and multiple sites.

When choosing any alternate processing site, be sure to situate it far away enough from your primary location that it won't be affected by the same disaster that disables your primary site.

### Cold Sites

*Cold sites* are simply standby facilities large enough to handle the processing load of an organization and equipped with appropriate electrical and environmental support systems. They may be large warehouses, empty office buildings, or other similar structures. However, a cold site has no computing facilities (hardware or software) preinstalled with no active broadband communications links. Many cold sites do have at least a few copper telephone lines, and some sites may have standby links that can be activated with minimal notification.

---

### Cold Site Setup

A cold site setup is best depicted in the fictional work *Boiler Room*, which involves a chop-shop investment firm telemarketing bogus pharmaceutical investment deals to prospective clients. In this fictional case, the "disaster" is man made, but the concept is much the same, even if the timing is quite different.

Under threat of exposure and a pending law enforcement raid, the firm establishes a nearby building that is empty, save for a few banks of phones on dusty concrete floors in a mock-up of a cold recovery site. Granted, this work is both fictional and illegal, but it illustrates a very real and legitimate reason for maintaining a redundant fail-over recovery site for the purpose of business continuity.

Research the various forms of recovery sites, and then consider which among them is best suited for your particular business needs and budget. A cold site is the least expensive option and perhaps the most practical. A warm site contains the data links and preconfigured equipment necessary to begin restoring operations but no usable data or information. The most expensive option is a hot site, which fully replicates your existing business infrastructure and is ready to take over for the primary site on short notice.

---

The major advantage of a cold site is its relatively low cost—there's no computing base to maintain and no monthly telecommunications bill when the site is idle. However, the drawbacks of such a site are obvious—there is a tremendous lag time between the time the decision is made to activate the site and the time when that site is actually ready to support business operations. Servers and workstations must be brought in and configured. Data must be restored from backup tapes. Communications links must be activated or established. The time to activate a cold site is often measured in weeks, making timely recovery close to impossible and often yielding a false sense of security. It's also worth observing that the substantial time, effort, and expense required to activate and transfer operations to a cold site make this approach the most difficult to test.

## Hot Sites

A *hot site* is the exact opposite of the cold site. In this configuration, a backup facility is maintained in constant working order, with a full complement of servers, workstations, and communications links ready to assume primary operations responsibilities. The servers and workstations are all preconfigured and loaded with appropriate operating system and application software.

When choosing a facility, be sure it is far enough away from the original site so as not to be affected by the same disaster yet close enough that it doesn't take a full day's drive to reach it.

The data on the primary site servers is periodically or continuously replicated to corresponding servers at the hot site, ensuring that the hot site has up-to-date data. Depending on the bandwidth available between the sites, hot site data may be replicated instantaneously. If that is the case, operators could simply move operations to the hot site at a moment's notice. If it's not the case, disaster recovery managers have three options to activate the hot site:

- If there is sufficient time before the primary site must be shut down, they can force replication between the two sites right before the transition of operational control.

- If replication is impossible, managers may carry backup tapes of the transaction logs from the primary site to the hot site and manually reapply any transactions that took place since the last replication.

- If there are no available backups and it isn't possible to force replication, the disaster recovery team may simply accept the loss of some portion of the data.

The advantages of a hot site are obvious—the level of disaster recovery protection provided by this type of site is unsurpassed. However, the cost is *extremely* high. Maintaining a hot site essentially doubles an organization's budget for hardware, software, and services and requires the use of additional employees to maintain the site.

**WARNING**     If you use a hot site, never forget that it has copies of your production data. Be sure to provide that site with the same level of technical and physical security controls you provide at your primary site.

If an organization wants to maintain a hot site but wants to reduce the expense of equipment and maintenance, it might opt to use a shared hot site facility managed by an outside contractor. However, the inherent danger in these facilities is that they may be overtaxed in the event of a widespread disaster and be unable to service all clients simultaneously. If your organization considers such an arrangement, be sure to investigate these issues thoroughly, both before signing the contract and periodically during the contract term.

## Warm Sites

*Warm sites* occupy the middle ground between hot and cold sites for disaster recovery specialists. They always contain the equipment and data circuits necessary to rapidly establish operations. As it is in hot sites, this equipment is usually preconfigured and ready to run appropriate applications to support an organization's operations. Unlike hot sites, however, warm sites do not typically contain copies of the client's data. The main requirement in bringing a warm site to full operational status is the transportation of appropriate backup media to the site and restoration of critical data on the standby servers.

Activation of a warm site typically takes at least 12 hours from the time a disaster is declared. This does not mean that any site that can be activated in less than 12 hours qualifies as a hot site, however: Switchover times for most hot sites are often measured in seconds or minutes, and complete cutovers seldom take more than an hour or two.

However, warm sites avoid significant telecommunications and personnel costs inherent in maintaining a near-real-time copy of the operational data environment. As with hot sites and cold sites, warm sites may also be obtained on a shared facility basis. If you choose this option, be sure that you have a "no lockout" policy written into your contract guaranteeing you the use of an appropriate facility even during a period of high demand. It's a good idea to take this concept one step further and physically inspect the facilities and the contractor's operational plan to reassure yourself that the facility will indeed be able to back up the "no lockout" guarantee should push ever come to shove.

## Mobile Sites

*Mobile sites* are nonmainstream alternatives to traditional recovery sites. They typically consist of self-contained trailers or other easily relocated units. These sites include all the environmental control systems necessary to maintain a safe computing environment. Larger corporations sometimes maintain these sites on a "fly-away" basis, ready to deploy them to any operating location around the world via air, rail, sea, or surface transportation. Smaller firms might contract with a mobile site vendor in their local area to provide these services on an as-needed basis.

If your disaster recovery plan depends on a workgroup recovery strategy, mobile sites are an excellent way to implement that approach. They are often large enough to accommodate entire (small!) work groups.

Mobile sites are often configured as cold sites or warm sites, depending upon the disaster recovery plan they are designed to support. It is also possible to configure a mobile site as a hot site, but this is unusual because one seldom knows in advance where a mobile site will be deployed.

### Hardware Replacement Options

One thing to consider when determining mobile sites and recovery sites in general is hardware replacement supplies. There are basically two options for hardware replacement supplies. One option is to employ "in-house" replacement whereby you store extra and duplicate equipment at a different but nearby location (that is, a warehouse on the other side of town). (*In-house* here means you own it already, not that it is necessarily housed under the same roof as your production environment.) If you have a hardware failure or a disaster, you can immediately pull the appropriate equipment from your stash. The other option is an SLA-type agreement with a vendor to provide quick response and delivery time in the event of a disaster. However, even a 4-, 12-, 24-, or 48-hour replacement hardware contract from a vendor does not provide a reliable guarantee that delivery will actually occur. There are too many uncontrollable variables to rely upon this second option as your sole means of recovery.

## Service Bureaus

A *service bureau* is a company that leases computer time. Service bureaus own large server farms and often fields of workstations. Any organization can purchase a contract from a service bureau to consume some portion of their processing capacity. Access can be on site or remote.

A service bureau can usually provide support for all your IT needs in the event of a disaster, even desktops for workers to use. Your contract with a service bureau will often include testing and backups as well as response time and availability. However, service bureaus regularly oversell their actual capacity by gambling that not all their contracts will be exercised at the same time. Therefore, there is potential for resource contention in the wake of a major disaster. If your company operates in an industry-dense locale, this could be an important issue. You may need to select both a local and a distant service bureau to be sure to gain access to processing facilities during a real disaster.

## Multiple Sites

By splitting or dividing your outfit into several divisions, branches, offices, and so on, you create multiple sites and reduce the impact of a major disaster. In fact, the more sites you employ, the less impact a major disaster will have. However, for multiple sites to be effective, they must be far enough apart that a major disaster cannot affect too many of them simultaneously. One drawback of using multiple sites is that it increases the difficulty of managing and administering the entire company when it's spread across a large geographic area in numerous locations.

# Mutual Assistance Agreements

*Mutual assistance agreements (MAAs)*, also called *reciprocal agreements*, are popular in disaster recovery literature but are rarely implemented in real-world practice. In theory, they provide an excellent alternate processing option. Under an MAA, two organizations pledge to assist each other in the event of a disaster by sharing computing facilities or other technological resources. They appear to be extremely cost effective at first glance—it's not necessary for either organization to maintain expensive alternate processing sites (such as the hot sites, warm sites, cold sites, and mobile processing sites described in the previous sections). Indeed, many MAAs are structured to provide one of the levels of service described. In the case of a cold site, each organization may simply maintain some open space in their processing facilities for the other organization to use in the event of a disaster. In the case of a hot site, the organizations may host fully redundant servers for each other.

However, many drawbacks inherent to MAAs prevent their widespread use:

- MAAs are difficult to enforce. The parties trust each other to provide support in the event of a disaster. However, when push comes to shove, the nonvictim might renege on the agreement. A victim may have legal remedies available, but this doesn't help the immediate disaster recovery effort.

- Cooperating organizations should be located in relatively close proximity to each other to facilitate transportation of employees between sites. However, proximity means that both organizations may be vulnerable to the same threats. An MAA won't do you any good if an earthquake levels your city and destroys processing sites for *both* participating organizations.

- Confidentiality concerns often prevent businesses from placing their data in the hands of others. These may be legal concerns (such as in the handling of health-care or financial data) or business concerns (such as trade secrets or other intellectual property issues).

Despite these concerns, an MAA may be a good disaster recovery solution for an organization, especially if cost is an overriding factor. If you simply can't afford to implement any other type of alternate processing, an MAA might provide a degree of valuable protection in the event a localized disaster strikes your business.

# Database Recovery

Many organizations rely upon databases to process and track operations, sales, logistics, and other activities vital to their continued viability. For this reason, it's essential that you include database recovery techniques in your disaster recovery plans. It's a wise idea to have a database specialist on the DRP team who can provide input as to the technical feasibility of various ideas. After all, you shouldn't allocate several hours to restore a database backup when it's impossible to complete a restoration in less than half a day!

In the following sections, we'll cover the three main techniques used to create offsite copies of database content: electronic vaulting, remote journaling, and remote mirroring. Each one has specific benefits and drawbacks, so you'll need to analyze your organization's computing requirements and available resources to select the option best suited to your firm.

## Electronic Vaulting

In an *electronic vaulting* scenario, database backups are transferred to a remote site using bulk transfers. The remote location may be a dedicated alternative recovery site (such as a hot site) or simply an offsite location managed within the company or by a contractor for the purpose of maintaining backup data. If you use electronic vaulting, remember that there may be a significant time delay between the time you declare a disaster and the time your database is ready for operation with current data. If you decide to activate a recovery site, technicians will need to retrieve the appropriate backups from the electronic vault and apply them to the soon-to-be production servers at the recovery site.

**WARNING**   Be careful when considering vendors for an electronic vaulting contract. Definitions of electronic vaulting vary widely within the industry. Don't settle for a vague promise of "electronic vaulting capability." Insist upon a written definition of the service that will be provided, including the storage capacity, bandwidth of the communications link to the electronic vault, and the time necessary to retrieve vaulted data in the event of a disaster.

As with any type of backup scenario, be certain to periodically test your electronic vaulting setup. A great method for testing backup solutions is to give disaster recovery personnel a "surprise test," asking them to restore data from a certain day.

## Remote Journaling

With *remote journaling*, data transfers are performed in a more expeditious manner. Data transfers still occur in a bulk transfer mode, but they occur on a more frequent basis, usually once every hour if not more frequently. Unlike electronic vaulting scenarios, where database backup files are transferred, remote journaling setups transfer copies of the database transaction logs containing the transactions that occurred since the previous bulk transfer.

Remote journaling is similar to electronic vaulting in that transaction logs transferred to the remote site are not applied to a live database server but are maintained in a backup device. When a disaster is declared, technicians retrieve the appropriate transaction logs and apply them to the production database.

## Remote Mirroring

*Remote mirroring* is the most advanced database backup solution. Not surprisingly, it's also the most expensive! Remote mirroring goes beyond the technology used by remote journaling and electronic vaulting; with remote mirroring, a live database server is maintained at the backup site. The remote server receives copies of the database modifications at the same time they are applied to the production server at the primary site. Therefore, the mirrored server is ready to take over an operational role at a moment's notice.

Remote mirroring is a popular database backup strategy for organizations seeking to implement a hot site. However, when weighing the feasibility of a remote mirroring solution, be sure to take into account the infrastructure and personnel costs required to support the mirrored server as well as the processing overhead that will be added to each database transaction on the mirrored server.

# Recovery Plan Development

Once you've established your business unit priorities and have a good idea of the appropriate alternative recovery sites for your organization, it's time to put pen to paper and begin drafting a true disaster recovery plan. Don't expect to sit down and write the full plan in one sitting. It's likely that the DRP team will go through many evolutions of draft documents before reaching a final written document that satisfies the operational needs of critical business units and falls within the resource, time, and expense constraints of the disaster recovery budget and available manpower.

In the following sections, we explore some important items to include in your disaster recovery plan. Depending on the size of your organization and the number of people involved in the DRP effort, it may be a good idea to maintain multiple types of plan documents, intended for different audiences. The following list includes various types of documents worth considering:

- Executive summary
- Department-specific plans
- Technical guides for IT personnel responsible for implementing and maintaining critical backup systems
- Checklists for individuals on the disaster recovery team
- Full copies of the plan for critical disaster recovery team members

Using custom-tailored documents becomes especially important when a disaster occurs or is imminent. Personnel who need to refresh themselves on the disaster recovery procedures that affect various parts of the organization will be able to refer to their department-specific plans. Critical disaster recovery team members will have checklists to help guide their actions amid the chaotic atmosphere of a disaster. IT personnel will have technical guides helping them get the alternate sites up and running. Finally, managers and public relations personnel will have a simple document that walks them through a high-level view of the coordinated symphony that is an active disaster recovery effort without requiring interpretation from team members busy with tasks directly related to that effort.

Visit the Professional Practices library at www.drii.org/professionalprac/ to examine a collection of documents that explain how to work through and document your planning processes for BCP and disaster recovery. Other good standard documents in this area includes the BCI Good Practices Guideline (www.thebci.org/gpg/htm), ISO 27001 (www.27001-online.com), and NIST SP 800-34 (http://csrc.nist.gov/publications/PubsSPs.html).

## Emergency Response

A disaster recovery plan should contain simple yet comprehensive instructions for essential personnel to follow immediately upon recognizing that a disaster is in progress or is imminent. These instructions will vary widely depending upon the nature of the disaster, the type of personnel responding to the incident, and the time available before facilities need to be evacuated and/or equipment shut down. For example, instructions for a large-scale fire will be much more concise than the instructions for how to prepare for a hurricane that is still 48 hours away from a predicted landfall near an operational site. Emergency-response plans are often put together in the form of checklists provided to responders. When designing such checklists, keep one essential design principle in mind: Arrange the checklist tasks in order of priority, with the most important task first!

It's essential to remember that these checklists will be executed in the midst of a crisis. It is extremely likely that responders will not be able to complete the entire checklist, especially in the event of a short-notice disaster. For this reason, you should put the most essential tasks (that is, "Activate the building alarm") first on the checklist. The lower an item on the list, the lower the likelihood that it will be completed before an evacuation/shutdown takes place.

## Personnel Notification

A disaster recovery plan should also contain a list of personnel to contact in the event of a disaster. Usually, this includes key members of the DRP team as well as personnel who execute critical disaster recovery tasks throughout the organization. This response checklist should include alternate means of contact (that is, pager numbers, cell phone numbers, and so on) as well as backup contacts for each role should the primary contact be incommunicado or unable to reach the recovery site for one reason or another.

---

### The Power of Checklists

Checklists are invaluable tools in the face of disaster. They provide a sense of order amidst the chaotic events surrounding a disaster. Do what you must to ensure that response checklists provide first responders with a clear plan to protect life and property and ensure the continuity of operations.

A checklist for response to a building fire might include the following steps:

1.  Activate the building alarm system.

2.  Ensure that an orderly evacuation is in progress.

3.  After leaving the building, use a cellular telephone to call 911 to ensure that emergency authorities received the alarm notification. Provide additional information on any required emergency response.

4.  Ensure that any injured personnel receive appropriate medical treatment.

5.  Activate the organization's disaster recovery plan to ensure continuity of operations.

Be sure to consult with the individuals in your organization responsible for privacy before assembling and disseminating a telephone notification checklist. You may need to comply with special policies regarding the use of home telephone numbers and other personal information in the checklist.

The notification checklist should be supplied to all personnel who might respond to a disaster. This enables prompt notification of key personnel. Many firms organize their notification checklists in a "telephone tree" style: Each member of the tree contacts the person below them, spreading the notification burden among members of the team instead of relying on one person to make lots of telephone calls.

---

If you choose to implement a telephone tree notification scheme, be sure to add a safety net. Have the last person in each chain contact the originator to confirm that their entire chain has been notified. This lets you rest assured that the disaster recovery team activation is smoothly underway.

## Backups and Offsite Storage

Your disaster recovery plan (especially the technical guide) should fully address the backup strategy pursued by your organization. Indeed, this is one of the most important elements of any business continuity plan and disaster recovery plan.

Many system administrators are already familiar with various types of backups, so you'll benefit by bringing one or more individuals with specific technical expertise in this area onto the BCP/DRP team to provide expert guidance. There are three main types of backups:

**Full backups**   As the name implies, *full backups* store a complete copy of the data contained on the protected device. Full backups duplicate every file on the system regardless of the setting of the archive bit. Once a full backup is complete, the archive bit on every file is reset, turned off, or set to 0.

**Incremental backups**   *Incremental backups* store only those files that have been modified since the time of the most recent full or incremental backup. Only files that have the archive bit turned on, enabled, or set to 1 are duplicated. Once an incremental backup is complete, the archive bit on all duplicated files is reset, turned off, or set to 0.

**Differential backups**   *Differential backups* store all files that have been modified since the time of the most recent full backup. Only files that have the archive bit turned on, enabled, or set to 1 are duplicated. However, unlike full and incremental backups, the differential backup process does not change the archive bit.

The most important difference between incremental and differential backups is the time needed to restore data in the event of an emergency. If you use a combination of full and differential backups, you will need to restore only two backups—the most recent full backup and the most recent differential backup. On the other hand, if your strategy combines full backups with incremental backups, you will need to restore the most recent full backup as well as all incremental backups performed since that full backup. The trade-off is the time required to *create* the backups—differential backups don't take as long to restore, but they take longer to create than incremental ones.

The storage of the backup media is equally critical. It may be convenient to store backup media in or near the primary operations center to easily fulfill user requests for backup data, but you'll definitely need to keep copies of the media in at least one offsite location to provide redundancy should your primary operating location be suddenly destroyed.

## Using Backups

In case of system failure, many companies use one of two common methods to restore data from backups. In the first situation, they run a full backup on Monday night and then run differential backups every other night of the week. If a failure occurs Saturday morning, they restore Monday's full backup and then restore only Friday's differential backup. In the second situation, they run a full backup on Monday night and run incremental backups every other night of the week. If a failure occurs Saturday morning, they restore Monday's full backup and then restore each incremental backup in original chronological order (that is, Wednesday's, then Friday's, and so on).

Most organizations adopt a backup strategy that utilizes more than one of the three backup types along with a media rotation scheme. Both allow backup administrators access to a sufficiently large range of backups to complete user requests and provide fault tolerance while minimizing the amount of money that must be spent on backup media. A common strategy is to perform full backups over the weekend and incremental or differential backups on a nightly basis. The specific method of backup and all of the particulars of the backup procedure are dependent upon your organization's fault-tolerance requirements. If you are unable to survive minor amounts of data loss, then your ability to tolerate faults is low. However, if hours or days of data can be lost without serious consequence, then your tolerance of faults is high. You should design your backup solution accordingly.

## The Oft-Neglected Backup

Backups are probably the least practiced and most neglected preventive measure known to protect against computing disasters. A comprehensive backup of all operating system and personal data on workstations happens less frequently than for servers or mission-critical machines, but they all serve an equal and necessary purpose.

Carol, an information professional, learned this the hard way when she lost months of work following a natural disaster that wiped out the first floor at an information brokering firm. She never utilized the backup facilities built into her operating system or any of the shared provisions established by her administrator, Damon.

Damon has been there and done that, so he knows a thing or two about backup solutions. He has established incremental backups on his production servers and differential backups on his development servers, and he's never had an issue restoring lost data.

The toughest obstacle to a solid backup strategy is human nature, so a simple, transparent, and comprehensive strategy is the most practical. Differential backups require only two container files (the latest full backup and the latest differential) and can be scheduled for periodic updates at some specified interval. That's why Damon elects to implement this approach and feels ready to restore from his backups any time he's called upon to do so.

## Backup Media Formats

The physical characteristics and the rotation cycle are two factors that a worthwhile backup solution should track and manage. The physical characteristics involve the type of tape drive in use. This defines the physical wear placed on the media. The rotation cycle is the frequency of backups and retention length of protected data. By overseeing these characteristics, you can be assured that valuable data will be retained on serviceable backup media. Backup media has a maximum use limit; perhaps 5, 10, or 20 rewrites may be made before the media begins to lose reliability (statistically speaking). A wide variety of backup media formats exist:

- Digital Audio Tape (DAT)

- Quarter Inch Cartridge (QIC), commonly used in SOHO backups

- 8 mm tape, commonly used in Helical Scan tape drives but has been superseded by DLT

- Digital Linear Tape (DLT)

- Write Once, Read Many (WORM), a storage type often used to retain audit trails

- CDR/W media, usually requires faster file access than tape, useful for temporary storage of changeable data

There is increasing and widespread use of storage arrays as the backup medium of choice. With drives now 3 TB in size, tape and optical media can't really cope with data volume requirements anymore. Most enterprises use storage area networks (SANs) or network attached storage (NAS) for backup nowadays.

 Writeable CDs and DVDs as well as removable drives (Winchester, Zip, Jaz, and so forth) are considered inappropriate for network backup solutions, primarily because of their limited capacity but in some cases because of their speed or buffer underflow problems. Buffer underflow problems occurred before the advent of burn-proof software. *Underflow* happens when the write buffer of the drive empties during the writing process, which causes an error on the media, rendering it useless. However, these types of backup media are appropriate for end users to perform backups of limited sets of data from specific applications or for personal archiving purposes.

## Backup Best Practices

No matter what the backup solution, media, or method, you must address several common issues with backups. For instance, backup and restoration activities can be bulky and slow. Such data movement can significantly affect the performance of a network, especially during regular production hours. Thus, backups should be scheduled during the low peak periods (for example, at night).

The amount of backup data increases over time. This causes the backup (and restoration) processes to take longer each time and to consume more space on the backup media. Thus, you need to build sufficient capacity to handle a reasonable amount of growth over a reasonable amount of time into your backup solution. What is reasonable all depends on your environment and budget.

With periodic backups (that is, backups that are run every 24 hours), there is always the potential for data loss up to the length of the period. Murphy's law dictates that a server never crashes immediately after a successful backup. Instead, it is always just before the next backup begins. To avoid the problem with periods, you need to deploy some form of real-time continuous backup, such as RAID, clustering, or server mirroring.

## Tape Rotation

There are several commonly used tape rotation strategies for backups: the Grandfather-Father-Son (GFS) strategy, the Tower of Hanoi strategy, and the Six Cartridge Weekly Backup strategy. These strategies can be fairly complex, especially with large tape sets. They can be implemented manually using a pencil and a calendar or automatically by using either commercial backup software or a fully automated hierarchical storage management (HSM) system. An HSM system is an automated robotic backup jukebox consisting of 32 or 64 optical or tape backup devices. All the drive elements within an HSM system are configured as a single drive array (a bit like RAID).

Details about various tape rotations are beyond the scope of this book, but if you want to learn more about them, search by their names on the Internet.

# Software Escrow Arrangements

A *software escrow arrangement* is a unique tool used to protect a company against the failure of a software developer to provide adequate support for its products or against the possibility that the developer will go out of business and no technical support will be available for the product.

Focus your efforts on negotiating software escrow agreements with those suppliers you fear may go out of business because of their size. It's not likely that you'll be able to negotiate such an agreement with a firm such as Microsoft, unless you are responsible for an extremely large corporate account with serious bargaining power. On the other hand, it's equally unlikely that a firm of Microsoft's magnitude will go out of business, leaving end users high and dry.

If your organization depends upon custom-developed software or software products produced by a small firm, you may want to consider developing this type of arrangement as part of your disaster recovery plan. Under a software escrow agreement, the developer provides copies of the application source code to an independent third-party organization.

This third party then maintains updated backup copies of the source code in a secure fashion. The agreement between the end user and the developer specifies "trigger events," such as the failure of the developer to meet terms of a service-level agreement (SLA) or the liquidation of the developer's firm. When a trigger event takes place, the third party releases copies of the application source code to the end user. The end user can then analyze the source code to resolve application issues or implement software updates.

## External Communications

During the disaster recovery process, it will be necessary to communicate with various entities outside your organization. You will need to contact vendors to provide supplies as they are needed to support the disaster recovery effort. Your clients will want to contact you for reassurance that you are still in operation. Public relations officials may need to contact the media or investment firms, and managers may need to speak to governmental authorities. For these reasons, it is essential that your disaster recovery plan include appropriate channels of communication to the outside world in a quantity sufficient to meet your operational needs. Usually, it is not a sound business practice or recovery practice to use the CEO as your spokesperson during a disaster. A media liaison should be hired, trained, and prepared to take on this responsibility.

## Utilities

As discussed in previous sections of this chapter, your organization is reliant upon several utilities to provide critical elements of your infrastructure—electric power, water, natural gas, sewer service, and so on. Your disaster recovery plan should contain contact information and procedures to troubleshoot these services if problems arise during a disaster.

## Logistics and Supplies

The logistical problems surrounding a disaster recovery operation are immense. You will suddenly face the problem of moving large numbers of people, equipment, and supplies to alternate recovery sites. It's also possible that the people will be actually living at those sites for an extended period of time and that the disaster recovery team will be responsible for providing them with food, water, shelter, and appropriate facilities. Your disaster recovery plan should contain provisions for this type of operation if it falls within the scope of your expected operational needs.

## Recovery vs. Restoration

It is sometimes useful to separate disaster recovery tasks from disaster restoration tasks. This is especially true when a recovery effort is expected to take a significant amount of time. A disaster recovery team may be assigned to implement and maintain operations at the recovery site, while a salvage team is assigned to restore the primary site to operational capacity. Make these allocations according to the needs of your organization and the types of disasters you face.

 *Recovery* and *restoration* are separate concepts. In this context, recovery involves restoring business operations and processes to a working state. Restoration involves restoring a business facility and environment to a workable state.

The recovery team members have a very short time frame in which to operate. They must put the DRP into action and restore IT capabilities as swiftly as possible. If the recovery team fails to restore business processes within the MTD/RTO, then the company fails.

Once the original site is deemed safe for people, the salvage team members begin their work. Their job is to restore the company to its full original capabilities and, if necessary, to the original location. If the original location is no longer in existence, then a new primary spot is selected. The salvage team must rebuild or repair the IT infrastructure. Since this activity is basically the same as building a new IT system, the return activity from the alternate/recovery site to the primary/original site is itself a risky activity. Fortunately, the salvage team has more time to work than the recovery team.

The salvage team must ensure the reliability of the new IT infrastructure. This is done by returning the least-mission-critical processes to the restored original site to stress-test the rebuilt network. As the restored site shows resiliency, more important processes are transferred. A serious vulnerability exists when mission-critical processes are returned to the original site. The act of returning to the original site could cause a disaster of its own. Therefore, the state of emergency cannot be declared over until full normal operations have returned to the restored original site.

At the conclusion of any disaster recovery effort, the time will come to restore operations at the primary site and terminate any processing sites operating under the disaster recovery agreement. Your DRP should specify the criteria used to determine when it is appropriate to return to the primary site and guide the DRP recovery and salvage teams through an orderly transition.

# Training and Documentation

As with a business continuity plan, it is essential that you provide training to all personnel who will be involved in the disaster recovery effort. The level of training required will vary according to an individual's role in the effort and their position within the company. When designing a training plan, consider including the following elements:

- Orientation training for all new employees
- Initial training for employees taking on a new disaster recovery role for the first time

- Detailed refresher training for disaster recovery team members
- Brief refresher training for all other employees (can be accomplished as part of other meetings and through a medium like email newsletters sent to all employees)

Loose-leaf binders are an excellent way to store disaster recovery plans. You can distribute single-page changes to the plan without destroying a national forest!

The disaster recovery plan should also be fully documented. Earlier in this chapter, we discussed several of the documentation options available to you. Be sure you implement the necessary documentation programs and modify the documentation as changes to the plan occur. Because of the rapidly changing nature of the disaster recovery and business continuity plans, you might consider publication on a secured portion of your organization's intranet.

Your DRP should be treated as an extremely sensitive document and provided to individuals on a compartmentalized, need-to-know basis only. Individuals who participate in the plan should understand their roles fully, but they do not need to know or have access to the entire plan. Of course, it is essential to ensure that key DRP team members and senior management have access to the entire plan and understand the high-level implementation details. You certainly don't want this knowledge to rest in the mind of one individual.

Remember that a disaster may render your intranet unavailable. If you choose to distribute your disaster recovery and business continuity plans through an intranet, be sure you maintain an adequate number of printed copies of the plan at both the primary and alternate sites and maintain *only* the most current copy!

# Testing and Maintenance

Every disaster recovery plan must be tested on a periodic basis to ensure that the plan's provisions are viable and that it meets an organization's changing needs. The types of tests that you conduct will depend on the types of recovery facilities available to you, the culture of your organization, and the availability of disaster recovery team members. The five main test types—checklist tests, structured walk-throughs, simulation tests, parallel tests, and full-interruption tests—are discussed in the remaining sections of this chapter.

## Checklist Test

The *checklist test* is one of the simplest tests to conduct, but it's also one of the most critical. In this test, you simply distribute copies of disaster recovery checklists to the members of the disaster recovery team for review. This lets you accomplish three goals simultaneously:

- It ensures that key personnel are aware of their responsibilities and have that knowledge refreshed periodically.

- It provides individuals with an opportunity to review the checklists for obsolete information and update any items that require modification because of changes within the organization.

- In large organizations, it helps identify situations in which key personnel have left the company and nobody bothered to reassign their disaster recovery responsibilities. This is also a good reason why disaster recovery responsibilities should be included in job descriptions.

## Structured Walk-Through

A *structured walk-through* takes testing one step further. In this type of test, often referred to as a *table-top exercise*, members of the disaster recovery team gather in a large conference room and role-play a disaster scenario. Usually, the exact scenario is known only to the test moderator, who presents the details to the team at the meeting. The team members then refer to their copies of the disaster recovery plan and discuss the appropriate responses to that particular type of disaster.

## Simulation Test

*Simulation tests* are similar to the structured walk-throughs. In simulation tests, disaster recovery team members are presented with a scenario and asked to develop an appropriate response. Unlike with the tests previously discussed, some of these response measures are then tested. This may involve the interruption of noncritical business activities and the use of some operational personnel.

## Parallel Test

*Parallel tests* represent the next level in testing and involve relocating personnel to the alternate recovery site and implementing site activation procedures. The employees relocated to the site perform their disaster recovery responsibilities just as they would for an actual disaster. The only difference is that operations at the main facility are not interrupted. That site retains full responsibility for conducting the day-to-day business of the organization.

## Full-Interruption Test

*Full-interruption tests* operate like parallel tests, but they involve actually shutting down operations at the primary site and shifting them to the recovery site. For obvious reasons, full-interruption tests are extremely difficult to arrange, and you often encounter resistance from management.

## Maintenance

Remember that a disaster recovery plan is a living document. As your organization's needs change, you must adapt the disaster recovery plan to meet those changed needs to follow suit. You will discover many necessary modifications by using a well-organized and coordinated testing plan. Minor changes may often be made through a series of telephone conversations or emails, whereas major changes may require one or more meetings of the full disaster recovery team.

A disaster recovery planner should refer to the organization's business continuity plan as a template for its recovery efforts. This and all the supportive material must comply with federal regulations and reflect current business needs. Business processes such as payroll and order generation should contain specified metrics mapped to related IT systems and infrastructure.

Most organizations apply formal change management processes so that whenever the IT infrastructure changes, all relevant documentation is updated and checked to reflect such changes. Regularly scheduled fire drills and dry runs to ensure that all elements of the DRP are used properly to keep staff trained present a perfect opportunity to integrate changes into regular maintenance and change management procedures. Design, implement, and document changes each time you go through these processes and exercises. Know where everything is, and keep each element of the DRP working properly. In case of emergency, use your recovery plan. Finally, make sure the staff stays trained to keep their skills sharp—for existing support personnel—and use simulated exercises to bring new people up to speed quickly.

# Summary

Disaster recovery planning is critical to a comprehensive information security program. No matter how comprehensive your business continuity plan, the day may come when your business is interrupted by a disaster and you face the task of restoring operations to the primary site quickly and efficiently. Recall the old adage that "an ounce of prevention is worth a pound of cure." Spending the time and effort to develop a comprehensive disaster recovery plan greatly aids the process of recovering operations amidst a chaotic emergency.

An organization's disaster recovery plan is one of the most important documents under the purview of security professionals. It should provide guidance to the personnel responsible for ensuring the continuity of operations in the face of disaster. The DRP provides an orderly sequence of events designed to activate alternate processing sites while simultaneously restoring the primary site to operational status. Security professionals should ensure that adequate programs are in place so that those team members charged with disaster recovery duties are well trained for their roles under the plan.

# Exam Essentials

**Know the common types of natural disasters that may threaten an organization.** Natural disasters that commonly threaten organizations include earthquakes, floods, storms, fires, tsunamis, and volcanic eruptions.

**Know the common types of man-made disasters that may threaten an organization.** Explosions, electrical fires, terrorist acts, power outages, other utility failures, infrastructure failures, hardware/software failures, labor difficulties, theft, and vandalism are all common man-made disasters.

**Be familiar with the common types of recovery facilities.** The common types of recovery facilities are cold sites, warm sites, hot sites, mobile sites, service bureaus, and multiple sites. Be sure you understand the benefits and drawbacks for each such facility.

**Explain the potential benefits behind mutual assistance agreements as well as the reasons they are not commonly implemented in businesses today.** Mutual assistance agreements (MAAs) provide an inexpensive alternative to disaster recovery sites, but they are not commonly used because they are difficult to enforce. Organizations participating in an MAA may also be shut down by the same disaster, and MAAs raise confidentiality concerns.

**Know the five types of disaster recovery plan tests and the impact each has on normal business operations.** The five types of disaster recovery plan tests are checklist tests, structured walk-throughs, simulation tests, parallel tests, and full-interruption tests. Checklist tests are purely paperwork exercises, whereas structured walk-throughs involve a project team meeting. Neither has an impact on business operations. Simulation tests may shut down noncritical business units. Parallel tests involve relocating personnel but do not affect day-to-day operations. Full-interruption tests involve shutting down primary systems and shifting responsibility to the recovery facility.

# Written Lab

1. What are some of the main concerns businesses have when considering adopting a mutual assistance agreement?

2. List and explain the five types of disaster recovery tests.

3. Explain the differences between the three types of backup strategies discussed in this chapter.

# Answers to Written Lab

1.  Businesses have three main concerns when considering adopting a mutual assistance agreement. First, the nature of an MAA often necessitates that the businesses be located in close geographical proximity. However, this requirement also increases the risk that the two businesses will fall victim to the same threat. Second, MAAs are difficult to enforce in the middle of a crisis. If one of the organizations is affected by a disaster and the other isn't, the organization not affected could back out at the last minute, and the other organization is out of luck. Finally, confidentiality concerns (both legal and business related) often prevent businesses from trusting others with their sensitive operational data.

2.  There are five main types of disaster recovery tests:

    -   Checklist tests involve the distribution of recovery checklists to disaster recovery personnel for review.

    -   Structured walk-throughs are "table-top" exercises that involve assembling the disaster recovery team to discuss a disaster scenario.

    -   Simulation tests are more comprehensive and may impact one or more noncritical business units of the organization.

    -   Parallel tests involve relocating personnel to the alternate site and commencing operations there.

    -   Full-interruption tests involve relocating personnel to the alternate site and shutting down operations at the primary site.

3.  Full backups create a copy of all data stored on a server. Incremental backups create copies of all files modified since the last full or incremental backup. Differential backups create copies of all files modified since the last full backup without regard to any previous differential or incremental backups that may have taken place.

# Review Questions

1. What is the end goal of disaster recovery planning?
   A. Preventing business interruption
   B. Setting up temporary business operations
   C. Restoring normal business activity
   D. Minimizing the impact of a disaster

2. Which one of the following is an example of a man-made disaster?
   A. Tsunami
   B. Earthquake
   C. Power outage
   D. Lightning strike

3. According to the Federal Emergency Management Agency, approximately what percentage of U.S. states is rated with at least a moderate risk of seismic activity?
   A. 20 percent
   B. 40 percent
   C. 60 percent
   D. 80 percent

4. Which one of the following disaster types is not usually covered by standard business or homeowner's insurance?
   A. Earthquake
   B. Flood
   C. Fire
   D. Theft

5. In the wake of the September 11, 2001, terrorist attacks, what industry made drastic changes that directly impact DRP/BCP activities?
   A. Tourism
   B. Banking
   C. Insurance
   D. Airline

6. Which of the following statements about business continuity planning and disaster recovery planning is incorrect?

   A. Business continuity planning is focused on keeping business functions uninterrupted when a disaster strikes.

   B. Organizations can choose whether to develop business continuity planning or disaster recovery planning plans.

   C. Business continuity planning picks up where disaster recovery planning leaves off.

   D. Disaster recovery planning guides an organization through recovery of normal operations at the primary facility.

7. What does the term "100-year flood plain" mean to emergency preparedness officials?

   A. The last flood of any kind to hit the area was more than 100 years ago.

   B. The odds of a flood at this level are 1 in 100 in any given year.

   C. The area is expected to be safe from flooding for at least 100 years.

   D. The last significant flood to hit the area was more than 100 years ago.

8. In which one of the following database recovery techniques is an exact, up-to-date copy of the database maintained at an alternative location?

   A. Transaction logging

   B. Remote journaling

   C. Electronic vaulting

   D. Remote mirroring

9. What disaster recovery principle best protects your organization against hardware failure?

   A. Consistency

   B. Efficiency

   C. Redundancy

   D. Primacy

10. What business continuity planning technique can help you prepare the business unit prioritization task of disaster recovery planning?

    A. Vulnerability analysis

    B. Business impact analysis

    C. Risk management

    D. Continuity planning

11. Which one of the following alternative processing sites takes the longest time to activate?

    A. Hot site

    B. Mobile site

    C. Cold site

    D. Warm site

12. What is the typical time estimate to activate a warm site from the time a disaster is declared?

   A. 1 hour

   B. 6 hours

   C. 12 hours

   D. 24 hours

13. Which one of the following items is a characteristic of hot sites but not a characteristic of warm sites?

   A. Communications circuits

   B. Workstations

   C. Servers

   D. Current data

14. What type of database backup strategy involves maintenance of a live backup server at the remote site?

   A. Transaction logging

   B. Remote journaling

   C. Electronic vaulting

   D. Remote mirroring

15. What type of document will help public relations specialists and other individuals who need a high-level summary of disaster recovery efforts while they are underway?

   A. Executive summary

   B. Technical guides

   C. Department-specific plans

   D. Checklists

16. What disaster recovery planning tool can be used to protect an organization against the failure of a critical software firm to provide appropriate support for their products?

   A. Differential backups

   B. Business impact assessment

   C. Incremental backups

   D. Software escrow agreement

17. What type of backup involves always storing copies of all files modified since the most recent full backup?

   A. Differential backups

   B. Partial backup

   C. Incremental backups

   D. Database backup

18. What combination of backup strategies provides the fastest backup creation time?
    A. Full backups and differential backups
    B. Partial backups and incremental backups
    C. Full backups and incremental backups
    D. Incremental backups and differential backups

19. What combination of backup strategies provides the fastest backup restoration time?
    A. Full backups and differential backups
    B. Partial backups and incremental backups
    C. Full backups and incremental backups
    D. Incremental backups and differential backups

20. What type of disaster recovery plan test fully evaluates operations at the backup facility but does not shift primary operations responsibility from the main site?
    A. Structured walk-through
    B. Parallel test
    C. Full-interruption test
    D. Simulation test

# Answers to Review Questions

1.  C. Once a disaster interrupts the business operations, the goal of DRP is to restore regular business activity as quickly as possible. Thus, disaster recovery planning picks up where business continuity planning leaves off.

2.  C. A power outage is an example of a man-made disaster. The other events listed—tsunamis, earthquakes, and lightning strikes—are all naturally occurring events.

3.  D. As shown in Table 16.1, 41 of the 50 U.S. states are considered to have a moderate, high, or very high risk of seismic activity. This rounds to 80 percent to provide the value given in answer D.

4.  B. Most general business insurance and homeowner's insurance policies do not provide any protection against the risk of flooding or flash floods. If floods pose a risk to your organization, you should consider purchasing supplemental flood insurance under FEMA's National Flood Insurance Program.

5.  C. Although all the industries listed in the options made changes to their practices after September 11, 2001, the insurance industry's change toward noncoverage of acts of terrorism most directly impacts the BCP/DRP process.

6.  C. The opposite of this statement is true—disaster recovery planning picks up where business continuity planning leaves off. The other three statements are all accurate reflections of the role of business continuity planning and disaster recovery planning.

7.  B. The term *100-year flood plain* is used to describe an area where flooding is expected once every 100 years. It is, however, more mathematically correct to say that this labels indicates a 1 percent probability of flooding in any given year.

8.  D. When you use remote mirroring, an exact copy of the database is maintained at an alternative location. You keep the remote copy up-to-date by executing all transactions on both the primary and remote site at the same time.

9.  C. Redundant systems/components provide protection against the failure of one particular piece of hardware.

10. B. During the business impact assessment phase, you must identify the business priorities of your organization to assist with the allocation of BCP resources. You can use this same information to drive the DRP business unit prioritization.

11. C. The cold site contains none of the equipment necessary to restore operations. All of the equipment must be brought in and configured and data must be restored to it before operations can commence. This often takes weeks.

12. C. Warm sites typically take about 12 hours to activate from the time a disaster is declared. This is compared to the relatively instantaneous activation of a hot site and the lengthy (at least a week) time required to bring a cold site to operational status.

13. D. Warm sites and hot sites both contain workstations, servers, and the communications circuits necessary to achieve operational status. The main difference between the two alternatives is the fact that hot sites contain near real-time copies of the operational data and warm sites require the restoration of data from backup.

14. D. Remote mirroring is the only backup option in which a live backup server at a remote site maintains a bit-for-bit copy of the contents of the primary server, synchronized as closely as the latency in the link between primary and remote systems will allow.

15. A. The executive summary provides a high-level view of the entire organization's disaster recovery efforts. This document is useful for the managers and leaders of the firm as well as public relations personnel who need a nontechnical perspective on this complex effort.

16. D. Software escrow agreements place the application source code in the hands of an independent third party, thus providing firms with a "safety net" in the event a developer goes out of business or fails to honor the terms of a service agreement.

17. A. Differential backups involve always storing copies of all files modified since the most recent full backup regardless of any incremental or differential backups created during the intervening time period.

18. C. Any backup strategy must include full backups at some point in the process. Incremental backups are created faster than differential backups because of the number of files it is necessary to back up each time.

19. A. Any backup strategy must include full backups at some point in the process. If a combination of full and differential backups is used, a maximum of two backups must be restored. If a combination of full and incremental backups is chosen, the number of required restorations may be unlimited.

20. B. Parallel tests involve moving personnel to the recovery site and gearing up operations, but responsibility for conducting day-to-day operations of the business remains at the primary operations center.

# Chapter

# 17

# Law and Investigations

---

## THE CISSP EXAM TOPICS COVERED IN THIS CHAPTER INCLUDE:

✓ **Legal, Regulations, Investigations, and Compliance**

- Understand legal issues that pertain to information security internationally

  - Computer crime; licensing and intellectual property (e.g., copyright, trademark); import/export; trans-border data flow; privacy

- Understand and support investigations

  - Policy; incident handling and response; evidence collection and handling (e.g., chain of custody, interviewing); reporting and documenting

- Understand forensic procedures

  - Media analysis; network analysis; software analysis

- Understand compliance requirements and procedures

  - Regulatory environment; audits; reporting

✓ **Operations Security**

- Manage incident response

  - Detection; response; reporting; recovery; remediation

In the early days of computer security, information security professionals were pretty much left on their own to defend their systems against attacks. They didn't have much help from the criminal and civil justice systems. When they did seek assistance from law enforcement, they were met with reluctance by overworked agents who didn't have a basic understanding of how something that involved a computer could actually be a crime. The legislative branch of government hadn't addressed the issue of computer crime, and the executive branch thought they simply didn't have statutory authority or obligation to pursue those matters.

Fortunately, both our legal system and the men and women of law enforcement have come a long way over the past two decades. The legislative branches of governments around the world have at least attempted to address issues of computer crime. Many law enforcement agencies have full-time, well-trained computer crime investigators with advanced security training. Those that don't usually know where to turn when they require this sort of experience.

In this chapter, we'll cover the various types of laws that deal with computer security issues. We'll examine the legal issues surrounding computer crime, privacy, intellectual property, and a number of other related topics. We'll also cover basic investigative techniques, including the pros and cons of calling in assistance from law enforcement.

# Categories of Laws

Three main categories of laws play a role in our legal system. Each is used to cover a variety of different circumstances, and the penalties for violating laws in the different categories vary widely. In the following sections, we'll cover how criminal law, civil law, and administrative law interact to form the complex web of our justice system.

## Criminal Law

Criminal law forms the bedrock of the body of laws that preserve the peace and keep our society safe. Many high-profile court cases involve matters of criminal law; these are the laws that the police and other law enforcement agencies concern themselves with. Criminal law contains prohibitions against acts such as murder, assault, robbery, and arson. Penalties for violating criminal statutes fall in a range that includes mandatory hours of community service, monetary penalties in the form of fines (small and large), and deprivation of civil liberties in the form of prison sentences.

## Cops Are Smart!

A good friend of one of the authors is a technology crime investigator for the local police department. He often receives cases of computer abuse involving threatening emails and website postings.

Recently, he shared a story about a bomb threat that had been emailed to a local high school. The perpetrator sent a threatening note to the school principal declaring that the bomb would explode at 1 p.m. and warning him to evacuate the school. The author's friend received the alert at 11 a.m., leaving him with only two hours to investigate the crime and advise the principal on the best course of action.

He quickly began issuing emergency subpoenas to Internet service providers and traced the email to a computer in the school library. At 12:15 p.m., he confronted the suspect with surveillance tapes showing him at the computer in the library as well as audit logs conclusively proving that he had sent the email. The student quickly admitted that the threat was nothing more than a ploy to get out of school a couple of hours early. His explanation? "I didn't think there was anyone around here who could trace stuff like that."

He was wrong.

A number of criminal laws serve to protect society against computer crime. In later sections of this chapter, you'll learn how some laws, such as the Computer Fraud and Abuse Act, the Electronic Communications Privacy Act, and the Identity Theft and Assumption Deterrence Act (among others), provide criminal penalties for serious cases of computer crime. Technically savvy prosecutors teamed with concerned law enforcement agencies have dealt serious blows to the "hacking underground" by using the court system to slap lengthy prison terms on offenders guilty of what used to be considered harmless pranks.

In the United States, legislative bodies at all levels of government establish criminal laws through elected representatives. At the federal level, both the House of Representatives and the Senate must pass criminal law bills by a majority vote (in most cases) in order for the bill to become law. Once passed, these laws then become federal law and apply in all cases where the federal government has jurisdiction (mainly cases that involve interstate commerce, cases that cross state boundaries, or cases that are offenses against the federal government itself). If federal jurisdiction does not apply, state authorities handle the case using laws passed in a similar manner by state legislators.

All federal and state laws must comply with the document that dictates how the U.S. system of government works—the U.S. Constitution. All laws are subject to judicial review by regional courts with the right of appeal all the way to the Supreme Court of the United States. If a court finds that a law is unconstitutional, it has the power to strike it down and render it invalid.

Keep in mind that criminal law is a serious matter. If you find yourself involved—either as a witness, defendant, or victim—in a matter where criminal authorities become involved, you'd be well advised to seek advice from an attorney familiar with the criminal justice system and specifically with matters of computer crime. It's not wise to "go it alone" in such a complex system.

## Civil Law

Civil laws form the bulk of our body of laws. They are designed to provide for an orderly society and govern matters that are not crimes but require an impartial arbiter to settle between individuals and organizations. Examples of the types of matters that may be judged under civil law include contract disputes, real estate transactions, employment matters, and estate/probate procedures. Civil laws also are used to create the framework of government that the executive branch uses to carry out its responsibilities. These laws provide budgets for governmental activities and lay out the authority granted to the executive branch to create administrative laws (see the next section).

Civil laws are enacted in the same manner as criminal laws. They must pass through the legislative process before enactment and are subject to the same constitutional parameters and judicial review procedures. At the federal level, both criminal and civil laws are embodied in the United States Code (USC).

The major difference between civil laws and criminal laws is the way in which they are enforced. Usually, law enforcement authorities do not become involved in matters of civil law beyond taking action necessary to restore order. In a criminal prosecution, the government, through law enforcement investigators and prosecutors, brings action against a person accused of a crime. In civil matters, it is incumbent upon the person who thinks they have been wronged to obtain legal counsel and file a civil lawsuit against the person they think is responsible for their grievance. The government (unless it is the plaintiff or defendant) does not take sides in the dispute or argue one position or the other. The only role of the government in civil matters is to provide the judges, juries, and court facilities used to hear civil cases and to play an administrative role in managing the judicial system in accordance with the law.

As with criminal law, it is best to obtain legal assistance if you think you need to file a civil lawsuit or someone files a civil lawsuit against you. Although civil law does not impose the threat of imprisonment, the losing party may face severe financial penalties. You don't need to look any further than the nightly news for examples—multimillion-dollar cases against tobacco companies, major corporations, and wealthy individuals are filed every day.

## Administrative Law

The executive branch of our government charges numerous agencies with wide-ranging responsibilities to ensure that government functions effectively. It is the duty of these agencies to abide by and enforce the criminal and civil laws enacted by the legislative branch. However, as can be easily imagined, criminal and civil law can't possibly lay out rules and procedures that should be followed in any possible situation. Therefore, executive branch agencies have some leeway to enact administrative law, in the form of policies, procedures, and regulations that govern the daily operations of the agency. Administrative law covers topics as mundane as the procedures to be used within a federal agency to obtain a desk telephone to more substantial issues such as the immigration policies that will be used to enforce the laws passed by Congress. Administrative law is published in the Code of Federal Regulations, often referred to as the CFR.

Although administrative law does not require an act of the legislative branch to gain the force of law, it must comply with all existing civil and criminal laws. Government agencies may not implement regulations that directly contradict existing laws passed by the legislature. Furthermore, administrative laws (and the actions of government agencies) must also comply with the U.S. Constitution and are subject to judicial review.

In order to understand compliance requirements and procedures, it is necessary to be fully versed in the complexities of the law. From administrative law to civil law to criminal law (and, in some countries, even religious law), navigating the regulatory environment is a daunting task. The CISSP exam focuses on the generalities of law, regulations, investigations, and compliance. However, it is your responsibility to seek out professional help (i.e., an attorney) to guide and support you in your efforts to maintain legal and legally supportable security.

# Laws

Throughout these sections, we'll examine a number of laws that relate to information technology. By necessity, this discussion is U.S.-centric, as is the material covered by the CISSP exam. We'll look at several high-profile foreign laws, such as the European Union's data privacy act. However, if you operate in an environment that involves foreign jurisdictions, you should retain local legal counsel to guide you through the system.

**WARNING**   Every information security professional should have a basic understanding of the law as it relates to information technology. However, the most important lesson to be learned is knowing when it's necessary to call in an attorney: If you think you're in a legal "gray area," it's best to seek professional advice.

## Computer Crime

The first computer security issues addressed by legislators were those involving computer crime. Early computer crime prosecutions were attempted under traditional criminal law, and many were dismissed because judges thought that applying traditional law to this modern type of crime was too far of a stretch. Legislators responded by passing specific statutes that defined computer crime and laid out specific penalties for various crimes. In the following sections, we'll cover several of those statutes.

> The U.S. laws discussed in this chapter are federal laws. Almost every state in the union has enacted some form of legislation regarding computer security issues. Because of the global reach of the Internet, most computer crimes cross state lines and, therefore, fall under federal jurisdiction and are prosecuted in the federal court system. However, in some circumstances, state laws can be more restrictive than federal laws and impose harsher penalties.

## Computer Fraud and Abuse Act of 1984

Congress first enacted the Computer Fraud and Abuse Act (CFAA) in 1984, and it remains in force today, with several amendments. This law was carefully written to exclusively cover computer crimes that crossed state boundaries to avoid infringing upon states' rights and treading on thin constitutional ice. The major provisions of the act are that it is a crime to perform the following:

- Access classified information or financial information in a federal system without authorization or in excess of authorized privileges.
- Access a computer used exclusively by the federal government without authorization.
- Use a federal computer to perpetrate a fraud (unless the only object of the fraud was to gain use of the computer itself).
- Cause malicious damage to a federal computer system in excess of $1,000.
- Modify medical records in a computer when doing so impairs or may impair the examination, diagnosis, treatment, or medical care of an individual.
- Traffic in computer passwords if the trafficking affects interstate commerce or involves a federal computer system.

The CFAA was amended in 1986 to change the scope of the act. Instead of merely covering federal computers that processed sensitive information, the act was changed to cover all "federal interest" computers. This widened the coverage of the act to include the following:

- Any computer used exclusively by the U.S. government
- Any computer used exclusively by a financial institution
- Any computer used by the government or a financial institution when the offense impedes the ability of the government or institution to use that system
- Any combination of computers used to commit an offense when they are not all located in the same state

> When preparing for the CISSP exam, be sure you're able to briefly describe the purpose of each law discussed in this chapter.

## 1994 CFAA Amendments

In 1994, Congress recognized that the face of computer security had drastically changed since the CFAA was last amended in 1986 and made a number of sweeping changes to the act. Collectively, these changes are referred to as the Computer Abuse Amendments Act of 1994 and included the following provisions:

- Outlawed the creation of any type of malicious code that might cause damage to a computer system

- Modified the CFAA to cover any computer used in interstate commerce rather than just "federal interest" computer systems

- Allowed for the imprisonment of offenders, regardless of whether they actually intended to cause damage

- Provided legal authority for the victims of computer crime to pursue civil action to gain injunctive relief and compensation for damages

## Computer Security Act of 1987

After amending the CFAA in 1986 to cover a wider variety of computer systems, Congress turned its view inward and examined the current state of computer security in federal government systems. Members of Congress were not satisfied with what they saw and enacted the Computer Security Act (CSA) of 1987 to mandate baseline security requirements for all federal agencies. In the introduction to the CSA, Congress specified four main purposes of the act:

- To give the National Institute of Standards and Technology (NIST) responsibility for developing standards and guidelines for federal computer systems. For this purpose, NIST draws on the technical advice and assistance (including work products) of the National Security Agency where appropriate.

- To provide for the enactment of such standards and guidelines.

- To require the establishment of security plans by all operators of federal computer systems that contain sensitive information.

- To require mandatory periodic training for all people involved in management, use, or operation of federal computer systems that contain sensitive information.

This act clearly set out a number of requirements that formed the basis of federal computer security policy for many years. It also divided responsibility for computer security among two federal agencies. The National Security Agency (NSA), which formerly had authority over all computer security issues, now retained authority over classified systems. NIST gained responsibility for securing all other federal government systems and produces the 800 series of Special Publications related to computer security in the federal government. These are useful for all security practitioners and are available for free online at http://csrc.nist.gov/publications/PubsSPs.html.

## Federal Sentencing Guidelines

The Federal Sentencing Guidelines released in 1991 provided punishment guidelines to help federal judges interpret computer crime laws. Three major provisions of these guidelines have had a lasting impact on the information security community:

- The guidelines formalized the *prudent man rule*, which requires senior executives to take personal responsibility for ensuring the *due care* that ordinary, prudent individuals would exercise in the same situation. This rule, developed in the realm of fiscal responsibility, now applies to information security as well.

- The guidelines allowed organizations and executives to minimize punishment for infractions by demonstrating that they used due diligence in the conduct of their information security duties.

- The guidelines outlined three burdens of proof for *negligence*. First, there must be a legally recognized obligation of the person accused of negligence. Second, the person must have failed to comply with recognized standards. Finally, there must be a causal relationship between the act of negligence and subsequent damages.

## Paperwork Reduction Act of 1995

The Paperwork Reduction Act of 1995 requires that agencies obtain Office of Management and Budget (OMB) approval before requesting most types of information from the public. Information collections include forms, interviews, record-keeping requirements, and a wide variety of other things. The Government Information Security Reform Act (GISRA) of 2000 amended this act.

## National Information Infrastructure Protection Act of 1996

In 1996, Congress passed yet another set of amendments to the Computer Fraud and Abuse Act designed to further extend the protection it provides. The National Information Infrastructure Protection Act included the following main new areas of coverage:

- Broadens CFAA to cover computer systems used in international commerce in addition to systems used in interstate commerce

- Extends similar protections to portions of the national infrastructure other than computing systems, such as railroads, gas pipelines, electric power grids, and telecommunications circuits

- Treats any intentional or reckless act that causes damage to critical portions of the national infrastructure as a felony

## Government Information Security Reform Act of 2000

The Government Information Security Reform Act (GISRA) of 2000 amends the United States Code to implement additional information security policies and procedures. In the text of the act, Congress laid out five basic purposes for establishing the GISRA:

- To provide a comprehensive framework for establishing and ensuring the effectiveness of controls over information resources that support federal operations and assets

- To recognize the highly networked nature of the federal computing environment, including the need for federal government interoperability, and in the implementation of improved security management measures, to assure that opportunities for interoperability are not adversely affected

- To provide effective government-wide management and oversight of the related information security risks, including coordination of information security efforts throughout the civilian, national security, and law enforcement communities

- To provide for development and maintenance of minimum controls required to protect federal information and information systems

- To provide a mechanism for improved oversight of federal agency information security programs

The provisions of the GISRA continue to charge the National Institute of Standards and Technology and the National Security Agency with security oversight responsibilities for unclassified and classified information processing systems, respectively. However, GISRA places the burden of maintaining the security and integrity of government information and information systems squarely on the shoulders of individual agency leaders.

GISRA also creates a new category of computer system. A mission-critical system meets one of the following criteria:

- It is defined as a national security system by other provisions of law.

- It is protected by procedures established for classified information.

- The loss, misuse, disclosure, or unauthorized access to or modification of any information it processes would have a debilitating impact on the mission of an agency.

GISRA provides specific evaluation and auditing authority for mission-critical systems to the secretary of defense and the director of central intelligence. This is an attempt to ensure that all government agencies, even those that do not routinely deal with classified national security information, implement adequate security controls on systems that are absolutely critical to the continued functioning of the agency.

# Intellectual Property

America's role in the global economy is shifting away from a manufacturer of goods and toward a provider of services. This trend also shows itself in many of the world's large industrialized nations. With this shift toward providing services, intellectual property takes on an increasingly important role in many firms. Indeed, it is arguable that the most valuable assets of many large multinational companies are simply the brand names that we've all come to recognize, and company names such as Dell, Procter & Gamble, and Merck bring instant credibility to any product. Publishing companies, movie producers, and artists depend upon their creative output to earn their livelihood. Many products depend upon secret recipes or production techniques—take the legendary secret formula for Coca-Cola or the Colonel's secret blend of herbs and spices, for example.

These intangible assets are collectively referred to as *intellectual property*, and a whole host of laws exist to protect the rights of their owners. After all, it simply wouldn't be fair if a music store bought only one copy of each artist's CD and burned copies for all of its customers—that would deprive the artist of the benefits of their labor. In the following sections, we'll explore the laws surrounding the four major types of intellectual property—copyrights, trademarks, patents, and trade secrets. We'll also discuss how these concepts specifically concern information security professionals. Many countries protect (or fail to protect) these rights in different ways, but the basic concepts ring true throughout the world.

Some countries are notorious for violating intellectual property rights. The most notable example is China. China is world renowned for its blatant disregard of copyright and patent law. If you're planning to do business in this region of the world, you should definitely consult with an attorney who specializes in this area.

## Copyrights and the Digital Millennium Copyright Act

*Copyright* law guarantees the creators of "original works of authorship" protection against the unauthorized duplication of their work. Eight broad categories of works qualify for copyright protection:

- Literary works
- Musical works
- Dramatic works
- Pantomimes and choreographic works
- Pictorial, graphical, and sculptural works
- Motion pictures and other audiovisual works
- Sound recordings
- Architectural works

There is precedent for copyrighting computer software—it's done under the scope of literary works. However, it's important to note that copyright law protects only the expression inherent in computer software—that is, the actual source code. It does not protect the ideas or process behind the software. There has also been some question over whether copyrights can be extended to cover the "look and feel" of a software package's graphical user interface. Court decisions have gone in both directions on this matter; if you will be involved in this type of issue, you should consult a qualified intellectual property attorney to determine the current state of legislation and case law.

There is a formal procedure to obtain a copyright that involves sending copies of the protected work along with an appropriate registration fee to the U.S. Copyright Office. For more information on this process, visit the office's website at www.copyright.gov. However, it is important to note that officially registering a copyright is not a prerequisite for copyright enforcement. Indeed, the law states that the creator of a work has an automatic copyright from the instant the work is created. If you can prove in court that you were the creator of a work (perhaps by publishing it), you will be protected under copyright law. Official registration merely provides the government's acknowledgment that they received your work on a specific date.

Copyright ownership always defaults to the creator of a work. The exceptions to this policy are works for hire. A work is considered "for hire" when it is made for an employer during the normal course of an employee's workday. For example, when an employee in a company's public relations department writes a press release, the press release is considered a work for hire. A work may also be considered a work for hire when it is made as part of a written contract declaring it as such.

Current copyright law provides for a very lengthy period of protection. Works by one or more authors are protected until 70 years after the death of the last surviving author. Works for hire and anonymous works are provided protection for the shorter of 95 years from the date of first publication or 120 years from the date of creation.

In 1998, Congress recognized the rapidly changing digital landscape that was stretching the reach of existing copyright law. To help meet this challenge, it enacted the hotly debated Digital Millennium Copyright Act. The DMCA also serves to bring U.S. copyright law into compliance with terms of two World Intellectual Property Organization (WIPO) treaties.

The first major provision of the DMCA is the prohibition of attempts to circumvent copyright protection mechanisms placed on a protected work by the copyright holder. This clause was designed to protect copy-prevention mechanisms placed on digital media such as CDs and DVDs. The DMCA provides for penalties of up to $1,000,000 and 10 years in prison for repeat offenders. Nonprofit institutions such as libraries and schools are exempted from this provision.

The DMCA also limits the liability of Internet service providers when their circuits are used by criminals violating the copyright law. The DMCA recognizes that ISPs have a legal status similar to the "common carrier" status of telephone companies and does not hold them liable for the "transitory activities" of their users. To qualify for this exemption, the service provider's activities must meet the following requirements (quoted directly from the Digital Millennium Copyright Act of 1998, U.S. Copyright Office Summary, December 1998):

- The transmission must be initiated by a person other than the provider.
- The transmission, routing, provision of connections, or copying must be carried out by an automated technical process without selection of material by the service provider.
- The service provider must not determine the recipients of the material.
- Any intermediate copies must not ordinarily be accessible to anyone other than anticipated recipients, and must not be retained for longer than reasonably necessary.
- The material must be transmitted with no modification to its content.

The DMCA also exempts activities of service providers related to system caching, search engines, and the storage of information on a network by individual users. However, in those cases, the service provider must take prompt action to remove copyrighted materials upon notification of the infringement.

692    Chapter 17 · Law and Investigations

Congress also included provisions in the DMCA that allow the creation of backup copies of computer software and any maintenance, testing, or routine usage activities that require software duplication. These provisions apply only if the software is licensed for use on a particular computer, the usage is in compliance with the license agreement, and any such copies are immediately deleted when no longer required for a permitted activity.

Finally, the DMCA spells out the application of copyright law principles to the emerging field of *webcasting*, or broadcasting audio and/or video content to recipients over the Internet. This technology is often referred to as *streaming audio* or *streaming video*. The DMCA states that these uses are to be treated as "eligible nonsubscription transmissions." The law in this area is still under development, so if you plan to engage in this type of activity, you should contact an attorney to ensure that you are in compliance with current law.

## Trademarks

Copyright laws are used to protect creative works; there is also protection for *trademarks*, which are words, slogans, and logos used to identify a company and its products or services. For example, a business might obtain a copyright on its sales brochure to ensure that competitors can't duplicate its sales materials. That same business might also seek to obtain trademark protection for its company name and the names of specific products and services that it offers to its clients.

The main objective of trademark protection is to avoid confusion in the marketplace while protecting the intellectual property rights of people and organizations. As with copyright protection, trademarks do not need to be officially registered to gain protection under the law. If you use a trademark in the course of your public activities, you are automatically protected under any relevant trademark law and can use the ™ symbol to show that you intend to protect words or slogans as trademarks. If you want official recognition of your trademark, you can register it with the United States Patent and Trademark Office (USPTO). This process generally requires an attorney to perform a due diligence comprehensive search for existing trademarks that might preclude your registration. The entire registration process can take more than a year from start to finish. Once you've received your registration certificate from the USPTO, you can denote your mark as a registered trademark with the ® symbol.

One major advantage of trademark registration is that you may register a trademark that you intend to use but are not necessarily already using. This type of application is called an *intent to use* application and conveys trademark protection as of the date of filing provided that you actually use the trademark in commerce within a certain time period. If you opt not to register your trademark with the PTO, your protection begins only when you first use the trademark.

The acceptance of a trademark application in the United States depends on two main requirements:

- The trademark must not be confusingly similar to another trademark—you should determine this during your attorney's due diligence search. There will be an open opposition period during which other companies may dispute your trademark application.

- The trademark should not be descriptive of the goods and services that you will offer. For example, "Mike's Software Company" would not be a good trademark candidate because it describes the product produced by the company. The USPTO may reject an application if it considers the trademark descriptive.

In the United States, trademarks are granted for an initial period of 10 years and can be renewed for unlimited successive 10-year periods.

## Patents

*Patents* protect the intellectual property rights of inventors. They provide a period of 20 years during which the inventor is granted exclusive rights to use the invention (whether directly or via licensing agreements). At the end of the patent exclusivity period, the invention is in the public domain available for anyone to use.

Patents have three main requirements:

- The invention must be new. Inventions are patentable only if they are original ideas.

- The invention must be useful. It must actually work and accomplish some sort of task.

- The invention must not be obvious. You could not, for example, obtain a patent for your idea to use a drinking cup to collect rainwater. This is an obvious solution. You might, however, be able to patent a specially designed cup that optimizes the amount of rainwater collected while minimizing evaporation.

In the technology field, patents have long been used to protect hardware devices and manufacturing processes. There is plenty of precedent on the side of inventors in those areas. Recent patents have also been issued covering software programs and similar mechanisms, but the jury is still out on whether these patents will hold up to the scrutiny of the courts.

## Trade Secrets

Many companies have intellectual property that is absolutely critical to their business and significant damage would result if it were disclosed to competitors and/or the public—in other words, *trade secrets*. We previously mentioned two examples of this type of information from popular culture—the secret formula for Coca-Cola and Kentucky Fried Chicken's "secret blend of herbs and spices." Other examples are plentiful—a manufacturing company may want to keep secret a certain manufacturing process that only a few key employees fully understand, or a statistical analysis company might want to safeguard an advanced model developed for in-house use.

Two of the previously discussed intellectual property tools—copyrights and patents—could be used to protect this type of information, but with two major disadvantages:

- Filing a copyright or patent application requires that you publicly disclose the details of your work or invention. This automatically removes the "secret" nature of your property and may harm your firm by removing the mystique surrounding a product or by allowing unscrupulous competitors to copy your property in violation of international intellectual property laws.

- Copyrights and patents both provide protection for a limited period of time. Once your legal protection expires, other firms are free to use your work at will (and they have all the details from the public disclosure you made during the application process!).

There actually is an official process regarding trade secrets—by their nature you don't register them with anyone; you keep them to yourself. To preserve trade secret status, you must implement adequate controls within your organization to ensure that only authorized personnel with a need to know the secrets have access to them. You must also ensure that anyone who does have this type of access is bound by a nondisclosure agreement (NDA) that prohibits them from sharing the information with others and provides penalties for violating the agreement. Consult an attorney to ensure that the agreement lasts for the maximum period permitted by law. In addition, you must take steps to demonstrate that you value and protect your intellectual property. Failure to do so may result in the loss of trade secret protection.

Trade secret protection is one of the best ways to protect computer software. As discussed in the previous section, patent law does not provide adequate protection for computer software products. Copyright law protects only the actual text of the source code and doesn't prohibit others from rewriting your code in a different form and accomplishing the same objective. If you treat your source code as a trade secret, it keeps it out of the hands of your competitors in the first place. This is the technique used by large software development companies such as Microsoft to protect its core base of intellectual property.

---

### Economic Espionage Act of 1996

Trade secrets are very often the crown jewels of major corporations, and the U.S. government recognized the importance of protecting this type of intellectual property when Congress enacted the Economic Espionage Act of 1996. This law has two major provisions:

- Anyone found guilty of stealing trade secrets from a U.S. corporation with the intention of benefiting a foreign government or agent may be fined up to $500,000 and imprisoned for up to 15 years.

- Anyone found guilty of stealing trade secrets under other circumstances may be fined up to $250,000 and imprisoned for up to 10 years.

The terms of the Economic Espionage Act give true teeth to the intellectual property rights of trade secret owners. Enforcing this law requires that companies take adequate steps to ensure that their trade secrets are well protected and not accidentally placed into the public domain.

# Licensing

Security professionals should also be familiar with the legal issues surrounding software licensing agreements. Three common types of license agreements are in use today:

- *Contractual license agreements* utilize a written contract between the software vendor and the customer, outlining the responsibilities of each. These agreements are commonly found for high-priced and/or highly specialized software packages.

- *Shrink-wrap license agreements* are written on the outside of the software packaging. They commonly include a clause stating that you acknowledge agreement to the terms of the contract simply by breaking the shrink-wrap seal on the package.

- *Click-wrap license agreements* are becoming more commonplace than shrink-wrap agreements. In this type of agreement, the contract terms are either written on the software box or included in the software documentation. During the installation process, you are required to click a button indicating that you have read the terms of the agreement and agree to abide by them. This adds an active consent to the process, ensuring that the individual is aware of the agreement's existence prior to installation.

---

### Uniform Computer Information Transactions Act

The Uniform Computer Information Transactions Act (UCITA) is a federal law designed for adoption by each of the 50 states to provide a common framework for the conduct of computer-related business transactions. UCITA contains provisions that address software licensing. The terms of the UCITA give legal backing to the previously questionable practices of shrink-wrap licensing and click-wrap licensing by giving them status as legally binding contracts. UCITA also requires that manufacturers provide software users with the option to reject the terms of the license agreement before completing the installation process and receive a full refund of the software's purchase price.

---

Industry groups provide guidance and enforcement activities regarding software licensing. You can get more information from their websites. One major group is the Business Software Alliance (BSA) at www.bsa.org.

# Import/Export

The federal government recognizes that the very same computers and encryption technologies that drive the Internet and e-commerce can be extremely powerful tools in the hands of a military force. For this reason, during the Cold War, the government developed a complex set of regulations governing the export of sensitive hardware and software products to other nations. The regulations include the management of trans-border data flow of new technologies, intellectual property, and personally identifying information.

Until recently, it was very difficult to export high-powered computers outside the United States, except to a select handful of allied nations. The controls on exporting encryption software were even more severe, rendering it virtually impossible to export any encryption technology outside the country. Recent changes in federal policy have relaxed these restrictions and provided for more open commerce.

## Computer Export Controls

Currently, U.S. firms can export high-performance computing systems to virtually any country without receiving prior approval from the government. There are exceptions to this rule for countries designated by the Department of Commerce as Tier 3 countries. This includes countries such as India, Pakistan, Afghanistan, and many countries in the Middle East. The export of any computer that is capable of operating in excess of 0.75 weighted teraflops (a trillion floating-point operations per second) must be preapproved by the Department of Commerce.

 You can find a list of countries and their corresponding computer export tiers on the Department of Commerce's website at www.bis.doc.gov/hpcs.

The export of high-performance computers to any country currently on the Tier 4 list is prohibited. These countries include Cuba, Iran, Iraq, Libya, North Korea, Sudan, and Syria.

## Encryption Export Controls

The Department of Commerce's Bureau of Industry and Security sets forth regulations on the export of encryption products outside the United States. Under previous regulations, it was virtually impossible to export even relatively low-grade encryption technology outside the United States. This placed U.S. software manufacturers at a great competitive disadvantage to foreign firms that faced no similar regulations. After a lengthy lobbying campaign by the software industry, the president directed the Commerce Department to revise its regulations to foster the growth of the American security software industry.

Current regulations now designate the categories of retail and mass market security software. The rules now permit firms to submit these products for review by the Commerce Department, but the review will take no longer than 30 days. After successful completion of this review, companies may freely export these products.

# Privacy

The right to privacy has for years been a hotly contested issue in the United States. The main source of this contention is that the Constitution's Bill of Rights does not explicitly provide for a right to privacy. However, this right has been upheld by numerous courts and is vigorously pursued by organizations such as the American Civil Liberties Union (ACLU).

Europeans have also long been concerned with their privacy. Indeed, countries such as Switzerland are world renowned for their ability to keep financial secrets. Later in this chapter, we'll examine how the new European Union data privacy laws impact companies and Internet users.

## U.S. Privacy Law

Although there is no constitutional guarantee of privacy, a myriad of federal laws (many enacted in recent years) are designed to protect the private information the government maintains about citizens as well as key portions of the private sector such as financial, educational, and health-care institutions. In the following sections, we'll examine a number of these federal laws.

### Fourth Amendment

The basis for privacy rights is in the Fourth Amendment to the U.S. Constitution. It reads as follows:

> The right of the people to be secure in their persons, houses, papers, and effects, against unreasonable searches and seizures, shall not be violated, and no warrants shall issue, but upon probable cause, supported by oath or affirmation, and particularly describing the place to be searched, and the persons or things to be seized.

The direct interpretation of this amendment prohibits government agents from searching private property without a warrant and probable cause. The courts have expanded their interpretation of the Fourth Amendment to include protections against wiretapping and other invasions of privacy.

### Privacy Act of 1974

The Privacy Act of 1974 is perhaps the most significant piece of privacy legislation restricting the way the federal government may deal with private information about individual citizens. It severely limits the ability of federal government agencies to disclose private information to other persons or agencies without the prior written consent of the affected individual(s). It does provide for exceptions involving the census, law enforcement, the National Archives, health and safety, and court orders.

The Privacy Act mandates that agencies maintain only the records that are necessary for conducting their business and that they destroy those records when they are no longer needed for a legitimate function of government. It provides a formal procedure for individuals to gain access to records the government maintains about them and to request that incorrect records be amended.

### Electronic Communications Privacy Act of 1986

The Electronic Communications Privacy Act (ECPA) makes it a crime to invade the electronic privacy of an individual. This act updated the Federal Wiretap Act to apply to the illegal interception of electronic (in other words, computer) communications or to the intentional, unauthorized access of electronically stored data. It prohibits the interception

698 Chapter 17 • Law and Investigations

or disclosure of electronic communication and defines those situations in which disclosure is legal. It protects against the monitoring of email and voicemail communications and prevents providers of those services from making unauthorized disclosures of their content.

One of the most notable provisions of the ECPA is that it makes it illegal to monitor cellular telephone conversations. In fact, such monitoring is punishable by a fine of up to $500 and a prison term of up to five years.

### Communications Assistance for Law Enforcement Act (CALEA) of 1994

The Communications Assistance for Law Enforcement Act (CALEA) of 1994 amended the Electronic Communications Privacy Act of 1986. CALEA requires all communications carriers to make wiretaps possible for law enforcement with an appropriate court order, regardless of the technology in use.

### Economic and Protection of Proprietary Information Act of 1996

The Economic and Protection of Proprietary Information Act of 1996 extends the definition of property to include proprietary economic information so that the theft of this information can be considered industrial or corporate espionage. This changed the legal definition of theft so that it was no longer restricted by physical constraints.

### Health Insurance Portability and Accountability Act of 1996

In 1996, Congress passed the Health Insurance Portability and Accountability Act (HIPAA), which made numerous changes to the laws governing health insurance and health maintenance organizations (HMOs). Among the provisions of HIPAA are privacy and security regulations requiring strict security measures for hospitals, physicians, insurance companies, and other organizations that process or store private medical information about individuals.

The HIPAA privacy and security regulations are quite complex. You should be familiar with the broad intentions of the act, as described here. If you work in the health-care industry, you should consider devoting time to an in-depth study of this law's provisions.

HIPAA also clearly defines the rights of individuals who are the subject of medical records and requires organizations that maintain such records to disclose these rights in writing.

### Children's Online Privacy Protection Act of 1998

In April 2000, provisions of the Children's Online Privacy Protection Act (COPPA) became the law of the land in the United States. COPPA makes a series of demands upon websites that cater to children or knowingly collect information from children:

- Websites must have a privacy notice that clearly states the types of information they collect and what it's used for, including whether any information is disclosed to third parties. The privacy notice must also include contact information for the operators of the site.

- Parents must be provided with the opportunity to review any information collected from their children and permanently delete it from the site's records.

- Parents must give verifiable consent to the collection of information about children younger than the age of 13 prior to any such collection. Exceptions in the law allow websites to collect minimal information solely for the purpose of obtaining such parental consent.

## Gramm-Leach-Bliley Act of 1999

Until the Gramm-Leach-Bliley Act (GLBA) became law in 1999, there were strict governmental barriers between financial institutions. Banks, insurance companies, and credit providers were severely limited in the services they could provide and the information they could share with each other. GLBA somewhat relaxed the regulations concerning the services each organization could provide. When Congress passed this law, it realized that this increased latitude could have far-reaching privacy implications. Because of this concern, it included a number of limitations on the types of information that could be exchanged even among subsidiaries of the same corporation and required financial institutions to provide written privacy policies to all their customers by July 1, 2001.

## USA PATRIOT Act of 2001

Congress passed the Uniting and Strengthening America by Providing Appropriate Tools Required to Intercept and Obstruct Terrorism (USA PATRIOT) Act of 2001 in direct response to the September 11, 2001, terrorist attacks in New York City and Washington, D.C. The PATRIOT Act greatly broadened the powers of law enforcement organizations and intelligence agencies across a number of areas, including when monitoring electronic communications.

One of the major changes prompted by the PATRIOT Act revolves around the way government agencies obtain wiretapping authorizations. Previously, police could obtain warrants for only one circuit at a time, after proving that the circuit was used by someone subject to monitoring. Provisions of the PATRIOT Act allow authorities to obtain a blanket authorization for a person and then monitor all communications to or from that person under the single warrant.

Another major change is in the way the government deals with Internet service providers (ISPs). Under the terms of the PATRIOT Act, ISPs may voluntarily provide the government with a large range of information. The PATRIOT Act also allows the government to obtain detailed information on user activity through the use of a subpoena (as opposed to a wiretap).

Finally, the USA PATRIOT Act amends the Computer Fraud and Abuse Act (yes, another set of amendments!) to provide more severe penalties for criminal acts. The PATRIOT Act provides for jail terms of up to 20 years and once again expands the coverage of the CFAA.

## Family Educational Rights and Privacy Act

The Family Educational Rights and Privacy Act (FERPA) is another specialized privacy bill that affects any educational institution that accepts any form of funding from the federal government (the vast majority of schools). It grants certain privacy rights to students older than 18 and the parents of minor students. Specific FERPA protections include the following:

- Parents/students have the right to inspect any educational records maintained by the institution on the student.

- Parents/students have the right to request correction of records they think are erroneous and the right to include a statement in the records contesting anything that is not corrected.

- Schools may not release personal information from student records without written consent, except under certain circumstances.

## Identity Theft and Assumption Deterrence Act

In 1998, the president signed the Identity Theft and Assumption Deterrence Act into law. In the past, the only legal victims of identity theft were the creditors who were defrauded. This act makes identity theft a crime against the person whose identity was stolen and provides severe criminal penalties (up to a 15-year prison term and/or a $250,000 fine) for anyone found guilty of violating this law.

---

### Privacy in the Workplace

One of the authors of this book recently had an interesting conversation with a relative who works in an office environment. At a family Christmas party, the author's relative casually mentioned a story he had read online about a local company that had fired several employees for abusing their Internet privileges. He was shocked and couldn't believe that a company would violate their employees' right to privacy.

As you've read in this chapter, the U.S. court system has long upheld the traditional right to privacy as an extension of basic constitutional rights. However, the courts have maintained that a key element of this right is that privacy should be guaranteed only when there is a "reasonable expectation of privacy." For example, if you mail a letter to someone in a sealed envelope, you may reasonably expect that it will be delivered without being read along the way—you have a reasonable expectation of privacy. On the other hand, if you send your message on a postcard, you do so with the awareness that one or more people might read your note before it arrives at the other end—you do not have a reasonable expectation of privacy.

Recent court rulings have found that employees do not have a reasonable expectation of privacy while using employer-owned communications equipment in the workplace. If you send a message using an employer's computer, Internet connection, telephone, or other communications device, your employer can monitor it as a routine business procedure.

That said, if you're planning to monitor the communications of your employees, you should take reasonable precautions to ensure that there is no implied expectation of privacy. Here are some common measures to consider:

- Clauses in employment contracts that state the employee has no expectation of privacy while using corporate equipment

- Similar written statements in corporate acceptable use and privacy policies

- Logon banners warning that all communications are subject to monitoring

- Warning labels on computers and telephones warning of monitoring

As with many of the issues discussed in this chapter, it's a good idea to consult with your legal counsel before undertaking any communications-monitoring efforts.

## European Union Privacy Law

On October 24, 1995, the European Union Parliament passed a sweeping directive outlining privacy measures that must be in place for protecting personal data processed by information systems. The directive went into effect three years later in October 1998. The directive requires that all processing of personal data meet one of the following criteria:

- Consent
- Contract
- Legal obligation
- Vital interest of the data subject
- Balance between the interests of the data holder and the interests of the data subject

The directive also outlines key rights of individuals about whom data is held and/or processed:

- Right to access the data
- Right to know the data's source
- Right to correct inaccurate data
- Right to withhold consent to process data in some situations
- Right of legal action should these rights be violated

American companies doing business in Europe can obtain protection under a treaty between the European Union and the United States that allows the Department of Commerce to certify businesses that comply with regulations and offer them "safe harbor" from prosecution.

To qualify for the safe harbor provision, U.S. companies conducting business in Europe must meet seven requirements for the processing of personal information:

**Notice**   They must inform individuals of what information they collect about them and how the information will be used.

**Choice**   They must allow individuals to opt out if the information will be used for any other purpose or shared with a third party. For information considered sensitive, an opt-in policy must be used.

**Onward transfer**   Organizations can share data only with other organizations that comply with the safe harbor principles.

**Access**   Individuals must be granted access to any records kept containing their personal information.

**Security**   Proper mechanisms must be in place to protect data against loss, misuse, and unauthorized disclosure.

**Data Integrity**   Organizations must take steps to ensure the reliability of the information they maintain.

**Enforcement**   Organizations must make a dispute resolution process available to individuals and provide certifications to regulatory agencies that they comply with the safe harbor provisions.

For more information on the safe harbor protections available to American companies, visit the Department of Commerce's Safe Harbor website at www.export.gov/safeharbor/.

# Investigations

Every information security professional will, at one time or another, encounter a security incident that requires an investigation. In many cases, this investigation will be a brief, informal determination that the matter is not serious enough to warrant further action or the involvement of law enforcement authorities. However, in some cases, the threat posed or damage done will be severe enough to require a more formal inquiry. When this occurs, investigators must be careful to ensure that proper procedures are followed. Failure to abide by the correct procedures may violate the civil rights of those individual(s) being investigated and could result in a failed prosecution or even legal action against the investigator.

# Evidence

To successfully prosecute a crime, the prosecuting attorneys must provide sufficient evidence to prove an individual's guilt beyond a reasonable doubt. In the following sections, we'll explain the requirements that evidence must meet before it is allowed in court, the various types of evidence that may be introduced, and the requirements for handling and documenting evidence.

NIST's Guide to Integrating Forensic Techniques into Incident Response (SP 800-86) is a great reference and available at: www.csrc.nist.gov/publications/nistpubs/800-86/SP800-86.pdf.

## Admissible Evidence

There are three basic requirements for evidence to be introduced into a court of law. To be considered *admissible evidence*, it must meet all three of these requirements, as determined by the judge, prior to being discussed in open court:

- The evidence must be *relevant* to determining a fact.

- The fact that the evidence seeks to determine must be *material* (that is, related) to the case.

- The evidence must be *competent*, meaning it must have been obtained legally. Evidence that results from an illegal search would be inadmissible because it is not competent.

## Types of Evidence

Three types of evidence can be used in a court of law: real evidence, documentary evidence, and testimonial evidence. Each has slightly different additional requirements for admissibility.

### Real Evidence

*Real evidence* (also known as *object evidence*) consists of things that may actually be brought into a court of law. In common criminal proceedings, this may include items such as a murder weapon, clothing, or other physical objects. In a computer crime case, real evidence might include seized computer equipment, such as a keyboard with fingerprints on it or a hard drive from a hacker's computer system. Depending upon the circumstances, real evidence may also be *conclusive evidence*, such as DNA, that is incontrovertible.

### Documentary Evidence

*Documentary evidence* includes any written items brought into court to prove a fact at hand. This type of evidence must also be authenticated. For example, if an attorney wants to introduce a computer log as evidence, they must bring a witness (for example, the system administrator) into court to testify that the log was collected as a routine business practice and is indeed the actual log that the system collected.

Two additional evidence rules apply specifically to documentary evidence:

- The *best evidence rule* states that, when a document is used as evidence in a court proceeding, the original document must be introduced. Copies or descriptions of original evidence (known as *secondary evidence*) will not be accepted as evidence unless certain exceptions to the rule apply.

- The *parol evidence rule* states that, when an agreement between parties is put into written form, the written document is assumed to contain all the terms of the agreement and no verbal agreements may modify the written agreement.

If documentary evidence meets the materiality, competency, and relevancy requirements and also complies with the best evidence and parol evidence rules, it can be admitted into court.

---

### Chain of Evidence

Real evidence, like any type of evidence, must meet the relevancy, materiality, and competency requirements before being admitted into court. Additionally, real evidence must be authenticated. This can be done by a witness who can actually identify an object as unique (for example, "That knife with my name on the handle is the one that the intruder took off the table in my house and stabbed me with").

In many cases, it is not possible for a witness to uniquely identify an object in court. In those cases, a *chain of evidence* (also known as a *chain of custody*) must be established. This involves everyone who handles evidence—including the police who originally collect it, the evidence technicians who process it, and the lawyers who use it in court. The location of the evidence must be fully documented from the moment it was collected to the moment it appears in court to ensure that it is indeed the same item. This requires thorough labeling of evidence and comprehensive logs noting who had access to the evidence at specific times and the reasons they required such access.

When evidence is labeled to preserve the chain of custody, the label should include the following types of information regarding the collection:

- General description of the evidence

- Time, date the evidence was collected

- Exact location the evidence was collected from

- Name of the person collecting the evidence

- Relevant circumstances surrounding the collection

Each person who handles the evidence must sign the chain of custody log indicating the time they took direct responsibility for the evidence and the time they handed it off to the next person in the chain of custody. The chain must provide an unbroken sequence of events accounting for the evidence from the time it was collected until the time of the trial.

### Testimonial Evidence

*Testimonial evidence* is, quite simply, evidence consisting of the testimony of a witness, either verbal testimony in court or written testimony in a recorded deposition. Witnesses must take an oath agreeing to tell the truth, and they must have personal knowledge upon which their testimony is based. Furthermore, witnesses must remember the basis for their testimony (they may consult written notes or records to aid their memory). Witnesses can offer *direct evidence*: oral testimony that proves or disproves a claim based upon their own direct observation. The testimonial evidence of most witnesses must be strictly limited to direct evidence based upon the witness's factual observations. However, this does not apply if a witness has been accepted by the court as an expert in a certain field. In that case, the witness may offer an *expert opinion* based upon the other facts presented and their personal knowledge of the field.

Testimonial evidence must not be *hearsay evidence*. That is, a witness cannot testify as to what someone else told them outside court. Computer log files that are not authenticated by a system administrator can also be considered hearsay evidence.

## Evidence Collection

Collecting digital evidence is a tricky process and should be attempted only by professional forensic technicians. The International Organization on Computer Evidence (IOCE) outlined six principles to guide digital evidence technicians as they perform media analysis, network analysis, and software analysis in the pursuit of forensically recovered evidence:

- When dealing with digital evidence, all of the general forensic and procedural principles must be applied.
- Upon seizing digital evidence, actions taken should not change that evidence.
- When it is necessary for a person to access original digital evidence, that person should be trained for the purpose.
- All activity relating to the seizure, access, storage, or transfer of digital evidence must be fully documented, preserved and available for review.
- An individual is responsible for all actions taken with respect to digital evidence while the digital evidence is in their possession.
- Any agency that is responsible for seizing, accessing, storing, or transferring digital evidence is responsible for compliance with these principles.

# Investigation Process

When you initiate a computer security investigation, you should first assemble a team of competent analysts to assist with the investigation.

## Calling In Law Enforcement

One of the first decisions that must be made in an investigation is whether law enforcement authorities should be called in. This is actually a relatively complicated decision that should involve senior management officials. There are many factors in favor of calling in the experts. For example, the FBI now maintains a National Computer Crime Squad that includes individuals with the following qualifications:

- Degrees in the computer sciences

- Prior work experience in industry and academic institutions

- Basic and advanced commercial training

- Knowledge of basic data and telecommunications networks

- Experience with Unix and other computer operating systems

On the other hand, two major factors may cause a company to shy away from calling in the authorities. First, the investigation will more than likely become public and may embarrass the company. Second, law enforcement authorities are bound to conduct an investigation that complies with the Fourth Amendment and other legal requirements that may not apply if the organization conducted its own, private investigation.

---

### Search Warrants

Even the most casual viewer of American crime television is familiar with the question, Do you have a warrant? The Fourth Amendment of the U.S. Constitution outlines the burden placed upon investigators to have a valid search warrant before conducting certain searches and the legal hurdle they must overcome to obtain a warrant:

> The right of the people to be secure in their persons, houses, papers and effects, against unreasonable searches and seizures, shall not be violated, and no warrants shall issue, but upon probable cause, supported by oath or affirmation, and particularly describing the place to be searched, and the persons or things to be seized.

This amendment contains several important provisions that guide the activities of law enforcement personnel:

- Investigators must obtain a warrant before searching a person's private belongings, assuming that there is a reasonable expectation of privacy. There are a number of documented exceptions to this requirement, such as when an individual consents to a search, the evidence of a crime is in plain view, or there is a life-threatening emergency necessitating the search.

- Warrants can be issued only based upon probable cause. There must be some type of evidence that a crime took place and that the search in question will yield evidence relating to that crime. The standard of "probable cause" required to get a warrant is

> much weaker than the standard of evidence required to secure a conviction. Most warrants are "sworn out" based solely upon the testimony of investigators.
>
> - Warrants must be specific in their scope. The warrant must contain a detailed description of the legal bounds of the search and seizure.
>
> If investigators fail to comply with even the smallest detail of these provisions, they may find their warrant invalidated and the results of the search deemed inadmissible. This leads to another one of those American colloquialisms: "He got off on a technicality."

## Conducting the Investigation

If you elect not to call in law enforcement, you should still attempt to abide by the principles of a sound investigation to ensure the accuracy and fairness of your inquiry. It is important to remember a few key principles:

- Never conduct your investigation on an actual system that was compromised. Take the system offline, make a backup, and use the backup to investigate the incident.

- Never attempt to "hack back" and avenge a crime. You may inadvertently attack an innocent third party and find yourself liable for computer crime charges.

- If in doubt, call in expert assistance. If you don't want to call in law enforcement, contact a private investigations firm with specific experience in the field of computer security investigations.

- Usually, it's best to begin the investigation process using informal interviewing techniques. These are used to gather facts and determine the substance of the case. When specific suspects are identified, they should be questioned using interrogation techniques. Interviewing typically involves open-ended questions to gather information. Interrogation often involves closed-ended questioning with a specific goal in mind and is more adversarial in nature. Again, this is an area best left untouched without specific legal advice.

# Summary

Computer security necessarily entails a high degree of involvement from the legal community. In this chapter, you learned about a large number of laws that govern security issues such as computer crime, intellectual property, data privacy, and software licensing. You also learned about the procedures that must be followed when investigating an incident and collecting evidence that may later be admitted into a court of law during a civil or criminal trial.

Granted, computer security professionals cannot be expected to understand the intricate details of all of the laws that cover computer security. However, the main objective of this chapter is to provide you with the foundations of that knowledge. The best legal skill that a CISSP candidate should have is ability to identify a legally questionable issue and know when to call in an attorney who specializes in computer/Internet law.

# Exam Essentials

**Understand the differences between criminal law, civil law, and administrative law.** Criminal law protects society against acts that violate the basic principles we believe in. Violations of criminal law are prosecuted by federal and state governments. Civil law provides the framework for the transaction of business between people and organizations. Violations of civil law are brought to the court and argued by the two affected parties. Administrative law is used by government agencies to effectively carry out their day-to-day business.

**Be able to explain the basic provisions of the major laws designed to protect society against computer crime.** The Computer Fraud and Abuse Act (as amended) protects computers used by the government or in interstate commerce from a variety of abuses. The Computer Security Act outlines steps the government must take to protect its own systems from attack. The Government Information Security Reform Act further develops the federal government information security program.

**Know the difference between copyrights, trademarks, patents, and trade secrets.** Copyrights protect original works of authorship, such as books, articles, poems, and songs. Trademarks are names, slogans, and logos that identify a company, product, or service. Patents provide protection to the creators of new inventions. Trade secret law protects the operating secrets of a firm.

**Be able to explain the basic provisions of the Digital Millennium Copyright Act of 1998.** The Digital Millennium Copyright Act prohibits the circumvention of copy protection mechanisms placed in digital media and limits the liability of Internet service providers for the activities of their users.

**Know the basic provisions of the Economic Espionage Act of 1996.** The Economic Espionage Act provides penalties for individuals found guilty of the theft of trade secrets. Harsher penalties apply when the individual knows that the information will benefit a foreign government.

**Understand the various types of software license agreements.** Contractual license agreements are written agreements between a software vendor and user. Shrink-wrap agreements are written on software packaging and take effect when a user opens the package. Click-wrap agreements are included in a package but require the user to accept the terms during the software installation process.

**Explain the impact of the Uniform Computer Information Transactions Act on software licensing.** The Uniform Computer Information Transactions Act provides a framework for the enforcement of shrink-wrap and click-wrap agreements by federal and state governments.

**Understand the restrictions placed upon export of high-performance hardware and encryption technology outside the United States.** No high-performance computers or encryption technology may be exported to Tier 4 countries. The export of hardware capable of operating in excess of 0.75 weighted teraflops to Tier 3 countries must be approved by the Department of Commerce. New rules permit the easy exporting of "mass market" encryption software.

**Understand the major laws that govern privacy of personal information in both the United States and the European Union.** The United States has a number of privacy laws that affect the government's use of information as well as the use of information by specific industries, such as financial services companies and health-care organizations that handle sensitive information. The European Union has a more comprehensive directive on data privacy that regulates the use and exchange of personal information.

**Know the basic requirements for evidence to be admissible in a court of law.** To be admissible, evidence must be relevant to a fact at issue in the case, the fact must be material to the case, and the evidence must be competent, or legally collected.

**Explain the various types of evidence that may be used in a criminal or civil trial.** Real evidence consists of actual objects that can be brought into the courtroom. Documentary evidence consists of written documents that provide insight into the facts. Testimonial evidence consists of verbal or written statements made by witnesses.

# Written Lab

1. What are the key rights guaranteed to individuals under the European Union's directive on data privacy?

2. What are the three basic requirements that evidence must meet in order to be admissible in court?

3. What are some common steps that employers take to notify employees of system monitoring?

# Answers to Written Lab

1. Individuals have a right to access records kept about them and know the source of data included in those records. They also have the right to correct inaccurate records. Individuals have the right to withhold consent from data processors and have legal recourse if these rights are violated.

2. To be admissible, evidence must be reliable, competent, and material to the case.

3. Some common steps that employers take to notify employees of monitoring include clauses in employment contracts that state the employee should have no expectation of privacy while using corporate equipment, similar written statements in corporate acceptable use and privacy policies, logon banners warning that all communications are subject to monitoring, and labels on computers and telephones warning of monitoring.

# Review Questions

1.  Which criminal law was the first to implement penalties for the creators of viruses, worms, and other types of malicious code that cause harm to computer system(s)?

    **A.**  Computer Security Act

    **B.**  National Infrastructure Protection Act

    **C.**  Computer Fraud and Abuse Act

    **D.**  Electronic Communications Privacy Act

2.  Which law first required operators of federal interest computer systems to undergo periodic training in computer security issues?

    **A.**  Computer Security Act

    **B.**  National Infrastructure Protection Act

    **C.**  Computer Fraud and Abuse Act

    **D.**  Electronic Communications Privacy Act

3.  What type of law does not require an act of Congress to implement at the federal level but, rather, is enacted by the executive branch in the form of regulations, policies, and procedures?

    **A.**  Criminal law

    **B.**  Common law

    **C.**  Civil law

    **D.**  Administrative law

4.  Which federal government agency has responsibility for ensuring the security of government computer systems that are not used to process sensitive and/or classified information?

    **A.**  National Security Agency

    **B.**  Federal Bureau of Investigation

    **C.**  National Institute of Standards and Technology

    **D.**  Secret Service

5.  What is the broadest category of computer systems protected by the Computer Fraud and Abuse Act, as amended?

    **A.**  Government-owned systems

    **B.**  Federal interest systems

    **C.**  Systems used in interstate commerce

    **D.**  Systems located in the United States

6. What law protects the right of citizens to privacy by placing restrictions on the authority granted to government agencies to search private residences and facilities?

   **A.** Privacy Act

   **B.** Fourth Amendment

   **C.** Second Amendment

   **D.** Gramm-Leach-Bliley Act

7. Matthew recently authored an innovative algorithm for solving a mathematical problem, and he wants to share it with the world. However, prior to publishing the software code in a technical journal, he wants to obtain some sort of intellectual property protection. Which type of protection is best suited to his needs?

   **A.** Copyright

   **B.** Trademark

   **C.** Patent

   **D.** Trade secret

8. Mary is the cofounder of Acme Widgets, a manufacturing firm. Together with her partner, Joe, she has developed a special oil that will dramatically improve the widget manufacturing process. To keep the formula secret, Mary and Joe plan to make large quantities of the oil by themselves in the plant after the other workers have left. They want to protect this formula for as long as possible. What type of intellectual property protection best suits their needs?

   **A.** Copyright

   **B.** Trademark

   **C.** Patent

   **D.** Trade secret

9. Richard recently developed a great name for a new product that he plans to begin using immediately. He spoke with his attorney and filed the appropriate application to protect his product name but has not yet received a response from the government regarding his application. He wants to begin using the name immediately. What symbol should he use next to the name to indicate its protected status?

   **A.** ©

   **B.** ®

   **C.** ™

   **D.** †

10. What law prevents government agencies from disclosing personal information that an individual supplies to the government under protected circumstances?

   **A.** Privacy Act

   **B.** Electronic Communications Privacy Act

   **C.** Health Insurance Portability and Accountability Act

   **D.** Gramm-Leach-Bliley Act

11. What law formalizes many licensing arrangements used by the software industry and attempts to standardize their use from state to state?

    **A.** Computer Security Act

    **B.** Uniform Computer Information Transactions Act

    **C.** Digital Millennium Copyright Act

    **D.** Gramm-Leach-Bliley Act

12. The Children's Online Privacy Protection Act was designed to protect the privacy of children using the Internet. What is the minimum age a child must be before companies can collect personal identifying information from them without parental consent?

    **A.** 13

    **B.** 14

    **C.** 15

    **D.** 16

13. Which one of the following is not a requirement that Internet service providers must satisfy in order to gain protection under the "transitory activities" clause of the Digital Millennium Copyright Act?

    **A.** The service provider and the originator of the message must be located in different states.

    **B.** The transmission, routing, provision of connections, or copying must be carried out by an automated technical process without selection of material by the service provider.

    **C.** Any intermediate copies must not ordinarily be accessible to anyone other than anticipated recipients and must not be retained for longer than reasonably necessary.

    **D.** The transmission must be originated by a person other than the provider.

14. Which one of the following laws is not designed to protect the privacy rights of consumers and Internet users?

    **A.** Health Insurance Portability and Accountability Act

    **B.** Identity Theft Assumption and Deterrence Act

    **C.** USA PATRIOT Act

    **D.** Gramm-Leach-Bliley Act

15. Which one of the following types of licensing agreements does not require that the user acknowledge that they have read the agreement prior to executing it?

    **A.** Standard license agreement

    **B.** Shrink-wrap agreement

    **C.** Click-wrap agreement

    **D.** Verbal agreement

16. What industry is most directly impacted by the provisions of the Gramm-Leach-Bliley Act?

    **A.** Health care

    **B.** Banking

    **C.** Law enforcement

    **D.** Defense contractors

17. What is the standard duration of patent protection in the United States?

    **A.** 14 years from the application date

    **B.** 14 years from the date the patent is granted

    **C.** 20 years from the application date

    **D.** 20 years from the date the patent is granted

18. Which one of the following is not a valid legal reason for processing information about an individual under the European Union's data privacy directive?

    **A.** Contract

    **B.** Legal obligation

    **C.** Marketing needs

    **D.** Consent

19. What type of evidence must be authenticated by a witness who can uniquely identify it or through a documented chain of custody?

    **A.** Documentary evidence

    **B.** Testimonial evidence

    **C.** Real evidence

    **D.** Hearsay evidence

20. What evidentiary principle states that a written contract is assumed to contain all the terms of an agreement?

    **A.** Material evidence

    **B.** Best evidence

    **C.** Parol evidence

    **D.** Relevant evidence

# Answers to Review Questions

1.  C. The Computer Fraud and Abuse Act, as amended, provides criminal and civil penalties for those individuals convicted of using viruses, worms, Trojan horses, and other types of malicious code to cause damage to computer system(s).

2.  A. The Computer Security Act requires mandatory periodic training for all people involved in managing, using, or operating federal computer systems that contain sensitive information.

3.  D. Administrative laws do not require an act of the legislative branch to implement at the federal level. Administrative laws consist of the policies, procedures, and regulations promulgated by agencies of the executive branch of government. Although they do not require an act of Congress, these laws are subject to judicial review and must comply with criminal and civil laws enacted by the legislative branch.

4.  C. The National Institute of Standards and Technology (NIST) is charged with the security management of all federal government computer systems that are not used to process sensitive national security information. The National Security Agency (part of the Department of Defense) is responsible for managing those systems that do process classified and/or sensitive information.

5.  C. The original Computer Fraud and Abuse Act of 1984 covered only systems used by the government and financial institutions. The act was broadened in 1986 to include all federal interest systems. The Computer Abuse Amendments Act of 1994 further amended the CFAA to cover all systems that are used in interstate commerce, covering a large portion (but not all) of the computer systems in the United States.

6.  B. The Fourth Amendment to the U.S. Constitution sets the "probable cause" standard that law enforcement officers must follow when conducting searches and/or seizures of private property. It also states that those officers must obtain a warrant before gaining involuntary access to such property.

7.  A. Copyright law is the only type of intellectual property protection available to Matthew. It covers only the specific software code that Matthew used. It does not cover the process or ideas behind the software. Trademark protection is not appropriate for this type of situation. Patent protection does not apply to mathematical algorithms. Matthew can't seek trade secret protection because he plans to publish the algorithm in a public technical journal.

8.  D. Mary and Joe should treat their oil formula as a trade secret. As long as they do not publicly disclose the formula, they can keep it a company secret indefinitely.

9.  C. Richard's product name should be protected under trademark law. Until his registration is granted, he can use the ™ symbol next to it to inform others that it is protected under trademark law. Once his application is approved, the name becomes a registered trademark and Richard can begin using the ® symbol.

10. A. The Privacy Act of 1974 limits the ways government agencies may use information that private citizens disclose to them under certain circumstances.

11. B. The Uniform Computer Information Transactions Act (UCITA) attempts to implement a standard framework of laws regarding computer transactions to be adopted by all states. One of the issues addressed by UCITA is the legality of various types of software license agreements.

12. A. The Children's Online Privacy Protection Act (COPPA) provides severe penalties for companies that collect information from young children without parental consent. COPPA states that this consent must be obtained from the parents of children younger than the age of 13 before any information is collected (other than basic information required to obtain that consent).

13. A. The Digital Millennium Copyright Act does not include any geographical location requirements for protection under the "transitory activities" exemption. The other options are three of the five mandatory requirements. The other two requirements are that the service provider must not determine the recipients of the material and the material must be transmitted with no modification to its content.

14. C. The USA PATRIOT Act was adopted in the wake of the September 11, 2001, terrorist attacks. It broadens the powers of the government to monitor communications between private citizens and therefore actually weakens the privacy rights of consumers and Internet users. The other laws mentioned all contain provisions designed to enhance individual privacy rights.

15. B. Shrink-wrap license agreements become effective when the user opens a software package. Click-wrap agreements require the user to click a button during the installation process to accept the terms of the license agreement. Standard license agreements require that the user sign a written agreement prior to using the software. Verbal agreements are not normally used for software licensing but also require some active degree of participation by the software user.

16. B. The Gramm-Leach-Bliley Act provides, among other things, regulations regarding the way financial institutions can handle private information belonging to their customers.

17. C. U.S. patent law provides for an exclusivity period of 20 years beginning at the time the patent application is submitted to the Patent and Trademark Office.

18. C. Marketing needs are not a valid reason for processing personal information, as defined by the European Union privacy directive.

19. C. Real evidence must be either uniquely identified by a witness or authenticated through a documented chain of custody.

20. C. The parol evidence rule states that a written contract is assumed to contain all the terms of an agreement and cannot be modified by a verbal agreement.

# Chapter

# 18

# Incidents and Ethics

---

## THE CISSP EXAM TOPICS COVERED IN THIS CHAPTER INCLUDE:

✓ **Information Security Governance and Risk Management**

- Understand professional ethics

    - (ISC)[2] code of professional ethics; support organization's code of ethics

✓ **Legal, Regulations, Investigations, and Compliance**

- Understand legal issues that pertain to information security internationally

    - Computer crime; licensing and intellectual property (e.g., copyright, trademark); import/export; trans-border data flow; privacy

- Understand and support investigations

    - Policy; incident handling and response; evidence collection and handling (e.g., chain of custody, interviewing); reporting and documenting

- Understand forensic procedures

    - Media analysis; network analysis; software analysis

- Understand compliance requirements and procedures

    - Regulatory environment; audits; reporting

✓ **Operations Security**

- Manage incident response

    - Detection; response; reporting; recovery; remediation

In this chapter, we'll continue our discussion from Chapter 17, "Law and Investigations," regarding the Legal Regulations, Investigations, and Compliance domain of the Common Body of Knowledge (CBK) for the CISSP certification exam. This domain deals with topics and issues related to computer crime laws and regulations, investigative techniques used to determine whether a computer crime has been committed and to collect evidence when appropriate, and ethics issues and code of conduct for the information security practitioner.

The first step in deciding how to respond to a computer attack is to know if and when an attack has taken place. You must know how to determine that an attack is occurring, or has occurred, before you can properly choose a course of action. Once you have determined that an incident has occurred, the next step is to conduct an investigation and collect evidence to find out what has happened and determine the extent of any damage that might have been done. You must be sure you conduct the investigation in accordance with local laws and regulations.

# Major Categories of Computer Crime

There are many ways to attack a computer system and many motivations to do so. Information system security practitioners generally put crimes against or involving computers into different categories. Simply put, a *computer crime* is a crime (or violation of a law or regulation) that involves a computer. The crime could be against the computer, or the computer could have been used in the actual commission of the crime. Each of the categories of computer crimes represents the purpose of an attack and its intended result.

Any individual who violates one or more of your security policies is considered to be an *attacker*. An attacker uses different techniques to achieve a specific goal. Understanding the goals helps to clarify the different types of attacks. Remember that crime is crime, and the motivations behind computer crime are no different from the motivations behind any other type of crime. The only real difference may be in the methods the attacker uses to strike.

Computer crimes are generally classified as one of the following types:

- Military and intelligence attacks
- Business attacks
- Financial attacks
- Terrorist attacks
- Grudge attacks
- Thrill attacks

It is important to understand the differences among the categories of computer crime to best understand how to protect a system and react when an attack occurs. The type and amount of evidence left by an attacker is often dependent on their expertise. In the following sections, we'll discuss the different categories of computer crimes and the types of evidence you might find after an attack. This evidence can help you determine the attacker's actions and intended target. You may find that your system was only a link in the chain of network hops used to reach the real victim, making the trail harder to follow back to the true attacker.

# Military and Intelligence Attacks

*Military and intelligence attacks* are launched primarily to obtain secret and restricted information from law enforcement or military and technological research sources. The disclosure of such information could compromise investigations, disrupt military planning, and threaten national security. Attacks to gather military information or other sensitive intelligence often precede other, more damaging attacks.

An attacker may be looking for the following kinds of information:

- Military descriptive information of any type, including deployment information, readiness information, and order of battle plans
- Secret intelligence gathered for military or law enforcement purposes
- Descriptions and storage locations of evidence obtained in a criminal investigation
- Any secret information that could be used in a later attack

Because of the sensitive nature of information collected and used by the military and intelligence agencies, their computer systems are often attractive targets for experienced attackers. To protect from more numerous and more sophisticated attackers, you will generally find more formal security policies in place on systems that house such information. As you learned in Chapter 5, "Security Management Concepts and Principles," data can be classified according to sensitivity and stored on systems that support the required level of security. It is common to find stringent perimeter security as well as internal controls to limit access to classified documents on military and intelligence agency systems.

You can be sure that serious attacks to acquire military or intelligence information are carried out by professionals. Professional attackers are generally very thorough in covering their tracks. There is usually very little evidence to collect after such an attack. Attackers in this category are the most successful and the most satisfied when no one is aware that an attack occurred.

# Business Attacks

*Business attacks* focus on illegally obtaining an organization's confidential information. This could be information that is critical to the operation of the organization, such as a secret recipe, or information that could damage the organization's reputation if disclosed, such as personal information about its employees. The gathering of a competitor's confidential information, also called *industrial espionage*, is not a new phenomenon. Businesses have used illegal means to acquire competitive information for many years. The temptation to steal a competitor's trade secrets and the ease with which a savvy attacker can compromise some computer systems makes this type of attack attractive.

The goal of business attacks is solely to extract confidential information. The use of the information gathered during the attack usually causes more damage than the attack itself. A business that has suffered an attack of this type can be put into a position from which it might not ever recover. It is up to you as the security professional to ensure that the systems that contain confidential data are secure. In addition, a policy must be developed that will handle such an intrusion should it occur. (For more information on security policies, see Chapter 6, "Asset Value, Policies, and Roles.")

## Financial Attacks

*Financial attacks* are carried out to unlawfully obtain money or services. They are the type of computer crime you most commonly hear about in the news. The goal of a financial attack could be to steal credit card numbers, increase the balance in a bank account, or place "free" long-distance telephone calls. You have probably heard of individuals breaking into telephone company computers and placing free calls. This type of financial attack is called *phone phreaking*.

Shoplifting and burglary are both examples of financial attacks. You can usually tell the sophistication of the attacker by the dollar amount of the damages. Less-sophisticated attackers seek easier targets, but although the damages are usually minimal, they can add up over time.

Financial attacks launched by sophisticated attackers can result in substantial damages. Although phone phreaking causes the telephone company to lose the revenue of calls placed, serious financial attacks can result in losses amounting to millions of dollars. As with the attacks previously described, the ease with which you can detect an attack and track an attacker is largely dependent on the attacker's skill level.

## Terrorist Attacks

*Terrorist attacks* are a reality in modern society. Our increasing reliance upon information systems makes them more and more attractive to terrorists. Such attacks differ from military and intelligence attacks. The purpose of a terrorist attack is to disrupt normal life and instill fear, whereas a military or intelligence attack is designed to extract secret information. Intelligence gathering generally precedes any type of terrorist attack. The very systems that are victims of a terrorist attack were probably compromised in an earlier attack to collect intelligence. The more diligent you are in detecting attacks of any type, the better prepared you will be to intervene before more serious attacks occur.

Possible targets of a computer terrorist attack could be systems that regulate power plants or control telecommunications or power distribution. Many such control and regulatory systems are computerized and vulnerable to terrorist action. In fact, the possibility exists of a simultaneous physical and computerized terrorist attack. Our ability to respond to such an attack would be greatly diminished if the physical attack were simultaneously launched with a computer attack designed to knock out power and communications.

Most large power and communications companies have dedicated a security staff to ensure the security of their systems, but many smaller businesses that have systems connected to the Internet are more vulnerable to attacks. You must diligently monitor your systems to identify any attacks and then respond swiftly when an attack is discovered.

## Grudge Attacks

*Grudge attacks* are attacks that are carried out to damage an organization or a person. The damage could be in the loss of information or information processing capabilities or harm to the organization or a person's reputation. The motivation behind a grudge attack is usually a feeling of resentment, and the attacker could be a current or former employee or someone who wishes ill will upon an organization. The attacker is disgruntled with the victim and takes out their frustration in the form of a grudge attack.

An employee who has recently been fired is a prime example of a person who might carry out a grudge attack to "get back" at the organization. Another example is a person who has been rejected in a personal relationship with another employee. The person who has been rejected might launch an attack to destroy data on the victim's system.

 **Real World Scenario**

### The Insider Threat

It's common for security professionals to focus on the threat from outside an organization. Indeed, many of our security technologies are designed to keep unauthorized individuals out. We often don't pay enough (or much!) attention to protecting our organizations against the malicious insider, even though they often pose the greatest risk to our computing assets.

One of the authors of this book recently wrapped up a consulting engagement with a medium-sized subsidiary of a large, well-known corporation. The company had suffered a serious security breach, involving the theft of thousands of dollars and the deliberate destruction of sensitive corporate information. The IT leaders within the organization needed someone to work with them to diagnose the cause of the event and protect themselves against similar events in the future.

After only a very small amount of digging, it became apparent that they were dealing with an insider attack. The intruder's actions demonstrated knowledge of the company's

IT infrastructure as well as an understanding of which data was most important to the company's ongoing operations.

Additional investigation revealed that the culprit was a former employee who ended his employment with the firm on less-than-favorable terms. He left the building with a chip on his shoulder and an ax to grind. Unfortunately, he was a system administrator with a wide range of access to corporate systems, and the company had an immature deprovisioning process that failed to remove all of his access upon his termination. He simply found several accounts that remained active and used them to access the corporate network through a VPN.

The moral of this story? Don't underestimate the insider threat. Take the time to evaluate your controls to mitigate the risk that malicious current and former employees pose to your organization.

Your security policy should address the potential of attacks by disgruntled employees. For example, as soon as an employee is terminated, all system access for that employee should be terminated. This action reduces the likelihood of a grudge attack and removes unused access accounts that could be used in future attacks.

Although most grudge attackers are just disgruntled people with limited hacking and cracking abilities, some possess the skills to cause substantial damage. An unhappy cracker can be a handful for security professionals. Take extreme care when a person with known cracking ability leaves your company. At the least, you should perform a vulnerability assessment of all systems the person could access. You may be surprised to find one or more "back doors" left in the system. (For more on back doors, see Chapter 8, "Malicious Code and Application Attacks.") But even in the absence of any back doors, a former employee who is familiar with the technical architecture of the organization may know how to exploit its weaknesses.

Grudge attacks can be devastating if allowed to occur unchecked. Diligent monitoring and assessing systems for vulnerabilities is the best protection for most grudge attacks.

## Thrill Attacks

*Thrill attacks* are the attacks launched only for the fun of it. Attackers who lack the ability to devise their own attacks will often download programs that do their work for them. These attackers are often called *script kiddies* because they run only other people's programs, or scripts, to launch an attack.

The main motivation behind these attacks is the "high" of successfully breaking into a system. If you are the victim of a thrill attack, the most common fate you will suffer is a service interruption. Although an attacker of this type may destroy data, the main motivation is to compromise a system and perhaps use it to launch an attack against another victim.

One common type of thrill attack involves website defacements, where the attacker compromises a web server and replaces an organization's legitimate web content with other pages, often boasting about the attacker's skills. For example, an attacker operating under the pseudonym iSKORPiTX conducted more than 20,000 website defacements in 2006, replacing legitimate websites with his own pages containing the text "Hacked by iSKORPiTX."

## Evidence

Chapter 17 included general coverage of the topic of evidence. Remember that the term *evidence* refers to any hardware, software, or data that you can use to prove the identity and actions of an attacker. It's extremely important that you properly handle any and all evidence you collect after an attack, especially if you intend to use the information in court proceedings. You should realize that most computer evidence is intangible, meaning it is electronic and magnetically stored information that is vulnerable to erasure, corruption, and other forms of damage.

Your ability to recover damages in a court of law may depend solely on your diligence during the evidence collection process. In fact, your ability to determine the extent of an attack depends on your evidence collecting abilities. Once an attack has been identified, you should start the evidence collection process. Always assume an attack will result in a legal battle. It is far easier to take evidence collection seriously from the beginning than to later realize an attack was more severe than first thought and then try to go back and do it right. Following standard evidence collection procedures also ensures that you conduct your investigation in an orderly, scientific manner.

In most attacks, evidence of some kind is left. However, professional attackers may leave evidence that is so subtle that it is difficult or impossible to find. Another problem with evidence is that it is often time sensitive. Your logs probably roll over periodically and old information is lost. Do you know the frequency of your log purge routines? Some attacks leave traces in memory. The bulk of the evidence will be lost when you remove power from the system. Each step you take as you collect evidence should be deliberate and well documented.

You must know what your system baseline looks like and how it operates in a normal mode. Without this knowledge, you will be hard-pressed to recognize an attack or to know where to search for valuable evidence. Experienced security professionals learn how their systems operate on a daily basis and are comfortable with the regular operations of the system. The more you understand the "normal" state of your systems, the more an unusual event will stand out.

# Incident Handling

When an incident occurs, you must handle it in a manner that is outlined in your security policy and consistent with local laws and regulations. The first step in handling an incident properly is recognizing when one occurs. You should understand the following two terms related to incident handling:

**Event**   Any occurrence that takes place during a certain period of time

**Incident**   An event that has a negative outcome affecting the confidentiality, integrity, or availability of an organization's data

The most common reason incidents are not reported is that they are never identified. You could have many security policy violations occurring each day, but if you don't have a way of identifying them, you will never know. Therefore, your security policy should identify and list all possible violations and ways to detect them. It's also important to update your security policy as new types of violations and attacks emerge.

What you do when you find that an incident has occurred depends on the type of incident and scope of damage. Law dictates that some incidents must be reported, such as those that impact government or federal interest computers (a federal interest computer is one that is used by financial institutions and by infrastructure systems such as water and power systems) or certain financial transactions, regardless of the amount of damage. Most U.S. states now have laws that require organizations that experience an incident involving certain types of personally identifying information (for example, credit card numbers, Social Security numbers, and driver's license numbers) to notify affected individuals of the breach.

In addition to laws, many companies have contractual obligations to report different types of security incidents to business partners. For example, the Payment Card Industry Data Security Standard (PCI DSS) requires any merchant that handles credit card information to report incidents involving that information to their acquiring bank as well as law enforcement.

Next, we'll cover some of the different types of incidents and typical responses.

## Common Types of Incidents

We discussed the different types of attacks in Chapter 2, "Attacks and Monitoring." An incident occurs when an attack, or other violation of your security policy, is carried out against your system. There are many ways to classify incidents; here is a general list of categories:

- Scanning
- Compromises
- Malicious code
- Denial of service

These four areas are the basic entry points for attackers to impact a system. You must focus on each of these areas to create an effective monitoring strategy that detects system incidents. Each incident area has representative signatures that can tip off an alert security administrator that an incident has occurred. Make sure you know your operating system environment and where to look for the telltale signs of each type of incident.

## Scanning

*Scanning* attacks are reconnaissance attacks that usually precede another, more serious attack. They're comparable to a burglar "casing" a neighborhood for targets, looking for homes with unlocked doors or where nobody is home on guard. Attackers will gather as much information about your system as possible before launching a directed attack. Look for any unusual activity on any port or from any single address. For example, a high volume of Secure Shell (SSH) packets on port 22 may point to a systematic scan of your network.

Remember that simply scanning your system may not be illegal, depending upon your local laws. It can indicate that illegal activity will follow, so it is a good idea to treat scans as incidents and to collect evidence of scanning activity. You may find that the evidence you collect at the time the system is scanned could be the link you need later to find the party responsible for a later attack.

Because scanning is such a common occurrence, you definitely want to automate evidence collection. Set up your firewall to log rejected traffic and archive your log files. The logs may become large, but storage is cheap, and you should consider it a cost of doing business.

## Compromise

A system *compromise* is any unauthorized access to the system or information the system stores. A compromise could originate inside or outside the organization. To make matters worse, a compromise could come from a valid user. An unauthorized use of a valid user ID is just as much of a compromise incident as an experienced cracker breaking in from the outside. Another example of a system compromise is when an attacker uses a normal user account to gain the elevated privileges of a system administrator without authorization.

System compromises can be very difficult to detect. Most often, the data custodian notices something unusual about the data. It could be missing, altered, or moved; the time stamps could be different; or something else is just not right. The more you know about the normal operation of your system, the better prepared you will be to detect abnormal system behavior.

## Malicious Code

When *malicious code* is mentioned, you probably think of viruses and spyware. Although a virus is a common type of malicious code, it is only one type of several. (In Chapter 8, we discussed different types of malicious code.) Detection of this type of a malicious code incident comes from either an end user reporting behavior caused by the malicious code or an automated alert reporting that scanned code containing a malicious component has been found.

The most effective way to protect your system from malicious code is to implement virus and spyware scanners and keep the signature database up-to-date. In addition, your security policy should address the introduction of outside code. Be specific as to what code you will allow end users to install.

## Denial of Service

The final type of incident is a *denial of service (DoS)*. This type of incident is often the easiest to detect. A user or automated tool reports that one or more services (or the entire machine) is unavailable. Although they're simple to detect, avoidance is a far better course of action. It is theoretically possible to dynamically alter firewall rules to reject DoS network traffic, but in recent years the sophistication and complexity of DoS attacks make them extremely difficult to defend against. Because there are so many variations of the DoS attack, implementing this strategy is a nontrivial task.

A detailed discussion of DoS and distributed denial-of-service (DDoS) attacks appears in Chapter 8.

# Response Teams

Many organizations now have a dedicated team responsible for investigating any computer security incidents that take place. These teams are commonly known as computer incident response teams (CIRTs) or computer security incident response teams (CSIRTs). When an incident occurs, the response team has four primary responsibilities:

- Determine the amount and scope of damage caused by the incident.
- Determine whether any confidential information was compromised during the incident.
- Implement any necessary recovery procedures to restore security and recover from incident-related damages.
- Supervise the implementation of any additional security measures necessary to improve security and prevent recurrence of the incident.

---

 **Real World Scenario**

**The Gibson Research Denial-of-Service Attacks: Fun or Grudge?**

Steve Gibson is a well-known software developer and personality in the IT industry whose high visibility derives not only from highly regarded products associated with his company, Gibson Research, but also from his many years as a vocal and outspoken columnist for *Computer World* magazine. In recent years, he has become quite active in the field of computer security, and his site offers free vulnerability-scanning services and a variety of patches and fixes for operating system vulnerabilities. He operates a website at http://grc.com that has been the subject of numerous well-documented denial-of-service attacks. It's interesting to speculate whether such attacks are motivated by grudges (that is, by those who seek to advance their reputations by breaking into an obvious and presumably well-defended point of attack) or by fun (that is, by those with excess time on their hands who might seek to prove themselves against a worthy adversary without necessarily expecting any gain other than notoriety from their actions).

Gibson's website has in fact been subject to two well-documented denial-of-service attacks that you can read about in detail on his site:

- "Distributed Reflection Denial of Service": www.dsinet.org/files/textfiles/tcp-ip/ Distributed%20Reflection%20Denial%20of%20Service.pdf

- "The Strange Tale of the Denial of Service Attacks against GRC.COM": www.crime-research.org/library/grcdos.pdf

Although his subsequent anonymous discussions with one of the perpetrators involved seem to indicate that the motive for some of these attacks was fun rather than business damage or acting on a grudge, these reports are fascinating because of the excellent model they provide for incident handling and reporting.

These documents contain a brief synopsis of the symptoms and chronology of the attacks that occurred, along with short- and long-term fixes and changes enacted to prevent recurrences. They also stress the critical importance of communication with service providers whose infrastructures may be involved in attacks as they're underway. What's extremely telling about Gibson's report on the denial-of-service attacks is that he experienced 17 hours of downtime because he was unable to establish contact with a knowledgeable, competent engineer at his service provider who could help define the right kinds of traffic filters to stymie the floods of traffic that characterize denial-of-service attacks.

Gibson's analysis also indicates his thoroughness in analyzing the sources of the distributed denial-of-service attacks and in documenting what he calls "an exact profile of the malicious traffic being generated during these attacks." This information permitted his ISP to define a set of filters that blocked further such traffic from transiting the final T1 links from Gibson's Internet service provider to his servers. As his experience proves so conclusively, recognizing, analyzing, and characterizing attacks is absolutely essential to defining filters or other countermeasures that can block or defeat them.

As part of these duties, the team should facilitate a *postmortem review* of the incident within a week of the occurrence to ensure that key players in the incident share their knowledge and develop best practices to assist in future incident response efforts.

When putting together your incident response team, be sure to design a cross-functional group of individuals that represent the management, technical, and functional areas of responsibility most directly impacted by a security incident. Potential team members include the following:

- Representative of senior management
- Information security professionals
- Legal representatives
- Public affairs/communications representatives
- Engineering representatives (system and network)

## Incident Response Process

Many organizations use a three-step incident response process, consisting of the following phases:

1. Detection and identification
2. Response and reporting
3. Recovery and remediation

The next three sections outline each phase of the standard incident response process.

## Step 1: Detection and Identification

The incident identification process has two main goals: identifying incidents and notifying appropriate personnel. To successfully detect and identify incidents, a security team must monitor any relevant events that occur and notice when they meet the organization's defined threshold for a security incident. The key to identifying incidents is to detect abnormal or suspicious activity that may constitute evidence of an incident. Although you can detect many attacks by their characteristic signatures, experienced attackers know how to "fly under the radar." You must be very aware of how your system operates normally. *Abnormal* or *suspicious* activity is any system activity that does not normally occur on your system.

These are some of the tools and techniques you should monitor for events indicative of security incidents:

- Intrusion detection/prevention systems
- Antivirus software
- Firewall logs
- System logs
- Physical security systems
- File integrity monitoring software

Always use multiple sources of data when investigating an incident. Be suspicious of anything that does not make sense. Ensure that you can clearly explain any activity you see that is not normal for your system. If it just does not "feel" right, it could be the only clue you have to successfully intervene in an ongoing incident.

Once the initial evaluator identifies that an event or events meet the organization's security incident criteria, the evaluator must notify the incident response team. This notification concludes the incident detection and identification phase and initiates the response and reporting phase.

## Step 2: Response and Reporting

Once you determine that an incident has occurred, the next step is to choose an appropriate response. Your security policy should specify steps to take for various types of incidents. Always proceed with the assumption that an incident will end up in a court of law. Treat any evidence you collect as if it must pass admissibility standards. Once you taint evidence, there is no going back. You must ensure that the chain of evidence is maintained.

### Isolation and Containment

The first actions you take should be dedicated to limiting the exposure of your organization and preventing further damage. In the case of a potentially compromised system, you should disconnect it from the network to prevent intruders from accessing the compromised system and also to prevent the compromised system from affecting other resources on the network.

> In the isolation and containment phase of incident response, it is critical that you leave the system in a running state. Do not power down the system. Turning off the computer destroys the contents of volatile memory and may destroy evidence.

### Gathering Evidence

It is common to confiscate equipment, software, or data to perform a proper investigation. The manner in which the evidence is confiscated is important. The confiscation of evidence must be carried out in a proper fashion. There are three basic alternatives.

First, the person who owns the evidence could *voluntarily surrender* it. This method is generally appropriate only when the attacker is not the owner. Few guilty parties willingly surrender evidence they know will incriminate them. Less-experienced attackers may believe they have successfully covered their tracks and voluntarily surrender important evidence. A good forensic investigator can extract much "covered-up" information from a computer. In most cases, asking for evidence from a suspected attacker just alerts the suspect that you are close to taking legal action.

> In the case of an internal investigation, you will gather the vast majority of your information through voluntary surrender. Most likely, you're conducting the investigation under the auspices of a senior member of management who will authorize you to access any organizational resources necessary to complete your investigation.

Second, you could get a court to issue a *subpoena*, or court order, that compels an individual or organization to surrender evidence and then have the subpoena served by law enforcement. Again, this course of action provides sufficient notice for someone to alter the evidence and render it useless in court.

The last option is a *search warrant*. This option should be used only when you must have access to evidence without tipping off the evidence's owner or other personnel. You must have a strong suspicion with credible reasoning to convince a judge to pursue this course of action.

The three alternatives apply to confiscating equipment both inside and outside an organization, but there is another step you can take to ensure that the confiscation of equipment that belongs to your organization is carried out properly. It is common to have all new employees sign an agreement that provides consent to search and seize any necessary evidence during an investigation. In this manner, consent is provided as a term of the employment agreement. This makes confiscation much easier and reduces the chances of a loss of evidence while waiting for legal permission to seize it. Make sure your security policy addresses this important topic.

You should consider the following sources of data when determining what evidence to gather:

- Computer systems involved in the incident (both servers and workstations)

- Logs from security systems (such as intrusion detection, file integrity monitoring, and firewalls)

- Logs from network devices

- Physical access logs

- Other relevant sources of information specific to the incident under investigation

### Analysis and Reporting

Once you finish gathering evidence, you should analyze it to determine the most likely course of events leading up to your incident. Summarize those findings in a written report to management. In your report, you should be careful to delineate fact from opinion. It is acceptable to theorize about possible causes, but you should be certain to state which of your conclusions are based entirely on fact and which involve a degree of estimation.

## Step 3: Recovery and Remediation

After completing your investigation, you have two tasks remaining: restoring your environment to its normal operating state and completing a "lessons learned" process to improve how you handle future incidents.

### Restoration

The goal of the restoration process is to remediate any damage that may have occurred to the organization and limit the damage incurred by similar incidents in the future. These are some of the key actions you should take during this phase:

- Rebuild compromised systems, taking care to remediate any security vulnerabilities that may have contributed to the incident.

- Restore backup data, if necessary, to replace data of questionable integrity.
- Supplement existing security controls, if necessary, to fill gaps identified during the incident analysis.

Once you have completed the restoration process, your business should be back up and running in the state it was in prior to the incident (although in a more secure manner!).

### Lessons Learned

The final stage of the incident response process is to conduct a "lessons learned" session. During this important process, members of the incident response team review their actions during the incident and look for potential areas of improvement, both in their actions and in the incident response process. This hindsight review provides an important perspective on the success of your incident response process by analyzing its effectiveness during a real-world incident.

## Interviewing Individuals

During your incident investigation, you may find it necessary to speak with individuals who might have information relevant to your investigation. If you seek only to gather information to assist with your investigation, this is called an *interview*. If you suspect the person of involvement in a crime and intend to use the information gathered in court, this is called an *interrogation*.

Interviewing and interrogating individuals are specialized skills and should be performed only by trained investigators. Improper techniques may jeopardize the ability of law enforcement to successfully prosecute an offender. Additionally, many laws govern holding or detaining individuals, and you must abide by them if you plan to conduct private interrogations. Always consult an attorney before conducting any interviews.

## Incident Data Integrity and Retention

No matter how persuasive evidence may be, it can be thrown out of court if you somehow alter it during the evidence collection process. Make sure you can prove that you maintained the integrity of all evidence. (Chapter 17 includes more information on evidence rules.) But what about the integrity of data before it is collected?

You may not detect all incidents as they are happening. Sometimes an investigation reveals that there were previous incidents that went undetected. It is discouraging to follow a trail of evidence and find that a key log file that could point back to an attacker has been purged. Carefully consider the fate of log files or other possible evidence locations. A simple archiving policy can help ensure that key evidence is available upon demand no matter how long ago the incident occurred.

Because many log files can contain valuable evidence, attackers often attempt to sanitize them after a successful attack. Take steps to protect the integrity of log files and to deter their modification. One technique is to implement remote logging, where all systems on the network send their log records to a centralized log server that is locked down against attack and does not allow for the modification of data. This technique provides protection from post-incident log file cleansing. Administrators also often use digital signatures to prove that log files were not tampered with after initial capture. For more on digital signatures, see Chapter 10, "PKI and Cryptographic Applications."

Another important forensic technique is to preserve the original evidence. Remember that the very conduct of your investigation may alter the evidence you are evaluating. Therefore, it's always best to work with a copy of the actual evidence whenever possible. For example, when conducting an investigation into the contents of a hard drive, make an image of that drive, seal the original drive in an evidence bag, and then use the disk image for your investigation.

As with every aspect of security planning, there is no single solution. Get familiar with your system, and take the steps that make the most sense for your organization to protect it.

## Reporting Incidents

When should you report an incident? To whom should you report it? These questions are often difficult to answer. Your security policy should contain guidelines on answering both questions. There is a fundamental problem with reporting incidents. If you report every incident, you run the very real risk of being viewed as a noisemaker. When you have a serious incident, you may be ignored. Also, reporting an unimportant incident could give the impression that your organization is more vulnerable than is the case. This can have a serious detrimental effect on organizations that must maintain strict security. For example, daily incidents at your bank would probably not instill additional confidence in their security practices.

On the other hand, escalation and legal action become more difficult if you do not report an incident soon after discovery. If you delay notifying authorities of a serious incident, you will probably have to answer questions about your motivation for delaying. Even an innocent person could look as if they were trying to hide something by not reporting an incident in a timely manner.

As with most security topics, the answer is not an easy one. In fact, you are compelled by law or regulation to report some incidents. Make sure you know what incidents you must report. For example, any organization that stores credit card information must report any incident in which the disclosure of such information occurred.

Before you encounter an incident, it is wise to establish a relationship with your corporate legal personnel and the appropriate law enforcement agencies. Find out who the appropriate law enforcement contacts are for your organization and talk with them. When the time comes to report an incident, your efforts at establishing a prior working relationship will pay off. You will spend far less time in introductions and explanations if you already know the person with whom you are talking. It is a good idea to identify, in advance, a single point of contact in the organization that will act as your liaison with law enforcement. This provides two benefits. First, it ensures that law enforcement hears a single perspective from your organization and knows the "go-to" person for updates. Second, it allows the predesignated contact to develop working relationships with law enforcement personnel.

 One great way to establish technical contacts with law enforcement is to participate in the FBI's InfraGard program. InfraGard exists in most major metropolitan areas in the United States and provides a forum for law enforcement and business security professionals to share information in a closed environment. For more information, visit www.infragard.net.

Once you determine that you should report an incident, make sure you have as much of the following information as possible:

- What is the nature of the incident, how was it initiated, and by whom?

- When did the incident occur? (Be as precise as possible with dates and times.)

- Where did the incident occur?

- If known, what tools did the attacker use?

- What was the damage resulting from the incident?

You may be asked to provide additional information. Be prepared to provide it in as timely a manner as possible. You may also be asked to quarantine your system.

As with any security action you take, keep a log of all communication, and make copies of any documents you provide as you report an incident.

 For more information on incident handling, read NIST SP 800-61, Computer Security Incident Handling Guide, available at http://csrc.nist .gov/publications/nistpubs/800-61/sp800-61.pdf, and the Handbook for CSIRTs at www.cert.org/archive/pdf/csirt-handbook.pdf.

# Ethics

Security professionals hold themselves and each other to a high standard of conduct because of the sensitive positions of trust they occupy. The rules that govern personal conduct are collectively known as rules of *ethics*. Several organizations have recognized the need for standard ethics rules, or codes, and have devised guidelines for ethical behavior.

We present two codes of ethics in the following sections. These rules are not laws. They are minimum standards for professional behavior. They should provide you with a basis for sound, ethical judgment. As a profession, we expect all security professionals to abide by these guidelines regardless of their area of specialty or employer. Make sure you understand and agree with the codes of ethics outlined in the following sections.

# (ISC)² Code of Ethics

The governing body that administers the CISSP certification is the International Information Systems Security Certification Consortium (ISC)². The (ISC)² Code of Ethics was developed to provide the basis for CISSP behavior. It is a simple code with a preamble and four canons. The following is a short summary of the major concepts of the Code of Ethics.

All CISSP candidates should be familiar with the entire (ISC)² Code of Ethics because they have to sign an agreement that they will adhere to this code. We won't cover the code in depth, but you can find further details about the (ISC)²'s Code of Ethics at www.isc2.org/ethics. You need to visit this site and read the entire code.

## Code of Ethics Preamble

The Code of Ethics preamble is as follows:

- Safety of the commonwealth, duty to our principals, and to each other requires that we adhere, and be seen to adhere, to the highest ethical standards of behavior.

- Therefore, strict adherence to this code is a condition of certification.

## Code of Ethics Canons

The Code of Ethics includes the following canons:

**Protect society, the commonwealth, and the infrastructure.**   Security professionals have great social responsibility. We are charged with the burden of ensuring that our actions benefit the common good.

**Act honorably, honestly, justly, responsibly, and legally.**   Integrity is essential to the conduct of our duties. We cannot carry out our duties effectively if others within our organization, the security community, or the general public have doubts about the accuracy of the guidance we provide or the motives behind our actions.

**Provide diligent and competent service to principals.**   Although we have responsibilities to society as a whole, we also have specific responsibilities to those who have hired us to protect their infrastructure. We must ensure that we are in a position to provide unbiased, competent service to our organization.

**Advance and protect the profession.**   Our chosen profession changes on a continuous basis. As security professionals, we must ensure that our knowledge remains current and that we contribute our own knowledge to the community's common body of knowledge.

# Ethics and the Internet

In January 1989, the Internet Advisory Board (IAB) recognized that the Internet was rapidly expanding beyond the initial trusted community that created it. Understanding that misuse could occur as the Internet grew, IAB issued a statement of policy concerning the proper use of the Internet. The contents of this statement are valid even today. It is important that you know the basic contents of the document, titled "Ethics and the Internet," Request for Comments (RFC) 1087, because most codes of ethics can trace their roots back to this document.

The statement is a brief list of practices considered unethical. Where a code of ethics states what you should do, this document outlines what you should not do. RFC 1087 states that any activity with the following purposes is unacceptable and unethical:

- Seeks to gain unauthorized access to the resources of the Internet
- Disrupts the intended use of the Internet
- Wastes resources (people, capacity, computer) through such actions
- Destroys the integrity of computer-based information
- Compromises the privacy of users

---

### Ten Commandments of Computer Ethics

The Computer Ethics Institute created its own code of ethics. The Ten Commandments of Computer Ethics are as follows:

1. Thou shalt not use a computer to harm other people.

2. Thou shalt not interfere with other people's computer work.

3. Thou shalt not snoop around in other people's computer files.

4. Thou shalt not use a computer to steal.

5. Thou shalt not use a computer to bear false witness.

6. Thou shalt not copy proprietary software for which you have not paid.

7. Thou shalt not use other people's computer resources without authorization or proper compensation.

8. Thou shalt not appropriate other people's intellectual output.

9. Thou shalt think about the social consequences of the program you are writing or the system you are designing.

10. Thou shalt always use a computer in ways that ensure consideration and respect for your fellow humans.

There are many ethical and moral codes of IT behavior to choose from. Another system you should consider is the Generally Accepted Systems Security Principles (GASSP). You can find the full text of the GASSP system at www.infosectoday.com/Articles/gassp.pdf.

# Summary

Computer crimes are grouped into several major categories, and the crimes in each category share common motivations and desired results. Understanding what an attacker is after can help in properly securing a system.

For example, military and intelligence attacks are launched to acquire secret information that could not be obtained legally. Business attacks are similar except that they target civilian systems. Other types of attacks include financial attacks (phone phreaking is an example of a financial attack) and terrorist attacks (which, in the context of computer crimes, are attacks designed to disrupt normal life). Finally, there are grudge attacks, the purpose of which is to cause damage by destroying data or using information to embarrass an organization or person, and thrill attacks, launched by inexperienced crackers to compromise or disable a system. Although generally not sophisticated, thrill attacks can be annoying and costly.

An incident is a violation or the threat of a violation of your security policy. When an incident is suspected, you should immediately begin an investigation and collect as much evidence as possible because, if you decide to report the incident, you must have enough admissible evidence to support your claims.

The set of rules that govern your personal behavior is a code of ethics. There are several codes of ethics, from general to specific in nature, which security professionals can use to guide them. The (ISC)² makes the acceptance of its code of ethics a requirement for certification.

# Exam Essentials

**Know the definition of computer crime.** Computer crime is a crime (or violation of a law or regulation) that is directed against, or directly involves, a computer.

**Be able to list and explain the six categories of computer crimes.** Computer crimes are grouped into six categories: military and intelligence attack, business attack, financial attack, terrorist attack, grudge attack, and thrill attack. Be able to explain the motive of each type of attack.

**Know the importance of collecting evidence.**   As soon you discover an incident, you must begin to collect evidence and as much information about the incident as possible. The evidence can be used in a subsequent legal action or in finding the identity of the attacker. Evidence can also assist you in determining the extent of damage.

**Understand that an incident is any violation, or threat of a violation, of your security policy.**   Incidents should be defined in your security policy. Even though specific incidents may not be outlined, the existence of the policy sets the standard for the use of your system. An incident is any event that has a negative outcome affecting the confidentiality, integrity, or availability of an organization's data.

**Be able to list the four common types of incidents, and know the telltale signs of each.**   An incident occurs when an attack or other violation of your security policy is carried out against your system. Incidents can be grouped into four categories: scanning, compromises, malicious code, and denial of service. Be able to explain what each type of incident involves and what signs to look for.

**Know the importance of identifying abnormal and suspicious activity.**   Attacks will generate some activity that is not normal. Recognizing abnormal and suspicious activity is the first step toward detecting incidents.

**Know how to investigate intrusions and how to gather sufficient information from the equipment, software, and data.**   You must have possession of equipment, software, or data to analyze it and use it as evidence. You must acquire the evidence without modifying it or allowing anyone else to modify it.

**Know the three basic alternatives for confiscating evidence and when each one is appropriate.**   First, the person who owns the evidence could voluntarily surrender it. Second, a subpoena could be used to compel the subject to surrender the evidence. Third, a search warrant is most useful when you need to confiscate evidence without giving the subject an opportunity to alter it.

**Know the importance of retaining incident data.**   Because you will discover some incidents after they have occurred, you will lose valuable evidence unless you ensure that critical log files are retained for a reasonable period of time. You can retain log files and system status information either in place or in archives.

**Be familiar with how to report an incident.**   The first step is to establish a working relationship with the corporate and law enforcement personnel with whom you will work to resolve an incident. When you do have a need to report an incident, gather as much descriptive information as possible and make your report in a timely manner.

**Understand the importance of ethics to security personnel.**   Security practitioners are granted a very high level of authority and responsibility to execute their job functions. The potential for abuse exists, and without a strict code of personal behavior, security practitioners could be regarded as having unchecked power. Adherence to a code of ethics helps ensure that such power is not abused.

**Know the (ISC)² Code of Ethics and RFC 1087, "Ethics and the Internet."** All CISSP candidates should be familiar with the entire (ISC)² Code of Ethics because they have to sign an agreement that they will adhere to it. In addition, be familiar with the basic statements of RFC 1087.

# Written Lab

1. What are the major categories of computer crime?
2. What is the main motivation behind a thrill attack?
3. What is the difference between an interview and an interrogation?
4. What is the difference between an event and an incident?
5. Who are the common members of an incident response team?
6. What are the three phases of the incident response process?

# Answers to Written Lab

1.  The major categories of computer crime are military/intelligence attacks, business attacks, financial attacks, terrorist attacks, grudge attacks, and thrill attacks.

2.  Thrill attacks are motivated by individuals seeking to achieve the "high" associated with successfully breaking into a computer system.

3.  Interviews are conducted with the intention of gathering information to assist with your investigation. Interrogations are conducted with the intent of gathering evidence to be used in a criminal prosecution.

4.  An event is any occurrence that takes place during a certain period of time. Incidents are events that have negative outcomes affecting the confidentiality, integrity, or availability of your data.

5.  Incident response teams normally include representatives from senior management, information security professionals, legal representatives, public affairs/communications representatives, and technical engineers.

6.  The three phases of the incident response process are detection and identification, response and reporting, and recovery and remediation.

# Review Questions

1. What is a computer crime?
   - **A.** Any attack specifically listed in your security policy
   - **B.** Any illegal attack that compromises a protected computer
   - **C.** Any violation of a law or regulation that involves a computer
   - **D.** Failure to practice due diligence in computer security

2. What is the main purpose of a military and intelligence attack?
   - **A.** To attack the availability of military systems
   - **B.** To obtain secret and restricted information from military or law enforcement sources
   - **C.** To utilize military or intelligence agency systems to attack other nonmilitary sites
   - **D.** To compromise military systems for use in attacks against other systems

3. What type of attack targets proprietary information stored on a civilian organization's system?
   - **A.** Business attack
   - **B.** Denial-of-service attack
   - **C.** Financial attack
   - **D.** Military and intelligence attack

4. What goal is not a purpose of a financial attack?
   - **A.** Access services you have not purchased.
   - **B.** Disclose confidential personal employee information.
   - **C.** Transfer funds from an unapproved source into your account.
   - **D.** Steal money from another organization.

5. Which one of the following attacks is most indicative of a terrorist attack?
   - **A.** Alter sensitive trade secret documents.
   - **B.** Damage the ability to communicate and respond to a physical attack.
   - **C.** Steal unclassified information.
   - **D.** Transfer funds to other countries.

6. Which of the following would not be a primary goal of a grudge attack?
   - **A.** Disclose embarrassing personal information.
   - **B.** Launch a virus on an organization's system.
   - **C.** Send inappropriate email with a spoofed origination address of the victim organization.
   - **D.** Use automated tools to scan the organization's systems for vulnerable ports.

**7.** What are the primary reasons attackers engage in thrill attacks? (Choose all that apply.)

   **A.** Bragging rights

   **B.** Money from the sale of stolen documents

   **C.** Pride of conquering a secure system

   **D.** Retaliation against a person or organization

**8.** What is the most important rule to follow when collecting evidence?

   **A.** Do not turn off a computer until you photograph the screen.

   **B.** List all people present while collecting evidence.

   **C.** Never modify evidence during the collection process.

   **D.** Transfer all equipment to a secure storage location.

**9.** What would be a valid argument for not immediately removing power from a machine when an incident is discovered?

   **A.** All of the damage has been done. Turning the machine off would not stop additional damage.

   **B.** There is no other system that can replace this one if it is turned off.

   **C.** Too many users are logged in and using the system.

   **D.** Valuable evidence in memory will be lost.

**10.** What is the reason many incidents are never reported?

   **A.** It involves too much paperwork.

   **B.** Reporting too many incidents could hurt an organization's reputation.

   **C.** The incident is never discovered.

   **D.** Too much time has passed, and the evidence is gone.

**11.** What is an incident?

   **A.** Any active attack that causes damage to your system

   **B.** Any violation of a code of ethics

   **C.** Any crime (or violation of a law or regulation) that involves a computer

   **D.** Any event that adversely affects the confidentiality, integrity or availability of your data

**12.** If port scanning does no damage to a system, why is it generally considered an incident?

   **A.** All port scans indicate adversarial behavior.

   **B.** Port scans can precede attacks that cause damage and can indicate a future attack.

   **C.** Scanning a port damages the port.

   **D.** Port scanning uses system resources that could be put to better uses.

**13.** What type of incident is characterized by obtaining an increased level of privilege?

    **A.** Compromise

    **B.** Denial of service

    **C.** Malicious code

    **D.** Scanning

**14.** What is the best way to recognize abnormal and suspicious behavior on your system?

    **A.** Be aware of the newest attacks.

    **B.** Configure your IDS to detect and report all abnormal traffic.

    **C.** Know what your normal system activity looks like.

    **D.** Study the activity signatures of the main types of attacks.

**15.** If you need to confiscate a PC from a suspected attacker who does not work for your organization, what legal avenue is most appropriate?

    **A.** Consent agreement signed by employees

    **B.** Search warrant

    **C.** No legal avenue is necessary

    **D.** Voluntary consent

**16.** Why should you avoid deleting log files on a daily basis?

    **A.** An incident may not be discovered for several days and valuable evidence could be lost.

    **B.** Disk space is cheap, and log files are used frequently.

    **C.** Log files are protected and cannot be altered.

    **D.** Any information in a log file is useless after it is several hours old.

**17.** Which of the following conditions might require that you report an incident? (Choose all that apply.)

    **A.** Confidential information protected by government regulation was possibly disclosed.

    **B.** Damages exceeded $1,500.

    **C.** The incident has occurred before.

    **D.** The incident resulted in a violation of a law.

**18.** What are ethics?

    **A.** Mandatory actions required to fulfill job requirements

    **B.** Laws of professional conduct

    **C.** Regulations set forth by a professional organization

    **D.** Rules of personal behavior

**19.** According to the (ISC)$^2$ Code of Ethics, how are CISSPs expected to act?

    **A.** Honestly, diligently, responsibly, and legally

    **B.** Honorably, honestly, justly, responsibly, and legally

    **C.** Upholding the security policy and protecting the organization

    **D.** Trustworthy, loyally, friendly, courteously

**20.** Which of the following actions are considered unacceptable and unethical according to RFC 1087, "Ethics and the Internet"?

    **A.** Actions that compromise the privacy of classified information

    **B.** Actions that compromise the privacy of users

    **C.** Actions that disrupt organizational activities

    **D.** Actions in which a computer is used in a manner inconsistent with a stated security policy

# Answers to Review Questions

1. C. A crime is any violation of a law or regulation. The violation stipulation defines the action as a crime. It is a computer crime if the violation involves a computer either as the target or as a tool.

2. B. A military and intelligence attack is targeted at the classified data that resides on the system. To the attacker, the value of the information justifies the risk associated with such an attack. The information extracted from this type of attack is often used to plan subsequent attacks.

3. A. Confidential information that is not related to the military or intelligence agencies is the target of business attacks. The ultimate goal could be destruction, alteration, or disclosure of confidential information.

4. B. A financial attack focuses primarily on obtaining services and funds illegally.

5. B. A terrorist attack is launched to interfere with a way of life by creating an atmosphere of fear. A computer terrorist attack can reach this goal by reducing the ability to respond to a simultaneous physical attack.

6. D. Any action that can harm a person or organization, either directly or through embarrassment, would be a valid goal of a grudge attack. The purpose of such an attack is to "get back" at someone.

7. A, C. Thrill attacks have no reward other than providing a boost to pride and ego. The thrill of launching the attack comes from the act of participating in the attack (and not getting caught).

8. C. Although the other options have some merit in individual cases, the most important rule is to never modify, or taint, evidence. If you modify evidence, it becomes inadmissible in court.

9. D. The most compelling reason for not removing power from a machine is that you will lose the contents of memory. Carefully consider the pros and cons of removing power. After all is considered, it may be the best choice.

10. C. Although an organization would not want to report a large number of incidents (unless reporting them is mandatory), the reality is that many incidents are never discovered. The lack of well-trained users results in many incidents that are never recognized.

11. D. An incident is normally defined as any event that adversely affects the confidentiality, integrity, or availability of your data.

12. B. Some port scans are normal. An unusually high volume of port scan activity can be a reconnaissance activity preceding a more dangerous attack. When you see unusual port scanning, you should always investigate.

**13.** A.  Any time an attacker exceeds their authority, the incident is classified as a system compromise. This includes valid users who exceed their authority as well as invalid users who gain access through the use of a valid user ID.

**14.** C.  Although options A, B, and D are actions that can make you aware of what attacks look like and how to detect them, you will never successfully detect most attacks until you know your system. When you know what the activity on your system looks like on a normal day, you can immediately detect any abnormal activity.

**15.** B.  In this case, you need a search warrant to confiscate equipment without giving the suspect time to destroy evidence. If the suspect worked for your organization and you had all employees sign consent agreements, you could simply confiscate the equipment.

**16.** A.  Log files contain a large volume of generally useless information. However, when you are trying to track down a problem or an incident, they can be invaluable. Even if an incident is discovered as it is happening, it may have been preceded by other incidents. Log files provide valuable clues and should be protected and archived.

**17.** A, D.  You must report an incident when the incident resulted in the violation of a law or regulation. This includes any damage (or potential damage) to or disclosure of protected information.

**18.** D.  Ethics are simply rules of personal behavior. Many professional organizations establish formal codes of ethics to govern their members, but ethics are personal rules individuals use to guide their lives.

**19.** B.  The second canon of the (ISC)² Code of Ethics states how a CISSP should act, which is honorably, honestly, justly, responsibly, and legally.

**20.** B.  RFC 1087 does not specifically address the statements in A, C, or D. Although each type of activity listed is unacceptable, only the activity identified in option B is identified in RFC 1087.

# Chapter 19

# Physical Security Requirements

---

## THE CISSP EXAM TOPICS COVERED IN THIS CHAPTER INCLUDE:

✓ **Operations Security**

- Manage incident response
    - Detection; response; reporting; recovery; remediation

✓ **Physical (Environmental) Security**

- Participate in site and facility design considerations

- Support the implementation and operation of perimeter security (e.g., physical access control and monitoring, audit trails/access logs)

- Support the implementation and operation of internal security (e.g., escort requirements/visitor control, keys and locks)

- Support the implementation and operation of facilities security

    - Communications and server rooms; restricted and work area security; data center security; utilities and HVAC considerations; water issues (e.g., leakage, flooding); fire prevention, detection and suppression

- Support the protection and securing of equipment

Among numerous other topics, the Operations Security domain of the Common Body of Knowledge (CBK) for the CISSP certification exam deals with managing incident response as and when a security indicent occurs. It also delves into the mechanics of such a response, including detecting that an incident has occurred, and then responding to, reporting on, and recovering from or remediating its results.

The Physical (Environmental) Security domain of the Common Body of Knowledge (CBK) for the CISSP certification exam deals with topics and issues related to facility construction and location, the security features of a facility, forms of physical access control, types of physical security technical controls, and maintaining security by properly sustaining the environment and protecting human life.

The purpose of physical security is to protect against physical threats. The following physical threats are among the most common:

- Fire and smoke

- Water (rising/falling)

- Earth movement (earthquakes, landslides, volcanoes)

- Storms (wind, lightning, rain, snow, sleet, ice)

- Sabotage/vandalism

- Explosion/destruction

- Building collapse

- Toxic materials

- Utility loss (power, heating, cooling, air, water)

- Equipment failure

- Personnel loss (strikes, illness, access, transport)

This chapter explores each of these issues and discusses safeguards and countermeasures to protect against them. In many cases, you'll need a disaster recovery plan or a business continuity plan should a serious physical threat (such as an explosion, sabotage, or natural disaster) occur. Chapters 15, "Business Continuity Planning," and 16, "Disaster Recovery Planning," cover those topics in detail.

# Facility Requirements

It should be blatantly obvious if you've read the previous 18 chapters that without control over the physical environment, no collection of administrative, technical, or logical access controls can provide adequate security. If a malicious person can gain physical access to your facility or equipment, they can do just about anything they want, from destruction to disclosure or alteration. Physical controls are your first line of defense, and people are your last.

There are many aspects of and elements to implementing and maintaining physical security. A core or foundational element is selecting or designing the facility to house your IT infrastructure and your organization's operations. The process of selecting or designing a secure facility always starts with a plan.

## Secure Facility Plan

A secure facility plan outlines the security needs of your organization and emphasizes methods or mechanisms to employ to provide security. Such a plan is developed through a process known as *critical path analysis*. Critical path analysis is a systematic effort to identify relationships between mission-critical applications, processes, and operations and all the necessary supporting elements. For example, an e-commerce server used to sell products over the Web relies on Internet access, computer hardware, electricity, temperature control, storage facility, and so on.

When critical path analysis is performed properly, a complete picture of the interdependencies and interactions necessary to sustain the organization is produced. Once that analysis is complete, its results serve as a list of items to secure. The first step in designing a secure IT infrastructure is providing security for the basic requirements of the organization and its computers. These basic requirements include electricity, environmental controls (in other words, a building, air conditioning, heating, humidity control, and so on), and water/sewage.

Security staff should participate in site and facility design considerations. Otherwise, many important aspects of physical security essential for the existence of logical security may be overlooked. With security staff involved in the physical facility design, you can be assured that your long-term security goals as an organization will be supported not just by your policies, personnel, and electronic equipment, but by the building itself.

## Physical Security Controls

The security controls implemented to manage physical security can be divided into three groups: administrative, technical, and physical. Because these are the same categories used to describe access controls, it is vital to focus on the physical security aspects of these controls. *Administrative physical security controls* include facility construction and selection, site management, personnel controls, awareness training, and emergency response and procedures. *Technical physical security controls* include access controls; intrusion detection; alarms; closed-circuit television (CCTV); monitoring; heating, ventilating, and air conditioning (HVAC); power supplies; and fire detection and suppression. *Physical controls for physical security* include fencing, lighting, locks, construction materials, mantraps, dogs, and guards.

---

### Corporate vs. Personal Property

Physical security controls embrace both visible and invisible aspects in many ordinary business environments. You see them at the post office, at the corner store, and in certain areas of your own computing environment. They are so pervasive that some people choose where they live based on their presence, as in gated access communities or secure apartment complexes.

Alison is a security analyst for a major technology corporation that specializes in data management. This company includes an in-house security staff (guards, administrators, and so on) that is capable of handling physical security breaches.

Brad experienced an intrusion—into his personal vehicle in the company parking lot. He asks Alison whether she observed or recorded anyone breaking into and entering his vehicle, but this is a personal item and not a company possession, and she has no control or regulation over damage to employee assets.

This is understandably unnerving for Brad, but he understands that she's protecting the business and not his belongings. When or where would you think it would be necessary to implement security measures for both? The usual answer is anywhere business assets are or might be involved. Had Brad been using a company vehicle parked in the company parking lot, then perhaps Alison could make allowances for an incidental break-in involving Brad's things, but even then she isn't responsible for their safekeeping. On the other hand, where key people are also important assets (executive staff at most enterprises, security analysts who work in sensitive positions, heads of state, and so forth), protection and safeguards usually extend to embrace them and their belongings as part of asset protection and risk mitigation. Of course, if danger to employees or what they carry with them becomes a problem, securing the parking garage with key cards and installing CCTV monitors on every floor really begins to make sense. Simply put, if the costs of allowing break-ins to occur exceeds that of installing preventive measures, it's prudent to put them in place.

---

When designing physical security for an environment, focus on the functional order of controls. Security controls should be deployed so that initial attempts to access physical assets are deterred (in other words, boundary restrictions). If deterrence fails, then direct access to physical assets should be denied (for example, locked vault doors). If denial fails, your system needs to detect intrusion (for example, using motion detectors), and the intrusion should be delayed sufficiently to enable authorities to respond (for example, a cable lock on the asset). It's important to remember this order when deploying physical security controls: first deterrence, then denial, then detection, then delay.

## Site Selection

Site selection should be based on the security needs of the organization. Cost, location, and size are important, but addressing the requirements of security should always take precedence. When choosing a site on which to build a facility or selecting a preexisting structure, be sure to examine every aspect of its location carefully.

Securing assets depends largely on site security, which involves numerous considerations and situational elements. Site location and construction play a crucial role in the overall site selection process. Susceptibility to riots, looting, break-ins, and vandalism or location within a high-crime area are obviously all poor choices but cannot always be dictated or controlled. Environmental threats such as fault lines, tornado/hurricane regions, and close proximity to other natural disasters present significant issues for the site selection process as well because you can't always avoid such threats.

Proximity to other buildings and businesses is another crucial consideration. What sorts of attention do they draw, and how does that affect your operation or facility? Proximity to emergency-response personnel is another consideration, along with other elements. Some companies can afford to buy or build their own campuses to keep neighboring elements out of play and to enable tighter access control and monitoring. However, not every company can exercise this option and must make do with what's available and affordable instead.

At a minimum, ensure that the building is designed to withstand fairly extreme weather conditions and that it can deter or fend off overt break-in attempts. Vulnerable entry points such as windows and doors tend to dominate such analysis, but you should also evaluate objects (trees, shrubs, or man-made items) that can obscure break-in attempts.

## Visibility

Visibility is important. What is the surrounding terrain? Would it be easy to approach the facility by vehicle or on foot without being seen? The makeup of the surrounding area is also important. Is it in or near a residential, business, or industrial area? What is the local crime rate? Where are the closest emergency services located (fire, medical, police)? What unique hazards may be found in the vicinity (chemical plants, homeless shelters, universities, construction sites, and so on)?

## Accessibility and Perimeter Security

The accessibility to the building or campus location is also important. Single entrances are great for providing security, but multiple entrances are better for evacuation during emergencies. What types of roads are nearby? What means of transportation are easily accessible (trains, highway, airport, shipping)? What about traffic levels throughout the day?

Keep in mind that accessibility is also constrained by the need for perimeter security. The needs of access and use should meld and support the implementation and operation of perimeter security. The use of physical access controls and monitoring personnel and equipment entering and leaving as well as auditing/logging all physical events are key elements in maintaining overall organizational security.

## Natural Disasters

Another concern is the potential impact that natural disasters could make in the area. Is it prone to earthquakes, mudslides, sinkholes, fires, floods, hurricanes, tornadoes, falling rocks, snow, rainfall, ice, humidity, heat, extreme cold, and so on? You must prepare for natural disasters and equip your IT environment to either survive an event or be replaced easily.

## Facility Design

When designing the construction of a facility, you must understand the level of security that your organization needs. A proper level of security must be planned and designed before construction begins.

Important issues to consider include combustibility, fire rating, construction materials, load rating, placement, and control of items such as walls, doors, ceilings, flooring, HVAC, power, water, sewage, gas, and so on. Forced intrusion, emergency access, resistance to entry, direction of entries and exits, use of alarms, and conductivity are other important aspects to evaluate. Every element within a facility should be evaluated in terms of how it could be used for and against the protection of the IT infrastructure and personnel (for example, positive flows for air and water from inside a facility to outside its boundaries).

There's also a pretty well-established school of thought on "secure architecture" that's often called crime prevention through environmental design (CPTED). The guiding idea is to structure the physical environment and surroundings to influence individual decisions that potential offenders make before committing any criminal acts. The International CPTED Association is an excellent source for information on this subject (www.cpted.net), as is Oscar Newman's book *Creating Defensible Space*, published by HUD's Office of Policy Development and Research (free PDF download at www.defensiblespace.com/book.htm).

## Work Areas

The design and configuration of work areas and visitor areas should be considered carefully. There should not be equal access to all locations within a facility. Areas that contain assets of higher value or importance should have more restricted access. For example, anyone who enters the facility should be able to access the restrooms and the public telephone without going into sensitive areas, but only network administrators and security staff should have access to the server room. Valuable and confidential assets should be located in the heart or center of protection provided by a facility. In effect, you should focus on deploying concentric circles of physical protection. This type of configuration requires increased levels of authorization to gain access into more sensitive areas inside the facility.

Walls or partitions can be used to separate similar but distinct work areas. Such divisions deter casual shoulder surfing or eavesdropping (*shoulder surfing* is the act of gathering information from a system by observing the monitor or the use of the keyboard by the operator). Floor-to-ceiling walls should be used to separate areas with differing levels of sensitivity and confidentiality (where false or suspended ceilings are present, walls should cut these off as well to provide an unbroken physical barrier between more and less secure areas).

Each work area should be evaluated and assigned a classification just as IT assets are classified. Only people with clearance or classifications corresponding to the classification of the work area should be allowed access. Areas with different purposes or uses should be assigned different levels of access or restrictions. The more access to assets the equipment within an area offers, the more important become the restrictions that are used to control who enters those areas and what activities they are allowed to perform.

Your facility security design process should support the implementation and operation of internal security. In addition to the management of workers in proper work spaces, you should address visitors. Should there be an escort requirement for visitors, and what other forms of visitor control should be implemented? In addition to basic physical security tools such as keys and locks, mechanisms such as mantraps, video cameras, written logs, security guards, and RFID ID tags should be implemented.

## Server Rooms

Server rooms, server vaults, and IT closets are enclosed, restricted, and protected rooms where your mission-critical servers and network devices are housed. Centralized server rooms need not be human compatible. In fact, the more human incompatible a server room is, the more protection it will offer against casual and determined attacks. Human incompatibility can be accomplished by including Halotron, PyroGen, or other halon-substitute oxygen-displacement fire detection and extinguishing systems, low temperatures, little or no lighting, and equipment stacked with little room to maneuver. Server rooms should be designed to support optimal operation of the IT infrastructure and to block unauthorized human access or intervention.

Server rooms should be located at the core of the building. Try to avoid locating these rooms on the ground floor, the top floor, and the basement whenever possible. Additionally, the server room should be located away from water, gas, and sewage lines. These pose too large a risk of leakage or flooding, which can cause serious damage and downtime.

The walls of your server room should also have a one-hour minimum fire rating.

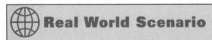

## Real World Scenario

### Making Servers Inaccessible

The running joke in the IT security realm is that the most secure computer is one that is disconnected from the network and sealed in a room with no doors or windows. No, seriously, that's the joke. But there's a massive grain of truth and irony in it as well.

Carlos operates security processes and platforms for a financial banking firm, and he knows all about one-way systems and unreachable devices. Sensitive business transactions occur in fractions of a second, and one wrong move could pose serious risks to data and involved parties.

In his experience, Carlos knows that the least accessible and least human-friendly places are his most valuable assets, so he stores many of his machines inside a separate bank vault. You'd have to be a talented burglar, a skilled safecracker, and a determined computer attacker to breach his security defenses.

Not all business applications and processes warrant this extreme sort of prevention. What security recommendations might you suggest to make a server more inconvenient or inaccessible, short of dedicating a vault? A basement with limited access or an interior room with no windows and only one entry/exit point makes an excellent substitute when an empty vault isn't available. The key is to select a space with limited access and then to establish serious hurdles to entry (especially unauthorized entry). CCTV monitoring on the door and motion detectors inside the space can also help maintain proper attention to who is coming and going.

## Visitors

If a facility employs restricted areas to control physical security, a mechanism to handle visitors is required. Often an escort is assigned to visitors, and their access and activities are monitored closely. Failing to track the actions of outsiders when they are allowed into a protected area can result in malicious activity against the most protected assets.

## Real World Scenario

### Deploying Physical Access Controls

In the real world, you will deploy multiple layers of physical access controls to manage the traffic of authorized and unauthorized individuals within your facility. The outermost layer will be lighting. The entire outer perimeter of your site should be clearly lit. This enables easy identification of personnel and makes it easier to notice intrusions and intimidate potential intruders. Just inside the lighted area, place a fence or wall designed to prevent intrusion. Specific controlled points along that fence or wall should be points for entry or exit. These should have gates, turnstiles, or mantraps all monitored by CCTV and security guards. Identification and authentication should be required at all entry points before entrance is granted.

Within the facility, areas of different sensitivity or confidentiality levels should be distinctly separated and compartmentalized. This is especially true for public areas and areas accessible to visitors. An additional identification/authentication process to validate the need to enter should be required when anyone moves from one area to another. The most sensitive resources and systems should be isolated from all but the most privileged personnel and located at the center or core of the facility.

# Forms of Physical Access Controls

You can deploy many types of physical access control mechanisms in an environment to control, monitor, and manage access to a facility. These range from deterrents to detection mechanisms.

The various sections, divisions, or areas within a site or facility should be clearly designated as public, private, or restricted. Each of these areas requires unique and focused physical access controls, monitoring, and prevention mechanisms. The following sections discuss many such mechanisms that may be used to separate, isolate, and control access to various areas within a site.

## Fences, Gates, Turnstiles, and Mantraps

A *fence* is a perimeter-defining device. Fences are used to clearly differentiate between areas that are under a specific level of security protection and those that aren't. Fencing can include a wide range of components, materials, and construction methods. It can consist of stripes painted on the ground, chain link fences, barbed wire, concrete walls, and even invisible perimeters using laser, motion, or heat detectors. Various types of fences are effective against different types of intruders:

- Fences 3 to 4 feet high deter casual trespassers.
- Fences 6 to 7 feet high are too hard to climb easily and deter most intruders, except determined ones.
- Fences 8 or more feet high with three strands of barbed wire deter even determined intruders.

A *gate* is a controlled exit and entry point in a fence. The deterrent level of a gate must be equivalent to the deterrent level of the fence to sustain the effectiveness of the fence as a whole. Hinges and locking/closing mechanisms should be hardened against tampering, destruction, or removal. When a gate is closed, it should not offer any additional access vulnerabilities. Keep the number of gates to a minimum. They can be manned by guards or not. When they're not protected by guards, use of dogs or CCTV is recommended.

A *turnstile* (see Figure 19.1) is a form of gate that prevents more than one person at a time from gaining entry and often restricts movement in one direction. It is used to gain entry but not to exit or vice versa. A turnstile is basically the fencing equivalent of a secured revolving door.

A *mantrap* is a double set of doors that is often protected by a guard (also shown in Figure 19.1) or some other physical layout that prevents piggybacking and can trap individuals at the discretion of security personnel. The purpose of a mantrap is to immobilize a subject until their identity and authentication is verified. If a subject is authorized for entry, the inner door opens, allowing entry into the facility or onto the premises. If a subject is not authorized, both doors remain closed and locked until an escort (typically a guard or a police officer) arrives to escort the subject off the property or arrest the subject for trespassing (this is called a *delay* feature). Often a mantrap includes a scale to prevent piggybacking or tailgating.

**FIGURE 19.1**   A secure physical boundary with a mantrap and a turnstile

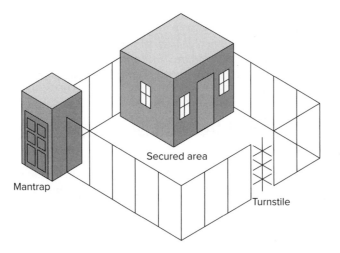

## Lighting

*Lighting* is a commonly used form of perimeter security control. The primary purpose of lighting is to discourage casual intruders, trespassers, prowlers, or would-be thieves who would rather perform their misdeeds in the dark. However, lighting is not a strong deterrent. It should not be used as the primary or sole protection mechanism except in areas with a low threat level.

Lighting should not illuminate the positions of guards, dogs, patrol posts, or other similar security elements. It should be combined with guards, dogs, CCTV, or some other form of intrusion detection or surveillance mechanism. Lighting must not cause a nuisance or problem for nearby residents, roads, railways, airports, and so on. It should also never cause glare or reflective distraction to guards, dogs, and monitoring equipment, which could otherwise aid attackers during break-in attempts.

The National Institute of Standards and Technology (NIST) standard for perimeter protection using lighting is that critical areas should be illuminated with 2 candle feet of power at a height of 8 feet. Another common issue for the use of lighting is the placement of the lights. Standards seem to indicate that light poles should be placed the same distance apart as the diameter of the illuminated area created by illumination elements. Thus, if a lighted area is 40 feet in diameter, poles should be 40 feet apart.

## Security Guards and Dogs

All physical security controls, whether static deterrents or active detection and surveillance mechanisms, ultimately rely upon personnel to intervene and stop actual intrusions and attacks. Security guards exist to fulfill this need. Guards can be posted around a perimeter or inside to monitor access points or watch detection and surveillance monitors. The real benefit of guards is that they are able to adapt and react to various conditions or situations. Guards can learn and recognize attack and intrusion activities and patterns, can adjust to a changing environment, and can make decisions and judgment calls. Security guards are often an appropriate security control when immediate situation handling and decision making onsite is necessary.

Unfortunately, using security guards is not a perfect solution. There are numerous disadvantages to deploying, maintaining, and relying upon security guards. Not all environments and facilities support security guards. This may be because of actual human incompatibility or the layout, design, location, and construction of the facility. Not all security guards are themselves reliable. Prescreening, bonding, and training do not guarantee that you won't end up with an ineffective or unreliable security guard.

Even if a guard is initially reliable, guards are subject to physical injury and illness, take vacations, can become distracted, are vulnerable to social engineering, and may become unemployable because of substance abuse. In addition, they sometimes focus on self-preservation instead of preserving security at the guarded facility. This may mean that security guards can offer protection only up to the point at which their life is endangered. Additionally, security guards are usually unaware of the scope of the operations within a facility and are therefore not thoroughly equipped to know how to respond to every situation. Finally, security guards are expensive.

Guard dogs can be an alternative to security guards. They can often be deployed as a perimeter security control. As a detection and deterrent, dogs are extremely effective. However, dogs are costly, require a high level of maintenance, and impose serious insurance and liability requirements.

## Keys and Combination Locks

Locks keep closed doors closed. They are designed and deployed to prevent access to everyone without proper authorization. A *lock* is a crude form of an identification and authorization mechanism. If you possess the correct key or combination, you are considered authorized and permitted entry. Key-based locks are the most common and inexpensive forms of physical access control devices. These are often known as *preset locks*. These types of locks are subject to picking, which is often categorized under a class of lock mechanism attacks called *shimming*.

 **Real World Scenario**

**Using Locks**

Keys or combination locks—which do you choose and for what purposes?

Ultimately, there will always be that forgetful element of users who just cannot be reminded enough. Elise constantly forgets her combination, and Francis can never remember to bring his security key card to work. Gino maintains a pessimistic outlook in his administrative style, so he's keen on putting combinations and key card accesses in all the right places.

Under what circumstances or conditions might you employ a combination lock, and where might you instead opt for a key or key card? What options put you at greater risk of loss if someone discovers the combination or finds the key? Can you be certain that these single points of failure do not significantly pose a risk to the protected assets?

Many organizations typically utilize separate forms of key or combination accesses throughout several areas of the facility. Key and key card access is granted at select shared entry points (exterior access into the building, access into interior rooms), and combination locks control access to individual entry points (storage lockers, file cabinets, and so on).

Programmable or combination locks offer a broader range of control than preset locks. Some programmable locks can be configured with multiple valid access combinations or may include digital or electronic controls employing keypads, smart cards, or cipher devices. For instance, an *electronic access control (EAC)* lock incorporates three elements: an electromagnet to keep the door closed, a credential reader to authenticate subjects and to disable the electromagnet, and a sensor to reengage the electromagnet when the door is closed.

Locks serve as an alternative to security guards as a perimeter entrance access control device. A gate or door can be opened and closed to allow access by a security guard who verifies your identity before granting access, or the lock itself can serve as the verification device that also grants or restricts entry.

## Badges

*Badges*, *identification cards*, and *security IDs* are forms of physical identification and/or electronic access control devices. A badge can be as simple as a name tag indicating whether you are a valid employee or a visitor. Or it can be as complex as a smart card or token device that employs multifactor authentication to verify and prove your identity and provide authentication and authorization to access a facility, specific rooms, or secured workstations. Badges often include pictures, magnetic strips with encoded data, and personal details to help a security guard verify identity.

Badges can be used in environments in which physical access is primarily controlled by security guards. In such conditions, the badge serves as a visual identification tool for the guards. They can verify your identity by comparing your picture to your person and consult a printed or electronic roster of authorized personnel to determine whether you have valid access.

Badges can also serve in environments guarded by scanning devices rather than security guards. In such conditions, a badge can be used either for identification or for authentication. When a badge is used for identification, it is swiped in a device, and then the badge owner must provide one or more authentication factors, such as a password, passphrase, or biological trait (if a biometric device is used). When a badge is used for authentication, the badge owner provides an ID, username, and so on and then swipes the badge to authenticate.

## Motion Detectors

A *motion detector*, or *motion sensor*, is a device that senses motion in a specific area. Many types of motion detectors exist, including infrared, heat, wave pattern, capacitance, photoelectric, and passive audio. An infrared motion detector monitors for significant or meaningful changes in the infrared lighting pattern of a monitored area. A heat-based motion detector monitors for significant or meaningful changes in the heat levels and patterns in a monitored area. A wave pattern motion detector transmits a consistent low ultrasonic or high microwave frequency signal into a monitored area and monitors for significant or meaningful changes or disturbances in the reflected pattern. A capacitance motion detector senses changes in the electrical or magnetic field surrounding a monitored object. A photoelectric motion detector senses changes in visible light levels for the monitored area. Photoelectric motion detectors are usually deployed in internal rooms that have no windows and are kept dark. A passive audio motion detector listens for abnormal sounds in the monitored area.

## Intrusion Alarms

Whenever a motion detector registers a significant or meaningful change in the environment, it triggers an alarm. An *alarm* is a separate mechanism that triggers a deterrent, a repellent, and/or a notification. Alarms that trigger deterrents may engage additional locks, shut doors, and so on. The goal of such an alarm is to make further intrusion or attack more difficult. Alarms that trigger repellants usually sound an audio siren or bell and turn on lights. These kinds of alarms are used to discourage intruders or attackers from continuing their malicious or trespassing activities and force them off the premises. Alarms that trigger notification are often silent from the intruder/attacker perspective but record data about the incident and notify administrators, security guards, and law enforcement. A recording of an incident can take the form of log files and/or CCTV tapes. The purpose of a silent alarm is to bring authorized security personnel to the location of the intrusion or attack in hopes of catching the person(s) committing the unwanted or unauthorized acts.

*Local alarm systems* must broadcast an audible (up to 120 decibel, or db) alarm signal that can be easily heard up to 400 feet away. Additionally, they must be protected from tampering and disablement, usually by security guards. For a local alarm system to be effective, there must be a security team or guards positioned nearby who can respond when the alarm is triggered. A *centralized alarm system* may not have a local alarm; a remote or centralized monitoring station is signaled when the alarm is triggered. *Auxiliary alarm systems* can be added to either local or centralized alarm systems. The purpose of an auxiliary alarm system is to notify local police or fire services when an alarm is triggered.

## Secondary Verification Mechanisms

When motion detectors, sensors, and alarms are used, secondary verification mechanisms should be in place. As the sensitivity of these devices increases, false triggers occur more often. Innocuous events such as the presence of animals, birds, bugs, or authorized personnel can trigger false alarms. Deploying two or more detection and sensor systems and requiring two or more triggers in quick succession to occur before an alarm is issued may significantly reduce false alarms and increase the certainty of sensing actual intrusions or attacks.

CCTV is a security mechanism related to motion detectors, sensors, and alarms. However, CCTV is not an automated detection-and-response system. CCTV requires personnel to watch the captured video to detect suspicious and malicious activities and to trigger alarms. Security cameras can expand the effective visible range of a security guard, therefore increasing the scope of the oversight. In many cases, CCTV is not used as a primary detection tool because of the high cost of paying a person to sit and watch the video screens. Instead, it is used as a secondary or follow-up mechanism that is reviewed after a trigger from an automated system occurs. In fact, the same logic used for auditing and audit trails is used for CCTV and recorded events. A CCTV is a preventative measure, while reviewing recorded events is a detective measure.

**Secondary Verification**

As illustrated in the previous real-world scenario, Gino was at constant risk of security breaches because Elise is constantly forgetting (and therefore writes down) every password, while Francis is habitually forgetful about the location of his key card. What happens when someone else comes into possession of either of these items and has knowledge of how or where to use them?

Gino's biggest advantage will be any secondary verification mechanisms he has established in the workplace. This may include a CCTV that identifies the face of the person who uses a key card for access or inputs a combination in some area designated under surveillance. Even videotape logs of ingress and egress through checkpoints can be helpful when it comes to chasing down accidental or deliberate access abuses.

With known "problem users" or "problem identities," many security systems can issue notifications or alerts when those identities are used. Depending on the systems that are available, and the risks that unauthorized access could pose, human follow-up may or may not be warranted. But any time Elise (or somebody who uses that identity) logs onto a system or any time Francis's key card is used, a floating or roving security guard could be dispatched to ensure that everything is on the up and up. Of course, it's probably also a good idea to have Elise's and Francis's managers counsel them on the appropriate use (and storage) of passwords and key cards, just to make sure they understand the potential risks involved too.

# Technical Controls

Technical controls most often employed as access control mechanisms to manage physical access include smart/dumb cards and biometrics. In addition to such controls, audit trails, access logs, and intrusion detection systems (IDSs) can serve as physical security mechanisms.

## Smart Cards

*Smart cards* are credit-card-sized IDs, badges, or security passes with an embedded magnetic strip, bar code, or integrated circuit chip. They can contain information about the authorized bearer that can be used for identification and/or authentication purposes. Some smart cards can even process information or store reasonable amounts of data in a memory chip. A smart card may be known by several phrases or terms:

- An identity token containing integrated circuits (ICs)
- A processor IC card
- An IC card with an ISO 7816 interface

Smart cards are often viewed as a complete security solution, but they should not be considered complete by themselves. As with any single security mechanism, smart cards are subject to weaknesses and vulnerabilities. Smart cards can fall prey to physical attacks, logical attacks, Trojan horse attacks, or social-engineering attacks.

*Memory cards* are machine-readable ID cards with a magnetic strip. Like a credit card, debit card, or ATM card, memory cards can retain a small amount of data but are unable to process data like a smart card. Memory cards often function as a type of two-factor control: The card is "something you have" and its PIN "something you know." However, memory cards are easy to copy or duplicate and are insufficient for authentication purposes in a secure environment.

## Proximity Readers

In addition to smart and dumb cards, proximity readers can be used to control physical access. A *proximity reader* can be a passive device, a field-powered device, or a transponder. The proximity device is worn or held by the authorized bearer. When it passes a proximity reader, the reader is able to determine who the bearer is and whether they have authorized access. A passive device reflects or otherwise alters the electromagnetic field generated by the reader. This alteration is detected by the reader.

The passive device has no active electronics; it is just a small magnet with specific properties (like antitheft devices commonly found on DVDs). A field-powered device has electronics that activate when the device enters the electromagnetic field that the reader generates. Such devices actually generate electricity from an EM field to power themselves (such as card readers that require only that the access card be waved within inches of the reader to unlock doors). A transponder device is self-powered and transmits a signal received by the reader. This can occur consistently or only at the press of a button (like a garage door opener or car alarm keyfob).

In addition to smart/dumb cards and proximity readers, physical access can be managed with radio frequency identification (RFID) or biometric access control devices. See Chapter 1, "Accountability and Access Control," for a description of biometric devices.

## Access Abuses

No matter what form of physical access control is used, a security guard or other monitoring system must be deployed to prevent abuse, masquerading, and piggybacking. Examples of abuses of physical access controls are propping open secured doors and bypassing locks or access controls. *Masquerading* is using someone else's security ID to gain entry into a facility. *Piggybacking* is following someone through a secured gate or doorway without being identified or authorized personally.

Audit trails and access logs are useful tools even for physical access control. They may need to be created manually by security guards. Or they can be generated automatically if sufficient automated access control mechanisms (such as smart cards and certain proximity readers) are in use. The time a subject requests entry, the result of the authentication process, and the length of time the secured gate remains open are important elements to include in audit trails and access logs. In addition to using the electronic or paper trail, consider monitoring entry points with CCTV. CCTV enables you to compare the audit trails and access logs with a visual recording of the events. Such information is critical to reconstruct the events for an intrusion, breach, or attack.

## Intrusion Detection Systems

*Intrusion detection systems* are systems—automated or manual—designed to detect an attempted intrusion, breach, or attack; the use of an unauthorized entry point; or the occurrence of some specific event at an unauthorized or abnormal time. Intrusion detection systems used to monitor physical activity may include security guards, automated access controls, and motion detectors as well as other specialty monitoring techniques.

Physical intrusion detection systems, also called *burglar alarms*, detect unauthorized activities and notify the authorities (internal security or external law enforcement). Physical intrusion detection systems can monitor for vibrations, movement, temperature changes, sound, changes in electromagnetic fields, and much more. The most common type of system uses a simple circuit (aka dry contact switches) comprising foil tape in entrance points to detect when a door or window has been opened.

An intrusion detection mechanism is useful only if it is connected to an intrusion alarm. An intrusion alarm notifies authorities about a breach of physical security. There are four types of alarms:

**Local alarm system**   An alarm sounds locally and can be heard up to 400 feet away.

**Central station system**   The alarm is silent locally, but offsite monitoring agents are notified so they can respond to the security breach. Most residential security systems are of this type. Most central station systems are well-known or national security companies, such as Brinks and ADT.

**Proprietary system**   This is the same thing as a central station system; however, the host organization has its own onsite security staff waiting to respond to security breaches.

**Auxiliary station**   When the security perimeter is breached, emergency services are notified to respond to the incident and arrive at the location. This could include fire, police, and medical services.

Two or more of these types of intrusion and alarm systems can be incorporated in a single solution. However, there are two aspects of any intrusion detection and alarm system that can cause it to fail: how it gets its power and how it communicates. If the system loses power, it will not function. Thus, a reliable detection and alarm system has a battery backup with enough stored power for 24 hours of operation.

If communication lines are cut, an alarm may not function and security personnel and emergency services will not be notified. Thus, a reliable detection and alarm system incorporates a *heartbeat sensor* for line supervision. A heartbeat sensor is a mechanism by which the communication pathway is either constantly or periodically checked with a test signal. If the receiving station detects a failed heartbeat signal, the alarm triggers automatically. Both measures are designed to prevent intruders from circumventing the detection and alarm system.

# Emanation Security

Many electrical devices emanate electrical signals or radiation that can be intercepted by unauthorized individuals. These signals may contain confidential, sensitive, or private data. Obvious examples of emanation devices are wireless networking equipment and mobile phones, but many other devices are vulnerable to interception. Other examples include monitors, modems, and internal or external media drives (hard drives, floppy drives, CDs, and so on). With the right equipment, unauthorized users can intercept electromagnetic or radio frequency signals (collectively known as *emanations*) from these devices and interpret them to extract confidential data.

## TEMPEST

Clearly, if a device emits a signal that someone outside your organization can intercept, some security protection is needed. The types of countermeasures and safeguards used to protect against emanation attacks are known as TEMPEST countermeasures. TEMPEST was originally a government research study aimed at protecting electronic equipment from the electromagnetic pulse (EMP) emitted during nuclear explosions. It has since expanded to a general study of monitoring emanations and preventing their interception. Thus, TEMPEST is now a formal name for a broad category of activities.

## Countermeasures

TEMPEST countermeasures include Faraday cages, white noise, and control zones. A *Faraday cage* is a box, mobile room, or entire building designed with an external metal skin, often a wire mesh that fully surrounds an area on all sides (in other words, front, back, left, right, top, and bottom). This metal skin is slightly electrified to produce a capacitor-like effect (which is why it's named after Faraday, a pioneer in the field of electromagnetism) that prevents electromagnetic signals (emanations) from exiting or entering the area that the cage encloses. Faraday cages are quite effective at blocking EM signals. In fact, inside an active Faraday cage, mobile phones do not work, and you can't pick up broadcast radio or television stations.

White noise simply means broadcasting false traffic at all times to mask and hide the presence of real emanations. White noise can consist of a real signal from another source that is not confidential, a constant signal at a specific frequency, a randomly variable signal (such as the white noise heard between radio stations or television stations), or even a jam signal that causes interception equipment to fail. White noise is most effective when created around the perimeter of an area so that it is broadcast outward to protect the internal area where emanations may be needed for normal operations.

*White noise* describes any random sound, signal, or process that can drown out meaningful information. This can vary from audible frequencies to inaudible electronic transmissions, and it may even involve the deliberate act of creating line or traffic noise to disguise origins or disrupt listening devices.

A third type of TEMPEST countermeasure, a *control zone*, is simply the implementation of either a Faraday cage or white noise generation in an environment where a specific area is protected while the rest is not. A control zone can be a room, a floor, or an entire building. Control zones are those areas where emanation signals are supported and used by necessary equipment, such as wireless networking, mobile phones, radios, and televisions. Outside the control zones, emanation interception is blocked or prevented through the use of various TEMPEST countermeasures.

# Environment and Life Safety

An important aspect of physical access control and maintaining the security of a facility is protecting the basic elements of the environment and protecting human life. In all circumstances and under all conditions, the most important aspect of security is protecting people. Thus, preventing harm to people is the most important goal for all security solutions.

## Personnel Safety

Part of maintaining safety for personnel is maintaining the basic environment of a facility. For short periods of time, people can survive without water, food, air conditioning, and power. But in some cases, the loss of these elements can have disastrous results, or they can be symptoms of more immediate and dangerous problems. Flooding, fires, release of toxic materials, and natural disasters all threaten human life as well as the stability of a facility. Physical security procedures should focus on protecting human life and then on restoring the safety of the environment and restoring the utilities necessary for the IT infrastructure to function.

People should always be your top priority. Only after personnel are safe can you consider addressing business continuity. Many organizations adopt occupant emergency plans (OEPs) to guide and assist with sustaining personnel safety in the wake of a disaster. The OEP provides guidance on how to minimize threats to life, prevent injury, and protect property from damage in the event of a destructive physical event. The OEP does not address IT issues or business continuity, just personnel and general property. The BCP and DRP address IT and business continuity and recovery issues.

## Power and Electricity

Power supplied by electric companies is not always consistent and clean. Most electronic equipment demands clean power to function properly. Equipment damage from power fluctuations is a common occurrence. Many organizations opt to manage their own power through various means. An *uninterruptible power supply (UPS)* is a type of self-charging battery that can be used to supply consistent clean power to sensitive equipment. Basically, a UPS functions by taking power in from the wall outlet, storing it in a battery, pulling power out of the battery, and then feeding that power to whatever devices are connected to it. By directing current through its battery, it is able to maintain a consistent clean power supply. A UPS has a second function, one that is often used as a selling point: A UPS provides continuous power even after the primary power source fails. A UPS can continue to supply power for minutes or hours, depending on its capacity and how much power the equipment attached to it needs.

Another means to ensure that equipment is not harmed by power fluctuations requires use of power strips with surge protectors. A surge protector includes a fuse that will blow before power levels change enough to cause damage to equipment. However, once a surge protector's fuse or circuit is tripped, current flow is completely interrupted. Surge protectors should be used only when instant termination of electricity will not cause damage or loss to the equipment. Otherwise, a UPS should be employed instead.

If maintaining operations for considerable time in spite of a brownout or blackout is a necessity, onsite electric generators are required. Such generators turn on automatically when a power failure is detected. Most generators operate using a fuel tank of liquid or gaseous propellant that must be maintained to ensure reliability. Electric generators are considered alternate or backup power sources.

The problems with power are numerous. Here is a list of terms associated with power issues you should know:

**Fault**   A momentary loss of power

**Blackout**   A complete loss of power

**Sag**   Momentary low voltage

**Brownout**   Prolonged low voltage

**Spike**   Momentary high voltage

**Surge**   Prolonged high voltage

**Inrush**   An initial surge of power usually associated with connecting to a power source, whether primary or alternate/secondary

**Noise**   A steady interfering power disturbance or fluctuation

**Transient**   A short duration of line noise disturbance

**Clean**   Nonfluctuating pure power

**Ground**   The wire in an electrical circuit that is grounded

A brownout is an interesting power issue because its definition references ANSI standards for power. Those standards allow for an 8 percent drop in power between the power source and the facility meter and a drop of 3.5 percent between the facility meter and the wall outlet before any prolonged instance of low voltage is labeled as a brownout. The ANSI standard further distinguishes that low voltage outside your meter is to be repaired by the power company, while an internal brownout is your responsibility.

## Noise

Noise can cause more than just problems with how equipment functions; it can also interfere with the quality of communications, transmissions, and playback. Noise generated by electric current can affect any means of data transmission that relies on electromagnetic transport mechanisms, such as telephone, cellular, television, audio, radio, and network mechanisms.

There are two types of *electromagnetic interference (EMI)*: common mode and traverse mode. *Common mode noise* is generated by a difference in power between the hot and ground wires of a power source or operating electrical equipment. *Traverse mode noise* is generated by a difference in power between the hot and neutral wires of a power source or operating electrical equipment.

*Radio frequency interference (RFI)* is another source of noise and interference that can affect many of the same systems as EMI. A wide range of common electrical appliances generate RFI, including fluorescent lights, electrical cables, electric space heaters, computers, elevators, motors, and electric magnets, so it's important to locate all such equipment when deploying IT systems and infrastructure elements.

Protecting your power supply and your equipment from noise is an important part of maintaining a productive and functioning environment for your IT infrastructure. Steps to take for this kind of protection include providing for sufficient power conditioning, establishing proper grounding, shielding all cables, and limiting exposure to EMI and RFI sources.

## Temperature, Humidity, and Static

In addition to power considerations, maintaining the environment involves control over the HVAC mechanisms. Rooms intended primarily to house computers should be kept at 60 to 75 degrees Fahrenheit (15 to 23 degrees Celsius). Humidity in a computer room should be maintained between 40 and 60 percent. Too much humidity can cause corrosion. Too little humidity causes static electricity. Even on nonstatic carpeting, if the environment has low humidity, it is still possible to generate 20,000-volt static discharges. As you can see in Table 19.1, even minimal levels of static discharge can destroy electronic equipment.

**TABLE 19.1**   Static voltage and damage

| Static Voltage | Possible Damage |
| --- | --- |
| 40 | Destruction of sensitive circuits and other electronic components |
| 1,000 | Scrambling of monitor displays |
| 1,500 | Destruction of data stored on hard drives |
| 2,000 | Abrupt system shutdown |
| 4,000 | Printer jam or component damage |
| 17,000 | Permanent circuit damage |

## Water

Water leakage and flooding should be addressed in your environmental safety policy and procedures. Plumbing leaks are not an everyday occurrence, but when they do happen, they can cause significant damage.

Water and electricity don't mix. If your computer systems come in contact with water, especially while they are operating, damage is sure to occur. Plus, water and electricity create a serious risk of electrocution for nearby personnel. Whenever possible, locate server rooms and critical computer equipment away from any water source or transport pipes. You may also want to install water detection circuits on the floor around mission-critical systems. Water detection circuits will sound an alarm and alert you if water is encroaching upon the equipment.

To minimize emergencies, be familiar with shutoff valves and drainage locations. In addition to monitoring for plumbing leaks, you should evaluate your facility's ability to handle severe rain or flooding in its vicinity. Is the facility located on a hill or in a valley? Is there sufficient drainage? Is there a history of flooding or accumulation of standing water? Is a server room in the basement or on the first floor?

## Fire Detection and Suppression

Fire detection and suppression must not be overlooked. Protecting personnel from harm should always be the most important goal of any security or protection system. In addition to protecting people, fire detection and suppression is designed to keep damage caused by fire, smoke, heat, and suppression materials to a minimum, especially as regards the IT infrastructure.

Basic fire education involves knowledge of the fire triangle (see Figure 19.2). The three corners of the triangle represent fire, heat, and oxygen. The center of the triangle represents the chemical reaction among these three elements. The point of the fire triangle is to illustrate that if you can remove any one of the four items from the fire triangle, the fire can be extinguished. Different suppression mediums address different aspects of the fire:

- Water suppresses the temperature.
- Soda acid and other dry powders suppress the fuel supply.
- $CO_2$ suppresses the oxygen supply.
- Halon substitutes and other nonflammable gases interfere with the chemistry of combustion and/or suppress the oxygen supply.

**FIGURE 19.2**    The fire triangle

When selecting a suppression medium, it is important to consider what aspect of the fire triangle it addresses, what this really represents, how effective the suppression medium usually is, and what impact the suppression medium will exert on your environment.

In addition to understanding the fire triangle, it is also helpful to understand the stages of fire. Fires go through numerous stages, and Figure 19.3 addresses the four most vital stages.

**Stage 1: The incipient stage**    At this stage, there is only air ionization but no smoke.

**Stage 2: The smoke stage**    In Stage 2, smoke is visible from the point of ignition.

**Stage 3: The flame stage**    This is when a flame can be seen with the naked eye.

**Stage 4: The heat stage**    At Stage 4, the fire is considerably further down the timescale to the point where there is an intense heat buildup and everything in the area burns.

**FIGURE 19.3**   The four primary stages of fire

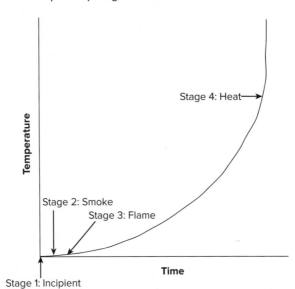

The earlier a fire is detected, the easier it is to extinguish and the less damage it and its suppression medium(s) can cause.

One of the basics of fire management is proper personnel awareness training. Everyone should be thoroughly familiar with the fire suppression mechanisms in their facility. Everyone should also be familiar with at least two evacuation routes from their primary work area and know how to locate evacuation routes elsewhere in the facility. Personnel should be trained in the location and use of fire extinguishers. Other items to include in fire or general emergency-response training include cardiopulmonary resuscitation (CPR), emergency shutdown procedures, and a pre-established rendezvous location or safety verification mechanism (such as voicemail).

   Most fires in a data center are caused by overloaded electrical distribution outlets.

## Fire Extinguishers

There are several types of fire extinguishers. Understanding what type to use on various forms of fire is essential to effective fire suppression. If a fire extinguisher is used improperly or the wrong form of fire extinguisher is used, the fire could spread and intensify instead of being quenched. Fire extinguishers are to be used only when a fire is still in the incipient stage. Table 19.2 lists the three common types of fire extinguishers.

**TABLE 19.2**   Fire extinguisher classes

| Class | Type | Suppression Material |
|-------|------|----------------------|
| A | Common combustibles | Water, soda acid (a dry powder or liquid chemical) |
| B | Liquids | $CO_2$, halon*, soda acid |
| C | Electrical | $CO_2$, halon* |
| D | Metal | Dry powder |

\* Halon or an EPA-approved halon substitute

Water cannot be used on Class B fires because it splashes the burning liquids and such liquids usually float. Water cannot be used on Class C fires because of the potential for electrocution. Oxygen suppression cannot be used on metal fires because burning metal produces its own oxygen.

## Fire Detection Systems

To properly protect a facility from fire requires installing an automated detection and suppression system. There are many types of fire detection systems. Fixed-temperature detection systems trigger suppression when a specific temperature is reached. The trigger is usually a metal or plastic component that is in the sprinkler head and melts at a specific temperature. Rate-of-rise detection systems trigger suppression when the speed at which the temperature changes reaches a specific level. Flame-actuated systems trigger suppression based on the infrared energy of flames. Smoke-actuated systems use photoelectric or radioactive ionization sensors as triggers.

Most fire detection systems can be linked to fire response service notification mechanisms. When suppression is triggered, such linked systems will contact the local fire response team and request aid using an automated message or alarm.

To be effective, fire detectors need to be placed strategically. Don't forget to place them inside dropped ceilings and raised floors, in server rooms, in private offices and public areas, in HVAC vents, in elevator shafts, in the basement, and so on.

As for suppression mechanisms used, they can be based on water or on a fire suppression gas system. Water is common in human-friendly environments, whereas gaseous systems are more appropriate for computer rooms where personnel typically do not reside.

## Water Suppression Systems

There are four main types of water suppression systems.

- A *wet pipe system* (also known as a *closed head system*) is always full of water. Water discharges immediately when suppression is triggered.

- A *dry pipe system* contains compressed air. Once suppression is triggered, the air escapes, opening a water valve that in turn causes the pipes to fill and discharge water into the environment.

- A *deluge system* is another form of dry pipe system that uses larger pipes and therefore delivers a significantly larger volume of water. Deluge systems are inappropriate for environments that contain electronics and computers.

- A *preaction system* is a combination dry pipe/wet pipe system. The system exists as a dry pipe until the initial stages of a fire (smoke, heat, and so on) are detected, and then the pipes are filled with water. The water is released only after the sprinkler head activation triggers are melted by sufficient heat. If the fire is quenched before sprinklers are triggered, pipes can be manually emptied and reset. This also allows manual intervention to stop the release of water before sprinkler triggering occurs.

Preaction systems are the most appropriate water-based system for environments that house both computers and humans together.

The most common cause of failure for a water-based system is human error, such as turning off a water source when a fire occurs or triggering water release when there is no fire.

## Gas Discharge Systems

Gas discharge systems are usually more effective than water discharge systems. However, gas discharge systems should not be used in environments in which people are located. Gas discharge systems usually remove the oxygen from the air, thus making them hazardous to personnel. They employ a pressurized gaseous suppression medium, such as $CO_2$, halon, or FM-200 (a halon replacement).

Halon is an effective fire suppression compound, but it degrades into toxic gases at 900 degrees Fahrenheit. Also, it is not environmentally friendly. The EPA has banned the manufacture of halon in the United States, but it can still be imported into that country. However, according to the Montreal Protocol, you should contact a halon recycling facility to make arrangements for refilling a discharged system instead of contacting a vendor or manufacturer directly. This action is encouraged so that already produced halon will be consumed and less new halon will be manufactured.

Owing to issues with halon, it is often replaced by a more ecologically friendly and less toxic medium. The following list itemizes various EPA-approved substitutes for halon:

- FM-200 (HFC-227ea)
- CEA-410 or CEA-308

- NAF-S-III (HCFC Blend A)

- FE-13 (HCFC-23)

- Argon (IG55) or Argonite (IG01)

- Inergen (IG541)

You can also replace halon substitutes with low-pressure water mists, but such systems are usually not employed in computer rooms or electrical equipment storage facilities. A low-pressure water mist is a vapor cloud used to quickly reduce the temperature in an area.

## Damage

Addressing fire detection and suppression includes dealing with possible contamination and damage caused by a fire. The destructive elements of a fire include smoke and heat, but they also include the suppression media, such as water or soda acid. Smoke is damaging to most storage devices. Heat can damage any electronic or computer component. For example, temperatures of 100 degrees Fahrenheit can damage storage tapes, 175 degrees can damage computer hardware (that is, CPU and RAM), and 350 degrees can damage paper products (through warping and discoloration).

Suppression media can cause short circuits, initiate corrosion, or otherwise render equipment useless. All these issues must be addressed when designing a fire response system.

 Don't forget that in the event of a fire, in addition to damage caused by the flames and your chosen suppression medium, members of the fire department may inflict damage using their hoses to spray water and their axes while searching for hot spots.

# Equipment Failure

No matter what the quality of the equipment your organization chooses to purchase and install might be, eventually it will fail. Understanding and preparing for this eventuality helps ensure the ongoing availability of your IT infrastructure and should help you to protect the integrity and availability of your resources.

Preparing for equipment failure can take many forms. In some non-mission-critical situations, simply knowing where you can purchase replacement parts for a 48-hour replacement timeline is sufficient. In other situations, maintaining onsite replacement parts is mandatory. Keep in mind that the response time in returning a system to a fully functioning state is directly proportional to the cost involved in maintaining such a solution. Costs include storage, transportation, prepurchasing, and maintaining onsite installation and restoration expertise. In some cases, maintaining onsite replacements is infeasible. For those cases, establishing a service-level agreement (SLA) with the hardware vendor is essential. An SLA clearly defines the response time a vendor will provide in the event of an equipment failure emergency.

Aging hardware should be scheduled for replacement and/or repair. The schedule for such operations should be based on the mean time to failure (MTTF) and mean time to repair (MTTR) estimates established for each device or upon prevailing best organizational practices for managing the hardware lifecycle. MTTF is the expected typical functional lifetime of the device given a specific operating environment. MTTR is the average length of time required to perform a repair on the device. A device can often undergo numerous repairs before a catastrophic failure is expected. Be sure to schedule all devices to be replaced before their MTTF expires.

When a device is sent out for repairs, you need to have an alternate solution or a backup device to fill in for the duration of the repair time. Often, waiting until a minor failure occurs before a repair is performed is satisfactory, but waiting until a complete failure occurs before replacement is an unacceptable security practice.

# Summary

If you don't have control over the physical environment, no amount of administrative or technical/logical access controls can provide adequate security. If a malicious person can gain physical access to your facility or equipment, they own it.

There are many aspects and elements involved in implementing and maintaining physical security. One core element is selecting or designing the facility to house your IT infrastructure and the operations of your organization. You must start with a plan that outlines the security needs for your organization and emphasizes methods or mechanisms to employ to provide such security. Such a plan is developed through a process known as *critical path analysis*.

The security controls implemented to manage physical security can be divided into three groups: administrative, technical, and physical. Administrative physical security controls include facility construction and selection, site management, personnel controls, awareness training, and emergency response and procedures. Technical physical security controls include access controls, intrusion detection, alarms, CCTV, monitoring, HVAC, power supplies, and fire detection and suppression. Examples of physical controls for physical security include fencing, lighting, locks, construction materials, mantraps, dogs, and guards.

There are many types of physical access control mechanisms that can be deployed in an environment to control, monitor, and manage access to a facility. These range from deterrents to detection mechanisms. They can be fences, gates, turnstiles, mantraps, lighting, security guards, security dogs, key locks, combination locks, badges, motion detectors, sensors, and alarms.

The technical controls most often employed as access control mechanisms to manage physical access include smart/dumb cards and biometrics. In addition to access control, physical security mechanisms can take the form of audit trails, access logs, and intrusion detection systems.

An important aspect of physical access control and maintaining the security of a facility is protecting the basic elements of the environment and protecting human life. In all circumstances and under all conditions, the most important goal of security is protecting people. Preventing harm is the utmost goal of all security solutions. Providing clean power sources and managing the environment are also important.

Fire detection and suppression must not be overlooked. In addition to protecting people, fire detection and suppression is designed to keep damage caused by fire, smoke, heat, and suppression materials to a minimum, especially in regard to the IT infrastructure.

# Exam Essentials

**Understand why there is no security without physical security.**   Without control over the physical environment, no amount of administrative or technical/logical access controls can provide adequate security. If a malicious person can gain physical access to your facility or equipment, they can do just about anything they want, from destruction to disclosure and alteration.

**Be able to list administrative physical security controls.**   Examples of administrative physical security controls are facility construction and selection, site management, personnel controls, awareness training, and emergency response and procedures.

**Be able to list the technical physical security controls.**   Technical physical security controls can be access controls, intrusion detection, alarms, CCTV, monitoring, HVAC, power supplies, and fire detection and suppression.

**Be able to name the physical controls for physical security.**   Physical controls for physical security are fencing, lighting, locks, construction materials, mantraps, dogs, and guards.

**Know the functional order of controls.**   These are denial, then deterrence, then detection, and then delay.

**Know the key elements in making a site selection and designing a facility for construction.**   The key elements in making a site selection are visibility, composition of the surrounding area, area accessibility, and the effects of natural disasters. A key element in designing a facility for construction is understanding the level of security needed by your organization and planning for it before construction begins.

**Know how to design and configure secure work areas.**   There should not be equal access to all locations within a facility. Areas that contain assets of higher value or importance should have restricted access. Valuable and confidential assets should be located in the heart or center of protection provided by a facility. Also, centralized server or computer rooms need not be human compatible.

**Understand how to handle visitors in a secure facility.**   If a facility employs restricted areas to control physical security, then a mechanism to handle visitors is required. Often an escort is assigned to visitors, and their access and activities are monitored closely. Failing to track the actions of outsiders when they are granted access into a protected area can result in malicious activity against the most protected assets.

**Know the three categories of security controls implemented to manage physical security and be able to name examples of each.**   The security controls implemented to manage physical security can be divided into three groups: administrative, technical, and physical. Understand when and how to use each, and be able to list examples of each kind.

**Know the common threats to physical access controls.**   No matter what form of physical access control is used, a security guard or other monitoring system must be deployed to prevent abuse, masquerading, and piggybacking. Abuses of physical access control are propping open secured doors and bypassing locks or access controls. Masquerading is using someone else's security ID to gain entry into a facility. Piggybacking is following someone through a secured gate or doorway without being identified or authorized personally.

**Understand the need for audit trails and access logs.**   Audit trails and access logs are useful tools even for physical access control. They may need to be created manually by security guards. Or they can be generated automatically if sufficiently automated access control mechanisms are in place (in other words, smart cards and certain proximity readers). You should also consider monitoring entry points with CCTV. Through CCTV, you can compare the audit trails and access logs with a visually recorded history of the events. Such information is critical to reconstructing the events of an intrusion, breach, or attack.

**Understand the need for clean power.**   Power supplied by electric companies is not always consistent and clean. Most electronic equipment demands clean power in order to function properly. Equipment damage because of power fluctuations is a common occurrence. Many organizations opt to manage their own power through several means. A UPS is a type of self-charging battery that can be used to supply consistent clean power to sensitive equipment. UPSs also provide continuous power even after the primary power source fails. A UPS can continue to supply power for minutes or hours depending on its capacity and the draw by equipment.

**Know the terms commonly associated with power issues.**   Know the definitions of the following: fault, blackout, sag, brownout, spike, surge, inrush, noise, transient, clean, and ground.

**Understand how to control the environment.**   In addition to power considerations, maintaining the environment involves control over the HVAC mechanisms. Rooms containing primarily computers should be kept at 60 to 75 degrees Fahrenheit (15 to 23 degrees Celsius). Humidity in a computer room should be maintained between 40 and 60 percent. Too much humidity can cause corrosion. Too little humidity causes static electricity.

**Know about static electricity.**    Even on nonstatic carpeting, if the environment has low humidity, it is still possible to generate 20,000-volt static discharges. Even minimal levels of static discharge can destroy electronic equipment.

**Understand the need to manage water leakage and flooding.**    Water leakage and flooding should be addressed in your environmental safety policy and procedures. Plumbing leaks are not an everyday occurrence, but when they occur, they often cause significant damage. Water and electricity don't mix. If your computer systems come in contact with water, especially while they are operating, damage is sure to occur. Whenever possible, locate server rooms and critical computer equipment away from any water source or transport pipes.

**Understand the importance of fire detection and suppression.**    Fire detection and suppression must not be overlooked. Protecting personnel from harm should always be the most important goal of any security or protection system. In addition to protecting people, fire detection and suppression is designed to keep damage caused by fire, smoke, heat, and suppression materials to a minimum, especially in regard to the IT infrastructure.

**Understand the possible contamination and damage caused by a fire and suppression.** The destructive elements of a fire include smoke and heat but also the suppression medium, such as water or soda acid. Smoke is damaging to most storage devices. Heat can damage any electronic or computer component. Suppression mediums can cause short circuits, initiate corrosion, or otherwise render equipment useless. All of these issues must be addressed when designing a fire response system.

# Written Lab

1. What kind of device helps to define an organization's perimeter, and also serves to deter casual trespassing?

2. What is the problem with halon-based fire suppression technology?

3. What kinds of potential issues can an emergency visit from the fire department leave in its wake?

# Answers to Written Lab

1. A fence is an excellent perimeter safeguard that can help to deter casual trespassing. Moderately secure installations work when the fence is 6 to 8 feet tall and will typically be cyclone (also known as chain link) fencing with the upper surface twisted or barbed to deter casual climbers. More secure installations usually opt for fence heights over 8 feet and often include multiple strands of barbed or razor wire strung above the chain link fabric to further deter climbers.

2. Although you will often see fire suppression information and texts reference fire suppression systems based on halon gas, which serve to starve a fire of oxygen by disrupting the chemical reaction between oxygen and combustible materials, halon is no longer approved by the U.S. EPA for new fire suppression systems, nor is manufacture of new halon gas encouraged for charging of such systems (the EPA seeks to exhaust existing stocks of halon to take this substance out of circulation). Halon is an ozone depleting substance, and production of halon 1301, halon 1211, and halon 2403 ceased in developed countries on December 31, 2003. Inert gases (such as nitrogen or argon), halocarbon gases (FE-13, FE-125, FM-200, FE-36, CEA-308, and CEA-410), and halocarbon generators are all recommended as substitutes. See http://www.berr.gov.uk/files/file29105.pdf for more information.

3. Any time water is used to respond to fire, flame, or smoke, water damage becomes a serious concern, particularly when water is released in areas where electrical equipment is in use. Not only can computers and other electrical gear be damaged or destroyed by water, so also can many forms of storage media become damaged or unusable. Also, when seeking hot spots to put out, firefighters often use axes to break down doors or cut through walls to reach them as quickly as possible. This, too, poses the potential for physical damage to or destruction of devices and/or wiring that may also be in the vicinity.

# Review Questions

1. Which of the following is the most important aspect of security?

   **A.** Physical security

   **B.** Intrusion detection

   **C.** Logical security

   **D.** Awareness training

2. What method can be used to map out the needs of an organization for a new facility?

   **A.** Log file audit

   **B.** Critical path analysis

   **C.** Risk analysis

   **D.** Inventory

3. What type of physical security controls focus on facility construction and selection, site management, personnel controls, awareness training, and emergency response and procedures?

   **A.** Technical

   **B.** Physical

   **C.** Administrative

   **D.** Logical

4. Which of the following is not a security-focused design element of a facility or site?

   **A.** Separation of work and visitor areas

   **B.** Restricted access to areas with higher value or importance

   **C.** Confidential assets located in the heart or center of a facility

   **D.** Equal access to all locations within a facility

5. Which of the following does not need to be true in order to maintain the most efficient and secure server room?

   **A.** It must be human compatible.

   **B.** It must include the use of nonwater fire suppressants.

   **C.** The humidity must be kept between 40 and 60 percent.

   **D.** The temperature must be kept between 60 and 75 degrees Fahrenheit.

6. What is a perimeter-defining device used to deter casual trespassing?

   **A.** Gates

   **B.** Fencing

   **C.** Security guards

   **D.** Motion detectors

**7.** Which of the following is a double set of doors that is often protected by a guard and is used to contain a subject until their identity and authentication is verified?

  **A.** Gate

  **B.** Turnstile

  **C.** Mantrap

  **D.** Proximity detector

**8.** What is the most common form of perimeter security devices or mechanisms?

  **A.** Security guards

  **B.** Fences

  **C.** CCTV

  **D.** Lighting

**9.** Which of the following is not a disadvantage of using security guards?

  **A.** Security guards are usually unaware of the scope of the operations within a facility.

  **B.** Not all environments and facilities support security guards.

  **C.** Not all security guards are themselves reliable.

  **D.** Prescreening, bonding, and training do not guarantee effective and reliable security guards.

**10.** What is the most common cause of failure for a water-based fire suppression system?

  **A.** Water shortage

  **B.** People

  **C.** Ionization detectors

  **D.** Placement of detectors in drop ceilings

**11.** What is the most common and inexpensive form of physical access control device?

  **A.** Lighting

  **B.** Security guard

  **C.** Key locks

  **D.** Fences

**12.** What type of motion detector senses changes in the electrical or magnetic field surrounding a monitored object?

  **A.** Wave

  **B.** Photoelectric

  **C.** Heat

  **D.** Capacitance

13. Which of the following is not a typical type of alarm that can be triggered for physical security?

   A. Preventive

   B. Deterrent

   C. Repellant

   D. Notification

14. No matter what form of physical access control is used, a security guard or other monitoring system must be deployed to prevent all but which of the following?

   A. Piggybacking

   B. Espionage

   C. Masquerading

   D. Abuse

15. What is the most important goal of all security solutions?

   A. Prevention of disclosure

   B. Maintaining integrity

   C. Human safety

   D. Sustaining availability

16. What is the ideal humidity range for a computer room?

   A. 20–40 percent

   B. 40–60 percent

   C. 60–75 percent

   D. 80–95 percent

17. At what voltage level can static electricity cause destruction of data stored on hard drives?

   A. 4,000

   B. 17,000

   C. 40

   D. 1,500

18. A Type B fire extinguisher may use all but which of the following suppression mediums?

   A. Water

   B. $CO_2$

   C. Halon or an acceptable halon substitute

   D. Soda acid

**19.** What is the best type of water-based fire suppression system for a computer facility?

 **A.** Wet pipe system

 **B.** Dry pipe system

 **C.** Preaction system

 **D.** Deluge system

**20.** Which of the following is typically not a culprit in causing damage to computer equipment in the event of a fire and a triggered suppression?

 **A.** Heat

 **B.** Suppression medium

 **C.** Smoke

 **D.** Light

# Answers to Review Questions

1.  A. Physical security is the most important aspect of overall security. Without physical security, none of the other aspects of security is sufficient.

2.  B. Critical path analysis can be used to map out the needs of an organization for a new facility. A critical path analysis is the process of identifying relationships between mission-critical applications, processes, and operations and all of the supporting elements.

3.  C. Administrative physical security controls include facility construction and selection, site management, personnel controls, awareness training, and emergency response and procedures.

4.  D. Equal access to all locations within a facility is not a security-focused design element. Each area containing assets or resources of different importance, value, and confidentiality should have a corresponding level of security restriction placed on it.

5.  A. A computer room does not need to be human compatible to be efficient and secure. Having a human-incompatible server room provides a greater level of protection against attacks.

6.  B. Fencing is a perimeter-defining device used to deter casual trespassing. Gates, security guards, and motion detectors do not define a facility's perimeter.

7.  C. A mantrap is a double set of doors that is often protected by a guard and used to contain a subject until their identity and authentication is verified.

8.  D. Lighting is the most common form of perimeter security devices or mechanisms. Your entire site should be clearly lit. This provides for easy identification of personnel and makes it easier to notice intrusions.

9.  A. Security guards are usually unaware of the scope of the operations within a facility, which supports confidentiality and helps reduce the possibility that a security guard will be involved in the disclosure of confidential information.

10. B. The most common cause of failure for a water-based system is human error. If you turn off the water source after a fire and forget to turn it back on, you'll be in trouble for the future. Also, pulling an alarm when there is no fire will trigger damaging water release throughout the office.

11. C. Key locks are the most common and inexpensive form of physical access control device. Lighting, security guards, and fences are all much more cost intensive.

12. D. A capacitance motion detector senses changes in the electrical or magnetic field surrounding a monitored object.

13. A. There is no such thing as a preventive alarm. Alarms are always triggered in response to a detected intrusion or attack.

**14.** B.  No matter what form of physical access control is used, a security guard or other monitoring system must be deployed to prevent abuse, masquerading, and piggybacking. Espionage cannot be prevented by physical access controls.

**15.** C.  Human safety is the most important goal of all security solutions.

**16.** B.  The humidity in a computer room should ideally be from 40 to 60 percent.

**17.** D.  Destruction of data stored on hard drives can be caused by 1,500 volts of static electricity.

**18.** A.  Water is never the suppression medium in Type B fire extinguishers because they are used on liquid fires.

**19.** C.  A preaction system is the best type of water-based fire suppression system for a computer facility.

**20.** D.  Light is usually not damaging to most computer equipment, but fire, smoke, and the suppression medium (typically water) are very destructive.

# Appendix

# About the Companion CD

---

**IN THIS APPENDIX:**

✓ What you'll find on the CD

✓ System requirements

✓ Using the CD

✓ Troubleshooting

# What You'll Find on the CD

The following sections are arranged by category and summarize the software and other goodies you'll find on the CD. If you need help with installing the items provided on the CD, refer to the installation instructions in the "Using the CD" section of this appendix.

## Sybex Test Engine

The CD contains the Sybex test engine, which includes the two bonus exams.

## Electronic Flashcards

These handy electronic flashcards are just what they sound like. One side contains a question or fill-in-the-blank, and the other side shows the answer.

## PDF of the Book

We have included an electronic version of the text in .pdf format. You can view the electronic version of the book with Adobe Reader.

## Adobe Reader

We've also included a copy of Adobe Reader so you can view PDF files that accompany the book's content. For more information on Adobe Reader or to check for a newer version, visit Adobe's website at www.adobe.com/products/reader/.

# System Requirements

Make sure your computer meets the minimum system requirements, shown in the following list. If your computer doesn't match up to most of these requirements, you may have problems using the software and files on the companion CD. For the latest and greatest information, please refer to the ReadMe file located at the root of the CD-ROM.

- A PC running Microsoft Windows 98, Windows 2000, Windows NT4 (with SP4 or later), Windows Me, Windows XP, Windows Vista, or Windows 7
- An Internet connection
- A CD-ROM drive

# Using the CD

To install the items from the CD to your hard drive, follow these steps:

1.  Insert the CD into your computer's CD-ROM drive. The license agreement appears.

> *Windows users*: The interface won't launch if you have autorun disabled. In that case, click Start ➢ Run (for Windows Vista or Windows 7, Start ➢ All Programs ➢ Accessories ➢ Run). In the dialog box that appears, type **D:\Start.exe**. (Replace *D* with the proper letter if your CD drive uses a different letter. If you don't know the letter, see how your CD drive is listed under My Computer.) Click OK.

2.  Read the license agreement, and then click the Accept button if you want to use the CD.

The CD interface appears. The interface allows you to access the content with just one or two clicks.

# Troubleshooting

Wiley has attempted to provide programs that work on most computers with the minimum system requirements. Alas, your computer may differ, and some programs may not work properly for some reason.

The two likeliest problems are that you don't have enough memory (RAM) for the programs you want to use or you have other programs running that are affecting installation or running of a program. If you get an error message such as "Not enough memory" or "Setup cannot continue," try one or more of the following suggestions and then try using the software again:

**Turn off any antivirus software running on your computer.**    Installation programs sometimes mimic virus activity and may make your computer incorrectly believe that it's being infected by a virus.

**Close all running programs.** The more programs you have running, the less memory is available to other programs. Installation programs typically update files and programs, so if you keep other programs running, installation may not work properly.

**Have your local computer store add more RAM to your computer.** This is, admittedly, a drastic and somewhat expensive step. However, adding more memory can really help the speed of your computer and allow more programs to run at the same time.

## Customer Care

If you have trouble with the book's companion CD-ROM, please call the Wiley Product Technical Support phone number at (800) 762-2974.

# Index

**Note to the reader:** Throughout this index **boldfaced** page numbers indicate primary discussions of a topic. *Italicized* page numbers indicate illustrations.

# The Absolutely Best CISSP Book/CD Package on the Market!

*Get ready for your Certified Information Systems Security Professional exam with the most comprehensive and challenging sample tests anywhere!*

The Sybex Test Engine features:

- All the review questions, as covered in each chapter of the book

- Challenging questions representative of those you'll find on the real exam

- Two full-length 250-question bonus exams available only on the CD

- An Assessment Test to narrow your focus to certain objective groups.

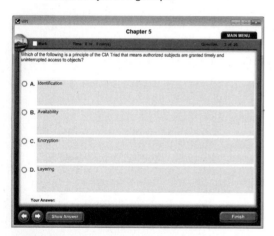

*Search through the complete book in PDF!*

- Access the entire *CISSP: Certified Information Systems Security Professional Study Guide, 5th Edition* complete with figures and tables, in electronic format.

- Search the *CISSP: Certified Information Systems Security Professional Study Guide, 5th Edition* chapters to find information on any topic in seconds.

- Also included in PDF format is a Glossary of key references.

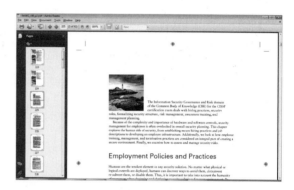

*Use the Electronic Flashcards to jog your memory and prep last minute for the exam!*

- Reinforce your understanding of key concepts with these hardcore flashcard-style questions.

- Now you can study for the CISSP exam any time, anywhere.

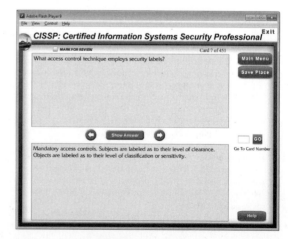